THE ENGLISH RENAISSANCE

This comprehensive anthology collects together primary texts and documents relevant to the literature, culture, and intellectual life in England between 1550 and 1660. Providing a combination of both well-known texts and forgotten texts that were influential at the time, *The English Renaissance* gives the reader an intimate first-hand knowledge of controversies, ideas, and views on all areas of cultural interest in early modern England.

The English Renaissance includes sections on:

- religion
- politics
- society and social life
- education
- literary and cultural theories
- science and magic
- gender and sexuality
- exploration and trade

This volume provides historical breadth within each section, demonstrating change and continuity and easy accessibility to rarely available texts in a single volume. *The English Renaissance* enables students to compare the ideology, content and rhetorical strategies of 'literary' and 'aesthetic' texts with 'historical' or 'political' events and texts.

Kate Aughterson is Senior Lecturer in English Literature at the University of Central England, and the editor of *Renaissance Woman: A Sourcebook* (Routledge, 1995).

THE ENGLISH RENAISSANCE

An anthology of sources and documents

Edited by
Kate Aughterson

London and New York

First published 1998
by Routledge
2 Park Square, Milton Park, Abingdon, Oxon, OX14 4RN

Simultaneously published in the USA and Canada
by Routledge
270 Madison Ave, New York NY 10016

First published in paperback in 2002

Routledge is an imprint of the Taylor & Francis Group

Transferred to Digital Printing 2005

Typeset in Baskerville by Routledge

British Library Cataloguing in Publication Data
A catalogue record for this book is available from the British Library

Library of Congress Cataloguing in Publication Data
The English Renaissance: an anthology of sources and documents/
edited by Kate Aughterson
Includes bibliographical references and index.
1. Great Britain – History –Tudors, 1485–1603 – sources.
2. Great Britain – History – Early Stuarts, 1603–1649 – sources. 3. Great Britain –
History – Commonwealth and Protectorate, 1649–1660 – sources. 4. Renaissance
– England – sources. I. Aughterson, Kate.
DA310. R46   1998
97–49601
942.05–dc 21
CIP

ISBN 0–415–18554–8 (Hbk)
ISBN 0–415–27115–0 (Pbk)

CONTENTS

Part 2 Politics

Part 3 Society and social life

Part 4 Education

Part 5 Literary and cultural theories

Part 6 Science and magic

Part 7 Gender and sexuality

CONTENTS

Part 8 Exploration and trade

CONTENTS

ACKNOWLEDGEMENTS

I would like to thank all my past students who asked the questions to which this book is a response, as well as all those students who read and commented on earlier versions of the texts in this book.

All the staff in the Bodleian Library, particularly those working in Duke Humphrey's, were unfailingly helpful, enthusiastic and efficient. The staff at the British Library's reproduction and photocopying department have been indispensable and always helpful. I am extremely grateful to them.

It has been a pleasure to work with the editorial staff at Routledge.

I am grateful to the University of Central England for granting me writing time to help complete the book, in the form of a semester's sabbatical.

I am also indebted to the indexing and proof-reading help, as well as personal support and advise, of Elizabeth Maddison.

PERMISSIONS

The author and publishers gratefully acknowledge permission from the following to quote copyright material: material from G.R. Elton, ed. *The Tudor Constitution* (1982, 2nd ed.), Cambridge University Press, pp. 425-8. The British Library, for permission to reproduce Thomas Digges's diagram of *A Perfect Description of the Celestial Orbs* (shelfmark: 718g52).

Every effort has been made to trace and acknowledge copyright holders, although this has not been possible in every case.

INTRODUCTION

In 1559, and in many subsequent years, the Queen issued a set of *Injunctions*, which accompanied in that year the Act of Uniformity, and in subsequent years, Visitations made by her Archbishops to inspect local Churches. This document is a comprehensive and fascinating social and political text: in a short space it encompasses, delineates and sets up ways of controlling all social, religious, political, intellectual and educational life. It demonstrates in what way both the local and national Church and its theology informed and structured all aspects of people's lives. Thus it sets out the *Homilies* (and their contents) which must be read to all people and requires regular recitation of the articles of faith. It provides for poor relief; local taxation; and the provision of reading the Bible in English for parishioners. It introduces regular parish record-keeping; ethical rules for the behaviour of priests; the regulation of who can and cannot preach in public; and of who can and cannot teach children. It orders the erasure of old Church monuments and icons, 'so that there remain no memory' of past catholicism. It establishes funds for poor scholars and a system of local administration of the morals of the community. It provides the mechanism for the censorship of all publications, for the suppression of religious dissent, for teaching grammar, for controlling the sale of goods, and for suppressing witchcraft.

Thus, just as the old icons and practices of the Roman Church were erased, so past systems of Church administration, function and belief had to be razed and reborn. *The Injunctions* are therefore one of the most central texts of the period: marking, as they do, the birth of the modern State and its ability to oversee and regulate our lives, through standardisation, taxation and accountable administrative systems. They thus actively dominated and affected all the different fields represented in this book, and demonstrate the centrality of Church and State, and their concomitant theology and ideology, in all areas of life. For that reason, they are set out here as the most appropriate introduction to the book's contents.

1

INJUNCTIONS GIVEN BY THE QUEEN'S MAJESTY (1559)

The first is that all Deans, Archdeacons, parsons, vicars and all other ecclesiastical persons shall faithfully keep and observe, and as far as in them may lie, shall cause to be observed and kept of other, all and singular laws and statutes made for the restoring to the crown the ancient jurisdiction over the state ecclesiastical, and abolishing of all foreign power repugnant to the same. And furthermore, all ecclesiastical persons having cure of soul, shall to the uttermost of their wit, knowledge and learning, purely, sincerely and without any colour of dissimulation, declare, manifest and open four times every year at the least, in their sermons and other collations, that all usurped and foreign power, having no establishment nor ground by the law of God, is for most just causes taken away and abolished: and that therefore no manner of obedience or subjection within her highness's realms and dominions is due unto any such foreign power. And that the Queen's power within her realms and dominions is the highest power under God, to whom all men within the same realms and dominions by God's laws owe most loyalty and obedience, afore and above all other powers and potentates in earth.

Besides this, to the intent that all superstition and hypocrisy crept into divers men's hearts may vanish away. They shall not set forth or extol the dignity of any images, relics or miracles, but declaring the abuse of the same, they shall teach that all goodness, health and grace ought to be both asked and looked for only of God, as of the very author and giver of the same and of none other.

Item, that they the persons above rehearsed shall preach in their Churches and every other cure they have, one sermon every month of the year at the least, wherein they shall purely and sincerely declare the word of God, and in the same exhort their hearers to the works of faith as mercy and charity, specially prescribed and commanded in Scripture: and that works derived by man's fantasies besides Scripture (as wandering of pilgrimages, setting up of candles, praying upon beads, or such like superstition) have not only no promise of reward in Scripture for doing of them, but contrariwise, great threatenings and maledictions of God, for that they be things tending to idolatry and superstition, which of all other offences God Almighty doth most detest and abhor, for that the same diminish most his honour and glory.

Item, that they the persons above rehearsed shall preach in their own persons once in every quarter of the year, at the least one sermon, being licensed specially thereunto, as is specified hereafter: or else shall read some *Homily* prescribed to be used by the Queen's authority, every Sunday at the least, unless some other preacher sufficiently licensed, as hereafter chance to come to the parish for the same purpose of preaching.

Item, that every holiday through the year when they have no sermon, they shall immediately after the Gospel, openly and plainly recite to their parishioners in the pulpit the paternoster, the creed, and the ten commandments in English, to the intent the people may learn the same by heart, exhorting all parents and householders to teach their children and servants the same as they are bound by the law of God and conscience to do.

Also that they shall provide within three months next after this visitation, at the charges of the parish, one book of the whole Bible of the largest volume in English: and within one twelve months next after the said visitation, the *Paraphrases* of Erasmus also in English upon the Gospels, and the same set by in some convenient place within the said Church, that they have cure of, whereas their parishioners may most commodiously resort unto the same, and read the same . . .

Also the said ecclesiastical persons shall in no wise at any unlawful time nor for any other cause than for their honest necessities, haunt or resort to any taverns or alehouses. And after their meals they shall not give themselves to drinking, or riot, spending their time idly by day or by night at dice, cards or tables playing, or any other unlawful games, but at all times as they shall have leisure, they shall hear or read somewhat of Holy Scripture, or shall occupy themselves with some other honest study or exercise, and that they shall always do the things which appertain to honesty, and endeavour to profit the common-wealth, having always in mind that they ought to excel all other in purity of life, and should be examples to the people to live well and Christianly.

Also that they shall admit no man to preach within any their cures but such as shall appear unto them to be sufficiently licensed thereunto by the Queen's Majesty, or the Archbishop of Canterbury, or the Archbishop of York . . .

Also that the parson, vicar or curate and parishioners of every parish within this realm shall in their Churches and Chapels keep one book or register wherein they shall write the day and year of every wedding, christening and burial made within the parish for their time, and so every man succeeding them likewise: and also therein shall write every person's name that shall be so wedded, christened, and buried. And for the safe-keeping of the same book, the parish shall be bound to provide of their common charges one sure coffer with two locks and keys. . .

Furthermore, because the goods of the Church are called the goods of the poor, and at these days nothing is less seen than the poor to be sustained with the same: all parsons, vicars, pensionaries, prebendaries, and other beneficed men within this deanery not being resident upon their benefices, which may dispend yearly twenty pounds or above, either within this deanery or elsewhere, shall distribute hereafter among their poor parishioners or other inhabitants, there in the presence of the churchwardens, or some other honest men of the parish, the forty part of the fruits and revenues of the said benefice, lest they be worthily noted of ingratitude . . .

And to the intent that learned men may hereafter spring the more for the execution of the premises, every parson, vicar, clerk or beneficed man within this deanery, having yearly to dispend in benefices and other promotions of the Church an hundred pounds, shall give £3.6s.8d. in exhibition to one scholar in any of the universities, and for as many £100 more as he may dispend, to so many scholars more shall give like exhibition in the university of Oxford or

Cambridge, or some grammar school, which after they have profited in good learning, may be partners of their patrons, cure and charge, as well in preaching as otherwise in execution of their offices, or may when need shall be otherwise profit the commonwealth with their counsel and wisdom . . .

Also that the said parsons, vicars and clerks shall once every quarter of the year read these Injunctions given unto them openly and deliberately before all their parishioners at one time, or any two several times in one day, to the intent that both they may be the better admonished of their duty and their said parishioners the more moved to follow the same for their part.

Also forasmuch by laws established every man is bound to pay his tithes, no man shall by colour of duty omitted in their curates, detain their tithes, and so requite one wrong with another, or be his own judge, but shall truly repay the same as he hath been accustomed to their parsons, vicars and curates without any restraint or diminution. And such lack or default as they can justly find in their parsons and curates, to call for reformation thereof at their ordinaries and other superiors, who upon complaint and due proof thereof, shall reform the same accordingly.

Also that every parson, vicar, curate and stipendiary priest being under the degree of a master of art shall provide and have of his own within three months after this visitation, the New Testament both in Latin and in English, with paraphrases upon the same, conferring the one with the other . . .

Also, that the vice of damnable despair may be clearly taken away and that firm belief and steadfast hope may be surely conceived of all their parishioners being in any danger, they shall learn and have always in a readiness, such comfortable places and sentences of Scripture as do set forth the mercy, benefits, and goodness of Almighty God towards all penitent and believing persons, that they may at all times, when necessity shall require, promptly comfort their flock with the lively word of God, which is the only stay of man's conscience . . .

Also that they shall take away, utterly extinct and destroy all shrines, covering of shrines, all tables, candlesticks, trundles, and rolls of ware, pictures, paintings and all other monuments of feigned miracles, pilgrimages, idolatry, and superstition, so that there remain no memory of the same in walls, glasses, windows, or elsewhere within their Churches and houses, preserving nevertheless or repairing both the walls and glass windows, and they shall exhort all their parishioners to do the like with their several houses.

And that the churchwardens at the common charge of the parishioners in every Church shall provide a comely and honest pulpit to be set in a convenient place within the same and to be there seemly kept for the preaching of God's word.

Also they shall provide and have within three months after this visitation a strong chest with a hole in the upper part thereof, to be provided at the cost and charge of the parish, having three keys, whereof one shall remain in the custody of the parson, vicar or curate, and the other two in the custody of the churchwardens, or any other two honest men to be appointed by the parish from year to year, which chest you shall set and fasten in a most convenient place to the intent the parishioners should put into it their oblations and alms for their poor neighbours . . .

Also because through lack of preachers in many places of the Queen's realms and dominions the people continue in ignorance and blindness, all parsons, vicars and curates shall read in their Churches every Sunday, one of the *Homilies* which are and shall be set forth for the same purpose by the Queen's authority in such sort as they shall be appointed to do in the preface of the same . . .

Item, that no man shall wilfully and obstinately defend or maintain any heresies, errors, or false doctrine contrary to the faith of Christ and his Holy Scripture.

Item, that no person shall use charms, sorceries, enchantments, witchcraft, soothsaying, or any such like devilish device, nor shall resort at any time to the same for counsel or help.

Item, that no person shall, neglecting their own parish Church, resort to any other Church in time of common prayer or preaching, except it be by the occasion of some extraordinary sermon in some parish of the same town.

Item, that no innholders, or alehouse keepers shall use to sell meat or drink in the time of common prayer, preaching, reading of the *Homilies* or Scriptures.

Item, that no persons keep in their houses abused images, tables, pictures, paintings, and other monuments of feigned miracles, pilgrimages, idolatry and superstition . . .

Item, that no man shall talk or reason of the holy scriptures rashly or contentiously, or maintain any false doctrine or error, but shall commune of the same when occasion is given reverently, humbly and in the fear of God, for his comfort and better understanding.

Item, that no man, woman or child, shall be otherwise occupied in the time of the service than in quiet attendance to hear, mark and understand that is read, preached, and ministered.

Item, that every schoolmaster and teacher shall teach the grammar set forth by King Henry the Eighth of noble memory, and continued in the time of King Edward the Sixth, and none other.

Item, that no man shall take upon him to teach but such as shall be allowed by the Ordinary and found meet as well for his learning and dexterity in teaching, as for sober and honest conversation and also for right understanding of God's true religion.

Item, that all teachers of children shall stir and move them to the love and due reverence of God's true religion, now truly set forth by published authority.

Item, that they shall accustom their scholars reverently to learn such sentences of Scriptures as shall be most expedient to induce them to all godliness . . .

Item, every parson, vicar and curate shall upon every holiday and every second Sunday in the year hear and instruct all the youth of the parish for half an hour at the least before evening prayer in the ten commandments, the articles of the belief and in the Lord's Prayer, and diligently examine them and teach the Catechism set forth in the *Book of Common Prayer*.

Item that the Ordinaries do exhibit unto our visitors their books or a true copy of the same, containing the causes why any person was imprisoned, famished or put to death for religion.

Item, that in every parish, three or four discreet men which tender God's glory and his true religion, shall be appointed by the Ordinaries diligently to see that all parishioners duly resort to their Church upon all Sundays and holidays, and there to continue the whole time of the godly service. And all such as shall be found slack or negligent in resorting to the Church, having no great nor urgent cause of absence, they shall straightly call upon them and after due monition, if they amend not, they shall denounce them to the Ordinary . . .

Item, because in all alterations and specially in rites and ceremonies there happeneth discords among the people, and thereupon slanderous words and railings whereby charity, the knot of christian society, is loosed: the Queen's Majesty, being most desirous of all other earthly things that her people should live in charity both towards God and man, and therein abound in good works, willeth and straightly commandeth all manner her subjects to forbear all vain and contentious disputations in matters of religion . . .

Item, because there is a great abuse in the printers of books, which for covetousness chiefly, regard not what they print, so they may have gain, whereby ariseth great disorder by publication of unfruitful, vain and infamous books and papers, the Queen's Majesty straightly chargeth and commandeth that no manner of person shall print any manner of book or paper of what sort, nature or in what language soever it be, except the same be first licensed by her Majesty by express words in writing, or by six of her Privy Council: or be perused and licensed by the Archbishops of Canterbury and York, the Bishop of London, the Chancellors of both Universities, the Bishop being Ordinary, and the Archdeacon also of the place where any such shall be printed, or by two of them, whereof the Ordinary of the place to be always one. And that the names of such that shall allow the same to be added in the end of every such work for a testimony of the allowance thereof. And because many pamphlets, plays, and ballads be oftentimes printed wherein regard would be had that nothing therein should be either heretical, seditious or unseemly for Christian ears: her Majesty likewise commandeth that no manner of persons shall enterprise to print any such except the same be licensed by such her Majesty's commissioners, or three of them, as be appointed by the City of London to hear and determine divers causes ecclesiastical tending to the execution of certain statutes made the last parliament for uniformity of order in religion. And if any shall sell or utter any manner of books or papers, being not licensed, as is above said: that the same party shall be punished by order of the said commissioners, as to the quality of the fault shall be thought meet. And touching all other books of matters of religion or policy or governance that hath been printed either on this side the seas, or on the other side, because the diversity of them is great, and that there needeth good consideration to be had of the particularities thereof: her Majesty refereth the prohibition or permission thereof to the order which her said commissioners within the City of London shall take and notify. According to the which, her Majesty straightly commandeth all manner her subjects and specially the wardens and company of Stationers to be obedient.

Provided that these orders do not extend to any profane authors and works in any language that hath been heretofore commonly received or allowed in any of the universities or schools, but the same may be printed and used as by good order they were accustomed.

This anthology is divided into eight parts, which each represent a significant aspect of early modern English life, as it was structured externally (for example through religion, politics, economics, social norms and education); or experienced internally (through theology, education, intellectual debates and theories, and sexual identity). Each part contains a selection of texts over the range of the whole early modern period to give a sense of the key issues and events which affected the nation and individuals' lives. Essential constraints on the length of this textbook have necessitated a policy of exclusion rather than inclusion. I have therefore included extracts of major statutory legislation, of central and national government policy, and printed material, at the partial expense of local practice and experience and manuscript sources: although I have aimed to include some examples of diaries, travelogues, prophecies and autobiography. The overall introduction to each part aims to provide a context for reading the subsequent texts, and cross-references these to texts elsewhere in the anthology. I thus suggest that no text should be read in isolation, and that there is no single intrepretive position or place for these texts. Short reading lists and further, published, primary reading is given at the end of the book to aid further enquiry. All the texts are briefly placed in their historical or published context at the head of the entry, and should be read in conjunction with the overall chronology at the end of the book.

Thus these texts can give a sense of continuity and change, of ideology and belief, and of social, economic and political practice and structure, in early modern England. In addition, all the texts may, and should, be read alongside other literary, theological, autobiographical, legal, political, geographical or private texts of the period as contextual aids in various scholarly disciplines.

TEXTUAL AND EDITORIAL POLICY

The texts included in this anthology have been edited and chosen according to the following principles:

1 First English editions have been used wherever possible.

2 Selections are chosen for their relevance to the book's overall concerns: where authors' arguments or examples are too long for complete inclusion, I have omitted parts of the text, indicating this by ellipses where the omission is only of a sentence or two; where the omission is of several paragraphs, I have used an asterisk.

3 Spelling, punctuation and lay-out have been modernised, but the original emphasis has been retained.

4 Marginal references in the original text have been included within square brackets in text.

5 Where authors use Latin or Greek and immediately translate the sense, I have omitted the Greek or Latin text; where they do not translate the original, I have placed a translation within square brackets.

6 Notes are placed at the end of the book.

RELIGION

INTRODUCTION

Religion was central to the structure, action, language, policing and validity of the Tudor State, whether Catholic or Protestant, in two crucial ways. First, on a political and ideological level, it was through the 'nationalisation' of the Church by Henry VIII and his successors that he helped define and extend the powers of the State: bringing it closer to our idea of the modern State and its various apparatuses with which it can survey and influence most areas of modern lives. Second, on the individual and social level, the Church provided the only totalising belief system and accompanying rituals which early modern people had to understand the world and their place in it. Thus, whether we talk about Catholics, Protestants, Arminians, Brownists, Baptists or Quakers, we need to remember that Christian faith structured and informed everyday lives in ways which it does not today. This is clear from many of the extracts in other parts of the book as well: for example, it structured the way in which ideas about society were formulated (part 3); the way in which science and its uses were articulated (part 6); and the European view of the colonisation of the Americas (part 8). Of course, theological differences between individual Churches, and between individual sects, could, and did, divide communities, families and States, and even change the structures of people's lives (see, for example, the accounts of Richard Fitz, James Naylor, Mary Cary and Anna Trapnel in this part). But before considering some such differences, it is useful to emphasise the place of the Church and of religion during this period in England.

Thus for most early modern English people between the 1530s and 1660, the local parish Church was their central source of information about politics, both nationally and locally; about ethics; about the appropriate annual rituals and holidays; for structuring behaviour about birth, marriage, sex and death; a source of taxation through the tithes; and for monitoring and regulating social and sexual behaviour, using the Church courts as a last resort. It was a relatively stable system: even during and after the Civil

War, when there was some pressure on priests and vicars to take oaths of loyalty to Parliament, most parish Churches continued to perform services according to the prescribed Elizabethan *Book of Common Prayer*, and over 60 per cent of pastors who had been in post in 1642, still were in 1649.[1] It is true that many of the complaints against the Church throughout the period, in Parliament and pamphlets, were aimed against some of these powers: those of tithing and the Church courts being raised most frequently (see the *Admonition to Parliament*, *The Root and Branch Petition* and Fell Fox). But they had been raised before the Reformation, and remained largely unchanged by it until the abolition of episcopacy by Parliament in 1643. The Church was also the monopoly provider of services equivalent to modern social services and education at all levels: through charitable acts and donations in the former case, and schools and universities in the latter. Although the monastic schools were greatly reduced through the dissolution of the monasteries, the universities were still run by churchmen, and all students had to study some theology. In addition, belief in an animate God helped explain the universe, bad harvests, sudden death, difficulties in childbirth, the good or bad luck of oneself or one's neighbours, sickness and health. Whilst there is much evidence that such beliefs were often more magical than specifically Christian, the Christian Church provided an external structure and rhetoric which gave meaning to the natural world.

However, the Reformation, although it was a less 'pure' version than that in Calvin's Geneva, did have a significant impact on England's culture and society. In general, the changes may be said to have been: the formation of a new self-consciously national Church, defined in partial contradistinction to Rome, with its concomitant local bureaucracies to enforce its policies; the development of a specifically protestant doctrine for the Church; an increased emphasis on individual salvation and personal reading of Scriptures, with a consequent emphasis on the mother tongue; an emphasis on the word of God, rather than the image of God and the saints; a more specifically intimate relationship between Church and State, with the monarch established as supreme governor of the Church, and the consequent increased influence of the nobles and monarch in appointing clergy to Church posts. Complete and intense individual commitment to the Protestant creed can be seen in Margaret Hoby's *Diary*, Foxe's account of George Eagles's marytrdom, as well as the later prophets and preachers of the Civil War period (1.7, 1.15, 1.24, 1.25 and 1.26). The frequency with which the Calvinist outlook informs writing in supposedly secular fields (such as literature, education, science and trade) demonstrates the effective spread of Protestant belief among the educated classes.

The nature of the English Reformation was twofold. It was a reformation that was primarily an act of State, and not a revolution from below as it was in Germany. But it combined this change of government with an intellectual and spiritual shift that was more radical: a reformed theology of individual grace. Thus the national Church may be said to have pulled in opposite ways from its inception. The tension between, on the one hand, a theology based on individual salvation and a Calvinist interpretive framework of the elect and the reprobate; and, on the other, an ideology of an inclusive national Church, which continually asserted the supremacy of the monarch and episcopacy, is what characterised the religious conflicts of the period.[2] For the most part, such tensions were held together within what has become known as the Elizabethan Settlement: the combination of the policies of The Acts of Uniformity and Supremacy (1.5 and 2.2); and the ambiguous wording of *The Book of Common Prayer* (1.3) on and *The Thirty Nine Articles* (1.8). In addition to these key texts, the Church and State's doctrine was expounded and defended in the book of *Homilies* (1.4 and 2.5) and the subsequent Church *Canons* published in 1604 (1.17), which mostly codified previous monarchical or Arch-episcopate Injunctions. Despite puritan and Arminian debates about exact meanings and interpretations of these texts, during James I's and Charles's reign, they continued in use until the outbreak of the Civil War in 1642, and in many places afterwards, despite the alternative offered in *The Directory of Worship*, proposed by Parliament as a replacement for the *Book of Common Prayer*, but never enforced by statute. In 1545, Henry VIII, in a speech made to his last Parliament, and pleading for religious unity and uniformity, explicitly acknowledged this tension as justification of the need for a supreme power:

You rail on bishops, speak slanderously of priests, and rebuke and taunt preachers, both contrary to good order and Christian fraternity. If you know surely that a bishop or preacher erreth, or teacheth perverse doctrine, come and declare it to some of our council, or to us . . . and be not judges yourselves of your own fantastical opinions. . . . And although you be permitted to read holy scripture, and to have the word of God in your mother tongue, you must understand that it is licensed you so to do, only to inform your conscience and to instruct your children and family, and not to dispute and make scripture a railing and a taunting stock against priests and preachers, as many light persons do. I am very sorry to hear how unreverently that most precious jewel the word of God is disputed, rhymed, sung and jangled in every alehouse and tavern contrary to the true meaning and doctrine of the same.[3]

The political attempt to restrict issues of conscience to private occasions, whilst public religion remained a matter of order, uniformity and ritual may be described as the theology of the Church of England, and is certainly what Archbishop Parker (1.9), Hooker (2.9) and later Laud (1.19) believed provided the foundation stones of the Church. However, for men and women who placed a different emphasis on the individual conscience, and read and interpreted the Bible accordingly, the political State and its power and actions became subordinate to the individual's conscience or belief: Ann Askew is one of the earliest examples of an assertion of this creed (1.7), and much of Foxe's *Book of Martyrs* explicitly defends such a position *vis à vis* the Catholic Church. The later practical preaching ministries and conversion work of Baptists, Quakers and other independent Churches (1.24–29), as well as the establishment of religious separatist communities in both England and New England, testify to the strength of this spiritual imperative.

The short- and long-term causes, as well as the significances, of the religious divide during the Civil War is a matter of fierce debate amongst historians.[4] The current consensus is that the Church of England successfully contained dissent through a combination of a general consensus on doctrine (a belief in predestinarianism) with a relatively flexible enforcement of the prescriptions on Church ritual (over the use of the cross in baptism; the placing of the communion table and so on). Thus whilst there were fierce debates within the Church about important issues: for example, Church government and presbyterianism in the 1570s and 1580s; Church vestments in the 1560s; and the regulation of preachers in the 1600s, none of these threatened the unity of the consensual Church. It was only during the 1620s, most particularly after the accession of Charles I, and his adoption of an aggressive uniformity campaign, coordinated by William Laud, first bishop of London and then archbishop of Canterbury after 1633, that the left wing of the Protestant Church began to feel their religious beliefs to be fundamentally threatened. Laud and others, aiming at uniformity and unity, brought back an emphasis on ceremonialism, vigorously prosecuted preachers who were not licensed by local bishops, urged local pastors to inform on non-church attenders, used the Court of High Commission to prosecute many more censures for treason (the most famous being the Prynne and Bastwick cases), and helped foster further appointments of Arminians (non-predestinarians) in the Church. These moves, combined as they were by Laud's semi-hysterical rhetoric against 'puritans' and their political populist threat to the State, alienated increasing numbers of men and women who had been moderate members of the Church, and forced them to articulate their beliefs as ideology: either in the form of explicit attacks on Laud's position and theology, or as separatist churches. Had either Charles or Laud been more politically aware, both of Church and State, the Civil War might have been something else altogether. The order of changes made by Laud and Charles, for example, were certainly no greater than those made by Henry VIII, or by Elizabeth I again after Mary I's reversal of Edward VI's Protestant measures. The nature of the reaction, therefore, was a combination of a greater national commitment to Protestantism, [5] increasing political tensions between court and country, and a monarch less skilled in the arts of compromise. Large-scale religious conflict, endemic within the nature of the Reformation philosophy from the very beginning, had by-passed England through political luck: the political, economic and social circumstances of the 1630s, however, brought the kind of civil war to England which had plagued and divided continental Europe for a century.

The interregnum brought with it a limited amount of religious toleration: first by default, since both censorship laws, Church courts and the licensing of preachers by bishops, all lapsed in 1642. The proliferation of sects, prophesiers and independent Churches, as well as the freedom of the press, began an unprecedented debate about religious beliefs, faith, spirituality and individual liberty, which severely frightened many Parliamentarians (see, for example, Anna Trapnel's or James Naylor's accounts of the magistrates' inquisitions of them). Presbyterian Church government [6] was approved, but so was a limited toleration of independent Churches (and see the *Instrument of Government*). Nevertheless, after the defeat of the Ranters in 1650 Parliament passed the Blasphemy Act which aimed at Church uniformity, with limited freedom of speech and worship. The restoration of Charles II in 1660 brought back the pre-1642 Church, mostly unreformed, and with clearer battle lines drawn between its doctrine and that of independent Churches, such as the Baptists or Quakers. The clutch of legislation, known collectively as *The Clarendon Code*, aimed to penalise severely any who did not conform to the re-established church (see 1.30). Margaret Fell Fox's eloquent appeal to the King (1.29) to maintain religious toleration in order to obtain political peace fell on deaf ears. Thus the centralising and hierarchical theology and ecclesiastical policies of Charles I and Laud triumphed in 1660: but only until 1688, when reaction against political absolutism brought about a quieter political and religious revolution than that of 1642–9.

1.1 THE BIBLE

1.1a *The Geneva Bible*

Until the translation of the Authorised Version (see 1.1b), *The Geneva Bible* was the most popular version among English Protestants and Churches. It provided the Calvinist interpretive structure for domestic biblical readings. The texts from Exodus, the Psalms, Isaiah and Paul's Epistle to the Romans were frequently cited in Genevan Reformation theology, sermons and catechisms. Text from: Geneva 1560 edition; notes given in square brackets are the original marginal annotations: preface; Old Testament: pp. 25r; 257^v–258^r, 299^r; New Testament, pp. 71^r; 73^r.

To the most virtuous and noble Queen Elizabeth, Queen of England, France and Ireland, Your humble subjects of the English church at Geneva, wish Grace and peace from God the Father through Jesus Christ our Lord.

For the word of God is an evident token of God's love and our assurance of his defence wheresoever it is obediently received; it is the trial of the spirits, and as the prophet saith, it is as a fire and hammer to break the stony hearts of them that resist God's mercies offered by the preaching of the same. Yea it is sharper than any two edged sword to examine the very thoughts and to judge the affections of the heart and to discover whatsoever lieth hid under hypocrisy and would be secret from the face of God and his Church. So that this must be the first foundation and groundwork, according whereunto the good stones of this building must be framed, and the evil tried out and rejected. [Ezra 4.1; 2 Tim. 4.10; Amos. 7.12; 3 John 9; Act. 19.24. *The necessity of God's word for the reforming of religion.* John 14.23; 1 John 4.1; Jer. 23.29; Ebr. 4.12; *The ground of true religion...*].

Now as he that goeth about to lay a foundation surely, first taketh away such impediments as might justly either hurt, let or deform the work: so is it necessary that your Grace's zeal appear herein, that neither the crafty persuasion of man, neither worldly policy, or natural fear dissuade you to root out, cut down and destroy these weeds and impediments which do not only deface your building but utterly endeavour, yea and threaten, the ruin thereof. For when the noble Josias enterprised the like kind of work, among other notable and many things he destroyed not only with utter confusion the idols with their appurtenances but also burnt (in sign of detestation) the idolatrous priests' bones upon their altars and put to death false prophets and sorcerers to perform the words of the law of God: and therefore the Lord gave him good success and blessed him wonderfully, so long as he made God's word his line and rule to follow, and enterprised nothing before he had enquired at the mouth of the Lord . . .

Last of all (most gracious Queen) for the advancement of this building and rearing up of the work, two things are necessary. First, that we have a lively and steadfast faith in Christ Jesus, who must dwell in our hearts as the only means and assurance of our salvation: for he is as the ladder that reacheth from the earth to heaven; he lifteth up his Church and setteth it in the heavenly places; he maketh us lively stones and buildeth us upon himself; he joineth us to himself as the members and body to the head: yea he maketh himself and his Church one Christ. The next is that our faith bring forth good fruits, so that our godly conversation may serve us as a witness to confirm our election [1 Pet. 2.5; 2 Cor. 12.12; 2 Pet. 1.10; Ephes. 4.1], and be an example to all others to walk as appertaineth to the vocation whereunto they are called: lest the word of God be evil spoken of and this building be stayed to grow up to a just height: which cannot be without the great provocation of God's just vengeance and discouraging of many thousands through all the world, if they should see that our life were not holy and agreeable to our profession.

Exodus 1.15–19

15. Moreover the King of Egypt commanded the midwives of the Hebrew women. . . 16. and said, when ye do the office of a midwife to the women of the Hebrews and see them on their stools, if it be a son, then ye shall kill him: but if

it be a daughter, then let her live. 17. Notwitstanding the midwives feared God, and did not as the King of Egypt commanded them, but preserved alive the men children. 18. Then the King of Egypt called for the midwives and said unto them, why have ye done thus, and have preserved alive the men children? 19. And the midwives answered Pharoah [*their disobedience herein was lawful, but their dissembling evil*], because Hebrew women are not as the women of Egypt: for they are lively and are delivered yer[1] the midwife come at them. 20. God therefore prospered the midwives and the people multiplied and were very mighty.

Psalm 105

He praiseth the singular grace of God who hath of all the people of the world chosen a peculiar people unto himself, and having chosen them, never ceaseth to do them good even for his promise's sake.

6. Ye seed of Abraham, his servant, ye children of Jacob which are his elect. 7. He is the Lord our God: his judgements are through all the earth. 8. He hath alway remembered his covenant and promise that he made to a thousand generations . . . 14. Yet suffered he no man to do them wrong, but reproved kings for their sakes, saying: 15. touch not mine anointed [*Those whom I have sanctified to be my people*], and do my prophets no harm [*meaning the old fathers to whom God showeth himself plainly, and who were setters forth of his word*]. 16. Moreover he called a famine upon the land and utterly brake the staff of bread [*Either by sending scarcity or by taking away the nourishment thereof*]. 17. But he sent a man before them: Joseph was sold for a slave. 18. They held his feet in the stocks, and he was laid in irons. 19. [*So long he suffered adversity as God had appointed, and till he had tried sufficiently his patience*] until his appointed time came, and the counsel of the Lord had tried him. 20. The king sent and loosed him: even the ruler of the people delivered him. . . 38. Egypt was glad at their departing [*for God's plagues caused them rather to depart with the Israelites than with their lives*]: for the fear of them had fallen upon them. 39. He spread a cloud to be a covering and fire to give light in the night. 40. They asked and he brought quails [*not for necessity, but for satisfying of their lust*] and he filled them with the bread of heaven. 41. He opened the rock and the waters flowed out and ran in the dry places like a river. 42. For he remembered his holy promise to Abraham his servant [*which he confirmeth to the posterity in whom, after a sort, the dead live and enjoy the promises*]. 43. And he brought forth his people with joy, and his chosen with gladness [*when the Egyptians lamented and were destroyed*]. 44. And gave them the lands of the heathen and they took the labours of the people in possession, 45. that they might keep his statutes and observe his laws. Praise ye the Lord. [*This is the end why God preserveth his church, because they should worship and call upon him in this world.*]

Isaiah 45.17–25

17. But Israel shall be saved in the Lord, with an everlasting salvation: shall not

be ashamed nor confounded world without end. 18. For thus saith the Lord (that created heaven, God himself, that formeth the earth and made it; he that prepared it, he created it not in vain, he formed it to be inhabited). I am the Lord and there is none other. 19. I have not spoken in secret, neither in a place of darkness in the earth: I said not in vain unto the seed of Jacob, seek you me: I the Lord do speak righteousness and declare righteous things . . . 25. The whole seed of Israel shall be justified and glory in the Lord.

Romans 3.10ff

10. As it is written, there is none righteous, no not one. 11. There is none that understandeth: there is none that seeketh God . . . 23. For there is no difference, for all have sinned and are deprived of the glory of God; 24. and are justified freely by his grace, through the redemption that is in Christ Jesus. 25. Whom God hath set forth to be a reconciliation through faith in his blood to declare his righteousness by the forgiveness of the sins that are passed through the patience of God.

Romans 8.28ff

28. Also we know that all things work together for the best unto them that love God, even to them that are called of his purpose. 29. For those which he knew before he also predestinate to be made like to the image of his Son, that he might be the first born among many brethren. [*He showeth by the order of our election that afflictions are means to make us like the son of God*] 30. Moreover whom he predestinate, them also he called, and whom he called, them also he justified, and whom he justified, them also he glorified. 31. What shall we then say to these things? If God be on our side, who can be against us?

1b *The King James Bible*

The 1611 translation was commissioned after the Hampton Court Conference to provide the first Bible santioned by the Church of England. It was dedicated to James I as head of the Church and State. Text from: The Authorised Version of 1611, fos A3v–B3.

The translators to the reader

Zeal to promote the common good, whether it be by devising any thing ourselves or revising that which hath been laboured by others, deserveth certainly much respect and esteem, but yet findeth but cold entertainment in the world. It is welcomed with suspicion instead of love . . .

But how shall men meditate in that which they cannot understand? How shall they understand that which is kept close in an unknown tongue? As it is written, *except I know the power of the voice, I shall be to him that speaketh, a barbarian, and he that speaketh, shall be a barbarian to me* [1 Cor. 14]. The Apostle excepteth no tongue; not Hebrew the ancientest; not Greek the most copious; not Latin the finest. Nature taught a natural man to confess that all of us, in those tongues which we do not understand, are plainly deaf; we may turn the deaf ear unto them. The Scythian counted the Athenian whom he did not understand, barbarous; so the Roman did the Syrian, and the Jew. . . . Therefore as one complaineth, that always in the senate of Rome, there was one or other that called for an interpreter: so lest the Church be driven to the like exigent, it is necessary to have translations in a readiness. Translation it is that openeth the window, to let in the light; that breaketh the shell, that we may eat the kernel; that putteth aside the curtain that we may look into the most holy place; that removeth the cover of the well, that we may come by the water, even as Jacob rolled away the stone from the mouth of the well, by which means the flocks of Laban were watered . . .

. . . Niceness in words was always counted the next step to trifling, and so was to be curious about names too; also that we cannot follow a better pattern for elocution than God himself; therefore he using divers words in his holy writ and indifferently for one thing in nature: we, if we will not be superstitious, may use the same liberty in our English versions out of Hebrew and Greek, for that copy or store He hath given us. Lastly we have on the one side avoided the scrupulosity of the Puritans, who leave the old Ecclesiastical words, and betake them to other, as when they put *washing* for *baptism*, and *congregation* instead of *Church*: as also on the other side we have shunned the obscurity of the Papists . . . whereof their late translation is full, and that of purpose to darken the sense, that since they must needs translate the Bible, yet by the language thereof it may be kept from being understood. But we desire that the Scripture may speak like itself, as in the language of Canaan, that it may be understood even of the very vulgar.

1.2 WILLIAM TYNDALE, *A PROLOGUE, SHOWING THE USE OF SCRIPTURE*

Tyndale urged a full translation of the Bible into English as early as 1528 when he was a young clergyman. He began his own translation, without Church authorisation, using the texts of Erasmus and Luther, and printing began in 1525 on the continent: it was banned in England in 1526, and burned at St. Paul's Cross, although within five years Henry VIII had set up a commission which agreed on the need for such a translation. Tyndale's commentaries on how to read the Scripture are exemplary of central Protestant tenets. Text from: *The Whole Works of William Tyndale*, edited by John Foxe, London 1573, pp. 3–5.

Though a man had a precious well, and a rich, yet if he wist not the value thereof, nor wherefore it served, he were neither the better, nor richer of a straw. Even so, though we read the Scripture and babble of it never so much, yet if we know not the use of it, and wherefore it was given, and what is therein to be sought, it profiteth us nothing at all. It is not enough therefore to read and talk of it only, but we must also desire God day and night instantly to open our eyes and to make us understand and feel, wherefore the Scripture was given, that we may apply the medicine of the Scripture, every man to his own sores, unless then we intend to be idle disputers, and brawlers about vain words, ever gnawing upon the bitter bark without, and never attaining unto the sweet pith within, and persecuting one another in defending of lewd imaginations and fantasies of our own inventions.

Paul in third of the second Epistle to Timothy saith, *that the Scripture is good to teach* (for that men ought to teach and not dreams of their own making, as the Pope doth) *and also to improve,* for the Scripture is the touchstone that trieth all doctrines, and by that we know the false from the true. And in the sixth to the Ephesians, he calleth it *the sword of the spirit,* by cause it killeth hypocrites and uttereth and improveth their false inventions. And in the fifteenth to the Romans he saith, *All that are written, are written for our learning, that we thorow patience and comfort of the Scripture, might have hope.* That is, the examples that are in the Scripture comfort us in all our tribulations and make us to put our trust in God and patiently to abide his leisure. And in the tenth of the first to the Corinthians, he bringeth in examples of the Scripture to fear us and to bridle the flesh, that we cast not the yoke of the law of God from our necks, and fall to lusting and doing of evil.

So know the Scripture is a light and showeth us the true way, both what to do and what to hope for. And a defence from all error, and a comfort in adversity that we despair not, and feareth us in prosperity that we sin not. Seek therefore in the Scripture as thou readest it, first the law, what God commandeth us to do. And secondly, the promises which God promiseth us again, namely in Christ Jesus our Lord. Then seek examples, first of comfort, how God purgeth all them that submit themselves to walk in his ways, in the purgatory of tribulation, delivering them yet at the latter end, and never suffering any of them to perish that cleave fast to his promises. And finally, note the examples which are written to fear the flesh, that we sin not. That is, how God suffereth the ungodly and wicked sinners that resist God and refuse to follow him, to continue in their wickedness, ever waxing worse and worse until their sin be so sore increased and so abominable that if they should longer endure, they would corrupt the very elect, but for the elects' sake God sendeth them preachers. Nevertheless, they harden their hearts against the truth and God destroyeth them utterly, and beginneth the world anew.

This comfort shalt thou evermore find in the plain text and literal sense. Neither is there any story so homely, so rude, yea or so vile (as it seemeth outward) wherein is not exceeding great comfort. And when some which seem to themselves great clerks, say: they wot not what more profit is in many gests of the Scripture, if they be read without an allegory, than in a tale of Robin Hood: say thou that they were written for our consolation and comfort, that we despair not, if such like happen unto us. We be not holier than Noah, though he were once drunk. Neither better beloved than Jacob, though his own son defiled his head. We be not holier than Lot, though his daughters through ignorance deceived him, nor peradventure holier than those daughters. Neither are we holier than David, though he brake wedlock, and upon the same committed abominable murder. All those men have witness of the Scripture that they pleased God and were good men, both before that those things chanced, and also after. Nevertheless, such things happened them for our example: not that we should counterfeit their evil, but if while we fight with ourselves, enforcing to walk in the law of God (as they did) we yet fall likewise, that we may despair not, but come again to the laws of God, and take better hold . . .

As thou readest therefore, think that every syllable pertaineth to thine own self, and suck out the pith of the Scripture, and arm thyself against all assaults. First note with strong faith the power of God in creating all of nought. Then mark the grievous fall of Adam, and of us all in him, through the light regarding of the commandment of God. In the third chapter God turneth him unto Abel and then to his offering, but not to Cain and his offering. Where thou seest that though the deeds of the evil appear outward as glorious as the deeds of the good, yet in the sight of God, which looketh on the heart, the deed is good because of the man, and not the man good because of his deed. In the sixth God sendeth Noah to preach to the wicked and giveth them space to repent: they were hard hearted, God bringeth them to nought, and yet saveth Noah: even by the same water by which he destroyeth them. Mark also what followed the pride of the building of the tower of Babel . . .

Finally see what God promised Joseph in his dreams. These promises accompanied him always, and went down with him even into the deep dungeon. And brought him up again. And never forsook him till all that was promised was fulfilled. These are examples written for our learning (as Paul saith) to teach us to trust in God in the strong fire of tribulation, and purgatory of our flesh. And that they which submit themselves to follow God should note and mark such things for learning and comfort is the fruit of the Scripture, and cause why it was written. And with such a purpose to read it is the way to everlasting life, and to those joyful blessings that are promised unto all nations in the seed of Abraham, which seed is Jesus Christ our Lord, to whom be honour and praise for ever and unto God our father through him. Amen.

1.3 THE BOOK OF COMMON PRAYER

The Book of Common Prayer contained the official order of service, the Church calendar, and the rules of ecclesiastical behaviour and conduct for both priest and people. The first edition of 1549 established the text, the order and dates of service that was to become the mainstay of the Church of England's practice. The 1552 edition was more radical, but the wording of the Holy Communion was amended in the 1559 edition (see below).

Each edition was prefaced with a full text of The Act of Uniformity (see 1.5). Text from: 1559 edition, London, preface, fos A3^v–A4^v fo. 125^r fo. 132^r 1552 edition, fos 120^v–123^v.

The preface

The people (by daily hearing of Holy Scripture read in the Church) should continually profit more and more in the knowledge of God and be the more inflamed with the love of his true religion. But these many years passed this godly and decent order of the ancient fathers hath been so altered, broken, and neglected by planting in uncertain stories, legends, responses, verses, vain repetitions, commemorations and synodals that commonly when any book of the Bible was begun, before three or four chapters were read out, all the rest are unread. . . . And moreover, whereas St. Paul would have such language spoken to the people in the Church, as they might understand and have profit by hearing the same: the service in this Church of England (these many years) hath been read in Latin to the people which they understood not, so that they have heard with their ears only: and their hearts, spirit and mind have not been edified thereby . . .

These inconveniences therefore considered: here is set forth such an order whereby the same shall be redressed. And for a readiness in this matter here is drawn out a calendar for that purpose which is plain and easy to be understanded, wherein (so much as may be) the reading of Holy Scripture is so set forth that all things shall be done in order, without breaking one piece thereof from another. For this cause be cut off anthems, responses, invitatories, and such like things, as did break the continual course of the reading of the Scripture. Yet because there is no remedy but that of necessity there must be some rules, therefore certain rules are here set forth, which as they be few in number so they be plain and easy to be understanded. So that here you have an order for prayer (as touching the reading of Holy Scripture) much agreeable to the mind and purpose of the old fathers and a great deal more profitable and commodious than that which of late was used. It is more profitable because here are left out many things whereof some be untrue, some uncertain, some vain and superstitious: and is ordained nothing to be read but the very pure word of God, the Holy Scriptures or that which is evidently grounded upon the same: and that in such a language and order as is most easy and plain for the understanding, both of the readers and hearers. It is also more commodious, both for the shortness thereof, and for the plainness of the order, and for that the rules be few and easy. Furthermore, by this order the curates shall need none other books for their public service but this book and the Bible, by the means whereof the people shall not be at so great charge for books, as in time past they have been . . .

Though it be appointed in the afore written preface that all things shall be read and sung in the church in the English tongue, to the end that the congregation may be thereby edified: yet it is not meant but when men say Matins and Evensong privately they may say the same in any language that they themselves do understand . . .

Of ceremonies: why some be abolished and some retained

. . . The most weighty cause of the abolishment of certain ceremonies was that they were so far abused, partly by the superstitious blindness of the rude and unlearned; and partly by the unsatiable avarice of such as sought more their own lucre than the glory of God, that the abuses could not well be taken away, the thing remaining still. But now as concerning those persons, which peradventure will be offended for that some of the old ceremonies are retained still: if they consider that without some ceremonies it is not possible to keep any order or quiet discipline in the church, they shall easily perceive just cause to reform their judgements. And if they think much that any of the old do remain and would rather have all devised anew, then such men granting some ceremonies convenient to be had, surely where the old may be well used, there they cannot reasonably reprove the old only for their age, without bewraying of their own folly. For in such a case they ought rather to have reverence unto them for their antiquity, if they will declare themselves to be more studious of unity and concord than of innovations and newfangledness which (as much as may be with the true setting forth of Christ's religion) is always to be eschewed . . .

* * *

The order for the administration of the Lord's Supper, or Holy Communion (1552)

So many as do intend to be partakers of the holy communion shall signify their names to the curate over night, or else in the morning, afore the beginning of morning prayer, or immediately after.

And if any of those be an open and notorious evil liver, so that the congregation by him is offended, or have done any wrong to his neighbours, by word or deed, the curate having knowledge thereof, shall call him and advertise him, in any wise not to presume to the Lord's table, until he have openly declared himself to have truly repented, and amended his former naughty life, that the congregation may thereby be satisfied, which afore were offended, and that he have recompensed the parties whom he hath done wrong unto, or at the least declare himself to be in full purpose so to do as soon as he conveniently may . . .

The table having at the communion time a fair white linen cloth upon it, shall stand in the body of the church, or in the chancel where morning prayer and evening prayer be appointed to be said. And the priest standing at the north side of the table shall say the Lord's Prayer with this collect following.

Almighty God unto whom all hearts be open, all desires known, and from whom no secrets are hid: cleanse the thoughts of our hearts by the inspiration of thy Holy Spirit that we may perfectly love thee and worthily magnify thy holy name: through Christ our Lord, Amen . . .

Then shall the minister first receive the communion in both kinds himself, and next deliver it to other ministers, if any be there present (that they may help the chief minister) and after to the people in their hands kneeling. And when he delivereth the bread he shall say:

Take and eat this in remembrance that Christ died for thee, and feed on him in thy heart by faith with thanksgiving.

And the minister that delivereth the cup shall say:

Drink this in remembrance that Christ's blood was shed for thee, and be thankful.

Then shall the priest say the Lord's Prayer, the people repeating him after every petition . . .

And to take away the superstition, which any person hath, or might have in the bread and wine, it shall suffice that the bread be such as is usual to be eaten at the table, with other meats, but the best and purest wheat bread that conveniently may be gotten. And if any of the bread or wine remain, the curate shall have it to his own use.

The bread and wine for the communion shall be provided by the curate and the churchwardens, at the charges of the parish, and the parish shall be discharged of such sums of money or other duties, which hitherto they have paid for the same, by order of their houses every Sunday.

And note that every parishioner shall communicate at least three times in the year, of which Easter to be one, and shall also receive the sacraments and other rites according to the order in this book appointed. And yearly at Easter every person shall reckon with his Parson, Vicar or Curate, or his or their deputy or deputies and pay to them, or him, all Ecclesiastical duties, accustomably due, then and at that time to be paid.

* * *

The order for the administration of the Lord's Supper, or Holy Communion: 1559

. . . And when he delivereth the bread he shall say:

The body of our Lord Jesu Christ which was given for thee, preserve thy body and soul into everlasting life; and take and eat this in remembrance that Christ died for thee and feed on him in thine heart by faith with thanksgiving.

And the minister that delivereth the cup shall say:

> *The blood of our Lord Jesu Christ which was shed for thee, preserve thy body and soul into everlasting life. And drink this in remembrance that Christ's blood was shed for thee and be thankful.*

* * *

Confirmation: wherein is contained a Catechism for children

It is thought good that none hereafter shall be confirmed, but such as can say in their mother tongue the articles of faith, the Lord's Prayer, and the ten commandments: and can also answer to such questions of this short catechism . . .

First, because that when children come to the years of discretion and have learned what their godfathers and godmothers promised for them in baptism, they may then themselves, with their own mouth and with their own consent, openly before the church, ratify and confess the same, and also promise that by the grace of God they will evermore endeavour themselves faithfully to observe and keep such things, as they by their own oath and confession have assented unto.

Secondly, forasmuch as confirmation is ministered to them that be baptised, that by imposition of hands and prayer, they may receive strength and defence against all temptation to sin, and the assaults of the world and the devil: it is most meet to be ministered when children come to that age, that partly by the frailty of their own flesh, partly by the assaults of the world and devil, they begin to be in danger to fall into sin.

1.4 *CERTAIN SERMONS OR HOMILIES*

The *Sermons* or *Homilies*, as the *Injunctions* (see Introduction and 5.4) and the *Canons* ordered, were provided for curates who were unlicensed to preach, who had to use the published homilies on prescribed Sundays. Text from: second edition, 1559, the preface; fos C1^r–C4^v.

Considering how necessary it is that the word of GOD, which is the only food of the soul and that most excellent light that we must walk by, in this our most dangerous pilgrimage should at all convenient times be preached unto the people, that thereby they may both learn their duty towards God, their prince and their neighbours according to the mind of the Holy Ghost expressed in the Scriptures. And also to avoid the manifold enormities which heretofore by false doctrine have crept into the Church of God, and how that all they which are appointed ministers have not the gift of preaching sufficiently to instruct the people which is committed unto them, whereof great inconveniences might rise and ignorance still be maintained, if some honest remedy be not speedily found and provided. The Queen's most excellent Majesty, tendering the sole health of

23

her loving subjects and the quieting of their consciences in the chief and principal points of Christian religion and willing also by the true setting forth and pure declaring of God's word, which is the principal guide and leader unto all godliness and virtue, to expel and drive away as well all corrupt, vicious and poisoned doctrines, tending to superstition and idolatry: hath by the advice of her most honourable counsellors, for her discharge in this behalf, caused a *Book of Homilies* . . . to be printed anew, wherein are contained certain wholesome and godly exhortations, to move the people to honour and worship almighty God, and diligently to serve him, everyone according to their degree, state and vocation. All which homilies her Majesty commandeth and straightly chargeth all parsons, vicars, curates and all other having spiritual cure, every Sunday and holy day in the year at the ministering of the holy communion, or if there be no communion ministered that day, yet after the Gospel and Creed, in such order and place as is appointed by the Book of Common Prayers, to read and declare to their parishioners plainly and distinctly one of the said homilies in such order as they stand in the book, except there be a sermon according as it is enjoined in the book of her highness's *Injunctions* . . .

An homily of the misery of all mankind, and of his condemnation to death everlasting by his own sin

The holy ghost, in writing the Holy Scripture, is in nothing more diligent than to pull down man's vainglory and pride, which of all vices is most universally grafted in all mankind, even from the first infection of our first father Adam. And therefore we read in many places of Scripture, many notable lessons against this old rooted vice, to teach us the most commendable virtue of humility, how to know ourselves, and to remember what be of ourselves. In the book of Genesis, Almighty God giveth us all a title and a name in our great grandfather Adam, which ought to admonish us all to consider what we be, whereof we be, from whence we came, and whither we shall: saying thus: in the sweat of thy face shalt thou eat thy bread, till thou be turned again into the ground: for out of it wast thou taken, inasmuch as thou art dust, and into dust shalt thou be turned again. Here (as it were in a glass) we may learn to know ourselves to be but ground, earth, and ashes, and that to earth and ashes we shall return . . .

. . . And the holy prophet Job having in himself great experience of the miserable and sinful estate of man, doth open the same to the world in these words: man (saith he) that is born of a woman, living but a short time, is full of manifold miseries, he springeth up like a flower, and fadeth again, vanishing away, as it were a shadow, and never continueth in one state [Job. 14]. And dost thou judge it meet (o, Lord) to open thine eyes upon such a one and to bring him to judgement with thee? Who can make him clean that is conceived of an unclean seed? And all men of their evilness and natural proneness were so universally given to sin that (as the Scripture saith [Genesis 5,6]) God repented that ever he made man. And by sin his indignation was so much provoked against the world that he drowned all the world with Noah's flood (except Noah himself and his little household). It is not without great cause that the Scripture of God doth so many times call all men here in this world by this word, earth. O, thou earth, earth, earth, saith Jeremiah: hear the word of the Lord. This our right name, vocation and title: earth, earth, earth, pronounced by the prophet, showeth what we be in deed, by whatsoever other style, title or dignity men do call us . . .

Thus we have heard how evil we be of ourselves, how of ourselves and by our selves we have no goodness, help, nor salvation; but, contrariwise, sin, damnation and death everlasting, which if we deeply weigh and consider, we shall the better understand the great mercy of God and how our salvation cometh only by Christ [2 Corinth. 3]. For in ourselves, as of our selves, we find nothing whereby we may be delivered from this miserable captivity into the which we were cast through the envy of the devil, by transgressing of God's commandment in our first parent Adam. We are all become unclean [Psalm. 1], but we all are not able to cleanse ourselves, nor to make one another of us clean [Ephes. 2]. We are by nature the children of God's wrath, but we are not able to make ourselves the children and inheritors of God's glory [1 Peter 2]. We are sheep that run astray, but we cannot of our own power come again to the sheepfold, so great is our imperfection and weakness. In ourselves therefore, may not we glory, which of ourselves are nothing but sinful: neither may we rejoice in any works that we do, which all be so unperfect and unpure that they are not able to stand before the righteous throne of God, as the holy prophet David saith: enter not into judgement with thy servant, O Lord, for no man that liveth shall be found righteous in thy sight.

1.5 AN ACT FOR THE UNIFORMITY OF COMMON PRAYER AND SERVICE IN THE CHURCH, AND THE ADMINISTRATION OF THE SACRAMENTS

The Acts of Uniformity and Supremacy were key statutory expressions of the new faith, the status of a national Church and its enforcement by the State. Text from: the 1559 *Book of Common Prayer* (see 1.3): 1. Eliz. cap. 2.

And further be it enacted by the Queen's highness, with the assent of the Lords and Commons, in this present Parliament assembled, and by authority of the same, that all and singular ministers, in any Cathedral or parish Church, or other place within this realm of England, Wales and the marches of the same, or other the Queen's dominions: shall from, and after the feast of the nativity of Saint John Baptist next coming be bounden to say and use the Matins, Evensong, celebration of the Lord's Supper and administration of each of the sacraments, and all their common and open prayer in such order and form as is mentioned in the said book, so authorised by Parliament in the said fifth and sixth year of the reign of King Edward the Sixth, with one alteration or addition of certain lessons to be used on every Sunday in the year, and the form of the Litany altered and corrected, and two sentences only added in the delivery of the sacrament to the communicants, and none other or otherwise. And that if any manner of parson, vicar or other whatsoever minister that ought or should sing or say common prayer mentioned in the said book, or minister the sacraments from and after the feast of the nativity of Saint John Baptist next coming, refuse to use the said common prayers, or to minister the sacraments in such Cathedral or parish Church, or other places, as he should use to minister the same, in such order and form as they be mentioned and set forth in the said book, or shall wilfully or obstinately standing in the same, use any other rite, ceremony, order, form or manner of celebrating of the Lord's Supper openly or privily, or Matins, Evensong, administration of the sacraments, or other open prayers than is mentioned and set forth in the said book . . . or shall preach, declare or speak anything in the derogation or depraving of the said book, or anything therein contained, or of any part thereof, and shall be thereof lawfully convicted, according to the laws of this realm, by verdict of twelve men, or by his own confession, or by the notorious evidence of the fact, shall lose and forfeit to the Queen's highness, her heirs and successors, for his first offence, the profit of all his spiritual benefices or promotions, coming or arising in one whole year next after this conviction. And also that the person so convicted, shall for the same offence suffer imprisonment by the space of six months without bail or mainprise . . .

And if the person that shall offend and be convict in form aforesaid, concerning any of the premises, shall not be beneficed, nor have any spiritual promotion: that then the same person so offending and convict shall for the first offence suffer imprisonment during one whole year next after his said conviction, without bail or maintenance. And if any such person, not having any spiritual promotion, after his first conviction, shall eftsoons offend in any thing concerning the premises, and that in form aforesaid, be thereof lawfully convicted that then the same person shall for his second offence suffer imprisonment during his life.

And it is ordained and enacted by the authority above said that if any person or persons whatsoever after the said feast of the nativity of Saint John Baptist next coming, shall in any interludes, plays, songs, rhymes or by other open words declare or speak any thing in the derogation, depraving or despising of the same book, or of anything therein contained, or any part thereof, or shall by open fact, deed, or by open threatenings, compel or cause, or otherwise procure or maintain any parson, vicar, or other minister, in any cathedral, or parish church, or in chapel, or in any other place to sing or say any common and open prayer, or to minister any sacrament otherwise, or in any other manner and form than is mentioned in the said book, or that by any of the said means shall unlawfully interrupt or let any parson, vicar, or other minister in any Cathedral or parish Church, Chapel or any other place to sing or say common and open prayer, or to minister the sacraments or any of them in such manner and form as is mentioned in the said book: that then every such person being thereof lawfully convicted in form above said shall forfeit to the Queen our sovereign lady, her heirs and successors, for the first offence a hundred marks . . . [and] all and every person and persons inhabiting within this realm or any other the Queen's Majesty's dominions shall diligently and faithfully, having no lawful or reasonable excuse to be absent, endeavour themselves to resort to their parish Church or Chapel accustomed, or upon reasonable let thereof, to some usual place where Common Prayer and such service of God shall be used in such time of let, upon every Sunday and other days ordained and used to be kept as holy days. And then and there to abide orderly and soberly during the time of the common prayer, preachings, or other service of God, there to be used and ministered upon pain of punishment by the censures of the church. And also upon pain that every person so offending shall forfeit for every such offence xii.d. to be levied by the churchwardens of the parish, where such offences shall be done, to the use of the poor of the same parish, of the goods, lands and tenements of such offender by way or distress. And for due execution thereof, the Queen's most excellent Majesty, the Lords Temporal and all the Commons in this present Parliament assembled doth in God's name earnestly require and charge all Archbishops, Bishops, and other ordinaries that they shall endeavour themselves to the uttermost of their knowledges, that the due and true execution hereof may be had throughout their diocese and charges, as they will answer before God for such evils and plagues wherewith Almighty God may justly punish his people for neglecting this good and wholesome law . . .

And it is ordained and enacted by the authority aforesaid that all and every Justices . . . Assize shall have full power and authority in every of their open and general sessions to enquire here and determine all, and all manner of, offences that shall be committed and done contrary to any article conveyed in this present act, within the limits of the Commission to them directed, and to make process for the execution of the same, as they may do against any person being indicted before them of trespass or lawfully convicted thereof.

1.6 JOHN JEWEL, *AN APOLOGY OR ANSWER IN DEFENCE OF THE CHURCH OF ENGLAND*

In 1562, Bishop Jewel was asked by Queen Elizabeth to publish a defence of the status and position of the new Church of England, most particularly for Catholic critics in Europe, although it also served as a statement of faith at home. Originally written in Latin, it was much translated into English during the sixteenth and seventeenth centuries. It provides a useful summary of the attacks made against the Church of England by the Catholic Church, as well as the typical mode of defence: a return to the primitive Church and the definition of right faith proven by minority suffering. The language and argument of this defence also informs the Acts of Uniformity and

Supremacy (see 1.5). Text from: trans. Lady Anne Bacon (née Cooke), 1562, pp. 2–5.

Who is ignorant that there were men in times past which accused the Holy Scriptures of lies, saying that they contained things plain contrary and repugnant one to another; and that the Apostles did dissent every one from another, and Paul from them all? And lest it should be too long to rehearse all, for that were infinite: who is ignorant how that our fathers which first began to acknowledge and to possess the name of Christ, were slanderously reported of? That they conspired together amongst themselves, and that in their secret assemblies they had consultations against the State over the commonwealth, and that even therefore their meetings were appointed before day in the dark, that they killed young children, filled themselves with man's flesh, and, like most evil beasts, drank men's blood. And how that, at the last, when the candles were out, they committed adultery and incest at adventure together, the brother with the sister, the son with the mother . . .

All these things in those days were spoken against the people of God, against Christ Jesus, against Paul, against Stephen, and against all those that in the primitive Church embraced the truth of the Gospel and were content to be called by the name of Christians, a name at those days very odious amongst the people. And albeit those things were not true, yet the devil thought it enough for him if at the least he could bring it to pass to cause them to be taken for true and that the Christians should be hated of all men, and by all men persecuted unto the death. Wherefore kings and princes, led by such persuasions, killed the prophets of God, even to the last man. Esau they condemned to the saw, Jeremy to be stoned, Daniel to the lions, Amos to the club, Paul to the sword, Christ to the cross, all Christian men to prisons, to tortures in horses' bellies, to the gallows, to rocks, to dives, to wild beasts, to fire. Yea, and they sticked not to make great bonfires of their living bodies, only for a light to serve them in the night season, and for a scorn, of whom they made none other account than as of most vile dung, and as of accursed persons appointed to be slain for sacrifice and to be a scorn of all the world. Thus, I say, the maintainers and professors of the truth hath been always dealt withal.

So much the more ought we that have taken upon us the profession of the Gospel of Jesus Christ, to take it in better part, if in the same quarrel we be handled after the same sort, and like as our forefathers in times past, so we at this day, without any our desert, only because we teach and profess the truth, are vexed with slanderous names, reproaches and lies.

Nowadays they cry everywhere that all we are heretics, that we are departed from the faith and that we with our new persuasions and wicked doctrine have broke the consent of the Church; that we do raise as it were out of hell, and restore to life again old heresies, and such as long ago were condemned. We sow abroad new sects and furious fancies, that never before were heard of; also that we now are divided into contrary factions and opinions and could never agree by any means among ourselves; that we are wicked men and make war after the manner of the giants (as the fable is) against God himself; and do live together without care or reverence of God; that we do despise all good deeds, and use no discipline of virtue, maintain no laws, no customs, no equity, no justice, no right; that we loose the bridle to all mischief and allure the people to all kind of licence and lust; that we go about and seek how all the states of monarchies and kingdoms might be overthrown, and that all things might be brought unto the rash government of the people, and to the rule of the unskilful multitude; that we have rebelliously withdrawn ourselves from the Catholic Church, and shaken the whole world with accursed schism, and have troubled the common peace and the general quietness of the Church; and that like as in times past Dathan and Abiron severed themselves from Moses and Aaron, so we at this day depart from the Pope of Rome without any sufficient and just cause. As for the authority of the ancient fathers and old councils, we do set at naught. All ancient ceremonies, such as our grandfathers and great grandfathers now many ages past, when better manners and better days did flourish, were approved, we have rashly and arrogantly abolished, and have brought into the Church by our own private authority, without any commandment of any holy and sacred general council, new rites and ceremonies; and that we have done all these things not for any respect of religion, but only of a desire to maintain strife and contention. As for them, they have changed utterly nothing at all, but all things even as they received them from the Apostles, and were approved by the most ancient fathers, so they have kept them from age to age.

1.7 JOHN FOXE, *ACTS AND MONUMENTS*

Foxe's *Book of Martyrs*, as it was more popularly known, was first published in 1563, and went through seven editions by 1631: in 1571 it was ordered to be set in all collegiate and Cathedral Churches. Many spiritual autobiographies refer to its central influence in spiritual comfort, as well as demonstrating its role in forming a national religious consciousness: Margaret Hoby (1.15) is one such example. Text from: first edition, 1563, fos 677b; 1,613b–1,615b.

The martyrdom of Ann Askew

Hitherto we have entreated of this good woman, now it remaineth that we touch somewhat as touching her end and martyrdom. She being born of such stock and kindred that she might have lived in great wealth and prosperity if she would rather have followed the world than Christ, but now she was so tormented that she could neither live long in so great distress, neither yet by the adversaries be suffered to die in secret. Wherefore the day of her execution was appointed and she was brought into Smithfield in a chair because she could not go on her feet, by means of her great torments, when she was brought unto the stake she was tied by the middle with a chain, that held up her body, when all things were thus prepared to the fire, the king's letters of pardon were brought whereby to offer her safeguard of her life if she would recant, which she would neither receive, neither yet vouchsafe once to look upon. Shaxton also was there present who openly that day recanting his opinions, went about with a long oration to cause her also to turn, against whom she stoutly resisted. Thus she being troubled so many manner of ways, and having passed through so many torments, having now ended the long course of her agonies, being compassed in with flames of fire, as a blessed sacrifice unto God, she slept in the Lord, in an.1546, leaving behind her a singular example of Christian constancy for all men to follow.

George Eagles

Among other martyrs of singular virtue and constancy, one George Eagles deserveth not the least admiration, but is so much the more to be commended for that he, having little learning or none, most manfully served and fought under the banner of Christ's Church.

. . . we ought to glorify God the more thereby in his holiness, which in so blind a time inspired him with the gift of preaching, and constancy of suffering, who after a certain time he had used the occupation of a tailor, being eloquent and of good utterance, gave and applied himself to the profit of Christ's Church . . .

Now when he had been profited Christ's Church in this sort by going about and preaching the Gospel a year or two, and especially in Colchester, and the quarters thereabout. . . . And albeit it was well known that poor Eagles never did anything seditiously against the Queen, yet to cloak an honest matter withal and to cause him to be the more hated of the people, they turned religion into a civil offence and crime, and though he defended his cause stoutly and boldly, making a full declaration of his religion or faith before the judges, yet could he not bring it to pass by any means but that he must needs be indicted (as is said) of treason . . .

With him were cast certain thieves also, and the next day when they were brought out to be executed with him, there happened a thing that did much declare the innocency and godliness of this man. For being led between two thieves to the place where he should suffer . . . one William Swallow of Chelmsford, a bailiff . . . did hackle off his head and sometime hit his neck and sometime his chin, and did foully mangle him, and so opened him. Notwithstanding this blessed martyr of Christ abode steadfast and constant in the very midst of his torments.

His head was set up at Chelmsford on the Market Cross, on a long pole, and there stood till the wind did blow it down, and lying certain days in the street tumbled about, one caused it to be buried in the Churchyard in the night. Also a wonderful work of God was it that he showed on this wicked Bailiff Swallow, who within short space after this was so punished that all the hair went well near off his head, his eyes as it were closed up and could scantly see, the nails of his fingers and toes went clean off.

1.8 *THE THIRTY-NINE ARTICLES*

In 1563 Parliament and Convocation met to discuss the religious settlement of 1559: and the series of articles printed here were agreed by the majority of convocation. Dissent to the articles from Protestants loyal to the crown marked the emergence of dissent within the Established Church between 'puritans' and moderates. The Articles were not made statute law until 1571, when agreement to the ambiguous wording on the Eucharist was finally achieved. Text from: first edition, 1571.

6. Of the sufficiency of the Holy Scriptures for salvation

Holy Scripture containeth all things necessary to salvation: so that whatsoever is not read therein, nor may be proved thereby, is not to be required of any man, that it should be believed as an article of the faith, or be thought requisite or necessary to salvation. In the name of the Holy Scripture, we do understand those canonical books of the Old and New Testament . . .

9. Of original or birth sin

Original sin standeth not in the following of Adam (as the Pelagians do vainly talk) but it is the fault and corruption of the nature of every man, that naturally is engendered of the offspring of Adam; whereby man is very far gone from original righteousness, and is of his own nature inclined to evil, so that the flesh lusteth always contrary to the spirit, and therefore in every person born into this world, it deserveth God's wrath and damnation. And this infection of nature doth remain, yea in them that are regenerated . . .

10. Of free will

The condition of man after the fall of Adam is such that he cannot turn and prepare himself by his own natural strength and good works, to faith and calling upon God. Wherefore we have no power to do good works pleasant and acceptable to God, without the grace of God by Christ preventing us: that we may have a good will; and working with us when we have that good will.

12. Of good works

Albeit that good works, which are the fruits of faith and follow after justification, cannot put away our sins; and endure the severity of God's judgement: yet are they pleasing and acceptable to God in Christ, and do spring out necessarily of a true and lively faith, insomuch, that by them a lively faith may be as evidently known, as a tree discerned by the fruit.

17. Of predestination and election

Predestination to life is the everlasting purpose of God, whereby (before the foundations of the world were laid) he hath constantly decreed by his counsel secret to us, to deliver from curse and damnation those whom he hath chosen in Christ out of mankind, and to bring them by Christ to everlasting salvation as vessels made to honour. Wherefore, they which be endued with so excellent a benefit of God, be called according to God's purpose by his spirit working in due season: they through grace obey the calling; they be justified freely; they be made sons of God by adoption; they be made like the image of his only begotten son Jesus Christ; they walk religiously in good works and at length by God's mercy they attain to everlasting felicity.

As the godly consideration of predestination, and our election in Christ is full of sweet, pleasant and unspeakable comfort to godly persons and such as feel in themselves the working of the spirit of Christ, mortifying the works of the flesh and their earthly members, and drawing up their mind to high and heavenly things, as well because it doth greatly establish and confirm their faith of eternal salvation to be enjoyed through Christ, as because it doth fervently kindle their love towards God: so, for curious and carnal persons, lacking the spirit of Christ, to have continually before their eyes the sentence of God's predestination, is a most dangerous downfall, whereby the Devil doth thrust them either into desperation, or into wretchedness of most unclean living, no less perilous than desperation . . .

19. Of the Church

The visible church of Christ is a congregation of faithful men, in the which the pure word of God is preached and the sacraments be duly ministered, according to Christ's ordinance in all those things that of necessity are requisite to the same . . .

20. Of the authority of the Church

The Church hath power to decree rites or ceremonies, and authority in controversies of faith: and yet it is not lawful for the Church to ordain anything that is contrary to God's word written, neither may it so expound one place of Scripture that it be repugnant to another. Wherefore, although the Church be a witness and a keeper of holy writ: yet, as it ought not to decree anything against the same, so besides the same, ought it not to enforce anything to be believed for necessity of salvation.

23. Of ministering in the congregation

It is not lawful for any man to take upon him the office of public preaching, or ministering the sacraments in the congregation, before he be lawfully called and sent to execute the same. And those we ought to judge lawfully called and sent, which be chosen and called to this work by men who have public authority given unto them in the congregation, to call and send ministers into the Lord's vineyard.

24. Of speaking in the congregation, in such a tongue as the people understandeth

It is a thing plainly repugnant to the word of God and the custom of the primitive church, to have public prayer in the church or to minister the sacraments in a tongue not to be understanded of the people.

25. Of the sacraments

Sacraments ordained of Christ be not only badges or tokens of Christian men's profession: but rather they be certain sure witnesses and effectual signs of grace and God's good will towards us, by the which he doth work invisibly in us, and doth not only quicken but also strengthen and confirm our faith in him.

There are two sacraments ordained of Christ our Lord in the Gospel, that is to say, baptism and the Supper of the Lord. Those five commonly called sacraments, that is to say, confirmation, penance, orders, matrimony and extreme unction, are not to be counted for sacraments of the gospel.

The sacraments were not ordained of Christ to be gazed upon, or to be carried about: but that we should duly use them . . .

32. Of the marriage of priests

Bishops, priests, and deacons are not commanded by God's law either to vow the estate of single life, or to abstain from marriage. Therefore it is lawful also for them as for all other Christian men to marry at their own discretion, as they shall judge the same to serve better to godliness.

33. Of excommunicate persons, how they are to be avoided

That person which by open denunciation of the Church is rightly cut off from the unity of the Church and excommunicated, ought to be taken of the whole multitude of the faithful as an heathen and publican until he be openly reconciled by penance, and received into the Church by a judge that hath authority thereunto.

34. Of the traditions of the Church

It is not necessary that traditions and ceremonies be in all places one or utterly like, for at all times they have been diverse and may be changed according to the diversity of the countries, times and men's manners, so that nothing be ordained against God's word. Whosoever through his private judgement willingly and purposely doth openly break the traditions and ceremonies of the Church, which be not repugnant to the word of God, and be ordained and approved by common authority, ought to be rebuked openly (that other may fear to do the like), as he that offendeth against the common order of the Church, and hurteth the authority of the magistrate, and woundeth the consciences of the weak brethren.

Every particular or national Church hath authority to ordain change and abolish ceremonies or rites of the Church ordained only by man's authority, so that all things be done to edifying.

38. Of Christian men's goods, which are not common

The riches and goods of Christians are not common, as touching the right, title, and possession of the same, as certain Anabaptists do falsely boast. Notwithstanding, every man ought of such things as he posesseth, liberally to give alms to the poor, according to his ability.

1.9 ARCHBISHOP PARKER, *THE ADVERTISEMENTS*

As Archbishop of Canterbury, Parker was asked by Elizabeth I to enforce greater conformity amongst clergy in matters of preaching, doctrine and dress. However, some clergy continued to resist his strictures, on the grounds that they were never officially sanctioned by the Queen. The text in many cases echoes the Queen's *Injunctions*, which were published with *The Book of Common Prayer*. Successive attempts by Archbishops to impose uniformity and order, from Parker to Laud, tended to provoke a 'puritan' reaction: in this case, debates about Church government, appropriate dress and ritual (see 1.12 and 1.13). Text from: first edition, 1566, fos A1ʳff.

Articles for doctrine and preaching

First that all they which shall be admitted to preach shall be diligently examined for their conformity in unity of doctrine, established by public authority; and admonished to use sobriety and discretion in teaching the people; namely in matters of controversy; and to consider the gravity of their office, and to foresee with diligence the matters which they will speak, to utter them to the edification of the audience.

Item, that they set out in their preaching the reverent estimation of the holy sacraments of baptism and the Lord's supper, exciting the people to the often and devout receiving of the Holy Communion of the body and blood of Christ in such form as is already prescribed in the *Book of Common Prayer*, and as it is further declared in a Homily concerning the virtue and efficacy of the said sacraments.

Item, that they move the people to all obedience, as well in observation of the orders appointed in the book of common service, as in the Queen's Majesty's *Injunctions*, as also of all other civil duties due for subjects to do . . .

Item, if any preacher or parson, vicar or curate so licensed, shall fortune to preach any matter tending to dissension or to the derogation of the religion and doctrine received, that the hearers denounce the same to the ordinaries, or the next bishop of the same place; but no man openly to contrary or to impugn the same speech so disorderly uttered. Whereby may grow offence and disquiet of the people; but shall be convinced and reproved by the ordinary after such agreeable order, as shall be seen to him according to the gravity of the offence. And that it be presented within one month after the words spoken . . .

Articles for administration of prayer and sacraments

First that the common prayer be said or sung decently and distinctly, in such place as the ordinary shall think meet for the largeness and straitness of the church and choir, so that the people may be most edified.

Item, that no parson or curate, not admitted by the bishop of the diocese to preach, do expound in his own cure, or elsewhere, any Scripture or matter of doctrine, or by the way of exhortation, but only study to read gravely and aptly without any glossing of the same, or any additions, the *Homilies* already set out, or other such necessary doctrine as is or shall be prescribed for the quiet instruction and edification of the people . . .

Item, that they shall decently cover with carpet, silk, or other decent covering, and with a fair linen cloth (at the time of the ministration) the communion table and to set the Ten Commandments upon the east wall, over the said table.

Item, that all communicants do receive kneeling and as is appointed by the laws of the realm and the Queen's Majesty's *Injunctions*.

Item, that the font be not removed, nor that the curate do baptise in parish churches in any basins, nor in any other form than is already prescribed . . .

Item, that on Sundays there be no shops open, nor artificers commonly going about their affairs worldly, and that in all fairs and common markets falling upon the Sunday, there be no showing of any wares before the service be done . . .

Articles for outward apparel of persons ecclesiastical

First that all archbishops and bishops do use and continue their customed apparel . . .

Item, that all inferior ecclesiastical persons shall wear long gowns of the fashion aforesaid, and caps as afore is prescribed.

Item, that all poor parsons, vicars and curates do endeavour themselves to conform their apparel in like sort so soon and as conveniently as their ability will serve to the same. Provided that their ability be judged by the bishop of the diocese . . .

Protestations to be made, promised, and subscribed by them that shall hereafter be admitted to any office, room or cure in any church or other place ecclesiastical

Imprimis, I shall not preach or publicly interpret, but only read that which is appointed by public authority, without special licence of the bishop under his seal.

I shall read the service appointed plainly, distinctly and audibly, that all the people may hear and understand.

I shall keep the register book according to the Queen's Majesty's Injunctions.

I shall use sobriety in apparel and especially in the church at common prayers, according to order appointed.

I shall move the parishioners to quiet and concord and not give them cause of offence, and shall help to reconcile them which be at variance, to my uttermost power.

I shall read daily at the least one chapter of the Old Testament, and one other of the New, with good advisement to the increase of my knowledge.

I do also faithfully promise in my person to use and exercise my office and place to the honour of God, to the quiet of the Queen's subjects within my charge, in truth, concord and unity; and also to observe, keep and maintain such order and uniformity in all external policy, rites, and ceremonies of the Church, as by the laws, good usages, and orders are already well provided and established.

I shall not openly intermeddle with any artificer's occupations, as covetously to seek a gain thereby, having in ecclesiastical living to the sum of twenty nobles or above by year.

1.10 *PAPAL BULL*

In 1570 the long threatened excommunication of Elizabeth was pronounced by Rome: it placed English Catholics in a difficult position, although most remained loyal to the Queen. Text translated by Elton, in *Tudor Constitution*, pp. 425–7.

1. . . . the number of the ungodly has so much grown in power that there is no place left in the world which they have not tried to corrupt with their most wicked doctrines; and among others, Elizabeth the pretended Queen of England and the servant of crime has assisted in this, with whom as in a sanctuary the most pernicious of all have found refuge. This very woman, having seized the crown and monstrously usurped the place of supreme head of the Church in all England, together with the chief authority and jurisdiction belonging to it, has

once again reduced this same kingdom, which had already been restored to the Catholic faith and to good fruits, to a miserable ruin.

2. Prohibiting with a strong hand the use of the true religion, which after its earlier overthrow by Henry VIII (a deserter therefrom) Mary, the lawful Queen of famous memory, had with the help of this See restored, she has followed and embraced the errors of the heretics. She has removed the royal council, composed of the nobility of England, and has filled it with obscure men, being heretics; oppressed the followers of the Catholic faith; instituted false preachers and ministers of impiety; abolished the sacrifice of mass, prayers, fasts, choice of meats, celibacy, and Catholic ceremonies; and has ordered that books of manifestly heretical content be propounded to the whole realm and that impious rites and institutions after the rule of Calvin, entertained and observed by herself, be also observed by her subjects . . .

3. We, seeing impieties and crimes multiplied one upon another, the persecution of the faithful and afflictions of religion daily growing more severe under the guidance and by the activity of the said Elizabeth . . . are compelled by necessity to take up against her the weapons of justice . . . we do out of the fullness of our apostolic power declare the foresaid Elizabeth to be a heretic and favourer of heretics, and her adherents in the matters aforesaid to have incurred the sentence of excommunication and to be cut off from the unity of the body of Christ.

4. And moreover [we declare] her to be deprived of her pretended title to the aforesaid crown and of all lordship, dignity and privilege whatsoever.

5. And also [declare] the nobles, subjects and people of the said realm, and all others who have in any way sworn oaths to her, to be forever absolved from such an oath and from any duty arising from lordship, fealty and obedience; and we do, by authority of these presents, so absolve them and so deprive the same Elizabeth of her pretended title to the crown and all other the abovesaid matters.

1.11 *AN ADMONITION TO PARLIAMENT*

In 1570 Thomas Cartwright, a popular puritan preacher and divine in Cambridge, in a series of lectures on the Acts of the Apostles, compared the English Church to the early Church, but attacked episcopacy, thus fuelling a debate in radical Protestant circles about the formal and hierarchial direction in which the Church of England seemed to be heading. *An Admonition to Parliament* presented these arguments directly to Parliament in 1572. Text from: W. H. Frere and C. E. Douglas, *Puritan Manifestos*, 1907, pp. 9–17.

May it therefore please your wisdoms to understand we in England are so far off from having a Church rightly reformed, according to the prescript of God's word that as yet we are not come to the outward face of the same. For to speak of that wherein all consent and whereupon all writers accord: the outward marks whereby a true Christian Church is known are preaching the word purely, ministering of the sacraments sincerely, and ecclesiastical discipline which consisteth in admonition and correction of faults severely. Touching the first, namely the ministry of the word, although it must be confessed that the substance of doctrine by many delivered is sound and good, yet herein it faileth that neither the minsters thereof are according to God's word proved, elected, called or ordained, nor the function in such sort so narrowly looked unto as of right it ought and is of necessity required . . .

. . . Now to the second point, which concerneth ministration of sacraments. In the old time, the word was preached before they were ministered; now it is supposed to be sufficient if it be read. Then, they were ministered in public assemblies, now in private houses. Then by ministers only, now by midwives and deacons equally . . To redress these, your wisdoms have to remove (as before) ignorant ministers . . . To join assistance of elders and other officers, that seeing men will not examine themselves, they may be examined and brought to render a reason of their hope . . . That people be appointed to receive the sacrament rather sitting for avoiding of superstition, than kneeling, having in it the outward show of evil from which we must abstain. That excommunication be restored to his old former force. That papists nor other, neither constrainedly nor customably, communicate in the mysteries of salvation. That both the sacrament of the Lord's supper and baptism also may be ministered according to the ancient purity and simplicity . . .

Let us now come to the third part, which concerneth ecclesiastical discipline. The offices that have to deal in this charge are chiefly three: ministers, preachers, or pastors, of whom before; seniors or elders; and deacons. Concerning seniors, not only their office, but their name also is out of this English Church utterly removed. Their office was to govern the church with the rest of the ministers, to consult, to admonish, to correct and to order all things appertaining to the state of the congregation. Instead of these seniors in every Church, the pope has brought in, and we yet maintain, the lordship of one man over many churches, yea over sundry shires. These seniors, then, because their charge was not overmuch, did execute their offices in their own persons without substitutes. Our lords bishops have their under-officers . . . and such like. Touching deacons, though their names be remaining, yet is the office foully perverted and turned upside-down, for their duty in the primitive Church was to gather the alms diligently and to distribute it faithfully, also for the sick and impotent persons to provide painfully, having ever a diligent care that the charity of godly men were not wasted upon loiterers and vagabonds. . . . The final end of this discipline is the reforming of the disordered, and to bring them to repentance and to bridle such as would offend. The chiefest part and last punishment of this discipline is excommunication, by the consent of the Church determined, if the offender be obstinate, which how miserably it hath been by the Pope's proctors and is by our new canonists abused, who seeth not? In the primitive Church it was in many men's hands: now one alone excommunicateth. In those days it was the last censure of the Church, and never went forth but for notorious crimes: now it is pronounced for every light trifle.

1.12 RICHARD FITZ, THE SEPARATIST *COVENANT*

Fitz was the minister of a congregation at St. Mark's in London, which covenanted its separation from the Church of England: he died in prison for offending against the terms of The Act of Uniformity. Text from: C. Burrage, *Early English Dissenters*, Cambridge, 1912, pp. 13–18.

The Covenant

Being thoroughly persuaded in my conscience by the working and by the word of the almighty, that these relics of Antichrist be abominable before the Lord our God.

And also for that by the power and mercy, strength and goodness of the Lord my God only, I am escaped from the filthiness and pollution of these detestable traditions, through the knowledge of our Lord and saviour Jesus Christ.

And last of all, inasmuch as by the working also of the Lord Jesus his holy spirit, I have joined in prayer and hearing God's word with those that have not yielded to this idolatrous trash, notwithstanding the danger for not coming to my parish church, etc.

Therefore I come not back again to the preachings, etc. of them that have received these marks of the Romish beast.

1. Because of God's commandment to go forward to perfection: Hebrew 6.1; 2 Corinth. 7.1; . . . Also to avoid them: Romans 16.17; Ephes. 5. verse 11 . . .

2. Because they are abominations before the Lord our God. Deut. 7 verse 25 and 26; Deutero. 13.17; Ezekiel. 14.6.

3. I will not beautify with my presence those filthy rags which bring the heavenly word of the eternal our Lord God into bondage, subjection and slavery.

4. Because I would not communicate with other men's sins. 2 John 9,10, 11;2 Corinth. 6.17. Touch no unclean thing etc. Sirach. 13.1.

5. They give offences, both the preacher and the hearers. Rom.16.17. Luke 17.1.

6. They glad and strengthen the Papists in their error and grieve the godly. Ezekiel. 13.21, 22.

7. They do persecute our saviour Jesus Christ in his members. Acts 9.4, 5; 2 Corinth. 1.5. Also they reject and despise our Lord and saviour Jesus Christ. Luke 10 verse.16. Moreover those labourers whom at the prayer of the faithful, the Lord hath sent forth in to his harvest, they refuse and also reject. Math. 9.38.

8. These popish garments, etc., are now become very idols in deed because they are exalted above the word of the Almighty.

9. I come not to them because they should be ashamed and so leave their

idolatrous garments etc. 2 Thess. 3.14. If any man obey not our sayings, note him.

God give us strength still to strive in suffering under the cross, that the blessed word of our God may only rule and have the highest place, to cast down strongholds, to destroy or overthrow policies or imaginations, and every high thing that is exalted against the knowledge of God, and to bring in to captivity or subjection every thought to the obedience of Christ, etc. 2 Corinth.10 verses 4 and 5, that the name and word of the eternal our Lord God may be exalted or magnified above all things. Psalm 138 verse 2.

Petition to Parliament

O England, if thou return, return unto me, saith the Lord.

Jerem. 4.1

We the poor afflicted and your humble and obedient subjects in the Lord, most earnestly desire that the word of our God may be set to reign and have the highest place to rule and reform all estates and degrees of men to build and plant his holy signs and true marks, to cut down, to root out, and utterly destroy, by the axe of the same his holy word all monuments of idolatry, to wit, that wicked canon law which is the only root out of the which these abominable branches do grow, as forked caps and tippets, surplices, copes, starch cakes, godfathers and godmothers, popish holy days, forbidding of marriages and meats, which the Holy Ghost our Almighty calleth doctrines of devils, as in the 1 Timothy.4 verses 3.4, more to destroy idols, temples and chapels which the papists or infidels have builded to the service of their gods. Our God hath straightly commanded and charged his people Israel chiefly the governors, as in Deuteronomy 16 verse 20 with the note; and so in them the magistrates of our time, not to use in his service, the manners, fashions or customs of the papists, but contrariwise utterly to destroy them, to consume them and abhor them Deut. 7 verse 26. Which holy commandment of the Almighty our God if it be not executed speedily the Lord's wrath will surely break out upon this whole realm of England . . . So we a poor congregation, whom God hath separated from the Churches of England, and from the mingled and false worshipping therein used, out of the which assemblies the Lord our only saviour hath called us, and still calleth, saying, come out from among them and separate yourselves from them, and touch no unclean thing, then will I receive you and I will be your God, and you shall be my sons and daughters, saith the Lord. 2 Corinth. 6 verses 17,18: so as God giveth strength at this day we do serve the Lord every sabbath day in houses and on the fourth day in the week we meet or come together weekly to use prayer, and exercise discipline on them which do deserve it, by the strength and sure warrant of the Lord's good word as in Matthew 18 verses 15, 16, 17,

18; 1 Corinth. 5. But woe unto this cursed canon law the gain whereof hath caused the bishops and clergy of England to forsake the right way and have gone astray . . . I behold another beast coming up out of the earth which had two horns like the llama, so this secret and disguised Antichrist, to wit this canon law with the branches and their maintainers, though not so openly, have by long imprisonment, pained and killed the Lord's servants (as our minister Richard Fitz), Thomas Bowland, deacon, one Partridge, and Giles Fowler, and besides them a great multitude which no man could number of all nations and people and tongues, as Rev. 7 verse 9, whose good cause and faithful testimony though we should cease to groan and cry unto our God to redress such wrongs and cruel handlings of his poor members, the very walls of the prisons about this city, as the Gatehouse, Bridewell, the Counters, the King's Bench, the Marshalsea, the White Lion, would testify God's anger kindled against this land for such injustice and subtle persecution.

. . . Lord, we most humbly beseech thee to strengthen the Queen's highness with his holy spirit, that in the thirteenth year of her reign she may cast down all high places of idolatry within her land, with the popish canon law and all the superstition and commandments of men, and to pluck up by the roots all filthy ceremonies pertaining to the same, and that her Highness may send forth princes and ministers and give them the book of the Lord, that they may bring home the people of God to the purity and truth of the apostolic Church. Then shall the fear of the Lord come upon every city and country.

1.13 JOHN ROGERS, *THE DISPLAYING OF AN HORRIBLE SECT*

During the 1560s and 1570s there was growing consternation at the development of radical, and sometimes separatist, Protestant groups in London and other large cities. The most notorious in the earlier period was the Family of Love, who were persecuted, particularly in East Anglia in the 1580s. Rogers's work aimed at both anatomising and demonising the groups' practices and faith. Text from: first edition, 1572, pp. 118–30.

First they be generally all unlearned, saving that some of them can read English, and that not very perfectly, and of them that can so read, they have chosen Bishops, Elders and Deacons.

2. Their Bishops, Elders or Deacons do call those that be of their sect together by the name of a congregation into one of their disciple's houses, which they call also a Raab, where they commonly meet, to the number of thirty or above, and their bishop or Deacon doth read unto the congregation the Scriptures, expounding the same according to his own sense.

3. When any person shall be received into their congregation they cause all their brethren to assemble and the Bishop or Elder, or both, doth declare unto

the new elected brother that if he will be content that all his goods shall be in common amongst the rest of all his brethren, he shall be received: whereunto he answering yea, then he is admitted with a kiss, viz. All the company, both men and women kiss him, one after another.

4. At their meeting, either to receive a new brother or to read the Scripture, they all have meat, drink and lodging at the cost and charges of the owner of the house, whom they call a Raab: and there they do remain as long as he hath good victuals for them, whereby sometimes they do lose their Raab, seeing himself so far overcharged with them.

5. They are called together ever in the night time, and commonly to such houses as be far from neighbours, one of them doth always warn another: and when they come to the house of meeting they knock at the door, saying: here is a brother in Christ, or a sister in Christ . . .

10. In the beginning of Queen Mary's time they would not come to the Church, thinking it damnable so to do. But within a year after they were changed from that opinion, openly declaring unto their brethren that they were all bound to come unto the church, and to do outwardly there, all such things as the law required then at their hands, upon pain of damnation, although inwardly they did profess the contrary.

11. They cannot abide any of their sect to pray, but those that be new received brethren whom they call weaklings; thinking it a great fault to the rest, whom they affirm to be perfect, to pray unto God, as they were importunate troublers and vexers of him, having no need to do so . . .

14. They may not say *God save anything*: for they affirm that all things are ruled by nature, and not directed by God.

15. They did prohibit bearing of weapons, but at the length perceiving themselves to be noted and marked for the same, they have allowed the bearing of staves . . .

18. When their wives are to be delivered of child, they must use the help of none other but of those that be of their sect: so that sometime the women are delivered in the fields, for that they would eschew the coming of others unto them: as one of them was, having no woman with her at her travel.

19. If any of their sect do die, the wife or husband that overliveth must marry again with one of their congregation, or else the offence is great: the marriage is made by the brethren, who bring them together sometime that dwell above a hundred miles asunder: as for example, Thomas Chandler of Woverse in the county of Surrey, had his wife fetched out of the Isle of Ely by two of the congregation: the man and the woman being utter strangers before they came together to be married.

20. They do divorce again themselves asunder if they cannot agree before certain of the congregation: as the said Chandler and his wife did, upon a misliking after they had been one year married together . . .

30. They hold that heaven and hell are present in this world amongst us, and that there is none other: and for proof thereof they allege the xvii of

Matthew, of Christ's transfiguration, that as the cloud removed Peter did see Elias and Moses: so if the cloud were removed away both heaven and hell should be visible unto us.

31. They hold that they are bound to give alms to none other persons but to those of their sect: and if they do they give their alms to the devil.

32. They hold that they ought not to bury the dead, upon this place of Scripture: *Let the dead bury the dead. . .*

36. They hold that all men that are not of their congregation or that are revolted from them to be dead.

37. They hold that no Bishop, or Minister should remain still in one place, but they ought always to be wandering from country to country . . .

43. They hold that there was a world before Adam's time, as there is now.

44. They hold that they ought to keep silence amongst themselves, that the liberty they have in the Lord may not be espied out of others.

45. They hold that no man should be put to death for his opinion, and therefore they condemn Master Cranmer and Master Ridley for burning Joan of Kent.

46. They cannot abide any exposition of Scriptures but their own, conferring one place of Scripture with another, and so to say their minds of it, without any other bodies' exposition . . .

51. They have certain sleights among them to answer any questions that shall be demanded of them, with deceiving the demandant: as, for example, if one of them be demanded how he believeth in the Trinity, he will answer: I am to learn of you, and so provoketh the demandment to show his opinion therein. Which done, he will say then, I do believe so, by the which words he meaneth that he believeth the demandant saith as he thinketh: but not that he thinketh so.

52. They do decree all men to be infants that are under the age of thirty years: so that if they be demanded whether infants ought to be baptised, they answer yea, meaning thereby that he is an infant until he attain to those years, at which time he ought to be baptised and not afore.

1.14 ROBERT SOUTHWELL, *AN HUMBLE SUPPLICATION TO HER MAJESTY*

In 1591, in an attempt to restrict Catholic ministries to England, Elizabeth issued a Proclamation against priests and seminaries. Southwell's plea, written in the same year in direct response, for tolerance towards the Catholic minority is an exemplary argument. Despite his plea, Parliament passed an act in the following year which excluded Catholics from all public office, and provided measure for the removal of their children after the age of 7. Southwell himself was arrested under the terms of the Act, tried and executed for treason. Text from: 1595 edition, pp. 6–7; 75–86.

All bonds both of nature and grace invite us to love God and our country more than our lives, and our neighbours as ourselves: which if we observe in the highest degree, we hope what other title soever we deserve we shall at the least be deemed not to swerve from the rules of native courtesy: we are in so mighty and warrantable proofs assured by all antiquity, that our Catholic faith is the only truth (to which all that have been, or shall be, saved, must owe their fidelity) that we think it a worthy purchase for the perseverance in the same to forfeit our best fortunes and engage our lives to the great cruelties, than by revolting from it to enter league with error and to make our souls the price of infernal pain.

* * *

Is not that very statute a most heavy oppression now, when the most of these Queen Mary's Fathers that are left are become so old and impotent that they cannot possibly supply Catholics' special necessities, to make it by law felony to receive young priests? Are not Catholics shortened by this means from such helps to which their conscience and religion bindeth them, a torment to virtuous minds, more afflictive than any outward punishment? Are not they by this tied to this wounding and bitter choice: either to live like heathens without the rites of Christian and necessary sacraments for their soul's health, or to purchase them at the rigorous price of hazarding their liberties, lives, lands and posterities, as in case of felony. In points also of our credit how deeply we are incurred in respect of our religion, how many experiences make it most manifest? We are made the common theme of every railing declaimer; abused without means or hope of remedy, by every wretch with most infamous names; no tongue so foresworn but it is of credit against us; none so true, but it is thought false in our defence; our slanders are common works for idle presses, and our credits are daily sold at the stationers' stalls, every libeller repairing his wants with impairing our honours, being sure that when all other matters fail, any pamphlets against us shall ever be welcomed. . . . If we keep hospitality we are censured to be too popular; if we forbear, we hoard up money for secret purposes; if we be merry, we are fed with foreign hopes; if sad, we are malcontent with the state at home; if we subscribe to Articles, it must be called hypocrisy; if we refuse, disloyalty; in some we are measured by the eyes and tongues of such whom we can no way please, but by being miserable; yea the very name of a Catholic, as they in their New Testament term it a Papist, is so known a vantage for everyone that either oweth them money, or offereth them injury, that they can neither claim their right, nor right their wrongs; but their adversaries straight leaving the main point, pleadeth against them for their recusancy. . . . And what is our recusancy, or refusal, to be present at their Protestants' service, but a mere matter of conscience? For as there is none so known or usual a way to distinguish any religion from other as the external rites and sacraments peculiar to every one, so can none more effectually deny his own than by making open confession of a contrary speech by his assistance and present at the solemnities and service proper to it. . . . For first there are twenty pounds by the month exacted of such as are to pay it after thirteen months by the year, an account unusual in all other causes, as the laws commonly read, printed and practised witnesseth, and multitudes of the unabler sorts of Catholics daily feel that all their goods and third part of their lands are seized on, for their recusancy that cannot yearly pay thirteen score pounds for the same. And this is so prescribed and performed with such rigour that it is in the leases of Protestants' hands, by a special proviso, ordained that recusants should not be so much as tenants to their own lands, so severely is their religion punished in that behalf: yea and this law hath been severely executed that whereas poor farmers and husbandmen had but one cow for themselves, and many children to live upon it, that for their recusancy hath been taken from them, and where both kine and cattle were wanting, they have taken their coverlets, sheets and blankets from their beds, their victuals and poor provision from their houses, not sparing so much as the very glass from their windows, when they found nothing else to serve their turns withal, which most pitiful abuses poor souls both in the north and other countries have been continually cumbered, no complaints taking place, where these outrages were rather commended for good services, than rebuked for misdemeanours. So irrevocably are we condemned to a servile bondage. And if Your Majesty did but know what other extreme penury and desolation they ordinarily feel, your merciful heart, never hardened to see lamentable spoils would rather have the laws repealed than the execution so intolerable.

1.15 LADY MARGARET HOBY, *DIARY*

Spiritual exercises and the personal relationship with God was the main focus of such private diaries. Included here are two examples of Margaret Hoby's account of her week. Despite appearances, the absence of other personal thoughts, external referents and meetings does not suggest she was unusually pious, or unusually solitary, merely that she was an effective practitioner of the puritan autobiographical mode, made most famous eighty years later by John Bunyan. Text from: *Diary of Lady Margaret Hoby*, edited D. Meads, 1930, pp.79–81; 91–2.

1598

Wednesday the 24 [November]

After private prayer I went about the house a while, then I wrote notes in my testament and after I had eaten my breakfast, I went abroad; after I came home I prayed and soon after when I had read of the Bible, I dined; after, I despatched some business in the house, then I took a lecture; after, I writ in my commonplace book, and then prayed with Mr. Rhodes, and went about the house awhile, and then returned to meditation and private prayer; then I studied a while for my lecture, and after went to supper; and after I heard a lecture, and then I read of the *Book of Martyrs* and so went to bed.

Thursday the 25

After private prayer and breakfast I did read a while for being not well, partly through mine own folly, which I humble pray the Lord to pardon; I went to dinner; after I writ some notes in my testament, and then took a lecture; after heard Everill read and then prayed, so went to supper, after to prayers, and then to bed.

Friday the 26

After private prayer I did eat my breakfast, read a long letter and writ another, then prayed and after went to dinner; after which I heard a great disputation between two preachers, then took a lecture; after talked with one that came to see me, and then went to prayer and examination; after, I went to supper, then to lecture and so to bed.

Saturday the 27

After private prayer I wrote to my Lord Ewer, then I took leave, with some conference, of some that came to see me, then I did eat my breakfast, and walked about till dinner time; after dinner I went about the house and then took my coach and went abroad; after I came home and took order for supper, I prayed privately and examined myself; then I looked and wrote in the household book, and so went to supper; after to lecture and then to bed.

The Lord's day the 28

After private prayers I wrote notes in my testament and did eat my breakfast; then to Church, after I came home to prayer and so to dinner; after which I talked with a woman that was to be divorced from her husband with whom she lived incestuously: then I went to Church and, after catechising and sermon, I walked abroad; then I meditated of the sermons, and read and spoke to Mrs. Ormstone of the chapter that was read in the morning; and so went to private prayer; after to supper, then to prayers and soon after to bed.

Monday the 29

After private prayer I did eat my breakfast, then I did go about the house till almost dinner time, then I prayed and then dined; after I had rested a while, I wrote my sermon,[3] and then took a lecture, and after, I heard prayer and a lecture, because in regard of men's dullness after meat and being winter, it was thought more convenient to be before supper; after, I prayed privately and then of the testament and so went to bed.

* * *

Friday the 21

After private prayer I did a little, and so went to Church; after the sermon I prayed, then dined, and in the afternoon was busy till 5 a clock; then I returned to private prayer and examination; after, supped; then heard public prayers and after that, prayed privately, having read a chapter of the Bible; and so went to bed.

Saturday the 22

After private prayer I did eat my breakfast, dispatched divers business in the house, prayed, and then read of the Bible, and so dined; after, I was busy about the house preparing divers things against the holy days, and at 5 a clock, I returned into my closet unto private examination and prayer; then I went to supper, after to the lecture, and lastly to private prayers and preparation to the supper of the Lord, by taking an account what breaches I had made in my faith, since I found that I had it, by repairing those by repentance, as also meditating what grace I had, what benefits God's spirit there did offer me, if I came rightly and worthily, both of person and usage; and so I went to bed.

The Lord's day; the 23

After I was ready I was called away to the Church, for which cause I was driven to prepare myself, in part, as I went to the holy exercises; after the sermon and sacraments I came home and prayed; after dinner I talked awhile, and then went to the afternoon sermon; after that I was busy till almost supper time, then I prayed and examined myself, then went to supper; after to public prayers and examination of the sermons, and after that talked a little and, when I had privately prayed, went to bed.

Monday the 24

After private prayers I did eat my breakfast; then I read of the Bible, prayed, walked a little abroad, dined; after served divers poor people with wheat and beefer,[4] then was busy in the kitchen until 5 a clock, and then examined myself and prayed; after, I went to supper, then heard the lecture, and so to bed.

Tuesday, being Christ's day: 25

After private prayer I read of the Bible, eat my breakfast and went to Church; then I come home and prayed; after dinner I went a while about the house, then I caused one to read unto me and, being not well, I did omit my ordinary exercise of prayer till after supper; then I heard repetition and prayers and after I had talked a while to little purpose, I went to examination and private prayers and so to bed.

* * *

The Lord's day 20 [January]

After private prayer I read a while and then did eat my breakfast; after, I went to the Church, then I came home and prayed, after dined; then I read in Perkins[5] till I went again to the Church, where I found the Lord to assist me most graciously from the malice of my enemy; after, till night, I kept company with Mr. Hoby who read a while of Cartwright's[6] book to me, then I went to private examination and prayer; then I went to supper, after to public prayers, then I walked a while and after prayed privately and so went to bed.

1.16 *THE MILLENARY PETITION*

This petition was submitted to James I by the bishops who wanted reform to move more swiftly, and hoped for a radical outcome of the Hampton Court Conference of 1604. Comparison with the *Canons* (1.17) published after the Conference indicates how few of their demands were met. Text from: Fuller, *Church History*, 1655, book x, pp. 21–3.

Our humble suit, then, unto your Majesty is that these offences following, some may be removed, some amended, some qualified.

1. In the Church service: that the cross in baptism, interrogatories ministered to infants, confirmation, as superfluous, may be taken away; baptism not to be ministered by women, and so explained; the cap and surplice not urged; that examination may go before the communion; that it be ministered with a sermon; that divers terms of priests and absolution and some other used, with the ring in marriage, and other such like in the book, may be corrected; the longsomeness of service abridged; Church songs and music moderated to better edification; that the Lord's day be not profaned; the rest upon holy days not so strictly urged; that there may be a uniformity of doctrine prescribed; no popish opinion to be any more taught or defended; no ministers charged to teach their people to bow at the name of Jesus; that the canonical Scriptures only be read in the Church.

2. Concerning Church ministers: that none hereafter be admitted into the ministry but able and sufficient men, and those to preach diligently and especially upon the Lord's day; that such as be already entered and cannot preach, may either be removed, and some charitable course taken with them for their relief, or else be forced according to the value of their livings to maintain preachers; that non-residency be not permitted; that King Edward's statute for the lawfulness of minister's marriages be revived; that ministers be not urged to subscribe, but according to the law, to the Articles of religion and the King's supremacy only.

3. For Church livings and maintenance: that bishops leave their commendams,[7] some holding parsonages, some prebends, some vicarages, with their bishoprics; that double-beneficed men may not be suffered to hold some two,

some three benefices with cure, and some two, three or four dignities besides; that impropriations annexed to bishoprics and colleges be demised only to the preachers' incumbents for the old rent . . .

4. For church discipline: that the discipline and excommunication may be administered according to Christ's own institution, or at the least, that enormities may be redressed, as namely, that excommunication come not forth under the name of lay persons, chancellors, officials, etc. that men be not excommunicated for trifles and twelve-penny matters; that none be excommunicated without consent of his pastor; that the officers be not suffered to extort unreasonable fees; that none having jurisdiction or registers' places, put out the same to farm; that divers popish canons (as for restraint of marriage at certain times) be reversed; that the longsomeness of suits in ecclesiastical courts (which hang sometimes two, three, four, five, six, or seven years) may be restrained; that the oath *ex officio*, whereby men are forced to accuse themselves, be more sparingly used; that licences for marriages without banns asked, be more cautiously granted.

1.17 *CONSTITUTIONS AND CANONS ECCLESIASTICAL*

The Canons were published in 1604, after the Hampton Court Conference confirmed the moderate and episcopate line of the Church of England, as it had been practised by the Elizabethan bishopric and parliaments. Their adherence to a hierarchical and ritualistic Church, and consequent rejection of presbyterianism was seen by some puritans as a significant step away from the principles of a Calvinist Church. Text from: the first edition of 1604: fos C1–C4; D3–4; F4^v–G2^r; I2–3.

1. The King's supremacy over the Church of England, in causes ecclesiastical to be maintained

As our duty to the King's most excellent Majesty requireth, we first decree and ordain that the Archbishop of Canterbury (from time to time), all Bishops of this province, all Deans, Archdeacons, Parsons, Vicars and all other ecclesiastical persons shall faithfully keep and observe and (as much as in them lieth) shall cause to be observed and kept of others, all and singular laws and statutes made for the restoring to the crown of this kingdom, the ancient jurisdiction over the State ecclesiastical, and abolishing of all foreign power repugnant to the same.

4. Impugners of the public worship of God established in the Church of England censured

Whosoever shall hereafter affirm that the form of God's worship in the Church *complained too catholic* (handwritten)

Anti Puritan (handwritten, left margin)

of England, established by the law and contained in the *Book of Common Prayer and Administration of Sacraments* is a corrupt, superstitious, or unlawful worship of God, or containeth anything in it that is repugnant to the Scriptures, let him be excommunicated *ipso facto*, and not restored but only by Bishop of the place, or Archbishop, after his repentences and public revocation of such his wicked errors.

9. Authors of schisms in the Church of England censured

Excomm. Those who seperate themselves (handwritten, left margin)

Whosoever shall hereafter separate themselves from the communion of saints as it is approved by the Apostles' rules, in the Church of England, and combine themselves together in a new brotherhood, accounting the Christians who are conformable to the doctrine, government, rites and ceremonies of the Church of England to be profane and unmeet for them to join with in Christian profession: let them be excommunicated . . .

11. Maintainers of conventicles censured

Whosoever shall hereafter affirm or maintain that there are within this realm other meetings, assemblies or congregations of the King's born subjects, than such as by the laws of this land are held and allowed, which may rightly challenge to themselves the name of true and lawful churches: let him be excommunicated and not restored . . .

12. Maintainers of constitutions made in conventicles censured

Whosoever shall hereafter affirm that it is lawful for any sort of ministers and lay persons, or either of them, to join together, and make rules, orders, or constitutions in causes ecclesiastical without the King's authority, and shall submit themselves to be ruled and governed by them: let them be excommunicated . . .

24. Copes to be worn in Cathedral churches by those that administer the communion

In all Cathedral and Collegiate Churches, the Holy Communion shall be administered upon principal feast days, sometimes by the Bishop if he be present, and sometimes by the Dean: and at sometimes by a Canon or Prebendary, the principal minister using a decent Cope . . .

45. Beneficed preachers being resident upon their livings to preach every Sunday

Every beneficed man allowed to be a preacher and residing on his benefice, having no lawful impediment, shall in his own cure, or in some other Church or Chapel where he may, conveniently near adjoining (where no preacher is) preach one sermon every Sunday of the year, wherein he shall soberly and sincerely divide the word of truth, to the glory of God, and to the best edification of the people.

46. Beneficed men not preachers to procure monthly sermons

Every beneficed man not allowed to be a preacher shall procure sermons to be preached in his cure once in every month at the least, by preachers lawfully licensed, if his living in the judgement of the Ordinary, will be able to bear it. And upon every Sunday when there shall not be a sermon preached in his Cure, he or his Curate shall read some one of the *Homilies* prescribed, or to be prescribed by authority, to the intents aforesaid.

49. Ministers not allowed preachers, may not expound

No person whatsoever not examined and approved by the Bishop of the Diocese, or not licensed as aforesaid, for a sufficient or convenient preacher, shall take upon him to expound in his own cure, or elsewhere, any Scripture or matter or doctrine; but shall only study to read plainly and aptly (without glozing or adding) the *Homilies* already set forth . . .

50. Strangers not admitted to preach without showing their licence

Neither the minister, churchwardens nor any other officers of the Church shall suffer any man to preach within their Churches or Chapels but such as by showing their licence to preach shall appear unto them to be sufficiently authorised thereunto.

75. Sober conversation required in ministers

No ecclesiastical persons shall at any time, other than for their honest necessities, resort to any taverns or alehouses, neither shall they board or lodge in any such places. Furthermore they shall not give themselves to any base or servile labour, or to drinking or riot, spending their time idly by day or by night playing at dice, cards or tables, or any other unlawful games: but at all times convenient, they shall hear or read somewhat of the Holy Scriptures, or shall occupy themselves with some other honest study or exercise, always doing the things which shall appertain to honesty and endeavouring to profit the Church of God, having always in mind that they ought to excel all others in purity of life, and should be examples to the people to live well and christianly under pain of ecclesiastical censures to be inflicted with severity, according to the qualities of their offences.

1.18 ARTHUR DENT, *THE PLAIN MAN'S PATHWAY TO HEAVEN*

This dialogue, in the form of a populist catechism, aims to convince the reader of the truth and force of Calvinist belief. The speakers are: Theologus (a divine), Philagathus (an honest man), Asunetus (an ignorant man) and Antilegon (a caviller). Dent's work was extremely popular, going through twenty-five impressions by 1640. Text from: first edition, 1601, pp. 5; 17–21; 259–93.

Philagathus	First then, I demand of you, in what state all men are born by nature?
Theologus	In the state of condemnation, as appeareth, Ephes. 2.3. We are by nature the children of wrath as well as others. And again it is written, *Behold I was born in iniquity and in sin hath my mother conceived me*, Psalm 51.5.
Philagathus	Is it every man's case? Are not dukes and nobles, Lords and Ladies, and the great potentates of the earth exempted from it?
Theologus	No, surely. It is the common case of all, both high and low, rich and poor, as it is written: *what is man that he should be clean, and he that is born of woman, that he should be just?* Job 15.14

* * *

Philagathus	Some think that courtesy, kindness, good nurture, good nature and good education are regeneration, and that courteous and good natured men must needs be saved.
Theologus	They are greatly deceived: for these things do not necessarily accompany salvation, but are to be found in such as are altogether profane and irreligious: yet we are to love such good outward qualities and the men in whom we find them.
Philagathus	What say you then to learning, wit and policy? Are not these things of the essence of religion and prove a regeneration?
Theologus	No, no: for they be external gifts which may be in the most wicked men, as in Papists, heathen poets and philosophers: yet we are greatly to reverence learned and wise men, although the new and inward work be not as yet wrought, for that is only of God, that is from above.
Philagathus	The common people do attribute much to learning and policy: for they will say that such a man is learned and wise, and knoweth the Scriptures as well as any of them all, and yet he doth not thus and thus.

Theologus	It is one thing to know the history and letter of the Scriptures, and another thing to believe and feel the power thereof in the heart, which is only from the sanctifying spirit, which none of the wise of this world can have . . .
Asunetus	What sound reason can you yield why such honest men should be condemned?
Theologus	Because many such are utterly void of all true knowledge of God and of his word. Nay, which is more, many of them despise the word of God and hate all the zealous professors of it. They esteem preachers but as prattlers, and sermons as good tales; they regard the Scriptures no more than their old shoes. What hope is there then, I pray you, that such men should be saved? Doth not the holy Ghost say: how shall we escape if we neglect so great salvation? Heb. 2.3 . . . for all experience showeth that they mind, dream and dote of nothing else day and night, but this world: this world, lands, and leases, grounds and livings, kine and sheep, and how to wax rich.

* * *

Philagathus	Set down then which be the most certain and infallible evidences of a man's salvation, against the which no exception can be taken.
Theologus	I judge these to be most sound and infallible:
	Assured faith in the promises. Act. 16.31.
	Sincerity of heart. Pro. 11.20; Joh. 1.47.
	The spirit of adoption. Rom. 8.14,15.
	Sound regeneration and sanctification. Joh. 3.3.1. Thess. 4.3.
	Inward peace. Rom. 5.1.
	Groundedness in the truth. Coll. 1.23.; 2.7.
	Continuance to the end. Math. 24.13. Joh. 8.3.
Philagathus	Now you come near the quick indeed: for in my judgement none of these can be found truly in any reprobate. Therefore I think no divine can take exception against any of these . . . and one thing more I do gather out of all your speech: to wit, that you do think that a man may be assured of his salvation even in this life.
Theologus	I do think so indeed. . . . The groundwork of our salvation is laid in God's eternal election, and in respect thereof it standeth fast and unmovable. As it is written: *the foundation of God standeth fast.* 2 Tim. 2.19. And again, *he is faithful that hath promised.* 1 Thess. 5. *Though we cannot believe, yet he abideth faithful.* 2 Tim. 2.13. So then as we know it certainly in ourselves by the consequences of election: so it standeth most firm in respect of God and his eternal and immutable decree. And a thousand infirmities, nay all the sins in the world, nor all the devils in hell, cannot overthrow God's election. For our Lord Jesus saith: *all that the Father hath given me, shall come*

unto me. Joh. 6.37. And again: *this is the Father's will that hath sent me, that of all which he hath given me, I should lose nothing, but should raise it up again at the last day.* John 6.39. And in another place our Saviour Christ saith: *my sheep hear my voice, and I know them, and they follow me, and I give unto them eternal life, and they shall never perish, neither shall any pluck them out of mine hand: my father which gave them me is greater than all, and none is able to take them out of my father's hand.* Joh. 10.27. We ought therefore to be as sure of our salvation as of any other thing which God hath promised, or which we are bound to believe: for to doubt thereof in respect of God's truth is blasphemous against the immutability of his truth.

Philagathus	But are there not some doubts at some times even in the very elect, and those which are grown to the greatest persuasion?
Theologus	Yes, verily. For he that never doubted, never believed: for whosoever believeth in truth feeleth sometimes doubtings and waverings. Even as the sound body feeleth many grudgings of diseases, which if he had not health he could not feel: so the sound soul feeleth some doubtings, which if it were not sound, it could not so easily feel: for we feel not corruption by corruption: but we feel corruption by grace: and the more grace we have, the more quick are we in the feeling of corruption . . .
Philagathus	Cannot the reprobates and ungodly be assured of their salvation?
Theologus	No. For the prophet saith: *there is no peace for the wicked.* Esay. 57.21. Then I reason thus: they which have not the inward peace, cannot be assured, but the wicked have not the inward peace, therefore they cannot be assured . . .
Philagathus	Is not the doctrine of the assurance of salvation a most comfortable doctrine?
Theologus	Yes doubtless. For except a man be persuaded of the favour of God and the forgiveness of sins, and consequently of his salvation, what comfort can he have in anything? . . .
Antilegon	Touching this point, I am flat of your mind: for I think verily a man ought to be persuaded of his salvation: and for mine own part, I make no question of it. I hope to be saved as well as the best of them all. I am out of fear for that: for I have such a steadfast faith in God that if there should be but two in the world saved, I hope I should be one of them.
Theologus	You are very confident indeed. You are persuaded before you know. I would your ground were as good as your vain confidence. . . . Even so what hope can you have to be saved, when you walk nothing that way, when you use no means, when you do all things that are contrary unto the same? For, alas there is nothing in you of those things which the Scriptures do affirm must be in all those that shall be saved. . . . You have no prayers in your family: no reading, no

54

singing of psalms, no instructions, exhortations, or admonitions, or any other Christian exercises. You make no conscience of the observation of the Sabbath; you use not the name of God with any reverence; you break out sometimes into horrible oaths and cursings; you make an ordinary matter of swearing by your faith and your troth. Your wife is irreligious, your children dissolute and ungracious; your servants profane and careless. You are an example in your own house of all atheism and conscienceless behaviour. You are a great gamester, a rioter, a spendthrift, a drinker, a common alehouse-haunter, and whore-hunter: and to conclude, given to all vice and naughtiness. Now then I pray you tell me, or rather let your conscience tell me, what hope you can have to be saved when you walk in no path of salvation? . . .

Antilegon   You would make a man mad. You put me out of my faith: you drive me from Christ. . . . If none can be saved by Christ but only those which are so qualified as you speak of, then Lord have mercy upon us: then the way to Heaven is very straight indeed and few at all shall be saved, for there be few such in the world.

Theologus   You are in no whit therein deceived: for when all comes to all, it is most certain that few shall be saved. Which thing I will show unto you both by scripture, reason and examples. . . . Our Lord Jesus saith: *enter in at the straight gate, for it is the wide gate and broad way that leadeth to destruction, and many there be which go in thereat, because the gate is straight and the way narrow that leadeth unto life, and few there be that find it.* Math. 7.13. Again he saith: *many are called, but few are chosen.* Math. 20.16. In another place we read of a certain man which came to our Saviour Christ and asked him of purpose, whether few should be saved. To whom our Lord Jesus answered thus: *strive to enter in at the straight gate: for many, I say unto you, will seek to enter in, and shall not be able.* Luke 13.24. In which answer, albeit our Saviour doth not answer directly to his question, either negatively or affirmatively: yet doth he plainly insinuate by his speeches that few shall be saved . . .

Philagathus   I pray you tell us how few, and to what scantling they may be reduced, whether one of an hundred, or one of a thousand, shall be saved.

Theologus   No man knoweth that, neither can I give you any direct and certain answer unto it. But I say that in comparison of the reprobate there shall be but a few saved: for all that profess the gospel are not the true Church before God. There be many in the Church which are not of the Church . . . the ninth to the Romans, where the Apostle saith: *all are not Israel, that are of Israel.* And again, Isaiah crieth concerning Israel: *though the number of the children of Israel were as the sand of the sea, yet but a remnant shall be saved. Rom.* 9.27 . . .

Philagathus   Doth not the knowledge of this doctrine discourage men from seeking after God?

55

Theologus   Nothing less. But rather it ought to awake us, and to stir up in us a greater care of our salvation, that we may be of the number of Christ's little flock, which make an end of their salvation in fear and trembling. . . . The greatest part shall perish: but all that shall be saved, shall be saved by his mercy. As it is written: *he will have mercy on whom he will have mercy: and whom he will he hardeneth*. Rom.9. And again: *it is not in him that willeth, or in him that runneth, but in God that showeth mercy*.

1.19 WILLIAM LAUD, *SPEECH DELIVERED IN THE STAR CHAMBER AT THE CENSURE OF JOHN BASTWICK, HENRY BURTON AND WILLIAM PRYNNE*

Laud's speech after the trial of Bastwick, Burton and Prynne, for the attacks made on bishops in their writing and preaching, was published at the insistence of Charles I and merely served to fuel popular resentment against Laud's attempts at reform, and the enforcement of uniformity through excommunications and the perceived abuse of the Star Chamber. It is a short summary of some of his views. Text from: first edition, 1637, pp. 4–13; 43–54.

And I can say it clearly and truly as in the presence of God, I have done nothing as a prelate, to the uttermost of what I am conscious, but with a single heart and with a sincere intention for the good government and honour of the Church and the maintenance of the orthodox truth and religion of Christ professed, established and maintained in this Church of England.

For my care of this Church, the reducing of into order, the upholding of the external worship of God in it, and the settling of it to the rules of its first reformation, are the causes (and the sole causes, whatever are pretended) of all this malicious storm, which hath lowered so black upon me, and some of my brethren. And in the meantime they which are the only or the chief innovators of the Christian world, having nothing to say, accuse us of innovation; they themselves and their complices in the meantime being the greatest innovators that the Christian world hath almost ever known. I deny not but others have spread more dangerous errors in the Church of Christ: but no men, in any age of it, have been more guilty of innovation than they, while they themselves cry out against it: *quis tulerit Gracchos?* . . .

Our main crime is (would they all speak out, as some of them do) that we are bishops; were we not so, some of us might be as passable as other men.

And a great trouble 'tis to them, that we maintain that our calling of bishops is *jure divino*, by divine right . . .

And I say farther, that from the Apostles' time, in all ages, in all places, the Church of Christ was governed by bishops; and lay-elders never heard of, till Calvin's newfangled device at Geneva.

Now this is made by these men, as if it were *contra Regem*, against the King, in right or in power.

But that's a mere ignorant shift; for our being bishops, *jure divino*, by divine right, takes nothing from the King's right or power over us. For though our office be from God and Christ immediately, yet may we not exercise that power, either of order or jurisdiction, but as God hath appointed us, that is not in his Majesty's or any Christian King's kingdoms, but by and under the power of the King given us so to do.

And were this a good argument against us as bishops, it must needs be good against priests and ministers too; for themselves grant that their calling is *jure divino*, by divine right; and yet I hope they will not say that to be priests and ministers is against the King or any his royal prerogatives.

Next suppose our callings as Bishops could not be made good *jure divino*, by divine right, yet *jure ecclesiastico*, by ecclesiastical right it cannot be denied. And here in England the Bishops are confirmed both in their power and means by Acts of Parliament. So that here we stand in as good case as the present laws of the realm can make us. And so we must stand till the laws shall be repealed by the same power that made them.

Now then suppose we had no other string to hold by (I say suppose this, but I can grant it not) yet no man can libel against our calling (as these men do) be it in pulpit, print or otherwise, but he libels against the King and the State, by whose laws we are established. Therefore all these libels so far forth as they are against our calling, are against the King and the law, and can have no other purpose than to stir up sedition among the people.

If they had any other intention or if they had any Christian or charitable desire to reform any thing amiss, why did they not modestly petition his Majesty about it, that in his princely wisdom he might set all things right, in a just and orderly manner? But this was neither their intention, nor way. For one clamours out of his pulpit, and all of them from the press, and in a most virulent and unchristian manner set themselves to make a heat among the people; and so by mutiny to effect that which by law they cannot. And, by most false and unjust calumnies to defame both our callings and persons. But for my part, as I pity their rage, so I heartily pray God to forgive their malice.

* * *

One thing sticks much in their stomachs, and they call it an innovation too. And that is bowing or doing reverence at our first coming into the Church, or at our nearer approaches to the holy table or the altar (call it whether you will). In which they will needs have it that we worship the holy table, or God knows what.

To this I answer, first that God forbid we should worship any thing but God himself.

Secondly that if to worship God when we enter into his house or approach his altar be an innovation, 'tis a very old one. . . . But this is the misery: 'tis superstition nowadays for any man to come with more reverence into a church than a tinker and his bitch come into an alehouse; the comparison is too homely, but my just indignation at the profaneness of the times makes me speak it . . .

The thirteenth innovation is the placing of the holy table altar-wise at the upper end of the chancel; that is the setting of it north and south and placing a rail before it to keep it from profanation, which Mr. Burton says is done to advance and usher in popery.

To this I answer that 'tis no popery to set a rail to keep profanation from that holy table: nor is it any innovation to place it at the upper end of the chancel, as the altar stood. And this appears both by the practice and by the command and canon of the Church of England.

First by the practice of the Church of England. For in the King's royal chapels and divers Cathedrals the holy table hath, ever since the Reformation, stood at the upper end of the choir, with the large or full side towards the people.

And though it stood in most parish Churches the other way, yet whether there be not more reason the parish Churches should be made conformable to the Cathedral and mother Churches, than the Cathedrals to them, I leave to any reasonable man to judge.

1.20 JOSEPH HALL, *EPISCOPACY BY DIVINE RIGHT*

Hall, Bishop of Exeter, addressed this to King Charles I, in public defence of the ecclesiastical government of the Church, and its validation of the divine right of monarchs and bishops, in the context of the contemporary debate between puritans and Laudians, and the contentious issues raised by *The Root and Branch Petition* (1.21). Text from: 1640 edition, London, part II, pp. 2–9.

The terms and state of the question, settled and agreed upon

It hath pleased the providence of God so to order it that as the Word itself, the Church; so the names of the offices belonging to it in their several comprehensions should be full of senses and variety of use and acception; and that in such manner, that each of them runs one into other, and oftentimes interchanges their appellations. A prophet, we know, is a foreteller of future things; an evangelist, in the natural sense of the word, is he that preaches the glad tidings of the Gospel; an apostle one of Christ's twelve great messengers to the world; a Bishop, an overseer of the Church; a presbyter some grave, ancient churchman; a deacon a servant, or minister in the church: yet all these in Scripture are so promiscuously used that a preacher is more than once termed a prophet; an evangelist an apostle; an apostle a bishop; an apostle a presbyter; a presbyter an apostle, as Romans 6.7; a presbyter a bishop; and lastly, an evangelist and bishop, a deacon or minister. For all these met in Timothy alone, who being Bishop of Ephesus, is with one breath charged to do the work of an evangelist and to fulfil his ministry. It could not be otherwise likely, but from this community of names there would follow some confusion of apprehensions, for since names were intended for distinction of things, where names are the same how can notions be distinguished? But howsoever it pleased the spirit of God in the first hatching of the evangelical Church to make use of these indistinct expressions, yet, all this while the offices were several, known by their several characters and employments. So as, the function and work of an apostle was one: viz, to plant the church and to ordain the governors of it; of a bishop another, to wit, to manage the government of his designed circuit and to ordain presbyters and deacons; of a presbyter another, namely to assist the Bishop and to watch over his several charges; of a deacon another (besides his sacred services) to order the stock of the church and to take care of the poor: yet all these agreed in one common service, which was the propagation of the gospel and the founding of God's Church . . .

Now we take episcopacy, as it is thus punctually differenced, in an eminence from the two inferior orders of presbyter and deacon: so as to define it, episcopacy is no other than a holy order of Church governors appointed for the administration of the Church. Or, more fully thus: episcopacy is an eminent order of sacred function, appointed by the holy ghost in the evangelical Church, for the governing and overseeing thereof; and for that purpose besides the administration of the word and sacraments, endued with power of imposition of hands and perpetuity of jurisdiction. Wherein we find that we shall meet two sorts of adversaries. The one are furiously and impetuously fierce, crying down episcopacy for an unlawful and anti-Christian State, not to be suffered in a truly evangelical church. . . . And such are the frantic separatists and semi-separatists of our time and nation, who are only swayed with mere passion and wilfully blinded with unjust prejudice. These are reformers of the new cut, which if Calvin or Beza were alive to see they would spit at, and wonder whence such an offspring should come. Men that defend and teach there is no higher ecclesiastical government in the world than that of a parish; that a parochial minister (though but of the blindest village in a country) is utterly independent and absolute, a perfect bishop within himself, and hath no superior in the Church upon earth, and doth no less inveigh even against the overruling power of classes, synods, etc., than of bishops. . . . The other is more mild and gentle and less unreasonable, not disallowing episcopacy in itself, but holding it to be lawful, useful, ancient; yet such as was by mere human device, upon wise and politic considerations, brought into the Church and so continued, and therefore upon like grounds alterable: with both these we must have to do. But since it is wind ill lost to talk reason to a madman, it shall be more than sufficient to confute the former of them, in giving satisfaction to the latter for, if we shall make it appear that episcopacy is not only lawful and ancient, but of no less than divine institution, those raving and black mouths are fully stopped, and those more easy and moderate opposites at once convinced. But before we offer to deal blows on either side, it is fit we should know how far we are friends, and upon what points this quarrel stands.

1.21 *THE ROOT AND BRANCH PETITION*

The Root and Branch Petition was addressed to the Commons, supposedly signed by 15,000 Londoners on 11 December 1640, and summarised the accumulated resentments towards Charles's twelve years of personal rule and Archbishop Laud's autocratic way with Church conformity. Within a week, the old *Canons* had been abolished and Laud impeached for high treason. Text from: *Historical Collections of Private Passages of State (London 1659–1701)*, vol. 5, edited by J. Rushworth, pp. 93–6.

To the Right Honourable the Commons House of Parliament

A particular of the manifold evils, pressures and grievances caused, practised and occasioned by the prelates and their dependants

1. The subjecting and enthralling all ministers under them and their authority, and so by degrees exempting them from the temporal power, whence follows:

2. The faint-heartedness of ministers to preach the truth of God, lest they should displease the prelates; as namely, the doctrine of predestination, of free grace, of perseverance, of original sin remaining after baptism, of the Sabbath, the doctrine against universal grace, election for faith foreseen, free will against Anti-Christ, non-residents, human inventions in God's worship; all which are generally withheld from the people's knowledge, because not relishing to the bishops.

3. The encouragement of ministers to despise the temporal magistracy, the nobles and gentry of the land, to abuse the subjects and live contentiously with their neighbours, knowing that they, being the bishops' creatures, shall be supported.

4. The restraint of many godly and able men from the ministry, and thrusting out of many congregations their faithful, diligent and powerful ministers, who lived peaceably with them, and did them good, only because they cannot in conscience submit to and maintain the bishops' needless devices; nay sometimes for no other cause but for their zeal in preaching or great auditories.

5. The suppressing of that godly design set on foot by certain saints, and sugared with many great gifts by sundry well affected persons for the buying of impropriations and placing of able ministers in them, maintaining of lectures and founding of free schools, which the prelates could not endure, lest it should darken their glories and draw the ministers from their dependence upon them.

6. The great increase of idle, lewd and dissolute, ignorant and erroneous men in the ministry, which swarm like the locusts of Egypt over the whole kingdom; and will they but wear a canonical coat, a surplice, a hood, bow at the

name of Jesus, and be zealous of superstitious ceremonies, they may live as they list, confront whom they please, preach and vent what errors they will, and neglect preaching at their pleasures without control.

7. The discouragement of many from bringing up their children in learning; the many schisms, errors and strange opinions which are in the Church; great corruptions which are in the universities; the gross and lamentable ignorance almost everywhere among the people; the want of preaching ministers in very many places both of England and Wales; the loathing of the ministry and the general defection to all manner of profaneness.

8. The swarming of lascivious, idle and unprofitable books and pamphlets, play books and ballads . . .

9. The hindering of godly books to be printed, the blotting out or perverting those which they suffer, all or most of that which strikes either at Popery or Arminianism, the adding of what or where pleaseth them, and the restraint of reprinting books formerly licensed, without relicensing.

10. The publishing and venting of Popish, Arminian and other dangerous books and tenets . . .

11. The growth of Popery and increase of Papists and Jesuits in sundry places, but especially about London since the Reformation; the frequent venting of crucifixes and popish pictures both engraven and printed and the placing of such in Bibles.

12. The multitude of monopolies and patents, drawing with them innumerable perjuries; the large increase of customs and impositions upon commodities, the ship-money, and many other great burthens upon the Commonwealth, under which all groan.

13. Moreover, the offices and jurisdictions of archbishops, lord bishops, deans, archdeacons, being the same way of Church government, which is in the Romish Church, and which was in England in the time of Popery, little change thereof being made (except only the head from whence it was derived), the same arguments supporting the Pope which do uphold the prelates, and overthrowing the prelates which do pull down the Pope; and other reformed churches having upon their rejection of the Pope, cast prelates out also . . .

14. The great conformity and likeness both continued and increased of our Church to the Church of Rome, in vestures, postures, ceremonies and administrations, namely as the bishops' rotchets and the lawn-sleeves, the four-cornered cap, the cope and surplice, the tippet, the hood and the canonical coat, the pulpits clothed, especially now of late, with the Jesuits' badge upon them every way.

15. The standing up at *Gloria Patri*, and at the reading of the Gospel, praying towards the east, the bowing at the name of Jesus, the bowing to the altar towards the east, cross in baptism, the kneeling at the communion.

16. The turning of the communion table altar-wise, setting images, crucifixes and conceits over them, and tapers and books upon them, and bowing or adoring to or before them . . . which is a plain device to usher in the mass . . .

19. The multitude of canons formerly made, wherein among other things excommunication, *ipso facto* is denounced for speaking of a word against the

devices above said, or subscription thereunto, though no law enjoined a restraint from the ministry without subscription and appeal is denied to any that should refuse subscription or unlawful conformity, though he be never so much wronged by inferior judges . . .

20. The countenancing plurality of benefices, prohibiting of marriages without their licence, at certain times almost half the year, and licensing of marriages without banns asking.

21. Profanation of the Lord's day, pleading for it, and enjoining ministers to read a Declaration[8] set forth (as 'tis thought) by their procurement of tolerating of sports upon that day, suspending and depriving many godly ministers for not reading the same only out of conscience, because it was against the law of God so to do, and no law of the land to enjoin it.

22. The pressing of the strict observance of the Saints' days, whereby great sums of money are drawn out of men's purses for working on them; a very high burthen on most people, who getting their living on their daily employments, must either omit them and be idle, or part with their money whereby many poor families are undone, or brought behindhand . . .

25. . . . The pride and ambition of the prelates being boundless, unwilling to be subject either to man or laws, they claim their office and jurisdiction to be *de jure divino*, exercise ecclesiastical authority in their own names and rights and under their own seals, and take upon them temporal dignities, places and offices in the commonwealth, that they may sway both swords.

26. Whence follows the taking commissions in their own courts and consistories, and where else they sit, in matters determinable of right at common law, the putting of ministers upon parishes without the patron's and people's consent . . .

28. The exercising of the oath *ex officio*, and other proceedings by way of inquisition, reaching even to men's thoughts, the apprehending and detaining of men by pursuivants, the frequent suspending and depriving of ministers, fining and imprisoning of all sorts of people, breaking up of men's houses and studies . . . and the doing of many other outrages, to the utter infringing of the laws of the realm and the subjects' liberties, and ruining of them, and their families; and of later time the judges of the land are so awed with the power and greatness of the prelates and other ways promoted that neither prohibition, *habeas corpus*, nor any other lawful remedy can be had or take place, for the distressed subjects in most cases; only papists, Jesuits, priests and other such as propagate popery or Arminianism are countenanced, spared and have much liberty; and from hence followed amongst others these dangerous consequences:

First, the general hope and expectation of the Romish party that their superstitious religion will ere long be fully planted in this kingdom again, and so they are encouraged to persist therein and to practise the same openly in divers places, to the high dishonour of God and contrary to the laws of the realm.

29. The discouragement and destruction of all good subjects, of whom are multitudes both clothiers, merchants and others, who being deprived of their ministers and overburdened with these pressures, have departed the kingdom, to

Holland and other parts, and have drawn with them a great manufacture of cloth and trading out of the land into other places where they reside, whereby wool, the great staple of the kingdom is become of small value, and vends not: trading is decayed, many poor people want work, seamen lose employment and the whole land is much impoverished, to the great dishonour of this kingdom and blemishment to the government thereof.

30. The present wars and commotions happened between his Majesty and his subjects of Scotland, wherein his Majesty and all his kingdoms are endangered and suffer greatly, and are like to become a prey to the common enemy, in case the wars go on, which we exceedingly fear will not only go on, but also increase, to an utter ruin of all unless the prelates with their dependences be removed out of England, and also they and their practices, who, as we under your Honour's favours do verily believe and conceive, have occasioned the quarrel.

1.22 THOMAS EDWARDS, *GANGRAENA*

Edwards was a presbyterian who sought to catalogue the sects and schisms which proliferated particularly after the 1642 breakdown of censorship and Church government. His aim was to demonstrate to Parliament the dangers of dividing the country, of depriving the nation of strong central government, and of libertarianism. Text from: the 1646 edition, pp. 10–12; 15; 18–36.

The prevailing of heresies and sects among us is not now to be discovered and published to the world: it hath not been all this time kept within our own walls and known only to ourselves, but hath been a long time known abroad and at home, and hath been declared by divers others, both in writing and preaching, before now: so that I shall not divulge any secret to the common enemy, all that I do is but to draw them into one, that we may see them as it were at once: our errors and schisms are spoken of far and near by enemies and friends. How many sermons have been preached before the honourable houses of Parliament and in other public places speaking of the errors of the time, which have been also printed long since by command of authority and exposed to the view of all? . . .

Secondly, supposing our errors to be known, which is fully proved in my first answer, I then secondly say 'tis so far from being unseasonable and inconvenient that 'tis most necessary that some ministers who are friends to the Reformation and zealots for the Parliament, should lay them open to the full, by testifying against them and disclaiming them that so our enemies may not say we favour and countenance them: and one of my great ends in this Tractate is to take away occasion from the common enemy to blaspheme the Reformation and speak ill of the Parliament, by our not owning them, but speaking as much against heresy, schism and all errors as any of them can.

* * *

Now the errors, heresies, blasphemies in this catalogue particularised may be referred to sixteen heads or sorts of sectaries, as namely: 1. Independents; 2. Brownists; 3. Chiliasts or Millenaries; 4. Antinomians; 5. Anabaptists; 6. Manifestarians or Arminians; 7. Libertines; 8. Familists; 9. Enthusiasts; 10. Seekers and Waiters; 11. Perfectists; 12. Socinians; 13. Arians; 14. Anti-trinitarians; 15. Anti-scripturists; 16. Sceptics and questionists, who question everything in matters of religion, namely all the Articles of Faith, and first principles of Christian religion: holding nothing positively nor certainly, saving the doctrine of pretended liberty of conscience for all, and liberty of prophesying.

* * *

The Catalogue of the errors, heresies, blasphemies is as follows:

1. That the Scriptures cannot be said to be the word of God, there is no word but Christ, the Scriptures are a dead letter, and no more to be credited than the writings of men: not divine, but human invention . . .

3. That the Scriptures are unsufficient and uncertain, there is no certainty to build any doctrine upon them, they are not an infallible foundation of faith . . .

8. That right reason is the rule of faith, and that we are to believe the Scriptures and the doctrine of the Trinity, incarnation, resurrection so far as we see them agreeable to reason, and no farther . . .

11. That God hath a hand in, and is the author of the sinfulness of his people; that he is the author not of those actions alone in and with which sin is, but of the very pravity, ataxy, anomy, irregularity and sinfulness itself which is in them . . .

20. That God loved not one man more than another before the world, neither is there an absolute particular election, but only general and conditional upon perseverance: and the Scripture nowhere speaks of reprobates or reprobation.

21. That the soul dies with the body, and all things shall have an end, but God only shall remain for ever . . .

32. That by Christ's death all the sins of all the men in the world, Turks, pagans, as well as Christians committed against the moral law and first covenant, are actually pardoned and forgiven, and this is the everlasting gospel . . .

50. That there is a perfect way in this life, not by word, sacraments, prayer and other ordinances, but by the experience of the spirit in a man's self.

51. That a man baptised with the holy ghost, knows all things even as God knows all things . . .

86. Infants rise not again because they are not capable of knowing God, and therefore not of enjoying him . . .

87. That the perfection and resurrection spoken of by Paul 1 Cor. 15.51, 52, 53, 54, 55, 56, 57, the hope set before us, the eternal inheritance, a city having foundations, whose builder and maker is God, are to be attained in the fullness and perfection of them now in this present time before the common death of the body.

88. That none of the souls of the saints go to heaven where Christ is, but heaven is empty of the saints till the resurrection of the dead.

89. There is no resurrection at all of the bodies of men after this life; nor no heaven nor hell after this life, nor no devils . . .

96. That many Christians in these days have more knowledge than the Apostles, and when the time is come that there shall be true Churches and ministry erected, they shall have greater gifts and do greater miracles than the Apostles ever did, because the Christian Church was but then in its infancy . . .

101. That the Scriptures nowhere speak of sacraments, name or thing . . .

105. 'Tis as lawful to break any of the ten commandments as to baptise an infant: yea, 'tis as lawful to commit adultery and murther, as to baptise a child.

106. That baptising belongs not to ministers only; all gifted brethren and preaching disciples (though no ministers) may baptise . . .

111. That Christ's words in the institution of his supper: *this is my body, and this is my blood* are to be understood literally . . .

114. That the Church of England and the ministry thereof is antichristian, yea of the devil, and that 'tis absolutely sinful and unlawful to hear any of their ministers preach in their assemblies . . .

123. No man hath more to do to preach the Gospel than another: but every man may preach the gospel as well as any.

124. That 'tis lawful for women to preach, and why should they not, having gifts as well as men? And some of them do actually preach, having great resort to them.

125. 'Tis a part of the Christian liberty of Christians, not to hear their own ministers, but to go and hear where they will, and whom they think they may profit most by.

126. That 'tis unlawful to worship God in places consecrated and in places where superstition and idolatry have been practised, as in our churches.

127. That men ought to preach and exercise their gifts without study and premeditation and not to think of what they are to say till they speak, because it shall be given them in that hour, and the Spirit shall teach them . . .

144. That there are revelations and visions in these times, yea to some they are more ordinary and shall be to the people of God generally within a while.

145. That the gift of miracles is not ceased in these times, but that some of the Sectaries have wrought miracles, and miracles have accompanied them in their baptism etc., and the people of God shall have power of miracles shortly . . .

148. That Christian magistrates have no power at all to meddle in matters of religion, or things ecclesiastical, but in civil only, concerning the bodies of men and goods of men . . .

151. That the Parliament having their power from, and being entrusted by, the people, the people may call them to an account for their actions and set them right and straight: and seeing this present Parliament doth engross law making and also law executing into their own hands, contrary both to reason and the

true meaning of the law, the free men of England ought not only to choose new members where they are wanting once every year but also to renew and enquire once a year after the behaviour and carriage of those they have chosen . . .

154. That 'tis lawful for a man to put away his wife upon indisposition, unfitness or contrariety of mind, arising from a cause in nature unchangeable, and for disproportion and deadness of spirit, or something distasteful and averse in the immutable bent of name; and man in regard of the freedom and eminency of his creation is a law to himself in this matter, being head of the other sex, which was made for him, neither need he near any judge therein but himself [*Milton's doctrine of divorce*].

156. That children are not bound to obey their parents at all, if they be ungodly.

157. That parents are not to catechise their little children, nor to set them to read the Scripture, or to teach them to pray, but must let them alone for God to teach them.

158. 'Tis unlawful for Christians to defend religion with the sword, or to fight for it when men come with the sword to take it away: religion will defend itself.

1.23 *THE SUSSEX CLUBMEN'S PETITION TO PARLIAMENT*

The Clubmen were groups of gentry who, during 1645, came together to plead for peace and neutrality in their area. The Sussex petition decries the religious developments under Parliament's rule. Text from: B. L. Tanner MS. 60, fo. 254.

A humble remonstrance of all the inhabitants in Chichester and Arundel Rapes, of the general grievances which were the cause of the late assembly, presented by the not engaged as well as the engaged party in the same

1. Imprimis the want of Church government whereby our Churches are decayed, God's ordinances neglected, orthodox ministers cast out without cause, and never heard; mechanics and unknown persons thrust in, who were never called as Aaron, but by a committeeman, whereby God and the Parliament are dishonoured and the people grieved.

2. Whereas for three years late past we have through much labour and God's blessing gained the fruit of the earth and had hoped to enjoy the same; but by free quarter and plunder of soldiers our purses have been exhausted, corn eaten up, cattle plundered, persons frighted from our habitations and by reason of the violence of the soldiers, our lives not safe; and have no power nor authority to resist the same, nor relieved or secured upon any complaints whereby we are disabled to pay our rents, just debts, or to maintain our wives and families from utter ruin and decay.

3. The insufferable, insolent, arbitrary power that hath been used amongst us, contrary to all our ancient known laws, or ordinances of Parliament, upon our persons and estates, by imprisoning our persons, imposing of sums of money, light horses and dragoons, and exacting of loans by some particular persons stepped into authority who have delegated their power to men of sordid condition whose wills have been laws and commands over our persons and estates, by which they have overthrown all our English liberties.

1.24 ABIEZER COPPE, *A FIERY FLYING ROLL*

Coppe was one of the more notorious Ranters, who preached in the Midlands and Berkshire: his faith and preaching asserted the inner spiritual light, the falsity of the visible Church, and the truth of God's revelation through his chosen vessels, such as Coppe. Both the violence and exuberance of his language and the political implications of his visions led to Parliament condemning the text for blasphemy in 1650, and ordering all copies to be burned. Text from: first edition, 1649, preface, chapters II, IV, VI.

Go up to London, to London that great city, write, write, write. And behold I writ, and lo a hand was sent to me, and a roll of a book was therein, which this fleshly hand would have put wings to, before the time. Whereupon it was snatched out of my hand and the roll thrust into my mouth; and I eat it up, and filled my bowels with it, where it was as bitter as wormwood; and it lay broiling and burning in my stomach, till I brought it forth in this form.

* * *

Thus, saith the Lord: be wise now therefore, O ye rulers etc.; be instructed etc.; kiss the sun, etc.; yea, kiss beggars, prisoners, warm them, feed them, clothe them, money them, relieve them, take them into your houses, don't serve them as dogs, without door etc.; own them, they are flesh of your flesh, your own brethren, your own sisters, every whit as good (and if I should stand in competition with you) in some degrees better than yourselves. Once more I say, own them, they are yourself, make them one with you, or else go howling into hell; howl for the miseries that are coming upon you, howl.

The very shadow of levelling, sword levelling, man levelling, frighted you (and who, like yourselves, can blame you, because it shook your kingdom?), but now the substantiality of levelling is coming.

The eternal God, the mighty Leveller, is coming; yea come; even at the door, and what will you do in that day?

* * *

God hath numbered thy kingdom and finished it.

And thou and all that join thee, or are (in the least degree) accessory to thy former or like intended pranks, shall most terribly and most strangely be plagued.

There is a little spark lies under (that huge heap of ashes) all thine honour, pomp, pride, wealth and riches, which shall utterly consume all that is uppermost, as it is written:

The Lord, the Lord of hosts shall send among his fat ones, leanness; and under his glory he shall kindle a burning, like the burning of a fire, and the light of Israel shall be for a fire, and his holy one of a flame, and it shall burn and devour his thorns and his briars in one day.

* * *

A terrible word and fatal blow from the Lord, upon the gathered Churches (so called) especially upon those that are styled Anabaptists.

He that hath an ear to hear, let him hear what the Spirit saith against the Churches:

Thus saith the Lord, woe to thee Bethaven, who callest thyself by the name Bethel, it shall be more tolerable (now in the day of judgement, for Tyre and Sidon) for those whom thou accountest and callest heathens, than for thee.

And thou, proud Lucifer, who exaltest thyself above all the stars of God in heaven, shalt be brought down into hell, it shall be more tolerable for Sodom and Gomorrah, for drunkards and whoremongers, than for thee. Publicans and harlots shall, publicans and hartlots do sooner enter into the kingdom of heaven than you. I'll give thee this fatal blow, and leave thee.

Thou hast affronted and defied the Almighty, more than the vilest of men (upon the face of the earth) and that so much the more, by how much the more thou takes upon thee the name of Saint, and ashamest it to thyself only, damning all those that are not of thy sect . . .

But when I came to proclaim (also) the great day of the Lord (among you) O, ye carnal Gospellers.

The devil (in you) roared out, who was tormented to some purpose, though not before his time.

He there showed both his fangs and paws, and would have torn me to pieces, and have eaten me up. Thy pride, envy, malice, arrogance, etc., was poured out like a river of brimstone, crying out, a blasphemer, a blasphemer, away with him. At length, threatening me, and being at last raving mad, some took hold of my cloak on one side, some on another, endeavouring to throw me from the place where I stood (to proclaim his Majesty's message) making a great uproar in a great congregation of people, till at length I wrapped up myself in silence (for a season) . . .

And to thine eternal shame and damnation (O, mother of witchcrafts who dwellest in gathered Churches), let this be told abroad: and let her FLESH be burned with FIRE. Amen, Hallelujah.

1.25 MARY CARY, *A NEW AND MORE EXACT MAP OR DESCRIPTION OF NEW JERUSALEM'S GLORY*

Cary was one of a small group of Fifth Monarchists who believed and preached that the Civil War and trial and execution of the King heralded the Coming of the Saints, prophesied in Revelations. In 1651 that vision had not yet been curtailed by the perceived failures of Parliament to deliver religious and social change. Text from: 1651 edition, pp. 51–7; 115–20.

And the kingdom and dominions and the greatness of the kingdom under the whole heaven shall be given unto the people of the Saints of the most high; whose kingdom is an everlasting kingdom and all dominions shall serve and obey him.

Daniel 7.27

The assertion which is laid down in these words is plain and clear, and needs no explanation at all, which is this.

That not only this kingdom of England and some few others, but all the kingdoms and dominions in the whole world, shall in a more peculiar and a more eminent manner than yet they have been, be subjected to the Lord Jesus Christ, and by him given to his Saints to possess.

This same truth likewise is positively asserted in the 13, 14, 15, 18, 21, and 22 verses of this chapter, in the 13 and 14 verses where the vision itself, of which the verses are an interpretation, is declared. There it is thus expressed: *I saw in the night vision, and behold one like the son of man came with the clouds of heaven, and came to he ancient of days, and they brought him near before him, and there was given him dominion and glory and a kingdom, that all people, nations and languages should serve him; his dominion is an everlasting dominion, which shall not pass away, and his kingdom that which shall not be destroyed . . .*

And what is in these verses said to be given to the Lord Jesus Christ is in the 18, 20, 21 and 27 verses said to be given to his Saints: for in the 18 verse it is said that *the saints of the most high should take the kingdom and possess the kingdom for ever, even for ever and ever . . .*

. . . The truth is that which is given to the head, is given to the members, that which is given to the husband, the wife must partake of: for there is nothing that he possesses which she hath not a right unto. And the Saints of Christ are the members of Christ, they are the Lamb's wife: and having given himself unto them, he will not withhold anything that is his from them: but when all the kingdoms and dominions under the whole heaven are given to him, they shall possess them with him . . .

And as it is clear here, so there are very many other Scriptures wherein it is as clearly asserted, several of which Scriptures I shall here produce, that out of the mouth of many witnesses it may be confirmed against all contradictions, which I shall the rather do because this doctrine is so much despised by profane men, who jeering at Saints, say these are the meek that must inherit the earth.

69

But first let me premise:

That though it be unquestionably true that the riches of this world, which hath been hitherto equally dispensed alike to all, shall in a very short time be abundantly given to the Saints of the most high; as Canaan's land was to Israel of old, which was but a shadow of what shall come to pass in the latter days. . . . The advanced Saints of God shall not in these days seek the wealth of the nations, but the nations themselves: as Paul expresses himself, 2 Cor. 11.14, *we seek not yours, but you*; that is, not their wealth, but their weal; not their treasure, but their safety; not their riches, but their happiness; not their outward things, but the salvation of their souls; and they that seek not these things, to wit the public weal and safety and happiness and salvation of all, but that do covet to treasure up most riches for themselves, and to poll and rob and cheat the people to enhance their own estates and make themselves great in the world, and their children gay and splendid amongst men, as do kings, princes and evil governors (not to mention some sorts of committee men) these shall become the basest and vilest among men, and their children be despised, and condemned for their sakes, especially if they walk in their steps. . . . It is heaven and not the earth, *it is the kingdom of God; and his righteousness that Saints will seek after, and these things shall be added unto them* [Math. 6.33].

* * *

But when God arises to shake terribly the earth and to visit the inhabitants thereof for their iniquity; especially for the cruelty and malice and inhumanity they have exercised against his own people, his peculiarly beloved ones, who bear his own stamp and image and name and nature; of whose souls he is the beloved, and who are the beloved of his soul. Then when he cometh to visit wicked men for these things and to own his own people (as he did the Israelites of old when he brought them out of Egypt), and to manifest to all the world that they are indeed his people, and that he will avenge their quarrel; and when he comes to rebuke, destroy and scatter the kings and the great ones of the earth for their sakes; and when he sets his people at perfect liberty and crowns them with gracious blessings and destroys all the nations that endeavour to injure them or disturb their peace. Then, I say, when the Lord doth these things, doth he appear in his glory; and so he did when he brought the Israelites out of Egypt, and so in a more glorious manner than ever will he do when he buildeth his Sion now in these latter days, wherein he hath spoken of doing greater things for them than ever hath been done from the beginning of the world, as will appear in the following discourse . . .

I have . . . showed that the King of England was one of those that was of one mind with the Beast, and that having one mind with the Beast, he persecuted the Saints and made war against them, and overcame them for a season as the Beast did.

I have showed also that the time of this prevalency of the Beast and the kings under him over the Saints and making war against them and overcoming them, was a limited, prefixed time, and that beyond it they could not go, nor have power to overcome the Saints after that time was expired . . .

I have also shown when that time expired, and that was the year 1645 . . .

In this year, as I have said, did the time of the prevalency of the Beast and his associates over the Saints cease; and though those enemies of the Saints do not cease to be, after this year, but they do and shall remain yet longer, yet they cease to overcome the Saints, and instead of prevailing they shall be prevailed against; and instead of overcoming, they shall be overcome by the Saints. . . . In that year 1645 did it come to a period, at the expiration whereof the Lord appeared in his glory and raised up his Saints out of their low condition, and gave them to overcome their enemies, and to go on by Jesus Christ their great Lord General, conquering and to conquer; causing them to tread down strength, to overcome the little horn, giving him into their hands, causing them to do justice upon him and his associates, and to overcome all that rise up against them. This hath already been done.

1.26 *ANNA TRAPNEL'S REPORT AND PLEA*

Trapnel was also a Fifth Monarchist, whose work was published after the failure of the Barebones Parliament: her visions, preaching and prophecies began early in 1654, and followed the pattern described here, of emerging after a trance-like state. Text from: first edition, 1654, pp. 20–2.

Then the Lord made his rivers flow, which soon broke down the banks of an ordinary capacity, and extraordinarily mounted my spirits into a praying and singing frame, and so they remained till morning light, as I was told, for I was not capable of that. But when I had done, and was a while silent, I came to speak weakly to those about me, saying, 'I must go to bed, for I am very weak'; and the men and women went away, and my friend that tended me, and some other maids, helped me to bed, where I lay till the afternoon, they said, silent. And that time I had a vision of the minister's wife stirring against me, and she was presented to me as one enviously bent against me, calling that falsity which she understood not. And I saw the clergymen and jurors contriving an indictment against me, and I saw myself stand before them; in a vision I saw this. And I sang with much courage, and told them I feared not them, nor their doings, for that I had not deserved such usage.

But while I was singing praises to the Lord, for his love to me, the justices sent their constable to fetch me who came and said he must have me with him. And he pulled and called me, they said that were by, but I was not capable thereof. They said he was greatly troubled how to have me to his master; they told him he had better obey God than man. And his hand shook, they said, while he was pulling me. Then some went to the justices to tell them I could not come. But they would not be pacified, some offered to be bound for my appearance next day, if I were in a capacity, but this was refused. They would have me out of my bed, unless some would take their oaths that it would endanger my life to be taken out of my bed, which none could do. . . . Then a friend persuaded them to see whether they could put me out of that condition, and told them I was never known to be put out of it; so they came. Justice Launce, now a Parliament man, was one of them, I was told. These justices that came to fetch me out of my bed, they made a great tumult, them and their followers, in the house, and some came upstairs crying, 'a witch, a witch!', making a great stir on the stairs. And a poor honest man rebuking such that said so, he was tumbled downstairs and beaten too by one of the justice's followers. And the justices made a great noise in putting out of my chamber where I lay, many of my friends, and they said if my friends would not take me up, they would have some should take me up. One of my friends told them that they must fetch their silk gowns to do it then, for the poor would not do it. And they threatened much, but the Lord overruled them. They caused my eyelids to be pulled up, for they said I held them fast, because I would deceive the people, they spake to this purpose. One of the justices pinched me by the nose and caused my pillow to be pulled from under my head, and kept pulling me and calling me; but I heard none of all this stir and bustle. Neither did I hear Mr. Welstead, which I was told called to the rulers, saying, 'a whip will fetch her up', and he stood at the chamber door talking against me, and said, 'she speaks nonsense'. The women said, 'Harken, for you cannot hear, there is such a noise'; then he listened, and said, 'Now she hears me speak, she speaks sense'. And this clergyman durst not come till the rulers came, for then, they say, the witches can have no power over them: so that one depends upon another, rulers upon clergy, and clergy upon rulers.

. . . The Lord kept me this day from their cruelty, which they had a good mind further to have let out against me. And that witch-trier woman of that town, some would fain have had come with her great pin which she used to thrust into witches to try them, but the Lord my God, in whom I trust, delivered me from their malice, making good that word to me in the psalms [76.10]: *the rage of man shall turn to thy praise and the remnant of rages thou wilt restrain.* Then further, to tell you how the Lord carried me in singing and prayer after they were gone two hours, as I was told, and then I came to myself; and being all alone, I blessed God for that quiet still day that I had.

1.27 JAMES NAYLOR, *A CAUTION TO ALL*

The publication by Quakers of their testimonies and the texts of examinations and indictments by magistrates of disturbances of the civil law served as effective propaganda for their supporters, as well as catechistic guides to their beliefs. Text from: *Naylor: A Collection of Sundry Books*, edited by George Whitehead, London, 1716, pp. 85–90; 11–16, dated 1653.

He that studies out eloquent words to please the ears of men and can talk against sin in words; but when they have done, join with the wicked in his wicked ways, as pride, covetousness, oppression, drunkenness, rioting and such like, and so become men-pleasers. These are prophets most fit for them that love their sins, and would not have their minds crossed. Micah saith [Micah 2.11] in his days that a liar and one that will prophesy of the wine and the strong drink, is a prophet most fit for his people: and these prophets shall never suffer persecution, nor ever turn any from their sins. But if any come with a true message from the Lord, and declare his judgements to come against all sin and filthiness, and witness against all the ways of the wicked, both in word and practice: then, away with such a fellow from the earth, it is not fit he should live, for he judgeth all but himself; send him to prison, or into his own country out of our coasts: what hath he to do here? Or, who sent him? Or, what is his authority? I love him not, for he never speaks good of us, but evil. O friend! Didst thou but know whom thou strivest against, thould'st tremble before him: *it is hard for thee to kick against the pricks* [King. 22.8], thou art not against man but God.

And this know, that no prophecy of old came by the will of man, but against the wills of all men in the world, both he that was sent and they to whom he was sent. But who hath resisted his will? For there is a necessity laid upon such as are sent by him; and woe unto them if they go not. And they who are thus sent are no hirelings, neither do they come with *what will you give me?* But they must witness forth freely what Christ hath revealed in them, though they suffer for it. But this call is not known to Babylon's merchants, who buy, sell and trade for money; neither is it known to the world, for if it were they would not hate and persecute it. But they that are sent by God have been hated in all ages, and it is the same now, else how should the scriptures be fulfilled [1 Cor. 2.8]? But, o man, take heed what thou doest: thy power is limited, though thou knowest it not: thou canst but kill the body and the soul shall live; thou canst but imprison the body, but the spirit is at liberty out of thy reach.

The examination of James Naylor, upon an indictment of blasphemy, at the sessions at Appleby, in January 1652

Justice Pearson   Put off your hats.

James Naylor   I do it not in contempt of authority, for I honour the power as it is of God, without respecting men's persons, it being forbidden in Scripture. He that respects persons commits sin, and is convinced of the law as a transgressor. . . .

If I see one in goodly apparel and a gold ring, and see one in poor and vile raiment, and say to him in fine apparel, sit thou in a higher place than the poor, I am partial and judged of evil thoughts.

Colonel Brigs   If thou wert in the Parliament house, wouldst thou keep it on?

James Naylor   If God should keep me in the same mind I am in now, I should.

Colonel Brigs   I knew thou wouldst condemn authority.

James Naylor   I speak in the presence of God, I do not condemn authority; but I am subject to the power as it is of God for conscience sake.

Justice Pearson   Now authority commands thee to put off thy hat, what sayest thou to it?

James Naylor Where God commands one thing, and man another, I am to obey God rather than man . . .

Colonel Brigs What profession wast thou of?

James Naylor A husbandman.

Colonel Brigs Wast thou a soldier?

James Naylor Yea, I was a soldier between eight and nine years.

Colonel Brigs Wast thou not at Burford among the Levellers?

James Naylor I was never there.

Colonel Brigs I charge thee by the Lord, that thou tell me whether thou wast or no.

James Naylor I was then in the north, and was never taxed for any mutiny, or any other thing, while I served the Parliament.

Colonel Brigs What was the cause of thy coming into these parts?

James Naylor If I may have the liberty, I shall declare it. I was at the plough, meditating on the things of God, and suddenly I heard a voice, saying unto me. *Get thee out from thy kindred, and from thy father's house.* And I had a promise given in with it, whereupon I did exceedingly rejoice that I had heard the voice of that God which I had professed from a child, but had never known him . . . and when I came at home, I gave up my estate, cast out my money, but not being obedient in going forth, the wrath of God was upon me, so that I was made a wonder to all; and none thought I would have lived. But (after I was made willing) I began to make some preparation, as apparel and other necessaries, not knowing whither I should go: but shortly afterward going a gate-ward with a friend from my own house, having on an old suit without any money, having neither taken leave of wife or children, not thinking then of any journey, I was commanded to go into the west, not knowing whether I should go, nor what I was to do there, but when I had been there a little while, I had given me what I was to declare and ever since I have remained, not knowing today what I was to do tomorrow.

Colonel Brigs What was the promise that thou hadst given?

James Naylor That God would be with me: which promise I find made good every day.

Colonel Brigs I never heard such a call as this, in our time.

James Naylor I believe thee.

Justice Pearson Is Christ in thee?

James Naylor I witness him in me, and if I should deny him before men, he would deny me before my father which is in heaven.

Justice Pearson Spiritual, you mean?

James Naylor Yea, spiritual . . .

Justice Pearson How comes it to pass that people quake and tremble?

James Naylor The Scriptures witness the same condition in the saints formerly, as David, Daniel, Habbakkuk, and divers others.

Justice Pearson Did they fall down?

James Naylor Yea, some of them did so . . . They must first be made spiritual, he cannot be seen with carnal eyes, for he is a spirit, and no flesh can see God and live . . .

Justice Pearson To the Word: what sayest thou to the Scriptures? Are they the word of God?

James Naylor They are a true declaration of the word, that was in them who spoke forth.

Higginson Is there not a written word?

James Naylor Where readest thou in the Scriptures that they are called the written word? The Word is spiritual, not seen with carnal eyes: but as for the Scriptures they are true and I witness them true, in measure fulfilled in me, as far as I am grown up.

Justice Pearson Why dost thou disturb the ministers in their public worships?

James Naylor I have not disturbed them in their public worships.

Justice Pearson Why dost thou speak against tithes, which are allowed by the states?

James Naylor I meddle not with the states, I speak against them that are hirelings, as they are hirelings: those that were sent of Christ never took tithes, nor yet sued any for wages.

Justice Pearson Dost thou think we are so beggarly as the heathens that we cannot afford our minister's maintenance? We give them it freely.

James Naylor They are the ministers of Christ who abide in the doctrine of Christ.

Justice Pearson But who shall judge? How shall we know them?

James Naylor By their fruits you shall know them; they that abide not in the doctrine of Christ make it appear they are not the ministers of Christ.

Justice Pearson That is true.

This Justice Pearson was convinced at this sessions by J. Naylor as he sat on the bench, one of his judges being that Anthony Pearson who afterwards writ the book called *The Great Case of Tithes*.

1.28 *INSTRUMENT OF GOVERNMENT*

The Instrument of Government emerged out of the chaos of the Barebones Parliament, which was dissolved in 1653 by members opposed to its radical bent. It confirmed Cromwell as Lord Protector, but subject to Parliament. The extract here shows some religious toleration was statutorily validated. Text from: *Acts and Ordinances of the Interregnum 1642–1660*, London, 1911, II, 820.

XXXV. That the Christian religion, as contained in the Scriptures, be held forth and recommended as the public profession of these nations; and that as soon as may be a provision, less subject to scruple and contention, and more certain than the present, be made for the encouragement and maintenance of able and painful teachers for instructing the people and for discovery and confutation of error, heresy, and whatever is contrary to sound doctrine. And that until such provision be made the present maintenance shall not be taken away nor impeached.

XXXVI. That to the Public Profession held forth none shall be compelled by penalties or otherwise; but that endeavours be used to win them by sound doctrine and the example of a good conversation.

XXXVII. That such as profess faith in God by Jesus Christ (though differing in judgement from the doctrine, worship or discipline publicly held forth) shall not be restrained from, but shall be protected in, the profession of the Faith and exercise of their religion, so as they abuse not this liberty to the civil injury of others, and to the actual disturbance of the public peace on their parts. Provided this liberty be not extended to popery nor prelacy, nor to such as, under the profession of Christ, hold forth and practise licentiousness.

1.29 MARGARET FELL FOX, *A DECLARATION AND AN INFORMATION FROM US PEOPLE OF GOD CALLED QUAKERS*

Fell Fox was an active and effective Quaker preacher, travelling the country on her missionary purpose, either alone or with her husband. The Quakers were particularly feared because of their lack of deference to any temporal power, their insistence on inner spirituality and for their physical symptoms when under the influence of the spirit (they quaked). This publication was addressed to the restored King and Parliament in 1660, pleading for toleration. Text from: 1660 edition.

We who are the people of God called Quakers, who are hated and despised and everywhere spoken against as people not fit to live, as they were that went before us, who were of the same spirit, power and life, and were as we are in that they were accounted as the off-scouring of all things, by that spirit and nature that is of the world, and so the Scripture is fulfilled, *he that is born of the flesh persecuteth him that is born of the spirit;* we have been a suffering people, under every power and change, and under every profession of religion that hath been, and born the outward power in the nation these twelve years, since we were a people, and being that through the old enemy which hath continually appeared against us, not only in the profane people of the nation, but also in the highest profession of sorts and sects of religion we have suffered under and been persecuted by them all. Even some persecuted and prisoned till death, others their bodies bruised till death; stigmatised, bored thorough the tongue, gagged in the mouth, stocked and whipped thorough towns and cities, our goods spoiled, our bodies two or three years imprisoned. . . . And this hath been the only ground and cause of our sufferings, because we obeyed the command of Christ, the author of our eternal salvation, and observed the Apostles' doctrine and practice and not for any other cause or end have our sufferings been, but for conscience sake, because we cannot bow to men's wills and worships, contrary to the command of Christ Jesus, our everlasting priest, king and prophet, whom we serve with our spirits and worship in that, which the world calls heresy.

. . . if ye did rightly understand our innocency and integrity, nakedness and singleness in our carriage towards all men upon the face of the earth, and if ye would but examine and search out our carriage and behaviour towards all men's persons, souls and estates, if these things were searched out and examined thorough the nations, and that no prejudice were let into your minds from other words, which proceed from secret envy, malice and hatred, and not from any just ground they have against us, but as it is from a contrary spirit and mind, as it was in the Jews against Christ, and in all others against the Apostles, so it is the same now against us; but this we commit to the Lord, who will plead over our cause and clear our innocency, who hath said *vengeance is mine*, and *I will repay it*, and now that they know we cannot swear, nor take an oath for conscience sake, but have suffered because we could not take them; now do the magistrates of several counties of the nation, through the suggestion of the priest's envy, which is inveterate against us, tender us an oath which they call the Oath of Allegiance, with several other Engagements, what their own wills can invent, on purpose to ensnare us, that upon the denial thereof they may cast us into prison, and have already cast several of us into prison at their own pleasure. We do therefore declare to take of all jealousies, fears and suspicions of our truth and fidelity to the King and these present governors, that our intentions and endeavours are and shall be good, true, honest, and peaceable towards them and that we do love, own and honour the King and these present governors so far as they do rule for God and his truth, and do not impose anything upon people's consciences, but let the Gospel have its free passage through the consciences of men, which we do not know that they have (by any law) as yet imposed. And if they grant liberty of conscience towards God and towards man, then we know that God will bless them, for want of which hath been the overthrow of all that went before them. We do not desire any liberty that may justly offend anyone's conscience, but the liberty we do desire is that we may keep our consciences clear and void of offence towards God and towards men, and that we may enjoy our civil rights and liberties of subjects as freeborn English men. And this we do in the presence of the Lord declare, not in flattering titles, but in reality and truth of our hearts, and shall manifest the same. Now that we may be clear in the presence of the living God, and of all just and moderate men that they may not have their hands in blood and persecution, as those have had that are gone before . . .

Given forth the 5th of the 4th month, 1660. Margaret Fell

1.30 *THE CLARENDON CODE*

On the restoration of Charles II in 1660, many of the religious and political reforms of the Commonwealth and Protectorate period were repealed. The clutch of legislation which restated the restrictions on worship, conformity, toleration, free speech, and freedom of movement were known collectively as *The Clarendon Code*, after their architect and Charles's principal adviser, Edward Hyde. The Corporation Act and the Act of Uniformity ensured both conformity and uniformity in the theological and political spheres, through a combination of effective policing and effective loyalty tests. Text from: *Statutes of the Realm*, V, 321–3.

The Act of Uniformity 1662

Whereas in the first year of the late Queen Elizabeth there was one uniform Order of Common Service and Prayer . . . and yet this notwithstanding, a great number of people in divers parts of this realm, following their own sensuality and living without knowledge and due fear of God, do wilfully and schismatically abstain and refuse to come to their parish churches . . . and whereas by the great and scandalous neglect of ministers in using the said order or liturgy so set forth and enjoined as aforesaid, great mischiefs and inconveniences during the times of the late unhappy troubles have arisen and grown, and many people have been led into factions and schisms, to the great decay and scandal of the reformed religion of the Church of England, and to the hazard of many souls . . .

Now in regard that nothing conduceth more to the settling of the peace of this nation (which is desired by all good men) nor to the honour of our religion and the propagation thereof, than a universal agreement in the public worship of Almighty God, and to the intent that every person within this realm may certainly know the rule to which he is to conform in public worship . . . all and singular ministers in any cathedral, collegiate, or parish Church or Chapel . . . shall be bound to say and use the Morning Prayer, Evening Prayer, celebration and administration of both the sacraments, and all other the public and common prayer in such order and form as is mentioned in the said book annexed and joined to this present act and entitled *The Book of Common Prayer* . . .

. . . that every parson, vicar or other minister whatsoever who now hath and enjoyeth any ecclesiastical benefice or promotion within this realm of England or places aforesaid, shall in the Church, Chapel or place of public worship belonging to his said benefice or promotion, upon some Lord's day before the feast of St. Bartholomew, 1662, openly, publicly and solemnly read the morning and evening prayer appointed to be read . . . and after such reading thereof shall openly and publicly before the congregation there assembled declare his unfeigned assent and consent to the use of all things in the said book contained and prescribed, in these words, and no other:

I, A. B. do declare my unfeigned assent and consent to all and everything contained and prescribed in and by the book entitled The Book of Common Prayer . . .

And that all and every such person who shall . . . neglect or refuse to do the same within the time aforesaid . . . shall *ipso facto* be deprived of all his spiritual promotions . . . the same as though the person or persons so offending or neglecting were dead . . .

And be it further enacted . . . that every dean, canon and prebendary of every cathedral or collegiate church, and all masters and other heads, fellows, chaplains and tutors of or in any college, hall, house of learning or hospital, and every public professor and reader in either of the universities and in every college elsewhere, and every parson, vicar, curate, lecturer and every other person in holy orders and every schoolmaster keeping any public or private schools, and every person instructing or teaching any youth in any house or private family as a tutor or schoolmaster . . . shall before the Feast Day of St. Bartholomew 1662, or at or before his or their respective admission or be incumbent or have possession aforesaid subscribe the Declaration or Acknowledgement following:

I, A. B. do declare that it is not lawful upon any pretence whatsoever to take arms against the king and that I do abhor that traitorous position of taking arms by his authority against his person or against those that are commissioned by him, and that I will conform to the liturgy of the Church of England as it is now by law established. And I do declare that I do hold there lies no obligation upon me or on any other person from the oath commonly called the Solemn League and Covenant to endeavour any change or alteration of government either in Church or State. And that the same was in itself an unlawful oath and imposed upon the subjects of this realm against the known laws and liberties of this kingdom.

2

POLITICS

INTRODUCTION

Populist myths about politics in the sixteenth and seventeenth centuries have tended to tell a simplified and misleading story of the gradual enlargement and encroachment of the State and its powers over the individual, epitomised in the successive conflicts between monarchs and parliaments. Parliamentary and individual liberty, freedom of speech and the modern political theory of a social contract (so the tale goes) were won through the Civil War and subsequent parliaments in their attacks on the monarch and absolutist political theory. These versions of history[1] essentially pit conservative monarchs and aristocracy against a radical libertarian Commons. The problems with such accounts is that they ask us to read history backwards: most particularly in order to explain rationally the conflicts of the Civil War years of 1642 to 1649, and the Glorious Revolution of 1688, as a principled and long-awaited revolution in thought and political development.

Revisionist historians, by contrast, have used local sources and parliamentary records to make two crucial, and now largely accepted, points. First, that Elizabethan parliaments, far from seeing the beginning of the 'high road to civil war', as Neale, Hill and others saw it, with the establishment of a 'puritan' parliamentary opposition and brake to royal prerogative, were remarkably consensual, tractable, well managed, and actively acquiescent in the dominant political philosophy, and were mainly divided according to machinations of court factions.[2] Second, that James I's parliaments, and even those of the early years of Charles I's reign, built on and maintained a political consensus which acknowledged the special nature and function of each of the political institutions of the English mixed monarchy: monarch, Lords and Commons, in which the common law protected the rights of the propertied individual.[3] Thus, for example, James I's articulation of the renowned 'divine right of kings' philosophy and the royal prerogative (2.14), despite appearing incredible to a nineteenth- or twentieth-century reader, was not disputed by the majority of his contemporaries and subjects; and he was extremely careful to phrase the articulation of his rights and duties in the context of the rights and duties of his subjects (see, for example, 2.14). In other words, such a theory of monarchy worked within and because of an overall framework of consensual belief in an ordered, hierarchical society in which most men and women knew their place (see Elyot and Smith, for example). Of course, threats to stability and matters of disagreement did disturb this system from time to time: most often about local matters such as grain shortages or local feuds: but on the whole large-scale political revolution and rebellion were anathema to the conservative, small-parish mentality of a pre-industrial age.

But such an account does not explain why such a revolution did occur in the 1640s. We need to ask why this apparently widespread political consensus did break down, and why so drastically? Contemporary answers of the time, not only those of the Long Parliament in 1642, and the army after 1647, but also royalist academic accounts (for example the Earl of Clarendon's account) blamed the actions and character of Charles I, who, from his accession in 1625, failed to understand the complexities of English politics and administration, as well as underestimating the growing attachment to and pride in a Protestant nationhood. He was accused of two mistakes: unlike his father James, when he was unable to negotiate money from Parliament, he resorted to taxes which were seen as extra-parliamentary and hence unconstitutional. Second, he sought to bring order and regularity to the Church in a way which was interpreted as proto-Catholic (see for example, *The Petition of Right*, *The Root and Branch Petition*, and *The Grand Remonstrance*). Real fears about the Catholic threat surfaced in England continually from the 1570s: and the fact that both James I and Charles I had married Catholic women, who maintained their own factions and followers at Court, was seen as an affront to English nationhood. Many accounts of local disturbances of the late 1630s and of 1640–2, before the outbreak of fighting, show that 'country' feeling quite quickly polarised into attacks made upon 'puritans' and 'papists' respectively: both used as terms of easy abuse without necessarily being accurate. Most revisionist and post-revisionist historians concur in allocating the final blame for the violent outbreak of civil war on a combination of Charles I's mismanagement and bad luck.[4] Where they disagree is in accounting for subsequent loyalties and the short- and long-term origins and significance of political and cultural disagreements.[5] Civil war was not the necessary outcome of conflict: but when it did result, after negotiations between King and Parliament broke down in 1642, allegiance was based upon a combination of traditional local feeling, religious conviction, the power and effectiveness of local power structures and their relationship to Parliament or monarch, and a greater amount of national political knowledge and opinion than some historians have acknowledged.[6]

The kinds of difficulties Charles I faced as a monarch were endemic to the early modern State, and shared not only by James I and Elizabeth I, and subsequently Cromwell, but also by other Western European monarchs of the period. These were: an inefficient system of local bureaucracy; no agreement, or even understanding, about national taxation needs; a divided kingdom;[7] a rapidly changing and increasingly expensive military technology; inflation; and religious divisions. The combination of all of these factors together with Charles I's apparent inability to follow through on consensus politics[8] reached a crisis point in the late 1630s and precipitated the Civil War. The tendency of contemporaries was to see this crisis point as simply one of constitutional conflict: one in which, on the one side the monarch was defending his rights to rule and raise an army in the interests of the nation (see 2.20), and on the other, the Commons were defending ancient rights of the liberty of property, expressed through the right of Parliament alone to raise and agree to taxes (expressed here in the *Petition of Right* and *The Grand Remonstrance*, 2.19, 2.20). Thus each party claimed to be entrenched in a conservative defence of ancient rights. What these contemporary accounts of events thus failed to do was to solve, or even suggest solutions to, the endemic problems besetting the State. Where political groups did attempt to provide solutions, these ranged between utopian programmes of minorities such as the Levellers (2.19) and the Diggers (2.23), and the machinery of government and taxation introduced by the Major Generals in 1656, which is attacked in *The Humble Petition and Advice* (2.27).

Of course in the same way as religion is not the story of 'faith by statute',[9] politics is not simply a narration of political events, of statute and proclamation, of faction and counter-faction, and the succession of kings. Nor is it all of these, with the addition of some political philosophy. As David Underdown writes:

> we might pause to ask what 'politics' actually meant for the English common people in the early seventeenth century. Politics involves those matters pertaining to the *polis*, the community. There was a politics of the kingdom, a politics of the shire, a politics of the town or village, all in various ways related to each other. People were engaged with these several levels of politics in different ways according to their place in society. The marginal landholders, cottagers and labourers were involved primarily in the third kind, and then only as subjects or victims of policies devised and implemented by others, except on the rare occasions when they combined in riotous protests serious enough to require the attention of the county governors, or even of King or Council.[10]

Yet local politics was on a continuum with monarch, Privy Council and Parliament: local administration was carried out through the Justices of Peace, in conjunction with local parish priests: as both the Acts of

Supremacy and Uniformity show (1.5, 2.2); and the cases found in Church court records and records of petty assizes demonstrate a continuity of concern with order and property rights.[11] Studies of local politics do suggest a growing cultural gap, not between 'court' and 'country',[12] but between conservative defenders of an older deferential culture of paternalism and hierarchy, and a newer culture of reform and godliness.[13] This cultural split, Underdown argues, becomes a political one. The later debate between Filmer's political philosophy of patriarchalism and Locke's of economic contractualism,[14] which became the dividing issue between Tories and Whigs respectively, after 1660, is thus genuinely prefigured in the existence of two cultures in the earlier seventeenth century. Thus, the language of the parliamentarians during the 1640s and 1650s, of liberty and property, does not just represent a continuity of a defence of parliamentary and common law rights dating back to the fifteenth century, but the discovery, in the context of an ongoing debate with royalists, of an ideology and its language (see for example, 2.18, 2.19). This latter discourse is not one of liberty, equality and fraternity (even the Levellers did not imagine such things), but one of individualism and property rights, contract and law. Liberty, as defined by parliamentarians, Levellers and later by Locke, was the liberty to own property; the liberty of the 'freeborn' Englishman: where both birth and gender crucially defined only a minority of the populace as fit to govern, whilst the rest were fit only to be subjects. As Sir Thomas Smith writes (2.7): 'These have no voice nor authority in our commonwealth and no account is made of them, but only to be ruled, not to rule other' (see 3.9).

2.1 THOMAS ELYOT, *THE GOVERNOR*

Elyot's defence of the traditional 'chain of being' political theory has a decided humanist meritocratic slant: knowledge and reason are the crucial distinguishing marks of the highest estate, and from these follow the honours and status given to governors. Hence it is a logical consequence of this philosophy that the remainder of the work is then devoted to educational philosophy and practice in a State. Education and politics are entwined for Elyot, as for many of his contemporary followers of Cicero and Plato. Text from: 1531 edition, chapters 1–4.

But now to prove, by example of those things that be within the compass of man's knowledge, of what estimation order is, not only among men, but also with God, albeit his wisdom, bounty and magnificence can be with no tongue or pen sufficiently expressed. Hath not he set degrees and estates in all his glorious works?

First, in his heavenly ministers, whom, as the church affirmeth, he hath constituted to be in divers degrees called hierarchies [Aquinas, *Summ. Theol.* pt. 1. cviii] . . .

Behold also the order that God hath put generally in all his creatures, beginning at the most inferior or base and ascending upward: he made not only herbs to garnish the earth, but also trees of a more eminent stature than herbs, and yet in the one and the other be degrees of qualities; some pleasant to behold, some delicate or good in taste, other wholesome and medicineable, some commodious and necessary. Semblably in birds, beasts and fishes. . . . But where any is found that hath many of the said properties, he is more set by than all the other and by that estimation the order of his place and degree evidently appeareth; so that every kind of trees, herbs, birds, beasts and fishes, beside their diversity of forms, have (as who saith) a peculiar disposition aproppered[1] unto them by God their creator: so that in everything is order, and without order may be nothing stable or permanent; and it may not be called order except it do contain in it degrees, high and base, according to the merit or estimation of the thing that is ordered . . .

. . . And therefore it appeareth that God giveth not to every man like gifts of grace, or of nature, but to some more, some less, as it liketh his divine majesty.

Nor they be not in common (as fantastical folks would have all things)[2], nor one man hath not all virtues and good qualities. Notwithstanding, forasmuch as understanding is the most excellent gift that man can receive in his creation, whereby he doth approach most nigh unto the similitude of God; which understanding is the principal part of the soul: it is therefore congruent and according, that, as one excelleth another in that influence, as thereby being next to the similitude of his maker, so should the estate of his person be advanced in degree or place where understanding may profit; which is also distributed into sundry uses, faculties and offices necessary for the living and governance of mankind. . . . Forasmuch as the said persons, excelling in knowledge whereby other be governed, be ministers for the only profit and commodity of them which have not equal understanding; where they which do exercise artificial science or corporal labour, do not travail for their superiors only, but also for their own necessity. So the husbandman feedeth himself and the cloth maker; the cloth maker apparelleth himself and the husband; they both succour other artificers; other artificers them; they and other artificers them that be governors. But they that be governors (as I before said) nothing do acquire by the said influence of knowledge for their own necessities, but do employ all the powers of their wits and their diligence to the only preservation of other their inferiors; among which inferiors also behoveth to be a disposition and order according to reason, that is to say that the slothful or idle person do not participate with him that is industrious and taketh pain, whereby the fruits of his labours should be diminished: wherein should be none equality, but thereof should proceed discourage and finally dissolution for lack of provision. Wherefore it can none otherwise stand with reason, but that the estate of the person in preeminence of living should be esteemed with his understanding, labour and policy: whereunto must be added an augmentation of honour and substance; which not only impresseth a reverence, whereof proceedeth due obedience among subjects, but also inflameth men naturally inclined to idleness or sensual appetite to covet like fortune, and for that cause to dispose them to study or occupation. Now to conclude my first assertion or argument: where all thing is common, there lacketh order; and where order lacketh, there all thing is odious and uncomely. And that have we in daily experience: for the pans and pots garnisheth well the kitchen, and yet should they be to the chamber none ornament . . .

That one Sovereign governor ought to be in a public weal

Like as to a castle or fortress sufficeth one owner or sovereign, and where any more be of like power and authority seldom cometh the work to perfection; or being already made, where the one diligently overseeth and the other neglecteth, in that contention all is subverted and cometh to ruin. In semblable wise doth a public weal that hath more chief governors than one. Example we may take of the Greeks, among whom in divers cities were divers forms of public weals governed by multitudes: wherein one was most tolerable where the governance and rule was alway permitted to them which excelled in virtue, and was in the Greek tongue called *Aristocratia* . . .

Another public weal was among the *Atheniensis*, where equality was of estate among the people, and only by their whole consent, their city and dominions were governed; which might well be called a monster with many heads; nor never it was certain nor stable; and often times they banished or slew the best citizens, which by their virtue and wisdom had most profited to the public weal. This manner of governance was called in Greek *democratia*. . . . Of these two governances none of them may be sufficient. For in the first, which consisteth of good men, virtue is not so constant in a multitude, but that some, being once in authority, be incensed with glory; some with ambition; other with covetous [*sic*] and desire of treasure or possessions; whereby they fall into contention, and finally, where any achieveth the superiority, the whole governance is reduced unto a few in number, which, fearing the multitude and their mutability, to the intent to keep them in dread to rebel, ruleth by terror and cruelty, thinking thereby to keep themself in surety: notwithstanding rancour coarcted[3] and long detained in a narrow room, at the last brasteth out with intolerable violence and bringeth all to confusion. . . . The popular estate, if it anything do vary from equality of substance or estimation, or that the multitude of people have over much liberty, of necessity one of these inconveniences must happen: either tyranny, where he that is too much in favour would be elevate and suffer none equality, or else into the rage of a communality, which of all rules is most to be feared. For like as the commons, if they feel some severity, they do humbly serve and obey, so where they embracing a licence refuse to be bridled, they fling and plunge; and if they once throw down their governor, they order everything without justice, only with vengeance and cruelty; and with incomparable difficulty and unneth[4] by any wisdom be pacified and brought again into order. Wherefore undoubtedly the best and most sure governance is by one King or Prince, which ruleth only for the weal of his people to him subject: and that manner of governance is best approved and hath longest continued and is most ancient. For who can deny but that all thing in heaven and earth is governed by one God, by one perpetual order, by one providence?

That in a public weal ought to be inferior governors called magistrates

There be both reasons and examples, undoubtedly infinite, whereby may be proved that there can be no perfect public weal without one capital and sovereign governor which may long endure or continue. But since one mortal man cannot have knowledge of all things done in a realm or large dominion and at one time discuss all controversies, reform all transgressions and exploit all consultations, concluded as well for outward as inward affairs: it is expedient and also needful that under the capital governor be sundry mean authorities, as it were aiding him in the distribution of justice in sundry parts of a huge multitude. . . . Such governors would be chosen out of that estate of men which be called worshipful, if among them may be founden a sufficient number, ornate with virtue and wisdom, meet for such purpose and that for sundry causes.

First it is of good congruence that they which be superior in condition or haviour, should have also preeminence in administration, if they be not inferior to other in virtue. Also they having of their own revenues certain whereby they have competent substance to live without taking rewards: it is likely that they will not be so desirous of lucre (whereof may be engendered corruption) as they which have very little, or nothing, so certain.

Moreover, where virtue is in a gentleman, it is commonly mixed with more sufferance, more affability, and mildness than for the more part it is in a person rural, or of a very base lineage; and when it happeneth otherwise, it is to be accounted loathsome and monstrous. Furthermore, where the person is worshipful, his governance, though it be sharp, is to the people more tolerable, and they therewith the less grudge, or be disobedient. Also such men, having substance in goods by certain and stable possessions, which they may apportionate to their own living, and bringing up of their children in learning and virtues, may (if nature repugn not) cause them to be so instructed and furnished toward the administration of a public weal, that a poor man's son only by his natural wit, without other adminiculation[5] or aid, never or seldom may attain to the semblable. Toward the which instruction I have, with no little study, and labours, prepared this work, as Almighty God be my judge, without arrogance or any spark of vainglory.

2.2 THE ACT OF SUPREMACY

The title of this Act exposits the Tudors' political aim and ideological method of claiming a return to an ancient and original theological and political purity, lost by the incursions of the Roman Church: 'An Act restoring to the Crown the ancient jurisdiction over the state ecclesiastical and spiritual and abolishing all foreign power repugnant to the same'. Text from: *Statutes of the Realm:* 1 Eliz. I, c.1.

. . . And to the intent that all usurped and foreign power and authority, spiritual and temporal, may for ever be clearly extinguished and never to be used nor obeyed within this realm or any other your Majesty's dominions or countries: may it please your Highness that it may be further enacted by the authority aforesaid that no foreign prince, person, prelate, State or potentate, spiritual or temporal, shall at any time after the last day of this session of Parliament use, enjoy or exercise any manner of power, jurisdiction, superiority, authority, pre-eminence or privilege spiritual or ecclesiastical within this realm . . . but from thenceforth the same shall be clearly abolished out of this realm and all other your Highness's dominions for ever: any statute, ordinance, custom, constitutions, or any other matter or cause whatsoever to the contrary in any wise notwithstanding.

And that also it may likewise please your Highness that it may be established and enacted by the authority aforesaid that such jurisdiction, privileges, superiorities and pre-eminences spiritual and ecclesiastical, as by any spiritual or ecclesiastical power or authority hath heretofore been or may lawfully be exercised or used for the visitation of the ecclesiastical state and persons, and for reformation, order and correction of the same and of all manner of errors, heresies, schisms, abuses, offences, contempts, and enormities, shall for ever by authority of this present Parliament be united and annexed to the imperial crown of this realm. And that your Highness, your heirs and successors, kings or queens of this realm, shall have full power and authority . . . to visit, reform, redress, order, correct and amend all such errors, heresies, schisms, abuses, offences, contempts and enormities whatsoever which by any manner spiritual or ecclesiastical power, authority or jurisdiction can or may lawfully be reformed, ordered, redressed, corrected, restrained or amended to the pleasure of Almighty God, the increase of virtue and the conservation of the peace and unity of this realm . . .

And for the better observation and maintenance of this act, may it please your Highness that it may be further enacted by the authority aforesaid that all and every archbishop, bishop and all and every other ecclesiastical person and other ecclesiastical officer and minister, of what estate, dignity, pre-eminence or degree soever he or they be or shall be, and all and every temporal judge, justicer, mayor and other lay or temporal officer and minister, and every other person having your Highness's fee or wages within this realm or any your Highness's dominions, shall make, take and receive a corporal oath upon the evangelist, before such person or persons as shall please your Highness, your heirs or successors, under the great seal of England to assign and name to accept and take the same according to the tenor and effect hereafter following, that is to say, *I, A. B., do utterly testify and declare in my conscience that the Queen's Highness is the only supreme governor of this realm and of all other her Highness's dominions and countries, as well in all spiritual or ecclesiastical things or causes as temporal, and that no foreign prince, person, prelate, State or potentate hath or ought to have any jurisdiction, power, superiority, pre-eminence or authority ecclesiastical or spiritual within this realm and therefore I do utterly renounce and forsake all foreign jurisdictions, powers, superiorities and authorities, and do promise that from henceforth I shall bear faith and true allegiance to the Queen's Highness, her heirs and lawful successors, and to my power shall assist and defend all jurisdictions, pre-eminences, privileges and authorities granted or belonging to the Queen's Highness, her heirs and successors, or united or annexed to the imperial crown of this realm: so help me God and by the contents of this Book. . . .*

. . . [And] if any person or persons dwelling or inhabiting within this your realm or in any other your Highness's realms or dominions . . . after the end of thirty days next after the determination of this session of this present Parliament shall by writing, printing, teaching, preaching, express words, deed or act; advisedly, maliciously and directly affirm, hold, stand with, set forth, maintain, or defend the authority, pre-eminence, power or jurisdiction, spiritual or ecclesiastical of any foreign prince, prelate, person, State or potentate whatsoever, heretofore claimed, used, or usurped within this realm or any dominion or country being within or under the power, dominion or obeisance of your Highness; or shall advisedly, maliciously and directly put in ure or execute anything for the extolling, advancement, setting forth, maintenance or defence of any such pretended or usurped jurisdiction, power, pre-eminence or authority, or any part thereof, that then every such person and persons so doing and offending, their abettors, aiders, procurers, and counsellors, being thereof lawfully convicted . . . [shall be] attainted according to the due order and course of the common laws of this realm.

2.3 JOHN KNOX, *THE FIRST BLAST OF THE TRUMPET AGAINST THE MONSTROUS REGIMENT OF WOMEN*

Knox, a strict calvinist, firmly believed that Mary Queen of Scots should not hold the Scottish throne, neither as a Catholic nor as a woman. His vitriolic blast was answered by Aylmer in defence of Elizabeth I's right to rule in England (see 2.4). Text from: first edition, 1558, pp. 2–5.

The first blast of the trumpet to awake women degenerate

To promote a woman to bear rule, superiority, dominion or empire above any realm, nation, or city is repugnant to nature, contumely to God, a thing most contrarious to his revealed will and approved ordinance, and finally it is the subversion of good order, of all equity and justice . . .

And first, where that I affirm the empire of a woman to be a thing repugnant to nature, I mean not only that God by the order of his creation hath spoiled women of authority and dominion, but also that man hath seen, proved and pronounced just causes why that it so should be. Man, I say, in many other cases blind, doth in this behalf see very clearly. For the causes be so manifest that they cannot be hid. For who can deny but it repugneth to nature, that the blind shall be appointed to lead and conduct such as do see? That the weak, the sick and impotent persons shall nourish and keep the whole and strong, and finally, that the foolish, mad and frenetic shall govern the discreet, and give counsel to such as be sober of mind? And such be all women compared unto man, in bearing of authority. For their sight in civil regiment is but blindness; their strength weakness; their counsel foolishness: and judgement frenzy, if it be rightly considered.

I except such as God, by singular privilege, and for certain causes known only to himself hath exempted from the common rank of women, and do speak of women as nature and experience do this day declare them. Nature, I say, doth paint them forth to be weak, frail, impatient, feeble and foolish; and experience hath declared them to be unconstant, variable, cruel, and lacking the spirit of counsel and regiment. And these notable faults have men in all ages espied in that kind, for the which not only they have removed women from rule and authority, but also some have thought that men subject to the counsel or empire of their wives were unworthy of all public office. For this writeth Aristotle in the second of his *Politics*: what difference shall we put, saith he, whether that women bear authority, or the husbands that obey the empire of their wives, be appointed to be magistrates? For what ensueth the one must needs follow the other, to wit: injustice, confusion, and disorder. The same author further reasoneth, that the policy or regiment of the Lacedemonians (who other ways amongst the Grecians were most excellent) was not worthy to be reputed nor accompted amongst the number of commonwealths that were well governed, because the magistrates and rulers of the same were too much given to please and obey their wives. What would this writer (I pray you) have said to that realm or nation where a woman sitteth crowned in Parliament amongst the midst of men. O, fearful and terrible are thy judgements (o, Lord) which thus hast abased man for his iniquity! I am assuredly persuaded that if any of those men, which illuminated only by the light of nature, did see and pronounce causes sufficient why women ought not to bear rule nor authority, should this day live and see a woman sitting in judgement, or riding from Parliament in the midst of men, having the royal crown upon her head, the sword and sceptre born before her, in sign that the administration of justice was in her power: I am assuredly persuaded . . . that such a sight should so astonish them, that they should judge the whole world to be transformed into Amazons, and that such a metamorphosis and change was made of all the men of that country, as poets do feign was made of the companions of Ulysses, or at least, that albeit the outward form of men remained, yet should they judge that their hearts were changed from the wisdom, understanding, and courage of men, to the foolish fondness and cowardice of women. Yea they should further pronounce that where women reign or be in authority, that there must needs vanity be preferred to virtue; ambition and pride to temperancy and modesty, and finally, that avarice the mother of all mischief must needs devour equity and justice. But lest that we shall seem to be of this opinion alone, let us hear what others have seen and decreed in this matter. In the rules of the law thus it is written: women are removed from all civil and public office, so that they neither may be judges, neither may they occupy the place of the magistrate, neither yet may they be speakers for others. The same is repeated in the third and the sixteenth books of the digests: where certain persons are forbidden, *ne pro alius postulent*, that is that they be no speakers nor advocates for others. And among the rest are women forbidden, and this cause is added, that they do not against their shamefastness intermeddle themselves with the causes of others, neither yet that women presume to use the offices due to men. The law in the same place doth further declare, that a natural shamefastness ought to be in womankind, which most certainly she loseth, whensoever she taketh upon her the office and estate of man.

2.4 JOHN AYLMER, *AN HARBOROW FOR FAITHFUL AND TRUE SUBJECTS*

Aylmer, a convinced Protestant, instructed Lady Jane Grey, spent Mary's reign in exile and returned on the accession of Elizabeth. He later became bishop of London. His argument, in refutation of Knox, in defence of woman's rule is that God's election is the most supreme law, and therefore may be equated to natural law. Text from: first edition, 1559, fos C3^v–C4; G4^{r-v}.

If it were unnatural for a woman to rule because she lacketh a man's strength, then old kings which be most meet to rule for wit and experience, because they lack strength, should be unmeet for the feebleness of the body. Yea, say you, God hath appointed her to be subject to her husband: . . . therefore she may not be the head. I grant that so far as pertaineth to the bands of marriage and the office of a wife, she must be a subject, but as a magistrate she may be her husband's head. For the Scripture saith not thine eye must be to the man, but to thy husband. Neither oweth every woman obedience to every man, but to her own husband. Well, if she be her husband's subject, she can be no ruler. That followeth not, for the child is the father's subject and the father the child's ruler, and as Aristotle saith (whom you so much urge) his rule is kinglike over his child. But the husband's is civil, then if the child by nature a subject may be by law a head, yea the head of his father, and his father his subject, why may not the woman be the husband's inferior in matters of wedlock, and his head in the guiding of the commonwealth? . . . If then they may govern men in the house by saint Paul's commission, and an household is a little commonwealth, as Socrates in Xenophon saith, then I cannot see how you can debar them of all rule, or conclude that to be heads of men is against nature. . . . But while you take this word nature too largely, you deceive yourself wittingly, thinking that because it is not so convenient, so profitable, or meet, therefore it is unnatural. But that is too large a scope. Wherefore that we may understand how far you stretch this word nature, I will ask you whether you take it as it is for the most part; or all together, that is universal. If you take it as it is in the order of nature, for the most part (as, it is natural for an old man to have white hairs in his age, or for a woman to bring forth one child at a burden) and then reason it is against nature for an old man to have black hairs, or against nature for a woman to bring forth two children or three at a burden: no man would allow your reasoning. For though the one be according to nature as it is for the most part, yet is not the other that happeneth sometime utterly against nature. In like manner, though it be for the most part seen that men and not women do rule commonwealths, yet when it happeneth sometime by the ordinance of God and course of inheritance that they bear rule, it is not to be concluded that it repugneth against nature: no more than the old man's black hairs, or the woman's two twins. So that you see that in this acception of nature, their rule cannot be against nature

* * *

The third reason of this argument is out of Saint Paul, whereby women be forbidden to speak in the congregation, for it is an unseemly thing for them to speak. This is marvellously amplified and urged, as though it were so sound, as no fault, nor crack could be found in it. This is the Hercules club that beateth all down before it. These be Sampson's locks that make him so strong, wherefore there must be taken some pains in the confuting of it. First therefore I lay this foundation, which I laid before, that Saint Paul, nor none of the rest of Christ's guard, meddle not with civil policy, no further than to teach obedience, nor have no commission thereunto in all the whole Scripture. And this being a great matter of policy, yea the greatest (for it containeth the whole) it cannot be within the compass of Paul's commission, and so followeth it that Paul either in this place meant no such matter as they gather: or if he did, he did it without the compass of his commission, but that is unlike. . . . And not only he debarred the women from prophesying, but also from any public function in the ecclesiastical jurisdiction. For in such as shall occupy the pulpit is required these things, that they be meet to teach, to reprove, and convince. In teaching is required gravity, learning and eloquence. In reproving, courage and sound judgement, and in convincing, arts, memory and much science. And because the bringing up of women is commonly such as they can not have these things (for they be not brought up in learning in schools, nor trained in disputations; or if they were yet because nature hath made them softer and milder than men; yet be they not such as are meet for that function). Therefore be they unmeet for this calling. For those that be preachers must be no milk-sops.

2.5 *AN EXHORTATION CONCERNING GOOD ORDER AND OBEDIENCE*

This Homily was substantially extended and revised in each successive edition of the *Homilies*: and ordered to be read by *The Book of Common Prayer, The Injunctions* and later the *Canons* (see part 1). Text from: 1559 edition, fos R4^r–S2^v; T1^r–^{v}.

Almighty God hath created and appointed all things in heaven, earth and waters in a most excellent and perfect order. In heaven he hath appointed distinct or several orders and states of archangels and angels. In earth he has assigned and appointed kings, princes, with other governors under them, all in good and necessary order. The water above is kept and raineth down in due time and season. The sun, moon, stars, rainbow, thunder, lightning, clouds and all birds of the air do keep their order. The earth, trees, seeds, plants, herbs, corn, grass, and all manner of beasts keep themselves in their order. All the parts of the whole year: as winter, summer, months, nights and days, continue in their order. All kinds of fishes in the sea, rivers and waters, with all fountains, springs, yea the seas themselves keep their comely course and order. And man himself also hath all his parts, both within and without, as: soul, heart, mind, memory, understanding, reason, speech withal and singular corporal members of his body in a profitable, necessary and pleasant order. Every degree of people, in their vocation, calling and office, hath appointed to them their duty and order. Some are in high degree, some in low; some kings and princes; some inferiors and subjects; priests and laymen; masters and servants; fathers and children; husbands and wives; rich and poor; and everyone have need of other, so that in all things is to be lauded and praised the goodly order of God, without the which no house, no city, no commonwealth can continue and endure or last. For where there is no right order there reigneth all abuse, carnal liberty, enormity, sin, and babylonical confusion. Take away kings, princes, rulers, magistrates, judges and such estates of God's order, no man shall ride or go by the highway unrobbed; no man shall sleep in his own house or bed unkilled; no man shall keep his wife, children and possessions in quietness; all things shall be common and there must needs follow all mischief and utter destruction, both of souls, bodies, goods and commonwealths. But blessed be God that we in this realm of England feel not the horrible calamities, miseries and wretchedness which all they undoubtedly feel and suffer that lack this godly order. And praised be God that we know the great excellent benefit of God showed towards us in this behalf. God hath sent us his high gift, our most dear sovereign Lady Queen Elizabeth with godly, wise and honourable council, with other superiors and inferiors in a beautiful order, and goodly. Wherefore let us subjects do our bounden duties, giving hearty thanks to God and praying for the preservation of this godly order. Let us all obey, even from the bottom of our hearts, all their godly proceedings, laws, statutes, proclamations, and injunctions, with all other godly orders. Let us consider the Scriptures of the Holy Ghost which persuade and command us all obediently to be subject. First and chiefly to the Queen's majesty, supreme head over all, and next to her honourable council, and to all other noble men, magistrates and officers, which by God's goodness be placed and ordered: for almighty God is the only author and provider of this forenamed state and order, as it is written of God in the book of Proverbs: *Through me Kings do reign: through me counsellors make just laws; through me do princes bear rule and all judges of the earth execute judgements. I am loving to them: they love me* [Proverbs 7] . . .

We read in the book of Deuteronomy that all punishment pertaineth to God, by this sentence: *vengeance is mine and I will reward* [Deut. 32]. But this sentence we must understand to pertain also to the magistrates, which do exercise God's room in judgement and punishing by good and godly laws here in earth. And the places of Scripture which seem to remove from among all Christian men judgement, punishment or killing, ought to be understand that no man of his own private authority may be judge over other, may punish or may kill. But we must refer all judgement to God, to kings and rulers, and judges under them, which be God's officers to execute justice and by plain words of Scripture have their authority and use of the sword granted from God, as we are taught by Saint Paul, the dear and chosen Apostle of our saviour Christ whom we ought diligently to obey, even as we would obey our saviour Christ if he were present. Thus Saint Paul writeth to the Romans [Rom. 13]: *let every soul submit himself unto the authority of the higher powers, for there is no power but of God:* the powers that be, be ordained of God; whosoever withstandeth the power, withstandeth the ordinance of God, but they that resist or withstand it shall receive to themselves damnation; for rulers are not fearful to them that do good, but to them that do evil . . .

Here let us all learn of Saint Paul, the chosen vessel of God that all persons having souls (he excepteth none, nor exempteth none, neither priest, Apostle, nor prophet, saith Chrisostom) do owe of bounden duty and even in conscience, obedience, submission and subjection to the high powers, which be set in authority by God, forasmuch as they be God's lieutenants, God's presidents, God's officers, God's commissioners, God's judges, ordained of God himself, of whom only they have all their power and all their authority. And the same Saint Paul threateneth no less pain than everlasting damnation to all disobedient persons, to all resisters, against this general and common authority, forasmuch as they resist not man, but God, not man's device and invention, but God's wisdom, God's order, power and authority.

. . . And here (good people) let us all mark diligently that it is not lawful for inferiors and subjects in any case to resist or stand against the superior powers. For Saint Paul's words are plain, that whosoever withstandeth shall get to themselves damnation, for whosoever withstandeth, withstandeth the ordinance of God. Our saviour Christ himself and his apostles received many and diverse injuries of the unfaithful and wicked men in authority: yet we never read that they or any of them caused any sedition or rebellion against authority. We read oft that they patiently suffered all troubles, vexations, slanders, pangs and pains, and death itself obediently, without tumult or resistance . . .

. . . It is an intolerable ignorance, madness and and wickedness for subjects to make any murmuring, rebellion, resistance, withstanding, commotion or insurrection against their most dear and most dread sovereign Lord and King, ordained and appointed of God's goodness for their commodity, peace and quietness. Yet let us believe undoubtedly, good Christian people, that we may not obey kings, magistrates or any other (though they be our own fathers) if they would command us to do anything contrary to God's commandments. In such a case we ought to say with the Apostles: we must rather obey God than man [Acts 3]. But nevertheless in that case we may not in any wise withstand violently or rebel against rulers or make any insurrection, sedition, or tumults, either by force of arms or other ways, against the anointed of the Lord or any of his appointed officers. But we must in such cases patiently suffer all wrongs and injuries, referring the judgement of our cause only to God . . .

And let no man think that he can escape unpunished that committeth treason, conspiracy or rebellion against his sovereign Lady, the Queen, though he commit the same never so secretly, either in thought, word or deed; never so privily in his privy chamber by himself, or openly communicating and consulting with other. For treason will not be hid: treason will out at length. God will have that most detestable vice opened and punished, for that it is so directly against his ordinance and against his high principle judge, and anointed in earth. The violence and injury that is committed against authority is committed against God, the commonwealth, and the whole realm.

2.6 GEORGE BUCHANAN, *DE JURE REGNI*

Buchanan's work in defence of a secular theory of State gained a European reputation as a revolutionary argument for resistance, whether political or religious. It was actually written in defence of the deposition of Mary Queen of Scots and dedicated by the author to King James VI. Text from: 1583 edition: pp. 15–25; 39–42; 127–31.

Dialogue between Thomas Maitland and George Buchanan

B.   Now, as in our bodies consisting of contrary elements, there are diseases, that is perturbations and some intestine tumults, even so there must be of necessity in these greater bodies, that is in cities, which also consist of various (yea and for the most part) contrary humours, or sorts of men, and these of different ranks, conditions and natures, and which is more, of such as cannot remain one hour together approving the same things, and surely such must needs soon dissolve and come to nought if one be not adhibited, who as a physician may quiet such disturbances and by a moderate and wholesome temperament confirm the infirm parts, and compesce[6] redundant humours, and so take care of all the members, that the weaker may not languish for want of nutrition, nor the stronger become luxuriant too much . . .

M. I am not very anxious about his name, for by what name soever he be called, I think he must be a very excellent and divine person, wherein the wisdom of our ancestors seemeth to have foreseen, who have adorned the thing in itself most illustrious with an illustrious name. I suppose you mean, *king*, of which word there is such an emphasis, that it holds forth before us clearly a function in itself very great and excellent.

B. You are very right, for we define God by that name. For we have no other more glorious name whereby we may declare the excellency of his glorious nature, nor more suitable whereby to signify his paternal care and providence towards us. What other name shall I collect which we translate to denote the function of a king? . . .

B. In the creation of a king, I think the ancients have followed this way, that if any among the citizens were of any singular excellency, and seemed to exceed all others in equity and prudence, as is reported to be done in bee-hives, they willingly conferred the government or kingdom on him. . . . But what if none such as we have spoken of should be found in the city?

M. By that law of nature, whereof we formerly made mention, equals neither can, nor ought to usurp dominion: for by nature I think it just that amongst these that are equal in all other things, their course of ruling and obeying should be alike.

B. What if a people, wearied with yearly ambition be willing to elect some certain person not altogether endowed with royal virtues, but either famous by his noble descent, or war-like valour?

M. Most lawful, for the people have power to confer the government on whom they please.

B. What if we shall admit some acute man, yet not endowed with suitable skill, for curing diseases? Shall we presently account him a physician, as soon as he is chosen by all?

M. Not at all, for by learning and the experience of many arts, and not by suffrages is a man made a physician . . .

B. You have hit the nail on the head, if this then were complete and perfect in any person, we might say he were a king by nature, and not by suffrages, and might resign over to him a free power over all things: but if we find not such a man, we shall also call him a king who doth come nearest to that eminent excellency of nature, embracing in him a certain similitude of a true king. . . . And because we fear he be not firm enough against inordinate affections, which may, and for the most part use to decline men from truth, we shall adjoin to him the law, as it were a colleague, or rather a bridler of his lusts.

M. You do not think, then, that a king should have an arbitrary power over all things?

B. Not at all: for I remember that he is not only a king, but also a man, erring in many things by ignorance, often failing willingly, doing many things by constraint: yea a creature easily changeable at the blast of every favour or frown, which natural vice a magistrate useth also to increase. . . . For when the lust of kings stood instead of laws, and men being vested with an infinite and immoderate power, did not contain themselves within bounds, but connived at many things out of favour, hatred or self-interest, the insolency of kings made laws to be desired. For this cause therefore laws were made by the people, and kings constrained to make use not of their own licentious wills in judgement, but of that right or privilege which the people had conferred upon them. For they were taught by many experiences that it was better that their liberty should be accredited to laws than to kings; whereas one might decline many ways from the truth, but the other being deaf both to entreaties and threats might still keep one and the same tenor. This one way of government is to kings prescribed, otherwise free, that they should conform their actions and speech to the prescripts of laws, and by the sanctions thereof divide rewards and punishments, the greatest bonds of holding fast together human society . . .

M. But when you concredit the helm of government rather to laws than to kings, beware I pray you, lest you make him a tyrant, whom by name you make a king, who with authority doth oppress and with fetters and imprisonment doth bind, and so let him be sent back to the plough again, or to his former condition, yet free of fetters.

B. Brave words: I impose no lord over him, but I would have it in the people's power, who gave him the authority over themselves, to prescribe to him a model of his government, and that the king may make use of that justice which the people gave him over themselves. This I crave. I would not have these laws to be by force imposed, as you interpret it, but I think that by a common council with the king, that should be generally established, which may generally tend to the good of all.

M. You will then grant this liberty to the people?

B. Even to the people indeed, unless perhaps you be of another mind.

M. Nothing seems less equitable. . . . You know that saying, *a beast with many heads*. You know, I suppose, how great the temerity and inconstancy of a people is.

B. I did never imagine that the matter ought to be granted to the judgement of the whole people in general, but that near to our custom a select number out of all estates may convene with the king in council. And then how soon an overturn by them is made, that it be deferred to the people's judgement.

M. I understand well enough your advice. But by this so careful a caution you seem to help yourself nothing. You will not have a king loosed from laws, why? Because, I think, within a man two most cruel monsters, lust and wrath, are in a continual conflict with reason. Laws have been greatly desired which might repress their boldness, and reduce them too much insulting, to regard a just government. Which will these counsellors given by the people do? Are they not troubled by the same intestine conflict? Do they not conflict with the same evils as well as the king? . . .

B. But I expect a far other thing than you suppose. Now I shall tell you why I do expect it. First, it is not altogether true what you suppose, viz. that the assembling together of a multitude is to no purpose, of which number there will perhaps be none of a profound wit: for not only do many see more and understand more than one of them apart, but also more than one, albeit he exceed their wit and prudence. For a multitude for the most part doth better judge of all things, than single persons apart. For every one apart have some particular virtues, which being united together make up one excellent virtue.

* * *

B. Now if a king do those things which are directly for the dissolution of society, for the continuance whereof he was created, how do we call him?
M. A tyrant, I suppose.
B. Now a tyrant hath not only no just authority over a people, but he is also their enemy. . . . Is there not a just and lawful war with an enemy for grievous and intolerable injuries?
M. It is for sooth a just war . . .
B. Now a lawful war being once undertaken with an enemy and for a just cause, it is lawful not only for the whole people to kill that enemy, but for every one of them . . . there be some tyrannies allowed by the free suffrages of a people, which we do honour with royal titles, because of the moderate administration. No man, with my will, shall put violent hand on any such, nor yet on any of those who even by force or fraud have acquired sovereignty, providing they use a moderate way in their government. Such amongst the Romans were Vespasian, Titus, Pertinax; Alexander amongst the Grecians and Hiero in Syracusa. Who albeit they obtained the government by force and arms, yet by their justice and equity deserved to be reckoned amongst just kings. Besides, I do only show what may be lawfully done, or ought to be done in this case, but do not exhort or attempt any such thing.

2.7 THOMAS SMITH, *DE REPUBLICA ANGLORUM*

Smith's delineation and classification of the structure of English society and its manner of governance is a lucid account of how power worked and was distributed in early modern England. Text from: first edition, 1583, pp. 34–47.

The most high and absolute power of the realm of England consisteth in the Parliament. For as in war, where the King himself in person, the nobility, the rest of the gentility and the yeomanry are, is the force and power of England: so in peace and consultation where the prince is to give life and the last and highest commandment; the barony for the nobility and higher; the knights, esquires, gentlemen and commons for the lower part of the commonwealth, the bishops for the clergy be present to advertise, consult and show what is good and necessary for the commonwealth, and to consult together and upon mature deliberation, every bill or law being thrice read and disputed upon in either House, the other two parts; first each a part and after the prince himself in presence of both the parties doth consent unto and alloweth. That is the prince's and whole realm's deed; whereupon justly no man can complain but must accommodate himself to find it good and obey it.

That which is done by this consent is called firm, stable and *sanctum*, and is taken for law. The Parliament abrogateth old laws, maketh new, giveth orders for things past and for things hereafter to be followed, changeth rights and possessions of private men, legitimateth bastards, establisheth forms of religion, altereth weights and measures, giveth forms of succession to the Crown, defineth of doubtful rights whereof is no law already made, appointeth subsidies, tallies, taxes and impositions, giveth most free pardons and absolutions, restoreth in blood and name, as the highest court, condemneth or absolveth them whom the prince will put to that trial. And, to be short, all that ever the people of Rome might do either in *Centuriatis comitiis* or *tributis*, the same may be done by the Parliament of England which representeth and hath the power of the whole realm, both the head and the body. For every Englishman is intended to be there present, either in person or by procuration and attorneys, of what pre-eminence, state, dignity, or quality soever he be, from the prince (be he King or Queen) to the lowest person in England. And the consent of the Parliament is taken to be every man's consent . . .

Of the monarch, King or Queen of England

The prince whom I now call, as I have often before, the monarch of England, King or Queen, hath absolutely in his power the authority of war and peace, to defy what prince it shall please him, and to bid him war, and again to reconcile himself and enter into league or truce with him at his pleasure, or the advice only of his privy council. His privy council be chosen also at the prince's pleasure out of the nobility or barony, and of the knights and esquires such and so many as he shall think good, who doth consult daily, or when need is, of the weighty matters of the realm to give therein to their prince the best advice they can. The prince doth participate to them all, or so many of them as he shall think good, such legations and messages as come from foreign princes, such letters or occurrents as be sent to himself or to his secretaries, and keepeth so many ambassades[7] and letters sent unto him secret as he will, although these have a particular oath for a counsellor touching faith and secrets administered unto them when they be first admitted into that company. So that herein the kingdom of England is far more absolute than either the dukedom of Venice is, or the kingdom of the Lacedemonians was. In war time and in the field, the prince hath also absolute power, so that his word is a law: he may put to death, or to other bodily punishment, whom he shall think so to deserve, without process of law or form of judgement. . . . This absolute power is called martial law, and ever was and necessarily must be used in all camps and hosts of men, where the time nor place do suffer the tariance of pleading and process, be it never so short, and the important necessity requireth speedy execution, that with more awe the soldier might be kept in more straight obedience, without which never captain can do anything valuable in the wars.

The prince useth also absolute power in crying and decreeing the money of the realm by his proclamation only. The money is always stamped with the prince's image and title. The form, fashion, manner, weight, fineness and baseness thereof is at the discretion of the prince. For whom should the people trust more in that matter than their prince, seeing the coin is only to certify the goodness of the metal and the weight, which is affirmed by the prince's image and mark? But if the prince will deceive them and give them copper for silver or gold, or enhance his coin more than it is worth, he is deceived himself, as well as he doth go about to deceive his subjects. For in the same sort they pay the prince his rents and customs. And in time they will make him pay rateably or more for meat, drink, and victuals for him and his, and for their labour; which experience doth teach us now in our days to be done in all regions. For there ever hath been and ever will be a certain proportion between the scarcity and plenty of other things, with gold and silver, as I have declared more at large in my book of money. For all other measures and weights, as well of dry things as of wet, they have accustomed to be established or altered by the Parliament, and not by the prince's proclamation only . . .

The prince giveth all the chief and highest offices or magistracies of the realm, be it of judgement or dignity, temporal or spiritual, and hath the tenths and first fruits of all ecclesiastical promotions, except in the universities and certain colleges, which be exempt.

All writs, executions and commandments be done in the prince's name. We do say in England the life and member of the Kings's subjects are the King's only, that is to say that no man hath *hault* nor *moyenne*[8] justice but the King, nor can hold plea thereof. And therefore all those pleas, which touch the life or the mutilation of man, be called pleas of the crown, nor can be done in the name of any inferior person than he or she that holdeth the crown of England. And likewise no man can give pardon thereof but the prince only . . .

The prince hath the wardship and first marriage of all those that hold lands of him in chief. And also the government of all fools natural, or such as be made by adventure of sickness, and so continue, if they be landed.

2.8 ELIZABETH TUDOR: SPEECHES TO PARLIAMENT

Many of Elizabeth I's speeches to Parliament were published during her lifetime, and were also recorded by the Parliamentary historian Sir Simonds D'Ewes. Two examples of her speeches here demonstrate her ability to affirm simultaneously her view and appease her critics. The first speech, not long after her ascent to the throne, was sent as a result of Parliament's petition that she should marry, on 10 February 1559. The second speech was made to the English troops at Tilbury, after the defeat of the Armada, but with the prospect of a land invasion still feared. Texts from: Sir Simonds D'Ewes, *A Complete Journal of the Parliaments ... of Queen Elizabeth* (1682), fos 107–8; and *Cabala* (1691) fos 94–5.

On marriage

As I have good cause, so do I give you all my hearty thanks for the good zeal and loving care you seem to have, as well towards me as to the whole estate of your country. Your petition, I perceive, consisteth of three parts, and my answer to the same shall depend of two.

And to the first part, I may say unto you that from my years of understanding sith I first had consideration of myself to be born a servant of Almighty God, I happily chose this kind of life in the which I yet live: which, I assure you, for mine own part hath hitherto best contented myself, and I trust, hath been most acceptable unto God. From the which, if either ambition of high estate offered to me in marriage by the pleasure and appointment of my prince ... or if eschewing the danger of mine enemies or the avoiding of the peril of death, whose messenger or rather a continual watchman, the prince's indignation was no little time daily before mine eyes (by whose means, although I know or justly may suspect, yet I will not now utter, or if the whole cause were in my sister herself, I will not now burthen her therewith because I will not charge the dead), if any of these, I say, could have drawn or dissuaded me from this kind of life I had not now remained in this estate wherein you see me. But so constant have I always continued in this determination (although my youth and words may seem to some hardly to agree together, yet is it most true), that at this day I stand free from any other meaning that either I have had in times past or have at this present; with which trade of life I am so thoroughly acquainted that I trust God, who hath hitherto therein preserved and led me by the hand, will not of His goodness suffer me to go alone.

For the other part, the manner of your petition I do well like, and take it in good part because it is simple and containeth no limitation of place or person. If it had been otherwise, I must needs have misliked it very much and thought it in you a very great presumption: being unfit and altogether unmeet for you to require them that may command; or those to appoint, whose parts are to desire; or such to bind and limit, whose duties are to obey; or to take upon you to draw my love to your liking, or to frame my will to your fantasy. For a guerdon[9] constrained and gift freely given can never agree together. Nevertheless, if any of you be in suspect, whensoever it may please God to incline my heart to another kind of life you may very well assure yourselves, my meaning is not to determine anything wherewith the realm may or shall have just cause to be discontented. And therefore put that clean out of your heads. For I assure you (what credit soever my assurance may have with you I cannot tell; but what credit it shall deserve to have, the sequel shall declare) I will never in that matter conclude anything that shall be prejudicial to the realm. For the well, good and safety whereof, I shall never shun to spend my life. And whomsoever my chance shall be to light upon, I trust he shall be such as shall be as careful for the realm and you: I will not say as myself, because I cannot so certainly determine of any other, but by myself he shall be such as shall be as careful for the preservation of the realm, and you, as myself. And albeit it might please Almighty God to continue me still in this mind to live out of the state of marriage, yet is it not to be feared: but He will so work in my heart and in your wisdom, as good provision by his help may be made whereby the realm shall not remain destitute of an heir that may be a fit governor, and peradventure more beneficial to the realm than such offspring as may come of me. For though I be never so careful of your well doing and mind ever so to be, yet may my issue grow out of kind and become perhaps ungracious. And in the end, this shall be for me sufficient: that a marble stone shall declare that a queen, having reigned such a time, lived and died a virgin. And here I end, and take your coming to me in good part and give unto you all my hearty thanks, more yet for your zeal and good meaning, than for your petition.

Speech to the troops at Tilbury

My loving people, we have been persuaded by some that are careful of our safety to take heed how we commit ourselves to armed multitudes for fear of treachery, but I assure you I do not desire to live to distrust my faithful and loving people. Let tyrants fear. I have always so behaved myself that, under God, I have place my chiefest strength and safeguard in the loyal hearts and goodwill of my subjects. And therefore I am come amongst you as you see at this time, not for my recreation and disport, but being resolved in the midst and heat of battle to live or die amongst you all, to lay down for my God and for my kingdom and for my people, my honour and my blood, even in the dust. I know I have the body but of a weak and feeble woman, but I have the heart and stomach of a king, and of a king of England too, and think foul scorn that Parma, or Spain, or any prince of Europe should dare to invade the borders of my realm. To which, rather than any dishonour shall grow by me, I myself will take up arms, I myself will be your general, judge and rewarder of every one of your virtues in the field. I know already for your forwardness you have deserved rewards and crowns, and we do assure you, in the word of a prince, they shall be duly paid to you.

2.9 RICHARD HOOKER, *THE LAWS OF ECCLESIASTICAL POLITY*

Hooker published the first parts of his work in 1593: famously, a reasoned defence of the theology of the Church of England, and the relationship between Church and State. Book 8 was not published until 1662, and is mildly critical of absolute monarchical influence in Church matters. Text from: 8.I.vii; II.xvi–xvii.

Wherefore to end this point, I conclude: first, that under dominions of infidels, the Church of Christ and their commonwealth were two societies independent. Secondly, that in those commonwealths where the bishop of Rome beareth sway, one society is both the Church and the commonwealth; but the bishop of Rome doth divide the body into two diverse bodies, and doth not suffer the Church to depend upon the power of any civil prince or potentate. Thirdly, that within this realm of England, the case is neither as in the one, nor as in the other of the former two: but from the state of pagans we differ in that with us one society is both the Church and commonwealth, which with them it was not; as also from the state of those nations which subject themselves to the bishop of Rome, in that our Church hath dependency upon the chief in our commonwealth, which it hath not under him. In a word, our estate is according to the pattern of God's own ancient elect people, which people was not part of them the commonwealth, and part of them the church of God, but the selfsame people whole and entire were both under one chief governor, on whose supreme authority they did all depend . . .

Without order there is no living in public society, because the want thereof is the mother of confusion, whereupon division of necessity followeth, and out of division, inevitable destruction. The Apostle [Luke 11.17] therefore giving instruction to public societies, requireth that all things be orderly done. Order can have no place in things unless it be settled amongst the persons that shall by office be conversant about them. And if things or persons be ordered, this doth imply that they are distinguished by degrees. For order is a gradual disposition.

The whole world consisting of parts so many, so different, is by this only thing upheld: he which framed them hath set them in order. Yea, the very deity itself both keepeth and requireth for ever this to be kept as a law, that wheresoever there is a coagmentation of many, the lowest be knit to the highest by that which being interjacent may cause each to cleave unto other, and so all to continue one.

This order of things and persons in public societies is the work of polity, and the proper instrument thereof in every degree is power; power being that ability which we have of ourselves or receive from others, for performance of any action. If the action which we are to perform be conversant about matter of mere religion, the power of performing it is then spiritual; and if that power be such as hath not any other to overrule it, we term it dominion or power supreme, so far as the bounds thereof do extend.

When therefore Christian kings are said to have spiritual dominion or supreme power in ecclesiastical affairs and causes, the meaning is that within their own precincts and territories they have authority and power to command even in matters of Christian religion, and that there is no higher nor greater that can in those causes over-command them, where they are placed to reign as kings.

But withal we must likewise note that their power is termed supremacy, as being the highest, not simply without exception of any thing. For what man is there so brain-sick as not to except in such speeches God himself, the king of all the kings of the earth? Besides, where the law doth give him dominion, who doubteth but that the king who receiveth it must hold it of, and under, the law? . . .

Touching that which is now in hand, we are on all sides fully agreed; first that there is not any restraint or limitation of matter for regal authority and power to be conversant in: but of religion whole, and of whatsoever cause thereto appertaineth, kings may lawfully have charge, they lawfully may therein exercise dominion, and use the temporal sword. Secondly that some kinds of actions conversant about such affairs are denied unto kings; as namely, actions of the power of order, and of that power of jurisdiction which is with it unseparably joined: power to administer the word and sacraments; power to ordain; to judge as an ordinary; to bind and loose; to excommunicate; and such like; thirdly, that even in these very actions which are proper unto dominion, there must be some certain rule whereunto kings in all their proceedings ought to be strictly tied . . .

It hath been declared already in general how the best established dominion is where the law doth most rule the king: the true effect whereof particularly is found well in ecclesiastical as civil affairs. In these the king, through his supreme power, may do great things and sundry himself, both appertaining unto peace and war, both at home by commandment and by commerce with States abroad, because so much the law doth permit. Some things on the other side, the king alone hath no power to do without consent of the Lords and Commons assembled in Parliament; the king of himself cannot change the nature of pleas, nor courts, no not so much as restore blood, because the law is a bar unto him; not any law divine or natural, for against neither it were, though kings of themselves might do both, but the positive laws of the realm have abridged therein, and restrained the king's power; which positive laws, whether by custom, or otherwise established without repugnancy unto the law of God and nature, ought no less to be of force even in the spiritual affairs of the Church.

2.10 NICHOLAS MACHIAVELLI, *THE PRINCE*

First published in Italian in 1516, despite (or perhaps because of) its notorious reputation, *The Prince* was only first translated into English in 1640: the translator assures his readers of his own sceptical readings of Machiavelli, by annotating some chapters at the end (see below). Text from: 1640 edition, trans. E. D. pp. 117–145 (chapters 15, 18, 19).

Many principalities and republics have been in imagination, which neither have been seen nor known to be indeed: for there is such a distance between how men do live and how men ought to live, that he who leaves that which is done, for that which ought to be done, learns sooner his ruin than his preservation, for that man who will profess his honesty in all his actions must needs go to ruin among so many that are dishonest. Whereupon it is necessary for a prince desiring to preserve himself to be able to make use of that honesty, and to lay it aside again as need shall require. Passing by then things that are only in imagination belonging to a prince, to discourse upon those that are really true: I say that all men, whensoever mention is made of them, and especially princes, because they are placed aloft in the view of all, are taken notice of for some of these qualities which procure them either commendations or blame: and this is that someone is held liberal; some miserable (miserable I say, nor covetous: for the covetous desire to have, though it were by rapine; but a miserable man is he that too much forbears to make use of his own); some free-givers, others extortioners; some cruel, other piteous; the one a league-breaker, another faithful; the one effeminate and of small courage, the other fierce and courageous; the one courteous, the other proud; the one lascivious, the other chaste; the one of fair dealing, the other wily and crafty; the one hard, the other easy; the one grave, the other light; the one religious, the other incredulous, and such like. I know that everyone will confess it were exceedingly praiseworthy for a prince to be adorned with all these above named qualities that are good: but because this is not possible, nor do human conditions admit such perfection in virtues, it is necessary for him to be so discreet, that he know how to avoid the infamy of those vices which would thrust him out of his state . . .

[*The second blemish in this our author's book I find in his fifteenth chapter: where he instructs his prince to use such an ambidexterity as that he may serve himself either of virtue or vice, according to his advantage, which in true policy is neither good in attaining the principality, nor in securing it when it is attained. For Politics presupposes Ethics, which will never allow this rule: as that a man might make this small difference between virtue and vice, that he may indifferently lay aside or take up the one or the other, and put in practice as best conduceth to the end he propounds himself.*] . . .

In what manner princes ought to keep their words

How commendable in a prince it is to keep his word, and live with integrity, not making use of cunning and subtlety, everyone knows well: yet we see by experience in these our days that those princes have effected great matters who have made small reckoning of keeping their words, and have known by their craft to turn and wind men about, and in the end have overcome those who have grounded upon the truth. You must then know there are two kinds of combating or fighting: the one by right of the laws, the other merely by force. That first way is proper to men, the other is also common to beasts: but because the first many time suffices not, there is a necessity to make recourse to the second; wherefore it behoves a prince to know how to make good use of that part which belongs to a beast, as well as that which is proper to a man. This part hath been covertly showed to princes by ancient writers, who say that Achilles and many others of those ancient princes were entrusted to Chiron the centaur, to be brought up under his discipline. The moral of this, having for their teacher one that was half a beast and half a man, was nothing else but that it was needful for a prince to understand how to make his advantage of the one and the other nature, because neither could subsist without the other. A prince then being necessitated to know how to make use of that part belonging to a beast, ought to serve himself of the conditions of the fox and the lion: for the lion cannot keep himself from snares, nor the fox defend himself against the wolves. He had need then be a fox, that he may beware of the snares and a lion that he may scare the wolves. Those that stand wholly upon the lion, understand not well themselves, and therefore a wise prince cannot, nor ought not, keep his faith given, when the observance thereof turns to disadvantage, and the occasions that made him promise, are past. For if men were all good, this rule would not be allowable; but being they are full of mischief, and would not make it good to thee, neither art thou tied to keep it with them; nor shall a prince ever want lawful occasions to give colour to this breach . . . and ordinarily things have best succeeded with him that hath been nearest the fox in condition. But it is necessary to understand how to set a good colour upon this disposition, and to be able to fain and dissemble throughly [*sic*]; and men are so simple and yield so much to the present necessities that he who hath a mind to deceive, shall always find another that will be deceived. I will not conceal any one of the examples that have been of late. Alexander the sixth never did anything else than deceive men, and never meant otherwise, and always found whom to work upon; yet never was there man would protest more effectually, nor aver anything with more solemn oaths, and observe them, less than he; nevertheless, his cosenages all thrived well with him, for he knew how to play this part cunningly. Therefore is there no necessity for a prince to be endued with all above written qualities, but it behoveth well that he seem to be so; or rather I will boldly say this, that having these qualities, and always regulating himself by them, they are hurtful; but seeming to have them, they are advantageous: as to seem pitiful, faithful, mild, religious and of integrity; and indeed to be so, provided withal thou beest of such a composition that if need require to use the contrary, thou canst, and knowest how to apply thyself thereto. And it suffices to conceive this, that a prince, and especially a new prince, cannot observe all those things for which men are held good: he being often forced, for the maintenance of his state, to do contrary to his faith, charity, humanity and religion: and therefore it behoves him to have a mind so disposed as to turn and take the advantage of all winds and fortunes and as formerly I said, not forsake the good, while he can: but to know how to make use of the evil upon necessity. A prince then ought to have a special care that he never let fall any words but what are all seasoned with the five above written qualities, and let him seem to him that sees and hears him all pity, all faith, all integrity, all humanity, all religion: nor is there anything more necessary for him to seem to have than this last quality. For all men in general judge thereof, rather by the sight than by the touch; for every man may come to the sight of him, few come to the touch and feeling of him; every man may come to see what thou seemest, few come to perceive and understand what thou art; and those few dare not oppose the opinion of many who have the majesty of State to protect them. And in all men's actions, especially those of princes wherein there is no judgement to appeal unto men, forbear to give their censures, till the events and ends of things. Let a prince therefore take the surest course he can to maintain his life and state: the means shall always be thought honourable and commended by everyone: for the vulgar is overtaken with the appearance and event of a thing; and for the most part of people, they are but the vulgar: the others that are but few, take place where the vulgar have no subsistence . . .

That princes should take care not to incur contempt or hatred

But because among the qualities whereof formerly mention is made, I have spoken of those of most importance, I will treat of the others more briefly under these qualities that a prince is to beware, as in part is above-said, and that he fly those things which cause him to be odious or vile: and whenever he shall avoid this, he shall fully have played his part, and in the other disgraces he shall find no danger at all. There is nothing makes him so odious, as I said, as his extortion of his subjects' goods, and abuse of their women, from which he ought to forbear; and so long as he wrongs not his whole people, neither in their goods, nor honours, they live content, and he hath only to strive with the ambition of some few: which many ways, and easily too, is restrained. To be held various, light, effeminate, faint-hearted, unresolved, these make him be condemned and thought base, which a prince should shun like rocks; and take a care that in all his actions there appear: magnanimity, courage, gravity, and valour; and that in all the private affairs of his subjects, he orders it so, that his word stand irrevocable: and maintain himself in such repute that no man may think either to deceive or wind and turn him about; that prince that gives such an opinion of himself is much esteemed. And against him who is so well esteemed, hardly are any conspiracies made by his subjects, or by foreigners any invasion, when once notice is taken of his worth and how much he is reverenced by his subjects. For a prince ought to have two fears, the one from within, in regard of his subjects; the other from abroad, in regard of his mighty neighbours: from these he defends himself by good arms and good friends.

2.11 EDMUND SPENSER, *A VIEW OF THE PRESENT STATE OF IRELAND*

Spenser was secretary to Lord Grey in 1580, and held other administrative posts in the English occupation of Ireland for the next eighteen years. He published his *View* in 1596, advocating the full colonisation of Ireland. Text from: *The Works of Edmund Spenser* edited by J. Morris, Macmillan, 1924, pp. 609–12; 618; 650–4; 674–8.

Discoursed by way of a dialogue between Eudoxus and Irenaeus

Eudoxus But if that country of Ireland, whence you lately came, be so goodly and commodious a soil as ye report, I wonder that no course is taken for the turning thereof to good uses, and reducing of that savage nation to better government and civility.

Irenaeus Marry, so there have been divers good plots devised and wise counsels cast already about reformation of that realm; but they say it is the fatal destiny of that land that no purposes, whatsoever are meant for her good, will prosper or take good effect, which, whether it proceed from the very genius of the soil or influence of the stars, or that Almighty God hath not yet appointed the time of her reformation, or that he reserveth her in this unquiet state still for some secret scourge, which shall by her come unto England, it is hard to be known, but yet much to be feared. . . . I will then, according to your advisement, begin to declare the evils which seem to me most hurtful to the common-weal of that land, and first those which I said were most ancient and long-grown. And they also are of three kinds: the first in laws, the second in customs, and the third in religion . . .

. . . there be many wide countries in Ireland in which the laws of England were never established nor any acknowledgement of subjection made . . .

Eudoxus Then by that acceptance of his sovereignty [Henry VIII] they also accepted of his laws. Why then should any other laws be now used amongst them?

Irenaeus True it is that thereby they bound themselves to his laws and obedience and in case it had been followed upon them, as it should have been, and a government thereupon presently settled amongst them agreeable thereunto, they should have been reduced to perpetual civility and contained in continual duty. But what boots it to break a colt, and to let him straight run loose at random? So were this people at first well handled, and wisely brought to acknowledge allegiance to the Kings of England; but being straight left unto themselves, and their own inordinate life and manners, they eftsoons forgot what before they were taught, and so soon as they were out of sight by themselves, shook off their bridles, and began to colt anew, more licentiously than before.

Eudoxus It is a great pity that so good an opportunity was omitted and so happy an occasion forestalled, that might have bred the eternal good of that land. But do they not still acknowledge that submission? . . .

Irenaeus They say no: for their ancestors had no estate in any their lands, seigneuries, or hereditaments, longer than during their own lives, as they allege. . . . It is the custom among all the Irish that presently after the death of any of their chief Lords or Captains, they do presently assemble themselves to a place generally appointed and known unto them, to choose another in his stead; where they do nominate and elect, for the most part, not the eldest son, nor any of the children of their Lord deceased, but the next to him of blood that is the eldest and worthiest; as commonly the next brother to him if he have any, or the next cousin german, or so forth, as any is elder in that kindred or sept, and then next to him they choose the next of blood to be Tanistih, who shall next succeed him in the said captainry, if he live thereunto. . . . I have heard that the beginning and cause of this ordinance amongst the Irish was specially for the defence and maintenance of their lands in their posterity, and for excluding of all innovation or alienation thereof unto strangers, and specially to the English. For when their Captain died, if the seigneury should descend to his child, and he perhaps an infant, another might peradventure step in between, or thrust him out by strong hand, being then unable to defend his right, or withstand the force of a foreigner; and therefore they do appoint the eldest of the kin to have the seigneury, for that he commonly is a man of stronger years and better experience to maintain the inheritance and to defend the country, either against the next bordering Lords, which use commonly to encroach one upon another, as each one is stronger, or against the English, which they think lie still in wait to wipe them out of their territories. . . . [Thus] they reserved their titles, tenures and seignories whole and sound to themselves, and for proof allege that they have ever sithence remained to them untouched, so as now to alter them should (say they) be a great wrong.

Eudoxus What remedy is there then, or means to avoid this inconvenience? For without first cutting off this dangerous custom, it seemeth hard to plant any sound ordinance, or reduce them to a civil government, since all their ill customs are permitted unto them.

Irenaeus Surely nothing hard: for by this Act of Parliament whereof we speak, nothing was given to King Henry which he had not before from his ancestors, but only the bare name of a King; for all other absolute power of principality he had in himself before derived from many former Kings, his famous progenitors and worthy conquerors of that land. . . . The Common Law appointeth that all trials, as well of crimes as title and rights, shall be made by verdict of a jury, chosen out of the honestest and most substantial free-holders. Now most all the free-holders of that realm are Irish, which when the cause shall fall betwixt an Englishman and an Irish, or between the Queen and any free-holder of that country, they make no more scruple to pass against an Englishman and the Queen, though it be to strain their oaths, than to drink milk unstrained. So that, before the jury go together, it is well known what the verdict will be. The trial hereof have I so often seen that I dare confidently avouch the abuse thereof. Yet is the law of itself, I say good; and the first institution thereof, being given to all natural Englishmen, very rightful, but now that the Irish have stepped into the rooms of the English (who are now become so heedful and provident to keep them out from henceforth that they make no scruple of conscience to pass against them) it is good reason that either that course of the law for trial be altered, or other provision for juries made.

* * *

Eudoxus   I pray you then, declare your mind at large, how you would wish that sword, which you mean to be used to the reformation of all those evils.

Irenaeus   The first thing must be to send over into that realm such a strong power of men as that shall perforce bring in all that rebellious rout of loose people, which either do now stand out in open arms, or in wandering companies do keep the woods, spoiling the good subject.

Eudoxus   You speak now, Irenaeus, of an infinite charge to her Majesty, to send over such an army as should tread down all that standeth before them on foot, and lay on the ground all the stiff-necked people of that land; for there is now but one outlaw of any great reckoning, to weet the Earl of Tyrone, abroad in arms, against whom you see what great charges she hath been at, this last year, in sending of men, providing of victuals and making head against him: yet there is little or nothing at all done, but the Queen's treasure spent, her people wasted, the poor country troubled, and the enemy nevertheless brought unto no more subjection than he was, or list outwardly to show, which in effect is none, but rather a scorn of her power, and an emboldening of a proud rebel, and an encouragement unto all like lewd disposed traitors that shall dare to lift up their heels against their sovereign lady. Therefore it were hard counsel to draw such an exceeding great charge upon her, whose event shall be so uncertain . . .

Irenaeus   At the beginning of those wars, and when the garrisons are well planted and fortified, I would wish a proclamation were made generally and to come to their knowledge: that what persons soever would within twenty days absolutely submit themselves (excepting only the very principals and ring-leaders) should find grace; I doubt not but upon the settling of those garrisons such a terror and near consideration of their perilous estate will be stricken into most of them, that they will covet to draw away from their leaders . . . but withal that good assurance may be taken for their true behaviour and absolute submission, and that they then be not suffered to remain any longer in those parts; no, nor about the garrisons, but sent away into the inner parts of the realm, and dispersed in such sort as they shall not come together, nor easily return if they would. For if they might be suffered to remain about the garrison and there inhabit, as they will offer to till the ground and yield a great part of the profit thereof, and of their cattle to the Colonel, wherewith they have heretofore tempted many, they would (as I have by experience known) be ever after such a gall and inconvenience unto them, as that their profit should not recompense their hurt: for they will privily relieve their friends that are forth; they will send the enemy secret advertisement of all their purposes and journeys which they mean to make upon them; they will also not stick to draw the enemy privily upon them, yea and to betray the fort itself by discovery of all her defects and disadvantages (if any be) to the cutting of all their throats. For avoiding whereof and many other inconveniences, I wish that they should be carried far from thence into some other parts, so that (as I said) they come in and submit themselves upon the first summons; but afterwards I would have none received, but left to their fortune and miserable end. My reason is, for that those which will afterwards remain without, are stout and obstinate rebels, such as will never be made dutiful and obedient, nor brought to labour or civil conversation, having once tasted that licentious life, and being acquainted with spoils and outrages, will ever after be ready for the like occasions, so as there is no hope of their amendment or recovery, and therefore needful to be cut off. . . . The end (I assure me) will be very short and much sooner than can be (in so great a trouble as it seemeth) hoped for, although there should none of them fall by the sword, nor be slain by the soldier, yet thus being kept from manurance and their cattle from running abroad, by this hard restraint they would quickly consume themselves and devour one another. The proof whereof I saw sufficiently ensampled in those late wars in Munster; for notwithstanding that the same was a most rich and plentiful country, full of corn and cattle, that you would have thought they would have been able to stand long, yet ere one year and a half they were brought to such wretchedness, as that any stony heart would have rued the same. Out of every corner of the woods and glens they came creeping forth upon their hands, for their legs could not bear them; they looked like anatomies of death, they spake like ghosts crying out of their graves; they did eat of the dead carrions, happy were they if they could find them; yea and one another soon after, insomuch as the very carcases they spared not to scrape out of their graves; and if they found a plot of water-cresses or shamrocks, there they flocked as to a feast for the time, yet not able long to continue therewithal; that in short space there were none almost left, and a most populous and plentiful country suddenly made void of man or beast; yet sure, in all that war there perished not many by the sword, but all by the extremity of famine which they themselves had wrought . . .

Eudoxus I do now well understand you. But now when all things are brought to this pass and all filled with this rueful spectacle of so many wretched carcasses starving, goodly countries wasted, so huge a desolation and confusion, as even I that do but hear it from you, and do picture it in my mind, do greatly pity and commiserate it, if it shall happen, that the state of this misery and lamentable images of things shall be told, and feelingly presented to her sacred Majesty, being by nature full of mercy and clemency, who is most inclinable to such pitiful complaints, and will not endure to hear such tragedies made of her people and poor subjects as some about her may insinuate; then she perhaps, for very compassion of such calamities, will not only stop the stream of such violence, and return to her wonted mildness, but also con them little thanks which have been the authors and counsellors of such bloody platforms.

* * *

Irenaeus Neither should their lands be taken away from them, nor the uttermost advantages enforced against them. But this by discretion of the commissioners should be made known unto them, that it is not her Majesty's meaning to use any such extremity, but only to reduce things into order of English law, and make them to hold their lands of her Majesty, and restore to her, her due services, which they detain out of those lands, which were anciently held of her. And that they should not only not be thrust out, but also have estates and grants of their lands now made to them from her Majesty, so as they should thenceforth hold them rightfully, which they now usurp most wrongfully; and yet withal I would wish that in all those Irish countries there were some land reserved to her Majesty's free disposition for the better containing of the rest, and intermeddling them with English inhabitants and customs, that knowledge might still be had by them, and of all their doings, so as no manner of practice or conspiracy should be had in hand amongst them, but notice should be given thereof by one means or other, and their practices prevented . . .

Eudoxus In truth, Irenaeus, this is more that ever I heard, that English-Irish there should be worse than the wild Irish: Lord! How quickly doth that country alter men's natures! It is not for nothing (I perceive) that I have heard that the Council of England think it no good policy to have that realm reformed or planted with English, lest they should grow as undutiful as the Irish, and become much more dangerous. . . .

If that be so (methinks) your late advisement was very evil, whereby you wished the Irish to be sowed and sprinkled with the English, and in all the Irish countries to have English planted amongst them, for to bring them English fashions, since the English be sooner drawn to the Irish than the Irish to the English: for as you said before, if they must run with the stream, the greater number will carry away the less: therefore (meseems) by this reason it should be better to part the Irish and English, than to mix them together.

Irenaeus   Not so, Eudoxus, for where there is no good stay of government and strong ordinances to hold them, there indeed the fewer will follow the more; but where there is due order of discipline and good rule, there the better shall go foremost, and the worse shall follow. And therefore now, since Ireland is full of her own nation, that may not be rooted out, and somewhat stored with English already, and more to be, I think it best by an union of manners and conformity of minds, to bring them to be one people, and to put away the dislikeful conceit both of the one and the other, which will be by no means better than by this intermingling of them. That neither all the Irish may dwell together, nor all the English, but by translating of them and scattering of them by small numbers amongst the English, not only to bring them by daily conversation unto better liking of each other, but also to make both of them less able to hurt. And therefore when I come to the tithing of them, I will tithe them one with another, and for the most part will make an Irish man the tithing man, whereby he shall take the less exception to partiality, and yet be the more tied thereby. But when I come to the Head-borough, which is the head of the Lathe, him I will make an Englishman, or an Irishman of no small assurance, as also when I come to appoint the Alderman, that is the head of that hundred, him will I surely choose to be an Englishman of special regard, that may be a stay and pillar of all the boroughs under him . . .

The next thing that I will do shall be to appoint to everyone that is not able to live of his free-hold, a certain trade of life, to which he shall find himself fittest and shall be thought ablest, the which trade he shall be bound to follow, and live only thereupon. All trades therefore, it is to be understood, are to be of three kinds: manual, intellectual and mixed. The first containing all such as needeth exercise of bodily labour to the performance of their profession; the other consisting only of the exercise of wit and reason; the third part partly of bodily labour and partly of wit, but depending most of industry and carefulness. Of the first sort be all handicrafts and husbandry labour. Of the second be all sciences, and those which are called the liberal arts. Of the third is merchandise and chaffery, that is buying and selling; and without all these three there is no commonwealth that can almost consist, or at the least be perfect.

But that wretched realm of Ireland wanteth the most principal of them, that is the intellectual; therefore in seeking to reform her state, it is specially to be looked unto. But because of husbandry, which supplieth unto us all necessary things for food, whereby we chiefly live, therefore it is first to be provided for. . . . And therefore since now we purpose to draw the Irish from desire of wars and tumults, to the love of peace and civility, it is expedient to abridge their great custom of herding, and augment their more trade of tillage and husbandry. As for other occupations and trades, they need not to be enforced to, but every man bound only to follow one that he thinks himself aptest for. For other trades of artificers will be occupied for very necessity, and constrained use of them; and so likewise will merchandise for the gain thereof; but learning and bringing up in liberal sciences, will not come of itself, but must be drawn on with straight laws and ordinances. And therefore it were meet that such an Act were ordained that all the sons of lords, gentlemen and such other as are able to bring them up in learning, should be trained up therein from their childhood. And for that end every parish should be forced to keep on petty schoolmaster adjoining to the parish church, to be the more in view, which should bring up their children in the first rudiments of letters. . . . In planting of religion thus much is needful to be observed, that it be not sought forcibly to be impressed into them with terror and sharp penalties, as now is the manner, but rather delivered and intimated with mildness and gentleness, so as it may not be hated afore it be understood, and their professors despised and rejected. For this I know that the most of the Irish are so far from understanding of the Popish religion, as they are of the Protestants' profession; and yet do they hate it though unknown, even for the very hatred which they have of the English and their government. Therefore it is expedient that some discreet ministers of their own countrymen be first sent amongst them, which by their mild persuasions and instructions, as also by their sober life and conversation, may draw them first to understand and afterwards to embrace the doctrine of their salvation.

2.12 FRANCIS BACON, *A DECLARATION OF THE PRACTICES AND TREASONS ATTEMPTED AND COMMITTED BY ROBERT LATE EARL OF ESSEX*

Essex was one of Bacon's patrons during the 1590s, and evidence suggests a close working relationship. Nevertheless, he was appointed to be one of the commissioners to prosecute Essex for his attempted rebellion against the Queen in 1601, after the failure of his campaign against the Irish under Tyrone. He wrote this account of the trial for publication immediately afterwards. It is a useful contemporary account of the relationship between Elizabeth I and one of her favourites. Text from: *The Life and Letters of Francis Bacon*, edited by Spedding *et al.*, 1857–74, vol. II, pp. 248–9.

The most partial will not deny but that Robert, late Earl of Essex was by her Majesty's manifold benefits and graces, besides oath and allegiance, as much tied to her Majesty as the subject could be to the sovereign; her Majesty having heaped upon him both dignities, offices and gifts in such measure as within the circle of twelve years or more there was scarcely a year of rest in which he did not obtain at her Majesty's hands some notable addition either of honour or profit.

But he on the other side, making these her Majesty's favours nothing else but wings for his ambition, and looking upon them not as her benefits but as his advantages, supposing that to be his own metal which was but her mark and impression, was so given over by God (who often punished ingratitude by ambition, and ambition by treason, and treason by final ruin), as he had long ago plotted it in his heart to become a dangerous supplanter of that seat whereof he ought to have been a principal supporter; in such sort as now every man of common sense may discern not only his last actual and open treasons, but also his former more secret practices and preparations towards those his treasons, and that without any gloss or interpreter but himself, and his own doings.

For first of all, the world can now expound why it was that he did aspire and had almost attained unto a greatness like unto the ancient greatness of the *praefectus praetorio* under the emperors of Rome, to have all men of war to make their sole and particular dependence upon him; that with such jealousy and watchfulness he sought to discountenance any one that might be a competitor to him in any part of that greatness; that with great violence and bitterness he sought to suppress and keep down all the worthiest martial men which did not appropriate their respects and acknowledgements only towards himself. All which did manifestly detect and distinguish that it was not the reputation of a famous leader in the wars which he sought (as it was construed a great while), but only power and greatness to serve his own ends; considering he never loved virtue nor valour in another, but where he thought he should be proprietary and commander of it, as referred to himself.

So likewise those points of popularity which every man took notice and note of, as his affable gestures, open doors, making his table and his bed so popularly places of audience to suitors, denying nothing when he did nothing, feeding many men in their discontentments against the Queen and the State, and the like, as they ever were since Absolon's time the forerunners of treasons following; so in him were they either the qualities of a nature disposed to disloyalty, or the beginnings and conceptions of that which afterwards grew to shape and form.

But as it were a vain thing to search the roots and first motions of treasons, which are known to none but God that discerns the heart, and the devil that gives the instigation; so it is more than to be presumed (being made apparent by the evidence of all the events following) that he carried into Ireland a heart corrupted in his allegiance and pregnant of those, or the like, treasons which afterwards came to light.

For being a man by nature of an high imagination, and a great promiser to himself as well as to others, he was confident that if he were once the first person in a kingdom, and a sea between the Queen's sea and his, and Wales the nearest land from Ireland, and that he had got the flower of the English forces into his hands (which he thought so to intermix with his own followers as the whole body should move by his spirit), and if he might also have absolutely into his hands *potestatem vitae et necis* [power of life and death] and *arbitrium belli et pacis* [judgement of peace and war] over the rebels in Ireland, whereby he might entice and make them his own, first by pardons and conditions, and after by hopes to bring them in place where they should serve for hope of better booties than cows, he should be able to make that place of Lieutenancy of Ireland as a rise or step to ascend to his desired greatness in England.

2.13 FRANCIS BACON, *A BRIEF DISCOURSE TOUCHING THE HAPPY UNION*

James I, on accession to the English throne, desired the formal legal establishment of a union of England, Scotland and Ireland, and appointed Bacon as one of the commissioners on the union in 1604. However, opposition to such a union was fiercely chauvinist in the English Parliament, and the furthest such a union proceeded under the early Stuarts was the flying of a union flag on British ships, and the mutual repeal of hostile laws. Bacon's carefully constructed analogies demonstrate an ability to both flatter and warn the king at once. Text from: *Life and Letters of Francis Bacon*, edited by Spedding *et al.*, 1857–74. vol. III, pp. 92–9.

Your Majesty is the first king that had the honour to be *lapis angularis*, to unite these two mighty and warlike nations of England and Scotland under one sovereignty and monarchy. It doth not appear by the records and monuments of any true history, nor scarcely by the fiction and pleasure of any fabulous narration or tradition of any antiquity that ever this island of Great Britain was united under one king before this day. And yet there be no mountains nor races of hills, there be no seas, nor great rivers, there is no diversity of tongue or language that hath invited or provoked this ancient separation or divorce. The lot of Spain was to have the several kingdoms of the continent (Portugal only except) to be united in an age not long past; and now in our age that of Portugal also, which was the last that held out, to be incorporate with the rest. The lot of France hath been much about the same time likewise to have reannexed to that crown the several duchies and portions which were in former times dismembered. The lot of this island is the last, reserved for your Majesty's happy times by the special favour and providence of God, who hath brought you Majesty to this happy conjunction with great consent of hearts, and in the strength of your years and in the maturity of your experience. It resteth therefore but that (as I promised) I set before your Majesty's princely consideration the grounds of nature touching the union and commixture of bodies and the correspondency which they have with the grounds of policy in the conjunction of States and kingdoms.

First, therefore, that position *vis unita fortior* [unity is the greater power], being one of the common notions of the mind, needeth not much to be induced or illustrated . . .

So we see waters and liquors in small quantity do easily putrefy and corrupt; but in large quantity subsist long, by reason of the strength they receive by union . . .

So then this point touching the force of union is evident. And therefore it is more fit to speak of the manner of union. Wherein again it will not be pertinent to handle one kind of union, which is union by victory; when one body doth merely subdue another and converteth the same into his own nature, extinguishing and expulsing what part soever of it it cannot overcome . . .

Now to reflect this light of nature upon matter of estate; there hath been put in practice in government these two several kinds of policy in uniting and conjoining States and kingdoms; the one to retain the ancient forms still severed, and only conjoined in sovereignty; the other to superinduce a new form agreeable and convenient to the entire estate. The former of these hath been more usual and is more easy; but the latter is more happy. For if a man do attentively revolve histories of all nations, and judge truly thereupon, he will make this conclusion, that there were never any States that were good commixtures but the Roman. Which because it was the best State of the world, and is the best example in this point, we will chiefly insist thereupon . . .

But that which is chiefly to be noted in the whole continuance of the Roman government, they were so liberal of their naturalisations, as in effect they made perpetual mixtures. For the manner was to grant the same not only to particular persons, but to families and lineages; and not only so, but to whole cities and countries; so as in the end it came to that, that Rome was *communis patria* [a nation of communities] as some of the civilians call it . . .

So likewise the authority of Nicholas Machiavelli seemeth not to be condemned; who enquiring the causes of the growth of the Roman empire doth give judgement, there was not one greater than this: that the State did so easily compound and incorporate with strangers . . .

Now to speak briefly of the several parts of that form, whereby estates and kingdoms are perfectly united; they are (besides the sovereignty itself) four in number; union in name, union in language, union in laws, and union in employments.

For name, though it seems but a superficial and outward matter, yet it carrieth much impression and enchantment. The general and common name of Graecia made the Greeks always apt to unite (though otherwise full of divisions amongst themselves) against other nations, whom they called barbarous. The Helvetian name is no small band to knit together their leagues and confederacies the faster. The common name of Spain (no doubt) hath been a special mean of the better union and conglutination of the several kingdoms of Castile, Aragon, Granada,

Navarra, Valentia, Catalonia and the rest, comprehending also now lately Portugal.

For language, it is not necessary to insist upon it; because both your Majesty's kingdoms are of one language, though of several dialects; and the difference is so small between them as promiseth rather an enriching of one language than a continuance of two . . .

For laws, it is a matter of curiosity and inconvenience to seek either to extirpate all particular customs or to draw all subjects to one place or resort of judicature or session. It sufficeth that there be a uniformity in the principal and fundamental laws both ecclesiastical and civil . . .

For manners, a consent in them is to be sought industriously, but not to be enforced. For nothing amongst people breeds so much pertinacy in holding their customs as sudden and violent offer to remove them.

2.14 JAMES STUART, *THE TRUE LAW OF FREE MONARCHIES*

On its first publication in 1599, the argument of this treatise was described on the title page as delineating: 'the mutual duty betwixt a free King and his natural subjects'. This work thus expresses James I's theory of the divine patriarchal nature of monarchy, framed within a consensual hierarchical social fabric. It was reissued on his accession to the throne in 1603. Text from: 1603 edition, fos B3ᵛ–B4ᵛ; C5ᵛ–D5ᵛ; D7.

And therefore in the coronation of our own Kings, as well as of every Christian monarchy, they give their oath, first to maintain the religion presently professed within their country, according to their laws, whereby it is established, and to punish all those that should press to alter or disturb the profession thereof.

And next, to maintain all the lowable and good laws made by their predecessors; to see them put in execution, and the breakers and violators thereof to be punished according to the tenor of the same; and lastly to maintain the whole country, and every State therein, in all their ancient privileges and liberties, as well against all foreign enemies, as among themselves; and shortly to procure the weal and flourishing of his people, not only in maintaining and putting to execution the old lowable laws of the country, and by establishing of new (as necessity and evil manners well require) but by all other means possible to foresee and prevent all dangers, that are likely to fall upon them, and to maintain concord, wealth, and civility among them, as a loving father, and careful watchman, caring for them more than for himself; knowing himself to be ordained for them, and they not for him; and therefore countable to that great God, who placed him as his lieutenant over them, upon the peril of his soul to procure that weal of both souls and bodies as far as in him lieth, of all them that are committed to his charge. And this oath, in the coronation is the clearest, civil and fundamental law, whereby the King's office is properly defined.

By the law of nature the King becomes a natural father to all his lieges at his coronation. And as the father of his fatherly duty is bound to care for the nourishing, education and virtuous government of his children: even so is the King bound to care for all his subjects. As all the toil and pain that the father can take for his children, will be thought light and well bestowed by him; so that the effect thereof redound to their profit and weal: so ought the Prince to do towards his people. As the kindly father ought to see all inconvenients and dangers that may arise towards his children, and though with the hazard of his own person press to prevent the same: so ought the King towards his people. As the father's wrath and correction upon any of his children that offendeth ought to be by a fatherly chastisement seasoned with pity, as long as there is any hope of amendment in them: so ought the King towards any of his lieges that offends in that measure.

And shortly, as the father's chief joy ought to be in procuring his children's well-fare, rejoicing at their weal, sorrowing and pitying at their evil, to hazard for their safety, to avail for their rest, wake for their sleep, and in a word, to think that his earthly felicity and life standeth and liveth more in them, nor in himself: so ought a good prince think of his people.

* * *

The Kings therefore in Scotland were before any estates or ranks of men within the same, before any Parliaments were holden, or laws made; and by them was the land distributed, which at the first was whole theirs, States erected and discerned, and forms of government devised and established. And so it follows of necessity that the Kings were the authors and makers of the laws and not the laws of kings . . .

And according to these fundamental laws already alleged, we daily see that in the Parliament, which is nothing else but the head court of the King and his vassals, the laws are but craved by his subjects and only made by him at their rogation, and with their advice. For albeit the King made daily statutes and ordinances, enjoining such pains thereto as he thinks meet, without any advice of Parliament or estates, yet it lies in the power of no Parliament to make any kind of law or statute without his sceptre be put to it, for giving it the force of a law. And although divers changes have been in other countries of the blood royal and kingly house, the kingdom being reft by conquest from one to another as in our neighbour country in England, which was never in ours . . .

And as ye see it manifest that the King is overlord of the whole land, so is he master over every person that inhabiteth the same, having power over the life and death of every one of them. For although a just prince will not take the life of any of his subjects without a clear law, yet the same laws whereby he taketh them are made by himself or his predecessors, and so the power flows always from himself. As by daily experience we see good and just princes will from time to time make new laws and statutes, adjoining the penalties to the breakers thereof, which, before the law was made, had been no crime to the subject to have committed. Not that I deny the old definition of a King and of a law which makes the King to be a speaking law and the law a dumb King. For certainly a King that governs not by this law can neither be countable to God for his administration nor have a happy and established reign. For albeit it be true that I have at length proved that the King is above the law, as both the author and giver of strength thereto, yet a good King will not only delight to rule his subjects by the law, but even will conform himself in his own actions thereunto, always keeping that ground that the health of the commonwealth be his chief law.

* * *

As likewise, although I have said a good King will frame all his actions to be according to the law: yet is he not bound thereto but of his good will, and for good example-giving to his subjects. For as in the law of abstaining from eating of flesh in Lenten, the King will, for example's sake, make his own house to observe the law: yet no man will think he needs to take a license to eat flesh. And though by our laws the bearing and wearing of hag-buts and pistols be forbidden, yet no man can find any fault in the King for causing his train to use them in any raid upon the borderers, or other malefactors or rebellious subjects. So, as I have already said, a good King, though he be above the law, will subject and frame his actions thereto, for example's sake to his subjects, and of his own free will, but not as subject or bound thereto.

Since I have so clearly proved then out of the fundamental laws and practice of this country, what right and power a King hath over his land and subjects, it is easy to be understood, what allegiance and obedience his lieges owe unto him. I mean always of such free monarchies as our King is, and not of elective Kings: and much less of such sort of governors as the Dukes of Venice are, whose aristocratic and limited governors is nothing like to free monarchies, although the malice of some writers hath not been ashamed to misknow any difference to be betwixt them. And if it be not unlawful to any particular Lord's tenants or vassals, upon whatsoever pretext to control and displace their master, and over lord . . . how much less may the subjects and vassals of their great overlord the King, control or displace him? And since in all inferior judgements in the land, the people may not upon any respect displace their magistrates, although but subaltern; for the people of a borough cannot displace their provost before the time of their election; nor in ecclesiastical policy the flock can upon any pretence displace the pastor, nor judge of him, yea even the poor schoolmaster cannot be displaced by his scholars: if these I say (whereof some are but inferior, subaltern, and temporal magistrates, and none of them equal in any sort to the dignity of a King), cannot be displaced for any occasion or pretext by them that are ruled by them: how much less is it lawful upon any pretext to control or displace the great provost and great school-master of the whole land: except by inverting the order of all law and reason, the commanded may be made to command their commander, the judged to judge their judge, and they that are governed, to govern their time about their lord and governor?

And the agreement of the law of nature in this our ground with the laws and constitutions of God and man already alleged, will by two similitudes easily appear. The King towards his people is rightly compared to a father of children, and to a head of a body composed of divers members. For as fathers, the good Princes and magistrates of the people of God acknowledged themselves to their subjects. And for all other well ruled commonwealths, the rule of *Pater patriae* was ever and is commonly used for Kings. And the proper office of a King towards his subjects agrees very well with the office of the head towards the body, and all members thereof. For from the head, being the seat of judgement, proceedeth the care and foresight of guiding and preventing all evil that may come to the body, or any apart thereof. The head cares for the body, so doth the King for his people. As the discourse and direction flows from the head, and the execution according thereunto belongs to the rest of the members, every one according to their office: so is it betwixt a wise prince and his people. As the judgement coming from the head may not only employ the members, every one in their own office, as long as they are able for it: but likewise in case any of them be affected with any infirmity must care and provide for their remedy, in case it be curable: and if otherwise, gar[10] cut them off for fear of infecting of the rest: even so is it betwixt the Prince and his people. And as there is ever hope of curing any diseased member by the direction of the head, as long as it is whole: but by the contrary, if it be troubled, all the members are partakers of that pain: so is it betwixt the Prince and his people.

2.15 JAMES STUART, SPEECH TO PARLIAMENT

James I's speech was in defence of his prerogative in 1610, but also in support of the concept of the constitutional 'King-in-Parliament' method of raising taxes, which many members had felt he threatened. Text from: *Works*, 1616, pp. 529–31.

The state of monarchy is the supremest thing upon earth; for Kings are not only God's lieutenants upon earth, and sit upon God's throne, but even by God himself they are called gods. There be three principal similitudes that illustrates the state of monarchy: one taken out of the word of God and the two other out of the grounds of policy and philosophy. In the Scriptures Kings are called gods and so their power after a certain relation compared to the divine power. Kings are also compared to fathers of families, for a King is truly *parens patriae* [the parent of his country], the politic father of his people. And lastly Kings are compared to the head of this microcosm of the body of man.

Kings are justly called gods for that they exercise a manner of resemblance of divine power upon earth. For if you will consider the attributes to God you shall see how they agree in the person of a King. God hath power to create or destroy, make or unmake, at his pleasure, to give life or send death, to judge all and to be judged nor accountable to none, to raise low things and to make high things low at his pleasure and to God are both soul and body due. And the like power have Kings: they make and unmake their subjects; they have power of raising and casting down; of life and death; judges over all their subjects and in all causes, and yet accountable to none but God only. They have power to exalt low things and abase high things, and make of their subjects like men at the chess, a pawn to take a bishop or a knight, and to cry up or down any of their subjects as they do their money. And to the King is due both the affections of the soul and the service of the body of his subjects . . .

A father may dispose of his inheritance to his children at his pleasure, yea, even disinherit the eldest upon just occasions and prefer the youngest, according to his liking; make them beggars or rich at his pleasure; restrain or banish out of his presence as he finds them give cause of offence; or restore them in favour again with the penitent sinners. So may the King deal with his subjects.

And lastly, as for the head of the natural body, the head hath the power of directing all the members of the body to that use which the judgement of the head thinks most convenient. It may apply sharp cures or cut off corrupt members, let blood in what proportion it thinks fit.

2.16 JOHN CHAMBERLAIN, *LETTERS* ON THE OVERBURY AFFAIR

The Overbury affair was just one of the many sexual and financial scandals that rocked the Jacobean court. The Countess of Essex claimed that her marriage to the Earl had never been consummated, and despite the opposition of the Essex faction, led by Thomas Overbury, obtained a divorce on these grounds, and swiftly married the King's then favourite, Robert Carr, Earl of Somerset. Several years later, it emerged that Overbury had been poisoned in order to secure his silence, and both Buckingham and the Countess were tried and found guilty. Texts from: Winwood Papers vol. 9; State Papers Domestic, Jac. I, 86:160; 87:25, 26, 51.

To Sir Ralph Winwood

London, June 10 1613

. . . Sir Thomas Overbury lies still by it [in the tower] and for ought I hear is like to do: . . . The divorce twixt the Earl of Essex and his lady is on foot, and hath been argued twice or thrice at Lambeth afore certain commissioners, but *a huis clos* [in secret]. The greatest difficulty is that though he be willing to confess his insufficiency towards her, yet he would have liberty to marry with any other, as being *maleficiatus* [impotent] only *ad illam* [to her]. Yet some lawyers are of opinion that if she will take her oath that he is impotent towards her, it will serve the turn, whereof it is thought she will make no bones as presuming that she is provided of a second, which I should never have suspected, but that I know he was with her three hours together within these two days, which makes me somewhat to stagger and to think that great folks, to compass their own ends, have neither respect to friends nor followers.

To Sir Dudley Carleton

London, June 23 1613

. . . The divorce now in question twixt the Earl of Essex and his lady is thought shall be decided one way or other the first day of July. The opinions are divers of the success, and the case is of so dangerous consequence that no doubt the commissioners will proceed with great wariness and maturity, for if such a gap be once let open, it will not be so easily stopped but that infinite inconveniences will follow. In the mean time the lady hath been visited and searched by some ancient ladies and midwives expert in those matters, who both by inspection and otherwise find her upon their oath a pure virgin: which some doctors think a strange asseveration, and make it more difficult than to be discerned. The world speaks liberally that my Lord of Rochester and she be in love one with another, which breeds a double question, whether that consideration be like to hinder or set it forward?

* * *

To Sir Dudley Carleton

London, May 18 1616

My very good Lord: I thought I should this day have given you an account of our intended arraignments, but the matter is once more deferred till Thursday and Friday next. The stage in the mids of Westminster Hall, with numbers of scaffolds round about was finished, the Lords assembled, and all things ready against Wednesday, when about Tuesday noon came order to put all off, whereby a great many that tarried of purpose after the term, were disappointed, and have since got themselves out of town with loss of their earnest for places, which at this time were grown to so extraordinary a rate, that four or five pieces (as they call them) was an ordinary price, and I know a lawyer that had agreed to given ten pound for himself and his wife for the two days, and fifty pound was given for a corner that could hardly contain a dozen. The cause of the stay is not certainly known, but this is certain that warning being given the Lady on Saturday to prepare for her trial against Wednesday, she fell that night to casting and scouring, and so continued till the next day very sick, whether it were that the apprehension wrought so violently with her, or that she had taken a dram. Some make this reason, others say that her Lord begins to relent, and makes show to reveal secrets of great importance. . . . In the mean time the peers attend here in town. Taverner was reprieved at the instant almost that he was to be executed and so was one Anderson a gentleman condemned for murder and other foul facts, and the world apprehends they shall live, which they take for a leading case for some that may follow. Yesterday was a woman condemned at the Sessions house for a lamentable murder of two of her own children: she dwelt at Acton and was a woman of good fashion both for means, shape and behaviour, but being a violent recusant and urged by her husband to conform herself, and to have her children otherwise educated, she took this course to rid them out of the world rather than to have them brought up in our religion.

To Sir Dudley Carleton

London, May 25 1616

My very good Lord: . . . I come tired from hearing a piece of the Earl of Somerset's arraignment, who I think is but now in the middest of his answer, the proceeding against him having continued ever since ten a clock in the morning, till five that he began to answer for himself, which how it will succeed I cannot certainly say, for he denies all, even his own letters, saying they be counterfeited, and will not be brought to write whereby to show the conformity of the character, but says it is against law that he should be put to it. He had pen and ink allowed him take notes, which is more than ever I knew any to have heretofore. I was there at six a clock in the morning and for ten shillings had a reasonable place but the weather is so hot and I grew so faint with fasting that I could hold out no longer: especially when I hear they had sent to provide torches, so that it is verily thought he will hold them till midnight, if the Lord Chancellor, who is High Steward for the time, be able to continue it. The Lady Winwood is there and more ladies and other great personages than ever I think were seen at any trial. . . .
His Lady was arraigned yesterday and made shorter work by confessing the indictment so that all was done and we at home before noon. She won pity by her sober demeanour, which in my opinion was more curious and confident than was fit for a Lady in such distress, yet she shed, or made show of, some few tears divers times. She was used with more respect than is usual, nothing being aggravated against her by any circumstance nor any invective used, but only touching the main offence of murder: as likewise it was said today to be the King's pleasure that no odious or uncivil speeches should be given: the general opinion is that she shall not die, and many good words were given to put her in hope of the King's mercy, wherein the Lord Steward with the rest of the peers promised their best mediation. The Earl of Essex was at her arraignment, but somewhat more privately than this day when he stood full in his face.

To Sir Dudley Carleton

London, June 8 1616

My very good Lord: when I wrote last I left the Earl of Somerset pleading for his life, but that he said for himself was so little that he was found guilty by all his peers: which did so little appal him that when he was asked what he could say why sentence should not be pronounced, he stood still upon his innocence and could hardly be brought to refer himself to the King's mercy: upon which terms he stands still, and having leave to write to the King, hath only required that his judgement of hanging should be changed to heading, and that his daughter might have such of his lands as the King doth not resume and reserve in his own hands. The Lady Knolles and some other friends had had access to the Lady divers times since her conviction, and carried her young daughter to her twice or thrice; but I hear not of any that comes at him. He hath been much urged and fair offered to confess the offence before his arraignment and since, but he stands firm in denial, though by all circumstances and most pregnant (yea almost infallible) probabilities he be more faulty and foul than any of the company, which makes the King marvel that all the rest that have gone before, having so frankly confessed the matter after their condemnation, he only should continue so confident. Whether this or any other reason be the cause of stay of execution, I know not, but they live yet and for ought I can learn, so are like to do many a day.

2.17 *THE PETITION OF RIGHT*

The 1628 Parliament was the first of Charles I's reign, and both its rocky passage and petitions convinced Charles I that it was impossible to rule effectively through Parliament. His alternative money-raising ventures, such as the forced loan and ship money, were seen as illegal assaults on the liberties of the property-owning freeholders and gentry, and merely served to fuel opposition to Charles I's policies and political practice. Text from: *Statutes of the Realm*, V, 23–4.

To the King's Most excellent Majesty

. . . whereas it is declared and enacted by a statute made in the time of the reign of King Edward the First . . . that no tallage or aid should be laid or levied by the king or his heirs in this realm without the good will and assent of the archbishops, bishops, earls, barons, knights, burgesses and other the freemen of the commonalty of this realm . . . by which the statutes before mentioned and other the good laws and statutes of this realm your subjects have inherited this freedom, that they should not be compelled to contribute to any tax, tallage, aid, or other like charge not set by common consent in Parliament.

II. Yet, nevertheless of late, divers commissions directed to sundry commissioners, in several counties with instructions have issued by means whereof your people have been in divers places assembled and required to lend certain sums of money unto your Majesty and many of them upon their refusal so to do have had an oath administered unto them not warrantable by the laws or statutes of this realm, and have been constrained to become bound to make appearance and give attendance before your Privy Council and in other places; and others of them have been therefore imprisoned, confined and sundry other ways molested and disquieted, and divers other charges have been laid and levied upon your people in several counties by lord lieutenants, deputy lieutenants, commissioners for musters, justices of the peace and others by command or direction from your Majesty or your Privy Council against the laws and free customs of the realm.

III. And where also by the statute called the Great Charter of the Liberties of England, it is declared and enacted that no freeman may be taken or imprisoned or be disseised of his freehold or liberties or his free customs or be outlawed or exiled or in any manner destroyed, but by the lawful judgement of his peers or by the law of the land.

IV. And in the eight and twentieth year of the reign of King Edward the Third it was declared and enacted by authority of Parliament, that no man, of what estate or condition that he be, should be put out of his land or tenement, not taken, nor imprisoned, nor disherited, nor put to death without being brought to answer by due process of law.

V. Nevertheless against the tenor of the said statutes and other the good laws and statutes of your realm to that end provided, divers of your subjects have of late been imprisoned without any cause shown; and when for their deliverance they were brought before your justices by your Majesty's writ of habeas corpus there to undergo and receive as the Court should order, and their Keepers commanded to certify the causes of their detainer, no cause was certified but that they were detained by your Majesty's special command . . .

VI. And whereas of late great companies of soldiers and mariners have been dispersed into divers counties of the realm, and the inhabitants against their will have been compelled to receive them into their houses, and there to suffer them to sojourn against the laws and customs of this realm, and to the great grievance and vexation of the people.

VII. And whereas also by authority of Parliament in the five and twentieth year of the reign of King Edward the Third it is declared and enacted that no man should be forejudged of life and limb against the form of the Great Charter and the law of the land; and by the said Great Charter and other the laws and statutes of this your realm, no man ought to be adjudged to death but by the laws established in this your realm, either by the customs of the same realm or by Act of Parliament, and whereas no offender of what kind soever is exempted from the proceedings to be used and punishments to be inflicted by the laws and statutes of this your realm; nevertheless of late time divers commissions under your Majesty's great seal have issued forth, by which certain persons have been assigned and appointed commissioners with power and authority to proceed within the land according to the justice of martial law against such soldiers or mariners or other dissolute persons joining with them as should commit any murder, robbery, felony, mutiny or other outrage or misdemeanour whatsoever, and by such summary course and order as is agreeable to martial law and is used in armies in time of war to proceed to the trial and condemnation of such offenders and them to cause to be executed and put to death according to the law martial.

By pretext whereof some of your Majesty's subjects have been by some of the said commissioners put to death, when and where, if by the laws and statutes of the land they had deserved death: by the same laws and statutes also they might and by no other ought to have been judged and executed . . .

VIII. They do therefore humbly pray your most excellent Majesty that no man hereafter be compelled to make or yield any gift, loan, benevolence, tax or such like charge without common consent by Act of Parliament, and that none be called to make answer or take such oath or to give attendance or be confined or otherwise molested or disquieted concerning the same or for refusal thereof. And that no freeman in any such manner as is before mentioned be imprisoned or detained. And that your Majesty would be pleased to remove the said soldiers and mariners, and that your people may not be so burdened in time to come.

2.18 *THE GRAND REMONSTRANCE*

The *Remonstrance* was an organised attempt by the reforming party in the Long Parliament, led by John Pym, to remind former opponents of the King's policies of the history of their grievances, in the wake of increased support for the King after the Irish rebellion. The *Remonstrance* passed the Commons by only eleven votes: but its passage marked the emergence of two distinct parties, in which a moderate constitutional party which supported the King developed. Text from: *Constitutional Documents of the Puritan Revolution*, edited by S. Gardiner, OUP, 1906, pp. 205–7, 222–4, 228–31.

The commons in this present Parliament assembled having with much earnestness and faithfulness of affection and zeal to the public good of this kingdom, and his Majesty's honour and service for the space of twelve months wrestled with great dangers and fears, the pressing miseries and calamities, the various distempers and disorders which had not only assaulted, but even overwhelmed and extinguished the liberty, peace, and prosperity of this kingdom, the comfort and hopes of all his Majesty's good subjects, and exceedingly weakened and undermined the foundation and strength of his own royal throne, do yet find an abounding malignity and opposition in those parties and factions who have been the cause of those evils and do still labour to cast aspersions upon that which hath been done, and to raise many difficulties for the hindrance of that which remains yet undone, and to foment jealousies between the King and Parliament, that so they may deprive him and his people of the fruit of his own gracious intentions and their humble desires of procuring the public peace, safety and happiness of this realm.

For the preventing of those miserable effects which such malicious endeavours may produce, we have thought good to declare the root and growth of these mischievous designs; the maturity and ripeness to which they have attained before the beginning of the Parliament; the effectual means which have been used for the extirpation of those dangerous evils, and the progress which hath therein been made by His Majesty's goodness and the wisdom of Parliament; the ways of obstruction and opposition by which that progress hath been interrupted; the courses to be taken for removing those obstacles, and for the accomplishing of our most dutiful and faithful intentions and endeavours of restoring and establishing the ancient honour, greatness and security of this Crown and nation.

The roots of all this mischief we find to be a malignant and pernicious design of subverting the fundamental laws and principals of government, upon which the religion and justice of this kingdom are firmly established. The actors and promoters hereof have been:

1. The Jesuited Papists who hate the laws as the obstacles of that change and subversion of religion which they so much long for;

2. The bishops and the corrupt part of the clergy, who cherish formality and superstition as the natural effects and more probable supports of their own ecclesiastical tyranny and usurpation.

3. Such councillors and courtiers as for private ends have engaged themselves to further the interests of some foreign princes or states to the prejudice of his Majesty and the State at home.

The common principles by which they moulded and governed all their particular counsels and actions were these:

First, to maintain continual differences and discontents between the King and the people, upon question of prerogative and liberty, that so they might have the advantage of siding with him, and under the notions of men addicted to his service, gain to themselves and their parties the places of greatest trust and power in the kingdom.

A second, to suppress the purity and power of religion and such persons as were best affected to it, as being contrary to their own ends, and the greatest impediment to that change which they thought to introduce.

A third, to conjoin those parties of the kingdom which were most propitious to their own ends and to divide those who were most opposite, which consisted in many particular observations . . .

A fourth, to disaffect the King to Parliaments by slander and false imputations, and by putting him upon other ways of supply, which in show and appearance were fuller of advantage than the ordinary course of subsidies, though in truth they brought more loss than gain both to the King and people, and have caused the great distractions under which we both suffer.

* * *

[The *Remonstrance* then lists 204 points of concern, commencing with an account of the political events since Charles I's first Parliament at Oxford in 1628.]

121. Another step of great advantage is this, the living grievances, the evil counsellors, and actors of these mischiefs have been so quelled . . .

123. The accusation and imprisonment of the Archbishop of Canterbury, of Judge Berkely, and;

124. The impeachment of divers other bishops and judges, that it is like not only to be an ease to the present times, but a preservation to the future.

125. The discontinuance of Parliaments is prevented by the Bill for a triennial Parliament, and the abrupt dissolution of this Parliament by another Bill, by which it is provided it shall not be dissolved or adjourned without the consent of both houses . . .

131. The canons and power of canon-making are blasted by the votes of both houses.

132. The exorbitant power of bishops and their courts are much abated, by some provisions in the Bill against the High Commission Court, the authors of the many innovations in doctrine and ceremonies . . .

137. Many excellent laws and provisions are in preparation for removing the inordinate power vexation and usurpation of bishops; for reforming the pride and idleness of many of the clergy; for easing the people of unnecessary ceremonies in religion; for censuring and removing unworthy and unprofitable ministers, and for maintaining godly and diligent preachers through the kingdom . . .

139. The establishing and ordering the King's revenue, that so the abuse of officers and superfluity of expenses may be cut off, and necessary disbursements for His Majesty's honour, the defence and government of the kingdom, may be more certainly provided for.

140. The regulating of courts of justice, and abridging both the delays and charges of law-suits.

141. The settling of some good courses for preventing the exportation of gold and silver and the inequality of exchanges between us and other nations for the advancing of native commodities, increase of our manufactures and well balancing of trade, whereby the stock of the kingdom may be increased, or at least kept from impairing, as through neglect hereof it hath done for many years last past.

142. Improving the herring fishing upon our coasts, which will be of mighty use in the employment of the poor, and a plentiful nursery of mariners for enabling the kingdom in any great action.

143. The oppositions, obstructions, and other difficulties wherewith we have been encountered and which still lie in our way with some strength and much obstinacy are these: the malignant party whom we have formerly described to be the actors and promoters of all our misery, they have taken heart again . . .

145. They have endeavoured to work in His Majesty ill impressions and opinions of our proceedings, as if we had altogether done our own work and not his; and had obtained from him many things prejudicial to the Crown, both in respect of prerogative and profit . . .

180. And now what hope have we but in God, when as the only means of our subsistence and power of reformation is under Him in the Parliament?

181. But what can we the Commons, without the conjunction of the House of Lords, and what conjunction can we expect there, when the Bishops and recusant lords are so numerous and prevalent that they are able to cross and interrupt our best endeavours for reformation, and by that means give advantage to this malignant party to traduce our proceedings?

182. They infuse into the people that we mean to abolish all Church government and leave every man to his own fancy for the service and worship of God, absolving him of that obedience which he owes under God unto his Majesty, whom we know to be entrusted with the ecclesiastical law as well as with the temporal, to regulate all the members of the Church of England, by such rules of order and discipline as are established by Parliament, which is his great council, in all affairs both in Church and State.

183. We confess our intention is, and our endeavours have been to reduce within bounds that exorbitant power which the prelates have assumed unto themselves, so contrary both to the Word of God and to the laws of the land, to which end we passed the Bill for the removing them from their temporal power and employments . . .

184. And we do here declare that it is far from our purpose or desire to let loose the golden reins of discipline and government in the Church, to leave private persons or particular congregations to take up what form of divine service they please, for we hold it requisite that there should be throughout the whole realm a conformity to that order which the laws enjoin according to the Word of God . . .

186. They have maliciously charged us that we intend to destroy and discourage learning, whereas it is our chiefest care and desire to advance it, and to provide a competent maintenance for conscionable and preaching ministers throughout the kingdom, which will be a great encouragement to scholars and a certain means whereby the want, meanness and ignorance, to which a great part of the clergy is now subject, will be prevented.

187. And we intended likewise to reform and purge the fountains of learning, the two universities, that the streams flowing from thence may be clear and pure, and an honour and comfort to the whole land . . .

195. For the better preservation of the laws and liberties of the kingdom, that all illegal grievances and exactions be presented and punished at the sessions and assizes.

196. And that Judges and Justices be very careful to give this in charge to the grand jury, and both the Sheriff and Justices to be sworn to the due execution of the *Petition of Right* and other laws.

197. That his Majesty be humbly petitioned by both Houses to employ such counsellors, ambassadors, and other ministers in managing his business at home and abroad as the Parliament may have cause to confide in, without which we cannot give His Majesty such supplies for support of his own estate, nor such assistance to the Protestant party beyond the seas, as is desired...

202. That all Councillors of State may be sworn to observe those laws which concern the subject in his liberty, that they may likewise take an oath not to receive or give reward or pension from any foreign Prince, but such as they shall within some reasonable time discover to the Lords of his Majesty's Council.

2.19 RICHARD OVERTON, *AN AGREEMENT OF THE PEOPLE*

Political debates within the army, which culminated in the Putney debates, were driven by the radical Levellers, led by Overton, Lillburn and Walwyn. The content of these debates ranged far wider than those within Parliament: this advocated widespread social, political and economic reform, albeit on behalf of small property owners. The *Agreement*, in an amended and extended form, was presented to Parliament in January 1649. Text from: first edition of 1648.

Having by our late labours and hazards made it appear to the world at how high a rate we value our just freedom and God having so far owned our cause as to deliver the enemies thereof into our hands, we do now hold ourselves bound in mutual duty to each other, to take the best care we can for the future to avoid both the danger of returning into a slavish condition and the chargeable remedy of another war. For as it cannot be imagined that so many of our countrymen would have opposed us in this quarrel, if they had understood their own good, so may we safely promise to ourselves that when our common rights and liberties shall be cleared, their endeavours will be disappointed that seek to make themselves our masters. Since therefore our former oppressions and scarce yet ended troubles have been occasioned either by want of frequent national meetings in council or by rendering those meetings ineffectual, we are fully agreed and resolved to provide that hereafter our representatives be neither left to an uncertainty for the time, nor made useless to the ends for which they are intended.

In order whereunto we declare:

1. That the people of England, being at this day very unequally distributed by counties, cities and boroughs for the election of their deputies in Parliament, ought to be more indifferently proportioned according to the number of the inhabitants, the circumstances, whereof for number, place and manner are to be set down before the end of this present Parliament.

2. That to prevent the many inconveniences apparently arising from the long continuance of the same persons in authority, this present Parliament be

dissolved upon or before the last day of September, which shall be in the year of our Lord 1648.

3. That the people do, of course, choose themselves a Parliament once in two years, viz. upon the first Thursday in every 2nd March, after the manner as shall be prescribed before the end of this Parliament, to begin to sit upon the first Thursday in April following, at Westminster, or such other place as shall be appointed from time to time, by the preceding Representatives, and to continue till the last day of September then next ensuing, and no longer.

4. That the power of this and all future Representatives of this nation is inferior only to theirs who choose them and doth extend, without the consent or concurrence of any other person or persons to the enacting, altering, and repealing of laws; to the erecting and abolishing of offices and Courts, to the appointing, removing and calling to account magistrates and officers of all degrees, to the making war and peace, to the treating with foreign States, and generally to whatsoever is not expressly or impliedly reserved by the represented to themselves. Which are as followeth:

i. That matters of religion and the ways of God's worship are not at all entrusted by us to any human power, because therein we cannot remit or exceed a tittle of what our consciences dictate to be the mind of God, without wilful sin: nevertheless the public way of instructing the nation (so it be not compulsive) is referred to their discretion.

ii. That the matter of impresting and constraining any of us to serve in the wars is against our freedom; and therefore we do not allow it in our Representatives; the rather because money (the sinews of war) being always at their disposal, they can never want numbers of men apt enough to engage in any just cause.

iii. That after the dissolution of this present Parliament, no person be at any time questioned for anything said or done in reference to the late public differences, otherwise than in execution of the judgements of the present Representatives or House of Commons.

iv. That in all laws made or to be made, every person may be bound alike, and that no tenure, estate, charter, degree, birth or place do confer any exemption from the ordinary course of legal proceedings, whereunto others are subjected.

v. That as the laws ought to be equal, so they must be good, and not evidently destructive to the safety and well-being of the people.

These things we declare to be our native rights, and therefore are agreed and resolved to maintain them with our utmost possibilities, against all opposition whatsoever; being compelled thereunto not only by the examples of our ancestors, whose blood was often spent in vain for the recovery of their freedom, suffering themselves through fraudulent accommodations to be still deluded of the fruit of their victories, but also by our own woeful experience, who, having long expected and dearly earned the establishment of these

native rights

132

certain rules of government, are yet made to depend for the settlement of our peace and freedom upon him that intended our bondage and brought a cruel war upon us.

2.20 CHARLES STUART, *HIS MAJESTY'S REASONS AGAINST THE PRETENDED JURISDICTION OF THE HIGH COURT*

This speech was prepared to be read at Charles I's trial, and published after his execution. Charles I defends the place of a monarch within the law and constitution, using a similar language of liberty and the defence of property as the parliamentarians. Text from: Muddiman, *The Trial of Charles I*, Edinburgh, 1928, pp. 231–2; 261–3.

There is no proceeding just against any man but what is warranted either by God's laws or the municipal laws of the country where he lives. Now I am most confident this day's proceedings cannot be warranted by God's law, for on the contrary the authority of obedience unto kings is clearly warranted and strictly commanded both in the Old and New Testaments . . . then for the law of the land, I am no less confident that no learned lawyer will affirm than an impeachment can lie against the King, they all going in his name. . . . Besides the law upon which you ground your proceedings must either be old or new: if old, show it; if new, tell what authority warranted by the fundamental laws of the land hath made it, and when. But how the House of Commons can erect a court of judicature, which was never one itself . . . I leave to God and the world to judge . . .

And admitting, but not granting that the people of England's commission could grant your pretended power, I see nothing you can show for that. For certainly you never asked the question of the tenth man in the kingdom. And in this way you manifestly wrong even the poorest ploughman, if you demand not his free consent. Nor can you pretend any colour for this your pretended commission without the consent at least of the major part of every man in England, of whatsoever quality or condition, which I am sure you never went about to seek, so far are you from having it. Thus you see I speak not for my own right alone, as I am your King, but also for the true liberty of all my subjects, which consists not in the power of government, but in living under such laws, such a government, as may give themselves the best assurance of their lives and the propriety of their goods . . .

I am against my will brought hither, where, since I am come, [I] cannot but to my power defend the ancient laws and liberty of this kingdom, together with my own just right. . . . Besides all this, the peace of the kingdom is not the least in my thoughts, and what hope of settlement is there so long as power reigns without rule or law, changing the whole frame of that government under which this kingdom hath flourished for many hundred years? . . . And believe it, the commons of England will not thank you for this change. For they will remember how happy they have been of late years under the reign of Queen Elizabeth, the king my father, and myself, until the beginning of these unhappy troubles, and will have cause to doubt that they shall be never so happy under any new. And by this time it will be too sensibly evident that the arms I took up were only to defend the fundamental laws of the kingdom against those who have supposed my power hath totally changed the ancient government.

King Charles his speech, made upon the scaffold at Whitehall Gate immediately before his execution

... I could hold my peace very well, if I did not think that holding my peace would make some men think I did submit to the guilt as well as the punishment. But I think it is my duty to God, first, and to my country, to clear myself both as an honest man and a good king, and a good Christian.

I shall begin first with my innocence. In truth I think it not very needful for me to insist long upon this, for all the world knows that I never did begin a war with the two Houses of Parliament. And I call God to witness, to whom, I must shortly make an account, that I never did intend for to encroach upon their privileges ...

Now for to show you that I am a good Christian. I hope there is a good man that will bear me witness that I have forgiven all the world, and even those in particular that hath been the chief cause of my death. Who they are, God knows, I do not desire to know: God forgive them. But this is not all, my charity must go further. I wish that they may repent, for indeed they have committed a great sin in that particular. I pray God, with St. Stephen, that this be not laid to their charge. Nay, not only so, but that they may take the right way to the peace of the Kingdom, for my charity commands me not only to forgive particular men, but my charity commands me to endeavour to the last gasp the peace of the kingdom ...

Now sirs, I must show you both how you are out of the way and will put you in a way. First, you are out of the way, for certainly all the way you ever had yet, as I could find by anything, is by way of conquest. Certainly this is an ill way, for conquest, sir, in my opinion, is never just, except there be a good just cause, either for matter of wrong or just title. And then if you go beyond it, the first quarrel that you have to it, that makes it unjust at the end that was just at the first. . . . Believe it, you will never do right, nor God will never prosper you, until you give God his due, the King his due (that is my successors) and the people their due. I am as much for them as any of you.

You must give God his due by regulating his Church (according to the Scripture), which is now out of order. . . . A national synod freely called, freely debating among themselves, must settle this, when that every opinion is freely and clearly heard.

For the King ... the laws of the land will clearly instruct you for that. Therefore because it concerns my own particular, I only give you a touch of it.

For the people. And truly I desire their liberty and freedom as much as anybody whomsoever. But I must tell you that their liberty and freedom consists in having of government: those laws by which their life and their goods may be most their own. It is not for having share in government, sir, that is nothing pertaining to them. A subject and a sovereign are clean different things. And therefore until they do that, I mean that you do put the people in that liberty as I say, certainly they will never enjoy themselves.

Sirs, it was for this that now I am come here. If I would have given way to an arbitrary way, for to have all the laws changed according to the power of the sword, I needed not to have come here. And therefore I tell you, and I pray God it be not laid to your charge, that I am the martyr of the people. . . . I have delivered my conscience. I pray God that you do take those courses that are best for the good of the kingdom and your own salvation.

2.21 AN ACT FOR THE ABOLISHING OF THE KINGLY OFFICE

The Act, which retrospectively made the trial and execution of the King legal, was passed on 17 March 1649. Text from: *Acts and Ordinances of the Interregnum, 1642–1660*, edited by C. H. Firth, and R. S. Rait, London, 1911: vol. II, pp. 18–20.

Whereas Charles Stuart, late King of England . . . hath by authority derived from Parliament been and is hereby declared to be justly condemned, adjudged to die and put to death for many treasons, murders and other heinous offences committed by him, by which judgement he stood and is hereby declared to be attainted to high treason, whereby his issue and posterity and all other pretending title under him, are become incapable of the said crowns, or of being king or queen of the said kingdom or dominions, or either or any of them; be it therefore enacted and ordained . . . by this present Parliament and by the authority thereof that all the people of England and Ireland . . . of what degree or condition soever, are discharged of all fealty, homage and allegiance which is or shall be pretended to be due unto any of the issue and posterity of the said late king, or any claiming under him . . .

And whereas it is and hath been found by experience that the office of a king in this nation and Ireland and to have the power thereof in any single person is unnecessary, burdensome and dangerous to the liberty, safety and public interest of the people, and that for the most part use hath been made of the regal power and prerogative to oppress and impoverish and enslave the subject, and that usually and naturally any one person in such power makes it his interest to encroach upon the just freedom and liberty of the people, and to promote the setting up of their own will and power above the laws, that so they might enslave these kingdoms to their own lust, be it therefore enacted and ordained by this present Parliament . . . that the office of a king in this nation shall not henceforth reside in or be exercised by any one single person and that no one person whatsoever shall or may have or hold the office, style, dignity, power or authority of king of the said kingdoms and dominions, or any of them . . .

And whereas by the abolition of the kingly office provided for in this act a most happy way is made for this nation (if God see it good) to return to its just and ancient right of being governed by its own Representatives or National Meetings in Council from time to time chosen and entrusted for that purpose by the people; it is therefore resolved and declared by the Commons assembled in Parliament, that they will put a period to the sitting of this present Parliament and dissolve the same so soon as may possibly stand with the safety of the people that hath betrusted them, and with what is absolutely necessary for the preserving and upholding the government now settled in the way of a commonwealth . . .

And it is hereby further acted and declared notwithstanding anything contained in this act, that no persons or persons of what condition and quality soever shall be discharged from the obedience and subjection which he and they owe to the government of this nation, as it is now declared, but all and every of them shall in all things render and perform the same, as of right is due unto the supreme authority hereby declared to reside in this and the successive representatives of the people of this nation, and in them, only.

2.22 AN ACT FOR SUBSCRIBING THE ENGAGEMENT

This was passed by the Rump Parliament in order to secure loyalty to the Commonwealth in central and local government: supposedly to be taken by all men over the age of eighteen. Text from: *Acts and Ordinances of the Interregnum, 1642–1660*, edited by C. H. Firth, and R. S. Rait, London, 1911, vol. II, p. 20.

2 January 1650

Whereas divers disaffected persons do by sundry ways and means oppose and endeavour to undermine this present government so that unless special care be taken a new war is likely to break forth, for the preventing whereof and also for the better uniting of this nation, as well against all invasions from abroad as the common enemy at home, and to the end that those which receive benefit and protection from this present government may give assurance of their living quietly and peaceably under the same, and that they will neither directly or indirectly contrive or practice anything to the disturbance thereof, the Parliament now assembled do enact and ordain . . . that all men whatsoever within the Commonwealth of England, of the age of eighteen years and upwards, shall as is hereafter in this present act directed, take and subscribe this Engagement following: viz. *I do declare and promise that I will be true and faithful to the Commonwealth of England as it is now established, without a king or a House of Lords.*

And for the due taking and subscribing thereof be it further enacted . . . that all and every person and persons that now hath or hereafter shall have, hold or enjoy any place or office of trust or profit, or any place or employment of public trust whatsoever within the said Commonwealth . . . that hath not formerly taken the said Engagement by virtue of any order or direction of Parliament, shall take and subscribe the said Engagement at or before the twentieth day of February, 1650 . . .

And it is further enacted and declared that all and every person or persons that expects benefit from the courts of justice of this Commonwealth and that either now are or hereafter shall be plaintiff or plaintiffs, demandant or demandants in any suit, plaint, bill, action, information, writ, demand, execution, or any other process whatsoever in any of the courts . . . shall take and subscribe and are hereby required to take and subscribe the aforesaid Engagement.

2.23 GERRARD WINSTANLEY, *THE LAW OF FREEDOM IN A PLATFORM*

Winstanley took direct action in April 1649 to establish a communal society at St. George's Hill in Surrey, by occupying waste land and issuing a manifesto to establish 'Digger' communities, which rejected the Leveller defence of private property (see 2.20). Despite the establishment of a couple of other such communities in the midlands, Diggers and Levellers were suppressed within the year. He addressed *The Law of Freedom* to Cromwell, and it may be read as a detailed delineation of his political ideas after the failure of the Diggers' direct action. Text from: Epistle to 1652 edition.

Sir,

God hath honoured you with the highest honour of any man since Moses's time, to be the head of a people who have cast out an oppressing Pharaoh. For when the Norman power had conquered our forefathers, he took the free use of our English ground from them, and made them his servants. And God hath made you a successful instrument to cast out that conqueror, and to recover our land and liberties again, buy your victories, out of that Norman hand.

That which is yet wanting on your part to be done is this, to see the oppressor's power to be cast out with his person; and to see that the free possession of the land and liberties be put into the hands of the oppressed commoners of England.

For the crown of honour cannot be yours, neither can those victories be called victories on your part, till the land and freedoms won, be possessed by them who adventured person and purse for them.

Now you know, Sir, that the kingly conqueror was not beaten by you only, as you are a single man, nor by the officers of the army joined to you; but by the hand and assistance of the commoners, whereof some came in person and adventured their lives with you; others stayed at home and planted the earth and payed taxes and free-quarter to maintain you that went to war.

So that whatsoever is recovered from the conqueror is recovered by a joint consent of the commoners; therefore it is all equity, that all the commoners who assisted you should be set free from the conqueror's power with you: as David's law was, *the spoil shall be divided between them who went to war and them who stayed at home.*

And now you have the power of the land in your hand, you must do one of these two things: first, either set the land free to the oppressed commoners who assisted you and paid the army their wages; and then you will fulfil the Scriptures and your own engagements, and so take possession of your deserved honour.

Or secondly, you must only remove the conqueror's power out of the King's hand into other men's, maintaining the old laws still; and then your wisdom and honour is blasted for ever, and you will either lose yourself, or lay the foundation of greater slavery to posterity than you ever knew . . .

The spirit of the whole creation (who is God) is about the reformation of the world, and he will go forward in his work. For if he would not spare kings who have sat so long at his right hand governing the world, neither will he regard you, unless your ways be found more righteous than the King's.

You have the eyes of the people all the land over, nay I think I may say all neighbouring nations over, waiting to see what you will do. And the eyes of your oppressed friends who lie yet under kingly power are waiting to have the possession given them of that freedom in the land which was promised by you, if in case you prevailed . . .

It may be you will say to me: what shall I do? I answer: you are in place and power to see all burdens taken off from your friends, the commoners of England. You will say: what are those burdens?

I will instance in some, both which I know in my own experience and which I hear the people daily complaining of and groaning under, looking upon you and waiting for deliverance.

Most people cry: *we have paid taxes, given free-quarter, wasted our estates and lost our friends in the wars, and the task-masters multiply over us more than formerly.* I have asked divers this question: why do you say so?

Some have answered me that promises, oaths, and engagements have been made as a motive to draw us to assist in the wars; that privileges of Parliament and liberties of subjects should be preserved, and that all Popery and episcopacy and tyranny should be rooted out; and these promises are not performed. Now there is an opportunity to perform them.

For first say they: *the current of succeeding Parliaments is stopped, which is one of the great privileges (and people's liberties) for safety and peace; and if that continue stopped, we shall be more offended by an hereditary Parliament than we were oppressed by an hereditary king.*

And for the commoners, who were called subjects while the kingly conqueror was in power, have not as yet their liberties granted them: I will instance them in order, according as the common whisperings are among the people.

For, they say: *the burdens of the clergy remains still upon us, in a threefold nature.*

First, if any man declare his judgement in the things of God, contrary to the clergy's report or the mind of some high officers, they are cashiered, imprisoned, crushed and undone, and made sinners for a word, as they were in the Pope's and bishop's days; so that though their names be cast out, yet their High Commission Court's power remains still, persecuting men for conscience's sake when their actions are unblamable.

Secondly, in many parishes there are old formal ignorant episcopal priests established; and some ministers who are bitter enemies to commonwealth's freedom and friends to monarchy, are established preachers, and are continually buzzing their subtle principles into the minds of the people, to undermine the peace of our declared commonwealth, causing a disaffection of spirit among neighbours, who otherwise would live in peace.

Thirdly the burden of tithes remains still upon our estates, which was taken from us by the kings and given to the clergy to maintain them by our labours; so that though their preaching fill the minds of many with madness, contention and unsatisfied doubting, because their imaginary and ungrounded doctrines cannot be understood by them, yet we must pay them large tithes for so doing. This is oppression.

Fourthly, if we go to the lawyer, we find him to sit in the conqueror's chair though the kings be removed, maintaining the king's power to the height; for in many courts and cases of law the will of a judge and lawyer rules above the letter of the law, and many cases and suits are lengthened to the great vexation of the clients, and to the lodging of their estates in the purse of the unbounded lawyer. So that we see, though other men be under a sharp law, yet many of the great lawyers are not, but still do act their will as the conqueror did; as I have heard some belonging to the law say: *what cannot we do?*

Fifthly, say they, if we look upon the customs of the law itself, it is the same it was in the king's day, only the name is altered; as if the commoners of England had paid their taxes, free-quarter and shed their blood not to reform but to baptise the law into a new name, from kingly law to State law; by reason whereof the spirit of discontent is strengthened, to increase more suits of law than formerly was known to be. And so, as the sword pulls down kingly power with one hand, the kings' old law builds up monarchy again with the other.

And indeed, the main work of reformation lies in this, to reform the clergy, lawyers and law; for all complaints of the land are wrapped up within them three, not in the person of a king . . .

Sixthly if we look into parishes, the burdens there are many.

First, for the power of lords of manors remains still over their brethren, requiring fines and heriots; beating them off the free use of the common land, unless their brethren will pay them rent; exacting obedience as much as they did, and more, when the King was in power . . .

Secondly, in parishes where commons lie, the rich Norman freeholders, or the new (more covetous) gentry, over-stock the commons with sheep and cattle, so that inferior tenants and poor labourers can hardly keep a cow, but half starve her. So that the poor are kept poor still, and the common freedom of the earth is kept from them, and the poor have no more relief than they had when the king (or conqueror) was in power.

Thirdly, in many parishes two or three of the great ones bears all the sway in making assessments, over-awing constables and other officers; and when time was to quarter soldiers, they would have a hand in that, to ease themselves and over-burden the weaker sort; and many times make large sums of money over and above the justice's warrant in assessments, and would give no account why; neither durst the inferior people demand an account, for he that spake should be sure to be crushed the next opportunity; and if any have complained to committees of justices, they have been either wearied out by delays and waiting, or else the offence hath been by them smothered up; so that we see one great man favoured another, and the poor oppressed have no relief.

Fourthly, there is another grievance which the people are much troubled at, and that is this: country people cannot sell any corn or other fruits of the earth in a market town but they must either pay toll or be turned out of town.

2.24 *THE INSTRUMENT OF GOVERNMENT*

The Instrument of Government was prepared for Cromwell after the failure of the Barebones Parliament to rule with consensus between its radical wing and the moderates. It strengthened the executive power, increased county membership in the Commons, and limited the franchise. Text from: *Acts and Ordinances of the Interregnum, 1642–1660*, edited by C. H. Firth and R. S. Rait, London, 1911, vol. II, pp. 813–22.

16 December 1653

I. That the supreme legislative authority of the Commonwealth of England, Scotland and Ireland, and the dominions thereunto belonging shall be and reside in one person, and the people assembled in Parliament; the style of the which person shall be, *the Lord Protector of the Commonwealth of England, Scotland and Ireland.*

II. That the exercise of the chief magistracy and the administration of the government over the said countries and dominions and the people thereof shall be in the Lord Protector, assisted with a Council the number whereof shall not exceed twenty-one nor be less than thirteen.

III. That all writs, processes, commissions, patents, grants and other things which now run in the name and style of the Keepers of the Liberties of England by Authority of Parliament, shall run in the name and style of the Lord Protector, from whom for the future shall be derived all magistracy and honours in these three nations; and shall have the power of pardons (except in case of murders and treason) and benefit of all forfeitures for the public use; and shall govern the said countries and dominions in all things by the advice of the Council and according to these presents and the laws.

IV. That the Lord Protector, the Parliament sitting shall dispose and order the militia and forces, both by sea and land, for the peace and good of the three nations by consent of Parliament; and that the Lord Protector with the advice and consent of the major part of the Council shall dispose and order the militia for the ends aforesaid in the intervals of Parliament.

V. That the Lord Protector, by the advice aforesaid, shall direct in all things concerning the keeping and holding of a good correspondency with foreign kings, princes, and States; and also, with the consent of the major part of the Council, have the power of war and peace.

VI. That the laws shall not be altered, suspended, abrogated, or repealed nor any new law made, nor any tax, charge or imposition laid upon the people but by common consent in Parliament (save only as is excepted in the 30th article).

VII. That there shall be a Parliament summoned to meet at Westminster upon the third day of September 1654, and that successively a Parliament shall be summoned once in every third year, to be accounted from the dissolution of the present Parliament.

VIII. That neither the Parliament to be next summoned, nor any successive Parliament, shall during the time of five months, to be accounted from the day of their first meeting, be adjourned, prorogued or dissolved without their own consent.

* * *

XXVII. That a constant yearly revenue shall be raised, settled and established for maintaining 10,000 horse and dragoons, and 20,000 foot in England, Scotland and Ireland, for the defence and security thereof, and also for a convenient number of ships for guarding of the seas; besides £200,000 per annum for defraying the other necessary charges of administration of justice, and other expenses of the government; which revenue shall be raised by the customs and the such other ways and means as shall be agreed upon by the Lord Protector and the Council, and shall not be taken away or diminished, nor the way agreed upon for raising the same altered but by the consent of the Lord Protector and the Parliament.

XXVIII. That the said yearly revenue shall be paid into the public treasury, and shall be issued out for the uses of aforesaid.

2.25 THOMAS HOBBES, *LEVIATHAN*

Hobbes wrote most of the *Leviathan* from exile in Paris, after the defeat of the King's forces in the early 1640s. His thesis of absolute sovereignty, although emerging originally from a monarchical position, applied as much to the Protectorate as to the Stuarts: the sovereign was defined as one who could protect his subjects and maintain recognition of his own position. Sovereignty was described philosophically as pragmatic expediency: the economic and social context now provided the rationale for political power, not divine right and heredity. Text from: first edition, 1651, chapter 17.

Of commonwealth

For the laws of nature (as justice, equity, modesty, mercy, and, in sum, doing to others as we would be done to) of themselves, without the terror of some power to cause them to be observed, are contrary to our natural passions, that carry us to partiality, pride, revenge and the like. And covenants without the sword are but words and of no strength to secure a man at all. Therefore notwithstanding the laws of nature (which everyone hath then kept, when he has the will to keep them, when he can do it safely) if there be no power erected, or not great enough for our security, every man will and may lawfully rely on his own strength and art, for caution against all other men. And in all places where men have lived by small families, to rob and spoil one another has been a trade, and so far from being reputed against the law of nature, that the greater spoils they gained, the greater was their honour; and men observed no other laws therein but the laws of honour; that is, to abstain from cruelty, leaving to men their lives, and instruments of husbandry. And as small families did then; so now do cities and kingdoms, which are but greater families (for their own security), enlarge their dominions, upon all pretences of danger, and fear of invasion, or assistance that may be given to invaders, endeavour as much as they can to subdue or weaken their neighbours by open force and secret arts, for want of other caution, justly; and are remembered for it in after ages with honour.

Nor is it the joining together of a small number of men that gives them this security; because in small numbers, small additions on the one side or the other make the advantage of strength so great as is sufficient to carry the victory; and therefore gives encouragement to an invasion. The multitude sufficient to confide in for our security is not determined by any certain number, but by comparison with the enemy we fear; and is the sufficient when the odds of the enemy is not of so visible and conspicuous moment to determine the event of war, as to move him to attempt.

And be there never so great a multitude, yet if their actions be directed according to their particular judgements and particular appetites, they can expect thereby no defence, nor protection, neither against a common enemy, nor against the injuries of one another. For being distracted in opinions concerning the best use and application of their strength, they do not help, but hinder one another; and reduce their strength by mutual opposition to nothing: whereby they are easily not only subdued by a very few that agree together, but also, when there is no common enemy, they make war upon each other for their particular interests. For if we could suppose a great multitude of men to consent in the observation of justice and other laws of nature, without a common power to keep them all in awe, we might as well suppose all mankind to do the same; and then there would be nor need to be any civil government or commonwealth at all, because there would be peace without subjection.

Nor is it enough for the security which men desire should last all the time of their life, that they be governed and directed by one judgement for a limited time, as in one battle or one war. For though they obtain a victory by their unanimous endeavour against a foreign enemy, yet afterwards when either they have no common enemy, or he that by one part is held for an enemy, is by another part held for a friend, they must needs by the difference of their interests dissolve, and fall again into a war amongst themselves.

It is true that certain living creatures, as bees and ants, live sociably one with another (which are therefore by Aristotle numbered amongst political creatures), and yet have no other direction than their particular judgements and appetites, nor speech whereby one of them can signify to another what he thinks expedient for the common benefit: and therefore some man may perhaps desire to know why mankind cannot do the same.

To which I answer, first, that men are continually in competition for honour and dignity, which these creatures are not; and consequently amongst men there ariseth on that ground envy and hatred, and finally war: but amongst these, not so.

Secondly, that amongst these creatures the common good differeth not from the private; and being by nature inclined to their private, they procure thereby the common benefit. But man, whose joy consisteth in comparing himself with other men can relish nothing but what is eminent.

Thirdly, that these creatures, having not (as man) the use of reason, do not see, nor think they see, any fault in the administration of their common business: whereas amongst men there are very many that think themselves wiser and abler to govern the public better than the rest; and these strive to reform and innovate, one this way, another that way; and thereby bring it into distraction and civil wars.

Fourthly, that these creatures though they have some use of voice in making known to one another their desires and other affections, yet they want the art of words, by which some men can represent to others that which is good in the likeness of evil; and evil in the likeness of good; and augment or diminish the apparent greatness of good and evil; discontenting men and troubling their peace at their pleasure.

Fifthly, irrational creatures cannot distinguish between injury and damage, and therefore as long as they be at ease, they are not offended with their fellows: whereas man is then most troublesome when he is most at ease, for then it is that he loves to show his wisdom, and control the actions of them that govern the commonwealth.

Lastly, the agreement of these creatures is natural; that of men is by covenant only, which is artificial: and therefore it is no wonder if there be somewhat else required (besides covenant) to make their agreement constant and lasting; which is a common power to keep them in awe and to direct their actions to the common benefit.

The only way to erect such a common power as may be able to defend them from the invasion of foreigners and the injuries of one another, and thereby to secure them in such sort as that by their own industry and by the fruits of the earth they may nourish themselves and live contentedly, is to confer all their power and strength upon one man, or upon one assembly of men that may reduce all their wills, by plurality of voices, unto one will; which is as much as to say, to appoint one man, or assembly of men, to bear their person; and every one to own and acknowledge himself to be author of whatsoever he that so beareth their person, shall act or cause to be acted in those things which concern the common peace and safety; and therein to submit their wills, everyone to his will, and their judgements to his judgement. This is more than consent, or concord; it is a real unity of them all, in one and the same person, made by covenant of every man with every man, in such manner as if every man should say to every man, *I authorise and give up my right of governing myself to this man, or to this assembly of men, on this condition: that thou give up thy right to him and authorise all his actions in like manner.* This done, the multitude so united in one person is called a commonwealth, in Latin, *civitas*. This is the generation of that great LEVIATHAN, or rather (to speak more reverently) of that mortal God to which we owe under the immortal God, our peace and defence. For by this authority, given him by every particular man in the commonwealth, he hath the use of so much power and strength conferred on him, that by terror thereof, he is enabled to form the wills of them all to peace at home, and mutual aid against their enemies abroad. And in him consisteth the essence of the commonwealth: which (to define it) is: *one person of whose acts a great multitude, by mutual covenants one with another, have made themselves every one the author, to the end he may use the strength and means of them all as he shall think expedient, for their peace and common defence.*

And he that carrieth this person is called sovereign, and said to have sovereign power, and everyone besides, his subject.

The attaining to this sovereign power is by two ways: one by natural force, as when a man maketh his children to submit themselves, and their children to his government, as being able to destroy them if they refuse; or by war subdueth his enemies to his will, giving them their lives on that condition. The other is when men agree amongst themselves to submit to some man, or assembly of men, voluntarily, on confidence to be protected by him against all others. This latter may be called a political commonwealth, or commonwealth by institution; and the former a commonwealth by acquisition.

2.26 JAMES HARRINGTON, *OCEANA*

Harrington dedicated his political thesis to Oliver Cromwell, but in the form of an attack on *Leviathan* and on government by aristocracy and privilege. Much of the work is a description of his fictional utopia, *Oceana*: but in his prefatory remarks he sets out his political philosophy, in which he argues that power should be circumscribed by law and property. Text from: first edition, 1656, pp. 1–7.

The preliminaries, showing the principles of government

... The most excellent describer of the commonwealth of Venice, divideth the whole series of government into two times or periods. The one ending with the liberty of Rome, which was the course of *empire*, as I may call it, of *ancient prudence* first discovered unto mankind by God himself in the fabric of the commonwealth of Israel, and afterward picked out of his footsteps in nature and unanimously followed by the Greeks and Romans. The other beginning with the arms of Caesar, which extinguishing liberty were the translation of ancient into modern prudence, introduced by those inundations of Huns, Goths, Vandals, Lombards, Saxons, which, breaking the Roman empire, deformed the whole face of the world with those ill features of government which at this time are become far worse in these western parts, except Venice ...

Relation being had unto these two times, government (to define it *de jure* or according to *ancient prudence*) is an art whereby a civil society of men is instituted and preserved upon the foundation of common right or interest, or (to follow Aristotle and Livy) it is the empire of laws and not of men.

And government (to define it *de facto* or according unto *modern prudence*), is an art whereby some man or some few men subject a city of a nation and rule it according unto his or their private interest: which because the laws in such cases are made according to the interest of a man or of some few families, may be said to be the empire of men, and not of laws.

The former kind is that which Machievell (whose books are neglected) is the only politician that hath gone about to retrieve, and that *Leviathan* (who would have his book imposed upon the universities) goes about to destroy. *For it is* (saith he) *another error of Aristotle's Politics that in a well ordered commonwealth not men should govern, but the laws: what man that hath his natural senses though he can neither write nor read does not find himself governed by them he fears, and believes can kill or hurt him when he obeyeth not? Or who believes that the law can hurt him, which is but words and paper, without the hands and sword of a man?* ...

... The principles of government, then, are in the goods of the mind or the goods of fortune. To the goods of the mind answers authority; to the goods of fortune, power or empire. Wherefore *Leviathan*, though he be right where he saith that riches are power, is mistaken where he saith that prudence or the reputation of prudence is power: for the learning or prudence of a man is no more power than learning or prudence of a book or author, which is properly authority: a learned writer may have authority though he have no power: and a foolish magistrate may have power though he have otherwise no esteem or authority ...

Empire is of two kinds, domestic and national; or foreign and provincial.

Domestic empire is founded upon dominion. Dominion is propriety real or personal, that is to say, in lands or in money and goods.

Lands, or the parts and parcels of a territory are held by the proprietor or proprietors, Lords or Lords of it, in some proportions and such (except it be in a city that hath little or no lands, and whose revenue is in trade) as is the proportion or balance of dominion or property in land, such is the nature of empire . . .

If the few or a nobility, or a nobility with the clergy be landlords, or overbalance the people unto the like proportion, it makes the Gothic balance . . . and the empire is mixed monarchy, as that of Spain, Poland, and late of Britain.

And if the whole people be landlords or hold the lands so divided among them that no one man or numbers of men within the compass of the few or aristocracy overbalance them, the empire (without the interposition of force) is a commonwealth.

If force be interposed in any of these three cases it must either frame the government unto the foundation, or the foundation unto the government, or holding the government not according unto the balance, it is not natural, but violent: and therefore if it be at the devotion of a Prince, it is tyranny; if at the devotion of the few, oligarchy; or if in the power of the people, anarchy. Each of which confusions, the balance standing otherwise, is but of short continuance because against the nature of the balance which, not destroyed, destroyeth that which opposeth it.

But there be certain other confusions which being rooted in the balance are of longer continuance and of greater horror, as first, where a nobility holdeth half the property, or above that proportion, and the people the other half, in which case without altering the balance, there is no remedy but the one must eat out the other: as the people did the nobility in Athens, and the nobility the people in Rome. Secondly, when a Prince holdeth about half the dominion, and the people the other half, which was the case of the Roman emperors, planted partly upon their military colonies and partly upon the senate and the people, the government becometh a very shambles both of the princes and the people. Somewhat of this nature are certain governments at this day, which are said to subsist by confusion. In this case to fix the balance is to entail misery: but in the three former not to fix it is to loose the government. Wherefore it being unlawful in Turkey that any should posses land but the Grand Seigneur, the balance is fixed by the law and that empire firm. Nor, though the Kings often fell, was the throne of Oceana known to shake until the statute of alienations broke the pillars by giving way unto the nobility to sell their estates. . . . This kind of law, fixing the balance in lands, is called agrarian, and was first introduced by God himself, who divided the land of Canaan unto his people by lots, and is of such virtue that wherever it hath held, that government hath not altered, except by consent as in that unparalleled example of the people of Israel, when being in liberty they would needs choose a king. But without an agrarian, government, whether monarchical, aristocratical or popular, hath no long lease . . . unto propriety producing empire it is required that it should have some certain root or foothold, which, except in land, it cannot have, being otherwise as it were upon the wing.

Nevertheless, in such cities as subsist most by trade and have little or no land, as Holland and Genoa, the balance of treasure may be equal unto that of land in the cases mentioned.

But *Leviathan* . . . hath caught hold of the public sword, unto which he reduceth all manner and matter of government; as where he affirms *the opinion that any monarch receiveth his power by covenant, that is to say, upon conditions, to proceed from the not understanding the easy truth, that covenants, being words and breath, have no power to oblige, contain, constrain, or protect any man, but what they have from the public sword* [part II, ch. 18]. But as he said of the law that without this sword it is but paper, so he might have thought of this sword that without an hand it is but cold iron. The hand which holdeth this sword is the militia of a nation; and the militia of a nation is either an army in the field, or ready for the field upon occasion. But an army is a beast that hath a great belly and must be fed; wherefore, this will come unto what pastures you have, and what pastures you have will come unto the balance of propriety, without which the public sword is but a name or a mere spitfrog.

2.27 *THE HUMBLE PETITION AND ADVICE*, 1657

The Humble Petition of 1657 attempted to strengthen the perceived weaknesses of the constitutional position established by the *Instrument of Government* (2.24), through the addition of a second legislative chamber, and the confirming of Cromwell's permanent and hereditary right to the Lord Protectorship. Text from: *Acts and Ordinances of the Interregnum, 1642–1660*, edited by C. H. Firth and R. S. Rait, London, 1911, vol. II; pp. 1,048–56.

1. That your Highness will be pleased by and under the name and style of Lord Protector of the Commonwealth of England, Scotland and Ireland and the dominions and territories thereunto belonging, to hold and exercise the office of chief magistrate of these nations and to govern according to this petition and advice in all things therein contained and in all other things according to the laws of these nations and not otherwise; that your Highness will be pleased during your lifetime to appoint and declare the person who shall, immediately after your death succeed you in the government of these nations.

2. That your Highness will, for the future be pleased to call Parliaments consisting of two houses (in such manner and way as shall be more particularly afterwards agreed and declared in this Petition and Advice) once in three years at furthest, or oftener, as the affairs of the nation shall require, that being your Great Council, in whose affection and advice yourself and this people will be most happy.

3. That the ancient and undoubted liberties and privileges of Parliament (which are the birthright and inheritance of the people, and wherein every man is interested) be preserved and maintained . . .

4. That those who have advised, assisted or abetted the rebellion of Ireland and those who do or shall profess the Popish religion, be disabled and made incapable for ever to be elected, or to give any vote in the election of any member to sit or serve in Parliament . . .

5. That your Highness will consent that none be called to sit and vote in the other house but such as are not disabled, but qualified according to the qualifications mentioned in the former article, being such as shall be nominated by your Highness and approved by this House, and that they exceed not seventy in number . . . and that as any of them do die, or be legally removed, no new ones be admitted to sit and vote in their rooms but by the consent of the House itself. That the other House do not proceed in any civil causes, except in writs of error, in cases adjourned from inferior courts into the Parliament for difficulty, in cases of petitions against proceedings in Courts of equity, and in cases of privileges of their own Houses; that they do not proceed in any criminal cases whatsoever against any person criminally, but upon an impeachment of the Commons assembled in Parliament and by their consent; that they do not proceed in any cause, either civil or criminal, but according to the known laws of the land, and the due course and custom of Parliament . . .

8. That none may be admitted to the Privy Council of your Highness or successors, but such as are of known piety and undoubted affection to the rights of these nations, and a just Christian liberty in matters of religion, nor without consent of the Council to be afterwards approved by both Houses of Parliament, and shall not afterwards be removed except but by consent of Parliament . . .

9. And that the Chancellor, Keeper or Commissioners of the Great Seal of England, the Treasurer or Commissioners of the treasury there, the admiral, the chief governor of Ireland, the Chief Justices of both the benches and the Chief Baron in England and Ireland, the Commander-in-chief of the forces in Scotland and such officers of State there as by Act of Parliament in Scotland, are to be approved by Parliament, and the judges of Scotland hereafter to be made, shall be approved of by both Houses of Parliament.

10. And whereas your Highness out of your zeal to the glory of God and the propagation of the Gospel of the Lord Jesus Christ, hath been pleased to encourage a godly ministry in these nations, we earnestly desire that such as do openly revile them or their assemblies, or disturb them in the worship or service of God, to the dishonour of God, scandal of good men, or breach of the peace may be punished according to law; and where the laws are defective, that your Highness will give consent to such laws as shall be made in that behalf.

11. That the true Protestant Christian religion, as it is contained in the Holy Scriptures of the Old and New Testament, and no other, be held forth and asserted for the public profession of these nations.

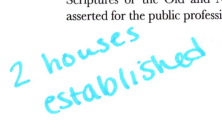

2.28 *THE DECLARATION OF BREDA*

On the request of General Monk and with the acquiescence of the recalled Long Parliament, Charles II engaged in secret negotiations to ascend the throne. The *Declaration* aimed at reconciliation. Text from: *Lords Journals*, XI, pp. 7–8.

April 4 1660

To all our loving subjects, of what degree or quality soever, greeting.

If the general distraction and confusion which is spread over the whole kingdom doth not awaken all men to a desire and longing that those wounds which have so many years together been kept bleeding, may be bound up, all we can say will be to no purpose; however, after this long silence, we have thought it our duty to declare how much we desire to contribute thereunto; and that as we can never give over the hope, in good time, to obtain possession of that right which God and nature hath made our due, so we do make it our daily suit to the Divine Providence that He will, in compassion to us and our subjects, after so long misery and sufferings, remit and put us into a quiet and peaceable possession of that our right, with as little blood and damage to our people as is possible; nor do we desire more to enjoy what is ours than all our subjects may enjoy what by law is theirs, by a full and entire administration of justice throughout the land, and by extending our mercy where it is wanted and deserved.

And to the end that the fear of punishment may not engage any, conscious to themselves of what is past, to a perseverance in guilt for the future, by opposing the quiet and happiness of their country, in the restoration both of king, peers and people to their just, ancient and fundamental rights, we do, by these presents declare that we do grant a free and general pardon, which we are ready, upon demand, to pass under our Great Seal of England, to all our subjects, of what degree or quality soever who, within forty days after the publishing hereof, shall lay hold upon this our grace and favour and shall, by any public act, declare their doing so, and that they return to the loyalty and obedience of good subjects; excepting only such persons as shall hereafter be excepted by Parliament. Those only excepted, let all our loving subjects, how faulty soever, rely upon the word of a King, solemnly given by this present Declaration, that no crime whatsoever committed against us or our royal father before the publication of this, shall ever rise in judgement or be brought in question against any of them, to the least endamagement of them, either in their lives, liberties or estates, or (as far forth as lies in our power) so much as to the prejudice of their reputations, by any reproach or term of distinction from the rest of our best subjects; we desiring and ordaining that henceforth all notes of discord, separation and difference of parties be utterly abolished among all our subjects, whom we invite and conjure to a perfect union among themselves, under our protection, for the resettlement of our just rights and theirs in a free Parliament, by which, upon the word of a King, we will be advised.

And because the passion and uncharitableness of the times have produced several opinions in religion, by which men are engaged in parties and animosities against each other (which when they shall hereafter unite in a freedom of conversation, will be composed and better understood) we do declare a liberty to tender consciences, and that no man shall be disquieted or called in question for differences of opinion in matter of religion, which do not disturb the peace of the kingdom; and that we shall be ready to consent to such an Act of Parliament as, upon mature deliberation, shall be offered to us for the full granting that indulgence.

And because, in the continued distractions of so many years and so many and great revolutions, many grants and purchases of estates have been made to and by many officers, soldiers and others, who are now possessed of the same, and who may be liable to actions at law upon several titles, we are likewise willing that all such differences and all things relating to such grants, sales and purchases, shall be determined in Parliament, which can best provide for the just satisfaction of all men who are concerned.

And we do further declare that we will be ready to consent to any Act or Acts of Parliament to the purposes aforesaid, and for the full satisfaction of all arrears due to the officers and soldiers of the army under the command of General Monk, and that they shall be received into our service upon as good pay and conditions as they now enjoy.

3

SOCIETY AND
SOCIAL LIFE

INTRODUCTION

In 1548 the radical poet and writer Robert Crowley addressed the House of Commons with a petition, which explicitly linked the religious reformation with social reformation in a discourse which was both old and new (3.1). Thus, he emphasises the Pauline injunctions to the Thessalonians 'that no man be suffered to eat but such as would labour in their vocation and calling'. This was frequently used by Calvin and later English Protestant writers to make what they saw as a crucial distinction between the 'deserving' and 'undeserving' poor: a distinction later enshrined in the succession of English poor laws during the sixteenth century, culminating in the comprehensive one of 1598 (3.12). Nevertheless, Crowley actually goes on to critique the literal application of 2 Thessalonians 3, when taken out of its original context. His full statement reads as follows:

> Take me not here that I should go about by these words to persuade men to make all things common: for if you do you mistake me. For I take God to witness that I mean no such things. But with all mine heart I would wish that no man were suffered to eat, but such as would labour in their vocation and calling, according to the rule that St. Paul gave to the Thessalonians. But yet I would wish that the possessioners would consider who gave them their possessions and how they ought to bestow them. And then (I doubt not) it should not need to have all things made common.
>
> For what needeth it the servant of the household to desire to have their masters' goods common, so long as the steward ministereth unto every man the thing that is needful for him?

Crowley argues that reformed religion should return to the practice and purity of the early apostolic Church, where all members were stewards of the Lord, and not 'possessioners'. But rather than placing this apparently radical view of property and society in the context of a general social or political communism (as the Diggers were to do a century later: 2.23), he places it within a quite conventional Tudor, even feudal, view of society: in which household management was part of a continuum with political structure and allegiance, a hierarchy of men and women who all knew their proper place and duties (see the *Exhortation Concerning Good Order and Obedience*, 2.5, and Thomas Smith, 3.9). This combination of social philanthropy and political conservativism was the social philosophy of older (Catholic) views on charity; the basis of English patriarchalism for several subsequent centuries; and the necessary cement of the 'deferential society'.[1] As the *Homilies* show (1.4, 2.5, 7.7), knowing one's exact social place meant owing obedience to someone above one in the social hierarchy which Smith delineates (3.9): and the many Elizabethan and Stuart expressions of fear about social and political disorder and vagrancy sprang from anxiety about threats to the culture of deference. The frequency of the articulation of a political and social philosophy of hierarchy may suggest that its hegemony was perceived as being under threat. Certainly, much of the literature about vagrancy interpreted the growth of unemployed itinerancy not as a genuine and needy search for work, but as the beginnings of possible revolution.

Thus we can see from Crowley's words the twin pillars on which early modern society and social life hung: a social structure in which deference and place defined identity, power and work, maintained through a social policy of minimal welfare and maximum regulation. The social structure is described most precisely by Thomas Smith (3.9), who allows some flexibility in the apparently rigid status hierarchy, when he acknowledges that definitions of 'gentry' are fluid. The regulatory and statutory framework by which order was maintained is represented here in three very different examples. First, by the 'medieval' looking Statutes of Apparel (here reiterated in a 1574 Proclamation, 3.4), which demonstrate an ostensibly crude way of signifying and demanding the control of social behaviour and deference. Second, the Statute of Artificers (3.5) may also be said to look backwards to a medieval economy in which entrance to skilled craft jobs was restricted, and employment regulated and policed through local parish and manorial power bases. Its attempt to restrict wages, training, labour movement and skills illustrates both the contemporary fear of 'masterless men', set loose from the economic, social and political order, and the somewhat clumsy political and economic philosophy with which they were able to deal with it. During this period, there was no generally agreed economic philosophy of 'free trade' which could explain the sharp rise in unemployment or the phenomenon of an increasingly national economy, and hence, consequently, no concerted use of capital or borrowing to fund economic expansion. Third, the Poor Law (3.12) tried to systematise the provision of welfare and the payment for it by locating provision and payment in the parish, with the responsibility for raising and assessing the taxes placed upon local Justices of Peace. In this way the Elizabethan Privy Council attempted to make provision for poverty, whilst preventing itinerancy and vagrancy. They certainly achieved the former aim, at least until the impact of the Industrial Revolution in the late eighteenth century: but unemployment and 'vagrancy' remained an endemic problem, particularly in times of dearth such as the 1590s and the mid 1620s.

The myth of 'merrie England', of static idyllic rural life in a pre-industrial age[2] is one that has been comprehensively demystified by a combination of different historical approaches over the past thirty years. Thus historical demography has been able to demonstrate the huge population increase over the period: almost doubling between 1550 and 1650, from three million to five and a quarter million[3], as well as looking at migration to towns and cities. London grew from a small enclave enclosed in the city walls of 120,000 residents in 1550, to a sprawling metropolis of 375,000 people in 1650, despite the fact that deaths always exceeded baptism records. There could be no more graphic expression of the simultaneous threat and attraction of the dangerous city than the combination of those figures.

Studies of local parishes and litigation[4] have demonstrated the fragility of local order and consensus, and its dependence on the power and allegiance of the 'middling sort' to the gentry and status quo. Whilst, for the most part, such consensus was maintained, it was at the expense of the growth of an under class excluded from social and economic development.[5] Studies of cases before Church and assize courts,[6] which were continually regulating social behaviour and mores, have shown that men and women were often quick to slander, could be slow to acquiesce to authority, and recalcitrant in obedience to Church and State. Studies of wage and price fluctuations have shown us that underemployment and very real poverty affected the majority of the population.[7] Finally the study of patterns of age expectancy, famine and mortality from illnesses such as influenza, dysentery, smallpox and other more common diseases have illuminated the harshness and uncertainty of life for early modern women and men. The very real threat of plague, for example, hung over cities, towns and villages for the whole of the early modern period. It had a 60–85 per cent death rate for those contracting it, and the figures of deaths in London during some of its most virulent visitations are staggering: in 1563 it killed 20,000 people; in 1593 18,000 in the inner suburbs alone; in 1603, 30,000; and in 1625 40–50,000. This represents over 10 per cent of the total population: and those who died were more likely to be the poor, since they did not have the resources to leave the city.

Early modern England was then a place where 'contrasting communities'[8] begin to differentiate themselves: the invocation of the myth of the seamless social order seems increasingly inaccurate and desperate. These contrasts were not only of different economic areas (wood pasture and arable) and of cultural attitudes (of deference and godly reform)[9] but also of city and village; of court and city; of 'court' and 'country'; of rich and poor; the 'possessioners' and the dispossessed.

3.1 ROBERT CROWLEY, *AN INFORMATION AND PETITION AGAINST THE OPPRESSORS OF THE POOR COMMONS OF THIS REALM*

Crowley's address to the Commons in 1548 sets the tone and terms of the debate about poverty and social responsibility for the Elizabethan period. Text from: 1548 edition, fos A3ᵛff.

To the most honourable Lords of the Parliament with the commons of the same: their most humble and daily orator Robert Crowley wisheth the assistance of God's holy spirit

But as for the oppression of the poor, which is no less needful to be communed of and reformed than the other, I fear me we will be passed over with silence, or if it be communed of, I can scarcely trust that any reformation can be had, unless God do now work in the hearts of the possessioners of this realm, as he did in the primitive church when the possessioners were contented and very willingly to sell their possessions and give the price thereof to be common to all the faithful believers. Take me not here that I should go about by these words to persuade men to make all things common: for if you do, you mistake me. For I take God to witness I mean no such thing. But with all mine heart I would wish that no man were suffered to eat, but such as would labour in their vocation and calling, according to the rule that St. Paul gave to the Thessalonians [2 Thess. 3]. But yet I would wish that the possessioners would consider who gave them their possessions and how they ought to bestow them. And then (I doubt not) it should not need to have all things made common.

For what needeth it the servant of the household to desire to have their masters' goods common, so long as the steward ministereth unto every man the thing that is needful for him?

If the possessioners would consider themselves to be but stewards, and not lords over their possessions, this oppression would soon be redressed. But so long as this persuasion sticketh in their minds: *it is mine own: who shall warn me to do with mine own as me self listeth?* it shall not be possible to have any redress at all. For if I may do with my own as me listeth, then may I suffer my brother, his wife and his children to lie in the street, except he will give me more rent for mine house than ever he shall be able to pay. Then may I take his goods for that he oweth me and keep his body in prison, turning out his wife and children to perish, if God will not move some man's heart to pity them: and yet keep here my coffers full of gold and silver.

If there were no God then would I think it lawful for men to use their possessions as they list; or if God would not require an account of us for the bestowing
of them, I would not greatly gainsay though they took their pleasure of them
whiles they lived here. But forasmuch as we have a God, and he hath declared
unto us by the Scriptures that he hath made the possessioners but stewards of his
riches, and that he will hold a straight account with them for the occupying and
bestowing of them, I think no Christian ears can abide to hear that more than
Turkish opinion . . .

Now harken you possessioners and you rich men lift up your ears, ye stewards
of the Lord, mark what complaints are laid against you in the high court of the
living God. Lord (saith the prophet) hast thou forsaken us? Dost thou hide thy
self in the time of our trouble? Whiles the wicked wax proud, the poor man is
afflicted and troubled. Would to God the wicked might feel the same things that
they invent for other. . . . Behold you engrossers of farms and tenements, behold
I say, the terrible threatenings of God whose wrath you cannot escape. The voice
of the poor (whom you have with money thrust out of house and home) is well
accepted in the ears of the Lord, and hath stirred up his wrath against you. He
threateneth you most horrible plagues . . .

For when you have multiplied your rents to the highest so that ye have made
all your tenants your slaves to labour and toil and bring to you all that may be
ploughen and digged out of your grounds, then shall death suddenly strike you,
then shall God withdraw his comfortable grace from you, then shall your
conscience prick you, then shall you think with desperate Cain that your sin is
greater than that it may be forgiven, for your own conscience shall judge you
worthy no mercy, because you have showed no mercy. Yea, the same enemy that
hath kindled and doth yet maintain in you this mischievous, outrageous and
unsatiable covetousness, shall then be as busy to put you in mind of the words of
Christ, saying, the same measure that you have made unto other, shall be now
made unto you.

You have showed no mercy: how can you look then for mercy? O, noble
counsellors, be merciful to yourselves. Destroy not your own souls to enrich your
heirs; enlarge not your earthly possession with the loss of the eternal inheritance;
learn to know the estate that God hath called you unto, and to live according to
your profession; know that you are all ministers in the common weal, and that
the portion which you are born unto, or that your prince giveth you, is your
estate; know that your office is to distribute, and not to scrape together on heaps.
God hath not set you to survey his lands, but to play the stewards on his household of this world, and to see that your poor fellow servants lack not their
necessaries.

Consider that you are but ministers and servants under the Lord our God,
and that you shall render a straight account of your administration. Stand not so
much in your own conceit, glorying in the worthiness of your blood, for we are
all one man's children, and have (by nature) like right to the riches and treasures
of this world whereof our natural father, Adam, was made Lord and King.

Which of you can say for himself any natural cause why he should possess the treasure of this world, but that the same cause may be found in him also whom you make your slave? By nature (therefore) you can claim nothing but that which you shall get with the sweat of your faces. That you are lords and governors therefore, cometh not by nature, but by the ordinance and appointment of God. Know then that he hath not called you to the wealth and glory of this world: but hath charged you with the great and rude multitude.

And if any of them perish through your default, know then for certainty that the blood of them shall be required at your hands. If the impotent creatures perish for lack of necessaries, you are the murderers for you have their inheritance and do not minister unto them. If the sturdy fall to stealing, robbing and receiving: then are you the causes thereof, for you dig in, enclose, and withhold from them the earth out of which they should dig and plough their living. For as the Psalmist writeth: *all the heaven is the Lord's: but as for the earth, he hath given it to the children of men* [Psalm 113].

The whole earth therefore (by birthright) belongeth to the children of men. They are all inheritors thereof indifferently by nature . . .

What a sea of mischiefs have flowed out of this, more than Turkey the tyranny: what honest householders have been made followers of other not so honest men's tables; what honest matrons have been brought to the needy rock and cards; what men children of good hope in the liberal sciences and other honest qualities (whereof this realm hath great lack) have been compelled to fall some to handicrafts and some to day labour to sustain their parents' decrepit age and miserable poverty; what froward and stubborn children have hereby shaken off the yoke of goodly chastisement, running headlong into all kinds of wickedness and finally garnished gallow trees; what modest, chaste and womanly virgins have for lack of dowry been compelled either to pass over the days of their youth in ungrate servitude or else to marry perpetual miserable poverty; what immodest and wanton girls have hereby been made sisters of the Bank[1] (the stumbling stock of all frail youth), and finally most miserable creatures lying and dying in the streets full of all plagues and penury; what universal destruction chanceth to this noble realm by this outrageous and unsatiable desire of the surveyors of lands: I report me to you (most Christian counsellors) which are here assembled from all parts of this noble realm, to consult for the wealth of all the members of the same.

On the other side, there be certain tenants not able to be landlords and yet after a sort they counterfeit landlords, by obtaining leases in and upon grounds and tenements and so raise fines, incomes and rents: and by such pillage pick out a portion to maintain a proud port, and all by pilling and polling of the poor commons that must of necessity seek habitations at their hands.

That this is true, I report me to my Lord the Mayor and other the head officers of the City of London who (if they be not ignorant of the state of the city) can witness with me that the most part; yea, I think nine of the ten parts, of the houses in London be set and let by them that have them by lease: and not by the owners . . .

For what discommodity is it to the head, shoulders, the arms and other the upper members of the body, being already sufficiently clothed, to put on the legs and feet a pair of hose and shoes to defend them also from the injuries of the weather and other hurts that might chance unto them in their travailing to carry the body from place to place, for his commodity and pleasure? Verily in mine opinion that body is far unworthy to have either legs or feet that will let them go bare, having wherewith to cover them.

Even so, you being the chief members of this noble realm and having in your hands the wonderful and incomparable riches of the same, what should it grieve you to depart with some portion thereof, that the inferior members thereof may at all times be able to do their ministry and office accordingly?

Once remember that as the body without the inferior parts is but lame and as a block unwieldy, and must, if it will remove from place to place, creep upon the hands, even so you, if ye had not the poor members of this realm to till the ground and do your other drudgery, no remedy, you must needs do it yourselves . . .

Other things there be whereby the poor members of Christ in this noble realm are oppressed whereof I have made no mention. . . . I mean the great extortion and usury that reigneth freely in this realm and seem to be authorised by Parliament within these three years last past.

The clergy of the City of London have for their part obtained by Parliament authority to over tenths. . . . No couple can be married but these men must have a duty, as they call it. No woman may be purified, but they and their idle ministers must have some duties of her. None can be buried but they will have a slice. Not three months before the beginning of this present Parliament I had just occasion to be at the payment of this duty for the burying of an honest poor man, whose friends were willing to have his body reverently laid in the ground and according to the custom, gave warning to the curate that they would bring the dead body to the church, desiring him that he would do his duty and to be there to receive it, and according to the custom, to lay it in the ground. But this raven, smelling the carrion, could not but reveal it to the other carrion birds of the same church, and so would needs come altogether in a flock to fetch their prey, with cross and holy water, as they were wont to do, notwithstanding the King's injunctions and late visitation. The friends of the dead man refused all this and required to have no more but the common coffin to put the body in, agreeing to pay to the keeper thereof his accustomed duty, and in like manner to the grave maker and the four poor men to carry the body so that the whole charges had been but 7d.

But when the corpse was buried, without either cross or holy water stick, dirge or Mass, with prayers of as small devotion as any poor curate could say, yet must we needs pay 7d. more. That is to say, 1d. to the curate, which he called an head pedy [*sic*], and 6d. to two clerks that we had no need of.

This was done in Sepulchre's parish in the City of London. And it shall please any of this noble assembly to try the truth of this: I will verify it wheresoever I shall be called, even in the presence of all the idle ministers of the same church.

3.2 JOHN AWDELEY, *THE FRATERNITY OF VAGABONDS*

Awdeley's pamphlet was part of a popular genre which both celebrated and castigated the culture and methods of a criminal underclass. Text from: 1561 edition, fos A2^r–B2^r.

The company of cozeners and shifters

A courtesy man is one that walketh about the back lanes in London in the day time, and sometime in the broad streets in the night season: and when he meeteth with some handsome young man cleanly apparelled, or some other citizen, he maketh humble salutations, and low courtesy, and showeth him that he hath a word or two to speak with his mastership. This child can behave himself mannerly, for he will desire him that he talketh withal, to take the upper hand, and show him much reverence and at last (like his familiar acquaintance) will put on his cap, and walk side by side and talk on this fashion. O, Sir, you seem to be a man, and one that favoureth men, and therefore I am the more bolder to break my mind unto your good Mastership. Thus it is, Sir, there are a certain of us (though I say it, both tall and handsome men of our hands) which have come lately from the wars, and (as God knoweth) have nothing to take to, being both masterless and moneyless, and knowing no way whereby to earn a penny. And further, whereas we have been wealthily brought up, and we also have been had in good estimation, we are ashamed now to declare our misery, and to fall a craving as common beggars: and as for to steal and rob (God is our record) it striketh us to the heart, to think of such a mischief that ever any handsome man should fall into such a danger for this worldly trash; which if we had to suffice our want and necessity, we should never seek thus shamefast to crave of such good pitiful men as you seem to be, neither yet so dangerously to hazard our lives for so vile a thing. Therefore, good Sir, as you seem to be a handsome man your self, and also such a one as pitieth the miserable case of handsome men, as now your eyes and countenance showeth to have some pity upon this my miserable complaint. So in God's cause I require your mastership, and in the behalf of my poor afflicted fellows, which though here in sight, they cry not with me to you, yet wheresoever they be, I am sure they cry unto God, to move the hearts of some good men to show forth their liberality in this behalf. All which, and I with them, crave now the same request at your good mastership's hand.

With these, or such like, words he frameth his talk. Now if the party (which he thus talketh withal) profereth him a penny or two pence, he taketh it, but very scornfully, and at last speaketh on this sort: Well, Sir, your good will is not to be refused, but yet you shall understand (good Sir) that this is nothing for them for whom I do thus shamefully entreat. Alas, Sir, it is not a groat or twelve pence I speak for, being such a company of servitors as we have been, yet nevertheless, God forbid I should not receive your gentle offer at this time, hoping hereafter, through your good motions to some such like good Gentlemen, as you be, that I, or some of my fellows in my place, shall find the more liberality.

These kind of idle vagabonds will go commonly well apparelled, without any weapon: and in, place where they meet together, as at their hostices or other places, they will bear the port of right good gentlemen, and some are the more trusted; but commonly they pay them with stealing a pair of sheets or coverlet, and so take their farewell early in the morning, before the master or dame be stirring.

3.3 CASTIGLIONE, *THE COURTIER*

The Courtier was the quintessential handbook on courtiership and much imitated by English writers. Its readership, however, unlike for example Peacham's *The Complete Gentleman* (see 3.21), was mainly courtiers and gentlemen who aspired to work at court. Text from: translation by Thomas Hoby, 1561, fo. 41^v; C2^v–E4^r; H2^r.

You then require me to write (what is to my thinking) the trade and manner of courtiers, which is most convenient for a gentleman that liveth in the court of princes, by the which he may have the knowledge how to serve them perfectly in every reasonable matter, and obtain thereby favour of them and praise of other men.

Finally of what sort he ought to be that deserveth to be called so perfect a courtier that there be no want in him . . .

Let us therefore at length settle ourselves to begin that that is our purpose and drift and (if be it possible), let us fashion such a courtier as the prince that shall be worthy to have him in his service, although his state be but small, may notwithstanding be called a mighty Lord.

* * *

Count Lewis I will have this our courtier therefore to be a gentleman born and of a good house. For it is a great deal less dispraise for him that is not born a gentleman to fail in the acts of virtue, than for a gentleman. If he swerve from the steps of his ancestors, he staineth the name of his family. And doth not only not get, but loseth that is already gotten. For nobleness of birth is, as it were, a clear lamp that showeth forth and bringeth into light works both good and bad, and inflameth and provoketh unto virtue as well with the fear of slander, as also with the hope of praise.

And whereas this brightness of nobleness doth not discover the works of the unnoble, they have a want of provocation and of fear of slander, and they reckon not themselves bound to wade any further than their ancestors did before them, whereas the noble of birth count it a shame not to arrive at the least at the bounds of their predecessors set forth unto them.

Therefore it chanceth always in a manner, both in arms and in all other virtuous acts, that the most famous men are gentlemen. Because nature in every thing hath deeply sowed that privy seed which giveth a certain force and property of her beginning, unto whatsoever springeth of it, and maketh it like unto herself.

As we see by example, not only in the race of horses and other beasts, but also in trees, whose slips and grafts always for the most part are like unto the stock of the tree they came from: and if at any time they grow out of kind, the fault is in the husbandman. And the like is in men if they be trained up in good nurture, most commonly they resemble them from whom they come, and oftentimes pass them, but if they have not one that can well train them up, they grow (as it were) wild and never come to their ripeness . . .

The courtier therefore, besides nobleness of birth, I will have him to be fortunate in this behalf, and by nature to have not only a wit and a comely shape of person and countenance, but also a certain grace, and (as they say) a hue, that shall make him at the first sight acceptable and loving unto whoso beholdeth him.

And let this be an ornament to frame and accompany all his acts and to assure men in his look such a one to be worthy the company and favour of every great man . . .

But to come to some particularity, I judge the principal and true profession of a Courtier ought to be in feats of arms, the which above all I will have him to practise lively, and to be known among other of his hardiness, for his achieving of enterprises, and for his fidelity toward him whom he serveth. And he shall purchase himself a name with these good conditions in doing the deeds in every time and place, for it is not for him to faint at any time in this behalf without a wondrous reproach.

And even as in women, honesty once stained doth never return again to the former estate: so the fame of a gentleman that carrieth weapon, if it once take a foil in any little point through dastardliness or any other reproach, doth evermore continue shameful in the world and full of ignorance . . .

And such a countenance as this is, will I have our courtier to have and not so soft and womanish as many procure to have, that do not only curl the hair and pick the brows, but also pamper themselves in every point like the most wanton and dishonest women in the world: and a man would think them in going, in standing, and in all their gestures so tender and faint that their members were ready to flee one from another, and their words they pronounce so drawningly, that a man would ween they were at that instant yielding up the ghost: and the higher in degree that men are they talk withal, the more they use such fashions.

These men, seeing nature (as they seem to have a desire to appear and to be) hath not made them women, ought not to be esteemed in place of good women, but like common harlots to be banished, not only out of princes' courts but also out of the company of gentlemen . . .

It is meet for him also to have the art of swimming, to leap, to run, to cast the stone: for beside the profit that he may receive of this in the wars, it happeneth to him many times to make proof of himself in such things, whereby he getteth a reputation, especially among the multitude, unto whom a man must sometime apply himself.

Also it is a noble exercise and meet for one living in court to play at tennis, where the disposition of the body, the quickness and nimbleness of every member is much perceived and almost whatsoever a man can see in all other exercises.

And I reckon vaulting of no less praise, which for all it is painful and hard, maketh a man more light and quicker than any of the rest. And beside the profit, if that lightness be accompanied with a good grace, it maketh (in my judgement) a better show than any of the rest.

If our courtier then be taught these exercises more than indifferently well, I believe he may set aside tumbling, climbing upon a cord and other such matters that taste somewhat of jugglers' craft and do little beseem a gentleman . . .

Notwithstanding, to fulfil your request in what I am able, although it be (in manner) in a proverb, that grace is not to be learned, I say unto you: who so mindeth to be gracious, or to have a good grace in the exercises of the body (presupposing first that he be not of nature unapt) ought to begin betimes and to learn his principles of cunning men.

The which thing how necessary a matter Philip King of Macedonia thought it, a man may gather in that his will was that Aristotle so famous a philosopher, and perhaps the greatest that ever hath been in the world, should be the man that should instruct Alexander his son in the first principles of letters . . .

And even as the bee in green meadows fleeth always about the grass, choosing out flowers: so shall our courtier steal his grace from them that to his seeming have it, and from each one, that parcel that shall be most worthy of praise. And not to do as a friend of ours, whom you all know, that though he resembled much Ferdinand the younger of Aragon, and regarded not to resemble him in any other point but in the often lifting up of his head, writhing therewithal a part of his mouth: the which custom the king had gotten by infirmity.

And many such there are that think that they do much, so they resemble a great man in somewhat, and take many times the thing in him that worst becometh him.

But I, imagining with myself often times how this grace cometh, leaving apart such as have it from above, find one rule that is most general, which in this part (methink) taketh place in all things belonging to a man in word or deed, above all other. And that is to eschew as much as a man may, and as a sharp and dangerous rock, affection or curiosity, and (to speak a new word) to use in everything a certain recklessness to cover art withal: and seem whatsoever he doth and saith, to do it without pain and (as it were) not minding it.

And of this do I believe grace is much derived, for in rare matters and well brought to pass, every man knoweth the hardness of them, so that a readiness therein maketh great wonder . . .

Therefore that may be said to be a very art that appeareth not to be art, neither ought a man to put more diligence in anything than in covering it: for in case it be open, it loseth credit clean and maketh a man little set by.

And I remember that I have read in my days that there were some most excellent orators, which among other their cares, enforced themselves to make every man believe that they had no sight in letters, and dissembling their cunning, made semblant their orations to be made very simply, and rather as nature and truth led them, than study and art: the which, if it had been openly known, would have put a doubt in the people's mind for fear lest he beguiled them.

You may see then how to show art, and such bent study taketh away the grace of everything . . .

This virtue therefore contrary to curiosity, which we for this time term recklessness, beside that it is the true fountain from the which all grace springeth, it bringeth with it also another ornament, which accompanying any deed that a man doth, how little soever it be, doth not only by and by open the knowledge of him that doth it, but also many times maketh it to be esteemed much more in effect than it is, because it imprinteth in the minds of the lookers-on an opinion that who can so slightly do well, hath a great deal more knowledge than indeed he hath: and if he will apply his study and diligence to that he doth, he might do it much better . . .

Likewise in dancing, one measure, one motion of a body that hath a good grace, not being forced, doth by and by declare the knowledge of him that danceth.

A musician, if in singing he roll out but a plain note, ending in a double relise with a sweet tune, so easily that a man would judge he did it at a venture, in that point alone he doth men to understand that his knowledge is far greater than it is in deed.

* * *

And how that ought to be in our courtier (leaving apart the precepts of so many wise philosophers that write in this matter and define the virtues of the mind, and so subtly dispute of the dignity of them) we will express in few words, applying to our purpose, that it is sufficient he be (as they term it commonly) an honest man and well meaning: for in this is comprehended the goodness, the wisdom, the manliness and the temperance of the mind, and all other qualities that belong to so worthy a name. And I reckon him only a true moral philosopher that will be good, and to that he needeth few other precepts than that will of his . . .

You know in great matters and adventures in wars, the true provocation is glory: and who so for lucre's sake or for any other consideration taketh it in hand (beside that he never doth anything worthy praise) deserveth not the name of a gentleman, but is a most vile merchant.

And every man may conceive it to be true glory that is stored up in the holy treasure of letters, except such unlucky creatures as have no taste thereof.

What mind is so faint, so bashful, and of so base a courage that in reading the acts and greatness of Caesar, Alexander, Scipio, Hanibal and so many other, is not incensed with a most fervent longing to be like them: and doth not prefer the getting of that perpetual fame, before the rotten life that lasteth two days? Which, in spite of death, maketh him live a great deal more famous than before . . .

. . . Return we again unto our courtier, whom in letters I will have to be more than indifferently well seen, at the least in those studies which they call Humanity, and to have not only the understanding of the Latin tongue, but also of the Greek, because of the many and sundry things that with great excellency are written in it.

Let him much exercise himself in poets and no less in orators and historiographers, and also in writing both rhyme and prose, especially in this our vulgar tongue. For beside the contentation that he shall receive thereby himself, he shall by this means never want pleasant entertainments with women which ordinarily love such matters.

And if by reason either of his other business beside, or of his slender study, he shall not attain unto that perfection that his writings may be worthy much commendation, let him be circumspect in keeping them close, lest he make other men to laugh at him. Only he may show them to a friend whom he may trust.

For at the least wise he shall receive so much profit that by that exercise he shall be able to give his judgement upon other men's doings. For it happeneth very seldom that a man not exercised in writing, how learned soever he be, can at any time know perfectly the labour and toil of writers, or taste of the sweetness and excellency of styles, and those inner observations that often times are found in them of old time . . .

Notwithstanding I will have our courtier to keep fast in his mind one lesson, and that is this: to be always wary, both in this and every other point, and rather fearful than bold, and beware that he persuade not himself falsely to know the thing he knoweth not in deed.

3.4 ELIZABETHAN SUMPTUARY LAWS

Proclamations were issued repeatedly during both Elizabeth I's and James I's reigns to re-enforce the Statutes of Apparel of 24 Henry VIII, c.13 (1523) and 1 & 2 Philip and Mary, c.2 (1555). Restrictions on behaviour, social and geographical movement and political hierarchy could be enforced through statutes on appropriate clothing: but after 1570 these statutes were less frequently invoked, as social mobility was accepted as the norm for the gentry and citizens, and as other methods of social control proved both necessary and more effective for the poorer sort. Text from: 1574 proclamation.

Greenwich 15 June 1574

The excess of apparel and the superfluity of unnecessary foreign wares thereto belonging now of late years is grown by sufferance to such an extremity that the manifest decay not only of a great part of the wealth of the whole realm generally is like to follow (by bringing into the realm such superfluities of silks, cloths of gold, silver and other most vain devices of so great cost for the quantity thereof, as of necessity the moneys and treasure of the realm is and must be yearly conveyed out of the same to answer the said excess), but also particularly the wasting and undoing of a great number of young gentlemen, otherwise serviceable, and others seeking by show of apparel to be esteemed as gentlemen, who, allured by the vain show of these things, do not only consume themselves, their goods and lands which their parents have left unto them, but also run into such debts and shifts as they cannot live out of danger of laws without attempting of unlawful acts, whereby they are not any ways serviceable to their country as otherwise they might be:

Which great abuses, tending both to so manifest a decay of the wealth of the realm and to the ruin of a multitude of serviceable young men and gentlemen and of many good families, the Queen's Majesty hath of her own princely wisdom so considered as she hath of late with great charge to her council commanded the same to be presently and speedily remedied both in her own court and in all other places of her realm, according to sundry good laws heretofore provided . . .

Wherefore her Majesty willeth and straightly commandeth all manner of persons in all places within 12 days after the publication of this present proclamation to reform their apparel according to the tenor of certain articles and clauses taken out of the said statutes and with some moderations annexed to this proclamation, upon pain of her highness's indignation and punishment for their contempts, and such other pains as in the said several statutes be expressed.

For the execution of which orders her Majesty first giveth special charge to all such as do bear office within her most honourable house to look unto it, each person in his degree and office, that the said articles and orders be duly observed, and the contrary reformed in her Majesty's court by all them who are under their office, thereby to give example to the rest of the realm; and further generally to all noblemen, of what estate or degree soever they be, and all and every person of her Privy Council, to all archbishops and bishops, and to the rest of the clergy according to their degrees, that they do see the same speedily and duly executed in their private households and families; and to all mayors and other head officers of cities, towns and corporations, to the chancellors of the universities, to governors of colleges, to the ancients and benchers in every the Inns-of-Court and Chancery, and generally to all that hath any superiority or government over and upon any multitude, and each man in his own household for their children and servants, that they likewise do cause the said orders to be kept by all lawful means that they can.

And to the intent the same might be better kept generally throughout all the realm, her Majesty giveth also special charge to all Justices of the Peace to inquire of the defaults and breaking of those orders in their quarter sessions, and to see them redressed in all open assemblies by all wise, godly and lawful means . . .

Men's apparel

None shall wear in his apparel any silk of the colour of purple, cloth of gold tissued, nor fur of sables, but only the King, Queen, King's mother, children, brethren and sisters, uncles and aunts; and except dukes, marquises and earls, who may wear the same in doublets, jerkins, linings of cloaks, gowns, and hose; and those of the Garter, purple in mantles only.

Cloth of gold, silver, tinselled satin, silk or cloth mixed or embroidered with any gold or silver; except all degrees above viscounts; and viscounts, barons and other persons of like degree, in doublets, jerkins, linings of cloaks, gowns and hose.

Woollen cloth made out of the realm, but in caps only; velvet, crimson or scarlet; furs, black genets, lucerns; embroidery or tailor's work having gold or silver or pearl therein: except dukes, marquises, earls and their children, viscounts, barons, and knights being companions of the Garter, or any person of the Privy Council.

Velvet in gowns, coats or other outermost garments; fur of leopards; embroidery with any silk: except men of the degrees above mentioned, barons' sons, knights and gentlemen in ordinary office attendant upon her majesty's person, and such as have been employed in embassages to foreign princes.

Caps, hats, hatbands, capbands, garters, boothose trimmed with gold or silver or pearl; silk netherstocks; enamelled chains, buttons, eaglets: except men of the degrees above mentioned, the gentlemen attending upon the Queen's person in her highness's privy chamber or in the office of the cupbearer, carver, sewer, esquire for the body, gentlemen ushers, or esquires of the stable.

Satin, damask, silk, camlet or taffeta, in gown, coat, hose or uppermost garments; fur whereof the kind groweth not within the Queen's dominions, except foins, grey genets and bodge: except the degrees and persons above mentioned, and men that may dispend £100 by the year, and so valued in the subsidy book.

Hat, bonnet, girdle, scabbard of swords, daggers etc.; shoes and pantoffles of velvet: except the degrees and persons above named and the son and heir apparent of a knight.

Silk other than satin, damask taffeta, camlet, in doublets; and sarcenet, camlet or taffeta in facing of gowns and cloaks, and in coats, jackets, jerkins, coifs, purses being not of colour scarlet, crimson, or blue; fur of foins, grey genets or other as the like groweth not in the Queen's dominions: except men of the degrees and persons above mentioned, son of a knight, or son and heir apparent of a man of 300 marks land by year, so valued in the subsidy books; and men that may dispend £40 by the year, so valued *ut supra* [as above] . . .

None shall wear in their trappings or harness of their horse any studs, buckles, or other garniture gilt, silvered or damasked; . . . nor any velvet in saddles or horse trappers: except the persons next before mentioned, and others of higher degrees; and gentlemen in ordinary, *ut supra*.

Note that the Lord Chancellor, Treasurer, President of the Council, Privy Seal may wear any velvet, satin, or other silks, except purple; furs, except black genet.

These may wear as they have heretofore used, viz. any of the king's council, justices of either bench, Barons of the Exchequer, Master of the Rolls, sergeants at law, Masters of the Chancery, of the Queen's Council, apprentices of law, physicians of the king, queen and prince, mayors and other head officers of any towns corporate, Barons of the five ports: except velvet, damask, satin of the colour crimson, violet, purple, blue.

Note that her Majesty's meaning is not, by this order, to forbid in any person the wearing of silk buttons, the facing of coats, cloaks, hats and caps, for comeliness only with taffeta, grosgrain, velvet or other silk, as is commonly used.

Note also that the meaning of this order is not to prohibit a servant from wearing any cognizance of his master or henchman, heralds, pursuivants at arms, runners at jousts, tourneys or such martial feats, and such as wear apparel given by the Queen, and such as shall have licence from the Queen for the same.

Women's apparel

None shall wear any cloth of gold, tissue, nor fur of sables: except duchesses, marquises and countesses in their gowns, kirtles, partlets and sleeves; cloth of gold, silver, tinselled satin, silk, or cloth mixed or embroidered with gold or silver . . . in linings of cowls, partlets and sleeves: except all degrees above viscountesses, and viscountesses, baronesses and other personages of like degrees in their kirtles and sleeves.

Velvet (crimson, carnation); furs (black genets, lucerns); embroidery or passement lace of gold or silver: except all degrees above mentioned, the wives of knights of the garter, and of the Privy Council, the ladies and gentlewomen of the privy chamber and bed chamber, and maidens of honour.

None shall wear any velvet in gowns, furs of leopards, embroidery of silk: except the degrees and persons above mentioned, the wives of baron's sons, or of knights.

Cowls, sleeves, partlets, and linings, trimmed with spangles or pearls of gold, silver, or pearl; cowls of gold or silver, or of silk mixed with gold or silver: except the degrees and person above mentioned; and trimmed with pearl, none under the degree of a baroness, or those of like degrees.

Enamelled chains, buttons, aglets, borders: except the degrees before mentioned.

Satin, damask, or tufted taffeta (in gowns, kirtles, or velvet in kirtles); fur whereof the kind groweth not within the Queen's dominions, except foins, grey genets, bodge and wolf: except the degrees and persons above mentioned, or the wives of those that may dispend £100 by the year, and so valued in the subsidy book.

Gowns of silk grosgrain, doubled sarcenet, camlet or taffeta, or kirtles of satin or damask: except the degrees and persons above mentioned and the wives of the sons and heirs of knights, and the daughters of knights, and of such as may dispend 300 marks by the year, so valued *ut supra*, and the wives of those that may dispend £40 by the year.

Gentlewomen attendant upon duchesses, marquises, countesses, may wear in their liveries given them by their mistresses, as the wives of those that may dispend £100 by the year, and are so valued *ut supra*.

Gentlewomen attendant upon viscounts' wives and barons' wives may wear in their liveries as the daughters of such as may dispend 300 marks by the year, and as the wives of those that may dispend £40, valued *ut supra*.

None shall wear any velvet, tufted taffeta, satin or any gold or silver in their petticoats: except wives of barons, knights of the order or councillors, ladies and gentlewomen of the privy chamber and bed chamber, and the maidens of honour.

Damask, taffeta or other silk in their petticoats: except, knights' daughters and such as be matched with them in the former article, who shall not wear a guard of any silk upon their petticoats.

Velvet, tufted taffeta, satin, nor any gold or silver in any cloak or safeguard: except the wives of barons, knights of the order, or councillors, ladies and gentlewomen of the privy chamber and bed chamber, and the maidens of honour and all degrees above them.

Damask, taffeta, or other silk in any cloak or safeguard: except knights' wives and the degrees and persons above mentioned.

No person under the degrees above specified shall wear any guard or welt of silk upon any petticoat, cloak or safeguard.

3.5 THE STATUTE OF ARTIFICERS

The Statute of Artificers of 1563 summarised all the legislation relating to employment and wages in the Elizabethan State. It is both extraordinarily comprehensive (covering the control of vagrant women, as well, for example) and economically interventionist; and combined with the Poor Law (see 3.12) provided the local and national machinery for a pre-industrial welfare state. It empowered wage and price setting, examples of which are given in extracts 3.14 and 3.16. Text from: *Statutes of the Realm* IV, pp. 414–22 [5 Elizabeth c.4].

An act containing divers orders for artificers, labourers etc.

Although there remain and stand in force presently a great number of acts and statutes concerning the retaining, departing, wages and orders of apprentices, servants, and labourers, as well in husbandry as in divers other arts, mysteries and occupations, yet, partly for the imperfection and contrariety that is found and do appear in sundry of the said laws, and for the variety and number of them, and chiefly for that the wages and allowances limited and rated in many of the said statutes are in divers places too small and not answerable to this time, respecting the advancement of prices of all things belonging to the said servants and labourers, the said laws cannot without the great grief and burden of the poor labourer and hired man, be put in due execution . . . [if] the substance of as many of the said laws as are meet to be continued, shall be digested and reduced into one sole law and statute, and in the same an uniform order prescribed and limited concerning the wages and other orders for apprentices, servants and labourers, there is good hope that it will come to pass that the same law, being duly executed, should banish idleness, advance husbandry, and yield unto the hired person both in the time of scarcity and in the time of plenty a convenient proportion of wages. Be it therefore enacted by the authority of this present Parliament . . .

. . . that no manner of person or persons after the foresaid last day of September now next ensuing, shall retain, hire, or take into service, or cause to be retained, hired or taken into service, by any means or colour, to work for any less time or term than for a whole year, in any of the sciences, crafts, mysteries or arts of clothiers, woollen cloth weavers, tuckers, fullers, cloth-workers, sheermen, dyers, hosiers, tailors, shoemakers, tanners pewterers, bakers, brewers, glovers, cutlers, smiths, farriers, curriers, saddlers, spurriers, turners, cappers, hatmakers or feltmakers, bowyers[2], fletchers, arrowhead makers, butchers, cooks or millers.

And be it further enacted that every person being unmarried and every other person under the age of thirty years that after the feast of Easter next shall marry and having been brought up in any of the said arts, crafts or sciences, or that hath used or exercised any other by the space of three years or more, and not having lands, tenements, rents, or hereditaments, copyhold or freehold, of one estate of inheritance or for term of any life or lives, of the clear yearly value of £10, and so allowed by two Justices of Peace of the county where he hath most commonly inhabited by the space of one whole year, and under their hands and seals, or by the mayor or other head officer of the city, borough or town corporate, where such person hath commonly dwelled by the space of one whole year, and two Aldermen . . . under their seals; nor being retained with any person in husbandry, or in any of the foresaid arts and sciences, according to this statute, nor lawfully retained in household, or in any office with any nobleman, gentleman, or others, according to the laws of this realm, nor having a convenient farm, or their holding in tillage, whereupon he may employ his labour, shall during the time that he or they shall so be unmarried, or under the said age of thirty years, upon request be made by any person using the art or mystery where the said person so requireth hath been exercised as is aforesaid, be retained and shall not refuse to serve, according to the tenor of this statute, upon the pain and penalty hereafter mentioned.

And be it further enacted that no person which shall retain any servant shall put away his or her said servant, and that no person retained according to this statute shall depart from his master, mistress or dame before the end of his or her term, upon the pain hereafter mentioned, unless it be for some reasonable and sufficient cause or matter to be allowed before two Justices of Peace, or one at the least, within the said county or before the mayor or other chief officer, of the city, borough or town corporate, wherein the said master, mistress or dame inhabiteth, to whom any of the parties grieved shall complain; which said justices or justice, mayor or chief officer, shall have and take upon them, or him the hearing and ordering of the matter between the said master, mistress or dame, and servant, according to the equity of the cause . . .

And be it further enacted by the authority aforesaid that every person betwixt the age of twelve years and sixty years, not being lawfully retained; nor apprenticed with any fisherman or mariner haunting the seas; not being in service with any rider or carrier of any corn, grain or meal for the provision of the city of London, nor in any city, town corporate or market town, in any of the arts or sciences limited or appointed by this statute, to have or take apprentices; nor being retained by the year or half year at the least, for the digging, seeking, finding, getting, melting, fining, working, trying or making of any silver, tin, lead, iron, copper, stone, sea coal, stone coal, moor coal, or chalk coal; nor being occupied in or about the making of any glass; nor being a gentleman born; nor being a student or scholar in any of the universities; or in any school; nor having lands, tenements, rents or hereditaments for term of life, or of one estate of inheritance, of the clear yearly value of 40s; nor being worth in goods and cattles to the value of £10; nor having a father and mother then living, or other ancestor, whose heir apparent he is, them having lands, tenements, or hereditaments of the yearly value of ten pounds or above, or goods or cattles of the value of £40; nor being a necessary or convenient officer, or servant lawfully retained, as is aforesaid, not having a convenient farm or holding whereupon he may lawfully employ his labour; nor being otherwise lawful retained, according to the true meaning of this statute: shall after the aforesaid last day of September now next ensuing by virtue of this statute, be compelled to be retained to serve in husbandry by the year with any person that keepeth husbandry, and will require any such person so to serve within the same shire where he shall be so required. And be it enacted that if any person after he hath retained any servant, shall put away any such servant at the end of his term without one quarter's warning given before the said end, as is above remembered, that then every such master, mistress or dame so offending, unless he or they be able to prove by two sufficient witnesses such reasonable and sufficient cause of putting away of their servant or servants during their term [be fined 40s]. . . . And if any servant retained according to the form of this statute, depart from his said master, mistress or dame's service, before the ends of his term, unless it be for some reasonable and sufficient cause to be allowed, as is aforesaid, or if any servant at the end of his term shall depart from his said master, mistress or dame's service without one quarter's warning given before the end of his said term in form aforesaid, and before two lawful witnesses, or if any person or persons compellable and bound to be retained to serve in husbandry, or in any other arts, sciences, or mysteries above remembered, by the year or otherwise, do on request made, refuse to serve, for the wages that shall be limited, rated and appointed according to the form of this statute, or promise or covenant to serve, and do not serve according to the tenor of the same: that then every servant so departing away, and every person so refusing to serve for such wages, upon complaint thereof made by the master, mistress or dame of the said servant, or by the party to or with whom the said refusal is made, or promise not kept, to two Justices of Peace of the county, or to the mayor or other head officer . . . upon such good proofs and good matter, as to their discretion shall be thought sufficient, to commit him or them to ward, there to remain without bail or mainprise, until the said servant or party so offending shall be bound to the party to whom the offence shall be made, to serve and continue with him for the wages that shall then be limited and appointed, according to the tenor and form of this statute, and to be discharged upon his delivery, without paying any fee to the gaoler, where he or they shall be so imprisoned.

And be it likewise enacted that none of the said retained persons in husbandry or in any of the arts or sciences above remembered, after the time of the retainer expired, shall depart forth of one city, town or parish to any other, nor out of the lathe, rape, wapentake, or hundred, nor out of the county or shire where he last served, to serve in any other city, town corporate, lathe, rape, wapentake, hundred, shire or county, unless he have a testimonial under the seal of the city or town corporate, or of the constable or constables, or other head officers, and of two other honest householders of the city, town or parish where he last served, declaring his lawful departure, and the name of the shire and the place where he dwelled last before his departure, according to the form expressed in this Act: which certificate or testimonial shall be written and delivered unto the said servant and also registered by the parson, vicar or curate of the parish where such master, mistress or dame doth or shall dwell . . .

And be it further enacted etc. that no person or persons that shall depart out of service shall be retained or accepted into any other service without showing before his retainer, such testimonial as is above remembered, to the chief officer of the town corporate and in every town and place, to the constable, curate, churchwarden or other head officer of the same, where he shall be retained to serve, upon the pain that every such servant departing without such certificate or testimonial, shall be imprisoned until he procure a testimonial or certificate the which if he cannot do within the space of twenty-one days next after the first day of his imprisonment, then the said person to be whipped and used as a vagabond, according to the laws in such cases provided. And that every person retaining any such servant without showing such testimonial or certificate, as is aforesaid, shall forfeit for every such offence £5. And if any such person shall be taken with any counterfeit or forged testimonial, then to be whipped as a vagabond.

And be it enacted that all artificers and labourers being hired for wages by the day or week, shall betwixt the midst of the months of March and September, be and continue at their work, at or before five of the clock in the morning, and not to depart until betwixt seven and eight of the clock at night (except it be in the time of breakfast, dinner or drinking, the which time at the most shall not exceed above two hours in the day: that is to say, at every drinking one half hour, for his dinner one hour and for his sleep, when he is allowed to sleep, (the which is from the midst of May to the midst of August) half an hour at the most, and at every breakfast one half hour; and all the said artificers and labourers between the midst of September and the midst of March shall be and continue at their work from the spring of the day in the morning until night of the same day, except it be in time afore appointed for breakfast and dinner. Upon pain to lose and forfeit one penny for every hour's absence, to be deducted and dafaulked [sic] out of his wages that should so offend.

And be it also enacted by the authority aforesaid that every artificer and labourer that shall be lawfully retained in or for the building of any church, house, ship, mill, or any other piece of work taken in great, in task or gross, or that shall hereafter take upon him to make or finish any such thing to work shall continue and not depart from the same, unless it be for not paying of his wages or hire agreed on, or otherwise lawfully taken or appointed to serve the Queen's majesty, her heirs or successors . . .

And be it further enacted that the Justices of Peace of every shire . . . and the sheriff of the county (if he conveniently may) and every mayor, bailiff, or other head officer within any city or town corporate . . . shall before the tenth day of June next coming and afterward yearly . . . assemble themselves together and they (so assembled) calling unto them such grave and discreet persons of the said county or of the said city or town corporate, as they shall think meet, and conferring together, respecting the plenty or scarcity of the time and other circumstances necessary to be considered, shall have authority by virtue hereof, within the limits and precincts of their several commissions, to limit, rate, and appoint the wages as well of such and so many of the said artificers, handicraftsmen, husbandmen, or any other labourer, servant or workman, whose wages in times past have been by any law or statute rated and appointed; as also the wages of all other labourers, artificers, workmen, or apprentices of husbandry, which have not been rated, as they the same Justices, mayors, or head officers within their several commissions or liberties shall think meet by their discretion to be rated, limited or appointed by the year or by the day, week, month or otherwise, with meat and drink, or without meat and drink, and what wages every workman and labourer shall take by the great for mowing, reaping, or threshing corn and grain, and for mowing or making of hay, or for ditching, paling, railing or hedging by the rod, perch, lug, yard, pole, rope or foot, or for any other kind of reasonable labour or service. And shall yearly before the 12th day of July, next after the said assessment and rates so appointed and made, certify the same, engrossed in parchment with the considerations and causes thereof, under their hands and seals, into the Queen's most honourable court of chancery: whereupon it shall be lawful to the Lord Chancellor of England or Lord Keeper of the great seal for the time being, upon declaration thereof to the Queens Majesty . . . to cause to be printed and sent down before the first day of September next after the said certificate into every county to the sheriff and Justices of Peace three, and to the said mayors, bailiffs and head officers, ten or twelve proclamations or more containing in every one of them the several rates appointed by the said Justices, and other head officers, as is aforesaid, with commandment by the said proclamations to all persons in the name of the Queen's Majesty . . . straightly to observe the same, and to all Justices, sheriffs, and other officers to see the same duly and severely observed upon the danger of the punishment and forfeitures limited and appointed by this statute. Upon receipt whereof the said sheriffs, Justices of Peace and the mayor and head officer in every city or town corporate shall cause the same proclamation to be entered of record by the clerk of the peace, or the clerk of the city or town corporate, and the said sheriffs, justices, and other the said mayor and head officers shall forthwith in open markets, upon the market days, before Michaelmas then ensuing, cause the same proclamation to be fixed in some convenient place of the said city and town . . .

And be it further enacted by the authority aforesaid that if any person after the said proclamation shall be so sent down and published, shall by any secret ways or means, directly or indirectly, retain or keep any servant, workman or labourer or shall give any more or greater wages or other commodity contrary to the true intent and purpose of this statute, or contrary to the rates or wages that shall be assessed or appointed in the said proclamations: that the very person that shall so offend, and be thereof lawfully convicted before any the Justices or other head officers above remembered, or either of the said presidents and counsels: shall suffer imprisonment by the space of ten days, without bail or mainprise, and shall lose and forfeit five pound of lawful money of England. And that every person that shall be so retained and take wages contrary to this statute or any branch thereof, or of the said proclamation, and shall be thereof convicted before the Justices aforesaid, or any two of them, or before the mayor or other head officer aforesaid: shall suffer imprisonment by the space of twenty-one days without bail or mainprise. And that every retainer, promise, gift, or payment of wages or other thing whatsoever contrary to the true meaning of this statute, and every writing and bond to be made for that purpose, shall be utterly void and of none effect. And be it enacted by the authority aforesaid that if any servant, workman or labourer, shall wilfully or maliciously make any assault or affray upon his master, mistress or dame, or upon any other that shall at the time of such assault or affray have the charge or oversight of any such servant, workman or labourer, or of the work wherein the said servant, workman or labourer is appointed or hired to work, and being thereof convicted before any two of the justices, mayor or head officer aforesaid, where the said offence is committed or before either of the said Lord Presidents and counsel before remembered, by confession of the said servant, workman or labourer, or by the testimony, witness and oath of two honest men: that then every such offender shall suffer imprisonment by the space of one whole year, or less by the discretion of the two justices of the peace, if it be without a town corporate, and if it be within a town corporate, by the discretion of the mayor or head officer of the same town corporate at the least. And if the offence shall require further punishment, so as it extend not to life nor limb . . .

Provided always and be it enacted by the authority aforesaid, that in the time of hay or corn harvest, the Justices of Peace, and every of them and also the constable or other head officer of every township upon request, and for the avoiding of the loss of any corn, grain or hay, shall and may cause all such artificers and persons as be meet to labour . . . to serve by the day for the mowing, reaping, shearing, getting, or inning of corn, grain, and hay, according to the skill and quality of the person, and that none of the said persons shall refuse so to do: upon pain to suffer imprisonment in the stocks by the space of two days and one night . . .

And be it further enacted by the authority aforesaid that two Justices of Peace, the mayor or other head officer of any city borough, or town corporate, . . . shall and may by virtue hereof, appoint any such woman, as is of the age of twelve years, and under the age of forty years and unmarried and forth of service, as they shall think meet to serve, to be retained or serve by the year, or by the week, or day, for such wages and in such reasonable sort and manner as they shall think meet. And if any such woman shall refuse so to serve, then it shall be lawful for the said Justices of Peace, mayor, or head officers to commit such woman to ward until she shall be bounden to serve, as is aforesaid.

And for the better advancement of husbandry and tillage, and to the intent that such as are fit to be made apprentices to husbandry may be bounden thereinto: be it enacted that every person being an householder and having and using half a ploughland at the least in tillage, may have and receive as an apprentice any person above the age of ten years, and under the age of eighteen years to serve in husbandry, until his age of twenty-one years at the least, or until the age of twenty-four years, as the parties can agree; and the said retainer and taking of an apprentice to be made and done by indenture. And be it enacted that every person being an householder and four and twenty years old at the least, dwelling or inhabiting, or which shall dwell and inhabit, in any city, town corporate, and using and exercising any art, mystery or manual occupation there, shall and may after the feast of Saint John Baptist next coming (during the time that he shall so dwell or inhabit in any such city or town corporate and use and exercise any such art, mystery or manual occupation) have and retain the son of any freeman, not occupying husbandry, nor being a labourer and inhabiting in the same, or in any other city or town that now is or after shall be and continue incorporate, to serve and be bound as an apprentice, after the custom and order of the city of London, for seven years at the least, so as the term and years of such apprentice do not expire or determine afore such apprentice shall be of the age of four and twenty years at the least. Provided always and be it enacted, that it shall not be lawful to any person dwelling in any city or town corporate, using or exercising any of the mysteries or crafts of a merchant, trafficking by traffic or trade into any parts beyond the sea, mercer, draper, goldsmith, ironmonger, embroiderer, or clothier, that doth or shall put cloth to making and sale, to take any apprentice or servant to be instructed or taught in any of the arts, occupations, crafts or mysteries which they or any other do use or exercise, except such servant or apprentice be his son, or else that the father or mother of such apprentice or servant shall have at the time of taking such apprentice or servant, lands, tenements, or other hereditaments, of the clear yearly value of forty shillings, of an estate of inheritance or freehold at the least to be certified under the hands of three Justices of Peace, of the shire or shires where the said lands, tenements or other hereditaments do or shall lie . . .

And be it further enacted that from and after the said feast it shall be lawful to any person using or exercising the art or occupation of a smith, wheelwright, ploughwright, millwright, carpenter rough mason, plasterer, sawyer, lime burner, brickmaker, bricklayer, tiler, slater . . . tilemaker, linen weaver, turner, cooper, miller, earthen potters, woollen weaver, weaving housewives (of household cloth only and none other cloth), fuller or otherwise called tucker or walker, burner or oak and woodashes, thatcher or shingler, wheresoever he or they shall dwell or inhabit: to have or receive the son of any person as apprentice in manner and form aforesaid, to be taught and instituted in these occupations only and in none other: albeit the father or mother of such any such apprentice have not any lands, tenements or hereditaments. And be it further enacted by the authority aforesaid that after the first day of May next coming, it shall not be lawful to any person or persons other than such as now do lawfully exercise any art, mystery or manual occupation, to set up, occupy, use or exercise any craft, mystery or occupation now used or occupied within the realm of England or Wales except he shall have been brought up therein seven years at the least as an apprentice in manner and form above said, nor to set any person on work in such mystery, art, or occupation, being not a workman at this day, except he shall have been an apprentice as is aforesaid, shall or will become a journeyman, or hired by the year, upon pain that every such person willingly offending or doing the contrary, shall forfeit and lose for every default forty shillings for every month. . . . Provided always that this act or anything therein contained or mentioned shall not be prejudicial or hurtful to the cities of London and Norwich, or to the lawful liberties, usages, customs, or privileges of the same cities, for or concerning the having or taking of any apprentice or apprentices, but that the citizens and freemen of the same cities shall and may take, have and retain apprentices there, in such manner and form as they might lawfully have done before the making of this statute.

3.6 THOMAS TUSSER, *A HUNDRED GOOD POINTS OF HUSBANDRY*

Tusser's work on husbandry and housewifery was immensely popular, and of practical use to the small-scale domestic rural unit, which made up the majority of the population. Text from: 1570 edition: pp. 4ff.

The description of husbandry

Of husband doth husbandry challenge the name,
Of husbandry husband doth likewise the same.
Where housewife and housewifery joineth with these,
There wealth in abundance is gotten with ease.

The name of a husband, what is to say?
Of wife and of household the band and the stay.
Some husbandly thriveth that never had wife,
Yet scarce a good husband in goodness of life.

The husband is he that to labour doth fall,
The labour of him I do husbandry call.
If thrift by that labour be any way caught,
Then is it good husbandry, else is it naught.

So household and householdry I do define,
For folk and the goods that in house be of thine.
Housekeeping to them as a refuge is set,
Which like as it is, so report it doth get.

Thus household and housewifery lovers must be,
With husband and housewife: yea, further we see,
Housekeeping and husbandry (if they be good)
Must love one another as cousins in blood.

The ladder to thrift

1. To take thy calling thankfully,
To shun the path to beggary.

2. To grudge in youth no drudgery
To come by penny luckily.

3. To get more to it wittily,
To keep thy gettings covertly.

4. To spend at first but niggardly,
To lay for age continually.

5. To hark to profit earnestly,

To curry favel willingly.

6. To get good plot to occupy
To store and use it husbandly.

7. To get good wife for company,
To live in wedlock honestly.

8. To store thy house with householdry,
To make provision thriftily.

9. To join to wife good family,
To keep no more but needfully.

10. To govern household skilfully,
To suffer none live idly.

11. To courage wife in housewifery,
To use well doers genteelly.

12. To buy and sell with policy,
To meddle not with pilfery.

13. To keep thy touch substantially,
To make thy bonds advisedly.

14. To use thy neighbour neighbourly,
To use no friend deceitfully.

15. To take good heed of surety,
To love to live at liberty.

16. To hate to live unthriftily,
To stop thy mouth from perjury.

17. To win thy foe by honesty,
To undermine his subtlety.

18. To answer stranger courteously,
To keep thy doings secretly.

19. To do thy doings orderly,
To play the subject subjectly.

20. To trouble no man wilfully,
To hinder no man wittingly.

21. To offer no man villainy,
To stay a mischief speedily.

22. To keep that thine is, manfully,
To live by all men quietly.

23. To think well in adversity,
To do well in prosperity.

24. To get good love and amity,
To help relieve the poverty.

25. To keep good hospitality.
To hate all prodigality.

26. To keep thyself from malady,
To ease thy sickness speedily.

27. These be the steps unfainedly
To climb to thrift by husbandry.

3.7 JOHN STOWE, *A SURVEY OF THE CITIES OF LONDON AND WESTMINSTER*

John Stowe, an historian and chronicler of his own times, compiled and synthesised the writings and observations of others, including Hall and Holinshed, but also earlier writers such as the twelfth-century Fitzstephens. Stowe weaves their observations with his own occasional comments about the late 1590s. Text from: 1598, pp. 62–71, 412–15.

Men of trades and sellers of wares in this city have oftentimes since changed their places, as they have found their best advantage. For whereas mercer and haberdashers used to keep their shops in West Cheap, of later time they held them on London Bridge, where partly they yet remain. The goldsmiths of Gutherton's Lane and Old Exchange are now for the most part removed into the south side of West Cheap, the pepperers and grocers of Soper's Lane are now in Bucklesbury, and other places dispersed. The drapers of Lombard Street and of Cornhill are seated in Candlewick Street and Watling Street; the skinners from St. Mary Pellipers, or at the Axe, into Budge Row and Wallbrook; the stockfish-mongers in Thames Street; wet fishmongers in Knightriders Street and Bridge Street; the ironmongers of Ironmongers Lane and Old Jury into Thames Street; the vintners from the Vintry into divers places. But the brewers for the most part remain near to the friendly water of Thames; the butchers in East Cheap, St. Nicholas Shambles, and the Stocks Market; the hosiers of old time in Hosier Lane, near unto Smithfield, are since removed into Cordwainer Street, the upper part thereof by Bow Church, and last of all into Birchoveries Lane by Cornhill; the shoemakers and curriers of Cordwainer Street removed, the one to St. Martin's le Grand, the other to London Wall, near unto Moorgate; the founders remain by themselves in Lothbury; cooks or pastellers, for the more part in Thames Street, the other dispersed into divers parts; poulterers of late removed out of the Poultry, betwixt the Stocks and the great conduit in Cheap, into Grass Street and St. Nicholas Shambles; bowyers from Bowyers Row by

Ludgate into divers places, and almost worn out with the fletchers; paternoster makers of old time, or bede-makers, and text-writers, are gone out of Paternoster Row, and are called Stationers of Paul's Churchyard; patten makers of St. Margaret, Pattens Lane, clean worn out; labourers every work day are to be found in Cheap, about Soper's Land End; horse-counters and sellers of oxen, sheep, swine and the like remain in their old market of Smithfield . . .

But now in our time, instead of these enormities [plagues mentioned by Fitzstephen], others are come in place no less meet to be reformed; namely . . . encroachments on the highways, lanes and common grounds in and about this city . . .

Then the number of cars, drays, carts and coaches, more than hath been accustomed, the streets and lanes being straitened, must needs be dangerous, as daily experience proveth . . .

Nicholas West, Bishop of Ely, in the year 1532, kept continually in his house an hundred servants, giving to the one half of them 53s.4d. the piece yearly, to the other half each 40s. the piece; to every one for his winter gown four yards of broadcloth, and for his summer coat three yards and a half; he daily gave at his gates, besides bread and drink, warm meat to two hundred poor people . . .

The late Earl of Oxford, father to him that now liveth, hath been noted within these forty years to have ridden into this city and to his house by London Stone, with eighty gentlemen in a livery of Reading tawny, and chains of gold about their necks, before him, and one hundred tall yeomen, in the like livery, to follow him without chains, but all having his cognisance of the blue boar embroidered on their left shoulder.

These, as all other of their times, gave great relief to the poor. I myself, in that declining time of charity, have oft seen at the Lord Cromwell's gate in London more than two hundred persons served twice every day with bread, meat and drink sufficient; for he observed that ancient and charitable custom, as all prelates, noblemen, or men of honour and worship, his predecessors, had done before him . . .

On the holy days in summer the youths of this city have in the field exercised themselves in leaping, dancing, shooting, wrestling, casting of the stone or ball etc.

And for defence and use of the weapon, there is a special profession of men that teach it. . . . The youths of this city have also used on holy days after evening prayer at their master's doors, to exercise their wasters and bucklers; and the maidens, one of them playing on a timbrel, in sight of their masters and dames, to dance for garlands hung athwart the streets; which open pastimes in my youth being now suppressed, worse practices within doors are to be feared. As for the baiting of bulls and bears, they are to this day much frequented, namely in Bear gardens, on the Bank's side, wherein be prepared scaffolds for beholders to stand upon. Sliding upon the ice is now but children's play; but in hawking and hunting many grave citizens at this present have great delight, and do rather want leisure than goodwill to follow it . . .

Now for sports and pastimes yearly used.

First in the feast of Christmas, there was in the King's house, wheresoever he was lodged, a lord of misrule, or master of merry disports, and the like had ye in the house of every nobleman of honour or good worship, were he spiritual or temporal. Amongst the which the Mayor of London and either of the sheriffs had their several lords of misrule, ever contending without quarrel or offence who should make the rarest pastimes to delight the beholders. These lords, beginning their rule on Alhollon[3] eve, continued the same till the morrow after the feast of the purification, commonly called Candlemas Day. In all which space there were fine and subtle disguisings, masks and mummeries, with playing at cards for counters, nails and points, in every house more for pastime than for gain . . .

In the week before Easter had ye great shows made for the fetching in of a twisted tree, or with, as they termed it, out of the woods into the King's house; and the like into every man's house of honour and worship.

In the month of May, namely on May-day in the morning, every man, except impediment, would walk into the sweet meadows and green woods, there to rejoice their spirits with the beauty and savour of sweet flowers, and with the harmony of birds, praising God in their kind; and for example hereof, Edward Hall hath noted that King Henry VIII, as in the third of his reign, and divers other years, so namely in the seventh of his reign, on May-day in the morning, with Queen Katherine his wife, accompanied with many lords and ladies, rode a-maying from Greenwich to the high ground of Shooter's Hill, where, as they passed by the way they espied a company of tall yeomen, clothed all in green, with green hoods, and bows and arrows, to the number of two hundred; one being their chieftain, was called Robin Hood, who required the King and his company to stay and see his men shoot; whereunto the King granting, Robin Hood whistled, and all the two hundred archers shot off, loosing all at once; and when he whistled again they likewise shot again; their arrows whistled by craft of the head, so that the noise was strange and loud, which greatly delighted the King, Queen and their company. Moreover, this Robin Hood desired the King and Queen with their retinue, to enter the greenwood, where in harbours made of boughs and decked with flowers, they were set and served plentifully with venison and wine by Robin Hood and his men, to their great contentment, and had other pageants and pastimes, as ye may read in my said author.

I find also that in the month of May, the citizens of London of all estates, lightly in every parish, or sometimes two or three parishes joining together, had their several mayings and did fetch in maypoles, with divers warlike shows, with good archers, morris dancers and other devices, for pastime all the day long; and toward the evening they had stage plays and bonfires in the streets . . .

These great mayings and may-games made by the governors and masters of this city, with the triumphant setting up of the great shaft (a principal maypole in Cornhill, before the parish church of St. Andrew, therefore called Undershaft) by means of an insurrection of youths against aliens on May-day 1517, the ninth of Henry VIII, have not been so freely used as afore, and therefore I leave them.

Hospitals in this city and suburbs thereof that have been of old time, and now presently are, I read of these as followeth

Hospital of St. Mary, in the parish of Barking church, that was provided for poor priests and others, men and women in the city of London that were fallen into frenzy or loss of their memory, until such time as they should recover, was since suppressed and given to the hospital of St. Katherine by the Tower . . .

St. Bartholomew, in Smithfield, an hospital of great receipt and relief for the poor, was suppressed by Henry VIII, and again by him given to the city, and is endowed by the citizens' benevolence . . .

St. James in the field was an hospital for leprous virgins of the City of London, founded by citizens for that purpose, and suppressed by King Henry VIII . . .

St. Katherine, by the Tower of London, an hospital with a master, brethren and sisters and almswomen, founded by Matilda, wife to King Stephen; not suppressed, but in force as before . . .

St. Mary Bethlehem, without Bishopsgate, was an hospital founded by Simon Fitzmary, a citizen of London, to have been a priory, and remaineth for lunatic people, being suppressed and given to Christ's Hospital . . .

St. Thomas in Southwark, being an hospital of great receipt for the poor, was suppressed, but again newly founded and endowed by the benevolence and charity of the citizens of London . . .

The hospital, or almshouse called God's house, for thirteen poor men, with a college, called Whittington College, founded by Richard Whittington, mercer, and suppressed; but the poor remain and are paid their allowance by the mercers.

Christ's Hospital in Newgate Market. of a new foundation in the Grey Friar's Church by King Henry VIII; poor fatherless children be there brought up and nourished at the charges of the citizens.

Bridewell, now an hospital, or house of correction, founded by Edward VI, to be a workhouse for the poor and idle persons of the city, wherein a great number of vagrant persons be now set at work, and relieved at the charges of the citizens.

3.8 PHILIP STUBBES, *ANATOMY OF ABUSES*

Philip Stubbes wrote ballads prior to the *Anatomy of Abuses*, which became immensely successful with two editions in 1583. Subsequent writings had a purely devotional stance. The work satirises social life in Ailgna (a barely disguised Anglia), and is hence a good benchmark for contemporary moral debates about social change. The dialogue is between Spudeaus and Philoponus. Text from: 1583 second edition, fos D7^v–F6.

Spudeaus   The state and condition of that land must needs be miserable, and in time grow to great scarcity and dearth, where is such vain prodigality and excess of all things used.

Philoponus   Their shirts, which all in a manner do wear (or if the nobility or gentry only did wear them, it were some deal more tolerable) are either of cameric, holland, lawn, or else of the finest cloth that may be got. And of these kinds of shirts everyone now doth wear alike; so as it may be thought our forefathers have made their bands and ruffs (if they had any at all) of grosser cloth, and baser stuff than the worst of our shirts are made of nowadays. And these shirts (sometimes it happeneth) are wrought throughout with needle work of silk and such like, and curiously stitched with open seam, and many other knacks besides, more than I can describe. . . . This their curiosity and niceness in apparel (as it were) transnatureth them, maketh them weak, tender, and infirm, nor able to abide such sharp conflicts and blustering storms, as many other people, both abroad far from them and in their confines nigh to them, do daily sustain. . . . And when they wore shirts of hemp or flax (but now these are too gross, our tender stomachs cannot easily digest such rough and crude meats), men were stronger than we, healthfuller, fairer complexioned, longer living, and finally, ten times harder than we, and able to bear out any sorrow or pains whatsoever. For be sure this pampering of our bodies makes them weaker, tenderer and nesher[4] than otherwise they would be if they were used to hardness and more subject to receive any kind of infection or malady. And rather abbreviate our days by many years than extenuate our lives one minute of an hour.

Spudeaus   I think no less: for how strong men were in times past, how long they lived and how healthful they were before such niceness and vain, pampering curiosity was invented, we may read and many that live at this day can testify. But now through our fond toys and nice inventions we have brought ourselves into such pusillanimity and effeminate condition as we may seem rather nice dames and young girls than puissant agents or manly men, as our forefathers have been.

Philoponus   Their doublets are no less monstrous than the rest: for now the fashion is to have them hang down to the middest of their thighs, or at least to their privy members, being so hard-quilted and stuffed, bombasted and sewed as they can very hardly either stoop down or decline themselves to the ground, so stiff and sturdy they stand about them. Now what handsomeness can be in these doublets which stand on their bellies like, or much bigger than, a man's codpiece (so as their bellies are thicker than all their body's beside) let wise men judge . . .

In times past kings (as old historiographers in their books yet extant do record) would not disdain to wear a pair of hosen of a noble, ten shillings or a mark price, with all the rest of their apparel after the same rate: but now it is a small matter to bestow twenty nobles, ten pound, twenty pound, forty pound yea a hundred pound of one pair of breeches . . .

Then have they nether-stocks to these gay hosen, not of cloth (though never so fine) for that is thought too base, but of Guernsey worsted, silk thread and such like, or else at the least the finest yarn that can be, and so curiously knit with open seam down the leg, with quirks and clocks about the ankles, and sometime (haply) interlaced with gold or silver threads, as is wonderful to behold. And to such insolence and outrage it is now grown that everyone (almost) though otherwise very poor, having scarce forty shillings of wages by the year, will be sure to have two or three pair of these silk netherstocks, or else of the finest yarn that may be got . . .

Spudeaus   I have seldom heard the like, I think verily that Satan prince of darkness and father of pride, is let loose in the land, else it could never so rage as it doth. For the like pride (I am fully persuaded) is not used under the sun, of any nation or people how barbarous soever: wherefore woe be to this age and thrice accursed be these days which bring forth such sour fruits and unhappy are that people whom Satan hath so bewitched and captived in sin. The Lord hold his hand of mercy over us.

Philoponus   To these netherstocks, they have corked shoes, pinsnets and fine pantofles,[5] which bear them up a finger or two from the ground, whereof some be of white leather, some of black, and some of red; some of black velvet, some of white, some of red, some of green; raced, carved, cut and stitched all over with silk, and laid on with gold, silver and such like. Yet notwithstanding to what good uses serve these pantofles, except it be to wear in a private house, or in a man's chamber to keep him warm? . . . Their coats and jerkins, as they be diverse in colours, so be they diverse in fashions. For some be made with colours, some without; some close to the body, some loose, covering the whole body down to the thigh, like bags or sacks that were drawn over them, hiding the dimensions and proportions of the body; some are buttoned down the breast, some under the arm, and some down the back; some with flaps over the breast, some without; some with great sleeves, some with small and some with none at all; some pleated and crested behind, and curiously gathered, some not so. . . . But if they would consider that their clothes (except those that they wear upon their backs) be none of theirs, but the poor's, they would not heap up their presses and wardrobes as they do. Do they think it is lawful for them to have millions of sundry sorts of apparel, lying rotting by them, when as the poor members of Jesus Christ die at their doors for want of clothing? . . . There is a certain city in Ailgna called Munidnol,[6] where as the poor lie in the streets, upon pallets of straw and well if they have that too, or else in the mire and dirt, as commonly it is seen, having neither house to put in their heads, covering to keep them from the cold, nor yet to hide their shame withal, penny to buy them sustenance, nor anything else, but are permitted to die in the streets like dogs or beasts without any mercy or compassion showed to them at all. And if any be sick of the plague (as they call it) or any other disease, their masters and mistresses are so impudent (being it should seem at a league with Satan, a covenant with hell, and as it were obliged themselves by obligation to the devil never to have to do with the works of mercy) as straightway they throw them out of their doors. And so being carried forth either in carts or otherwise, and thrown in the streets), there they end their days most miserably.

* * *

The women of Ailgna use to colour their faces with certain oils, liquors, unguents and waters made to that end whereat they think their beauty is greatly decored: but who seeth not that their souls are thereby deformed and they brought deeper into the displeasure and indignation of the Almighty, at whose voice the earth doth tremble and at whose presence the heavens shall liquify and melt away? Do they think thus to adulterate the Lord his workmanship and to be without offence? . . .

If an artificer or craftsman should make anything belonging to his art or science and a cobbler should presume to correct the same: would not the other think himself abused, and judge him worthy of reprehension? And think thou (o, woman) to escape the judgement of God, who hath fashioned thee to his glory, when thy great and more than presumptuous audacity dareth to alter and change his workmanship in thee? Thinkest thou that thou can make thyself fairer than God who made us all? These must needs be their inventions, or else they would never go about to colour their faces, with such ibbersauces. And these being their inventions, what can derogate more from the majesty of God in his creation? For in this doing they do plainly convince the Lord of untruth in his word who saith he made man glorious after his own likeness and the fairest of all other terrestrial creatures. If he be thus fair then what need they to make them fairer? Therefore this their colouring of their faces importeth (as may by probable conjecture be presupposed) that they think themselves not fair enough and then must GOD needs be untrue in his word. . . . St. Cyprian amongst all the rest, saith a woman thorough painting and dyeing of her face, showeth herself to be more than whorish. For (saith he) she hath corrupted and defaced (like a filthy strumpet or brothel) the workmanship of God in her, what is this else, but to turn truth into falsehood . . .

Philoponus   Then followeth the trimming and tricking of their heads in laying out their hair to the show, which of force must be curled, frisled and crisped, laid out (a world to see) on wreaths and borders from one ear to an other. And lest it should fall down, it is under propped with forks, wires, and I cannot tell what, rather like grim stern monsters, than chaste Christian matrons. Then on the edges of their bolstered hair (for it standeth crested round about their frontiers and hanging over their faces like pendices with glass windows on every side) there is laid great wreaths of gold and silver curiously wrought and cunningly applied to the temples of their heads. And for fear of lacking anything to set forth their pride withal, at their hair thus wreathed and crested, are hanged bugles (I dare not say baubles), ouches,[7] rings, gold, silver, glasses, and such other gewgaws and trinkets; besides which, for that they be innumerable and I unskilful in women's terms, I cannot easily recount. But God give them grace to give over these vanities and study to adorn their heads with the incorruptible ornaments of virtue and true godliness. . . . If curling and laying out their natural hair were all (which is impious and at no hand lawful notwithstanding, for its is the ensign of Pride and the stern of wantonness to all that behold it) it were the less matter, but they are not simply content with their own hair, but buy other hair, dyeing it of what colour they list themselves: and this they wear in the same order as you have heard, as though it were their own natural hair: and upon the other side if any have hair which is not fair enough then will they dye it into divers colours, almost changing the substance into accidents, by their devilish and more than thrice cursed devices. So whereas their hair was given them as a sign of subjection and therefore they were commanded to cherish the same, now have they made (as it were) a *Metamorphosis* of it, making it an ornament of pride, and destruction to themselves for ever, except they repent . . .

Spudeaus   As in a *Chamelion* are said to be in all colours, save white, so I think, in these people are all things else, save virtue and Christian sobriety. *Proteus* that monster could never change himself into so many forms as these women do, belike they have made an obligation with hell and are at agreement with the devil, else they would never outrage thus, without either fear of God, or respect to their weak brethren whom herein they offend.

Philoponus The women also there have doublets and jerkins as men have here, buttoned up the breast and made with wings, welts, and pinions on the shoulder points, as man's apparel is, for all the world and though this be a kind of attire appropriate only to man, yet they blush not to wear it, and if they could as well change their sex, and put on the kind of man as they can wear apparel assigned only to man, I think they would as verily become men indeed as now they degenerate from godly sober women, in wearing this wanton, lewd kind of attire proper only to man.

It is written in the 22 of Deuteronomy that what man soever weareth women's apparel is accursed, and what woman weareth man's apparel is accursed also. Now, whether they be within the bands and limits of that curse, let them see to it themselves. Our apparel was given us as a sign distinctive to discern betwixt sex and sex, and therefore one to wear the apparel of another sex is to participate with the same, and to adulterate the verity of his own kind. Wherefore these women may not improperly be called *Hermaphroditi*, that is monsters of both kinds, half women, half men. . . . So that when they have all these goodly robes upon them, women seem to be the smallest part of themselves, not natural women, but artificial women, not women of flesh and blood, but rather puppets or mawmets of rags and clowts[8] compact together. So far hath this canker of pride eaten into the body of the commonwealth that every poor yeoman his daughter, every husbandman his daughter, and every cottager his daughter will not spare to flaunt it out, in such gowns, petticoats and kirtles, as these. And notwithstanding that their parents owe a brace of hundred pounds more than they are worth, yet will they have it *quo iure quae inuria*, either by hook or by crook, by right or wrong as they say, whereby it commeth to pass, that one can scarcely know who is a noble woman, who is an honourable, or worshipful woman, from them of meaner sort.

3.9 THOMAS SMITH, *DE REPUBLICA ANGLORUM*

Smith was professor of Greek at Cambridge University, and worked as an ambassador for Elizabeth I. In this work he delineates the structures of English political and social life, and compares them to Roman structures. Text from: 1583 edition, pp. 20–34.

Of the first part of gentlemen of England, called nobilitas maior

Dukes, marquises, earls, viscounts and barons either be created by the prince, or come to that honour by being the eldest sons, as highest and next in succession to their parents. For the eldest of duke's sons during his father's life is called an earl, and earl's son is called by the name of a viscount, or baron, or else according as the creation is. The creation I call the first donation and condition of the honour (given by the prince for good service done by him and advancement that the prince will bestow upon him), which with the title of that honour is commonly (but not always) given to him and to his heirs, males only: the rest of the sons of the nobility by the rigour of the law be but esquires, yet in common speech, all dukes' and marquises' sons, and the eldest son of an earl, be called Lords. . . . The barony or degree of Lords doth answer to the dignity of the senators of Rome, and the title of our nobility to their *patricii* . . .

Of the second sort of gentlemen, which may be called nobilitas minor, and first of knights

No man is a knight by succession, not the King or prince. And the name of prince in England betokeneth the King's eldest son or prince of Wales: although the King himself, his eldest son and all dukes be called by general name princes. But as in France the King's eldest son hath the title of Dauphine, and he or the next heir apparent to the crown is Mon sire, so in England the King's eldest son is called the prince. Knights therefore be not born but made, either before the battle to encourage them the more to adventure their lives, or after the conflict, as advancement for their hardiness and manhood already showed: or out of the war for some great service done, or some good hope through the virtues which do appear in them. And they are made either by the King himself, or by his commission and royal authority, given for the same purpose, or by his lieutenant in the wars, who hath his royal absolute power committed to him for that time. And that order seemeth to answer in part to that which the Romans called *equites romanos*, differing in some points and agreeing in other, as their commonwealth and ours do differ and agree. . . . *Equites Romani* were chosen *ex censu*, that is according to their substance and riches. So be the knights in England most commonly, according to the yearly revenue of their lands being able to maintain that estate. . . . The number of *equites* was uncertain and so it is of knights, at the pleasure of the prince. *Equites romani* had *equum publicum* [a horse paid for by the public]: the knights of England have not so, but find their own horse themselves in peace time, and most usually in wars.

Census equester [knightly property] was among the Romans at divers times of diverse value, but in England whosoever may dispend of his free lands £40 sterling of yearly revenue by an old law of England either at the coronation of the King, or marriage of his daughter, or at the dubbing of the prince, knight or some such great occasion, may be by the King compelled to take that order and honour, or to pay a fine, which many not so desirous of honour as of riches, had rather disburse . . .

When the Romans did write, *senatus populusque Romanus* [the senate and people of Rome], they seemed to make but two orders, that is of the senate and of the people of Rome, and so in the name of people, they contained *equites* and *plebem*: so when we in England do say the Lords and the Commons: the knights, esquires, and other gentlemen, with citizens, burgesses, and yeomen be accounted to make the commons. In ordaining of laws the senate of Lords of England is one house, where the archbishops and bishops also be, and the King or Queen for the time being as chief: the knights and all the rest of the gentlemen, citizens and burgesses which be admitted to consult upon the greatest affairs of the realm be in another house by themselves, and that is called the House of the Commons . . .

Of esquires

Escuier or esquire (which we call commonly squire) is a French word and beto-keneth *scutigerium* or *armigerium* [shield or arm bearer] and be all those which bear arms (as we call them) or armories (as they term them in French) which to bear is a testimony of the nobility or race from whence they do come. These be taken for no distinct order of the commonwealth, but do go with the residue of the gentlemen: save that (as I take it) they be those who bear arms, testimonies (as I have said) of their race, and therefore have neither creation nor dubbing . . .

Of gentlemen

Gentlemen be those whom their blood and race doth make noble and known . . . the Latins call them all *nobiles*, as the French, *nobles*. Nobilitas in Latin is defined, honour or title given, for that the ancestor hath been notable in riches or virtues or (in fewer words) old riches or prowess remaining in one stock. Which if the successors do keep and follow, they be *vere nobiles* [nobles in truth] . . . if they do not, yet the fame and wealth of their ancestors serve to cover them so long as it can, as a thing once gilded, though it be copper within, till the gilt be worn away . . .

But as other commonwealths were fain to do, so must all princes necessarily follow, that is, where virtue is, to honour it: and although virtue of ancient race be easier to be obtained, as well by the example of the progenitors, which encourageth, as also through ability of education and bringing up, which enableth, and the lastly enraced [*sic*] love of tenants and neighbours to such noblemen and gentlemen, of whom they hold and by whom, they do dwell, which pricketh forward to ensue in their fathers' steps. So if all this do fail (as it were great pity it should), yet such is the nature of all human things, and so the world is subject to mutability, that it doth many times fail: but when it doth, the prince and commonwealth have the same power that their predecessors had, and as the husbandman hath to plant a new tree where the old faileth, so hath the prince to honour virtue where he doth find it, to make gentlemen, esquires, knights, barons, earls, marquises and dukes where he seeth virtue able to bear that honour or merits and deserves it, and so it hath always been used among us.

But ordinarily the King doth only make knights and create barons or higher degrees: for as for gentlemen they be made good cheap in England. For whosoever studieth the laws of the realm, who studieth in the universities, who professeth liberal sciences, and to be short, who can live idly and without manual labour, and will bear the port, charge and countenance of a gentleman, he shall be called master, for that is the title which men give to esquires and other gentlemen, and shall be taken for a gentleman . . .

Whether the manner of England in making gentlemen so easily is to be allowed

A man may make doubt and question whether this manner of making gentlemen is to be allowed or no, and for my part I am of that opinion that it is not amiss. For first the prince loseth nothing by it, as he should do if it were as in France, for the yeomen or husbandman is no more subject to tail or tare[9] in England than the gentleman: no, in every payment to the King, the gentleman is more charged, which he beareth the gladlier and dareth not gainsay for to save and keep his honour and reputation. In any show or muster or other particular charge of the town where he is, he must open his purse wider and augment his portion above others, or else he doth diminish his reputation. As for their outward show, a gentleman (if he will be so accounted) must go like a gentleman, a yeoman like a yeoman, and a rascal like a rascal: and if he be called to the wars he must and will (whatsoever it cost him) array himself and arm him according to the vocation which he pretendeth: he must show also a more manly courage and tokens of better education, higher stomach and bountifuller liberality than others, and keep about him idle servants, who shall do nothing but wait upon him. So that no man hath hurt by it but himself, who hereby perchance will bear a bigger sail then he is able to maintain. For as touching the policy and government of the commonwealth, it is not those that have to do with it which will magnify themselves and go in higher buskins than their estate will bear: but they which are to be appointed are persons tried and well known, as shall be declared hereafter.

Of citizens and burgesses

Next to gentlemen be appointed citizens and burgesses, such as not only be free and received as officers within the cities, but also be of some substance to bear the charges. But these citizens and burgesses be to serve the commonwealth in their cities and boroughs, or in corporate towns where they dwell. Generally in the shires they be of none account, save only in the common assembly of the realm to make laws, which is called the Parliament. The ancient cities appoint four and each borough two, to have voices in it, and to give their consent or dissent in the name of the city or borough for which they be appointed.

Of yeomen

Those whom we call yeomen next unto the nobility, knights, and squires, have the greatest charge and doings in the commonwealth, or rather are more travailed to serve in it than all the rest; as shall appear hereafter. I call him a yeomen whom our laws do call *legalem hominem*, a word familiar in writs and inquests, which is a freeman born English, and may dispend of his own free land in yearly revenue to the sum of 40s. sterling. This maketh (if the just value were taken now to the proportion of moneys) £6 of our current money at this present. This sort of people confess themselves to be no gentlemen, but give the honour to all which be or take upon them to be gentlemen, and yet they have a certain pre-eminence and more estimation than labourers and artificers and commonly live wealthily, keep good houses, and do their business, and travail to acquire riches. These be for the most part farmers unto gentlemen, which with grazing, frequenting of markets, and keeping servants not idle as the gentleman doth, but such as get their own living and part of their master's, by these means do come to such wealth that they are able and daily do buy the lands of unthrifty gentlemen, and after setting their sons to the school at the universities, to the law of the realm, or otherwise leaving them sufficient lands whereon they may live without labour, do make their said sons by those means gentlemen. These be not called masters, for that (as I said) pertaineth to gentlemen only: but to their surnames men add goodman . . .

. . . these tend their own business, come not to meddle in public matters and judgements but when they are called, and glad when they are delivered therof, are obedient to the gentlemen and rulers, and in war can abide travail and labour as men used to it, yet wishing it soon at an end that they might come home and live of their own. When they are forth they fight for their lords of whom they hold their lands; for their wives and children; for their country and nation ; for praise and honour; against they come home and to have the love of their Lord and his children to be continued towards them and their children, which have adventured their lives to and with him and his. These are they which in the old world gat that honour to England, not that either for wit, conduction or for power they are or were ever to be compared to the gentlemen, but because they be so many in number, so obedient at the Lord's call, so strong of body, so hard to endure pain, so courageous to adventure with their Lord or Captain going with or before them, for else they be not hasty, nor never were, as making no profession of knowledge of war. These were the good archers in times past, and the stable troop of footmen that afeared all France, that would rather die all then once abandon the knight or gentlemen their captain, who at those days commonly was their Lord, and whose tenants they were, ready (besides perpetual shame) to be in danger of undoing themselves and all theirs if they should show any sign of cowardice or abandon the Lord, knight or gentlment of whom they held their living. And this have they amongst them from their forefathers told one to another . . .

Of the fourth sort of men, who do not rule

The fourth sort or class amongst us is of those which the old romans called *capite censŭ proletaris* or *opera*, or day labourers, poor husbandmen, yea merchants or retailers which have no free land: copyholders and all artificers, as tailors, shoemakers, carpenters, brickmakers, bricklayers, masons etc. These have no voice nor authority in our commonwealth and no account is made of them; but only to be ruled, not to rule other; and yet they be not altogether neglected. For in cities and corporate towns for default of yeomen, inquests and juries are empanelled of such manner of people. And in villages they be commonly made churchwardens, alerunners and many times constables, which office toucheth more the commonwealth and at the first was not employed upon such low and base persons.

3.10 THE LORD MAYOR AND THE ALDERMEN OF THE CITY OF LONDON'S LETTER TO THE PRIVY COUNCIL

The City authorities petitioned the Privy Council on a number of occasions to ban all stage plays: partly because of understandable concerns about public order and health, but also because they saw drama as inherently dangerous. Text from: Malone Society, *Collections*, Part I, i, 1907, pp. 78–80.

To the Lords against stage plays

Our humble duties remembered to your good lordships and the rest. We have signified to your Honours many times heretofore the great inconvenience which we find to grow by the common exercise of stage plays. We presumed to do, as well in respect of the duty we bear towards her Highness for the good government of this her city, as for conscience's sake, being persuaded . . . that neither in polity nor in religion they are to be suffered in a Christian commonwealth, specially being of that frame and matter as usually they are, containing nothing but profane fables, lascivious matters, cozening devices, and scurrilous behaviours, which are so set forth as that they move wholly to imitation and not to the avoiding of those faults and vices which they represent. Among other inconveniences it is not the least that they give opportunity to the refuse sort of evil-disposed and ungodly people, that are within and about this City, to assemble themselves and to make their matches for all their lewd and ungodly practices; being as heretofore we have found, by the examination of divers apprentices and other servants who have confessed unto us that the said stage-plays were the very places of their rendezvous, appointed by them to meet with such other as were to join with them in their designs and mutinous attempts; being also the ordinary places for masterless men to come together and to recreate themselves. For avoiding whereof we are now again most humble and earnest suitors to your Honours to direct your letters as well to ourselves as to the Justices of Peace of Surrey and Middlesex for the present stay and final suppressing of the said stage-plays, as well at the Theatre, Curtain and Bankside, as in all other places in and about the City. Whereby we doubt not but th' opportunity and the very cause of many disorders being taken away, we shall be more able to keep the worse sort of such evil and disordered people in better order than heretofore we have been. . . . From London the 28th of July 1597.

The inconveniences that grow by stage-plays about the City of London

1. They are a special cause of corrupting their youth, containing nothing but unchaste matters, lascivious devices, shifts of cozenage, and other lewd and ungodly practices, being so as that they impress the very quality and corruption of manners which they represent, contrary to the rules and art prescribed for the making of comedies even among the heathen, who used them seldom, and at certain set times, and not all the year long, as our manner is. Whereby such as frequent them, being of the base and refuse sort of people, or such young gentlemen as have small regard of credit or conscience, draw the same into imitation and not the avoiding the like vices which they represent.

2. They are the ordinary places for vagrant persons, masterless men, thieves, horse-stealers, whoremongers, cozeners, coney-catchers, contrivers of treason, and other idle and dangerous persons to meet together and to make their matches, to the great displeasure of Almighty God and the hurt and annoyance of her Majesty's people; which cannot be prevented nor discovered by the governors of the City for they are out of the City's jurisdiction.

3. They maintain idleness in such persons as have no vocation, and draw apprentices and other servants from their ordinary works and all sorts of people from the resort unto sermons and other Christian exercises, to the great hindrance of trades, and profanation of religion established by her Highness within this realm.

4. In the time of sickness it is found by experience that many, having sores and not yet heart-sick, take occasion hereby to walk abroad and to recreate themselves by hearing a play. Whereby others are infected, and themselves also many things miscarry.

3.11 JOSEPH HALL, *VIRGIDEMIARUM*

Joseph Hall wrote and published his satires early in his career, in 1598. The satires anatomise the extravagancies and follies of London life in the late 1590s. Hall went on to a distinguished career in the Church, as Bishop of Exeter, and wrote *Episcopacy by Divine Right*, in defence of the Laudian Church (1.20). Text from: 1599 edition, Books III and IV.

Book 3: satire iii

The courteous citizen bad me to his feast,
With hollow words and overly request:
Come will ye dine with me this holy day?
I yielded, though he hop'd I would say nay:
For had I maiden'd it, as many use,
Loath for to grant, but loath to refuse:
Alack, Sir, I were loath, *another day:*
I should but trouble you: pardon me if you may.
No pardon should I need; for to depart,
He gives me leave, and thanks too, in his heart,
Two words for money: Derbyshirean wife:
(That's one too many) is a naughty guise.
Who looks to double biddings to a feast,
May dine at home for an importune guest.
I went, then saw and found the great expense,
The fare and fashion of our citizens.
O: Cleopatrical: what wanteth there
For curious cost and wondrous choice of cheer?
Beef, that erst Hercules held for finest fare;
Pork, for the fat Boaetian, or the hare
For Martial: fish for the Venetian,
Goose liver for the likerous Roman,
Th'Athenian's goat, quail, Iolan's cheer,
The hen for Esculape, and the Parthian deer,
Grapes for Arcesilas, figs for Plato's mouth,
And chestnuts fair for Amaryllis' tooth.
Hadst thou such cheer? Wer't thou ever there before?
Never: I thought so: nor come there no more.
Come there no more, for so meant all that cost,
Never hence take me for thy second host.
For whom he means to make an often guest,
One dish shall serve, and welcome make the rest.

Book IV: satire ii

Old drivelling Lolio drudges all he can,
To make his eldest son a gentleman;
Who can despair that sees another thrive,
By loan of twelve pence to an oyster wife?
When a crazed scaffold, and a rotten stage,
Was all rich Naevius his heritage.
Nought spendeth he for fear, nor spares for cost
And all he spends and spares besides is lost. . .

* * *

Who cannot shine in tissues and pure gold,
That hath his lands and patrimony sold?
Lolio's side coat is rough Pampilian,
Gilded with drops that down the bosom ran,
White Carsy hose, patched on either knee,
The very emblem of good husbandry.
And a knit nightcap, made of coarsest twine,
With two long labels buttoned to his chin;
So rides he mounted on the market day
Upon a straw stuff'd panel all the way;
With a mount charg'd with household merchandise,
With eggs or white meat, from both dairies;
And with that buys he roast for Sunday noon,
Proud how he made that week's provision:
Else he is stall-fed on the worky day
With brown bread crusts softened in sodden whey . . .
Good man! Him list not spend his idle meals,
In quincing plovers or in winning quails;
Nor root in Cheapside baskets earn[10] and late
To set the first tooth in some novel cate.[11]
Let sweet-mouth'd Mercia bid what crowns she please
For half red cherries or green garden peas,
Or the first artichokes of all the year,
To make so lavish cost for so little cheer:
When Lolio feasteth in his revelling fit
Some starved pullen scours the rusted spit,
For else how should his son maintained be
At Inns of Court of the Chancery?
There to learn law and courtly carriage,
To make amends for his mean parentage,
Where he unknown and ruffling as he can,
Goes current each-where for a gentleman.
What brokers lousy wardrobe cannot reach,
With tissued panes to prank each peasant's breech? . .
Old Lolio sees and laugheth in his sleeve,
At the great hope they and his state do give,
But that which glads and makes him proud'st of all,
Is when the brabbling neighbours on him call,
For counsel in some crabbed case of law,
Or some indentment, or some bond to draw;
His neighbour's gooses hath grazed on his lea,
What action mought be enter'd in the plea?

So new fallen lands have made him in request,
That now he looks as lofty as the best.
And well done Lolio, like a thrifty sire,
'Twere pity but thy son should prove a squire.
How I foresee in many ages past,
When Lolio's caitiff name is quite defaced,
Thine heir, thine heir's heir, and his heir again,
From out the loins of careful Lolian,
Shall climb up to the chancel pews on high
And rule and reign in their rich tenancy;
When perch'd aloft to perfect their estate
They rack the rents unto a treble rate;
And hedge in all the neighbour common lands,
And clog their slavish tenant with commands;
Whiles they, poor souls, with feeling sighs complain,
And wish old Lolio were alive again;
And praise his gentle soul and wish it well.
And of his friendly facts full often tell.
His father dead: tush, no it was not he:
He finds records of his great pedigree,
And tells how first his famous ancestor
Did come in long since with the conqueror.
Nor hath some bribed herald first assign'd
His quartered arms and crest of gentle kind,
The scottish barnacle (I might choose)
That of a worm doth wax a winged goose;
Natheless, some hungry squire for hope of good,
Matches the Church's son into gentle blood,
Whose son more justly of his gentry boasts
Than who were born at two pied-painted posts,
And had some traunting merchant to his sire,
That trafficked both by water and by fire.
O times! Since ever Rome did Kings create
Brass gentlemen and Caesar laureates.

3.12 AN ACT FOR THE RELIEF OF THE POOR

Much concern was expressed throughout the sixteenth century about increased vagrancy and poverty, both from those wishing for more charitable provision, and from those who believed it was a sign of a degenerate social group. It was clear that a more efficient system was required, both in terms of secure funding and in terms of effective provision. The Poor Law, as it has become known, set up a national statutory system which was administered and funded by local parishes and taxes, but monitored by

Justices of Peace and local aldermen, who were accountable to central government. It was first enacted in 1598, but consolidated in 1601. Text from: *Statutes of the Realm*, London, 1810–28: IV, pp. 896ff.

Be it enacted by the authority of this present Parliament that the churchwardens of every parish and four substantial householders there . . . who shall be nominated yearly in Easter week under the hand and seal of two or more Justices of the Peace in the same county . . . dwelling in or near the same parish, shall be called overseers of the poor of the same parish; and they or the greater part of them, shall take order from time to time, by and with the consent of two or more such Justices of Peace, for setting to work of the children of all such whose parents shall not by the said persons be thought able to keep and maintain their children, and also all such persons married or unmarried as, having no means to maintain them, use no ordinary and daily trade of life to get their living by; and also to raise weekly or otherwise by taxation of every inhabitant and every occupier of lands in the said parish in such competent sum and sums of money as they shall think fit, a convenient stock of flax, hemp, wool, thread, iron and other necessary ware and stuff to set the poor on work, and also competent sums of money for and towards the necessary relief of the lame, impotent, old, blind, and such other among them being poor and not able to work, and also for the putting out of such children to be apprentices, to be gathered out of the same parish according to the ability of the said parish; and to do and execute all other things, as well for the disposing of the said stock as otherwise concerning the premises, as to them shall seem convenient. Which said churchwardens and overseers so to be nominated, or such of them as shall not be let by sickness or other just excuse, to be allowed by two such Justices of Peace or more, shall meet together at the least once every month in the Church of the said parish, upon the Sunday in the afternoon after divine service, there to consider of some good course to be taken and of some meet orders to be set down in the premises; and shall, within four days after the end of their year . . . make and yield up to such two Justices of Peace a true and perfect account of all sums of money by them received . . . upon pain that every one of them absenting themselves without lawful cause as aforesaid from such monthly meeting for the purpose aforesaid, or being negligent in their office or in the execution of the orders aforesaid, being made by and with the assent of the said Justices of Peace, to forfeit for every such default, 20s.

And be it also enacted that, if the said Justices of Peace do perceive that the inhabitants of any parish are not able to levy among themselves sufficient sums of money for the purposes aforesaid . . . the said justices shall and may tax, rate and assess as aforesaid any other of other parishes, or out of any parish within the hundred where the said parish is . . . [and] pay such sum and sums of money to the churchwardens and overseers of the said poor parish for the said purposes as the said Justices shall think fit, according to the intent of this law. And if the said hundred shall not be thought to the said Justices able and fit to relieve the said several parishes not able to provide for themselves as aforesaid, then the

Justices of Peace at their general quarter sessions, or the greater number of them, shall rate and assess as aforesaid . . . other parishes . . . as in their discretion shall seem fit . . .

And to the intent that necessary place of habitation may more conveniently be provided for such poor impotent people, be it enacted by the authority aforesaid that it shall and may be lawful for the said churchwardens and overseers, or the greater part of them, by the leave of the lord or lords of the manor whereof any waste or common within their parish is, or shall be, parcel . . . to erect, build and set up, . . . in such waste or common, at the general charge of the parish, or otherwise of the hundred or county as aforesaid . . . convenient houses of dwelling for the said impotent poor; and also to place inmates or more families than one in one cottage or house . . .

And be it further hereby enacted that the mayors, bailiffs, or other head officers of every corporate town within this realm, being Justice or Justices of Peace, shall have the same authority by virtue of this act within the limits and precincts of their corporations as well out of sessions as at their sessions, as is herein limited, prescribed and appointed to any of the Justices of Peace in the county for all the uses and purposes in this act prescribed, and no other Justice of Peace to enter or meddle there . . .

And forasmuch as all begging is forbidden by this present act, be it further enacted by the authority aforesaid that the Justices of Peace of every county or place corporate, or the more part of them, in their general sessions to be holden next after the end of this session of Parliament, or in default thereof at the quarter sessions to be holden after the feast of Easter next, shall rate every parish to such a weekly sum of money as they shall think convenient; so as no parish be rated above the sum of sixpence, nor under the sum of an halfpenny weekly to be paid, and so as the total sum of such taxation of the parishes in every county amount not above the rate of twopence for every parish in the said county. Which sums so taxed shall be yearly assessed by the agreement of the parishioners within themselves, or in default thereof, by the churchwardens and constables of the same parish, or the more part of them, or in default of their agreement, by the order of such Justice or Justices of Peace as shall dwell in the same parish or, if none be there dwelling, in the next parts adjoining.

3.13 PROCLAMATION PROHIBITING ACCESS TO COURT BECAUSE OF PLAGUE

Proclamations from the monarch were a frequent means of enforcing order and policy, and did not require the assent of Parliament or the force of statute. Such proclamations are a good index to contemporary social and political concerns. The three below relate to prohibitions against travel in times of plague, price controls and vagrancy. Text from: STC 8223.

Hampton Court 12 October 1592

The Queen's Majesty, upon good consideration that her court may (with God's favour) be the better preserved from the infection of sickness in this time, commandeth that no manner persons but such as have cause to remain or come to her court for their ordinary attendance upon her Majesty's person, or to do service in her court, shall make their repair to her court, or within two miles of the same; upon pain to be committed to prison for their contempt. And where by her Majesty's commandment there are certain orders made who and how many shall be commanded to attend for the service of her Majesty, either for her chamber, or for her household, or for attendance upon her councillors, or other her Majesty's ordinary servants in court, and that no more shall be allowed to follow the court, or to enter into the same:

Her Majesty straightly chargeth both her councillors and her principal officers of her chamber, and of her household that they see the same orders duly observed, and that such as shall break the same orders may be sharply punished. And considering the term of St. Michael which should have begun at Westminster the 9th of this month is adjourned as by her proclamation is notified, her Majesty also commandeth that all private suitors shall forbear to come to the court where her Majesty shall reside until the 20th November next . . . upon pain of imprisonment.

Finally her Majesty commandeth that no manner of person allowed to attend in her court shall repair to London or to the suburbs or places within two miles of the city without special licence of the councillor or other officer under whom he serveth, in writing, to be showed to any officer that shall seek to impeach him; upon pain to be imprisoned by attachment of the knight marshal or of his officers, if the party shall not show in writing sufficient warrant both for his going and returning.

Her Majesty also straightly chargeth and commandeth the knight marshal of her household that he shall cause due search to be made of all vagabonds commonly called rogues that shall haunt about the court or in any places within the verge, and them to apprehend and commit either to the Marshelsea, or to deliver them to the next constables to be sent to the common jails next to the place where they shall be apprehended, there to be ordered and punished according to the laws provided for such offenders.

3.14 PRICING PROCLAMATION

During and after the war with Spain, the economic and social tensions arising from the quartering of soldiers in local communities are clearly evidenced in this Proclamation. Text from: STC 8173.

St. James, 7 August 1588, 30 Elizabeth I

The Queen's most excellent Majesty, being minded in this dangerous time to entertain a certain number of captains and soldiers for the guarding of her royal person and defense of this her realm to be under the government and lieutenancy of the right honourable the Lord Chamberlain, hath thought it requisite, for the better and more easy relief of the said army, by this her highness's proclamation straightly to charge and command that all and every person and persons, of whatsoever estate or degree he or they be of, do observe and keep such rates and prices for all kinds of victuals, horse meat, lodging and other necessaries as from time to time shall be rated and priced by the clerk of the market of her highness's most honourable household, or his lawful deputy or deputies, and the jury before him or them, by virtue of his office sworn and charged; which rates and prices shall accordingly (during the time of such attendance upon her Majesty's person) be set up and declared upon her highness's court gates, and in every town, village, parish, and hamlet where the said captains and soldiers or any of them are to be placed, within the circuit of twenty miles every way distant from her highness's court . . .

A limitation of such rates and prices of grain, victuals, horse meat, lodgings and other things, as by virtue of this proclamation here above expressed are to be sold and uttered as well within all manner of liberties as without:

First, a quarter best wheat, clean and sweet in the market	20s.
and a quarter second wheat in the market	16s.
Item, a quarter third wheat, or best rye in the market	12s.
and a quarter second rye in the market	10s.8d.
Item, a quarter best barley in the market	10s.8d.
and a quarter second barley in the market	9s.4d.
Item, a quarter best malt, clean and sweet in the market	11s.4d.
and a quarter second malt in the market	10s.
Item, a quarter beans or peas in the market	12s.
Item, a quarter best oats in the market	6s.8d.
Item, a bushel of the same oats within every house	13d.

* * *

Item, a thirdendeal of the best ale or beer within and without every house	1d.
and a full quart of good single ale or beer within and without every house	½d.
Item, a pound of butter, sweet and new, the best in the market	3d.
and a pound of barrel or salt butter in shop or in market	2½d.
Item, a pound of good Essex cheese in the shop or in market	1½d.
and a pound of good Suffolk cheese in shop or in market	1½d.
Item, seven eggs the best in the market	2d.

and three of the same eggs within every house	1d.
Item, a stone best beef at the butchers, weighing eight pound	12d.
and a stone second beef at the butchers	11d . . .
Item, a fat pig the best in the market	14d.
and a lean or second pig in the market	8d.
Item, a couple capons the best in the market	20d . . .

Item, that every soldier or other persons being placed and appointed
in the band within the circuit of twenty miles distant from her
highness's court under the right honourable Lord Chamberlain,
her Majesty's lieutenant of the same band and army, and
receiving her Majesty's pay by 8d. the day, having to dinner or
supper good wheaten bread and drink, beef, mutton or veal boiled,
and pig, beef, mutton, veal or lamb roasted, or otherwise upon the
fishdays, to have good wheaten bread and good drink, salt fish or
ling, eggs, butter, peas or beans buttered, and so having competent
and sufficient thereof for the sustenation of their bodies, every man
to pay for his meal   3d.

Item, a pound of tallow candles made of wick	3½d.
Item , a featherbed for one man one night and so depart	3½d.

Item, a featherbed with necessary apparel thereunto for one man
alone by the week   6d.

and the like featherbed and furniture by the week for two lying together	8d.
Item, a mattress or flockbed for one or two together by the week	3d.

Item, three horse loaves at the bakers every one loaf weighing
18 ounces troy   1d . . .

Item, every hundredweight of good sweet hay weighing 112 pounds
avoirdupois with carriage   8d . . .

Item, hay and litter day and night, for one horse within every inn   3½d.

and the like hay and litter, day and night, for one horse within
every other house being no inn   3d.

Item, good grass for one horse all day and night and so depart	2d.
and the like good grass for one horse alone by the week	8d . . .
Item, 100 good faggots keeping the assize, with carriage	4s.4d.
and three of the same faggots within every house	2d.
Item, a quarter of charcoals containing 8 bushels, with carriage	14d.

Item, a vacant or empty room, either chamber room or stable,
by the whole week   4d.

3.15 VAGRANCY PROCLAMATION

Many proclamations were issued about vagrancy prior to the Act for the
Relief of the Poor (3.12), most of which make a distinction between the
deserving and the undeserving. In this case, returning soldiers from France,
after one of the defensive forays against the Catholic League, evidently

created and fuelled social unrest. Text from: STC 8210.

Richmond 5 November 1591

The Queen's Majesty understanding of the common wandering abroad of a great multitude of her people, whereof the most part pretend that they have served in the wars of late on the other side of the seas, though in truth it is known that very many of them either have not served at all, or have not been licensed to depart from the places of their service as they ought to have been, but have run away from their service and therefore they are justly to be punished and not to be relieved; some others are such as have indeed served and fallen into sickness, and therefore licensed to depart towards their countries from whence they were levied, and do deserve relief; to the intent all her Majesty's officers of Justice in every place where these sorts of people shall resort may know what her Majesty's most gracious pleasure is for the usage of the said persons, both to punish the offenders and to relieve the sick soldiers and such as have truly served and are licensed to depart to their countries: she commandeth that such discretion be used betwixt the unlawful vagrant persons and the soldiers now lawfully dismissed from their services, that all such vagrant persons as neither have been brought to sickness nor lameness by the said late service, and that shall not be able to show sufficient passport for their dismission, shall be taken and apprehended wheresoever they may be found, as persons vagabond, and so to be punished. And if any of them shall allege that they have been in her Majesty's pay on the other side the seas and cannot show sufficient passport from the lord general, or some of the principal officers of the army, then to be taken and committed to prison and to be indicted as felons, and to suffer for the same as soldiers being in her Majesty's pay that have run away and left the service traitorously. And for the rest that have served as soldiers and can show their lawful passports, they ought to be relieved by some charitable means to conduct them into their country with commendation of public letters from the Justices of the Peace where they shall be found, to all other ministers both spiritual and temporal, both to grant them reasonable relief and aid for their passage, and to be particularly relieved by the parishes or hundreds from whence they were levied during the time of their infirmities and sickness, as in conscience they ought, and so to be placed with their former masters as by her Majesty's late directions to the counties hath been ordered and appointed; and nevertheless, with special pains to be added to the same letters of commendations of passports, that if they shall be found to wander abroad out of the ordinary ways mentioned in their passports, that then they are to be punished as vagabonds.

And her Majesty letteth it to be known that order is given by her that her treasurer of wars hath and shall make payment in every port where any such shall arrive, coming with lawful passport, of such sums of money as shall be convenient to conduct them to the places from which they were levied. . . . And furthermore, for the repressing of the great number of mighty and able vagrant persons now wandering abroad under pretence of begging as soldiers, although indeed they are known to commit open robberies upon her Majesty's poor subjects and travellers by the way: her Majesty straightly chargeth all her lieutenants of every county within the realm, having sufficient warrant by their commission to execute martial law upon such offenders against the public peace and state of the realm, to appoint some special persons within their jurisdictions to travel within the counties as provost marshals, and to give directions to the Justices of the Peace to assist the provost marshal for the apprehension of all such notable offenders, and to commit them to prison thereupon to be executed as by the laws of the realm they shall deserve.

3.16 LONDON WAGES

This allocation of wages rates in London gives a good picture of the range and hierarchy of occupations in the city, as well as their economic status. Text from: *Lords Journals*, 22, 197.

Westminster 24 August 1588

Having a special care and regard to the high and very chargeable prices of victual, fuel, raiment and apparel both linen and woollen, and also of house rents and other special and accidental charges wherewith artificers and labourers dwelling within the said city are very many and sundry times, after their power and substance charged and burdened with the residue of the citizens of the same city.

To the best and most skilful workmen, journeymen, and hired servants of any the companies hereunder named:

Clothworkers by the year with meat and drink	£5
Fullers by the year with meat and drink	£5
Shearmen by the year with meat and drink	£5
Dyers by the year with meat and drink	£6 13s.4d.
Tailors hosier by the year with meat and drink	£4
Drapers, being hosiers, by the year with meat and drink	£4
Shoemakers by the year with meat and drink	£4
Pewterers by the year with meat and drink	£3 6s.8d.
Whitebakers by the year with meat and drink	£4 13s.4d.
Brewers by the year with meat and drink	£10
The underbrewer by the year with meat and drink	£6
The foredrayman by the year with meat and drink	£6
The miller by the year with meat and drink	£6
The other draymen by the year with meat and drink	£3 6s.8d.

The tunman by the year with meat and drink	£3 6s.8d.
Alebrewers by the year with meat and drink	£6,
by the day with meat and drink	8d.
Saddlers by the year with meat and drink	£4
Turners by the year with meat and drink	£4 6s.8d.
Cutlers by the year with meat and drink	£4 6s.8d.
Blacksmiths by the year with meat and drink	£6
Curriers by the year with meat and drink	£6 . . .
Brownbakers by the year with meat and drink	£3 6s.8d.
Farriers by the year with meat and drink	£4
Glovers by the year with meat and drink	£3 6s.8d.
Cappers by the year with meat and drink	£4 13s.4d.
Hatmakers and feltmakers by the year with meat and drink	£4 13s.4d.
Butchers by the year with meat and drink	£6
Cooks by the year with meat and drink	£6

To the workmen, journeymen or hired servants of any the companies hereunder named:

Goldsmiths by the year with meat and drink £5, by the week 3s.4d., by the day 7d; without meat and drink by the week 6s., by the day 12d.

Skinners by the year with meat and drink £4, by the week 3s.4d., by the day 8d.; without meat and drink by the week 6s., by the day 13d.

Painter stainers by the year with meat and drink £4, by the week 4s., by the day 9d.; without meat and drink by the year £8, by the week 6s.8d., by the day 13d. . . . .

Linen weavers by the year with meat and drink £4, by the day 6d.; without meat and drink by the day 10d. . . . .

Glaziers with meat and drink by the day 9d.; without meat and drink by the day 13d. . . . .

Longbow stringmakers by the year with meat and drink £4, by the day 8d.; without meat and drink by the day 12d.

Founders by the year with meat and drink £5, by the day 12d.; without meat and drink by the day 16d. . . . .

Barbers by the year with meat and drink £3; by the week 20d.

Carmen by the week with meat and drink 2s.6d.

Watermen by the year with meat and drink 40s., by the week 12d., by the day 4d.; without meat and drink by the week 3s., by the day 7d.

Porters with meat and drink by the day 8d.; without meat and drink by the day 12d.

Carpenters with meat and drink by the week 4s.6d., by the day 9d.; without meat and drink by the week 6s.2d., by the day 13d.; his apprentice that hath served three years with meat and drink by the week 3s.4d., by the day 7d.; without meat and drink by the week 5s., by the day 11d.

Sawyers with meat and drink by the week 4s., by the day 8d.; without meat and drink by the week 6s., by the day 12d.; to him that saweth 100 [board feet] with meat and drink by the day 10d.; without meat and drink by the day 20d.

Common labourers with meat and drink by the day 5d.; without meat and drink by the day 9d.

3.17 EXTRAVAGANCE AT COURT

The notoriety of James Hay's extravagance in courtly entertainment and conspicuous consumption merits its inclusion, however exaggerated, since it was cited by contemporaries as worthy of note. Osborne's accounts of the Jacobean court are notoriously exaggerated; but it is here counterbalanced by Chamberlain. Texts from: *Francis Osborne: Secret History of the Court of James I*, 2 vols, edited by W. Scott, Edinburgh, 1811, i, 270–3; *State Papers Domestic*. Jac. I, xc, 79; 165. (old dates).

Francis Osborne

In the meantime, the reason King James was so poorly followed, especially in his journeys, was his partiality used towards the Scots, which hung like horseleeches on him till they could get no more, falling then off by retiring into their own country, or living at ease, leaving all chargeable attendance to the English. The harvest of the love and honour he reaped being suitable to the ill husbandry he used in the unadvised distribution of his favours. For of a number of empty vessels he filled to complete the measure of our infelicity, few proved of use to him, unless such as, by reason of their vast runnings out, had daily need of a new supply. And amongst these the Earl of Carlisle [James Hay] was one of the quorum, that brought in the vanity of ante-suppers, not heard of in our forefather's time, and for ought I have read, or at least remember, unpractised by the most luxurious tyrants. The manner of which was to have the board covered at the first entrance of the guests with dishes as high as a tall man could well reach, filled with the choicest and dearest viands sea or land could afford; and all this, once seen, and having feasted the eyes of the invited, was in a manner thrown away, and fresh set to the same height, having only this advantage of the other, that it was hot. I cannot forget one of the attendants of the King, that at a feast made by this monster in excess, eat to his single share a whole pie, reckoned to my lord at ten pounds, being composed of amber-grease, magisterial of pearl, musk, etc. Yet was so far (as he told me) from being sweet in the morning, that he almost poisoned his whole family, flying himself like a satyr from his own stink. And after such suppers, huge banquets no less profuse, a waiter returning his servant home with a cloak-bag full of dried sweet-meats and confects, valued to his lordship at more than ten shillings the pound. I am cloyed with the repetition of this excess, no less than scandalised at the continuance of it.

John Chamberlain, Letters

The French ambassador and his company were feasted at Whitehall on Sunday, and yesterday at Tiballs and last night had a great supper at the Lord Mayor's (who, poor man has been at death's door these six or seven weeks). The Duke of Lennox feasted him before the King, and this night he is solemnly invited by the Lord Hay to the wardrobe to a supper and a masque, where the Countess of Bedford is to be Lady and mistress of the feast, as she is of the managing of his love to the Earl of Northumberland's younger daughter, with whom he is far engaged in affection and finds such acceptance both at her hands and her mother's, that it is though it will prove a match. But (*pour retourner a nos moutons*), this feasting begins to grow to an excessive rate, the very provision of cates for this supper arising to more than £600, wherein we are too apish to imitate the French monkeys in such monstrous waste: for supping with Master Controller on Thursday (who, by the way desires very much you would excuse his long silence with promise of amends), he told me that the Lord Hay at his last being in France among many other great banquets made him had three whereof the least cost £1,000 sterling, the rest £1,300 and £1,500. But if there fall out any thing at these banquets worth the knowledge, you shall have it in my next. Sir Edward Sackville, Sir Harry Rich, Sir George Goring and Sir Thomas Badger are the principal persons in his masque. The Queen's French musicians (whereof she hath more than a good many) made her a kind of masque or antic at Somerset House on Wednesday night last . . . From London this 22th of February 1616.

Your Lordship's to command,
John Chamberlain

To the right honourable Sir Dudley Carleton knight, Lord Ambassador for his Majesty in the United Provinces at the Hague

My very good Lord,

. . . The Frenchmen are gone after their great entertainment, which was too great for such petty companions, specially that of the Lord Hay, which stood him in more than £2,200, being rather a profusion and spoil than reasonable or honourable provision, as you may guess at the rest by this scantling: of seven score pheasants, twelve partridges in a dish throughout, twelve whole salmons, and whatsoever else that cost or curiosity could procure in like superfluity: besides the workmanship and inventions of thirty cooks for twelve days. But the ill luck was that the chief and most desired guest was away, for the younger Lady Sidney with her sister the Lady Lucy Percy going some two or three days before the feast to visit their father in the Tower, after some few caresses he dismissed his daughter Sidney to go home to her husband, and to send her sister's maid to attend her . . .

From London this 8th March 1616

3.18 WILLIAM GOUGE, *OF DOMESTICAL DUTIES*

Gouge was a renowned puritan preacher, whose work *Of Domestical Duties* was first published in 1622, and went through several revised editions. Here Gouge argues that the family is the basic model for social and political structures: but that the distinction between private and public roles determines individuals' place in society, all within a Protestant philosophical framework which advocates individual vocations. Text from: 1634 edition, pp. 17–23.

Of the lawfulness of private functions in a family

Ephesians chapter 5 verse 22

Among other particular callings the Apostle maketh choice of those which God hath settled in private families, and is accurate in reciting the several and distinct orders thereof. For a family consisteth of these three orders: husbands, wives; parents, children; masters, servants: all which he reckoneth up; yea he is also copious and earnest in urging the duties which appertain to them. Whence we may infer that the private vocations of a family, and functions appertaining thereto, are such as Christians are called unto by God, and in the exercising whereof, they may and must employ some part of their time. For can we think that the Holy Ghost, (who, as the philosophers speak of nature, doth nothing in vain) would so distinctly set down these private duties and so forcibly urge them, if they did not well become and nearly concern Christians? All the places in Scripture which require family duties are proofs of the truth of this doctrine.

The reasons of the doctrine are clear: for the family is a seminary of the Church and commonwealth. It is a bee-hive in which is the stock and out of which are sent many swarms of bees: for in families are all sorts of people bred and brought up; and out of families are they sent into the Church and commonwealth. The first beginning of mankind and of his increase was out of a family. For first did God join in marriage Adam and Eve, made them husband and wife, and then gave them children: so as husband and wife, parent and child (which are parts of a family) were before magistrate and subject, minister and people, which are the parts of a commonwealth and a Church. When by the general deluge all public societies were destroyed, a family, even the family of Noah, was preserved, and out of it kingdoms and nations again raised. That great people of the Jews which could not be numbered for multitude, was raised out of the family of Abraham. Yea, even to this day have all sorts of people come from families and so shall to the end of the world. Whence it followeth that a conscionable performance of the domestical and household duties tend to the good ordering of Church and commonwealth, as being means to fit and prepare men thereunto.

Besides, a family is a little Church, and a little commonwealth, at least a lively representation thereof, whereby trial may be made of such as are fit for any place of authority, or of subjection in the Church or commonwealth. Or rather it is a school wherein the first principles and grounds of government and subjection are learned: whereby men are fitted to greater matters in Church or commonwealth. Whereupon the apostle declareth that a Bishop that cannot rule his own house is not fit to govern the Church. So may we say of inferiors that cannot be subject in a family, they will hardly be brought to yield such subjection as they ought in Church or commonwealth: instance Absolom and Adoniah, David's sons.

This is to be noted for satisfaction of certain weak consciences who think that if they have no public calling, they have no calling at all; and thereupon gather that all their time is spent without a calling. Which consequence, if it were good and sound, what comfort in spending their time should most women have, who are not admitted to any public function in Church or commonwealth? Or servants, children and others who are wholly employed in private affairs of the family? But the forenamed doctrine showeth the unsoundness of that consequence. Besides, who knoweth not that the preservation of families tendeth to the good of the Church and commonwealth? So as a conscionable performance of household duties in regard of the end and fruit thereof, may be accounted a public work. Yea, if domestical duties be well and thoroughly performed, they will be even enough to take up a man's whole time. If a master of a family be also an husband of a wife, and a father of children, he shall find work enough; as by those particular duties which we shall afterwards show to belong unto masters, husbands and parents, may easily be proved. So a wife likewise, if she also be a mother and a mistress, and faithfully endeavour to do what by virtue of those callings she is bound to do, shall find enough to do. As for children, under the government of their parents, and servants in a family, their whole calling is to be obedient to their parents and masters, and to do what they command them in the Lord. Wherefore, if they who have no public calling be so much the more diligent in the functions of their private callings, they shall be as well accepted of the Lord, as if they had public offices.

Yet many there be, who having no public employment, think they may spend their time as they list, either in idleness or in following their vain pleasures and delights, day after day, and so cast themselves out of all calling. Such are many masters of families who commit all the care of their house either to their wives or to some servant, and misspend their whole time in idleness, riotousness and voluptuousness. Such are many mistresses, who spend their time in lying a bed, attiring themselves, and gossiping. Such are many young gentlemen, living in their father's houses, who partly through too much indulgence and negligence of their parents, and partly through their own headstrong affections and rebellious will, run without restraint whither their corrupt lusts lead them. These, and other such like to these, though by God's providence they be placed in callings, in warrantable callings, and in such callings as minister unto them matter enough of employment, yet make themselves to be of no calling . . .

Now to return to the point, though it be so that governors have the heaviest burden laid on their shoulders, yet inferiors that are under subjection think their burden the heaviest, and are loathest to bear it, and most willing to cast it away. For naturally there is in everyone much pride and ambition, which as dust cast on the eyes of their understanding, putteth out the sight thereof, and so maketh them affect superiority and authority over others, and to be stubborn under the yoke of subjection: which is the cause that in all ages, both by divine and also by human laws, penalties and punishments of divers kinds have been ordained to keep inferiors in compass of their duty: and yet (such is the pride of man's heart) all will not serve. What age, what place ever was there, which hath not just cause to complain of subjects' rebellion, servants' stubbornness, children's disobedience, wives' presumption? Not without cause therefore doth the apostle first declare the duties of inferiors.

3.19 FRANCIS BACON, *ESSAYS OR COUNSELS CIVIL AND MORAL*

Bacon's *Essays* utilise commonplace phrases about social matters: and are thus useful indices for educated opinion. Text from: 1625 edition, fos H3ᵛ–12,ᵛ.

Of great place

Men in great place are thrice servants: servants of the sovereign or State; servants of fame and servants of business. So as they have no freedom, neither in their persons, nor in their action, nor in their times. It is a strange desire to seek power and to lose liberty; or to seek power over others and to lose power over a man's self. The rising unto place is laborious, and by pains men come to greater pains; and it is sometimes base, and by indignities, men come to dignities. The standing is slippery and the regress is either a downfall or at least an eclipse, which is a melancholy thing. . . . In the discharge of thy place, set before thee the best examples; for imitation is a globe of precepts. And after a time set before thee thine own example; and examine thyself strictly, whether thou didst not best at first. Neglect not also the examples of those that have carried themselves ill in the same place; not to set off thyself by taxing their memory, but to direct thyself what to avoid. Reform, therefore, without bravery or scandal of former times and persons; but yet set it down to thyself as well to create good precedents, as to follow them. Reduce things to the first institution, and observe wherein and how they have degenerate; but yet ask counsel of both times; of the ancient time what is best; and of the latter time, what is fittest. Seek to make thy course regular, that men may know beforehand what they may expect; but be not too positive and peremptory; and express thyself well when thou digressest from thy rule. Preserve the right of thy place, but stir not questions of jurisdiction: and rather assume thy right in silence and *de facto*, than voice it with claims and challenges. Preserve likewise the rights of inferior places; and think it more honour to direct in chief than to be busy in all. Embrace and invite helps and advices touching the execution of thy place; and do not drive away such as bring thee information, as meddlers, but accept of them in good part. The vices of authority are chiefly four: delays, corruption, roughness and facility. For delays: give easy access; keep times appointed; go through with that which is in hand; and interlace not business but of necessity. For corruption: do not only bind thine own hands or thine servants' hands from taking, but bind the hands of suitors also from offering. For integrity used doth the one; but integrity professed and with a manifest detestation of bribery, doth the other. And avoid not only the fault, but the suspicion. Whosoever is found variable and changeth manifestly without manifest cause, giveth suspicion of corruption. Therefore always when thou changest thine opinion or course, profess it plainly and declare it, together with the reasons that move thee to change; and do not think to steal it. A servant or a favourite, if he be inward, and no other apparent cause of esteem, is commonly thought but a by-way to close corruption. For roughness, it is a needless cause of discontent: severity breedeth fear, but roughness breedeth hate: even reproofs from authority ought to be grave and not taunting. As for facility, it is worse than bribery. For bribes come but now and then; but if importunity or idle respects lead a man, he shall never be without. As Solomon saith: *to respect persons is not good: for such a man will transgress for a piece of bread.* It is most true that was anciently spoken: *a place showeth the man*: and it showeth some to the better and some to the worse . . . honour is, or should be, the place of virtue; and as in nature things move violently to their place and calmly in their place, so virtue in ambition is violent, in authority, settled and calm. All rising to great place is by a winding stair and if there be factions, it is good to side a man's self whilst he is in the rising, and to balance himself when he is placed. Use the memory of thy predecessor fairly and tenderly; for if thou dost not, it is a debt will sure be paid when thou art gone. If thou have colleagues, respect them and rather call them when they look not for it, than exclude them when they have reason to look to be called. Be not too sensible or too remembering of thy place in conversation and private answers to suitors, but let it rather be said: *when he sits in place he is another man.*

3.20 *DECLARATION CONCERNING SPORTS*

In 1633 Charles I reissued this proclamation which had been made by his father in 1618, which insisted that sports and other festivities could take place on Sundays after Church. It was one of the issues of contention for puritan opponents of a perceived relaxing of reformed standards in the Church and its administration. Text from: 1633 proclamation.

By the King

Our dear father of blessed memory, in his return from Scotland, coming through Lancashire, found that his subjects were debarred from lawful recreations upon

Sundays after evening prayers ended, and upon Holy days; and he prudently considered that, if these times were taken from them, the meaner sort that labour hard all the week should have no recreations at all to refresh their spirits; and after his return he further saw that his loyal subjects in all other parts of his kingdom did suffer in the same kind, though perhaps not in the same degree; and did therefore in his princely wisdom publish a declaration to all his loving subjects concerning lawful sports to be sued at such times, which was printed and published by his royal commandment in the year 1618, in the tenor which hereafter followeth:

... Whereas we did justly in our progress through Lancashire rebuke some puritans and precise people and took order that the like unlawful carriage should not be used by any of them hereafter, in the prohibiting and unlawful punishing of our good people for using their lawful recreations and honest exercises upon Sundays and other holy days, after the afternoon sermon or service, we now find that two sorts of people wherewith that country is much affected, we mean papists and puritans, have maliciously traduced and calumniated those our just and honourable proceedings; and therefore lest our reputation might upon the one side (though innocently) have some aspersion laid upon it, and that upon the other part our good people in that country be misled by the mistaking and misinterpretation of our meaning we have therefore thought good hereby to clear and make our pleasure to be manifested to all our good people in those parts.

It is true that at our first entry to this crown and kingdom we were informed and that too truly, that our county of Lancashire abounded more in popish recusants than any county of England, and thus hath still continued since, to our great regret, with little amendment, save that now of late in our last riding through our said country, we find both by the report of the judges, and of the bishop of that diocese, that there is some amendment now daily beginning, which is no small contentment to us.

The report of this growing amendment amongst them made us the more sorry when with our own ears we heard the general complaint to our people that they were barred from all lawful recreation and exercise upon the Sunday's afternoon, after the ending of all divine service, which cannot but produce two evils: the one the hindering of the conversion of many, whom their priests will take occasion hereby to vex, persuading them that no honest mirth or recreation is lawful or tolerable in our religion, which cannot but breed a great discontentment in our people's hearts, especially such as are peradventure upon the point of turning; the other inconvenience is that this prohibition barreth the common and meaner sort of people from using such exercise as may make their bodies more able for war, when we or our successors shall have occasion to use them; and in place thereof sets up filthy tipplings and drunkenness and breeds a number of idle and discontented speeches in their ale-houses. For when shall the common people have leave to exercise, if not upon the Sundays and holy days, seeing they must apply their labour and win their livings in all working days?

Our express pleasure therefore is that the laws of our kingdom and canons of the church be as well observed in that county as in all other places of this our kingdom; and on the other part that no lawful recreation shall be barred to our good people which shall not tend to the breach of our aforesaid laws and canons of our Church; which to express more particularly, our pleasure is, that the bishop and all other inferior churchmen and churchwardens shall for their parts be careful and diligent both to instruct the ignorant and convince and reform them that are misled in religion, presenting them that will not conform themselves, but obstinately stand out, to our judges and justices; whom we likewise command to put the law in due execution against them.

Our pleasure likewise is that the bishop of that diocese take the like strait order with all the puritans and precisians within the same, either constraining them to conform themselves or to leave the county, according to the laws of our kingdom and canons of our Church, and so to strike equally on both hands against the condemners of our authority and adversaries of our Church; and as for our good people's recreation, our pleasure is likewise that after the end of divine service, our good people be not disturbed, letted or discouraged from any lawful recreation, such as dancing, either men or women; archery for men; leaping, vaulting, or any other harmless recreation; nor from having May-games, Whitsun-ales, and Morris-dances; and the setting up of may-poles and other sports therewith used; so as the same be had in due and convenient time, without impedient or neglect of divine service, and that women shall have leave to carry rushes to the church for the decorating of it, according to their old custom; but withal we do here account still as prohibited all unlawful games to be used upon Sundays only, as bear and bull-baitings, interludes and at all times in the meaner sort of people, by law forbidden, bowling.

And likewise we bar from this benefit and liberty all such known as recusants, either men or women, as will abstain from coming to church or divine service, being therefore unworthy of any lawful recreation after the said service that will not first come to the church and serve God; prohibiting in like sort the said recreations to any that, though they conform in religion, are not present in the church at the service of God, before their going to the said recreations. Our pleasure likewise is that they to whom it belongeth in office shall present and sharply punish all such, as in abuse of this our liberty, will use these exercises before the end of all divine services for that day; and we likewise straitly command that every person shall resort to his own parish church to hear divine service, and each parish by itself to use the said recreation after divine service; prohibiting likewise any offensive weapons to be carried or used in the said times of recreation; and our pleasure is that this our declaration shall be published by order from the bishop of the diocese, through all parish churches and that both our judges of the circuit and our Justices of the Peace be informed thereof.

3.21 HENRY PEACHAM, *THE ART OF LIVING IN LONDON*

Published in 1642, Peacham explains the purpose of his work in his title page: 'or a caution how gentlemen, countrymen, and strangers, drawn by occasion of business, should dispose themselves in the thriftiest way, not only in the city, but in all other populous places. As also, a direction to the poorer sort that come thither to seek their fortunes.' Thus it figured itself as one of the many self-help manuals for the burgeoning 'middling sort' in London. Text from: 1642 edition, pp. 1–16.

It is a greater piece of skill to live in a populous place, where multitudes of people reside, than in a solitary and private place among a few. Yet some natures are so carried and led away with variety of acquaintance and company that it is a death unto them to live by and to themselves, which indeed is the happiest life of all and hath ever been most contenting and pleasing to the best and wisest men.

Now our most populous places are cities, and among us London . . . the city whither all sorts reside, noble and simple, rich and poor, young and old, from all places and countries, either for pleasure (and let me add besides, to save the charge of housekeeping in the country); or for profit, as lawyers to the terms, countrymen and women to Smithfield and the markets; or for necessity, as poor young men and maids to seek services and places, servingmen, masters; and some others, all manner of employment.

Now the city being like a vast sea full of gusts, fearful dangerous shelves and rocks, ready at every storm to sink and cast away the weak and unexperienced bark with her fresh-water soldiers, as wanting her compass and her skilful pilot, myself, like another Columbus or Drake, acquainted with her rough entertainment and storms have drawn you this chart or map for your guide as well out of mine own as my many friends' experiences.

Who therefore soever shall have occasion to come to the city for the occasions before mentioned, the first thing he is to do is to arm himself with patience and to think that he is entered into a wood where there is as many briers as people, everyone as ready to catch hold of your fleece as yourself . . . so imagine a populous city could not live nor subsist (like the stomach) except it have help and nourishment from the other parts and members. Therefore the first rule I give you, next to the due observation of God and the Sabbath and at other times, is the choice of your company and acquaintance. For according to that every man finds his own valuation high or low. That is, we are esteemed to be such as we keep company withal, as well in estate as condition. If you cannot find such fitting for you, apply yourself to your friends, if you have any, or the friends of your friend. If you have not them either (I speak to the meaner and more inferior), be sure that you take your lodging at least in some honest house of credit, whether it be inn, alehouse, or other private house, which I could rather wish because in the other the multiplicity of resort and company of all sorts will draw you to much needless and vain expense, as in pots of beer or ale, tobacco, perhaps cards, dice, the shovelboard table etc.

But first of all have an eye to, and a care of, your main business or the end of your coming to town; as it were, at what mark you would shoot your arrow;

which being thoroughly considered, for your purse sake pursue it with all expedition. For the city is like a quicksand: the longer you stand upon it, the deeper you sink, if here money or means to get it be wanting.

But imagine you have money of your own, and come here only for your pleasure, as being tired and weary of your country. If you husband it not thriftily you may quickly take a nap upon penniless-bench: so many are the occasions here offered that are ready every hour to pick your purse: as perpetual visits of vain and useless acquaintance; necessitous persons ever upon borrowing hand with you; clothes in the fashion; this or that new play; play at ordinaries; tavern feasts and meetings; horse and coach hire, beside those brittle commodities they carry; boat hire to Kingston, Windsor and other places; with the like. For an antidote to these several poisons, let me prescribe to my city-country gentlemen these receipts or remedies.

First, being come to the city, avoid idleness, which commonly draws after a train of many vices. I call idleness keeping your chamber, consuming the day lying in bed; or, risen, in walking up and down from street to street, to this or that gentleman's chamber, having no business at all, and cannot meet with useful company. Let the Bible and other books of piety such as treat of philosophy, natural or moral, history, the mathematics, as arithmetic, geometry, music, sometimes heraldry, and the like, be your chief company. For you shall find books no flatterers, nor expensive in your converse with them. Besides, you shall meet with those who can instruct you in all those arts which Tully calls *venales*, which are taught for money, as the mathematics themselves, dancing, fencing, riding, painting and the like.

Next, have a care of saving and improving your money to the best, as who would bespeak a supper or a dinner at all adventure at a tavern, and not know the price of every dish, as the Italians and other nations do, while they laugh at our English for their vain profuseness and simplicity, who, when the dinner is ended, must stand to the courtesy of a nimble-tongued drawer or a many-ringed whistling mistress, whether they or you should be masters of your money. Besides, one dish, well-dressed, gives a good stomach more and better content than a variety of twenty.

And above all things beware of beastly drunkenness. . . . Drinking begets challenges and quarrels, and occasioneth the death of many, as is known by almost daily experience. Hence are Newgate, the Counters and other prisons filled with our young heirs and swaggering gallants, to the sorrow of their friends and joy of their gaolers. . . . There is less danger in outdoor recreations then, as shooting, bowls, riding, tennis etc.

Next, let every man beware of play and gaming, as cards, especially dice, at ordinaries and other places: for in the city there are many who, when they live only by cheating, are so cunning that they will so strip a young heir or novice but lately come to town, and woodcock-like so pull his wings that he shall in a short time never be able to fly over ten acres of his own land.

These and the like errors are the cause why so many fair estates, being near or not very far from the city have been so often bought and sold. And the truth is, very few have held out in a name to the third generation.

Let a moneyed man or gentleman especially beware in the city . . . your silken and gold-laced harlots [are] everywhere, especially in the suburbs to be found. These have been and are daily the ruin of thousands. And if they happen to allure and entice him, which is only to cheat him and pick his pocket to boot, with the bargain she makes . . .

Let him also in the city have a special care whom he entertains into his service. Let him or they have friends of acquaintance who may undertake for them, but not at all adventure every straggler. What says old Tusser in his book of good husbandry?

> Take runagate Robin to pity his need,
> And look to be filched as sure as thy creed.

And if you bring one with you out of the country, except you have a great eye over him, he will quickly be corrupted in the city with much acquaintance. Then shall you help yourself to bed; see your horse starved in the stable and never rubbed; your linen lost at the laundresses; in a word, yourself everywhere neglected. Think it therefore no disgrace in a city inn to see your horse everyday yourself, and to see him well meated, rubbed and watered. He shall make you amends in your journey: . . . the master's eye makes the horse fat. Besides, remember what Solomon saith: 'the righteous man regardeth the life of his beast, but the ungodly have cruel hearts'. I saw, I remember, a carrier flay his horse alive, being able to go on the way no further, his too heavy burden having broken his back, insomuch that he tumbled raw in his own skin.

Next let the gentleman living in the city have a care to keep himself out of debt. Let him owe as little as he can to his tailor for following the fashion, than which there can be no greater misery. For then if he walks abroad he is ready to be snapped up at every lane's end by sergeants, marshall's men or bailies,[12] or, keeping his chamber, let him stir never so little, be betrayed by some false knave or other. In the meantime his creditors if they be of the inferior sort, nay, their scolding and clamorous wives and every saucy apprentice will be ready to disgrace him. And if arrested he shall be hailed to prison many times like a dog if he returns but the least ill word. If he be a landed man, let him take heed of usurers and their factors of whom he shall find as much mercy in cities as an oxcheek from a butcher's cur . . .

. . . Walking abroad take heed with what company you sort yourself withal. If you are a countryman, and but newly come to town, you will be smelt out by some cheaters or other, who will salute, call you by your name, which perhaps one of their company meeting you in another street, hath learned, by way of mistaking you for another man, which is an old trick, carry you to a tavern, saying they are akin to someone dwelling near you etc. But all tricks of late years have been so plainly discovered and are so generally known almost to every child that their practice is out of date and now no great fear of them . . .

Now for such as are of the poorest condition and come to the city, compelled by necessity to try their fortunes, to seek services or other means to live. Let them presently provide themselves, if they can (for here is employment for all hands that will work), or return home again before they find or feel the extremity of want. Here are more occasions to draw them into ill courses than there, as being constrained to steal and to shorten their days; to seek death in the error of their lives, as Solomon saith; young maids, who never knew ill in their lives, to be enticed by impudent bawds to turn common whores; and the like. But if they can provide themselves and take honest courses, by the blessing of God they may come to as great preferment as aldermen and aldermen's wives. For poverty of itself is no vice, but by accident. Whom hath the city more advanced than poor men's children? The city itself being the most charitable place of the whole, and having done more good deeds than half the land beside. In a word, for a conclusion, let me give all comers, not only to London, but all other populous places, this only rule, never to be forgotten, which is: to serve God, avoid idleness, to keep your money and to beware of ill company.

4

EDUCATION

INTRODUCTION

The European humanist movement, with its twin emphasis on scholarship and service to a powerful State, with an educational philosophy of renewing classical Latin, reviving ancient texts, and rigorous learning alongside peda-gogic and ethical aims of preparing boys for public service, reached England in the late fifteenth century. The curriculum by which humanist educational aims were realised was based on studies of classical (mostly Ciceronian) texts, which inculcated and developed the humanist ideal combination of wisdom and eloquence. Colet and Erasmus, for example, founded St. Paul's School in 1510, the first grammar school endowed with a specifically humanist charter. Its statutes emphasise the combination of classical and Christian aims which grammar schools of the period shared:

> I would there were always taught good literature, both Latin and Greek, and good authors such as have the very Roman eloquence joined with wisdom, specially Christian authors that wrote with wisdom and clean and chaste Latin, either in verse or prose for my intent is by this school specially to increase knowledge and worshipping of God.

Grammar schools were endowed and founded during this period with remarkable frequency: 281 between 1558 and 1642; and £220,600 was spent on endowments in the first forty years of the seventeenth century.[1] This expansion, together with the concomitant growth of the two universities (from about 400 pupils in 1550, to over 1,000 in 1630, a participation rate of about 2.5 per cent)[2] is evidence of a learning society. Laurence Stone has claimed that these kinds of figures constituted an 'educational revolution': the continuation of a historiographical tradition which linked the advent of printing and humanism with the cultural renaissance, the Reformation and a growing middle class.[3]

Whilst there is intrinsically nothing flawed about this argument, it does not address several important issues, many relating to the interpretation of evidence. First, student numbers fell in universities after 1660, suggesting that the attraction of education had been something of an elite fad. Second, university records prior to the mid sixteenth century were not kept regularly, and growth after 1550 does not tell us about the numbers of students in 1500 or 1450: more accurate record keeping and standardisation can easily be misread as proof of a change in provision. Third, the curriculum actually became more conservative, or at least was unable to respond to demands for a more utilitarian curriculum, with its rigid emphasis on Latin, Greek and Hebrew (see Bacon, Milton, Webster, for example). Fourth, we have no accurate numbers for schools which were not endowed because they generally did not need to keep records. There were other schools available: 'petty' schools which taught both boys and girls to read and write in English; and writing schools, which took boys after they learned to read at 7 or 8 (for example see Ascham and Hoole), but the picture we have of these schools is always anecdotal.[4] Fifth, we know very little about the standard of teaching and learning during the period: much of the evidence cited by educational theorists of the period, such as Ascham, Bacon or Milton, suggests a more brutalised scholarly regime than the godly and classical ideals expressed in school statutes can tell. Sixth, we need to test Stone's model against literacy figures and figures on the social status of educational participation. And seventh, the education of women and girls was treated as of a different order to that of boys and men. These last two points need some further elaboration.

The use of literacy figures must be approached with some caution: where men and women could sign their names, this does not mean that they could read, say, the Bible. However, there is evidence that reading was taught before writing, in which case indicators of signing ability may underestimate the literacy level.[5] It is also probably true to argue that reading was more important in this society than writing: the ability to read apprenticeship documents or manorial rolls in a legal dispute, for example, or to read the Bible for personal salvation and illumination, were more important than the ability to write out one's own documents or keep a private spiritual autobiography.[6] With these provisos in mind, David Cressy has assembled evidence from 6,000 signatures in ecclesiastical courts from 1530 until 1750, and used statistical models to extrapolate from that: he found a rising literacy rate from 20 per cent of men (and 5 per cent of women) in 1550, to 30 per cent and 10 per cent respectively in 1650, and 45 per cent and 25 per cent in 1715. These overall figures, however, mask where the literacy rise occurs, both in terms of geography and status. Thus, for example, nearly all the gentry were literate by 1550; but only 40 per cent of the yeomanry; 20 per cent of tradesmen; and between 10 and 20 per cent of husbandmen. Figures for these first two social groups had grown to 60 per cent and 50 per cent respectively by 1715, whilst those for husbandmen remained static. In addition, although London and major towns had a high literacy rate, other geographical indices show no precise or regular link between economic development and literacy levels.[7] The picture, then, from these figures, is one of some polarisation between men and women; and between the gentry and middling sort, and the illiterate poor. However, as I have suggested, there is supplementary evidence which mitigates this stark picture. Thus, for example, the figures for the sale and production of popular texts such as almanacs and chap books, show us an avid reading populace:[8] around 400,000 almanacs were sold annually, about one copy for every twelve members of the population.[9] In addition Bible ownership was widespread.[10] The cultural incentives to read were many: not just economic need and Protestant religious enthusiasm, but social reassurance, a desire for self-improvement and illumination, and a search for good entertainment. Contemporary commentators remarked upon the increase in literacy and education: usually associating increased literacy with increased disorder. Thus, the Duke of Newcastle wrote to Charles II in 1660 advising him that educational deprivation amongst his subjects would ensure obedience:

The Bible in English under every weaver's and chambermaid's arms hath done us much hurt. That which made it one way is the universities, abounds with too many scholars. Therefore if every college had but half the number, they would be better fed and as well taught. But that which hath done us most hurt is the abundance of grammar schools and Inns of court. . . . And there are so many schools now, as most read. So indeed there should be, but such a proportion as to serve the church and moderately the law and merchants, and the rest for the labour, for else they run out to idle and unnecessary people that becomes a factious burden to the commonwealth. For when most was unlettered, it was much a better world both for peace and war.

(J. Thirsk, ed. *The Restoration*, Longman 1976, 170–1)

The belief that education was a force for social and political change on the one hand, or a force for entrenched conservativism on the other also informed much of the scientific and radical writing of the period of the interregnum.[11]

This perception of the dangerous nature of educational development informed society's views on the education of both the labouring poor and of women: the humanist revolution was very specifically gendered. Whilst many grammar schools developed statutes specifically offering scholarships to the sons of poor craftsmen, husbandmen, to orphans and those receiving parish relief,[12] at the same time they began specifically to exclude girls from entrance, either in the form of a total ban, or from the age of nine.[13] Additionally, as we can see in Mulcaster (4.5), the curriculum for

217

girls was limited to their perceived social function of mother and wife, unless birth had ordained an exceptional role: such as that of Queen. Even the high profile women educated by and associated with prominent English humanists, such as Margaret More or Lady Ann Cooke, expressed their learning through the conventional feminine codes of the period of chastity, obedience and silence. Thus their work consisted in translating rather than writing native English fiction; focusing on religious works; and was published (where they did publish) anonymously or through their husbands. This situation only began to change towards the end of the early modern period (see 4.14).

Educational philosophy and practice, then, may be said to have matched the concept of 'fitness for purpose', where purpose was defined exactly by social status. The deferential society, as described in part 3, was maintained and perpetuated through the educational system, allowing some movement into the gentry class (as Thomas Smith says in 3.9), through education. Yet, if anything, the social composition of universities and grammar schools became more narrow as the early modern period drew to a close. Thus, for example, Westminster School, St. Paul's and Eton became the preserve of the rich gentry; and although in the late sixteenth century over 50 per cent of students at Oxford and Cambridge were classified as 'plebeian',[14] this proportion had fallen to 32 per cent a hundred years later, as university education became socially fashionable, and a means of making useful social and political alliances.

Finally, although educational discourse emphasises the need for an educated society, its focus was not on the needs of the seventeenth-century economy and polis: but on fifth-century Athens or republican and imperial Rome. Wherever curriculum reform was mooted, for example by Humphreys, Bacon or Comenius, it was not taken up either by the State or by individual schools, until the end of the seventeenth century. Thomas Gresham left money in his will for the establishing of Gresham's College in London, which aimed to teach practical subjects such as physics, astronomy, mathematics and navigation.[15] These subjects were only available at Oxford and Cambridge through extra-curricula instruction,[16] although professorships in geometry, astronomy, anatomy and natural philosophy were established at Oxford in 1619 under the pressure of men associated with Gresham's such as Henry Briggs and William Oughtred.

Thus the 'educational revolution', if it did occur, was not one sanctioned by either the State or the majority of the elite: what we see during this period is the establishment of a grammar school culture which, whatever its origins, eventually became both socially, politically and intellectually elitist and explicitly non-utilitarian. The absence of a well-regarded technical school tradition and the tendency towards 'academic drift' is lamented here in Dell and Webster (4.11, 4.12). This has been a constant theme in educational writing ever since.

4.1 **THOMAS ELYOT, *THE GOVERNOR***

Elyot's text was the quintessential humanist tract on education, and its place in social life: thus, despite its early date, it was frequently cited and used during the whole sixteenth century. See 2.1 for a description of the political and textual background. Text from: first edition, 1531, chapters 4, 5, 10.

Forasmuch as all noble authors do conclude and also common experience proveth that where the governors of realms and cities be founden adorned with virtues, and do employ their study and mind to the public weal, as well to the augmentation thereof as to the establishing and long continuance of the same: there a public weal must needs be both honourable and wealthy. To the intent that I will declare how such personages may be prepared, I will use the policy of a wise and cunning gardener, who purposing to have in his garden a fine and precious herb, that should be to him and all other repairing thereto, excellently commodious or pleasant, he will first search throughout his garden where he can find the most mellow and fertile earth, and therein will he put the seed of the herb to grow and be nourished; and in most diligent wise attend that no weed be suffered to grow or approach nigh unto it; and to the intent it may thrive the faster, as soon as the form of an herb once appeareth, he will set a vessel of water by it, in such wise that it may continually distil on the root sweet drops; and as it springeth in stalk, under set it with some thing that it break not, and alway keep it clean from weeds. Semblable order will I ensue in the forming the gentle wits of noblemen's children, who, from the wombs of their mother shall be made . . . apt to the governance of a public weal.

First, they unto whom the bringing up of such children apperteineth ought again the time their mother shall be of them delivered, to be sure of a nurse which should be of no servile condition or vice notable. For as some ancient writers do suppose oftentimes the child sucketh the vice of his nurse with the milk of her pap. And also observe that she be of mature or ripe age, not under twenty years, or above thirty, her body also being clean from all sickness or deformity, and having her complexion most of the right and pure sanguine. Forasmuch as the milk thereof coming excelleth all other, both in sweetness and substance. Moreover to the nurse should be appointed another woman of approved virtue, discretion and gravity who shall not suffer in the child's presence, to be showed any act or tache[1] dishonest, or any wanton or unclean word to be spoken; and for that cause all men, except physicians only, should be excluded and kept out of the nursery. Perchance some will scorn me for that I am so serious, saying that there is no such damage to be feared in an infant, who for tenderness of years hath not the understanding to discern good from evil. And yet no man will deny but in that innocency he will discern milk from butter, and bread from pap, and ere he can speak he will with his hand or countenance signify which he desireth. And I verily do suppose that in the brains and hearts of children which be members spiritual, whiles they be tender, and the little slips of reason begin in them to burgeon, there may hap by evil custom some pestiferous dew of vice to pierce the said members . . .

. . . Wherefore not only princes, but also all other children, from their nurses' paps are to be kept diligently from the hearing or seeing any vice or evil tache. And incontinent as soon as they can speak, it behoveth with most pleasant allurings to instil in them sweet manners and virtuous custom. Also to provide for them such companions and playfellows, which shall not do in his presence any reproachable act or speak any unclean word or oath, nor to advance him with flattery, remembering his nobility, or any other like thing wherein he might glory, unless it be to persuade him to virtue, or to withdraw him from vice, in the remembering to him the danger of his evil example. For noble men more grievously offend by their example than by their deed. Yet often remembrance to them of their estate may happen to radicate[2] in their hearts intolerable pride, the most dangerous poison to nobleness: wherefore there is required to be therein much cautel[3] and soberness.

The order of learning that a nobleman should be trained in before he come to the age of seven years

Some old authors hold opinion that before the age of seven years a child should not be instructed in letters, but those writers were either Greeks or Latins, among whom all doctrine and sciences were in their maternal tongues; by reason whereof they saved all that long time which at this days is spent in understanding perfectly the Greek or Latin. Wherefore it requireth now a longer time to the understanding of both. Therefore that infelicity of our time and country compelleth us to encroach somewhat upon the years of children, and specially of noblemen, that they may sooner attain to wisdom and gravity than private persons, considering as I have said, their charge and example, which above all things is most to be esteemed. Notwithstanding, I would not have them enforced by violence to learn, but according to the counsel of Quintilian to be sweetly allured thereto with praises and such pretty gifts as children delight in. And their first letters to be painted or limned[4] in a pleasant manner, wherein children of gentle courage have much delectation. And also there is no better elective to noble wits than to induce them into a contention with inferior companions, they sometime purposely suffering the more noble children to vanquish and as it were, giving to them place and sovereignty, though indeed the inferior children have more learning. But there can be nothing more convenient than by little and little to train and exercise them in speaking of Latin: informing them to know first the names in Latin of all things that cometh in sight; and to name all the parts of their bodies; and giving them somewhat that they covet or desire, in most gentle manner to teach them to ask it again in Latin. And if by this means they may be induced to understand and speak Latin, it shall afterward be less grief to them in a manner, to learn anything, where they understand the language wherein it is written. And as touching grammar, there is at this day better introductions and more facile than ever before were made, concerning as well Greek as Latin, if they be wisely chosen. And it shall be no reproach to a nobleman to instruct his own children, or at the least ways to examine them, by the way of dalliance or solace, considering that the emperor Octavius Augustus disdained not to read the works of Cicero and Virgil to his children and nephews. And why should not noblemen rather so do than teach their children how at dice and cards they may cunningly lose and consume their own treasure and substance? Moreover teaching representeth the authority of a prince. . . . It shall be expedient that a nobleman's son, in his infancy, have with him continually only such as may accustom him by little and little to speak pure and elegant Latin. Semblably, the nurses and other women about him, if it be possible, to do the same; or at the least way, that they speak none English but that which is clean, polite, perfectly and articulately pronounced, omitting no letter or syllable, as foolish women oftentimes do of a wantonness, whereby divers noblemen and gentlemen's children (as I do at this day know) have attained corrupt and foul pronunciation . . .

After that a child is come to seven years of age, I hold it expedient that he be taken from the company of women; saving that he may have, one year or two at the most, an ancient and sad matron, attending on him in his chamber, which shall not have any young women in her company. For, though there be no peril of offence in that tender and innocent age, yet in some children, nature is more prone to vice than to virtue, and in the tender wits be sparks of voluptuosity, which, nourished by any occasion or object, increase oftentimes into so terrible a fire that therewith all virtue and reason is consumed. Wherefore to eschew that danger, the most sure counsel is to withdraw him from all company of women, and to assign unto him a tutor which should be an ancient and worshipful man, in whom is approved to be much gentleness, mixed with gravity, and as nigh as can be, such one as the child, by imitation following, may grow to be excellent. And if he be also learned, he is the more commendable . . .

The office of a tutor is first to know the nature of his pupil, that is to say, whereto he is most inclined or disposed, and in what thing he setteth his most delectation or appetite.

* * *

What order should be in learning, and which authors should be first read

Now let us return to the order of learning apt for a gentleman. Wherein I am of the opinion of Quintilian that I would have him learn Greek and Latin authors both at one time; or else to begin with Greek, forasmuch as that it is hardest to come by: by reason of the diversity of tongues which be five in number; and all must be known or else uneth any poet can be well understand. And if a child do begin therein at seven years of age, he may continually learn Greek authors three years, and in the meantime use the Latin tongue as a familiar language, which in a nobleman's son may well come to pass, having none other persons to serve him or keeping him company, but such as can speak Latin elegantly. And what doubt is there but so may he as soon speak good Latin as he may do pure French . . .

Grammar being but an introduction to the understanding of authors, if it be made too long or exquisite to the learner, it in a manner mortifieth his courage; and by that time he cometh to the most sweet and pleasant reading of old authors, the sparks of fervent desire of learning is extinct with the burden of grammar, like as a little fire is soon quenched with a great heap of small sticks: so that it can never come to the principal logs where it should long burn in a great pleasant fire.

Now to follow my purpose: after a few and quick rules of grammar, immediately or interlacing it therewith, would be read to the child, Aesop's fables in Greek; in which argument children much do delight. And surely it is a much pleasant lesson, and also profitable, as well for that it is elegant and brief (and notwithstanding it hath much variety in words and therewith much helpeth to the understanding of Greek) as also in those fables is included much moral and politic wisdom . . .

The next lesson would be some quick and merry dialogues, elect out of Lucian, which be without ribaldry or too much scorning, for either of them is exactly to be eschewed, specially for a nobleman, the one annoying the soul, the other his estimation concerning his gravity. The comedies of Aristophanes may be in the place of Lucian . . .

I could rehearse divers other poets which for matter and eloquence be very necessary, but I fear me to be too long from noble Homer, from whom as from a fountain proceeded all eloquence and learning. For in his books be contained and most perfectly expressed, not only the documents martial and discipline of arms, but also incomparable wisdoms and instructions for politic governance of people; with the worthy commendation and laud of noble princes, wherewith the readers shall be so all inflamed that they most fervently shall desire and covet by the imitation of their virtues, to acquire semblable glory. For the which occasion, Aristotle, most sharpest witted and excellent learned philosopher, as soon as he had received Alexander from King Philip his father, he before any other thing taught him the most noble works of Homer . . .

Finally (as I have said) this noble Virgil, like to a good nurse, giveth to a child, if he will take it, everything apt for his wit and capacity: wherefore he is in the order of learning to be preferred before any other author Latin. I would set next unto him two books of Ovid, the one called *Metamorphoses*, which is as much to say as, changing of men into other figure or form; the other is entitled, *De Fastis*, where the ceremonies of the gentiles and specially the Romans, be expressed: both right necessary for the understanding of other poets. . . . Wherefore in this place, let us bring in Horace, in whom is contained much variety of learning and quickness of sentence.

This poet may be interlaced with the lesson of *Odysseus* of Homer, wherein is declared the wonderful prudence and fortitude of Ulysses in his passage from Troy. And if the child were induced to make verses by the imitation of Virgil and Homer, it should minister to him much delectation and courage to study: nor the making of verses is not discommended in a noble man: since the noble Augustus and almost all the old emperors made books in verse.

The two noble poets Silius and Lucan, be very expedient to be learned: for the one setteth out the emulation in qualities and prowess of two noble and valiant captains . . .

Hesiodus, in Greek, is more brief than Virgil where he writeth of husbandry, and doth not rise so high in philosophy, but is fuller of fables, and therefore is more illecebrous.[5]

And here I conclude to speak of any more of poets, necessary for the childhood of a gentleman: forasmuch as these, I doubt not, will suffice until he pass the age of thirteen years. In which time childhood declineth, and reason waxeth ripe, and deprehendeth things with a more constant judgement. Here I would should be remembered that I require not that all these works should be thoroughly read of a child in this time, which were almost impossible. But I only desire that they have, in every of the said books, so much instruction that they may take thereby some profit.

Then the child's courage, inflamed by the frequent reading of noble poets, daily more and more desireth to have experience in those things that they so vehemently do commend in them, that they write of . . .

And when a man is comen to mature years, and that reason in him is confirmed with serious learning and long experience, then shall he, in reading tragedies, execrate and abhor the intolerable life of tyrants . . .

The most commodious and necessary studies succeeding ordinarily the lesson of poets

After that fourteen years be passed of a child's age, his master, if he can, or some other, studiously exercised in the art of an orator, shall first read to him somewhat of that part of logic that is called *Topica*, either of Cicero or else of that noble clerk of Almayne, which late flowered called Agricola: whose work prepareth invention, telling the places from whence an argument for the proof of any matter may be taken with little study; and that lesson with much and diligent learning, having mixed therewith none other exercise, will in the space of half a year be perfectly kenned. Immediately after that, the art of Rhetoric would be semblably taught, either in Greek out of Hermogenes, or of Quintilian in Latin . . .

Isocrates, concerning the lessons of orators is everywhere wonderful profitable, having almost as many wise sentences as he hath words: and with that is so sweet and delectable to read that after him, almost all other seem unsavoury and tedious; and in persuading as well a prince as a private person to virtue . . .

Demosthenes and Tully, by the consent of all learned men have preeminence and sovereignty over all orators; the one reigning in wonderful eloquence in the public weal of the Romans, which had empire and dominion of all the world; the other of no less estimation in the city of Athens, which of long time was accounted the mother of sapience, and the palace of muses and all liberal sciences. Of which two orators may be attained not only eloquence, excellent and perfect, but also precepts of wisdom and gentle manners: with most commodious examples of all noble virtues and policy. Wherefore the master, in reading them, must well observe and express the parts and colours of rhetoric in them contained, according to the respects of that art before learned.

The utility that a nobleman shall have by reading these orators is that when he shall hap to reason in council or shall speak in a great audience, or to strange ambassadors of great princes, he shall not be constrained to speak words sudden and disordered, but shall bestow them aptly and in their places . . .

Also to prepare the child to understanding of histories, which, being replenished with the names of countries and towns unknown to the reader, do make the history tedious or else the less pleasant, so if they be in any wise known, it increaseth an inexplicable delectation. It shall be therefore, and also for refreshing the wit, a convenient lesson to behold the old tables of Ptolemy wherein all the world is painted, having first some introduction into the sphere, whereof now of late be made very good treatises and more plain and easy to learn than was wont to be.

Albeit there is none so good learning as the demonstration of cosmography by material figures and instruments, having a good instructor. And surely this lesson is both pleasant and necessary. For what pleasure is it in one hour to behold those realms, cities, seas, rivers and mountains that uneth in an old man's life cannot be journeyed and pursued; what incredible delight is taken in beholding the diversities of people, beasts, fowls, fishes, trees, fruits and herbs; to know the sundry manners and conditions of people . . .

Surely if a nobleman do thus seriously and diligently read histories, I dare affirm there is no study or science for him of equal commodity and pleasure, having regard to every time and age.

By the time that the child do come to seventeen years of age, to the intent his courage be bridled with reason, it were needful to read unto him, some works of philosophy, specially that part that may inform him unto virtuous manners, which part of philosophy is called moral. Wherefore there would be read to him, for an introduction, two the first books of the work of Aristotle called *Ethicae*, wherein is contained the definitions and proper significations of every virtue; and that to be learned in Greek, for the translations that we yet have be but a rude and gross shadow of the eloquence and wisdom of Aristotle. Forthwith would follow the work of Cicero called in Latin *De Officiis*, whereunto yet is no proper English word to be given: but to provide for it some manner of exposition, it may be said in this form: 'of the duties and manners appertaining to men'. But above all other, the works of Plato would be most studiously read when the judgement of man is come to perfection, and by the other studies is instructed in the form of speaking that philosophers used. Lord God, what incomparable sweetness of words and matter shall he find in the said works of Plato and Cicero, wherein is joined gravity with delectation, excellent wisdom with divine eloquence, absolute virtue with pleasure incredible, and every place is so enforced with profitable counsel, joined with honesty, that those three books be almost sufficient to make a perfect and excellent governor. The proverbs of Solomon with the books of Ecclesiastes and Ecclesiasticus be very good lessons.

4.2 THOMAS HOBY 'PREFACE' TO *THE COURTIER*

Hoby's translation of *The Courtier* brought the already renowned and influential Castiglione home to an eager English audience for several generations after its publication in English in 1561: his aim was the education of young men into the modes and manners of courtiership (see also 3.4). Text from: preface to first edition, 1561.

To the right honourable the Lord Henry Hastings, son and heir apparent to the noble Earl of Huntington

. . . To princes and great men it [*The Courtier*] is a rule to rule themselves, that rule others, and one of the books that a noble philosopher exhorted a certain king to provide him, and diligently to search for in them he should find written such matters, that friends durst not utter unto kings; to men grown in years, a pathway to the beholding and musing of the mind, and to whatsoever else is meet for that age; to young gentlemen, an encouraging to garnish their minds with moral virtues and their bodies with comely exercises, and both the one and the other with honest qualities to attain unto their noble end; to ladies and gentlewomen, a mirror to deck and trim themselves with virtuous conditions, comely behaviours and honest entertainment toward all men; and to them all in general, a storehouse of most necessary implements for the conversation, use, and training up of man's life with courtly demeanours. Were it not that the ancientness of time, the degree of a consul, and the eloquence of Latin style in these our days bear a great stroke, I know not wither in the invention and disposition of the matter, as Castilio hath followed Cicero, and applied to his purpose sundry examples and pithy sentences out of him, so he may in feat conveyance and like trade of writing, be compared to him. But well I wot, for renown among the Italians, he is not inferior to him. Cicero an excellent orator, in three books of an Orator unto his brother, fashioneth such a one as never was, nor yet is like to be. Castilio, an excellent courtier, in three books of a Courtier, unto his dear friend, fashioneth such a one as is hard to find and perhaps unpossible. . . . Both Cicero and Castilio profess they follow not any certain appointed order of precepts or rules, as is used in the instruction of youth, but call to rehearsal matters debated in their times to and fro in the disputation of most eloquent men and excellent wits in every worthy quality, the one company in the old time assembled in Tusculane, and the other of late years in the new palace of Urbino. . . . In this point (I know not by what destiny) Englishmen are much inferior to most of all other nations. For where they set their delight and bend themselves with an honest strife of matching others to turn into their mother tongue, not only the witty writings of other languages, but also of all the philosophers and all sciences, both Greek and Latin, our men ween it sufficient to have a perfect knowledge, to no other end but to profit themselves, and (as it were) after much pains in breaking up a gap, bestow no less to close it up again, that others may with like travail follow after. And where our learned men for the most part hold opinion to have the sciences in the mother tongue hurteth memory and hindereth learning, in my opinion they do full ill consider from whence the Grecians first and afterward the Latins set their knowledge. And without wading to any further reasons that might be alleged, if they will mark well the truth, they shall see at this day where the sciences are most turned into the vulgar tongue, there are best learned men. . . . So that to be skilful and exercised in authors translated is no less to be called learning than is the very same in the Latin or Greek tongue. Therefore the translation of Latin or Greek authors doth not only not hinder learning, but furthereth it, yea, it is learning itself, and a great stay to youth, and the noble end to which they ought to apply their wits, that with diligence and study have attained a perfect understanding, to open a gap for others to follow their steps; and a virtuous exercise for the unlatined to come by learning and to fill their mind with the moral virtues and their bodies with civil conditions; that they may both talk freely in all company, live uprightly, though there were no laws, and be in a readiness against all kind of worldly chances that happen, which is the profit that cometh of Philosophy. And he said well that was asked the question: how much the learned differed from the unlearned: 'so much' (quoth he) 'as the well broken and ready horses, from the unbroken'. Wherefore I wot not how our learned men in this case can avoid the saying of Isocrates, to one that among sundry learned discourses at table never spake a word: 'if thou be unlearned thou doest wisely: but if thou be learned, unwisely'. As who should say, learning is ill bestowed where others be not profited by it. As I therefore have to my small skill bestowed some labour about this piece of work, even so could I wish with all my heart, profound learned men in the Greek and Latin should make the like proof and every man store the tongue according to his knowledge and delight above other men, in some piece of learning, that we alone of the world may not be still counted barbarous in our tongue as in time out of mind we have been in our manners. And so shall we perchance in time become as famous in England, as the learned men of other nations have been and presently are.

4.3 THOMAS BECON, *THE CATECHISM*

Becon's *Catechism* was both comprehensive and popular, covering almost

any social, political, educational or theological duty and issue of the day.
Text from: *Works*, 1561, fos 517^r–523^r; 538^r–542^v.

Of the office and duty of fathers and mothers toward their children

First of all, whosoever intendeth to have good, godly and virtuous children, and
the continuance of them and of their posterity upon the earth, it is necessary
that he be wary and circumspect in choosing his wife, and also in ordering his
own life. And forasmuch as the man is the principal part, it shall be expedient
that he himself live in the fear of God, and garnish his life with all kind of godly
virtues, that he may be an example of godliness and honesty to so many as are
under him . . .

Secondly, when God hath blessed Christian parents with children, the father
shall provide that the infants in convenient time and place be consecrated to God
by holy baptism and offered to God by fervent prayer; at the which time and
place, it is the duty of a godly father to be present and diligently to note what is
there promised for the children, both by him and by other, that he may train and
bring them up according to the vow and promise there made.

Thirdly, it is the duty of a good and natural mother not to put forth her children to other women to be nourished, fostered and brought up with strange
milk, except very necessity compel her; but to nurse them herself, yea, and that
with her own milk . . .

Fourthly, in the time of nursing the infants, the father and mother must provide
that no bodily harm chance to the children, either by fire, water, overlaying or
otherwise, but that they be kept warily and diligently, both by night and day . . .

Fifthly, when the little children begin to learn to speak, the parents must diligently take heed that neither they themselves nor any other by the reason of
niceness or wantonness learn them to stammer, to lisp, and to pronounce their
words by halves; but let them teach their young ones to speak plainly and
distinctly, and to utter every word and syllable truly and perfectly. . . . So soon as
the children be able to speak plainly, let them even from their cradles be taught
to utter, not vain, foolish and wanton, but grave, sober and godly words: as God,
Jesus Christ, faith, love, hope, patience, goodness, peace etc. And when they be
able to pronounce whole sentences, let the parents teach their children such
sentences as may kindle in them a love toward virtue and an hatred against vice
and sin. . . . It shall be profitable to teach them the Lord's Prayer, the articles of
the Christian faith, and the ten commandments, with such other wholesome
doctrine as is contained in the Catechism or principles of Christian religion, that
even from their very young and tender age, they may learn to drink in godliness.
It is also the duty of faithful parents to teach their children to say grace both at
dinner and supper . . .

Sixthly, forasmuch as children be naturally given to play and are desirous of
pastimes, it shall be convenient that such pastimes and plays be devised for them

as may not hurt their tender bodies, nor yet infect the mind with any lewdness. In their pastimes the parents must take heed that one of them hurt not another; again, that they use no swearing, no vain talk nor babbling, but use a certain kind of gravity and modesty, even in the midst of all their most pleasant pastimes and merry conceits, that gravity, sobriety, and modesty may grow up with them even from the very cradles; all lightness, lewdness and wantonness of manners utterly repelled and laid aside.

Seventhly, the parents also must take heed with whom they do accompany their young ones, both in earnest studies and in merry pastimes. For as great profit is to be gotten of company keeping with honest and godly persons, so likewise by keeping fellowship with the wicked and naughty packs, all evils are possessed . . .

Eighthly, it is the duty of godly and Christian parents to teach their children good manners, yea and that even in their very tender age and young years, lest they prove rude and barbarous in their behaviour, and so become savage people and unprofitable members of the Christian commonweal. Let them first of all be taught that whensoever God, Christ or the Holy Ghost be named of them, or of other in their presence, they show some outward reverence, either by putting off their cap, or else by bowing their knee. . . . Let them also be taught to reverence their elders, to rise against them, to make curtsey unto them, to put off their caps, and to give them the way. If any man speak unto them, let them salute them again, and uncover their heads. If any man talk with them, let them stand right up, hold up their heads and look them in the face with a modest and cheerful countenance, mixed with gravity . . .

Ninthly, when the children come to the age of six or seven years, let the parents provide that they be sent to school, yea and that unto such a schoolmaster as feareth God, is learned, well mannered and is able with discretion to judge of the nature and capacity of the children, and so according to the same, to teach, instruct, trade, rule and govern them. But in this education and bringing up of the children in good letters, this must be provided, that the children be not after the common custom of schools, continually nousled[6] in reading and learning heathen and pagan writers, of whom many times is drunken in more wickedness than godliness, more sin than virtue. . . . For those schools wherein nothing is taught but the doctrine of paganism are more meet for the youth of the Turks and of the Saracens and of such other miscreants and castaways, than for the children of the Christians. Neither can I see what great profit can come to a Christian commonweal of such schools . . .

Furthermore, that the children may learn these things the more commodiously, it is the duty of parents to prepare for them not idle and wanton, not vain and trifling books, but wholesome, holy and godly books, as the New Testament of our saviour Christ Jesu; the parables of Solomon; the book of Jesus the son of Syrach, and such like: that they may be trained and brought up in them, and by this means drink in the knowledge of godliness from their young and tender years. It shall profit also very much unto true godliness that the children be brought unto the Church to hear the godly psalms, prayers and chapters that be there read, but specially to hear the sermons and preachings of God's word; and when they come home to require of them an account of such things as they have heard in the Church, but namely concerning the sermon . . .

Tenthly, after the children have consumed certain years in the school of godliness, virtue and learning, it is convenient that the parents do now consider with themselves to what kind of honest and godly exercise they will put their children, that they may be able hereafter to live as good and profitable members of the commonweal, and by their own industry and labour to get their living, yea and to have also whereof to give unto the needy. For God hath appointed no man to be idle in this world, but every man to eat his own bread in the labour of his own hands, and to drink his own drink in the sweat of his own brows. And who knoweth not what a sure patrimony and strong defence against the cruel darts of poverty and beggary, an honest and good occupation is? . . . A man having an occupation shall be able to live, wheresoever he become. Therefore shall it be wisdom for godly parents to determine with themselves betimes how they will bestow their children, that they may be able afterward to live. If any of their children shall be found apt in time to come to be spiritual ministers in the church of God, pastors and preachers; or to be schoolmasters; or magistrates in the public weal; then shall it be convenient that they continue still in their studies and be sent unto some university, where they may exercise themselves in such kind of learning as shall be most meet for that vocation which they intend afterward openly to profess unto the glory of God, and unto the profit of their country. The residue of their children let the parents appoint to some honest and virtuous occupation, that they may be able afterward truly and honestly to live of themselves; and by no means suffer them to live idly . . .

Of the office and duty of schoolmasters

Son   First, forasmuch as the most noble treasures and most precious jewels of the Christian commonweal are committed to a schoolmaster to be kept and preserved in safety, yea, to be kept and preserved in such sort that he may render them home again much more noble, precious and glorious than he received them. . . . It is the office and duty of a good and godly schoolmaster first of all, and above all things, to instil into the minds of the young Christian children true persuasions of God, and of his holy religion according to this commandment of Christ: *first of all seek the kingdom of God, and the righteousness thereof;* that even from their tender infancy and as the proverb is, from the very cradles they may drink in that new sweet wine of Christs' gospel; while they yet are new and sweet bottles, not corrupt with the filthy savours of old Adam, nor made drunken with the poisonful wine of the whore of Babylon, that stinking strumpet and blasphemous bawd; yea, that murthering mother of whoredom and all abominations of the earth, which is guilty of the blood of the prophets and of the saints and of all that are slain upon the earth. And that the schoolmaster may do this thing the more aptly and with the greater fruit, it shall be convenient that he read unto his scholars some godly and learned Catechism, containing the principles or chief points of Christian religion, and that he exercise them in the same daily, diligently searching whether they truly understand the things which they read. If they understand them not, so is it the duty of a good schoolmaster to declare it unto them, and to show them the true understanding of all things, lest they pronounce after the manner of a parrot without any understanding, and profit nothing by their studies . . .

After that the schoolmaster hath diligently exercised his scholars in the doctrine of the Catechism, so that now they understand the principles of Christian religion, it shall greatly profit unto the increase of godly knowledge if he once a day read into them a lesson out of the New Testament of our Saviour Jesus Christ . . . yet forasmuch as tender wits are not to be acumbered with many things, lest they be there dulled, where they ought to be quickened; it shall be good that the schoolmaster do acquaint his scholars principally with these parcels of the New Testament: that is to say, with the Gospel of Saint Matthew and of Saint John, and with those Epistles which Saint Paul wrote to the Romans and to the Galatians. For whoso understandeth these parcels well, he shall easily understand the residue of the New Testament, yea of the whole Bible. For in them is contained whatsoever is taught in the whole Scripture necessary for our salvation . . .

And in these their lessons, as occasion shall serve, let them sometime handle and set forth unto them some common place of the Holy Scripture, as of God, of God's word, of the law, of the gospel, of faith, of charity, of hope, of good works, of our justification by Christ, of baptism, of the Lord's supper, of remission of sins, of the last judgement, of the resurrection, of the everlasting joys of the faithful, of the endless pains of the unfaithful, etc. Likewise let them sometime entreat of some better virtue or of some vice. And in the treatise of virtue, let them declare how acceptable it is to God, and how God in all ages hath blessed them that have practised that virtue in their life and conversation, whether it be humility, modesty, sobriety, concord, peace, patience or any other virtue. Let them allege certain histories concerning that matter out of the Holy Scriptures that the scholars by this means may be the better acquainted with the word of God, and be the sooner brought unto the love and practice of the same virtue. When they shall entreat of any kind of sin, let them paint and set forth the abomination of that sin, how horrible and grievous it is in the sight of God, how pestiferous, noisome and hurtful it is to man, how grievously it hath been plagued and punished in every age, and how the practisers of that sin have always come unto a most miserable end in this world, as they may speak nothing of the intolerable pains which they now suffer. . . . These things shall marvellously kindle and stir up the minds of the scholars, both unto the love of virtue, and also unto the hate of vice, and shall so plant godliness in their young and tender breasts, that as they grow in age so likewise shall they increase in all godliness and virtue, and never depart from it, so long as they live: so greatly doth it profit to be acquainted with good things from the tender years . . .

Moreover forasmuch as the education and bringing up of a child doth either make or mar him, whether it be in religion, doctrine or manners; it shall be necessary that a good and godly schoolmaster enarm the breasts of his scholars against all heresies and wicked opinions with the sound and wholesome doctrine of the Holy Scripture: yea, and that so much the more because this our age is most miserably vexed with divers and sundry damnable sects, as Papists, Anabaptists, Arians, Davidians, Adamites, Libertines, Epicures etc. . . .

Father After that the schoolmaster have diligently planted the religion of Christ in the tender breasts of the children by teaching them the word of God: what is then his duty to do?

Son To teach them good letters, I mean, poets, orators, historiographers, philosophers, etc. Not that they should be mates with God's word, but rather handmaids unto it, and serve to set forth the honour and glory thereof. For unto this end ought all liberal sciences to be studied and learned: even that they might not depress but avaunce the true religion of God. For eloquence without godliness is as a ring in a swine's snout: yea all arts and sciences not coupled with the love of religion are rather instruments of wickedness than of godliness: and as Tully saith, to give to a lewd man eloquence without wisdom is none other thing than to give unto him armours to destroy the commonweal. But in reading these kinds of authors to his disciples, the schoolmaster must diligently take heed that he read those only to his scholars that be most profitable, and contain in them no matter that may either hinder the religion of God, or the innocency of manners. Some writers in many places of their works are wanton and unhonest, as Martial, Catullus, Tibullus, Propertius, Cornelius, Gallus, and such like. Some wicked and ungodly, as Lucian, etc. From the reading of these and such like filthy writers, [it] is convenient that the youth do abstain, lest by the reading of them they make shipwreck both of their faith and manners and in their tender years drink in such corruption as shall be noisome unto them all their life after. For as he saith, *evil words corrupt good manners* [1 Cor. 15]. The very heathen were so wary and circumspect in the virtuous and honest bringing up of their youth that they by no means would suffer the breasts of their children to be infected with the reading of unclean and wanton writers, although never so wise, learned and eloquent. . . . They esteemed eloquence nothing in comparison of virtue and honesty. Eloquence is to be embraced, but not with the loss of virtue. All things ought to give place to virtue, and to innocency of life. Plato that most divine and noble philosopher also expelled all poets out of his commonweal, as persons occupied about vain, false, lying and wanton matters, unworthy to be read of such as tender the advancement of virtue. Was not the poet Ovid banished of Augustus Caesar for the books which he made, *De Arte Amandi?*

4.4 ROGER ASCHAM, *THE SCHOOLMASTER*

Ascham was a Greek scholar, and tutor to Elizabeth I when she was a girl. As with many other humanist scholars, he went on to serve the crown directly, as Latin Secretary to both Mary I and Elizabeth I. His educational curriculum combines classical learning with outdoor sports, in a supportive and non-violent pedagogic framework. Text from: first edition, 1570, pp. 1^r–30^v.

With this way of good understanding the matter, plain construing, diligent parsing, daily translating, cheerful admonishing, and heedful amending of faults; never leaving behind just praise for well doing, I would have the scholar brought up withal . . .

All this while, by mine advice, the child shall use to speak no Latin. . . . For good understanding must first be bred in the child, which being nourished with skill and use of writing (as I will teach more largely hereafter) is the only way to bring him to judgement and readiness in speaking: and that in far shorter time (if he follow constantly the trade of this little lesson) than he shall do by common teaching of the common schools in England . . .

I do gladly agree with all good schoolmasters in these points: to have children brought to good perfectness in learning; to all honesty in manners; to have all faults rightly amended; to have every vice severely corrected; but for the order and way that leadeth rightly to these points, we somewhat differ. For commonly many schoolmasters, some as I have seen, more as I have heard tell, be of so crooked a nature as when they meet with a hard-witted scholar, they rather break him than bow him, rather mar him than mend him. For when the school-master is angry with some other matter, then will he soonest fall to beat his scholar, and though he himself should be punished for his folly, yet he must beat some scholar for his pleasure: though there be no cause for him to do so, nor yet fault in the scholar to deserve so . . .

Socrates, whose judgement in Plato [7 *De Republica*] is plainly this in these words . . . in English thus: *no learning ought to be learned with bondage*. For bodily labours, wrought by compulsion, hurts not the body: but any learning learned by compulsion tarrieth not long in the mind. . . . Fond schoolmasters neither can understand nor will follow this good counsel of Socrates, but wise riders in their office can and will do both: which is the only cause that commonly the young gentlemen of England go so unwillingly to school and run so fast to the stable. For in very deed, fond schoolmasters by fear do beat into them the hatred of learning, and wise riders, by gentle allurements do breed up in them the love of riding. They find fear and bondage in schools; they feel liberty and freedom in the stables . . .

Yet some will say that children of nature love pastime and mislike learning, because in their kind, the one is easy and pleasant, the other hard and wearisome; which is an opinion not so true as some men ween. For the matter lieth not so much in the disposition of them that be young, as in the order and manner of bringing up by them that be old; nor yet in the difference of learning and pastime. For, beat a child if he dance not well, and cherish him though he learn not well, ye shall have him unwilling to go to dance, and glad to go to his book. Knock him always when he passeth his shaft ill, and favour him again, though he fault at his book, ye shall have him very loath to be in the field and very willing to be in the school. Yea, I say more, and not of myself, but by the judgement of those from whom few wisemen will gladly dissent, that if ever the nature of man be given at any time more than other to receive goodness, it is in innocency of young years, before that experience of evil have taken root in him. For the pure clean wit of a sweet young babe is like the newest wax, most able to receive the best and fairest printing: and like a new bright silver dish never occupied, to receive and keep clean any good thing that is put into it.

And thus, will in children, wisely wrought withal, may easily be won to be very well willing to learn. And wit in children, by nature, namely memory, the only key and keeper of all learning, is readiest to receive and surest to keep any manner of thing that is learned in youth . . .

But if will and wit, by farder age, be once allured from innocency, delighted in vain sights, filled with foul talk, crooked with wilfulness, hardened with stubbornness, and let loose to disobedience, surely it is hard with gentleness, but impossible with severe cruelty, to call them back to good frame again. For where the one perchance may bend it, the other shall surely break it, and so instead of some hope, leave an assured desperation and shameless contempt of all goodness . . .

. . . I wish as much now to have young men brought up in good order of living, and in some more severe discipline, than commonly they be. We have lack in England of such good order as the old noble Persians so carefully used: whose children to the age of twenty-one years were brought up in learning and exercises of labour, and that in such place where they should neither see that was uncomely, nor hear that was unhonest; yea, a young gentleman was never free to go where he would, and do what he list himself, but under the keep and by the counsel of some grave governor, until he was either married or called to bear some office in the commonwealth.

And see the great obedience that was used in old time to fathers and governors. No son, were he never so old in years, never so great of birth, though he were a king's son, might not marry but by his father and mother's also consent. . . . Our time is so far from that old discipline and obedience, as now, not only young gentlemen, but even very girls dare without all fear, though not without open shame, where they list and how they list, marry themselves in spite of father, mother, God, good order and all. The cause of this is that youth is least looked unto when they stand most need of good keep and regard. It availeth not to see them well taught in young years, and after when they come to lust and youthful days, to give them licence to live as they lust themselves. For if ye suffer the eye of a young gentleman once to be entangled with vain sights, and the ear to be corrupted with fond or filthy talk the mind shall quickly fall sick and soon vomit and cast up all the wholesome doctrine that he received in childhood, though he were never so well brought up before. And being once englutted with vanity, he will straight way loath all learning and all good counsel to the same. And the parents for all their great cost and charge, reap only in the end the fruit of grief and care . . .

And to say all in short, though I lack authority to give counsel, yet I lack not good will to wish, that the youth in England, specially gentlemen, and namely nobility, should be by good bringing up, so grounded in judgement of learning, so founded in love of honesty, as when they should be called forth to the execution of great affairs in service of their prince and country, they might be able to use and to order all experiences were they good, were they bad, and that according to the square, rule and line of wisdom, learning and virtue.

And I do not mean by all this my talk that young gentlemen should always be pouring on a book and by using good studies should leave honest pleasures and haunt no good pastime. . . . Therefore I would wish that beside some good time, fitly appointed and constantly kept, to increase by reading the knowledge of the tongues and learning, young gentlemen should use and delight in all courtly exercises and gentlemen like pastimes. And good cause why: for the self same noble city of Athens, justly commended of me before, did wisely and upon great consideration, appoint the muses Apollo and Pallas to be patrons of learning to their youth. For the muses, besides learning, were also ladies of dancing, mirth and minstrelsy: Apollo was god of shooting and author of cunning playing upon instruments. Pallas also was lady mistress in wars. Whereby was nothing else meant but that learning should be always mingled with honest mirth and comely exercises; and that war also should be governed by learning and moderated by wisdom . . .

Therefore to ride comely, to run fair at the tilt or ring, to play at all weapons, to shot fair in the bow, or surely in gun, to vaunt lustily, to run, to leap, to wrestle, to swim, to dance comely, to sing and play of instruments cunningly, to hawk, to hunt, to play at tennis, and all pastimes generally, which be joined with labour, used in open place and on daylight, containing either some fit exercise for war, or some pleasant pastime for peace, be not only comely and decent, but also very necessary for a courtly gentleman to use . . .

To join learning with comely exercises, Conto Baldessar Castiglione in his book *Cortegiane* doth trimly teach, which book, advisedly read and diligently followed, but one year at home in England would do a young gentleman more good, I wiss, than three years travel abroad spent in Italy. . . . He that by living and travelling in Italy, bringeth home into England out of Italy, the religion, the learning, the policy, the experience, the manners of Italy. That is to say, for religion, papistry or worse; for learning, less, commonly, than they carried out with them; for policy a factious heart, a discoursing head, a mind to meddle in all men's matters; for experience, plenty of new mischiefs never known in England before; for manners, variety of vanities and change of filthy living. These be the enchantments of Circes, brought out of Italy to mar men's manners in England:

much, by example of ill life, but more by precepts of fond books of late translated out of Italian into English, sold in every shop in London, commended by honest titles the sooner to corrupt honest manners; dedicated over-boldly to virtuous and honourable personages the easilier to beguile simple and honest wits. It is pity that those which have authority and charge to allow and disallow books to be printed, be no more circumspect herein than they are. Ten sermons at St. Paul's cross do not so much good for moving men to true doctrine as one of those books do harm, with enticing men to ill living.

4.5 RICHARD MULCASTER, *POSITIONS*

Mulcaster was headmaster of Merchant Taylors' School, and dedicated this work to Elizabeth I. It aims at being a comprehensive treatise on methodology and curriculum. Text from: first edition, 1581, pp.14–47; 166–214 (chapters 4, 5,38, 39).

What time were best for the child to begin to learn

The first question that of any necessity cometh in place seemeth to be at what years children be to be put to school: for neither would they be deferred so long for leasing of their time, nor hastened on too soon, for hindering of their health. The rule therefore must be given according to the strength of their bodies, and the quickness of their wits jointly . . .

What things they be wherein children are to be trained

. . . Amongst these my country's most familiar principles, reading offereth her self first in the entry, chosen upon good ground, continued upon great proof, enrolled among the best, and the very foremost of the best, by her own effects, as very many so very profitable. For whether you mark the nature of the thing, while it is in getting, or the goodness of thereof, when it is gotten, it must needs be the first and the most fruitful principle in training of the mind. For the letter is the first and simplest impression in the trade of teaching, and nothing before it. The knitting and jointing whereof groweth on very infinitely, as it appeareth most plainly by daily spelling and continual reading, till partly by use, and partly by argument, the child get the habit and cunning to read well, which being once gotten, what a cluster of commodities doth it bring withal? Whatsoever any other, for either profit or pleasure, of force or free will, hath published to the world by pen or print, for any end or to any use, it is by reading all made to serve us: in religion to love and fear God; in law to obey and please men; in skill to entertain knowledge; in will to expel ignorance; to do all in all as having by it all helps to do all things well. . . . I wish the child to have his reading thus perfect and ready, in both English and the Latin tongue very long before he dream of his Grammar.

Of the which two, at whether it were better to begin, by some accident of late it did seem somewhat doubtful, but by nature of the tongue the verdict is given up. For while our religion was restrained to the Latin, it was either the only, or the onliest principle in learning to learn to read Latin, as most appropriate to that effect, which the Church then esteemed on most.

But now we are returned home to our English abce as most natural to our soil and most proper to our faith, the restraint being repealed and we restored to liberty, we are to be directed by nature and property to read that first which we speak first, and to care for that most which we ever use most, because we need it most; and to begin our first learning there where we have most helps to learn it best, by familiarity of our ordinary language, by understanding all usual arguments by continual company of our own countrymen, all about us speaking English, and none uttering any words but those, which we ourselves are well acquainted with, both in our learning and living . . .

Next to reading followeth writing, in some reasonable distance after, because it requireth some strength of the hand, which is not so soon stayed nor so stiff to write, as the tongue is stirring and ready to read. . . . And writing itself hath profited so much since it hath been perfected, as it now proves the prop to remembrance; the executor of most affairs; the deliverer of secrets; the messager of meanings; the inheritance of posterity, whereby they receive whatsoever is left them; in law to live by; in letters to learn; in evidence to enjoy. To come by this thing so much commended, so as it may bring forth all her effects readily and roundly, these notes must be kept: that the master learn himself and teach his scholar a fair letter and a fast, for plainness and speed; that the matter of his example be pithy and proper to enrich the memory with profitable provision; and that the learning to write be not left off until it be very perfect; because writing being once perfectly gotten doth make a wonderful riddance in the rest of our learning . . .

Some controversy before the thing be considerately thought on, but none after, may arise about this next, which is to draw with pen or pencil, a cousin germane to fair writing, and of the self same charge. For pen and penknife, ink and paper, compass and ruler, a desk and a dust box, will set them both up, and in these young years, while the finger is flexible, and the hand fit for frame, it will be fashioned easily. And commonly they that have any natural towardness to write well, have a knack of drawing too, and declare some evident conceit in nature bending that way . . .

For the setting of colours, I do not much stand in, howbeit if any dexterity that way do draw the child on, it is an honest man's living, and I dare not commend that famous fellowship which is so renowned for handling the pencil . . .

Music maketh up the sum, and is divided into two parts, the voice and the instrument, whereof the voice resembleth reading, as yielding that to the ear, which it seeth with the eye.

That young maidens are to be set to learning

And to prove they [girls] are to be trained, I find four special reasons, whereof any one, much more all, may persuade any their most adversary, much more me, which am for them tooth and nail. The first is the manner and custom of my country, which allowing them to learn will be loath to be contraried by any of her countrymen. The second is the duty which we owe unto them, whereby we are charged in conscience not to leave them lame in that which is for them. The third is their own towardness, which God by nature would never have given them to remain idle or to small purpose. The fourth is the excellent effects in that sex when they have had the help of good bringing up: which commendeth the cause of such excellency, and wisheth us to cherish that tree whose fruit is both so pleasant in taste and so profitable in trial . . .

But now having granted them the benefit and society of our education, we must assign the end, wherefore the train shall serve, whereby we may apply it the better. Our own[7] train is without restraint for either matter or manner, by cause our employment is so general in all things: theirs is within limit, and so must their train be. If a young maiden be to be trained in respect of marriage, obedience to her head and the qualities which look that way must needs be her best way. If in regard of necessity to learn how to live, artificial train must furnish out her trade. If in respect of ornament to beautify her birth and to honour her place, rarities in that kind and seemly for that kind do best beseem such. If for government, not denied them by God and devised them by men, the greatness of their calling doth call for great gifts, and general excellencies for general occurrences. Wherefore having these different ends always in eye, we may point them their train in different degrees . . .

As concerning those which are to be trained, and when they are to begin their train, this is my opinion. The same restraint in cases of necessity, where they conveniently cannot, and the same freedom in cases of liberty, when they commodiously may, being reserved to parents in their daughters which I allowed them in their sons, and the same regard to the weakness and strength of their wits and bodies, the same care for their womanly exercises, for help of their health, and strength of their limbs, being remitted to their considerations which I assigned them in their sons. I do think the same time fit for both, not determinable by years but by ripeness of wit to conceive without tiring, and strength of body to travel without wearying. For though the girls seem commonly to have a quicker ripening in wit than boys have, for all that seeming, yet it is not so. Their natural weakness which cannot hold long, delivers very soon, and yet there be as prating boys as there be prating wenches. Besides their brains be not so much charged, neither with weight nor with multitude of matters, as boys heads be: and therefore like empty cask they make the greater noise. As those men which seem to be very quick witted by some sudden pretty answer, or some sharp reply, be not always most burdened, neither with letters nor learning. . . . As for bodies the maidens be more weak, most commonly even by nature, as of a moonish influence, and all our whole kind is weak of the mother side, which when she was first made even then weakened the man's side. Therefore great regard must be had to them, no less, nay rather more, than to boys in that time. For in process of time, if they be of worth themselves, they may so match as the parent may take more pleasure in his sons by law, than in his heirs by nature. They are to be the principal pillars in the upholding of households, and so they are likely to prove, if they prove well in training. The dearest comfort that man can have if they incline to good: the nearest corrosive if they tread awry. And therefore charily to be cared for, bearing a jewel of such worth in a vessel of such weakness.

* * *

For the matter, what shall they learn? Thus I think, following the custom of my country, which in that that is usual doth lead me on boldly and in that also which is most rare, doth show my path to be already trodden. So that I shall not need to err, if I mark but my guide well. Where rare excellencies in some women do but show us some one or two parents' good success in their daughters' learning, there is neither precedent to be fetched nor precept to be framed. For precepts be to conduct the common, but these singularities be above the common: precedents be for hope, those pictures pass beyond all hope. And yet they serve for proof to proceed by in way of argument, that women can learn if they will and may learn what they list, when they bend their wits to it. To learn to read is very common, where convenientness doth serve, and writing is not refused, where opportunity will yield it.

Reading, if for nothing else it were, as for many things else it is, is very needful for religion, to read that which they must know, and ought to perform, if they have not whom to hear in that matter which they read: or if their memory be not steadfast, by reading to revive it. If they hear first and after read of the self same argument, reading confirms their memory. Here I may not omit many and great contentments, many and sound comforts, many and manifold delights, which those women that have skill and time to read, without hindering their housewifery, do continually receive by reading of some comfortable and wise discourses penned either in form of history or for direction to live by.

As for writing, though it be discommended for some private carriages (wherein we men also, no less than women bear oftentimes blame, if that were a sufficient exception why we should not learn to write), it hath his commodity where it filleth in match, and helps to enrich the good man's mercery.[8] Many good occasions are oftentimes offered, where it were better for them to have the use of their pen for the good that comes by it, than to wish they had it when the default is felt: and for fear of evil, which cannot be avoided in some, to avert that good which may be commodious to many.

Music is much used, where it is to be had, to the parent's delight, while the daughter be young. . . . I meddle not with needles nor yet with housewifery, though I think it and know it, to be a principal commendation in a woman: to be able to govern and direct her household, to look to her house and family, to provide and keep necessaries, though the goodman pay, to know the force of her kitchen, for sickness and health in her self and her charge: because I deal only with such things as be incident to their learning. Which seeing the custom of my country doth permit, I may not mislike, nay I may wish it with warrant, the thing being good and well beseeming their sex.

* * *

Where the question is how much a woman ought to learn, the answer may be, so much as shall be needful. If that also come in doubt the return may be either so much as her parents conceive of her in hope, if her parentage be mean; or provide for her in state, if her birth bear a sail.[9] For if the parents be of calling and in great account, and the daughters capable of some singular qualities, many commendable effects may be wrought thereby, and the young maidens being well trained are very soon commended to right honourable matches, whom they may well beseem and answer much better, their qualities in state having good correspondence with their matches of state, and their wisdoms also putting to helping hand, for the procuring of their common good. . . . This *how much* consisteth either in perfecting of those forenamed four, reading well, writing fair, singing sweet, playing fine, beyond all cry and above all comparison, that pure excellency in things but ordinary may cause extraordinary liking: or else in skill of languages annexed to these four, that more good gifts may work more wonder. . . . These women, which we see in our days to have been brought up in learning, do rule this conclusion. That such personages as be born to be princes, or matches to great peers, or to furnish out such trains, for some peculiar ornaments to their place and calling, are to receive this kind of education in the highest degree, that is convenient for their kind. But princely maidens above all, because occasion of their height[10] stands in need of such gifts, both to honour themselves and to discharge the duty which the countries, committed to their hands, do daily call for: and besides what match is more honourable than when desert for rare qualities doth join itself with highness in degree? I fear no workmanship in women to give them geometry and her sister sciences, to make them mathematicals, though I mean them music: nor yet bars to plead at, to leave them the laws: nor urinals to look on to lend them some physic, though the skill of herbs hath been the study of nobility, by the Persian story, and much commended in woman: nor pulpits to preach in to utter their divinity . . . and for direction of their life they must be afforded some, though not as preachers and leaders, yet as honest performers and virtuous livers. Philosophy would furnish their general discourses, if their leisure could entend[11] it: but the knowledge of some tongues either of substance in respect of deeper learning, or account for the present time, may very well be wished them, and those faculties also which do belong to the furniture of speech, may be very well allowed them, because tongues be most proper where they do naturally arm.

* * *

Now there is nothing left to end this treatise of young maidens but where and under whom they are to learn, which question will be sufficiently resolved, upon consideration of the time how long they are to learn, which time is commonly till they be about thirteen or fourteen years old, wherein as the matter which they must deal withal cannot be very much in so little time, so the perfecting thereof requireth much travail, though their time be so little, and there would be some show afterward wherein their training did avail them. They that may continue some long time at learning, through the state and ability of their parents, have also their time and place suitable appointed by the foresight of their parents. So that the time resting in private forecast, I cannot reduce it to general precept, but only thus far, that in perfectness it may show how well it was employed.

Of the training up of young gentlemen

In the last title I did declare at large how young maidens in each degree were to be advanced in learning, which methought was very incident to my purpose, because they be counter-branches to us in the kind of mortal and reasonable creatures and also for that in each degree of life they be still our masters, and sometime our mistresses, through the benefit of law and honourableness of birth. Now considering they join allway with us in number and nearness, and sometime exceed us in dignity and calling, as they communicate with us in all qualities, and all honours even up to the sceptre, so why ought they not in any wise but be made communicants with us in education and train, to perform that part well which they are to play, for either equality with us, or sovereignty above us? Here now ensueth another title of marvellous importance for the kind of people whereof I am to entreat: because their state is still in the superlative and the greatest executions be theirs by degree . . .

. . . Education is the bringing up of one, not to live alone, but amongst others (because company is our natural cognizance) whereby he shall be best able to execute those doings in life which the state of his calling shall employ him unto, whether public abroad, or private at home, according unto the direction of his country whereunto he is born and oweth his whole service. All the functions here be public and regard everyone, even where the things do seem to be most private, because the main direction remaineth in the public, and the private must be squared, as it will best join with that: and yet we restrain education to private, all whose circumstances be singular to one. As if he that were brought up alone, should also ever live alone. . . . [But] how can education be private? It abuseth the name, as it abuseth the thing . . .

To knit up this question therefore of private and public education, I do take public to be simply the better: as being more upon the stage, where faults be more seen, and so sooner amended, as being the best means both for virtue and learning, which follow in such sort as they be first planted. What virtue is private? Wisdom to foresee, what is good for a desert? Courage to defend, where there is no assailant? Temperance to be modest, where none is to challenge? Justice to do right, where none is to demand it? What learning is for aloneness? Did it not come from collection in public dealings, and can it show her force in private affairs, which seem afraid of the public? Compare the best in both kinds, there the odds will appear. If ye compare a private scholar of a very fine capacity and worthy the open field, so well trained by a diligent and discreet master as that train will yield; with a blockhead brought up under a public teacher not of the best sort; or if in comparison ye match a toward private teacher with a weak public master, ye say somewhat to the persons but smally to the thing, which in equality shows the difference, in inequality deceives the doubter . . .

But to the education of gentlemen and gentlemanly fellows. What time shall I appoint them to begin to learn? Their wits be as the common, their bodies ofttimes worse. The same circumstance, the same consideration for time must direct all degrees. What thing shall they learn? I know none other, neither can I appoint better, than that which I did appoint for all. The common and private concur herein. Neither shall the private scholar go any faster on, nay perhaps not so fast, for all the help of his whole master, than our boys shall, with the bare help, that is in number and multitude, every boy being either a master for his fellow to learn by, or an example to set him on, to better him if he be negligent, to be like him if he be diligent.

Only this, young gentlemen must have some choice of peculiar matter, still appropriate unto them, because they be to govern under their prince in principal places: those virtues and virtuous lessons must be laid still before them, which do appertain to government, to direct others well, and belong to obedience to guide themselves wisely . . .

These things gentlemen have, and are much bound to God for them, which may make them prove excellent, if they use them well: great ability to go thorough withal, where the poorer must give over ere he come to the end; great leisure to use liberty, where the meaner must labour; all opportunities at will, where the common is restrained; so that singularity in them if, it be missed, discommends them, because they have such means and yet miss; if it hit in the meaner, it makes their account more, because their means was small, but their diligence exceeding . . .

As for rich men which being no gentlemen, but growing to wealth by what means soever, will counterfeit gentlemen in the education of their children, as if money made equality, and the purse were the preferrer, and no further regard; which condemn the common from which they came, which cloister up their youth as boding further state; they be in the same case for ability, though far behind for gentility. But as they came from the common, so they might with more commendation continue their children in that kind, which brought up the parents and made them so wealthy, and not to impatronise themselves unto a degree too far beyond the dunghill. For of all the means to make a gentleman, it is the most vile, to be made for money. Because all other means bear some sign of virtue, this only mean is too bad a mean, either to match with great birth, or to mate great worth. For the most part it is miserably scraped to the murthering of many a poor maggot, while lively cheese is lusty cheer, to spare expenses, that Jack may be a gentleman. . . . These people by their general trades will make thousands poor; and for giving one penny to any one poor of those many thousands, will be counted charitable. They will give a scholar some petty poor exhibition to seem to be religious, and under a slender veil of counterfeit liberality, hide the spoil of the ransacked poverty. And though they do not profess the impoverishing of purpose, yet their kind of dealing doth pierce as it passeth . . .

But ere I begin to deal with any of these points, once for all I must recommend unto them exercise of the body, and chiefly such as besides their health shall best serve their calling and place in their country. Whereof I have said, methink, sufficiently before. And as those qualities, which have I set out for the general train in their perfection being best compassed by them, may very well beseem a gentlemanly mind; so may the exercises without all exception, either to make a healthful body, seeing our mould is all one; or to prepare them for service, wherein their use is more. Is it not for a gentleman to use the chase and hunt? Doth their place reprove them if they have skill to dance? Is the skill in sitting of an horse no honour at home, no help abroad? Is the use of their weapon with choice, for their calling, any blemish unto them? For all these and what else beside, there is furniture for them, if they do but look back, and the rather for them, because in deed those great exercises be most proper to such persons, and not for the meaner.

4.6 FRANCIS BACON, *THE ADVANCEMENT OF LEARNING*

Bacon's *Advancement of Learning*, dedicated to James I in the hope that the monarch would patronise some of Bacon's educational schemes, attempts to survey and condemn contemporary learning, educational methods and achievements, at the same time as clearing a space for a new secular learning, whose primary aim should be utilitarian. There are traces of his interest in empirical discovery. Text from: 1605 edition, pp. 17^r–21^r.

Now I proceed to those errors and vanities which have intervened among the studies themselves of the learned, which is that which is principal and proper to the present argument . . .

There be therefore chiefly three vanities in studies, whereby learning hath been most traduced. For those things we do esteem vain which are either false or frivolous, those which either have no truth or use; and those persons we esteem vain, which are either credulous or curious; and curiosity is either in matter or words: so that in reason, as well as in experience there fall out to be these three distempers (as I may term them) of learning: the first fantastical learning; the second, contentious learning; and the last, delicate learning, vain imaginations, vain altercations and vain affections; and with the last I will begin. Martin Luther, conducted (no doubt) by an higher providence, but in discourse of reason, finding what a province he had undertaken against the Bishop of Rome and the degenerate traditions of the Church, and finding his own solitude, being no ways aided by the opinions of his own time, was enforced to awake all antiquity and to call former times to his succours to make a party against the present time: so that the ancient authors, both in divinity and in humanity, which had long time slept in libraries, began generally to be read and revolved. This by consequence did draw on a necessity of a more exquisite travail in the languages original, wherein those authors did write, for the better understanding of those authors and the better advantage of pressing and applying their words. And thereof grew again a delight in their manner of style and phrase, and an admiration of that kind of writing; which was much furthered and precipitated by the enmity and opposition that the propounders of those primitive but seeming new opinions had against the schoolmen; who were generally of the contrary part, and whose writings were altogether in a different style and form; taking liberty to coin and frame new terms of art to express their own sense, and, to avoid circuit of speech, without regard to the pureness, pleasantness, and (as I may call it) lawfulness of the phrase or word. And again, because the labour then was with the people . . . for the winning and persuading of them there grew of necessity in chief price and request eloquence and variety of discourse, as the fittest and forciblest access into the capacity of the vulgar sort: so that these four causes concurring, the admiration of ancient authors, the hate of the schoolmen, the exact study of languages, and the efficacy of preaching, did bring in an affectionate study of eloquence and copie of speech, which then began to flourish. This grew speedily to an excess, for men began to hunt more after words than matter; more after the choiceness of the phrase and the round and clean composition of the sentence, and the sweet falling of the clauses, and the varying and illustration of their works with tropes and figures than after the weight of matter, worth of subject, soundness of argument, life of invention or depth of judgement . . .

The second which followeth is in nature worse than the former: for as substance of matter is better than beauty of words, so contrariwise vain matter is worse than vain words. . . . Surely, like as many substances in nature which are solid do putrify and corrupt into worms; so it is the property of good and sound knowledge to putrify and dissolve into a number of subtle, idle, unwholesome and (as I may term them) vermiculate questions, which have indeed a kind of quickness and life of spirit, but no soundness of matter or goodness of quality. This kind of degenerate learning did chiefly reign amongst the schoolmen; who having sharp and strong wits and abundance of leisure, and small variety of reading, but their wits being shut up in the cells of a few authors (chiefly Aristotle their dictator), as their persons were shut up in the cells of monasteries and colleges, and knowing little history, either of nature or time, did out of no great quantity of matter and infinite agitation of wit spin out unto us those laborious webs of learning which are extant in their books. For the wit and mind of man, if it work upon matter, which is the contemplation of the creatures of God, worketh according to the stuff, and is limited thereby; but if it work upon itself, as the spider worketh his web, then it is endless, and brings forth indeed cobwebs of learning, admirable for the fineness of thread and work, but of no substance or profit . . .

For the third vice or disease of learning, which concerneth deceit or untruth, it is of all the rest the foulest: as that which doth destroy the essential form of knowledge, which is nothing but a representation of truth.

* * *

For the method of tradition,[12] I see it hath moved a controversy in our time.[13] But as in civil business, if there be a meeting and men fall at words, there is commonly an end of the matter for that time, and no proceeding at all; so in learning, where there is much controversy, there is many times little inquiry. For this part of knowledge of method seemeth to me to be so weakly inquired as I shall report it deficient.

Method hath been placed and that not amiss, in logic, as a part of judgement. For as the doctrine of syllogisms comprehendeth the rules of judgement upon that which is invented, so the doctrine of method containeth the rules of judgement upon that which it is to be delivered; for judgement preceedeth delivery, as it followeth invention.[14] Neither is the method or the nature of the tradition material only to the use of knowledge, but likewise to the progression of knowledge: for since the labour and life of one man cannot attain to perfection of knowledge, the wisdom of the tradition is that which inspireth the felicity of continuance and proceeding. And therefore the most real diversity of method is of method referred to use, and method referred to progression: whereof the one may be termed magistral, and the other of probation.

The latter whereof seemeth to be a *via deserta et interclusa* [a road deserted and closed off]. For as knowledges are now delivered there is a kind of contract of error between the deliverer and the receiver. For he that delivereth knowledge, desireth to deliver it in such form as may be best believed, and not as may be best examined; and he that receiveth knowledge desireth rather present satisfaction, than expectant inquiry; and so rather not to doubt, than not to err: glory making the author not to lay open his weakness, and sloth making the disciple not to know his strength.

De methodo sincera sive ad filios scientiarum [of the true method of the sciences, or the method of delivery to posterity]. But knowledge that is delivered as a thread to be spun on, ought to be delivered and intimated, if it were possible, in the same method wherein it was invented: and so is it possible of knowledge induced . . . a man may revisit and descend unto the foundations of his knowledge and consent; and so transplant it into another, as it grew in his own mind.

For it is in knowledges as it is in plants: if you mean to use the plant, it is no matter for the roots; but if you mean to remove it to grow, then it is more assured to rest upon roots than slips; so the delivery of knowledges (as it is now used) is as of fair bodies of trees without the roots; good for the carpenter, but not of the planter. But if you will have sciences grow, it is less matter for the shaft or body of the tree, so you look well to the taking up of the roots. Of which kind of delivery the method of mathematics, in that subject, hath some shadow: but generally I see it neither put in ure, nor put in inquisition, and therefore note it for deficient.

4.7 HENRY PEACHAM, *THE COMPLETE GENTLEMAN*

Peacham's writings were aimed equally at an aspiring gentry as at the gentry (see 3.21), and were social how-to books for the upwardly mobile seventeenth-century man or woman. Text from: 1622 edition, pp. 18–37.

Of the dignity and necessity of learning in princes and nobility

Since learning then is an essential part of nobility, as unto which we are beholden for whatsoever dependeth on the culture of the mind; it followeth that who is nobly born, and a scholar withal, deserveth double honour . . . for hereby as an ensign of the fairest colours, he is afar discerned and winneth to himself both love and admiration, heighting[15] with skill his image to the life, making it precious and lasting to posterity . . .

Rome saw her best days under her most learned kings and emperors; as Numa, Augustus, Titus, Antoninus, Constantine, Theodosius, and some other. Plutarch giveth the reason: *learning* (saith he) *reformeth the life and manners*, and affordeth the wholesomest advice for the government of a commonwealth . . .

Of the time of learning, duty of masters, and what the fittest method to be observed

As the spring is the only fitting seed time for grain, setting and planting in garden and orchard: so youth, the April of man's life, is the most natural and convenient season to scatter the seeds of knowledge upon the ground of the mind . . .

How many excellent wits we have in this land that smell of the cask, by neglecting their young time when they should have learned . . . who grown to years of discretion and solid understanding, deeply bewail their mis-spent or misguided youth with too late wishing (as I have heard many) that they had lost a joint, half their estates, so that they had been held to their books when they were young. The most (and without cause) lay the fault upon bad masters to say truth, it is a general plague and complaint of the whole land; for, for one discreet and able teacher, you shall find twenty ignorant and careless, who (among so many fertile and delicate wits as England affordeth) whereas they make one scholar, they mar ten.

The first and main error of masters is want of discretion, when in such variety of natures as different as their countenances, the master never laboureth to try the strength of every capacity by itself, which . . . must have the rule fitted to it, not that brought to the rule: for as the selfsame medicines have several operations, according to the complexions they work upon, so one and the self-same method agreeth not with all alike: some are quick of capacity and most apprehensive, others of as dull; some of a strong memory, others of as weak; yet may that dullard or bad memory (if he be observed) prove as good . . .

A second oversight nigh akin to the former is indiscretion in correction, in using all natures alike, and that with immoderation, or rather plain cruelty . . .

The noble, generous and best natures are won by commendation, enkindled by glory, which is *fax mentis honestae* [a thing of an honest mind], to whom conquest and shame are a thousand tortures. Of which disposition for the most part are our young nobility and gentlemen well born, inheriting with their being the virtue of their ancestors; which even in this tender greenness of years will bewray itself, as well in the school as abroad at their play and childish recreations . . .

In Germany the school is, and as the name importeth it ought to be, merely *ludus literarius* [a game of letters], a very pastime of learning, where it is a rare thing to see a rod stirring: yet I heartily wish that our children of England were but half so ready in writing and speaking Latin, which boys of ten and twelve years old will do so roundly, and with so neat a phrase and style, that many of our masters would hardly mend them; having only for their punishment shame, and for their reward praise . . .

Some affect, and severer schools enforce, a precise and tedious strictness, in long keeping the scholars by the walls, as from before six in the morning, till twelve, or past; so likewise in the afternoon; which beside the dulling of the wit, and dejecting the spirit . . . breedeth in him afterward a kind of hate and care-lessness of study when he cometh to be *sui iuris*, at his own liberty (as experience proveth by many who are sent from severe schools unto the universities), withal, over-loading his memory and taking off the edge of his invention, with over heavy tasks in themes, verses etc. To be continually pouring on the book (saith Socrates) hurteth and weakeneth the memory very much; affirming learning to be sooner attained unto by the ear in discourse and hearing than by the eye in continual reading. I verily believe the same, if we had instructors and masters at hand, as ready as books. For we see by experience those who have been blind from their birth, to retain more by hearing than others by their eyes, let them read never so much . . .

Wherefore I cannot but commend the custom of their schools in the Low Countries, where for the avoiding of this tedious sitting still and irksome pouring on the book all day long, after the scholar hath received his lecture, he leaveth the school for an hour, and walketh abroad with one or two of his fellows, either into the field, or up among the trees upon the rampire, [16] as in Antwerp, Breda, Utrecht, etc., where they confer and recreate themselves till time calls them in to repeat, where perhaps they stay an hour; so abroad again and thus at their pleasure the whole day . . .

A fourth error is the contrary . . . too much carelessness and remissness in not holding them in at all, or not giving them in the school that due attendance they ought: so that every day is play-day with them, bestowing the summer in seeking birds-nests, or haunting orchards; the winter in keeping at home for cold, or abroad all day with the bow, or the birding piece: they make as little conscience in taking, as their master in giving their learning . . .

But these diseases whereunto some of them are very subject, are humour and folly (that I may say nothing of the gross ignorance and insufficiency of many) whereby they become ridiculous and contemptible both in the school and abroad. Hence it comes to pass that in many places, especially in Italy, of all professions that of *Pedentaria* is held in basest repute; the schoolmaster almost in every comedy being brought upon the stage, to parallel the *Zani* or *Pantalon*[17] . . .

I knew one who in winter would ordinarily in a cold morning whip his boys over for no other purpose than to get himself a heat; another beat them for swearing, and all the while swears himself with horrible oaths: he would forgive any fault saving that.

I had, I remember myself, near St. Albans in Hertfordshire, where I was born, a master who by no entreaty would teach any scholar he had farther than his father had learned before him: as if he had only learned but to read English, the son, though he went with him seven years, should go no further. His reason was they would then prove fancy rogues and control their fathers: yet these are they that oftentimes have our hopeful gentry under their charge and tuition, to bring them up in science and civility.

Beside, most of them want that good and direct method whereby in shortest time and with least labour, the scholar may attain unto perfection: some teaching privately, use a Grammar of their own making, some again none at all; the most Lilly's,[18] but preposterously posted over, that the boy is in his quantity of syllables before he knoweth the quality of any one part of speech; for he profiteth no more than he mastereth by his understanding. Nor is it my meaning that I would all masters to be tied to one method, no more than all the shires of England to come up to London by one highway: there be many equally alike good . . .

. . . They cannot commonly err if they shall imitate the builder, first to provide the scholar with matter, then cast to lay a good foundation. I mean a solid understanding of the Grammar, every rule made familiar and fast, by short and pleasant examples, let him bring his matter into form, and by little and little raise the frame of a strong and well-knit style both in writing and speaking; and what doth harm in all other building is here most profitable and needful, that is translation. For I know nothing that benefitteth a scholar more than that: first by translating out of Latin into English, which, laid by for some time, let him translate out of English into Latin again, varying as often as he can both his words and phrases . . .

Of the duty of parents in their childrens' education

Neither must all the blame lie upon the schoolmaster, fond and foolish parents have oft as deep a share in this precious spoil, as he whose cockering and apish indulgence (to the corrupting of the minds of their children, disabling their wits, effeminating their bodies) how bitterly doth Plato tax and abhor? For avoiding of which, the law of Licurgus commanded children to be brought up, and to learn in the country, far from the delicacy of the city; and the Brutii in Italy, a people bordering upon Lucania, following the custom of the Spartans, sent their children after the age of fourteen away to be brought up in fields and forests among shepherds and herdsmen, without any to look unto them, or to wait upon them; without apparel, or bed to lie on, having nothing else than milk or water for their drink, and their meat such as they could kill or catch . . .

If many of our young youths and gallants were directed in this manner, mercers might save some paper and city laundresses go make caudles with their saffrons and eggs; dicing houses and ten shillings ordinaries let their large rooms to fencers and puppet players, and many a painted piece betake herself to a wheel or the next hospital. But nowadays parents either give their children no education at all (thinking their birth or estate will bear out that); or if any, it leaveth so slender an impression in them, that like their names cut upon a tree, it is overgrown with the old bark by the next summer. Beside, such is the most base and ridiculous parsimony of many of our gentlemen (if I may so term them) that if they can procure some poor Bachelor of Art from the university to teach their children, say grace and serve the cure of an impropriation, who wanting means and friends, will be content upon the promise of ten pounds a year at his first coming, to be pleased with five; the rest to be set off in hope of the next advowson (which perhaps was sold before the young man was born), or if it chance to fall in his time, his Lady or Master tells him, indeed Sir, we are beholden unto you for your pains, such a living is lately fallen, but I had before made a promise of to my butler, or bailiff, for his true and extraordinary service . . .

But touching parents, a great blame and imputation (how justly I know not) is commonly laid upon the mother, not only for her over-tenderness, but in winking at their lewd courses, yea more in seconding and giving them encouragement to do wrong . . .

Nor will I affirm that it is her pleasure the chambermaid should be more curious in fitting his ruff, than his master in refining his manners.

Nor that it is she that filleth the cistern of his lavish expense, at the university or Inns of Court; that after four or five years spent, he returns home as wise as Ammonius his ass that went with his master every day to the school to hear Origen and Porphyry read philosophy.

But albeit many parents have been diligent enough this way, and good masters have likewise done their parts, and neither want of will or ability of wit in their children to become scholars, yet (whether out of an over-weening conceit of their towardness, a pride to have their sons out-go their neighbours, or to make them men before their times) they take them from school, as birds out of the nest ere they be fledged, and send them so young to the university, that scarce one among twenty proveth ought. For as tender plants too soon or often removed, begin to decay and die at the root, so these young things of twelve, thirteen or fourteen that have no more care than to expect the next carrier, and where to sup on Fridays and fasting nights; no further thought of study than to trim up their studies with pictures, and place the fairest books in openest view, which poor lads, they scarce ever opened or understand not . . .

Others again, if they perceive any wildness or unsteadiness in their children, are presently in despair, and out of all hope of them for ever proving scholars, or fit for anything else; neither consider the nature of youth nor the effect of time, the physician of all. But to mend the matter, send them either to the court to serve as pages, or into France or Italy to see fashions and mend their manners, where they become ten times worse. These of all other, if they be well-tempered prove the best metal: yea Tully as of necessity desireth some abundant rankness, or superfluity of wit in that young man he would choose to make his orator of: I wish in a young man something to spare, and which I might cut off . . .

And some of a different humour will determine even from the A, B, C what calling their children shall take upon them, and force them even in despite of nature. . . . And certainly it is a principal point of discretion in parents to be thoroughly acquainted with and observe the disposition and inclination of their children, and indeed for every man to search into the addiction of his genius and not to wrest nature, as musicians say, out of her key . . .

Much less have parents nowadays that take care to take the pains to instruct and read to their children themselves, which the greatest princes and noblest personages have not been ashamed to do. Octavius Augustus Caesar read the works of Cicero and Virgil to his children and nephews himself . . .

The three daughters of ever-famous Sir Thomas More were by their father so diligently held to their book (notwithstanding he was so daily employed being Lord Chancellor of England) that Erasmus saith he found them so ready and perfect in Livy that the worst scholar of them was able to expound him quite through without any stop, except some extraordinary and difficult place. . . . I shall not need to remember within memory, those four sisters, the learned daughters of Sir Anthony Cooke, and rare poetesses, so skilful in Latin and Greek, beside many other their excellent qualities, eternised already by the golden pen of the prince of poets of our time;[19] with many other incomparable ladies and gentlewomen in our land, some yet living.

4.8 THOMAS POWELL, *TOM OF ALL TRADES*

Powell's satirical representation of the Northamptonshire man's tale of how to bring up his sons and daughters is deliberately parodic. Nevertheless, the educational consequences for the middling and lower sort of the social and economic necessity of finding boys a trade, and girls a husband are humorously depicted here. Text from: first edition, 1631, pp. 46–9.

For their portions, I showed you before, how and when to raise them. That is, by the marriage of your eldest son, or out of that part of your personal estate which you may spare without prejudice of yourself.

For their breeding: I would have their breeding like to the Dutch woman's clothing, tending to profit only and comeliness.

Though she never have a dancing school master, a French tutor nor a Scotch tailor, to make her shoulders of the breadth of the Bristow causeway, it makes no matter. For working in curious Italian pearls, or French borders, it is not worth the while. Let them learn plain works of all kind, so that take heed of too open seaming. Instead of song and music, let them learn cookery and laundry. And instead of reading Sir Philip Sidney's *Arcadia*, let them read the grounds of good housewifery. I like not a female poetress at any hand. Let greater personages glory their skill in music, the posture of their bodies, their knowledge in languages, the greatness and freedom of their spirits: and their arts in arraigning of men's affections, at their flattering faces. This is not the way to breed a private gentleman's daughter.

If the mother of them be a good housewife, and religiously disposed, let her have the bringing up of one of them. Place the other two forth betimes, and before they can judge of a good manly leg.

The one in the house of some good merchant, or citizen of civil and religious government, the other in the house of some lawyer, some judge, or well reported Justice or gentleman of the country, where the servingman is not too predominant. In any of these she may learn what belongs to her improvement, for sempstrie, for confectionery, and all requisites of housewifery. She shall be sure to be restrained of all rank company and unfitting liberty; which are the overthrow of too many of their sex.

There is a pretty way of breeding young maids in an exchange shop, or St. Martins le grand. But many of them get such a foolish crick with carrying the bandbox under their apron to gentlemen's chambers, that in the end it is hard to distinguish whether it be their belly or their bandbox makes such a goodly show.

And in a trade where a woman is sole chapman, she claims such a preeminence over her husband, that she will not be held to give him an account of her dealings, either in retail, or wholesale at any rate.

The merchant's factor, and citizen's servant of the better sort, cannot disparage your daughters with their society . . .

Your daughter at home will make a good wife for some good yeoman's eldest son, whose father will be glad to crown his sweating frugality, with alliance to such a house of gentry.

4.9 JOHANN COMENIUS, *A REFORMATION OF SCHOOLS*

Comenius was one of a group of Protestant reformers who advocated a revolution in educational curriculum and methods. He was a follower of Bacon, and corrresponded with Pym and other parliamentarians over the possibility of enacting these reforms in the Commonwealth. His vision that empiricism will classify and explain all physical phenomena is combined with a belief that millenarian biblical prophecies are about to be fulfilled. Text from: 1642 edition, translated by Samuel Hartlib, pp. 24–9.

I desire the learned to pardon me, of whose labours I now presume to show my judgement. The most exact encyclopedias, or sums of art, which I could ever lay my eyes upon, seemed to me like a chain neatly framed of many links, but nothing comparable to a perpetual mover, so artificially made with wheels that it turns itself; or like a pile of wood, very neatly laid in order with great care and diligence, but nothing like unto a tree arising from its living roots, which by its inbred virtue spreads itself into boughs and leaves and yieldeth fruit. But that which we desire is to have a living tree with living roots and living fruits of all the Arts and Sciences, I mean Pansophy, which is a lively image of the universe, every way closing and agreeing with itself, everywhere quickening itself and covering itself with fruit. That is (to reflect a little to our former intentions) we would have such a book of Pansophy compiled which might be:

I.   A solid breviary of universal learning;
II.   A clear light for human understanding;
III.   An exact and stable rule of truth;
IV.   A certain and directive register of the affairs of our life;
V.   And lastly, an happy ladder leading us to God himself.

Or (that I may otherwise express my desires) I think that seeing God hath ordered all things in number, measure and weight, we ought also to take care:

I.   That all things that are, were, or shall be throughout the world may be numbered and summed up, that nothing escape our knowledge;
II.   That the just proportion of all things, as well in respect of the universe, as also among themselves, may be laid open before our eyes.
III.   That the weights of causes may be evident and extant among us, whereby we may make exact trial of the truth of all things.

The first will make learning to be universal, which is our first intention. The

251

second will make it clear and distinct, which we also earnestly seek. And the third will be a means to have it true and solid, which is our chief desire.

I say, we would have such a book compiled, which alone, instead of all, should be the spense[20] and store-house of universal learning; in which nothing should be wanting, and by reading whereof, wisdom should of its own accord, spring up in men's minds, by reason of the clear, distinct and perpetual coherence of all things arising out of their true veins and roots, that every thing may plainly appear to be as it is said to be, and that it can be no otherwise than it is, in regard of the immutable truth of things everywhere interwoven with itself. But all this we would have done compendiously because we must have respect to the shortness and frailty of our lives; and in a popular style, which may bring light and not darkness into the understanding; and lastly, solidly by a perpetual connection of causes and effects; because we seek for a true and firm foundation of truth, and not for any forged and false props of opinions, that so all things which may be known (whether natural, moral or artificial, or even metaphysical) may be delivered like unto mathematical demonstrations, with such evidence and certainty that there may be no room left for any doubt to arise. By which means, not only such things as are will be certainly and truly known, but also the flood-gates of infinite devices, deductions and inventions will be set wide open.

O, how much are these things to be desired! What an improvement and bettering would this be of our mortality! For seeing books are the instruments of transplanting wisdom, and an instrument perfectly good, or a rule without any default, keeps the workman's hand from going awry: if such an instrument of learning and teaching universal wisdom, as we have projected and described, were extant among us, it would be beneficial, not only for the dextrous fashioning and instructing of youth (which Melanchthon[21] in one place saith is an harder matter than the taking of Troy), but also for the opening of a way, whereby all the sons of men may readily attain unto the true knowledge and conceptions of things, that they may be wise both in beholding the works of God, and ordering of their own.

As for the darkness of errors, it would flee amain from the face of so clear a light; and men, being busied only about solidities, and bending through assured and certain ways unto serious ends, would easier leave off those dissentions, strifes and wars, wherewith the world is now confused. . . . For by God's goodness this would be the means to heal up those wounds in schools, Churches, and commonwealths and to restore peace to the Christian world, that not only all Christian nations might flourish in the studies of true wisdom and piety, but even infidels themselves might partake of the same light and be won to the embracing of Christianity in this divinely revealed way of truth. And so at last we should see (what God's sacred oracles have foretold, shall at length come to pass) that the earth shall be filled with the knowledge of the Lord, as the waters cover the sea, Isa. 11.9. And that the Lord shall be king over all the earth, and there shall be but one Lord, and his name one, Zach. 14.9. And that the way of Sion shall be so plain that even fools shall not err therein, Isa. 35.8. Which is the same that another prophet hath foretold, that in the last days the mountain of the house of the Lord shall be established in the top of the mountains, and it shall be exalted above the hills and people shall flow unto it. And many nations shall come and say, come and let us go up to the mountain of the Lord, that he may teach us of his ways. And afterward: and they shall beat their swords into ploughshares, and spears into pruning hooks; nation shall not lift up a sword against nation, neither shall they learn war any more, Micah. 4.1. Take pity upon us, o Lord, and let thy peace rest upon Jerusalem: let thy glory arise over us, that the nations may walk in thy light.

But may such things be hoped for? Certainly we must not despair of them, if this guide and director of human understanding be once framed, whereby men's minds may be infallibly led by continual degrees and in open light from the groundworks and fundamentals, unto the highest tops of things. For if we come once by this means to behold the theatre of God's wisdom, men's minds cannot but be filled with joy and gladness, so that they will call one unto another, come and let us go up to the mountain of the Lord, that he may teach us of his ways. Now that such a director (or perfect method of Pansophy) is not to be despaired of, we have these persuasions.

First, although things may seem infinite and innumerable in respect of their multitude, not to be measured in regard of their diverse disproportions; and unsearchable by reason of that depth wherein truth is plunged; yet it is most certain that all things are beneath man and subject to his understanding. For all things are made for his sake, but in an inferior degree: he therefore being the last accomplishment of the creation and the absolute image of his creator, containing in himself only the perfections of all other things, which should he not at last habituate himself to the contemplation of himself and all things else? . . . All things else are made in number, weight and measure, Wisd. 11.20. Isa. 40.12. They are therefore to be numbered, measured, and weighed until this universal harmony do clearly appear unto us.

Secondly, God hath made all things well, as the Scripture saith, but everything in his time, that is, by degrees. Is it then in vain that God hath set the world in men's hearts, that is, a desire to find out those things which he worketh from the beginning to the end? Eccles. 3.11. It would be in vain, if that desire could not obtain its end. But we must not ascribe any frustraneous actions unto that sovereign welcome.

Thirdly, we have already great store of provision hereto, those books and monuments of men's diligence, compiled with great care and industry. Can we think that all these have done nothing? That cannot be, in regard (as I have showed already) of the supreme governor of all things, who will not suffer anything, even errors themselves, to be in vain. Let us grant therefore that they have erred and been deceived in most things, yet God who is the eternal and unchangeable foundation of truth will surely order the matter so, that even errors themselves will at last perforce be made subservient to the farther discovering and establishing of truth. Now it is manifest that many things are already found out, and why should we not hope that the rest will follow? It is no small matter that Euclides, Archimedes and others have brought the knowledge of Quantities to such evidence and perfection that even miracles may be effected by numbers, measures and weights. It is not a thing of nothing that hermetical physicians and others have, by means of Chemistry, found how to extract the qualities out of natural bodies, and to separate even the very essences of things. It is a matter of moment, which the Lord Verulam[22] hath effected in his excellent *Novum Organum*, where he shows the infallible way of making a narrow search into the natures of things . . .

For if everyone hath formerly had his own sharpness of wit, his own rules of proceeding, and his own weights of judgement; what might not be effected if all these wits were united into one, their laws into one, and their judgements into one? The more candles, the greater light . . .

We have also an express promise concerning the latter times that *many shall run to and fro, and knowledge shall be increased*, Dan. 12.4. Many have already passed to and fro, and have searched out (in this our age more than ever) both heaven and earth, seas and islands, even the whole kingdom of nature; as also the Holy Scriptures, and those divine oracles after a various manner. And what remains then, but that the other part of the prophecy should also take its turn to be fulfilled?

4.10 JOHN MILTON, *OF EDUCATION*

Milton's tract on education was published in 1644 in the form of a letter to Samuel Hartlib, who was translating Comenius's work in England. Text from: 1644 edition, pp. 1ff.

Master Hartlib,

I am long since persuaded that to say and do ought worth memory and imitation, no purpose or respect should sooner move us than simply the love of God and of mankind. Nevertheless, to write now the reforming of education, though it be one of the greatest and noblest designs that can be thought on, and for the want whereof this nation perishes, I had not yet at this time been induced but by your earnest entreaties and serious conjurements, as having my mind diverted for the present in the pursuance of some other assertions, the knowledge and use of which cannot but be a great furtherance to the enlargement of truth and honest living with much more peace[23] . . .

The end, then, of learning, is to repair the ruins of our first parents by regaining to know God aright, and out of that knowledge to love him, imitate him, to be like him, as we may the nearest, by possessing our souls of true virtue, which, being united to the heavenly grace of faith, makes up the highest perfection. But because our understanding cannot in this body found itself but on sensible things, nor arrive so clearly to the knowledge of God and things invisible as by orderly conning over the visible and inferior creature, the same method is necessarily to be followed in all discreet teaching.

And seeing every nation affords not experience and tradition enough for all kind of learning, therefore we are chiefly taught the languages of those people who have at any time been most industrious after wisdom; so that language is but the instrument conveying to us things useful to be known. And though a linguist should pride himself to have all the tongues that Babel cleft the world into, yet if he have not studied the solid things in them as well as the words and lexicons, he were nothing so much to be esteemed a learned man as any yeoman or tradesman competently wise in his mother-dialect only.

Hence appear the many mistakes which have made learning generally so unpleasing and so unsuccessful. First we do amiss to spend seven or eight years merely in scraping together so much miserable Latin and Greek as might be learned otherwise easily and delightfully in one year. And that which casts our proficiency therein so much behind is our time lost in too oft idle vacancies given both to schools and universities; partly in a preposterous exaction, forcing the empty wits of children to compose themes, verses, and orations, which are the acts of ripest judgement and the final work of a head filled by long reading and observing, with elegant maxims and copious invention.

These are not matters to be wrung from poor striplings, like blood out of the nose, or the plucking of untimely fruit; besides the ill habit which they get of wretched barbarising against the Latin and Greek idiom with their untutored Anglicisms, odious to read, yet not to be avoided without a well-continued and judicious conversing among pure authors digested, which they scarce taste . . .

And for the usual method of teaching arts, I deem it to be an old error of universities, not yet well recovered from the scholastic grossness of barbarous ages, that, instead of beginning with arts most easy (and those be such as are most obvious to the sense), they present their young unmatriculated novices at first coming with the most intellective abstractions of logic and metaphysics . . .

I shall detain you no longer in the demonstration of what we should not do, but straight conduct you to a hillside where I will point you out the right path of a virtuous and noble education; laborious indeed at the first ascent, but else so smooth, so green, so full of goodly prospect and melodious sounds on every side, that the harp of Orpheus was not more charming. I doubt not but ye shall have more ado to drive our dullest and laziest youth, our stocks and stubs, from the infinite desire of such a happy nurture, than we have now to haul and drag our choicest and hopefullest wits to that asinine feast of sow thistles and brambles which is commonly set before them as all the food and entertainment of their tenderest and most docible age. I call therefore a complete and generous education, that which fits a man to perform justly, skilfully, and magnanimously all the offices, both private and public, of peace and war. And how all this may be done between twelve and one and twenty, less time than is now bestowed in pure trifling at grammar and sophistry, is to be thus ordered:

First, to find out a spacious house and ground about it fit for an academy and big enough to lodge one hundred and fifty persons, whereof twenty or thereabout may be attendants, all under the government of one who shall be thought of desert sufficient and ability either to do all, or wisely to direct and oversee it done. This place should be at once both school and university, not needing a remove to any other house of scholarship, except it be some peculiar college of law or physic, where they mean to be practitioners; but as for those general studies which take up all our time from Lilly to the commencing, as they term it, master of art, it should be absolute. After this pattern, as many edifices may be converted to this use as shall be needful in every city throughout this land, which would tend much to the increase of learning and civility everywhere. This number, less or more, thus collected, to the convenience of a foot-company or interchangeably two troops of cavalry, should divide their day's work into three parts as it lies orderly: their studies, their exercise, and their diet.

For their studies, first they should begin with the chief and necessary rules of some good grammar, either that now used, or any better; and while this is doing, their speech is to be fashioned to a distinct and clear pronunciation, as near as may be to the Italian, especially in the vowels . . .

Next, to make them expert in the usefullest parts of grammar, and withal to season them and win them early to the love of virtue and true labour, ere any flattering seducement or vain principle seize them wandering, some easy and delightful book of education should be read to them, whereof the Greeks have store, as Cebes, Plutarch, and other Socratic discourses; but in Latin we have none of classical authority extant, except the two or three first books of Quintilian . . .

But here the main skill and groundwork will be to temper them such lectures and explanations upon every opportunity, as may lead and draw them in willing obedience, inflamed with the study of learning and the admiration of virtue, stirred up with high hopes of living to be brave men and worthy patriots, dear to God and famous to all ages; that they may despise and scorn all their childish and ill-taught qualities, to delight in manly and liberal exercises; which he who hath the art and proper eloquence to catch them with, what with mild and effectual persuasions, and what with the intimation of some fear if need be, but chiefly by his own example, might in a short space gain them to an incredible diligence and courage, infusing into their young breasts such an ingenuous and noble ardour as would not fail to make many of them renowned and matchless men.

At the same time, some other hour of the day might be taught them the rules of arithmetic, and soon after the elements of geometry, even playing, as the old manner was. After evening repast, till bed-time their thoughts would be best taken up in the easy grounds of religion and the story of Scripture.

The next step would be to the authors of agriculture, Cato, Varro and Columella, for the matter is most easy; and if the language is difficult, so much the better; it is not a difficulty above their years. And here will be an occasion of inciting and enabling them hereafter to improve the tillage of their country, to recover the bad soil, and to remedy the waste that is made of good; for this was one of Hercules's praises.

Ere half these authors be read (which will soon be with plying hard and daily) they cannot choose but be masters of an ordinary prose; so that it will be then seasonable for them to learn in any modern author the use of the globes and all the maps, first with the old names, and then with the new; or they might then be capable to read any compendious method of natural philosophy; and at the same time might be entering into the Greek tongue, after the same manner as was before prescribed for the Latin; whereby the difficulties of grammar being soon overcome, all the historical physiology of Aristotle and Theophrastus are open before them and, as I may say, under contribution. The like access will be to Vitruvius, to Seneca's *Natural Questions*, to Mela, Celsus, Pliny or Solinus. And having thus past the principles of arithmetic, geometry, astronomy and geography, with a general compact of physics, they may descend in mathematics to the instrumental science of trigonometry, and from thence to fortification, architecture, enginery, or navigation. And in natural philosophy they may proceed leisurely from the history of meteors, minerals, plants, and living creatures as far as anatomy . . . .

To set forward all these proceedings in nature and mathematics, what hinders but that they may procure as oft as shall be needful, the helpful experience of hunters, fowlers, fishermen, shepherds, gardeners, apothecaries; and in other sciences, architects, engineers, mariners, anatomists, who doubtless would be ready, some for reward, and some to favour such a hopeful seminary. And this would give them such a real tincture of natural knowledge, as they shall never forget, but daily augment with delight. Then also those poets which are now counted most hard will be both facile and pleasant, Orpheus, Hesiod, Theocritus . . . and in Latin, Lucretius, Manilius and the rural part of Virgil.

By this time years and good general precepts will have furnished them more distinctly with that act of reason which in ethics is called proairesis, that they may with some judgement contemplate upon moral good and evil. Then will be required a special reinforcement of constant and sound indoctrinating to set them right and firm, instructing them more amply in the knowledge of virtue and hatred of vice . . .

Being perfect in the knowledge of personal duty, they may then begin the study of economics. And either now, or before this, they may have easily learned at any odd hour the Italian tongue. And soon after, but with wariness and good antidote, it would be wholesome enough to let them taste some choice comedies, Greek, Latin, or Italian; those tragedies also that treat of household matters . . .

The next move must be to the study of politics, to know the beginning, end and reasons of political societies, that they may not, in a dangerous fit of the commonwealth, be such poor shaken, uncertain reeds, of such a tottering conscience as many of our great councillors have lately shown themselves; but steadfast pillars of the State. After this they are to dive into the grounds of law and legal justice, delivered first and with best warrant by Moses, and as far as human prudence can be trusted, in those extolled remains of Grecian law-givers,

Lycurgus, Solon, Zaleucus, Charondas; and thence to all the Roman edicts and tables, with their Justinian; and so down to the Saxon and common laws of England and the statutes.

Sundays also, and every evening, may now be understandingly spent in the highest matters of theology and Church history, ancient and modern; and ere this time, at a set hour the Hebrew tongue might have been gained, that the Scriptures may be now read in their own original . . .

And now lastly, will be the time to read with them those organic arts which enable men to discourse and write perspicuously, elegantly and according to the fitted style of lofty, mean or lowly. Logic, therefore, so much as it is useful, is to be referred to this due place, with all her well-couched heads and topics, until it be time to open her contracted palm into a graceful and ornate rhetoric taught out of the rule of Plato, Aristotle, Phalereus, Cicero, Hermogenes, Longinus.

To which poetry would be made subsequent, or indeed rather precedent, as being less subtle and fine, but more simple, sensuous and passionate; I mean not here the prosody of a verse which they could not but have hit on before among the rudiments of grammar, but that sublime art which in Aristotle's *Poetics*, in Horace and the Italian commentaries of Castlevetro, Tasso, Mazzoni and others, teaches what the laws are of a true epic poem, what of a dramatic, what of a lyric, what decorum is, which is the grand masterpiece to observe. This would make them soon perceive what despicable creatures our common rhymers and play-writers be; and show them what religious, what glorious and magnificent use might be made of poetry both in divine and human things.

4.11 WILLIAM DELL, *A TRIAL OF SPIRITS*

Dell was an educational reformer who argued that the higher educational system should be separated from the Church, both in terms of the curriculum and from its administrative control. Text from: 1653 edition, pp. 26–30; appendix.

The right reformation of learning: school and universities

I conceive it meet that the civil power of chief magistrates should take great care of the education of youth, as one of the greatest works that concerns them and as one of the worthiest things they can do in the world: inasmuch as what the youth now is, the whole commonwealth will shortly be.

To this end it is meet that schools, if wanting, be erected through the whole nation, and that not only in cities and great towns, but also as much as may be, in all lesser villages. And that the authority of the nation take great care that godly men especially have the charge of greater schools; and also that no women be permitted to teach little children in villages, but such as are the most sober and grave; and that the magistrate afford to all this work all suitable encouragement and assistance.

That in such schools they first teach them to read their native tongues which they speak without teaching; and then presently as they understand, bring them to read the Holy Scriptures; which though for the present they understand not, yet they may, through the blessing of God, come to understand them afterwards.

That in cities and greater towns, where are the greater schools and the greater opportunities to send children to them, they teach them also the Latin and Greek tongues and the Hebrew also, which is the easiest of them all and ought to be in great account with us for the Old Testament's sake. And it is most heedfully to be regarded that in teaching youth the tongues, to wit, the Greek and Latin, such heathenish authors be most carefully avoided, be their language never so good, those writings are full of the fables, vanities, filthiness, lasciviousness, idolatries and wickedness of the heathen . . .

It may be convenient also that there may be some universities or colleges for the instructing of youth in the knowledge of the liberal arts, beyond grammar and rhetoric; as in logic . . . but the mathematics especially are to be had in good esteem in universities, as arithmetic, geometry, geography and the like, which as they carry no wickedness in them, so are they besides very useful to human society and the affairs of this present life.

There may be also in these universities or colleges allowed the study of physic and of the law according to that reformation which a wise and godly authority will cause them to pass under, both being now exceedingly corrupt and out of order, both for practice and fees.

But why these universities or colleges should be only at Cambridge and Oxford, I know no reason. Nay, if human learning be so necessary to the knowledge and teaching of the Scriptures as the universities pretend, they surely are without love to their brethren who would have these studies thus confined to these places, and do swear men to read and teach them nowhere else: certainly it is most manifest that these men love their own private gain more than the common good of the people. . . . The universities usually have been places of great licentiousness and profaneness; whereby it often comes to pass that parents sending them children far from them, young and hopeful, have for all their care and cost, after several years, received them back again with their tongues and arts, proud; profane, wicked, abominable and incorrigible wretches. Wherefore, doubtless it would be more suitable to a commonwealth (if we become so in deed and not in word only) and more advantageous to the good of all the people, to have universities or colleges, one at least, in every great town or city in the nation, as in London, York, Bristol, Exeter, Norwich and the like; and for the State to allow these colleges an honest and competent maintenance, for some godly and learned men to teach the tongues and arts under a due reformation. And this the State may the better do by provision out of every county or otherwise. . . . The people having colleges in their own cities, near their own houses, may maintain their children at home whilst they learn in the schools, which would be indeed the greatest advantage to learning that can be thought of.

It should also be considered whether it be according to the word of God that youth should spend their time only in reading of books whilst they are well, strong and fit for business. . . . To remedy which great evil . . . it may be so ordered that the youth . . . spend some part of the day in learning or study, and the other part of the day in some lawful calling; or one day in study and another in business, as necessity or occasion shall require . . .

And if this course were taken . . . twenty would learn then, where one learns now; and also by degrees, many men on whom God shall please to pour forth his spirit, may grow up to teach the people, whilst yet they live in an honest calling and employment, as the Apostles did . . .

And by this means may the chargeable and burdensome maintenance of the ministers by degrees be taken away and the Church of Christ and the very nations themselves be supplied with a more faithful Christian and spiritual ministry than now it hath, at a far less rate.

A testimony from the word against divinity degrees in the university

Thus doth the university through power received from antichrist give men, chiefly for money, divinity degrees; and through those degrees it gives authority and privilege to Bachelors in Divinity to expound part of the Scriptures, and to Doctors to expound and profess all the Scriptures; and they that gain these degrees to themselves are, as there is good reason, the great men in account with the university, how destitute soever they be of the faith and spirit of the gospel . . .

I cannot choose but give in my testimony against this glorious and gainful privilege of the universities . . . creating them masters in that mystery which none can teach but God himself, and which none can learn but true believers, who are born of God and his true disciples. . . . Degrees in divinity, for I meddle with none else, given by the universities to their children are plainly and grossly antichristian being most manifestly contrary to the word of the Gospel and the light that shines in the New Testament.

4.12 JOHN WEBSTER, *ACADEMIARUM EXAMEN: OR THE EXAMINATION OF THE ACADEMIES*

Webster concentrates, as does Dell, on proposed reforms to the university curriculum: arguing that economic and political needs should determine curriculum content, not the models and aspirations of ancient Greece and Rome. Text from: first edition, 1653, pp. 9; 91–5.

There are three things concerning Academies that do obviously offer themselves to our examination: first that learning which is the subject of their labours; secondly their method in the teaching and delivering it unto others; thirdly their constitutions and customs of which we shall speak in order, and first of that learning which they subjectively handle. For they very proudly and vaingloriously pretending to make men Doctors in divers sciences and Masters and Bachelors in or of Arts, it will be very necessary to consider what these sciences and arts are, in or of which men are by them made masters, lest it prove that when men vainly boast and imagine that they are Masters of arts, they be Masters of none, but rather ignorant of all, or the most.

* * *

1. Though in one Academy there be usually divers colleges or houses, yet must all the scholars in those several places be tied to one method and carried on in one way, nay even bound to the same authors and hardly allowed so much liberty and difference, as is between Aristotle and Ramus's Logic. As though they in the way of their teaching had arrived at the highest point of perfection, which could no way be improved, or no other as profitable could be discovered and found out, and so are all forced like carriers' horses to follow one another in the accustomed path, though it be never so uneven or impassable.

2. Their scholastic exercises are but slenderly, negligently and slothfully performed, their public acts (as they call them, though but verbal digladiations) being kept but four times in the year, that is in the terms, which if one should tell them in plain terms are but usually idle terms, as though time of all other things here below were not to be accounted most precious, and that there can be no such detriment done unto youth as to lose or mis-spend it.

3. Their custom is injurious and prejudicial to all those that desire to make a speedy progress in learning, nay unequal and disproportionable in itself, namely to tie men to a set number of years or acts before they can receive their Laureation, or take their degrees; as though all were of one capacity or industry, or all equally able at their matriculation; and so the slothful and painful, the most capable and most blockish, should be in the same equal time have an equal honour, which is both disproportionable and unjust. For some will attain to more in one year than some in three, and therefore why should they not be respected according to their merits and proficiency, and not bound to draw in an unequal yoke? And what matter were it whether a man had been there one month or seven years, so he had the qualification required, and did *subire examen* [undergo examination] and perform the duties of the place . . .

4. Their custom is no less ridiculous and vicious in their histrionical personation in the performance of their exercises, being full of childishness and scurrility, far from the gravity and severity of the Pythagorean school, where a five years' silence was enjoined; using so much lightness as more befits stage-players than diligent searchers of science, by scoffing and jeering, humming and hissing, which shows them like those animals they imitate, nay rather hurtful geese than laborious bees that seek to gather into their hives the sweet honey of learning and knowledge.

5. What is there in all their exercises but mere notions and quarrelsome

disputations, accustoming themselves to no better helps for searching into nature's abstruse secrets than the Chimeras of their own brains and converse with a few paper idols? As though these alone were sufficient keys to open the cabinet of nature's rich treasury, without labour and pains, experiments and operations, trials and observations! Surely if he that intends to prove a proficient in the knowledge of agriculture should only give himself over to contemplation and reading the books of such as have written in that subject, and never put his hand to the plough, nor practise the way of tilling and sowing, would he ever be a good husbandman or understand thoroughly what pertains thereunto? Surely not, and no more can they be good naturalists that do but only make a mould and idea in their heads, and never go out by industrious searches and observant experiments to find out the mysteries contained in nature.

6. Their custom is no less worthy of reprehension that in all their exercises they make use of the Latin tongue, which though it may have custom and long continuance to plead its justification, and that it is used to bring youth to the ready exercise of it, being of general reception almost through the whole world: yet it is as clearly answered that custom without reason and benefit becomes injurious, and though it make them ready in speaking Latin, while they treat of such subjects as are usually handled in the schools, yet are they less apt to speak it with facility in negotiations of far greater importance; and in the meantime the way to attain knowledge is made more difficult, and the time more tedious, and so we almost become strangers to our own mother tongue, loving and liking foreign languages as we do their fashions, better than our own: so that while we improve theirs, our own lies altogether uncultivated, which doubtless would yield as plentiful an harvest as others if we did as much labour to advance it . . . and therefore were the Romans so careful to propagate their language in other nations, and to prohibit the Greek language or any other to be spoken in their public contentions; and so likewise Pythagoras, Plato and Aristotle did teach in their own mother tongues, and Hippocrates, Galen, Euclid and others writ in the vulgar language of their own nation; and yet we, neglecting our own, do fool-ishly admire and entertain that of strangers which is no less a ridiculous than prejudicial custom.

7. Another is no less faulty and hurtful than the precedent, and that is their too much admiring of, and adhering to, antiquity or the judgement of men that lived in ages far removed from us, as though they had known all things, and left nothing for the discovery of those that came after in subsequent ages. . . . And indeed we usually attribute knowledge and experience to men of the most years, and therefore these being the latter ages of the world should know more, for the grandeavity of the world ought to be accounted for antiquity, and so to be ascribed to our times, and not to the junior age of the world, wherein those that we call the ancients did live . . .

8. They usually follow another hurtful custom not unlike to this preceding, which is too much to bind in themselves with the universality of opinions and multiplicity of voices, as though it were not better to stand single and alone with

truth, than with error to have the company of the multitude, or as though the multitude could not err, or that the greater number must necessarily be in the truth: when, as the wiseman saith, the number of fools are infinite . . .

9. Consonant to this is that other of their adhering to authority, especially of one man, namely Aristotle, and so do *jurare in verbi magistri* [swear in the words of the master], when according to their own tenets, arguments drawn from authority are numbered among the weakest, and what could Aristotle know more than all other that his opinion should be received as oracles? He both might, and did, err as well as other mortals; and may not we as justly recede from him as he from his master Plato, and the rest of the ancient philosophers? Is it any thing but a just liberty that we ought to maintain, and pursue, thereby to be admitted into the court of Lady Verity? For which all chains ought to be broken, and all fetters to be filed off.

4.13 CHARLES HOOLE, *A NEW DISCOVERY OF THE OLD ART OF TEACHING SCHOOL*

Hoole aimed to survey contemporary provision of education, from petty schools upwards, and provide a guide for parents and teachers as to the most appropriate schooling for their children and pupils. Text from: 1659 edition, 1–30; 220–94.

The petty school

My aim being to discover the old art of teaching school and how it may be improved in every part suitable to the years and capacities of children as are now commonly taught . . .

Whereas then it is useful in cities and greater towns to put children to school about four or five years of age, and in country villages, because of further distance, not till about six or seven; I conceive the sooner a child is put to school, the better it is: both to prevent ill habits, which are got by play and idleness, and to ensure him betimes to affect learning and well doing. Not to say how the great uncertainty of parents' lives should make them careful of their children's early education, which is like to be the best part of their patrimony, whatever good thing else they may leave them in this world.

I observe that betwixt three and four years of age a child hath great propensity to peep into a book, and then is the most seasonable time (if conveniences may be had otherwise) for him to begin to learn: and though perhaps then he cannot speak so very distinctly, yet the often pronunciation of his letters will be a means to help his speech, especially if one take notice in what organ or instrument he is most defective, and exercise him chiefly in those letters which belong unto it.

Now there are five organs or instruments of speech in the right hitting of which as the breath moveth from within through the mouth, a true pronunciation of every letter is made: viz, the lips, the teeth, the tongue, the roof of the mouth, and the throat. According to which if one rank the twenty-four letters of our English alphabet, he shall find that A, E, I, O, U, proceed by degrees from the throat, along betwixt the tongue and the roof of the mouth to the lips contracted . . .

The usual way to begin with a child when he is first brought to school is to teach him to know his letters in the horn-book, where he is made to run over all the letters in the alphabet . . .

How a child might be taught to read any English book perfectly

The ordinary way to teach children to read is, after they have got some knowledge of their letters, and a smattering of some syllables and words in the horn-book, to turn them into the ABC or primer, and therein to make them name the letters and spell the words, till by often use they can pronounce (at least) the shortest words at the first sight.

This method takes with those of prompter wits, but many more of more slow capacities, not finding anything to affect them, and so make them heed what they learn, go on remissly from lesson to lesson and are not much more able to read when they have ended their book, than when they begun it. Besides, the ABC being now (I say) generally thrown aside and the ordinary primer not printed, and the very fundamentals of Christian religion (which were wont to be contained in those books and were commonly taught children at home by heart before they went to school) with sundry people (almost in all places) slighted, the matter which is taught in most books now in use, is not so familiar to them and therefore not so easy for children to learn.

But to hold still to the sure foundation, I have caused the Lord's Prayer (sect. 20), the Creed (sect. 21) and the ten commandments (sect. 23) to be printed in the Roman character that a child having learned already to know his letters and how to spell, may also be initiated to read by them, which he will do the more cheerfully if he be also instructed at home to say them by heart.

As he reads these, I would have a child name what words he can at the first sight, and what he cannot, to spell them and to take notice what pauses and numbers are in his lesson. And to go them often over, till he can tell any title in them, either in or without the book. . . . For thus learning to read English perfectly, I allow two or three years' time, so that at seven or eight years of age a child may begin Latin.

It is a fond conceit of many that have either not attained or by their own negligence have utterly lost the use of the Latin tongue, to think it altogether unnecessary for such children to learn it as are intended for trades, or to be kept as drudges at home, or employed about husbandry. For first there are but few children (in their playing years and before they can be capable of any serious employment in the meanest calling that is) may be so far grounded in the Latin as to find that little smattering they have of it to be of singular use to them, both for the understanding of the English authors (which abound nowadays with borrowed words) and the holding discourse with a sort of men that delight to flaunt it in Latin.

Secondly, besides I have heard it spoken to the great commendation of some countries, where care is had for the well education of children, that every peasant (almost) is able to discourse with a stranger in the Latin tongue: and why may not we here in England obtain the like praise, if we did but as they continue our children at the Latin school, till they be well acquainted with that language and thereby better fitted for any calling?

Thirdly, and I am sorry to add, that the non-improvement of children's time after they can read English any whit well, throweth open a gap to all loose kind of behaviour, for being then (as it is too commonly to be seen, especially with the poorer sort) taken from the school and permitted to run wilding up and down without any control, they adventure to commit all manner of lewdness and so become a shame and dishonour to their friends and country.

If these or the like reasons therefore might prevail to persuade them that have a prejudice against Latin, I would advise that all children might be put to the grammar school, so soon as they can read English well, and suffered to continue at it till some honest calling invite them thence: but if not, I would wish them rather to forbear it than to become there an hindrance to others whose work it is to learn that profitable language.

Of the founding of a petty school

The petty school is the place where indeed the first principles of all religion and learning ought to be taught, and therefore rather deserveth that more encouragement should be given to the teachers of it, than that it should be left as a work for poor women, or others whose necessities compel them to undertake it as a mere shelter from beggary . . .

Yet if anyone be desirous to contribute towards such an eminent work of charity, my advice is that he erect a school and dwelling house together, about the middle of a market town or some populous country village, and accommodate it with a safe yard adjoining to it, if not with an orchard or garden, and that he endow it with a salary of at least twenty pounds per annum in consideration whereof all such poor boys as can conveniently frequent it may be taught *gratis*, but the more able sort of neighbours may pay for children's teaching, as if the school was not free; for they will find it no small advantage to have such a school amongst them.

Such a yearly stipend and convenient dwelling with a liberty to take young children to board, and to make what advantage he can best by other scholars, will invite a man of good parts to undertake the charge and excite him to the diligent and constant performance of his duty especially if he be chosen into the place by three or four honest and discreet trustees, that may have power also to remove him from thence if by his uncivil behaviour or gross neglect, he render himself uncapable to perform so necessary a service to the Church and commonwealth.

* * *

And as before I have hinted somewhat touching the erecting of petty schools (whereof there is great need, especially in London) so I will here presume (and I hope it will prove no offence) to publish what I have often seriously thought, and sometimes spoken with some men's approbation touching the most convenient founding of a grammar school, that if it shall please God to stir up any man's spirit to perform so pious a work, he may do it to the best advantage for the improvement of piety and learning. For when I see in many places of this land what vast sums have been expended (even of late) in erecting stately houses and fencing large parcels of ground for orchards and gardens and the like, and how destitute for the most part they stand, and remain without inhabitants, I am too too apt to think that those persons which have undergone so great a charge to so little purpose would willingly have disbursed as much money upon a public good, did they but rightly know how to do it: since thereby their name and memory will be more preserved, especially if they have no children or posterity of their own to provide for.

But to return to the contrivance of a school, which is to be in many things (as I have mentioned) above the ordinary way of schooling, yet gradually distant from and subordinate to university colleges, which would thence also take a further rise towards perfection in all kinds of study and action. For the better grounded a scholar is in the principles of useful matters when he comes to the university, the great progress he will make there in their superstructures, which require more search and meditation: so that at last he will be able to discover many particulars which have not yet been found out by others, who (perhaps) have not gone so rationally to work as he may do, having obtained the whole encyclopedia of learning to help him in all sorts of books.

Such a school then as may be fit for the education of all sorts of children (for we have seen the very poorest to have come to dignities of preferment by being learned) should be situated in a city or town of great concourse and trading, whose inhabitants are generally addicted and sufficiently accommodated to entertain tablers,[24] and are unanimously well affected towards piety, learning and virtue. The place should be healthfully and pleasantly seated in a plentiful country, where the ways on all sides are most commonly fair and convenient passage to be had from remoter parts, both by land and by water.

The school house should be a large and stately building, placed by itself about the middle of the outside of a town, as near as may be to the Church, and not far from the fields where it may stand in a good air and be free from all annoyances. It should have a large piece of ground adjoining to it, which should be divided into a paved court to go round about the school, a fair orchard and garden with walks and arbours, and a spacious green close for scholars' recreations; and to shelter the scholars against rainy weather, and that they may not injure the school in times of play, it were good if some part of the court were shedded or cloistered over.

The school house should be built three storeys high, whereof the middle-most, for more freedom of the air should be the highest above head, and so spacious that it may contain (at least) 500 scholars together without thronging one another. It should be so contrived with folding doors made betwixt every form, as that upon occasion it may be all laid open into one room, or parted into six, for more privacy of hearing every form without noise or hindrance one of another. There should be seats made in the school, with desks before them, whereon every scholar may work and lay his book, and these should be so placed that a good space may be left in the middle of the school, so as six men abreast may walk up and down from form to form. The usher's pews should be set at the head ends of every form so as they may best see and hear every particular boy. And the master's chair should be so raised at the upper end of the school as that he may be able to have every scholar in his eye and to be heard of all when he hath occasion to give any common charge or instruction. There may be shelves made round about the school and boxes for every scholar to put his books in, and pins whereon they may hang their hats, that they be not trodden (as is usual) underfeet. Likewise every form should have a repository near unto it wherein to lay such subsidiary books as are most proper for its use. The lowest storey may be divided into several rooms, proportioned according to the uses for which they are intended, whereof one should be for a writing school, another for such languages as are to be taught at spare hours, and a third as a petty school for such children as cannot read English perfectly, and are intended for the grammar school. A fourth room may be reserved for laying in wood and coals and the rest made use on for ushers or scholars to lodge in, or the like occasion as the master shall think best to dispose them to the furtherance of his school. In the uppermost storey, there should be a fair pleasant gallery wherein to hang maps and set globes, and to lay up such rarities as can be gotten in presses or drawers, that the scholars may know them. There should likewise be a place provided for a school library, and the rest may be made use of as lodging rooms . . .

Though in many schools I observe six a clock in the morning to be the hour for children to be fast at their book, yet in most, seven is the constant time, both in winter and summer, against which hour, it is fit every scholar should be ready at the school. And all they that come before seven should be permitted to play about the school till the clock strike on condition they can say their parts at the master's coming in; else they are not to play at all, but to settle to their books as soon as they come . . .

The common time of dismissing scholars from school in the fore-noons is eleven a clock every day, and in the afternoons, on Mondays, Wednesdays and Fridays, five a clock, but on Tuesday afternoons, four; and on Thursdays, three . . .

The granting of a playday is to be referred wholly to the discretion of the master, who must in this be as fearful to work his scholars' hindrance and the school's discredit as willing by such a courtesy to gratify his deserving friends . . .

In places of great resort, and where often solicitation is used to be made for play (especially by mothers that come to visit their children which are tabled at school) it were good that a piece of an afternoon were designed constantly afore-hand, on which (in case any suit should be made) the scholars might have leave to play; but if not, that they be held to their books . . .

I should here add something touching those usual customs which are yet on foot in most places, of scholars excluding or shutting out the master once a year, and capitulating with him about orders to be observed, or the like; but foras-much as I see they differ very much and are of late discontinued in many schools, I will only mention how they may be carried on where they yet remain without any contest or disturbance till at last they die of themselves.

1. Therefore there should be no exclusion till after Saint Andrew's day, and that the master know of it before-hand, that all things may be ordered hand-somely to the credit of the school.

2. That at the time of exclusion, the scholars behave themselves merrily and civilly about the school, without injuring one another or making use of any weapons, whereby to endanger themselves or do harm to anything in the school.

3. That the heads of each form consult with their fellows what things they would desire of the master, and that they bring their suits to the highest scholar in the school, that he may prefer them to the master writ fairly in Latin, to receive his approbation or dislike of them in a mild way of arguing.

4. That the master do not molest or come among his scholars all the while they are drawing up their petition about school-orders, nor trouble himself concerning them more than to hear that they keep good rule.

5. That every scholar prepare all his exercises according to his form, to be ready to be hanged out before the school doors or windows (or rather to be hanged over his place within the school) against the master's coming.

6. That the master notice that all things are prepared for his coming, go quietly to the school, being accompanied with some of the scholars' parents and after he have before witnesses subscribed to their petition at the door, to enter into the school in a peaceable and loving manner and receive from his scholars (and also make to them) a short congratulatory oration and so dismiss them to play.

By thus doing a master shall both prevent his scholars behaving themselves against him, in such rude and tumultuous manner as hath formerly been used; and give them and their parents no occasion to grudge at him for seeming to take upon him too abruptly to break old use and custom, which so long as it becometh an encouragement to their learning, may the better be indulged to young scholars whilst no evil consequences attend it. It is yet a custom retained in some schools in the country for scholars to make a potation or general feast once a year (and that before Shrovetide), towards defraying the charge whereof, every one bringeth so much money as his parents think good to allow him, and giveth it to the master to be expended in a dinner orderly provided for them, or in some kind of banqueting manner, which children are commonly more delighted withal.

4.14 ANNA MARIA VAN SCHURMAN, *THE LEARNED MAID*

Van Schurman was a German scholar, renowned across Europe for her learning and correspondence with eminent philosophers and scientists of the mid-seventeenth century. She was an adherent of the educational theories of Comenius, who argued for a broader curriculum than the humanists had done. Her writing influenced the work of Bathsua Makin, who ran a school after the restoration. Text from: first edition, 1659, fos 1ff.

Whether a maid may be a scholar

First of the subject; and first that our maid be endued at least with an indifferent good wit, and not unapt for learning.

Secondly that she be provided of necessaries and not oppressed with want: which exception I therefore put in, because few are so happy as to have parents to bread them up[25] in studies, and teachers are chargeable.

Thirdly, that the condition of the times, and her quality be such, that she may have spare hours from her general and special calling, that is from the exercises of piety and household affairs. To which end will conduce, partly her immunity from cares and employments in her younger years, partly in her elder age either celibate, or the ministry of handmaids, which are wont to free the richer sort of matrons also from domestic troubles.

Fourthly, let her end be not vain glory and ostentation, or unprofitable curiosity, but beside the general end, God's glory and the salvation of her own soul; that both herself may be the more virtuous and the more happy, and that she may (if that charge lie upon her) instruct and direct her family, and also be useful, as much as may be, to her whole sex.

Next limitations of the predicate,[26] scholarship, or the study of letters I so limit, that I clearly affirm all honest discipline, the circle and crown of liberal arts and sciences (as the proper and universal good and ornament of mankind) to be convenient for the head of our christian maid; yet so that according to the dignity and nature of every art and science and according to the capacity and condition of the maid herself, all in their order, place and time succeed each other in the learning of them, or be commodiously joined. But especially, let regard be had unto those arts which have nearest alliance to theology and the moral virtues, and are principally subservient to them. In which number we reckon grammar, logic, rhetoric, especially logic, fitly called the key of all sciences; and then physics, metaphysics, history and also the knowledge of languages, chiefly of Hebrew and Greek. All which may advance to the more facile and full understanding of Holy Scripture: to say nothing now of other books. The rest, i.e. mathematics (to which is also referred music), poesy, picture, and the like, not illiberal arts, may obtain the place of pretty ornaments and ingenious recreations.

Lastly those studies which pertain to the practice of the law, military discipline, oratory in the church, court, university, as less proper and less necessary we do not very much urge. And yet we in no wise yield that our maid should be excluded from the scholastic knowledge or theory of those; especially not from understanding the most noble doctrine of the politics, or civil government.

And when we say a maid may be a scholar, it is plain we do not affirm learning to be a property, or a thing requisite and precisely needful to eternal salvation: no, nor as such a good thing which maketh to the very essence of happiness in this life: but as a mean, and very useful, conferring much to the integrity and perfection thereof: and as that, which by the contemplation of excellent things will promote us to a higher degree in the love of God, and everlasting felicity.

5

LITERARY AND CULTURAL THEORIES

INTRODUCTION

The year before Elizabeth I's accession to the throne, in 1557, a London publisher produced a collection of poems entitled, *Songs and Sonnets, written by the right honourable Lord Henry Howard late Earl of Surrey, and other* (5.1). On the face of it such a publication might have found small favour: its title thus advertising the work of a renowned rebel, executed in Henry VIII's reign for treasonous displaying of his claim to royal arms. But Surrey was celebrated for a different kind of politics in the collection of his poems: the politics of courtliness in the tradition of Castiglione and the renaissance Italian city States. Surrey himself had made this connection quite explicit in the unusual full-length portrait he commissioned of himself in 1546 in an Italianate renaissance setting. The painting itself is over seven feet high. His Italian costume and raffish look dominate the painting: he stands in an arched doorway, the arch of which is surrounded by carved neo-classical sculptures and putti, the larger figures holding the Earl's arms. Beyond and behind the Earl is a darkened landscape. Thus renaissance Italy is appropriated and naturalised by Surrey, who not only appears to dwell naturally in this environment, but is physically larger than anything else in the painting.[1] In the collection made by Tottel the self-aggrandisement and elitism of Surrey's own publicity is missing, and in the preface has been transposed into both a covert critique of English cultural isolation and a manifesto for cultural education through translation and publication.

This short statement is part of a wider, continuing cultural debate in England at the time, emerging out of humanism and contact with continental scholars, both literary and religious. The debate, often characterised as one simply about the English language and translation,[2] began between

271

scholars at Cambridge, many of whom had close contacts with, or were members of, the government and Privy Council of Edward VI's reign. In many ways, the debate could be described as being one about rival definitions of 'Englishness': both cultural and political beliefs and attitudes were intertwined on each side of the debate, and this interconnection remained crucial in the subsequent hundred years.

On the one hand there were those cultural extremists like John Cheke who argued that the distinctiveness of the English Protestant reformation was such that all continental influence, of language, religion or politics, should be eschewed, and that the purity of the English reformation could only be maintained by excising all foreign influences, of language, religion or fashions. On the other were those cultural integrationists, who saw England as dislocated from the main intellectual and cultural European developments of the previous two hundred years, and were anxious to join what they saw as the creative and cultural vanguard. They argued that many of the humanist discoveries and changes were not intrinsically linked to the Catholic Church, but rather to secular knowledge and developments (see, for example Elyot, Ascham or Hoby), and that English culture should therefore beg, steal and borrow from classical Greek or Roman, or renaissance Italian or French, in order to catch up.

For the latter group the continental humanist revolution combined the actual rediscovery of ancient classical texts with the development of rigorous historical textual editing practices. For them the rediscovery of the content of much of the writings of Aristotle, Plato, Cicero, Tacitus, Lucretius and others was a stimulus to a new articulation of ideas about politics, writing, ethics and science. Theories of the role of the State, and the place of the learned elite within that State, particularly those articulated in the writing of Cicero and Plato, were influential in humanist writings from Petrarch onwards.[3] There were two traditions developed from these writings: the first of which was strongly and assertively republican (directly linking Ciceronian rhetorical practice with the freedom of the pre-imperial Roman State); and the second was celebratory of a strong nation or city State, whatever its political form.

Thus, on the one side Castiglione's *The Courtier* was written in celebration of the court of Urbino in the early sixteenth century, modelled its form and content on Ciceronian and Platonic dialogues, and put forward an almost depoliticised model of appropriate courtiership in a modern State. The ideal of the playful and pleasurable courtier in intellectual and adulatory thrall to its prince, with the hard-earned knowledge and the naked realities of the court's power bases well hidden, was an attractive ideological expression of the increasingly centralised nation States of Europe.[4] For Castiglione, the good courtier was a good rhetorician, a good poet, and an effective flatterer or, as Puttenham argues, a good dissembler (see 5.2 and 5.10). Poetic and other entertainments were part of the necessary repertoire for a courtier: and theories of courtiership are interwoven with theories about poetry, and vice versa (see, for example, Sidney, Spenser and Pettie here). On the other side, defences of an indigenous and distinctive culture continued to be made, and were often the basis for critiques of political absolutism.[5] In Scotland, the tradition of using native dialects in contradistinction to Italianate borrowing was a specifically political act against Roman superstition. In addition, some puritan or strongly Protestant writers, such as Cheke, but also Spenser, for example, used native linguistic and generic traditions to assert a distinctive English and overtly Protestant culture, politics and religion.[6] Some writers in this tradition believed that all fictional or imagistic writing or icons were as evil and magic as the Catholic mass: and consequently, as the Protestant faith should return to the purity of the word and the literal understanding of the Bible: so should all cultural practices. Stubbes and Gosson are the most renowned and extreme examples of this tradition.

Nevertheless, Castiglione was, and remained, a strong model for the articulation of a renewed cultural nationalism combined with strong allegiance to a political absolutism. This current of thought, in which cultural productions and texts celebrated and playfully exhorted the court and its adherents to cultural humanist norms, was a strong influence in both educational and courtly circles.[7] Tottel's final sentence shows the focus of literary reading and writing (at least of these Englished Petrarchan sonnets) to be this civilising and normalising function:

> If perhaps some mislike the stateliness of style removed from the rude skill of common ears: I ask help of the learned to defend their learned friends, the authors of this work: and I exhort, the unlearned, by reading to learn to be more skilful and to purge that swinelike grossness, that maketh the sweet marjoram not to smell to their delight.

The educated are asked to defend the elite style as the new cultural norm: the uneducated to conform to it; and that style is defined as naturalised Latinate and Italianate. This elite cultural theory is one which informs and moulds the native tradition which continues through the writings of Puttenham, Sidney, Campion, Jonson and Milton: an integrationist model of English cultural and literary models and functions which meshes well with modern and postmodern literary theories, such as those, for example of the intertextual nature of all cultural products.

One of the features of literary theories in this period is that they are theories about the place of writing or poetry within culture. Although they do articulate internal theories about genre, style and metre, they do so within an overall, predominantly consensual view of the place of writing within society. This has best been described as a rhetorical culture: one in which the theory and practice of rhetoric is central to the way political society conceives of itself.[8] As we have seen in part 4, the educational curriculum, and the aims which it set itself, were based on classical models of the study and practice of the key texts of rhetoric (Cicero and Quintilian), where rhetoric was the theoretical and practical study of language in the market place of law and politics. Rhetoric handbooks provided both a theoretical place for language performance in the world, and models of how that performance should be structured according to audience, place and generic function.[9] Puttenham's work (5.10) is a good example of this in English. Cicero's *On the Orator* was one of the central texts of grammar school curricula, and its influence can easily be discerned in the texts of Sidney and Jonson. Cicero wrote:

> For the one point in which we have our very greatest advantage over the brute creation is that we hold converse with one another, and can reproduce our thought in word. . . . To come, however, at length to the highest achievements of eloquence, what other power could have been strong enough either to gather scattered humanity into one place, or to lead it out of its brutish existence in the wilderness up to our present condition of civilisation as men and as citizens, or after the establishment of social communities, to give shape to laws, tribunals and civic rights? . . . My assertion is this: that the wise control of the complete orator is that which chiefly upholds not only his own dignity, but the safety of countless individuals and of the entire state.
>
> (I.viii)

For Cicero, as for Sidney or Spenser, Daniel or Milton, the orator was the good political man, whose writing and speaking was intimately linked to the civilised and civilising nature of the State. Even Bacon, who attacked the rhetorical nature of humanist culture, weighing 'words' as more important than 'things', makes an understanding of the workings and deceptions of language (the idols of the market place) a necessary prior condition to a scientific understanding of the world.

There are several major distinctive consequences for cultural theories of the period of this rhetorical outlook. First was that all writing, whether fictional or historical, political or playful, occurred in a social environment. Thus, although Sidney, for example, claims a particularly elevated role for poetry (see 5.9), it shares its rhetorical function with many other forms of writing: history, philosophy and politics. Second, a further consequence is that textual theories tend also to be affective: readers' or listeners' responses are part of the measure of the success of a text. Third, texts tend to be dialectical: presenting dialogic or multi-faceted modes of writing and discourse which enable readers and listeners to think and act in a social context, but also to judge the 'right' answer to particular dilemmas.[10] Finally, where the political State did not allow the full expression of the

Ciceronian cultural imperative (that is, that the orator can critique the State as well as create it), there was a tendency for rhetorical textual theory to turn in on itself and formulate theories of cultural production as play: a tendency that can be seen in both Castiglione, and in the Ovidian and erotic fashions of the 1590s.

Most texts which articulate literary theories tend to utilise one of, or a combination of, several classical forbears: Aristotle's *Poetics*, Horace's *Ars Poetica* for references to educating and pleasing, or Plato's dialogues for neo-Platonic developments on ideal representation and poetic fury (for example, *Ion or Phaedrus*). Two apparently contradictory notions of the function and work of the poet co-existed at this time. One, of the poet as creator, perhaps most eloquently expressed by Sidney; and the other, of poet as imitator, which also threads itself through Sidney's work. Yet these two ideas, originating as they do from divergent and contradictory sources, tended to be fused in renaissance theory and practice, into a neo-Platonic, neo-Aristotelian expression, in which creativity, through the poetic imagination, could 'imitate' Platonic forms or ideas, as well as nature itself (see Ascham and Jonson, 5.5, 5.20). Theories of imitation included the notion that imitation of classical genres and modes was the route to cultural enlightenment and expression: but as we can see from the writings of Daniel, Johnson and Milton here (5.17, 5.20 and 5.24), their articulation of the theory of imitation was rather a dual one of the place of genres within particular societies, and of an acknowledgement of historical differences between one society and its epics, and the next. Theories of imitation thus became theories of difference.[11] Similarly, despite Wotton's plea to introduce Italianate architectural trends into English landscapes, he articulates this plea as a synthesis of native and foreign traditions (5.22).

Finally, as Milton's *Areopagitica* (5.23) and the royal *Injunctions* (5.4) make clear, this is a period when censorship and patronage dictate what can and cannot be written and published, played and portrayed.[12] All publications and dramatic performances had to be licensed by either the Master of the Revels or the ecclesiastical authorities, through the monopoly of the Stationer's Company. Between the 1586 *Injunctions* (see 5.4) and the breakdown of Church authority in 1640–1, there was no legal printing outside of Oxford, Cambridge and London.[13] Milton's articulation of the now established view that freedom of speech is the mark of a civilised society is one which was not generally accepted in his time: and we need to remember that despite the liberal and utopian expressions of the noble critical place of rhetoric in a civilised State to which Jonson, Sidney and Spenser give voice, their own writings and those of their contemporaries were occasionally suppressed, altered or amended by the censors. Thus, not only was their cultural theory dependent upon their social and political theories; but their cultural practices were dependent upon the wealth and position of their patrons or themselves, the prevailing view of the monarch and the Church, and the censor's pen. In addition, as Jonson makes clear in his *Discoveries* (5.20), and the innumerable prefaces to poetic collections show, the patronage, finance and protection of a powerful lord was the only way to ensure a market for one's writing. As deference and protection were part of the social and political fabric, so they were of the cultural market place.

5.1 TOTTEL'S *SONGS AND SONNETS*

Tottel published the first printed collection of Wyatt's and Surrey's sonnets in 1557, prefaced with the following address to readers. Text from: preface to first edition, 1557.

The printer to the reader

That to have well written in verse, yea and in small parcels, deserveth great praise, the works of divers Latins, Italians, and other, do prove sufficiently. That our tongue is able in that kind to do as praiseworthily as the rest, the honourable style of the noble Earl of Surrey and the weightiness of the deep-witted Sir Thomas Wyatt the elder's verse, with several graces in sundry good English writers do show abundantly. It resteth now (gentle reader) that thou think it not evil done to publish, to the honour of the English tongue, and for profit of the studious of English eloquence, those works which the ungentle hoarders up of such treasure have heretofore envied thee. And for this point (good reader) thine own profit and pleasure, in these presently, and in more hereafter, shall answer for my defence. If perhaps some mislike the stateliness of style removed from the rude skill of common ears: I ask help of the learned to defend their learned friends, the authors of this work: and I exhort, the unlearned, by reading to learn to be more skilful and to purge that swinelike grossness, that maketh the sweet marjoram not to smell to their delight.

5.2 JOHN CHEKE 'PREFACE' TO HOBY'S *THE COURTIER*

Hoby prefaced his edition of *The Courtier* (first published in 1561, see 5.3), with Cheke's letter to him on the English language. Text from: *The Courtier*, trans. T. Hoby, first edition, 1561, preface.

I am of this opinion that our own tongue should be written clean and pure, unmixed and unmangled with borrowing of other tongues, wherein if we take not heed by time, ever borrowing and never paying, she shall be fain to keep her house as bankrupt. For then doth our tongue naturally and praisably utter her meaning when she borroweth no counterfeitness of other tongues to attire herself withal; but useth plainly her own, with such shift as nature, craft, experience and following of other excellent doth lead her unto, and if she want at any time (as being unperfect she must) yet let her borrow with such bashfulness that it may appear that if either the mould of our own tongue could serve us to fashion a word of our own, or if the old denizened words could content and ease this need, we would not boldly venture of unknown words. This I say not for reproof of you who have scarcely and necessarily used where occasion serveth a strange word so, as it seemeth to grow out of the matter and to be sought for: but for mine own defence.

5.3 CASTIGLIONE, *THE COURTIER*

For an account of the significance of Castiglione's work in English courtly and educational circles, see part 3. Text from: Hoby's translation, 1561, pp. 45ff.

That therefore which is the principal matter and necessary for a courtier to speak and write well, I believe is knowledge. For he that hath not knowledge and the thing in his mind that deserveth to be understood, can neither speak nor write it.

Then must he couch in a good order that he hath to speak or to write, and afterward express it well with words: the which (if I be not deceived) ought to be apt, chosen, clear, and well applied, and (above all) in use also among the people: for very such make the greatness and gorgeousness of an oration; so he that speaketh have a good judgement and heedfulness withal, and the understanding to pick such as be of most proper signification . . .

I doubt, said the Lord Morello, if this courtier speak with such fineness and gravity among us, there will be some that will not understand him.

Nay, everyone shall understand him, answered the Count, for fineness hindereth not the easiness of understanding.

Neither will I have him to speak always in gravity, but of pleasant matters, of merry conceits, of honest devices, and of jests according to the time and in all notwithstanding after a pithy manner and with readiness and variety without confusion, neither shall he in any part show vanity or childish folly.

And when he shall then commune of a matter that is dark and hard, I will have him both in words and sentences well pointed, to express his judgement, and to make every doubt clear and plain after a certain diligent sort without tediousness.

Likewise (when he shall see time) to have the understanding to speak with dignity and vehemency and to raise those affections which our minds have in them, and to inflame or stir them according to the matter: sometime with a simplicity of such meekness of mind that a man would ween nature herself spake to make them tender and (as it were) dronken with sweetness: and with such conveyance of easiness, that whoso heareth him may conceive a good opinion of himself and think that he also with very little ado might attain to that perfection; but when he cometh to the proof, shall find himself far wide.

I would have our courtier to speak and write in that sort and not only choose

gorgeous and fine words out of every part of Italy, but also I would judge him
worthy praise to use some of those terms both French and Spanish, which by our
custom have been admitted. . . . Sometime I would have him take certain words
in another signification than that is proper to them, and wresting them to his
purpose (as it were) graft them like a graft of a tree in a more lucky stock to
make them more sightly and fair, and (as it were) draw the matters to the sense of
the very eyes, and (as they say) make them felt with hand, for the delight of him
that heareth or readeth.

Neither would I have him to stick to forge new also, and with new figures of
speech, deriving them featly from the Latins, as the Latins in old time derived
from the Grecians . . .

And (as you know) there were also read, and much set by in Rome, many
writers of barbarous nations.

But we more precise a great deal than they of old time, do bind ourselves
with certain new laws out of purpose: and having the broad, beaten way before
our eyes, seek through gaps to walk in unknown paths. For in our own tongue,
whose office is (as all others) to express well and clearly the conceits of the mind,
we delight in darkness and calling it the vulgar tongue, will use in it words that
are not only not understood of the vulgar people, but also of the best sort of
men, and those men of learning; and are not used in any part; not regarding
that all good writers of old time blamed such words as were refused of custom,
the which you (in my mind) do not well know: forasmuch as you say if any vice
of speech be taken up of any ignorant persons, it ought not to be called a
custom, nor received for a rule of speech . . .

Do you not know that figures of speech which give such grace and brightness to
an oration, are all the abuse of grammar rules: but yet are received and confirmed
by use? Because men are able to make no other reason but that they delight, and
to the very senses of our ears it appeareth they bring a life and sweetness.

And this believe I is good custom, which the Romans, the Neapolitans, the
Lombards and the rest are as apt to receive as the Tuscans. Truth it is, in every
tongue some things are always good, as easiness to be understood, a good order,
variety, picked sentences, clauses well framed: and on the other side, affectation
and the other contrary to these, are to be shunned.

But of words, some there are that last a good time, and afterward wax stale
and clean lose their grace: other some take force and creep into estimation.

For as the seasons of the year make leaves and fruits to fall, and afterward
garnish the trees afresh with other: even so doth time make those first words to fall,
and use maketh other to spring afresh, and giveth them grace and estimation, until
they in like sort consumed by little and little with the envious biting of time, come
to their end, because at the last both we and whatsoever is ours are mortal.

5.4 *INJUNCTIONS GIVEN BY THE QUEEN'S MAJESTY*

The Injunctions were published with the *Book of Common Prayer*, and updated every year or so during Elizabeth I's reign. They deal with the proper observation of the Acts of Uniformity and Supremacy and the *Thirty Nine Articles*, as well as with the issue of censorship. Thus it delineates how all published material had to be approved by the appropriate authority. The last clause of the 1559 *Injunctions* is given below. Text from: 1559 edition.

Item, because there is a great abuse in the printers of books, which for covetousness chiefly, regard not what they print, so they may have gain, whereby ariseth great disorder by publication of unfruitful, vain and infamous books and papers, the Queen's Majesty straightly chargeth and commandeth that no manner of person shall print any manner of book or paper of what sort, nature or in what language soever it be, except the same be first licensed by her Majesty by express words in writing, or by six of her Privy Council: or be perused and licensed by the Archbishops of Canterbury and York, the Bishop of London, the Chancellors of both Universities, the Bishop being Ordinary, and the Archdeacon also of the place where any such shall be printed, or by two of them, whereof the Ordinary of the place to be always one. And that the names of such that shall allow the same to be added in the end of every such work for a testimony of the allowance thereof. And because many pamphlets, plays, and ballads be oftentimes printed wherein regard would be had that nothing therein should be either heretical, seditious or unseemly for Christian ears: her Majesty likewise commandeth that no manner of person shall enterprise to print any such except the same be licensed by such her Majesty's commissioners, or three of them, as be appointed by the City of London to hear and determine divers causes ecclesiastical tending to the execution of certain statutes made the last Parliament for uniformity of order in religion. And if any shall sell or utter any manner of books or papers, being not licensed, as is above said: that the same party shall be punished by order of the said commissioners, as to the quality of the fault shall be thought meet. And touching all other books of matters of religion or policy or governance that hath been printed either on this side the seas, or on the other side, because the diversity of them is great, and that there needeth good consideration to be had of the particularities thereof: her Majesty refereth the prohibition or permission thereof to the order which her said commissioners within the City of London shall take and notify. According to the which, her Majesty straightly commandeth all manner her subjects and specially the wardens and company of stationers to be obedient.

Provided that these orders do not extend to any profane authors and works in any language that hath been heretofore commonly received or allowed in any the universities or schools, but the same may be printed and used as by good order they were accustomed.

5.5 ROGER ASCHAM, *THE SCHOOLMASTER*

Ascham's account of imitation is a paradigm of how poetic and fictional writing of the English renaissance proceeded, as well as being a marker for the key educational curricula and cultural texts of the learned elite of the time (see also 4.4). Text from: 1570 edition, fos 45ᵛff.

Imitation is a faculty to express lively and perfectly that example which ye go about to follow. And of itself it is large and wide: for all the works of nature in a manner be examples for art to follow.

But to our purpose: all languages, both learned and mother tongues, be gotten, and gotten only by imitation. For as ye use to hear, so ye learn to speak: if ye hear no other, ye speak not your self; and whom ye only hear, of them ye only learn.

And therefore, if ye would speak as the best and wisest do, ye must be conversant where the best and wisest are; but if you be born or brought up in a rude country, ye shall not choose but speak rudely; the rudest man of all knoweth this to be true.

Yet nevertheless the rudeness of common and mother tongues is no bar for wise speaking. For in the rudest country and most barbarous mother language, many be found can speak very wisely; but in the Greek and Latin tongue, the two only learned tongues, which be kept not in common talk, but in private books, we find always wisdom and eloquence, good matter and good utterance, never or seldom asunder. For all such authors as be fullest of good matter and right judgement in doctrine be likewise always most proper in words, most apt in sentence, most plain and pure in uttering the same.

And, contrariwise, in those two tongues, all writers, either in religion or any sect of philosophy, whosoever be found fond in judgement of matter, be commonly found as rude in uttering their mind. For stoics, anabaptists, and friars, with epicures, libertines and monks, being most like in learning and life, are no fonder and pernicious in their opinions than they be rude and barbarous in their writings. They be not wise therefore that say, *what care I for a man's words and utterance, if his matter and reasons be good?* Such men say so, not so much of ignorance, as either of some singular pride in themselves or some special malice or other, or for some private and partial matter, either in religion or other kind of learning. For good and choice meats be no more requisite for healthy bodies, than proper and apt words be for good matters, and also plain and sensible utterance for the best and deepest reasons; in which two points standeth perfect eloquence, one of the fairest and rarest gifts that God doth give to man.

Ye know not what hurt ye do to learning that care not for words but for matter, and so make a divorce betwixt the tongue and the heart. For mark all ages, look upon the whole course of both the Greek and Latin tongue, and ye shall surely find that when apt and good words began to be neglected and properties of those two tongues to be confounded, then also began ill deeds to spring, strange manners to oppress good orders, new and fond opinions to strive with old and true doctrine, first in philosophy, and after in religion, right judgement of all things to be perverted, and so virtue with learning is condemned, and study left off: of ill thoughts cometh perverse judgement, of ill deeds springeth lewd talk. Which four misorders, as they mar man's life, so destroy they good learning withal . . .

But to return to imitation again: there be three kinds of it in matters of learning.

The whole doctrine of comedies and tragedies is a perfect imitation, or fair lively painted picture of the life of every degree of man. Of this imitation, writeth Plato at large in 3. *De Rep.*, but it doth not much belong at this time to our purpose.

The second kind of imitation is to follow for learning of tongues and sciences the best authors. Here riseth amongst proud and envious wits a great controversy, whether one or many are to be followed; and if one, who is that one: Seneca or Cicero; Salust or Caesar; and so forth in Greek and Latin.

The third kind of imitation belongeth to the second, as when you be determined whether ye will follow one or more, to know perfectly and which way to follow, that one; in what place; by what mean and order; by what tools and instruments ye shall do it; by what skill and judgement ye shall truly discern whether ye follow rightly or no . . .

But if a man would take his pain also when he hath laid two places of Homer and Virgil, or of Demosthenes and Tully together, to teach plainly withal after this sort:

1. Tully retaineth thus much of the matter, these sentences, these words;
2. This and that he leaveth out, which he doth wittily to this end and purpose.
3. This he addeth here.
4. This he diminisheth there.
5. This he ordereth thus, with placing that here, not there.
6. This he altereth and changeth either in property of words, in form of sentence, in substance of the matter, or in one or other convenient circumstance of the author's present purpose.

In these few rude English words are wrapped up all the necessary tools and instruments, wherewith true imitation is rightly wrought withal in any tongue . . .

This foresaid order and doctrine of imitation would bring forth more learning and breed up truer judgement than any other exercise that can be used, but not for young beginners, because they shall not be able to consider duly thereof. And truly, it may be a shame to good students, who, having so fair examples to follow, as Plato and Tully, do not use so wise ways in following them for the obtaining of wisdom and learning as rude ignorant artificers do for gaining a small commodity. For surely the meanest painter useth more wit, better art, greater diligence in his shop in following the picture of any mean man's face than commonly the best students do, even in the university, for the attaining of learning itself.

* * *

But now when men know the difference and have the examples, both of the best and of the worst, surely to follow rather the Goths in rhyming than the Greeks in true versifying were even to eat acorns with swine, when we may freely eat wheat bread amongst men. Indeed, Chaucer, Thomas Norton of Bristow, my Lord of Surrey, M. Wyatt, Thomas Phaer, and other gentlemen in translating Ovid, Palingenius and Seneca have gone as far to their great praise as the copy they followed could carry them; but if such good wits and forward diligence had been directed to follow the best examples and not have been carried by time and custom to content themselves with that barbarous and rude rhyming, amongst their other worthy praises, which they have justly deserved, this had not been the least, to be counted amongst men of learning and skill more like unto the Grecians than unto the Gothians in handling of their verse.

Indeed, our English tongue, having in use chiefly words of one syllable which commonly be long, doth not well receive the nature of *carmen heroicum*, because *dactylus*, the aptest foot for that verse, containing one long and two short, is seldom therefore found in English; and doth also rather stumble than stand upon monosyllables.

5.6 MARGARET TYLER, *THE MIRROR OF PRINCELY DEEDS AND KNIGHTHOOD*

Tyler translates a Spanish romance and articulates a defence of woman writers in a masculine literary culture. Text from: first edition, 1578, fos A3ʳ.

M.T. To the reader

Thou hast here, gentle reader, the discourse of Trebatio, an emperor in Greece: whether a true history of him indeed, or a feigned fable, I wot not, neither did I greatly seek after it in the translation, but by me it is done into English for thy profit and delight. The chief matter therein contained is of exploits of wars and the parties therein named are especially renowned for their magnanimity and courage. The author's purpose appeareth to be this, to animate thereby, and to set on fire the lusty courages of young gentlemen to the advancement of their line by ensuing such like steps. The first tongue wherein it was penned was the Spanish, in which nation by common report, the inheritance of worldly commendation hath to this day rested. The whole discourse in respect of the end not unnecessary; for the variety and continual shift of fresh material, very delightful; in the speeches short and sweet; wise in sentence, and wary in the provision of contrary accidents. For I take the grace thereof to be rather in the reporter's device than in the truth of this report, as I would that I could so well impart with thee that delight which myself find in reading the Spanish: but seldom is the tale carried clean from another's mouth. Such delivery as I have made I hope thou wilt friendly accept, the rather for that it is a woman's work, though in a story profane, and a matter more manlike than becometh my sex. But as for the manliness of the matter, thou knowest that it is not necessary for every trumpeter or drumster in the war to be a good fighter: they take wages only to incite others, though themselves have privy maims and are thereby recureless. So, gentle reader, if my travail in Englishing this author may bring thee to a liking of the virtues herein commended, and by example thereof in thy prince's and country's quarrel to hazard thy person, and purchase good name: as for hope of well deserving myself that way, I neither bend myself thereto, nor yet fear the speech of people if I be found backward: I trust every man holds not the plough which would the ground were tilled: and it is no sin to talk of Robin Hood, though you never shot in his bow: or be it that the attempt were bold to intermeddle in arms, so as the ancient Amazons did, and in this story Claridiana doth,[1] and in other stories not a few, yet to report of arms is not so odious, but that it may be born withal, not only in you men which your selves are fighters, but in us women, to whom the benefit in equal part appertaineth of your victories, either for that the matter is so commendable that it carrieth no discredit from the homeliness of the speaker, or for that it is so generally known, that it fitteth every man to speak thereof, or for that it jumpeth with this common fear on all parts of war and invasion. The invention, disposition, trimming, and what else in this story, is wholly another man's, my part none therein but the translation, as it were only in giving entertainment to a stranger, before this time unacquainted with our country guise. Marry the worse perhaps is this, that amongst so many strangers as daily come over, some more ancient and some but new set forth, some penning matters of great weight and sadness in divinity, or other studies, the profession whereof more nearly beseemeth my years, other some discoursing of matters more easy and ordinary in common talk, wherein a gentlewoman may honestly employ her travail. I have notwithstanding made countenance only to this gentleman, whom neither his personage might sufficiently commend itself unto my sex, nor his behaviour (being light and soldier like) might in good order acquaint itself with my years. So that the question now ariseth of my choice, not of my labour, wherefore I preferred this story before matter of more importance? For answer whereto, gentle reader, the truth is, that as the first motion to this kind of labour came not from myself, so was this piece of work put upon me by others, and they which first counselled me to fall to work, took upon them also to be my taskmasters and overseers, lest I should be idle and yet because the refusal was in my power, I must stand to answer for my easy yielding, and may not be unprovided of excuse, wherein if I should allege for myself, that matters of less worthiness by as aged years have been taken in hand, and that daily new devices are published in songs, sonnets, interludes, and other discourses, and yet are born out without reproach, only to please the humour of some men. I think I should make no good plea therein, for besides that I should find thereby so many known enemies, as known men have been authors of such idle conceits, yet would my other adversaries be never the rather quieted: for they would say that as well the one as the other were all naught, and though peradventure I might pass unknown amongst a multitude, and not be the only gaze or odd party in my ill doing, yet because there is less merit of pardon if the fault be excused as common, I will not make that my defence which cannot help me, and doth hinder other men. But my defence is by example of the best, amongst which many have dedicated their labours, some stories, some of war, some physic, some law, some as concerning government, some divine matters, unto diverse ladies and gentlewomen. And if men may and do bestow such of their travails upon gentlewomen, then may we women read such of their works as they dedicate unto us, and if we may read them, why not further wade in them to the search of a truth? And then much more, why not deal by translation in such arguments, especially this kind of exercise, being a matter of more heed than of deep invention or exquisite learning? And they must needs leave this as confessed that in their dedications they mind not only to borrow names of worthy personages, but the testaments also for their further credit, which neither the one may demand without ambition, nor the other grant without over-lightness. If women be excluded from the view of such works as appear in their name, or if glory only be sought in our common inscriptions, it mattereth not whether the parties be men or women, whether alive or dead. But to return, whatsoever the truth is, whether that women may not at all discourse in learning, for men lay in their claim to be sole possessioners of knowledge, or whether they may in some manner, that is by limitation or appointment in some kind of learning, my persuasion hath been thus, that it is all one for a woman to pen a story as for a man to address his story to a woman. But amongst all my ill-willers, some I hope are not too straight that they would enforce me necessarily either not to write or to write of divinity. Whereas neither durst I trust mine own judgement sufficiently, if matter of controversy were handled, nor yet could I find any book in that tongue, which would not breed offence to some, but I perceive some may be rather angry to see their Spanish delight turned to an English pastime. . . . What natures such men be of, I list not greatly dispute, but my meaning hath been to make other partners of my liking, as I doubt not gentle reader, but if it shall please thee after serious matters to sport thyself with this Spaniard, that thou shalt find in him the just reward of malice and cowardice, with the good speed of honesty and courage, being able to furnish thee with sufficient store of foreign example to both purposes. And as in such matters which have been rather devised to beguile time, than to breed matter of sad learning, he hath ever born away that price, which could season such delights with some profitable reading: so shalt thou have this stranger an honest man when need serveth, and at other times either a good companion to drive out a weary night, or a merry jest at the board. And thus much concerning this present story, that it is neither unseemly for a woman to deal in, neither greatly requiring a less staid age than mine is. But of these two points gentle reader I thought to give thee warning, lest perhaps understanding of my name and years, thou mightest be carried into a wrong suspect of my boldness and rashness, from

284

which I would gladly free myself by this plain excuse, and if I may deserve thy good favour by like labour, when the choice is mine own, I will have a special regard of thy liking. So I wish thee well.

5.7 STEPHEN GOSSON, *THE SCHOOL OF ABUSE*

Gosson's main focus here is an attack on theatre and populist culture in London, first published in 1579 (see also 3.10). Text from: Ed. E. Arber, English Reprints, 1868, pp. 29–33; 45.

Plutarch complaineth that ignorant men, not knowing the majesty of ancient music, abuse both the ears of the people and the art itself with bringing sweet comforts into theatres, which rather effeminate the mind, as pricks unto vice, than procure amendment of manners, as spurs to virtue. Ovid, the high martial of Venus's field, planteth his main battle in public assemblies, sendeth out his scouts to theatres to descry the enemy, and instead of vaunt curriers,[2] with instruments of music, playing, singing and dancing, gives the first charge. Maximus Tyrius holdeth it for a maxim that the bringing of instruments to theatres and plays was the first cup that poisoned the commonwealth . . . they that never go out of their houses, for regard of their credit, nor step from the university for love of knowledge, seeing but slender offences and small abuses within their own walls, will never believe that such rocks are abroad, nor such horrible monsters in playing places . . .

. . . I cannot think that city to be safe that strikes down her percullises, rams up her gates, and suffereth the enemy to enter the postern. Neither will I be persuaded that he is in any way likely to conquer affection, which breaketh his instruments, burneth all his poets, abandons his haunt, muffleth his eyes, as he passeth the street and resorts to theatres to be assaulted. Cooks did never show more craft in their junkets to vanquish the taste, nor painters in shadows to allure the eye, than poets in theatres to wound the conscience.

There set they abroad strange comforts of melody to tickle the ear; costly apparel to flatter the sight; effeminate gesture to ravish the sense and wanton speech to whet desire to inordinate lust. Therefore of both barrels, I judge cooks and painters the better hearing, for the one extendeth his art no further than to the tongue, palate and nose, the other to the eye; and both are ended in outward sense, which is common to us with brute beasts. But these by the privy entries of the ear, slip down into the heart and with gunshot of affection gall the mind, where reason and virtue should rule the roost . . .

Consider with thyself (gentle reader) the old discipline of England, mark what we were before, and what we are now: leave Rome a while, and cast thine eye back to thy predecessors, and tell me how wonderfully we have been changed since we were schooled with these abuses. Dion saith that English men could suffer watching and labour, hunger and thirst, and bear of all storms with head and shoulders; they used slender weapons, went naked, and were good soldiers;

they fed upon roots and barks of trees; they would stand up to the chin many days in marshes without victuals; and they had a kind of sustenance in time of need, of which if they had taken but the quantity of a bean, or the weight of a pease, they did neither gape after meat, nor long for the cup a great while after. The men in valour not yielding to Scythia, the women in courage passing the Amazons. The exercise of both was shooting and darting, running and wrestling, and trying such masteries as either consisted in swiftness of feet, agility of body, strength of arms or martial discipline. But the exercise that is now among us is banqueting, playing, piping and dancing, and all such delights as may win us to pleasure, or rock us asleep.

O, what a wonderful change is this? Our wrestling at arms is turned to wallowing in ladies' laps; our courage to cowardice; our running to riot; our bows into bowls; and our darts to dishes. We have robbed Greece of gluttony, Italy of wantonness, Spain of pride, France of deceit, and Dutchland of quaffing. Compare London to Rome, and England to Italy, you shall find the theatres of the one, the abuses of the other, to be rife among us. . . . In our assemblies at plays in London, you shall see such heaving and shoving, such itching and shouldering to sit by women; such care for their garments that they be not trod on; such eyes to their laps, that no chips light in them; such pillows to their backs that they take no hurt; such masking in their ears, I know not what; such giving them pippins to pass the time; such playing at foot shunt without cards; such ticking, such toying, such smiling, such winking, and such manning them home when the sports are ended that it is a right comedy to mark their behaviour, to watch their conceits. . . . If this were as well noted as ill seen; or as openly punished as secretly practised, I have no doubt but the cause would be feared to dry up the effect, and these pretty rabbits very cunningly ferreted from their burrows. For they that lack customers all the week, either because their haunt is unknown, or the constables and officers of their parish watch them so narrowly that they dare not queatch;[3] to celebrate the sabbath, flock to theatres and there keep a general market of bawdry; not that any filthiness in deed is committed within the compass of that ground, as was done in Rome, but that every wanton and his paramour, every man and his mistress, every John and his Joan, every knave and his queen, are there first acquainted and cheapen the merchandise in that place, which they pay for elsewhere as they can agree.

* * *

Dicers and carders because their abuses are as commonly cried out on, as usually shown, have no need of a needless discourse, for every man seeth them and they stink almost in every man's nose. Common bowling alleys are privy moths that eat up the credit of many idle citizens, whose gains at home are not able to weigh down their losses abroad, whose shops are so far from maintaining their play, that their wives and children cry out for bread and go to bed supperless oft in the year.

5.8 WILLIAM WEBBE, *A DISCOURSE OF ENGLISH POETRY*

Webbe utilises many of the commonplaces of poetic theory of the period, but additionally translates Horace's Epistle to Pison, with its delineation of the rules of decorum, and insists upon the civilising and humanising function of poets. Text from: first edition, 1586, appendix.

Here follow the canons or general cautions of poetry, prescribed by Horace . . . in his epistle *Ad Pisones de Arte Poetica*

First, let the invention be meet for the matter, not differing or strange or monstrous. For a woman's head, a horse neck, the body of a divers coloured bird, and many members of sundry creatures compact together, whose legs ending like a fish's tail, this in a picture is a wonderful deformity; but if there be such diversity in the frame of a speech, what can be more uncomely or ill favoured?

2. The ornaments or colours must not be too many, nor rashly adventured on; neither must they be used everywhere and thrust into every place.

3. The propriety of speech must be duly observed, that weighty and great matters be not spoken slenderly, or matters of length too briefly . . .

4. In poetical descriptions the speech must not exceed all credit, nor anything feignedly brought in against all course of nature.

5. The disposing of the work must be such that there be no offence committed, as it were by too exquisite diligence . . .

6. He that taketh in hand to write any thing must first take heed that he be sufficient for the same: for often unwary fools through their rashness are over-took with great want of ability.

7. The ornament of a work consisteth in words and in the manner of the words, are either simple or mixed, new or old, proper or translated. In them all good judgement must be used and ready wit. The chiefest grace is in the most frequented words, for the same reason holdeth in words as doth in coins, that the most used and tried are best esteemed.

8. The kind of verse is to be considered and aptly applied to the argument in what measure is most meet for every sort. The most usual kinds are four: the heroic, elegiac, iambic and lyric.

9. One must use one kind of speech alike in all writings. Sometimes the lyric riseth aloft, sometime the comical. To the tragical writers belong properly the big and boisterous words. Examples must be interplaced according fitly to the time and place.

10. Regard is to be had of affections: one thing becometh pleasant persons, another sad; another wrathful, another gentle, which must all be heedfully respected . . .

11. Every person must be fitted accordingly and the speech well ordered;

wherein are to be considered the dignity, age, sex, fortune, condition, place, country etc. of each person.

12. The persons are either to be feigned by the poets themselves, or borrowed of others . . . again everyone must observe . . . fitness: as it is meet and agreeable everywhere for a man to be stout, a woman fearful, a servant crafty, a young man gentle.

13. Matters which are common may be handled by a poet as they may be thought proper to himself alone . . .

14. Where many things are to be taken out of ancienter tongues, as the Latins took much out of the Greeks, the words are not so precisely to be followed, but that they be altered according to the judgement and will of the imitator . . .

15. The beginning must not be foolishly handled, that is, strangely or too long.

16. The proposition or narration: let it not be far fetched or unlikely; and in the same, forget not the differences of ages and persons.

17. In a comedy it is not needful to exhibit all the actions openly, as such as are cruel, unhonest, or ugly; but such things may better be declared by some meet and handsome words after what sort they are supposed to be done.

18. If a comedy have more acts than five, it is tedious; if fewer, it is not sufficient. It fitteth not to bring in the persons of Gods but in very great matters. Cicero saith, when the tragedy writers cannot bring their matters to good pass, they run to God. Let not more persons speak together than four, for avoiding confusion. The *chori* must be well garnished and set forth, wherein either men are admonished, or reprehended, or counselled unto virtue. Such matter must be chosen for the chorus as may be meet and agreeable to that which is in hand. As for instruments and singing, they are relics of old simplicity. For the music commonly used at theatres and the licentiousness of their songs, which together with their wealth increased among the Romans, is hurtful to discipline and good manners.

19. In a *satyr* the clownish company and rural Gods are brought in to temperate the heaviness of tragedies with some mirth and pastime. In jesting it must be observed that it be not lascivious or ribald-like, or slanderous; which precept holdeth generally in all sorts of writings . . .

20. The feet are to be applied proper to every kind of verse and therein a poet must not use too much licence or boldness . . .

21. In compiling of verses, great care and circumspection must be used. Those verses which be made extempore are of no great estimation: those which are unartificial are utterly repelled as too foolish . . .

22. Arts have their increasings even as other things, being natural: so have tragedies which were first rudely invented by Thespis, at last were much adorned by Aeschylus: at the first they were practised in villages of the country, afterwards brought to stages in great cities.

23. Some arts do increase, some do decay by a certain natural course. The

old manner of comedies decayed by reason of slandering which therein they used against many, for which there was a penalty appointed, lest their bitterness should proceed too far: in place of which, among the Latins, came the *Satyrs* . . .

24. A poet should not content himself only with others' inventions, but himself also by the example of old writers should bring something of his own industry which may be laudable . . .

25. Heedfulness and good composition maketh a perfect verse, and that which is not so may be reprehended. The faculty of a good wit exceedeth art.

26. A poet, that he may be perfect, hath need to have knowledge of that part of philosophy which informeth the life to good manners. The other which pertaineth to natural things is less plausible, hath fewer ornaments and is not so profitable.

27. A poet to the knowledge of philosophy should also add greater experience, that he may know the fashions of men and dispositions of people. This profit is got by travelling, that whatsoever he writeth he may so express and order it that his narration may be formable.

28. The end of poetry is to write pleasant things and profitable. Pleasant it is which delighteth by being not too long or uneasy to be kept in memory, and which is somewhat likely and not altogether forged. Profitable it is which stirreth up the minds to learning and wisdom.

5.9 PHILIP SIDNEY, *AN APOLOGY FOR POETRY*

Sidney's *Apology* was published in 1595, after his death. It synthesises elegantly renaissance neo-classical poetic theories, combining Aristotelian imitative theory with neo-Platonic ideas about poets as second creators. It was widely read and cited by writers for the subsequent hundred years. Text from: 1595 edition, fos 10ff.

So as Amphion was said to move stones with his poetry to build Thebes; and Orpheus to be listened to by beasts, indeed stony and beastly people: so among the Romans were Livius, Andronicus and Ennius; so in the Italian language the first that made it aspire to be a treasure house of science were the poets Dante, Boccace and Petrach; so in our English were Gower and Chaucer.

After whom, encouraged and delighted with their excellent fore-going, others have followed to beautify our mother-tongue, as well in the same kind as in other arts. This did so notably show itself that the philosophers of Greece durst not a long time appear to the world but under the masks of poets. So Thales, Empedolces and Parmenides sang their natural philosophy in verses: so did Pythagoras and Phocilides their moral counsels; so did Tirteus in war matters and Solon in matters of policy: or rather, they being poets did exercise their delightful vein in those points of highest knowledge, which before them lay hid to the world. For that wise Solon was directly a poet it is manifest, having written in verse the notable fable of the Atlantic island, which was continued by Plato.

And truly, even Plato, whosoever well considereth, shall find that in the body of his work, though the inside and strength were philosophy, the skin as it were and beauty depended most of poetry, for all standeth upon Dialogues, wherein he feigneth many honest burgesses of Athens to speak of such matters that, if they had been set on the rack they would never have confessed them. Besides, his poetical describing the circumstances of their meetings, as the well ordering of a banquet, the delicacy of a walk, with interlacing mere tales . . . which who knoweth not to be flowers of poetry did never walk in to Apollo's garden.

And even historiographers (although their lips sound of things done and verity be written in their fore-heads) have been glad to borrow both fashion and perchance weight of poets. So Herodotus entitled his history by the name of the nine muses; and both he and all the rest that followed him either stole or usurped of poetry their passionate describing of passions, the many particularities of battles, which no man could affirm, or, if that be denied me, long orations put in the mouths of great kings and captains, which it is certain they never pronounced. So that, truly, neither philosopher nor historiographer could at the first have entered into the gates of popular judgements if they had not taken a great passport of poetry, which in all nations at this day, where learning flourisheth not, is plain to be seen . . .

Among the Romans a poet was called *vates*, which is as much as a diviner, forseer, or prophet, as by his conjoined words, vaticinium, and vaticiniari is manifest: so heavenly a title did that excellent people bestow upon this heart-ravishing knowledge. And so far were they carried into the admiration thereof, that they thought in the chanceable hitting upon any such verses great foretokens of their following fortunes were placed. Whereupon grew the word of *sortes virgilianae*, when by sudden opening Virgil's book, they lighted upon any verse of his making . . .

And may not I presume a little further to show the reasonableness of this word *vates*, and say that the holy David's Psalms are a divine poem? If I do, I shall not do it without the testimony of great learned men, both ancient and modern: but even the name Psalms will speak for me, which being interpreted, is nothing but songs . . .

There is no art delivered to mankind that hath not the works of nature for his principal object, without which they could not consist, and on which they so depend, as they become actors and players, as it were, of what nature will have set forth. So doth the astronomer look upon the stars, and by that he seeth, setteth down what order nature hath taken therein. So do the geometrician and arithmetician in their diverse sorts of quantities. So doth the musician in times tell you which by nature agree, which not. The natural philosopher thereon hath his name, and the moral philosopher standeth upon the natural virtues, vices and passions of man; and 'follow nature,' saith he, 'therein and thou shall not err'. The lawyer saith what men have determined. The historian what men have done. The grammarian speaketh only of the rules of speech; and the rhetorician and logician considering what in nature will soonest prove and persuade, thereon give artificial rules, which still are compassed within the circle of a question, according to the proposed matter. The physician weigheth the nature of a man's body, and the nature of things helpful or hurtful unto it. And the metaphysic, though it be in the second and abstract notions, and therefore be counted supernatural, yet doth he indeed build upon the depth of nature. Only the poet, disdaining to be tied to any such subjection, lifted up with the vigour of his own invention, doth grow in effect another nature, in making things either better than nature bringeth forth, or quite anew, forms such as never were in nature, as the heroes, demigods, Cyclops, Chimeras, Furies and such like: so as he goeth hand in hand with nature, not enclosed within the narrow warrant of her gifts, but freely ranging only within the zodiac of his own wit.

Nature never set forth the earth in so rich tapestry as divers poets have done, neither with pleasant rivers, fruitful trees, sweet smelling flowers, nor whatsoever else may make the too much loved earth more lovely. Her world is brazen, the poets only deliver a golden. But let those things alone and go to man, for whom as the other things are, so it seemeth in him her uttermost cunning is employed, and know whether she have brought forth so true a lover as Theagines, so constant a friend as Pilades, so valiant a man as Orlando, so right a prince as Xenophon's Cyrus, so excellent a man every way as Virgil's Aeneas. Neither let this be jestingly conceived because the works of the one be essential, the other in imitation or fiction: for any understanding knoweth the skill of the artificer standeth in that Idea or fore-conceit of the work, and not in the work itself. And that the poet hath that idea is manifest, by delivering them forth in such excellency as he hath imagined them. Which delivering forth also is not wholly imaginative, as we are wont to say by them that build castles in the air; but so far substantially it worketh, not only to make a Cyrus, which had been but a particular excellency as nature might have done, but to bestow a Cyrus upon the world, to make many Cyruses if they will learn aright why and how that maker made him.

Neither let it be deemed too saucy a comparison to balance the highest point of man's wit with the efficacy of nature: but rather give right honour to the heavenly maker of that maker, who, having made man to his own likeness, set him beyond and over all the works of that second nature, which in nothing he showeth so much as in poetry, when with the force of a divine breath, he bringeth things forth far surpassing her doings, with no small argument to the incredulous of that first accursed fall of Adam: sith our erected wit maketh us know what perfection is, and yet our infected will keepeth us from reaching unto it. But these arguments will by few be understood, and by fewer granted . . .

Poesy therefore is an art of imitation: for so Aristotle termeth it in his word, *mimesis*, that is to say a representing, counterfeiting, or figuring forth: to speak metaphorically, a speaking picture: with this end, to teach and delight. Of this have been three several kinds.

The chief both in antiquity and excellency were they that did imitate the inconceivable excellencies of God. Such were David in his Psalms, Solomon in his Song of Songs, in his Ecclesiastes and Proverbs, Moses and Deborah in their hymns, and the writer of Job. . . . In this kind, though in a full wrong divinity, were Orpheus, Amphion, Homer in his hymns and many other, both Greeks and Romans: and this poesy must be used by whosoever will follow St. James his counsel in singing Psalms when they are merry: and I know is used with the fruit of comfort by some, when in sorrowful pangs of their death-bringing sins, they find the consolation of the never-leaving goodness.

The second kind is of them that deal with matters philosophical; either moral, as Tirteus, Phocilides, and Cato; or natural, as Lucretius and Virgil's *Georgics,* or astronomical, as Manilius and Pontanus; or historical, as Lucan: which who mislike, the fault is in their judgements quite out of taste, and not in the sweet food of sweetly uttered knowledge.

But because this second sort is wrapped within the fold of the proposed subject, and takes not the course of his own invention, whether they properly be poets or no, let Grammarians dispute: and go to the third, indeed right poets, of whom chiefly this question ariseth: betwixt whom and these second is such a kind of difference as betwixt the meaner sort of painters (who counterfeit only such faces as are set before them) and the more excellent who having no law but wit, bestow that in colours upon you which is fittest for the eye to see: as the constant though lamenting look of Lucretia when she punished in herself another's fault; wherein he painteth not Lucretia whom he never saw, but painteth the outward beauty of such a virtue. For these third be they which most properly do imitate to teach and delight, and to imitate, borrow nothing of what is, hath been, or shall be: but range, only reined with learned discretion, into the divine consideration of what may be and should be. These be they that as the first and most noble sort, may justly be termed *vates,* so these are waited on in the excellentest languages and best understandings, with the fore described name of poets: for these indeed do merely make to imitate and imitate both to delight and teach, and delight to move men to take that goodness in hand, which without delight they would fly as from a stranger; and teach, to make them know that goodness whereunto they are moved, which being the noblest scope to which ever any learning was directed, yet want there not idle tongues to bark at them . . .

Now therefore it shall not be amiss first to weigh this latter sort of poetry by his works and then by his parts: and if in neither of these anatomies he be condemnable, I hope we shall obtain a more favourable sentence. This purifying of wit, this enriching of memory, enabling of judgement, and enlarging of conceit, which commonly we call learning, under what name soever it come forth, or to what immediate end soever it be directed, the final end is to lead and draw us to as high a perfection as our degenerate souls, made worse by their clayey lodgings, can be capable of. This, according to the inclination of the man, bred many formed impressions. For some that thought this felicity principally to be gotten by knowledge, and no knowledge to be so high and heavenly as acquaintance with the stars, gave themselves to astronomy; others persuading themselves to be demigods if they knew the causes of things, became natural and supernatural philosophers; some an admirable delight drew to music; and some the certainty of demonstration to the mathematics: but all, one and other, having this scope: to know, and by knowledge to lift up the mind from the dungeon of the body to the enjoying his own divine essence. But when by the balance of experience it was found that the astronomer looking to the stars might fall into a ditch; that the enquiring philosopher might be blind in himself; and the mathematician might draw forth a straight line with a crooked heart; then lo, did proof, the over-ruler of opinions, make manifest that all these are but serving sciences, which as they have each a private end in themselves, so yet are they all directed to the highest end of the mistress knowledge.

* * *

For suppose it be granted (that which I suppose with great reason may be denied) that the philosopher in respect of his methodical proceeding, doth teach more perfectly than the poet, yet do I think that no man is so much *philophilosophos* as to compare the philosopher in moving with the poet.

And that moving is of a higher degree than teaching, it may by this appear, that it is well nigh the cause and the effect of teaching. For who will be taught if he be not moved with desire to be taught? And what so much good doth teaching bring forth (I speak still of moral doctrine) as that it moveth one to do that which it doth teach? For, as Aristotle saith, it is not *gnosis* but *praxis* must be the fruit. And how *praxis* cannot be without being moved to practice, it is no hard matter to consider.

The philosopher showeth you the way, he informeth you of the particularities as well of the tediousness of the way, as of the pleasant lodging you shall have when your journey is ended, as of the many by-turnings that may divert you from your way. But this is to no man but to him that will read him, and read him with attentive, studious painfulness. Which constant desire, whosoever hath in him, hath already past half the hardness of the way, and therefore is beholding to the philosopher but for the other half . . .

Now therein of all sciences (I speak still of human and according to the human conceits) is our poet the monarch. For he doth not only show the way, but giveth so sweet a prospect into the way as will entice any man to enter into it. Nay, he doth, as if your journey should lie through a fair vineyard, at the first give you a cluster of grapes, that, full of that taste, you may long to pass further. He beginneth not with obscure definitions, which must blur the margent with interpretations and load the memory with doubtfulness; but he cometh to you with words sent in delightful proportion, either accompanied with, or prepared for, the well-enchanting skill of music; and with a tale, forsooth, he cometh unto you, with a tale which holdeth children from play and old men from the chimney corner. And pretending no more, doth intend the winning of the mind from wickedness to virtue: even as the child is often brought to take most wholesome things by hiding them in such other as have a pleasant taste: which if one should begin to tell them the nature of aloes or rhubarb they should receive, would sooner take their physic at their ears than at their mouth. So is it in men (most of which are childish in the best things, till they be cradled in their graves): glad they will be to hear the tales of Hercules, Achilles, Cyrus and Aeneas; and hearing them, must needs hear the right description of wisdom, valour and justice; which, if they had been barely, that is to say, philosophically set out, they would swear they be brought to school again.

That imitation whereof poetry hath the most conveniency to nature of all other, insomuch that, as Aristotle saith, those things which in themselves are horrible, as cruel battles, unnatural monsters, are made in poetical imitation delightful. Truly, I have known men that even with reading *Amadis de Gaul* (which God knoweth wanteth much of a perfect poesy) have found their hearts moved to the exercise of courtesy, liberality, and especially courage. Who readeth Aeneas carrying old Anchises on his back, that wisheth not it were his fortune to perform so excellent an act?

* * *

Now then go we to the most important imputations laid to the poor poets: for ought I can yet learn they are these. First that there being many other more fruitful knowledges a man might better spend his time in them than in this. Secondly, that it is the mother of lies. Thirdly that it is the nurse of abuse, infecting us with many pestilent desires; with a Siren's sweetness, drawing the mind to the serpent's tail of sinful fancy. And herein especially, comedies give the largest field to err, as Chaucer saith: how both in other nations and in ours before poets did soften us, we were full of courage, given to martial exercises, the pillars of man-like liberty and not lulled asleep in shady idleness with poets' pastimes. And lastly, and chiefly, they cry out with an open mouth, as if they out shot Robin Hood, that Plato banished them out of his Commonwealth. Truly, this is much, if there be much truth in it. First to the first: that a man might better spend his time is a reason indeed: but it doth (as they say) but *petere principium* [seek the original] for if it be, as I affirm, that no learning is so good as that which teacheth and moveth to virtue, and that none can both teach and move thereto so much as poetry, then is the conclusion manifest that ink and paper cannot be to a more profitable purpose employed. . . . To the second therefore, that they should be the principal liars, I answer paradoxically but truly. I think truly, that of all writers under the sun the poet is the least liar; and though he would, as a poet can scarcely be a liar. The astronomer with his cousin the geometrician can hardly escape, when they take upon them to measure the height of the stars. How often, think you, do the physicians lie when they aver things good for sickness, which afterwards send Charon a great number of souls drowned in a potion before they come to his ferry? And no less of the rest, which take upon them to affirm. Now, for the poet, he nothing affirms, and therefore never lieth. For, as I take it, to lie is to affirm that to be true which is false. So as the other artists and especially the historian, affirming many things, can in the cloudy knowledge of mankind, hardly escape from many lies. But the poet (as I said before) never affirmeth ... in truth not labouring to tell you what is, or is not, but what should or should not be; and therefore though he recount things not true, yet because he telleth them not for true, he lieth not ... so think I none so simple would say that Aesop lied in the tales of his beasts: for who thinks that Aesop writ it for actually true were well worthy to have his name chronicled among the beasts he writeth of. What child is there that, coming to a play, and seeing Thebes written in great letters upon an old door, doth believe that it is Thebes? ...

Their third is how much it abuseth men's wit, training it to wanton sinfulness and lustful love: for indeed that is the principal, if not the only abuse I can hear alleged. They say the comedies rather teach than reprehend amorous conceits. They say the lyric is larded with passionate sonnets; the elegiac weeps the want of his mistress; and that even to the heroical, Cupid hath ambitiously climbed. Alas, love, I would thou couldst as well defend thyself as thou canst offend others. I would those, on whom thou dost attend, could either put thee away, or yield good reason why they keep thee. But grant love of beauty to be a beastly fault (although it be very hard, sith only man and no beast hath that gift to discern beauty). Grant that lovely name of love to deserve all hateful reproaches (although even some of my masters the philosophers spent a great deal of their lamp-oil in setting forth the excellency of it). Grant, I say, whatsoever they will have granted: that not only love, but lust, but vanity, but (if they list) scurrility, posseseth many leaves of the poet's books: yet think I, when this is granted, they will find their sentence may with good manners put the last words foremost, and not say that poetry abuseth man's wit, but that man's wit abuseth poetry.

For I will not deny but that man's wit may make poesy (which should be *eikstatike*, which some learned have defined: figuring forth good things) to be *phantastike*: which doth, contrariwise infect the fancy with unworthy objects. As the painter, that should give to the eye either some excellent perspective, or some fine picture, fit for building or fortification, or containing in it some notable example, as Abraham sacrificing his son Isaac, Judith killing Holofernes, David fighting with Goliath, may leave those and please an ill-pleased eye with wanton shows of better hidden matters. But what, shall the abuse of a thing make the right use odious? Nay, truly, though I yield that poesy may not only be abused, but that being abused by the reason of his sweet charming force, it can do more hurt than any other army of words, yet shall it be so far from concluding that the abuse should give reproach to the abused: that contrariwise it is a good reason that whatsoever, being abused doth most harm, being rightly used (and upon the right use each thing conceiveth his title) doth most good.

5.10 GEORGE PUTTENHAM, *THE ART OF ENGLISH POESY*

Puttenham's work is more rhetorical handbook than a defence of poetry. It includes large sections on different figures and poetic forms. His explicit account of the political role of poets and poetry is unusually forthright. Text from: first edition, 1589, Book I, chaps 1, 4, 8, 17, 18; Book II, chap. 1; Book III, chaps 1, 3, 4, 25.

A poet is as much to say as a maker. . . . Such as (by way of resemblance and reverently) we may say of God; who without any travail to his divine imagination made all the world of nought, nor also by any pattern or mould, as the Platonics with their Ideas do fantastically suppose. Even so the very poet makes and contrives out of his own brain both the verse and matter of his poem, and not by any foreign copy or example, as doth the translator, who therefore may well be said a versifier but not a poet. The premises considered, it giveth to the name and profession no small dignity and preeminence, above all other artificers, scientific or mechanical. And nevertheless, without any repugnancy at all, a poet may in some sort be said a follower or imitator, because he can express the true and lively of every thing is set before him, and which he taketh in hand to describe: and so in that respect is both a maker and a counterfeiter: and poesy an art not only of making but also of imitation. And this science in his perfection cannot grow but by some divine instinct, the Platonics call it *furor*, or by excellency of nature and complexion, or by great subtility of the spirits and wit; or by much experience and observation of the world and course of kind; or peradventure by all or most part of them. Otherwise how was it possible that Homer, being but a poor private man, and, as some say, in his later age blind, should so exactly set forth and describe, as if he had been a most excellent captain or general, the order and array of battles, the conduct of whole armies, the sieges, and assaults of cities and towns? Or, as some great prince's majordomo and perfect surveyor in court, the order, sumptuousness and magnificence of royal banquets, feasts, weddings and interviews? Or, as a politician, very prudent and much inured with the private and public affairs, so gravely examined the laws and ordinances civil, or so profoundly discourse in matters of estate and forms of all politic regiment? Finally how could he so naturally paint out the speeches, countenance and manners of princely persons and private, to wit the wrath of Achilles, the magnanimity of Agamemnon, the prudence of Menaleus, the prowess of Hector, the majesty of King Priam, the gravity of Nestor, the policies and eloquence of Ulysses, the calamities of the distressed queens, and valiance of all the captains and adventurous knights in those lamentable wars of Troy?

* * *

How poets were the first philosophers . . .

Utterance also and language is given by nature to man for persuasion of others and aid of themselves, I mean the first ability to speak. For speech itself is artificial and made by man, and the more pleasing it is, the more it prevaileth to such purpose as it is intended for: but speech by metre is a kind of utterance more cleanly couched and more delicate to the ear than prose is, because it is more current and slipper upon the tongue, and withal tunable and melodious, as a kind of music, and therefore may be termed a musical speech or utterance, which cannot but please the hearer very well. Another cause is for that is briefer and more compendious and easier to bear away and be retained in memory, than that which is contained in multitude of words and full of tedious ambage and long periods. It is beside a manner of utterance more eloquent and rhetorical than the ordinary prose, which we use in our daily talk, because it is decked and set out with all manner of fresh colours and figures, which maketh that it sooner inveigleth the judgement of man and carrieth his opinion this way and that, whither soever the heart by impression of the ear shall be most affectionately bent and directed. . . . So as the poets were also from the beginning the best persuaders, and their eloquence the first rhetoric of the world, even so it became that the high mysteries of the gods should be revealed and taught by a manner of utterance and language of extraordinary phrase and brief and compendious, and above all others sweet and civil as the metrical is. The same also was meetest to register the lives and noble gests of princes, and of the great monarchs of the world, and all other the memorable accidents of time, so as the poet was also the first historiographer. Then, forasmuch as they were the first observers of all natural causes and effects in the things generable and corruptible, and from thence mounted up to search after the celestial courses and influences, and yet penetrated further to know the divine essences and substance separate, as is said before, they were the first astronomers and philosophists and metaphysics. Finally, because they did altogether endeavour themselves to reduce the life of man to a certain method of good manners, and made the first differences between virtue and vice, and then tempered all these knowledges and skills with the exercise of a delectable music by melodious instruments, which withal served them to delight their hearers, and to call the people together by admiration to a plausible and virtuous conversation, therefore were they the first philosophers' ethic and the first artificial musicians of the world. Such were Linus, Orpheus, Amphion and Museus, the most ancient poets and philosophers of whom there is left any memory by the profane writers. King David also and Solomon his son and many other of the holy prophets wrate in metres, and used to sing them to the harp, although to many of us, ignorant of the Hebrew language and phrase, and not observing it, the same seem but a prose.

* * *

In what reputation poets and poesy were in old time

In all former ages and in the most civil countries and commonwealths, good poets and poesy were highly esteemed and much favoured of the greatest princes. For proof whereof we read how much Amyntas, King of Macedonia, made of the tragical poet Euripedes; and the Athenians of Sophocles; in what price the noble poems of Homer were holden with Alexander the Great, insomuch as every night they were laid under his pillow, and by day were carried in the rich jewelled coffer of Darius, lately before vanquished by him in battle, and not only Homer, the father and prince of all poets, was so honoured by him, but for his sake all other meaner poets. . . . And in later times, how much were Jehan de Mehune and Guilaume de Loris made of by the French kings; and Geoffrey Chaucer, father of our English poets, by Richard the Second. . . . Nor this reputation was given them in ancient times altogether in respect that poesy was a delicate art, and the poets themselves cunning princepleasers, but for that also they were thought for their universal knowledge to be very sufficient men for the greatest charges in their commonwealths, were it for counsel or for conduct; whereby no man need to doubt but that both skills may very well concur and be most excellent in one person. For we find that Julius Caesar, the first emperor, and a most noble captain, was not only the most eloquent orator of his time, but also a very good poet, though none of his doings therein be now extant. And Quintius Catulus, a good poet; and Cornelius Gallus, treasurer of Egypt; and Horace the most delicate of all the Roman lyrics, was thought meet and by many letters of great instance provoked to be secretary of estate to Augustus the emperor, which nevertheless he refused for his unhealthfulness sake, and being a quiet minded man and nothing ambitious of glory. . . . So as the poets seemed to have skill not only in the subtleties of their art but also to be meet for all manner of functions civil and martial, even as they found favour of the times they lived in, insomuch as their credit and estimation generally was not small. But in these days, although some learned princes may take delight in them, yet universally it is not so. For as well poets as poesy are despised and the name become of honourable, infamous; subject to scorn and derision, and rather a reproach than a praise to any that useth it: for commonly whoso is studious in the art or shows himself excellent in it, they call him in disdain a *fantastical*; and a light headed or fantastical man, by conversion, they call a poet. And this proceeds through the barbarous ignorance of the time and pride of many gentlemen and others whose gross heads not being brought up or acquainted with any excellent art, nor able to contrive or in manner conceive any matter of subtlety in any business or science, they do deride and scorn it in all others as superfluous knowledges and vain sciences. . . . And peradventure in this iron and malicious age of ours princes are less delighted in it, being over earnestly bent and affected to the affairs of empire and ambition, whereby they are as it were enforced to endeavour themselves to arms and practices of hostility, or to entend to the right policing of their States, and have not one hour to bestow upon any other civil or debatable art of natural or moral doctrine, nor scarce any leisure to think one good thought in perfect and godly contemplation, whereby their troubled minds might be moderated and brought to tranquillity. So as it is hard to find in these days of noblemen nor gentlemen any good mathematician or excellent musician, or notable philosopher, or else a cunning poet, because we find few great princes much delighted in the same studies. . . . In other ages it was not so, for we read that Kings and princes have written great volumes and published them under their own regal titles. As to begin with Solomon, the wisest of Kings, Julius Caesar the greatest of emperors, Hermes Trismegistus, the holiest of priests and prophets.

* * *

Of the places where their interludes or poems dramatic were represented to the people

As it hath been declared, the satyrs were first uttered in their hallowed places within the woods, where they honoured their god under the open heaven, because they had no other housing fit for great assemblies. The old comedies were played in the broad streets, upon wagons or carts uncovered, which carts were floored with boards and made for removable stages to pass from one street of their towns to another, where all the people might stand at their ease to gaze upon the sights. Their new comedies or civil interludes were played in open pavilions or tents of linen cloth or leather, half displayed that the people might see. Afterward when tragedies came up, they devised to present them upon scaffolds or stages of timber, shadowed with linen or leather as the other, and these stages were made in the form of a semicircle, whereof the bow served for the beholders to sit in, and the string or forepart was appointed for the floor or place where the players uttered and had in it sundry little divisions by curtains as traverses to serve for several rooms where they might repair unto and change their garments and come in again, as their speeches and parts were to be renewed. Also there was place appointed for musicians to sing or to play upon their instruments at the end of every scene, to the intent the people might be refreshed and kept occupied. This manner of stage in half circle the Greeks called *theatrum*, as much to say as a beholding place, which was also in such sort contrived by benches and greeces to stand or sit upon, as no man should impeach another's sight. But as civility and withal wealth increased, so did the mind of man grow daily more haughty and superfluous in all his devises, so as for their theatres in half circle they came to be by the great magnificence of the Roman princes and people sumptuously built with marble and square stone in form all round and were called *amphitheatres*, whereof as yet appears one among the ancient ruins of Rome, built by Pompeius Magnus, for capacity to receive at ease fourscore thousand persons, as it is left written, and so curiously contrived as every man might depart at his pleasure, without any annoyance to other. It is also to be known that in those great amphitheatres were exhibited all manner of other shows and disports for the people, as their fence plays, or digladiations of naked men, their wrestlings, runnings, leapings, and other practices of activity and strength; also their baitings of wild beasts, as elephants, rhinoceros, tigers, leopards, and others, which sights much delighted the common people, and therefore the places required to be large and of great content.

Of the shepherds or pastoral poesy . . .

Some be of the opinion, and the chief of those who have written in this art among the Latins, that the pastoral poesy, which we commonly call by the name of Eclogue and Bucolic, a term brought in by the Sicilian poets, should be the first of any other, and before the Satyr, Comedy or Tragedy because, say they, the shepherds' and haywards' assemblies and meetings when they kept their cattle and herds in the common fields and forests was the first familiar conversation and their babble and talk under bushes and shady trees the first disputation and contentious reasoning and their fleshly heats growing of ease the first idle wooings, and their songs made to their mates or paramours either upon sorrow or jollity of courage the first amorous musics; sometime also they sang and played on their pipes for wagers, striving who should get the best game and be counted cunningest. All this I do agree unto, for no doubt the shepherds' life was the first example of honest fellowship, their trade the first art of lawful acquisition or purchase, for at those days robbery was a manner of purchase. . . . But for all this I do deny that the Eclogue should be the first and most ancient form of artificial poesy, being persuaded that the poet devised the Eclogue long after the other dramatic poems, not of purpose to counterfeit or represent the rustical manner of loves and communication, but under the veil of homely persons and in rude speeches to insinuate and glance at greater matters and such as perchance had not been safe to have been disclosed in any other sort, which may be perceived by the Eclogues of Virgil, in which are treated by figure matters of greater importance than the loves of Tityrus and Corydon.

* * *

Of proportion poetical

It is said by such as profess the mathematical sciences that all things stand by proportion and that without it nothing could stand to be good or beautiful. The doctors of our theology, to the same effect, but in other terms, say that God made the world by number, measure and weight; some for weight say tune, and peradventure better. For weight is a kind of measure or of much convenience with it; and therefore in their descriptions be always coupled together *statica et metrica*, weight and measures. . . . And this our proportion poetical resteth in five points: staff, measure, concord, situation and figure.

* * *

Of ornament poetical

. . . [Is] the fashioning of our maker's language and style, to such purpose as it may delight and allure as well the mind as the ear of the hearers with a certain novelty and strange manner of conveyance, disguising it no little from the ordinary and accustomed; nevertheless making it nothing the more unseemly or misbecoming, but rather decenter and more agreeable to any civil ear and understanding. And as we see in these great madames of honour, be they for personage or otherwise never so comely and beautiful, yet if they want their courtly habiliments or at leastwise such other apparel as custom and civility have ordained to cover their naked bodies, would be half ashamed or greatly out of countenance to be seen in that sort.

* * *

How ornament poetical is of two sorts

This ornament then is of two sorts, one to satisfy and delight the ear only by a goodly outward show set upon the matter with words and speeches smoothly and tunably running, another by certain intendments or sense of such words and speeches inwardly working a stir to the mind. That first quality the Greeks call *enargia*, of this word, *argos*, because it giveth a glorious lustre and light. This latter they call *energia*, of *ergon* because it wrought with a strong and virtuous operation. And figure breedeth them both, some serving to give gloss only to a language, some to give it efficacy by sense; and so by that means some of them serve the ear only, some serve conceit only and not the ear . . .

Of language

. . . When I say language I mean the speech wherein the poet or maker writeth, be it Greek or Latin, or as our case is, the vulgar English, and when it is peculiar unto a country, it is called the mother speech of that people: the Greeks term it *idioma*: so is ours at this day the Norman English. Before the conquest of the Normans it was the Anglesaxon, and before that the British, which, as some will, is at this day the Welsh, or as others affirm, the Cornish. I for my part think neither of both, as they be now spoken and pronounced. This part in our maker or poet must be heedily looked unto, that it be natural, pure, and the most usual of all his country; and for the same purpose, rather that which is spoken in the King's court or in the good towns and cities within the land, than in the marches and frontiers, or in port towns, where strangers haunt for traffic sake, or yet in universities where scholars use much peevish affectation of words out of the primitive languages, or finally in any uplandish village or corner of a realm, where is no resort but of poor, rustical or uncivil people: neither shall he follow the speech of a craftsman or carter, or other of the inferior sort, though he be inhabitant or bred in the best town and city in this realm, for such persons do abuse good speeches by strange accents or ill-shapen sounds and false orthography. But he shall follow generally the better brought up sort, such as the Greeks call *charientes*, men civil and graciously behavioured and bred. Our maker therefore at these days shall not follow *Piers Plowman* nor Gower nor Lydgate, nor yet Chaucer, for their language is now out of use with us; neither shall he take the terms of northern-men, such as they use in daily talk, whether they be noble men or gentlemen or of their best clerks, all is a matter; nor in effect any speech used beyond the river of Trent, though no man can deny but that theirs is the purer English Saxon at this day, yet it is not so courtly nor so current as our southern English is; no more is the far western man's speech. Ye shall therefore take the usual speech of the court, and that of London and the shires lying about London within 60 miles, and not much above.

* * *

That the good poet or maker ought to dissemble his art

And now (most excellent Queen) having largely said of poets and poesy and about what matters they be employed . . . and so have apparelled him to our seeming in all his gorgeous habiliments, and pulling him first from the cart to the school, and from thence to the court, and preferred him to your Majesty's service, in that place of great honour and magnificence to give entertainment to princes, ladies of honour, gentlewomen and gentlemen, and by his many moods of skill to serve the many humours of men thither haunting and resorting, some by way of solace, some of serious advice, and in matters as well profitable as pleasant and honest. We have in our humble conceit sufficiently performed our promise or rather duty to your Majesty in the description of this art, so always as we leave him not unfurnished of one piece that best beseems that place of any other, and may serve as a principal good lesson for all good makers to bear continually in mind in the usage of this science; which is, that being now lately become a courtier he show not himself a craftsman, and merit to be disgraded and with scorn sent back again to the shop or other place of his first faculty and calling; but that so wisely and discreetly he behave himself as he may worthily retain the credit of his place and profession of a very courtier, which is, in plain terms, cunningly to be able to dissemble. . . . Or perhaps rather that he could dissemble his conceits as well as his countenances, so as he never speak as he think, or think as he speaks, and that in any matter of importance his words and his meaning very seldom meet: for so as I remember it was concluded by us setting forth the figure *allegoria*, which therefore not impertinently we call the courtier, or figure of fair semblant? Or is it not perchance more requisite our courtly poet do dissemble not only his countenances and conceits, but also all his ordinary actions of behaviour, or the most part of them, whereby the better to win his purposes and good advantages? . . .

Which parts nevertheless we allow not now in our English maker, because we have given him the name of an honest man, and not of an hypocrite: and therefore leaving these manner of dissimulations to all base-minded men, and of vile nature or mystery, we do allow our courtly poet to be a dissembler only in the subtleties of his art, that is, when he is most artificial, so to disguise and cloak it as it may not appear, nor seem to proceed from him by any study or trade of rules, but to be his natural; nor so evidently to be descried as every lad that reads him shall say he is a good scholar: but will rather have him to know his art well, and little to use it.

302

And yet peradventure in all points it may not be so taken but in such only as may discover his grossness or his ignorance by some scholarly affectation; which thing is very irksome to all men of good training and specially to courtiers. And yet for all that our maker may not be in all cases restrained, but that he may both use and also manifest his art to his great praise, and need no more be ashamed thereof than a shoemaker to have made a cleanly shoe, or a carpenter to have built a fair house.

... [The poet] is not, as the painter, to counterfeit the natural by the like effects and not the same; nor, as the gardener, aiding nature to work both the same and the like; nor, as the carpenter, to work effects utterly unlike: but even as nature herself working by her own peculiar virtue and proper instinct and not by example or meditation or exercise as all other artificers do, is then most admired when he is most natural and least artificial: and in the feats of his language and utterance, because they hold as well of nature to be suggested and uttered, as by art to be polished and reformed. Therefore shall our poet receive praise for both, but more by knowing of his art than by unseasonable using it, and be more commended for his natural eloquence than for his artificial, and more for his artificial well dissembled, than for the same overmuch affected and grossly or undiscreetly bewrayed, as many makers and orators do.

5.11 THOMAS NASHE, *THE ANATOMY OF ABSURDITY*

Nashe was a prolific writer of satire: here he attacks hack poetry and argues the case for an ethical and philosophical poetic theory. Text from: first edition, 1589, pp. 298–320.

Hence come our babbling ballads, and our new found songs and sonnets, which every red-nosed fiddler hath at his finger's end, and every ignorant ale knight will breath forth over the pot, as soon as his brain waxeth hot. Be it a truth which they would tune, they interlace it with a lie or two to make metre, not regarding verity so they may make up the verse: not unlike to Homer who cared not what he feigned so he might make his countrymen famous. But as the straightest things being put into water seem crooked, so the crediblest truths, if once they come within compass of these men's wits seem tales. Were it that the infamy of their ignorance did redound only upon themselves, I could be content to apply my speech otherwise than to their Appuleain ears; but sith they obtain the name of our English poets and thereby make men think more basely of the wits of our country, I cannot but turn them out of their counterfeit livery and brand them in the forehead that all men may know their falsehood. . . . It were to be wished that the acts of the virtuous and the praise of the virtuous were by public edict prohibited: by such men's merry mouths to be so odiously extolled as rather breeds detestation than admiration, loathing than liking. What politic counsellor or valiant soldier will joy or glory of this, in that some stitcher, weaver, spendthrift or fiddler hath shuffled or slubbered up a few ragged rhymes in the memorial of the one's prudence or the other's prowess? It makes the learned sort to be silent, when as they see unlearned sots so insolent.

... Such kind of poets were they that Plato excluded from his common-wealth, and Augustine banished *ex civitate dei* [from the city of God], which the Romans derided and the Lacedaemonians scorned, who would not suffer one of Archilochus's books to remain in their country; and amiss it were not if these which meddle with the art they know not, were bequeathed to Bridewell, there to learn a new occupation: for as the basilisk with his hiss driveth all other serpents from the place of his abode, so these rude rhythmers with their jarring verse alienate all men's minds from delighting in numbers' excellence, which they have so defaced . . .

But lest I should be mistaken as an enemy to poetry, or at least not taken as a friend to that study, I have thought good to make them privy to my mind by expressing my meaning. I account of poetry as of a more hidden and divine kind of philosophy, enwrapped in blind fables and dark stories, wherein the principles of more excellent arts and moral precepts of manners, illustrated with divers examples of other kingdoms and countries, are contained: for amongst the Grecians there were poets before there were any philosophers, who embraced entirely the study of wisdom, as Cicero testifieth in his *Tusculanes*: whereas he saith that of all sorts of men poets are most ancient, who, to the intent they might allure men with a greater longing to learning, have followed two things, sweetness of verse and variety of invention, knowing that delight doth prick men forward to the attaining of knowledge, and that true things are rather admired if they be included in some witty fiction, like to pearls that delight more if they be deeper set in gold. Wherefore seeing poetry is the very same with philosophy, the fables of poets must of necessity be fraught with wisdom and knowledge, as framed of those men which have spent all their time and studies in the one and in the other. For even as in vines the grapes that are fairest and sweetest are couched under the branches that are broadest and biggest, even so in poems, the things that are most profitable are shrouded under the fables that are most obscure . . .

As these men offend in the impudent publishing of witless vanity, so others overshoot themselves as much another way, in senseless stoical austerity, accounting poetry impiety and witty folly. . . . These men condemn them of lasciviousness, vanity and curiosity, who under feigned stories include many profitable moral precepts, describing the outrage of unbridled youth having the rein in their own hands, the fruits of idleness, the offspring of lust, and how available good educations are unto virtue. In which their preciser censure they resemble them that cast away the nut for mislike of the shell, and are like to those which loath the fruit for the leaves, accounting the one sour because the other is bitter. It may be some dreaming dunce, whose bald affected eloquence making his function odious, better beseeming a privy than a pulpit, a misterming clown in a comedy, than a chosen man in the ministry, will cry out that it breeds a scab to the conscience to peruse such pamphlets, being indeed the display of their duncery, and breeding a mislike of such tedious dolts' barbarism by the view of their rhetorical invention. Such trifling studies, say they, infect the mind and corrupt the manners, as though the mind were only conversant in such toys, or should continually stay where the thoughts by chance do stray. The sunbeams touching the earth remain still from whence they came; so a wise man's mind, although sometimes by chance it wandereth here and there, yet it hath recourse in staid years to that it ought. But grant the matter to be fabulous: is it therefore frivolous? . . .

I would not have any man imagine that in praising of poetry I endeavour to approve Virgil's unchaste Priapus, or Ovid's obscenity: I commend their wit, not their wantonness, their learning, nor their lust; yet even as the bee out of the bitterest flowers and sharpest thistles gathers honey, so out of the filthiest fables may profitable knowledge be sucked and selected. Nevertheless, tender youth ought to be restrained for a time from the reading of such ribaldry, lest, chewing over wantonly the ears of summer corn, they be choked with the haun before they can come at the kernel.

5.12 GEORGE PETTIE, *GUAZZO'S CIVIL CONVERSATION*

Pettie's translation of the Italian *Civil Conversation* was another contribution to courtier literature; here he defends the importance of translation for English culture. Text from: first edition, 1581: fos i–iii.

The preface to the readers

. . . Those which mislike that a gentleman should publish the fruits of his learning, are some curious gentlemen who think it most commendable in a gentleman to cloak his art and skill in everything, and to seem to do all things of his own mother wit, as it were: not considering how we deserve no praise for that which God or nature hath bestowed upon us, but only for that which we purchase by our own industry; and if you shall chance to enter into reasoning with them, they will at the second word make protestation that they are no scholars; whereas notwithstanding they have spent all their time in study. Why gentlemen is it a shame to show to be that, which it is a shame not to be? In divers things, nothing so good as learning, you are desirous to seem to be that which you are not; and in learning, the best thing of all others, are you afeard to show to be that which you are? Alas you will be but ungentle gentlemen if you be no scholars: you will do your prince but simple service; you will stand your country but in slender stead; you will bring yourselves but to small preferment, if ye be no scholars. Can you counsel your prince wisely, foresee dangers providently, govern matters of State discretely, without learning? No, experience must then be your guide, which will be but a blind one; it must be your schoolmaster, but you shall find it a dangerous one. To come lower, can you discourse with strangers, inquire the state of foreign countries, give entertainment to ambassadors, being no scholars? No surely, unless it be with dumb shows, and signs: like as of late a pleasant gentleman (who could have spoken sufficiently if he had been put to it) being amongst others commanded to ride to meet an ambassador, that was coming to court, at his return a noble man asked him merrily what he said to the ambassador when he met him? Nothing (said he) but kissed my horse's mane and came my way. To come lowest of all, can you so much as tell your mistress a fine tale, or delight her with pleasant device, being unlearned? No, it must needs either be altogether unsavoury or else seasoned with the salt of others: and whether think you it more shame that you should show to have of your own, or that she should know you filch from others? You know Caesar was a brave gentleman, but yet he was a scholar, but yet he wrote books, but yet he came in print. Marcus Aurelius was an emperor, but he was learned and set forth learned works. Therefore gentlemen, never deny yourselves to be scholars, never be ashamed to show your learning: confess it, profess it, embrace it, honour it: for it is it which honoureth you; it is only it which maketh you men; it is only it which maketh you gentlemen . . .

There are some others yet who will set light by my labours because I write in English; and those are some nice travellers, who return home with such queasy stomachs, that nothing will down with them but French, Italian or Spanish, and though a work be but meanly written in one of those tongues, and finely trans- lated into our language, yet they will not stick far to prefer the original before the translation . . . but they consider not the profit which cometh by reading things in their own tongue, whereby they shall be able to conceive the matter much sooner, and bear it away far better than if they read it in a strange tongue, whereby also they shall be enabled to speak, to discourse, to write, to indite, properly, fitly, finely and wisely; but the worse is they think that impossible to be done in our tongue, for they count it barren; they count it barbarous; they count it unworthy to be accounted of; and, which is worse, as I myself have heard some of them, they report abroad that our country is barbarous, our manners rude, and our people uncivil. . . . But for our country, I am persuaded that those which know it and love it, will report it for the civilest country in the world; and if it be thought to be otherwise by strangers, the disorders of those travellers abroad are the chief cause of it. . . . For at home it is well known that we live in laws as orderly, in manners as decently, in apparel as comely, in diet as delicately, in lodging as curiously, in buildings as sumptuously, in all things as abundantly and every way as civilly as any nation under heaven. For the barbarousness of our tongue, I will likewise say that it is much the worse for them. . . . For take the Latin words from the Spanish tongue, and it shall be as barren as most part of their country; take them from the Italian, and you take away in a manner the whole tongue; take them from the French, and you mar the grace of that; yea take from the Latin itself the words derived from the Greek, and it shall not be so flowing and flourishing as it is. Wherefore I marvel how our English tongue hath cracked its credit, that it may not borrow of the Latin, as well as other tongues: and if it have been broken, it is but of late, for it is not unknown to all men how many words we have fetched from thence within these few years, which if they should be all counted ink-pot terms, I know not how we should speak anything without blacking our mouths with ink: for what words can be more plain than this word, *plain*? And yet what can come more near to the Latin? What more manifest than *manifest*? And yet in a manner Latin. What more common than *rare*; or less rare than *common*; and yet both of them coming of the Latin? But you will say long use hath made these words current: and why may not use do as much for these words which we shall now derive? Why should not we do as much for the posterity, as we have received of the antiquity?

5.13 EDMUND SPENSER, 'LETTER OF THE AUTHOR', PREFACED TO *THE FAERIE QUEENE*

Spenser's 'Letter' was annexed to the first edition of *The Faerie Queene* in 1590, and set out a theory of allegory. Text from: 1611 edition, fos q1^r–q2^r.

To the right noble and valorous Sir Walter Raleigh

Sir, knowing how doubtfully all allegories may be construed, and this book of mine which I have entitled *The Faerie Queene*, being a continued allegory or dark conceit, I have thought good as well for avoiding of jealous opinions and misconstructions, as also for your better light in reading thereof (being so by you commanded) to discover unto you the general intention and meaning, which in the whole course thereof I have fashioned, without expressing of any particular purposes or by-accidents therein occasioned. The general end therefore of all the book is to fashion a gentleman or noble person in virtuous and gentle discipline: which for that I conceived should be most plausible and pleasing being coloured with an historical fiction, the which the most part of men delight to read, rather for variety of matter than for profit of the example. I chose the history of King Arthur as most fit for the excellency of his person, being made famous by many men's former works, and also furthest from the danger of envy and suspicion of present time. In which I have followed all the antique poets historical: first Homer, who in the persons of Agamemnon and Ulysses hath ensampled a good governor and a virtuous man, the one in his *Iliad*, the other in his *Odysseus*; then Virgil, whose like intention was to do in the person of Aeneas; after him Ariosto comprised them both in his Orlando; and lately Tasso dissevered them again and formed both parts in two persons, namely that part which they in philosophy call ethic, or virtues of a private man, coloured in his Rinaldo; the other named politic in his Godfredo. By example of which excellent poets I labour to portrait in Arthur, before he was king, the image of a brave knight, perfected in the twelve private moral virtues. . . . To some I know this method will seem displeasant, which had rather have good discipline delivered plainly in way of precepts, or sermoned at large, as they use, than thus cloudily enwrapped in allegorical devices. But such, meseem, should be satisfied with the use of these days, seeing all things accounted by their shows and nothing esteemed of that is not delightful and pleasing to common sense. For this cause is Xenophon preferred before Plato, for that the one in the exquisite depth of his judgement formed a commonwealth such as it should be, but the other in the person of Cyrus and the Persians fashioned a government such as might best be. So much more profitable and gracious is doctrine by example than by rule. So have I laboured to do in the person of Arthur, whom I conceive after his long education by Timon, to whom he was by Merlin delivered to be brought up so soon as he was born of the Lady Igraine to have seen in a dream or vision the Fairy Queen, with whose excellent beauty ravished, he awaking resolved to seek her out, and so being by Merlin armed and by Timon thoroughly instructed, he went to seek her forth in Fairyland. In that Fairy Queen I mean glory in my general intention, but in my particular I conceive the most excellent and glorious person of our sovereign the Queen, and her kingdom in fairyland. And yet in some places else I do otherwise shadow her. For considering she beareth two persons, the one of a most royal queen or empress, the other of a most virtuous and beautiful lady, this latter part in some places I do express in Belphoebe, fashioning her name according to your own excellent conceit of Cynthia (Phoebe and Cynthia being both names of Diana). So in the person of Prince Arthur I set forth magnificence in particular, which virtue for that (according to Aristotle and the rest) it is the perfection of all the rest, and containeth in it them all. . . . Of which these three books contain three [knights representing virtues]: the first of the knight of the Redcross, in whom I express holiness; the second of Sir Guyon, in whom I set forth temperance; the third of Britomartis, a lady knight, in whom I picture chastity. But because the beginning of the whole work seemeth abrupt and as depending upon other antecedents, it needs that ye know the occasion of these three knights' several adventures. For the method of a poet historical is not such as of an historiographer. For an historiographer discourseth of affairs orderly as they were done, accounting as well the times as the actions: but a poet thrusteth into the middest, even where it most concerneth him, and there recoursing to the things forepast and divining of things to come, maketh a pleasing analysis of all.

5.14 JOHN HARRINGTON, 'PREFACE' TO *ORLANDO FURIOSO*

One erotic chapter of Harrington's translation of *Orlando Furioso* had circulated at court before its publication, which increased its notoriety once published. Harrington used the preface to defend his work against charges of lubriciousness, and here he gives an example of how to read any text allegorically. Text from: first edition, 1591, preface.

The ancient poets have indeed wrapped as it were in their writings divers and sundry meanings, which they call the senses or mysteries thereof. First of all for the literal sense (as it were the utmost bark or rind) they set down in manner of an history the acts and notable exploits of some person's worthy memory; then in the same fiction as a second rind and somewhat more fine, as it were nearer to the pith and marrow, they place the moral sense profitable for the active life of man, approving virtuous actions and condemning the contrary. Many times also under the selfsame words they comprehend some true understanding of natural philosophy or sometimes of politic government, and now and then of divinity: and these same senses that comprehend so excellent knowledge we call the allegory which Plutarch defineth to be when one thing is told and by that another is understood. Now let any man judge if it be a matter of mean art or wit to contain in one historical narration, either true or feigned, so many, so diverse, and so deep conceits: but for making the matter more plain I will allege an example thereof.

Perseus son of Jupiter is feigned by the poets to have slain Gorgon, and after that conquest achieved, to have flown up to heaven. The historical sense is this, Perseus, the son of Jupiter . . . slew Gorgon, a tryant in that country (Gorgon in Greek signifieth earth) and was for his virtuous parts exalted by men up into heaven. Morally it signifieth this much: Perseus a wise man, son of Jupiter, endued with virtue from above, slayeth sin and vice, a thing base and earthly signified by Gorgon, and so mounteth up to the sky of virtue. It signifies in one kind of allegory thus much: the mind of man being gotten by God and so the child of God killing and vanquishing the earthliness of this Gorgonical nature, ascendeth up to the understanding of heavenly things, of high things, of eternal things, in which contemplation consisteth the perfection of man: this is the natural allegory, because man [is] one of the chief works of nature. It hath also a more high and heavenly allegory, that the heavenly nature, daughter of Jupiter, procuring with her continual motion corruption and mortality in the inferior bodies, severed itself at last from these earthly bodies, and flew up on high and there remaineth for ever. It hath also another theological allegory: that the angelical nature, daughter of the most high God, the creator of all things, killing and overcoming all bodily substance signified by Gorgon, ascended into heaven.

5.15 PHILEMON HOLLAND, 'PREFACE' TO *PLINY'S NATURAL HISTORY*

Holland was one of the most prolific of Elizabethan and Jacobean translators, and later became master of the Free School in Coventry. Here he defends both classical learning and its modernisation, through translation. Text from: first edition, 1601, preface.

Now albeit my intention and only scope was to do a pleasure unto them that could not read these authors in the original: yet needs I must confess that even myself have not only gained thereby increase of the Latin tongue (wherein these works were written), but also grown to further knowledge of the matter and argument therein contained. For this benefit we reap by studying the books of such ancient authors: that the oftener we read them over, the more still we find and learn in them. . . . Well may the newest songs and last devised plays delight our eyes at the first, and for the present ravish our senses, like as hoary and early summer fruits content our taste and please the appetite; but surely it is antiquity that hath given grace, vigour and strength to writings, even as age commendeth the most generous and best wines. In which regard and upon this experience of mine own, I nothing doubt but they also whom I might justly fear as hard censors of these my labours, will not only pity me for my pains, but also in some measure yield me thanks in the end; when either by the light of the English (if they be young students) they shall be able more readily to go away with the dark phrase and obscure construction of the Latin; or (being great scholars and taking themselves for deep critics), by conferring the one with the other, haply to espy wherein I have tripped, they shall by that means peruse once again and consequently gather new profit out of that author whom peradventure, they had laid by for many years as sufficiently understood. When some benefit (I say) shall accrue to them likewise by this occasion, I less dread their fearful doom, to which so wilfully I have exposed myself. Well I wist that among the Athenians, order was taken by law that an interlude newly acted should be heard with silence and applause, which custom as it was respective and favourable to the first endeavours of the actors, so it implied an inevitable danger of hissing out and utter disgrace if afterwards they chanced to miss and fail in their parts. Having showed myself once before upon the stage, presuming upon this privilege and the courtesy of the theatre, I might have now sitten still and so rested. In mounting up thus soon again I may seem either in the assured confidence of mine own worthiness, to proclaim a challenge to all men's censures; or else upon a deep conceit of some general connivency make reckoning of an extraordinary and wonderful favour. . . . Moreover the title prefixed thereto, so universal as it is, to wit *The History of the World*, or *Reports of Nature*, imported no doubt that he first penned it for the general good of mankind. Over and besides the argument ensuing full of variety, furnished with discourse of all manners, not appropriate to the learned only, but accommodate to the rude peasant of the country; fitted for the painful artisan in town and city; pertinent to the bodily health of man, woman and child; and in one word, suiting with all sorts of people living in a society and commonweal. To say nothing of the precedent given by the author himself who indited the same, not with any affected phrase, but sorting well with the capacity even of the meanest and most unlettered; who also translated a good part thereof out of the Greek. What should I allege the example of former times, wherein the like hath evermore been approved and practised? Why should any man therefore take offence hereat, and envy this good to his natural country, which was first meant for the whole world? And yet some there be so gross as to give out that these and such like books ought not to be published in the vulgar tongue. It is a shame (quoth one) that Livy speaketh English as he doth: Latinists only are to be acquainted with him; as who should say, the soldier were to have recourse unto the university for military skill and knowledge; or the scholar to put on arms and pitch a camp. What should Pliny (saith another) be read in English, and the mysteries couched in his books divulged? As if the husbandman, the mason, carpenter, goldsmith, painter, lapidary, and engraver with other artificers were bound to seek unto great clerks or linguists for instructions in their several arts. Certes, such *Momi* [men asleep] as these, besides their blind and erroneous opinion, think not so honourably of their native country and mother tongue as they ought: who if they were so well affected that way as they should be, would wish rather and endeavour by all means to triumph now over the Romans in subduing their literature under the dent of the English pen, in requital of the conquest sometime over this island, achieved by the edge of their sword. As for our speech, was not Latin as common and natural in Italy as English here with us? And if Pliny faulted, but not deserved well of the Roman name, in laying abroad the riches and hidden treasures of nature in that dialect, or idiom which was familiar to the basest clown: why should any man be blamed for enterprising the semblable to the commodity of that country in which, and for which, he was born? Are we the only nation under heaven unworthy to taste of such knowledge? Or is our language so barbarous that it will not admit in proper terms a foreign phrase? I honour them in my heart, who having of late days trodden the way before me in Plutarch, Tacitus and others, have made good proof that as the tongue in an Englishman's head is framed so flexible and obsequent that it can pronounce naturally any other language; so a pen in his hand is able sufficiently to express Greek, Latin and Hebrew.

5.16 THOMAS CAMPION, *OBSERVATIONS IN THE ART OF ENGLISH POESY*

Campion's scholarly plea that English poetry should imitate the prosody of Latin poetry is an interesting footnote in the continued development of a distinctive English prosody. Daniels' *Defence* (5.17) makes the point. Text from: first edition, 1602, chapters 1–4, 10.

In treating of numbers in general

... The world is made by symmetry and proportion, and is in that respect compared to music, and music to poetry: for Terence saith, speaking of poets, *artem qui tractant musicam*, confounding music and poetry together. What music can there be where there is no proportion observed? Learning first flourished in Greece; from thence it was derived unto the Romans both diligent observers of the number and quantity of syllables, not in their verse only, but likewise in their prose. Learning, after the declining of the Roman empire and the pollution of their language through the conquest of the barbarians, lay most pitifully deformed till the time of Erasmus, Ruechlin, Sir Thomas More and other learned men of that age, who brought the Latin tongue again to light, redeeming it with much labour out of the hands of the illiterate monks and friars. . . . In those lack-learning times and in barbarised Italy began the vulgar and easy kind of poesy which is now in use throughout most parts of Christendom, which we abusively call rhyme and metre . . .

Declaring the unaptness of rhyme in poesy

I am not ignorant that whosoever shall by way of reprehension examine the imperfections of rhyme must encounter with many glorious enemies and those very expert and ready at their weapon, that can if need be extempore (as they say) rhyme a man to death. Besides there is grown a kind of prescription in the use of rhyme to forestall the right of true numbers, as also the consent of many nations, against all which it might seem a thing almost impossible and vain to contend. All this and more cannot yet deter me from a lawful defence of perfection, or make me any whit the sooner adhere to that which is lame and unbeseeming. For custom, I allege that ill uses are to be abolished, and that things naturally imperfect cannot be perfected by use. Old customs, if they be better, why should they not be recalled, as the yet flourishing custom of numerous poesy used among the Romans and Grecians? But the unaptness of our tongues and the difficulty of imitation disheartens us: again, the facility and popularity of rhyme creates as many poets as a hot summer flies.

. . . The ear is a rational sense and a chief judge of proportion; but in our kind of rhyming, what proportion is there kept where there remains such a confused inequality of syllables? Iambic and trochaic feet, which are opposed by nature, are by all rhymers confounded. . . . But the noble Grecians and Romans whose skilful monuments outlive barbarism, tied themselves to the strict observation of poetical numbers, so abandoning the childish titillation of rhyming . . .

Of our English numbers in general

There are but three feet which generally distinguish the Greek and Latin verses, the dactyl, consisting of one long syllable, and two short, as *vivere*; the trochee, of one long and one short, as *vita*; and the iambic of one short and one long, as *amor*. The spondee of two long and the tribrach of three short, the anapestic of two short and a long, are but as servants to the first. Divers other feet I know are by the grammarians cited, but to little purpose. The heroical verse that is distinguished by the dactyl hath been oftentimes attempted in our English tongue but with passing pitiful success; and no wonder, seeing it is an attempt altogether against the nature of our language. For both the concourse of our monosyllables make our verses unapt to slide, and also if we examine our polysyllables, we shall find few of them by reason of their heaviness, willing to serve in place of a dactyl. Thence it is that the writers of English heroics do so often repeat Amintas,

Olympus, Avernus, Erinnis, and suchlike borrowed words, to supply the defect of our hardly entreated dactyl. . . . There remain only the iambic foot, of which the iambic verse is framed, and the trochee, from which the trochaic numbers have their original. Let us now then examine the property of these two feet and try if they consent with the nature of our English syllables. And first for the iambics, they fall out so naturally in our tongue that if we examine our own writers we shall find they unawares hit oftentimes upon the true iambic numbers, but always aim at them as far as their ear without the guidance of art can attain unto, as it shall hereafter more evidently appear. The trochaic foot, which is but an iambic turned over and over, must of force in like manner accord in proportion with our British syllables, and so produce an English trochaical verse. Then having these two principal kinds of verses, we may easily out of them derive other forms, as the Latins and Greeks before us have done . . .

English Iambics pure

The more secure, the more the stroke we feel
Of unprevented harms; so gloomy storms
Appear the sterner, if the day be clear.

Th'English Iambic licentiate

Hark how these winds do murmur at thy flight.

The English trochee

Still where envy leaves, remorse doth enter.

Of the quantity of English syllables

The Greeks in the quantity of their syllables were far more licentious than the Latins. . . . But the English may very well challenge much more licence than either of them, by reason it stands chiefly upon monosyllables, which, in expressing with the voice, are of a heavy carriage, and for that cause, the dactyl, trybrach and anapestic are not greatly missed in our verses. But above all the accent of our words is diligently to be observed, for chiefly by the accent in any language the true value of the syllables is to be measured. Neither can I remember any impediment except position that can alter the accent of any syllable in our English verse. For though we accent the second of *Trumpington* short, yet is it naturally long, and so of necessity must be held of every composer. Wherefore the first rule that is to be observed is the nature of the accent, which we must ever follow.

The next rule is position, which makes every syllable long, whether the position happens in one or in two words, according to the manner of the Latins, wherein is to be noted that h is no letter.

Position is when a vowel comes before two consonants, either in one or two words. In one, as in *best*, *e* before *st* makes the word *best* long by position. In two words, as in *settled love*, *e* before *d* in the last syllable of the first word and *l* in beginning of the second makes *led* in *settled* long by position.

A vowel before a vowel is always short, as *flying, dying, going*, unless the accent alter it, in *denying*.

The diphthong in the midst of a word is always long, as *playing, deceiving.*

The synalaephus or elisions in our tongue are either necessary to avoid the hollowness and gaping in our verse, as *to* and *the, t'enchant, th'enchanter*, or may be used at pleasure as for *let us*, to say, *let's*, for *we will, we'll*; for *every, ev'ry* . . .

Also, because our English orthography (as the French) differs from our common pronunciation, we must esteem our syllables as we speak, not as we write; for the sound of them in a verse is to be valued and not their letters, as for *follow* we pronounce *follo*; for *perfect, perfit*, for *little, littel*, for *love sick, love-sok*; for *honour, honor*, for *money, mony*.

5.17 SAMUEL DANIEL, *A DEFENCE OF RHYME*

Daniel's *Defence* was written in refutation of Campion's (5.16), probably in 1603, and is a robust account of the role of custom and change in linguistic practice. Text from: *The Works of Samuel Daniel*, 1618, fos 1601ff.

The general custom and use of rhyme in this kingdom, noble Lord, having been so long (as if from a grant of nature) held unquestionable, made me to imagine that it lay altogether out of the way of contradiction, and was become so natural as we should never have had a thought to cast it off into reproach, or be made to think that it ill-became our language. But now I see when there is opposition made to all things in the world by words, we must now at length likewise fall to contend for words themselves, and make a question whether they be right or not. For we are told how that our measures go wrong, all rhyming is gross, vulgar, barbarous; which if it be so, we have lost much labour to no purpose; and for mine own particular, I cannot but blame the fortune of the times and mine own genius, that cast me upon so wrong a course, drawn with the current of custom and an unexamined example . . .

We could well have allowed of his numbers, had he not disgraced our rhyme, which both custom and nature doth most powerfully defend: custom, that is before all law, nature that is above all art. Every language hath her proper number or measure fitted to use and delight, which custom, entertaining by the allowance of the ear, doth indenize[4] and make natural. All verse is but a frame of words confined within certain measure, differing from the ordinary speech, and introduced the better to express men's conceits, both for delight and memory. Which frame of words consisting of *rithmus* or *metrum*, number or measure, are disposed into divers fashions, according to the humour of the composer and the set of the time. And these *rhythmi*, as Aristotle saith, are familiar amongst all nations and *e naturali et sponte fusa compositione*: and they fall as naturally already in our language as ever art can make them, being such as the ear of itself doth marshal in their proper rooms; and they of themselves will not willingly be put out of their rank and that in such a verse as best comports with the nature of our language. And for our rhyme (which is an excellency added to this work of measure, and a harmony far happier than any proportion antiquity could ever show us) doth add more grace and hath more of delight than ever bare numbers; howsoever they can be forced to run in our slow language, can possibly yield . . .

Methinks we should not so soon yield our consents captive to the authority of antiquity, unless we saw more reason; all our understandings are not to be built by the square of Greece and Italy. We are the children of nature as well as they; we are not so placed out of the way of judgement but that the same sun of discretion shineth upon us; we have our portion of the same virtues as well as of the same vices. . . . Time and the turn of things bring about these faculties according to the present estimation. . . . So that we must never rebel against use. . . . It is not the observing of *trochaiques* nor their *iambics* that will make our writings ought the wiser. All their poesy, all their philosophy is nothing, unless we bring the discerning light of conceit with us to apply it to use. It is not books, but only that great book of the world and the all overspreading grace of heaven that makes men truly judicial. Nor can it be but a touch of arrogant ignorance to hold this or that nation barbarous, these or those times gross; considering how this manifold creature man, wheresoever he stand in the world, hath always some disposition of worth; entertains the order of society; affects that which is most in use; and is eminent in some one thing or other that fits his humour and the times. The Grecians held all other nations barbarous but themselves; yet Pirrhus when he saw the well-ordered marching of the Romans, which made them see their presumptuous error, could say it was no barbarous manner of proceeding. The Goths, Vandals and Longobards, whose coming down like an inundation overwhelmed, as they say, all the glory of learning in Europe, have yet left us still their laws and customs as the originals of most of the provincial constitutions of Christendom, which well considered with their other courses of government may serve to clear them from this imputation of ignorance. And though the vanquished never yet spake well of the conqueror, yet even through the unsound coverings of malediction appear those monuments of truth, as argue well their worth and proves them not without judgement, though without Greek and Latin.

Will not experience confute us, if we should say the State of China, which never heard of anapestics, trochies, and tribrachs, were gross, barbarous and uncivil? And is it not a most apparent ignorance, both of the succession of learning in Europe and the general course of things to say: *that all lay pitifully deformed in those lack-learning times from the declining of the Roman empire till the light of the Latin tongue was revived by Reuchlin, Erasmus and More*? When for three hundred years before them, about the coming down of Tamburlain into Europe, Franciscus

Petrarcha (who then no doubt likewise found whom to imitate) showed all the best notions of learning, in that degree of excellency both in Latin, prose and verse, and in the vulgar Italian, as all the wits of posterity have not yet much over-matched him in all kinds to this day . . .

. . . And now in what case were this poor state of words, if in like sort another tyrant the next year should arise and abrogate these laws and ordain others clean contrary according to his humour, and say that they were only right, the other unjust? What disturbance were there here, to whom should we obey? Were it not far better to hold us fast to our old custom than to stand thus distracted with uncertain laws, wherein right shall have as many faces as it pleases passion to make it; that wheresoever men's affections stand, it shall still look that way? . . .

But yet notwithstanding all this which I have here delivered in the defence of rhyme, I am not so far in love with mine own mystery, or will seem so froward, as to be against the reformation and the better settling these measures of ours. Wherein there be many things I could wish were more certain and better ordered, though myself dare not take upon me to be a teacher therein, having so much need to learn of others. And I must confess that to mine own ear those continual cadences of couplets used in long and continued poems are very tiresome and unpleasing, by reason that still, methinks, they run on with a sound of one nature, and a kind of certainty which stuffs the delight rather than entertains it. But yet, notwithstanding, I must not out of mine own daintiness condemn this kind of writing, which peradventure to another may seem most delightful; and many worthy compositions we see to have passed with commendation in that kind. Besides, methinks, sometimes to beguile the ear with a running out, and passing over the rhyme, as no bound to stay us in the line where the violence of the matter will break through, is rather graceful than otherwise . . .

Next to this deformity [of imposing numbers on English verse] stands our affectation, wherein we always bewray ourselves to be both unkind and unnatural to our own native language, in disguising or forging strange or unusual words, as if it were to make our verse seem another kind of speech out of the course of our usual practice; displacing our words, or inventing new, only upon a singularity, when our own accustomed phrase, set in the due place, would express us more familiarly and to better delight than all this idle affectation of antiquity or novelty can ever do. And I cannot but wonder at the strange presumption of some men, that dare so audaciously adventure to introduce any whatsoever foreign words, be they never so strange, and of themselves, as it were, without a parliament, without any consent or allowance, establish them as free-denizens in our language. But this is but a character of that perpetual revolution which we see to be in all things that never remain the same: and we must herein be content to submit ourselves to the law of time, which in few years will make all that for which we now contend nothing.

5.18 WILLIAM CAMDEN, *REMAINS OF BRITAIN*

Camden's *Britannia* was first published in 1586, and expanded in the 1607 edition. He travelled Britain in search and confirmation of his antiquarian enterprise; in the preface to the 1607 edition, he outlines a scholarly methodology for historical research and writing. Text from: 1607 edition, fos q4^r–A1.

The author to the reader

Abraham Ortelius the worthy restorer of ancient geography, arriving here in England about thirty-four years past, dealt earnestly with me that I would illustrate this Isle of Britain or (as he said) that I would restore antiquity to Britain, and Britain to his antiquity; which was, as I understood, that I would renew ancientry, enlighten obscurity, clear doubts, and recall home verity by way of recovery, which the negligence of writers, and credulity of the common sort had in a manner proscribed and utterly banished from amongst us. A painful matter I assure you, and more than difficult, wherein what toil is to be taken, as no man thinketh, so no man believeth but he that hath made the trial. Nevertheless how much the difficulty discouraged me from it, so much the glory of my country encouraged me to undertake it. So while at one and the same time I was fearful to undergo the burden, and yet desirous to do some service to my country; I found two different affections, fear and boldness, I knew not how, conjoined in me. Notwithstanding by the most gracious direction of the Almighty, taking industry for my comfort, I adventured upon it and with all my study, care, cogitation, continual meditation, pain and travail, I employed myself thereunto when I had any spare time. I made search after the etymology of Britain, and the first inhabitants timorously, neither in so doubtful a matter have I affirmed ought confidently. For I am not ignorant that the first originals of nations are obscure, by reason of their profound antiquity, as things which are seen very deep and far remote: like as the courses, the reaches, the confluencies and the outlets of great rivers are well known, yet their first fountains and heads lie commonly unknown. I have succinctly run over the Roman's government in Britain, and the inundation of foreign people thereinto, what they were, and from whence they came: I have traced out the ancient divisions of these kingdoms, I have summarily specified the States and judicial courts of the same.

In the several counties I have compendiously set down the limits . . . what is the nature of the soil, which were places of greatest antiquity, who have been the Dukes, Marquises, Earls, Viscounts, Barons and some of the most signal and ancient families therein (for who can particulate all?). What I have performed, I leave to men of judgement. But time, the most sound and sincere witness will give the truest information, when envy which persecuteth the living, shall have her mouth stopped. Thus much give me leave to say, that I have in no wise neglected such things as are most material to search and sift out the truth. I have attained to some skill of the most ancient British and English-saxon tongues: I have travelled all over England for the most part; I have conferred with most skilful observers in each country; I have studiously read over our own country writers, old and new, all Greek and Latin authors, which have once made mention of Britain; I have had conference with learned men in other parts of Christendom; I have been diligent in the records of this realm; I have looked into most libraries, registers and memorials of Churches, cities and corporations; I have pored upon many an old roll, and evidence, and produced their testimony (as beyond all exceptions) when the cause required, in their very own words (although barbarous they be), that the honour of verity might in no wise be impeached . . .

. . . Truly it was my project and purpose to seek, rake out, and free from darkness such places as Caesar, Tacitus, Ptolomy, Antonine the Emperor, Notitia Provinciarum, and other antique writers have specified, and time hath overcast with mist and darkness by extinguishing, altering, and corrupting their old true names. In searching and seeking after these, as I will not avouch any uncertainties, so I do not conceal probabilities. That I have not found out every one although I have sought after them with painful and chargeable inquiry, let it be no imputation to me, as it is not to a spadiard[5] that worketh in the mines, who while he findeth and followeth the main veins, seeth not the hidden small fillets . . .

There are certain, as I hear, who take it impatiently that I have mentioned some of the most famous monasteries and their founders. I am sorry to hear it, and with their good favour will say thus much: they may take it as impatiently, and peradventure would have us forget that our ancestors were, and we are of the Christian profession; when as, there are not extant any other more conspicuous and certain monuments of their piety, and zealous devotion toward God. Neither were there any other seed gardens from whence Christian religion and good learning were propagated over this isle. Howbeit in corrupt ages some weeds grew out over-rankly . . .

As for obscurity, fables, extravagant digressions, I trust there is no cause to sue out my pardon. There will be no obscurity but to them which have not sipped the first elements of antiquity and our histories: upon fables I have no ways relied, and that I might not digress extravagantly. I have had often recourse to the title of my book (as Pliny adviseth) and eftsoons demanded of myself why I took pen in hand . . .

But lest I should run at random in my preface. To accomplish this work the whole main of my industry hath been employed for many years with a firm settled study of the truth and sincere antique faithfulness to the glory of God and my country. I have done dishonour to no nation; have descanted upon no man's name; I have impaired no man's reputation; I have impeached no man's credit, no not Geoffrey of Monmouth, whose history (which I would gladly support) is held suspected amongst the judicious. Neither have I assumed upon myself any possession of knowledge, but only that I have been desirous to know much. And so I right willingly acknowledge that I may err much, neither will I soothe and smooth my errors. Who, shooting all day long, doth always hit the mark? Many matters in this study are raked under deceitful ashes. There may be some escapes from memory, for who doth so comprehend particularities in the treasury of his memory, that he can utter them at his pleasure? There may be mistakings in regard of my unskilfulness, for who is so skilful that struggling with time in the foggy dark sea of antiquity, may not run upon rocks? It may be that I have been misled by the credits of authors and others whom I took to be most true and worthy of credit. *Neither is there verily* (as Pliny saith) *any easier slipping from truth than when a grave author warranteth an untruth.* Others may be more skilful and more exactly observe the particularities of the places where they are conversant. If they, or any other, whosoever, will advertise me wherein I am mistaken, I will amend it with manifold thanks; if I have, unwitting, omitted ought, I will supply it; if I have not fully explicated any point, upon their better information I will more clear it, if it proceed from good meaning and not from a spirit of contradiction and quarrelling, which do not befit such as are well bred and affect the truth. Meanwhile, let your kind courtesy, my industry, the common love of our common mother, our native country, the ancient honour of the British name obtain so much upon their entreaty that I may utter my judgement without prejudice to others.

5.19 AEMILIA LANYER, *SALVE DEUS REX JUDEAORUM*

Lanyer's preface to the reader precedes dedicatory poems to all the eminent literary women patrons of the early Jacobean period: her poem re-reads the history of Christ's life. Text from: 1611, fos F3rff.

To the virtuous reader

Often have I heard that it is the property of some women not only to emulate the virtues and perfections of the rest, but also by all their powers of ill-speaking to eclipse the brightness of their deserved fame. Now contrary to this custom, which men I hope unjustly lay to their charge, I have written this small volume, or little book for the general use of all virtuous ladies and gentlewomen of this kingdom; and in commendation of some particular persons of our own sex, such as for the most part are so well known to myself and others, that I dare undertake fame dares not to call any better. And this have I done to make known to the world that all women deserve not to be blamed, though some forgetting they are women themselves and in danger to be condemned by the words of their own mouths, fall into so great an error as to speak unadvisedly against the rest of their sex. Which if it be true, I am persuaded they can show their own imperfection in nothing more, and therefore could wish (for their own ease, modesties and credit) they would refer such points of folly to be practised by evil-disposed men, who forgetting they were born of women, nourished of women, and that if

319

it were not by the means of women they would be quite extinguished out of the world and a final end of them all, do like vipers deface the wombs wherein they were bred, only to give way and utterance to their want of discretion and goodness. Such as these were they that dishonoured Christ, his apostles and prophets, putting them to shameful deaths. Therefore we are not to regard any imputations that they undeservedly lay upon us no otherwise than to make use of them to our own benefits, as spurs to virtue, making us fly all occasions that may colour their vainest speeches to pass current. Especially considering that they have tempted even the patience of God himself, who gave power to wise and virtuous women, to bring down their pride and arrogancy. As was cruel Cesarus, by the discreet counsel of noble Deborah, judge and prophetess of Israel, and resolution of Jael, wife of Heber the Kenite; wicked Haman, by the divine prayers and prudent proceedings of beautiful Hester; blasphemous Holofernes by the invincible courage, rare wisdom and confident carriage of Judith; and the unjust judges by the innocency of chaste Susannah: with infinite others, which for brevity sake I will omit. As also in respect it pleased our Lord and saviour Jesus Christ, without the assistance of man, being free from original and all other sins, from the time of his conception till the hour of his death, to be begotten of a woman, born of a woman, nourished of a woman, obedient to a woman; and that he healed women, pardoned women, comforted women; yea, even when he was in his greatest agony and bloody sweat going to be crucified, and also in the last hour of his death took care to dispose of a woman; after his resurrection, appeared first to a woman, sent a woman to declare his most glorious resurrection to the rest of his disciples. Many other examples I could allege of divers faithful and virtuous women, who have in all ages, not only been confessors, but also endured most cruel martyrdom for their faith in Jesus Christ. All which is sufficient to enforce all good Christians and honourable minded men to speak reverently of our sex, and especially of all virtuous and good women. To the modest censures of both which, I refer these my imperfect endeavours, knowing that according to their own excellent dispositions, they will rather cherish, nourish, and increase the least spark of virtue where they find it, by their favourable and best interpretations, than quench it by wrong constructions. To whom I wish all increase of virtue, and desire their best opinions.

5.20 BEN JONSON, *DISCOVERIES*

Jonson's *Discoveries* were published posthumously in 1640 by his correspondent William Drummond. They were a collection of his thoughts and jottings on culture, politics, rhetoric, writing and poetry which he had kept as a commonplace book. Text from: first edition, 1640, ll.80–170; 710–70; 1,110–85; 1,320–50; 2,330–525; 3,130–50.

Learning needs rest: sovereignty gives it. Sovereignty needs council: learning affords it. There is such a consocation of offices between the prince and whom his favour breeds, that they may help to sustain his power, as he their knowledge. It is the greatest part of his liberality, his favour: and from whom doth he hear discipline more willingly, or the arts discoursed more gladly, than from those whom his own bounty and benefits have made able and faithful? . . .

The two chief things that give a man reputation in council are the opinion of his honesty and the opinion of his wisdom: the authority of those two will persuade when the same councils, uttered by other persons, less qualified, are of no efficacy or working.

Wisdom without honesty is mere craft and cozenage. And therefore the reputation of honesty must first be gotten; which cannot be but by living well. A good life is a main argument.

Next a good life, to beget love in the persons we council, by dissembling our knowledge of ability in ourselves, and avoiding all suspicion of arrogance; ascribing all to their instruction, as an ambassador to his master, or a subject to his sovereign; seasoning all with humanity and sweetness, only expressing care and solicitude. And not to council rashly, or on the sudden, but with advice and meditation. . . . For many foolish things fall from wise men if they speak in haste or be extemporal. It therefore behoves the giver of council to be circumspect, especially to beware of those with whom he is not thoroughly acquainted, lest any spice of rashness, folly, or self-love appear, which will be marked by new persons and men of experience in affairs.

And to the prince or his superior, to behave himself modestly and with respect. Yet free from flattery or empire; not with insolence or precept; but as the prince were already furnished with the parts he should have, especially in affairs of State . . .

I know nothing can conduce more to letters than to examine the writings of the ancients and not to rest in their sole authority, or take all upon trust from them, provided the plagues of judging and pronouncing against them be away: such as are envy, bitterness, precipitation, impudence and scurrile scoffing. For to all the observations of the ancients we have our own experience, which, if we will use and apply, we have better means to pronounce. It is true they opened the gates and made the way that went before us, but as guides, not commanders: *non domini nostri, sed duces fuere* [they were not our master, but leaders]. Truth lies open to all, it is no man's several.

* * *

But now nothing is good that is natural: right and natural language seems to have least of the wit in it: that which is writhed and tortured is counted the more exquisite. Cloth of bodkin or tissue must be embroidered, as if no face were fair that were not powdered or painted! No beauty to be had but in wresting and writhing our own tongue. Nothing is fashionable till it be deformed: and this is to write like a gentleman! All must be as affected and preposterous as our gallants' clothes, sweet bags and night dressings: in which you would think our men lay in, like ladies, it is so curious.

Nothing in our age, I have observed, is more preposterous than the running judgements upon poetry and poets, when we shall hear those things commended and cried up for the best writings, which a man would scarce vouchsafe to wrap any wholesome drug in: he would never light his tobacco with them! And those men almost named for miracles who yet are so vile that if a man should go about to examine and correct them, he must make all they have done but one blot. . . . Nay, if it were put to the question of the water-rhymer's works[6] against Spenser's, I doubt not but they would find more suffrages because the most favour common vices, out of a prerogative the vulgar have to lose their judgements and like that which is nought.

* * *

Cicero is said to be the only wit that the people of Rome had equalled to their empire. We have had many and in their several ages (to take in but the former seculum): Sir Thomas More, the elder Wyatt, Henry Earl of Surrey; Chaloner, Smith, Elyot, Bishop Gardiner, were for their times admirable, and the more because they began eloquence with us. Sir Nicholas Bacon was singular and almost alone in the beginning of Queen Elizabeth's time. Sir Philip Sidney and Mr. Hooker (in different matter) grew great masters of wit and language and in whom all vigour of invention and strength of judgement met. The Earl of Essex, noble and high, and Sir Walter Raleigh, not to be contemned either for judgement or style. Sir Henry Savile, grave and truly lettered, Sir Edwin Sandys, excellent in both; Lord Egerton, the Chancellor, a grave and great orator; and best when he was provoked. But his learned and able (though unfortunate) successor[7] is he who hath filled up all numbers, and performed that in our tongue which may be compared or preferred either to insolent Greece or haughty Rome. In short, within his view and about his times were all the wits born, that could honour a language or help study. Now things daily fall: wits grow downward and eloquence grows backward, so he may be named and stand as the mark and highest point of our language . . .

There cannot be one colour of the mind, another of the wit. If the mind be staid, grave and composed, the wit is so: that vitiated, the other is blown and deflowered. Do we not see, if the mind languish, the members are dull? Look upon an effeminate person: his very gait confesseth him. If a man be fiery, his motion is so: if angry, 'tis troubled and violent. So that we may conclude, wheresoever manners and fashions are corrupted, language is. It imitates the public riot. The excess of feasts and apparel are the notes of a sick state: and the wantonness of language, of a sick mind.

* * *

Flattery is a fine pick-lock of tender ears, especially of those whom fortune hath born high upon their wings, that submit their dignity and authority to it by a soothing of themselves, for indeed men could never be taken in that abundance

322

with the springs of others' flattery, if they began not there, if they did but remember how much more profitable the bitterness of truth were, than all the honey distilling from a whorish voice, which is not praise but poison. But now it is come to that extreme folly, or rather madness with some, that he that flatters them modestly or sparingly, is thought to malign them. If their friend consent not to their vices, though he do not contradict them, he is nevertheless an enemy. When they do all things the worst way, even then they look for praise. Nay, they will hire fellows to flatter them with suits and suppers, and to prostitute their judgements. They have livery-friends, friends of the dish and of the spit, that wait their turns as my lord has his feasts and guests.

I have considered, our whole life is like a play, wherein every man, forgetful of himself, is in travail with expression of another. Nay, we so insist in imitating others, as we cannot (when it is necessary) return to ourselves: like children that imitate the vices of stammerers so long, till at last they become such; and make the habit to another nature, as it is never forgotten.

* * *

Speech is the only benefit man hath to express his excellency of mind above other creatures, it is the instrument of society. Therefore Mercury, who is the president of language is called *deorum hominumque interpres* [the interpreter of gods and men]. In all speech, words and sense are as the body and the soul. The sense is as the life and soul of language, without which all words are dead. Sense is wrought out of experience, the knowledge of human life and actions, or of the liberal arts. . . . Words are the people's: yet there is a choice of them to be made. For *verborum delectus origo est eloquentiae* [delight in words is the origin of eloquence]. They are to be chose according to the persons we make speak or the things we speak of. Some are of the camp, some of the sheepcote, some of the pulpit, some of the bar etc. And herein is seen their elegance and propriety when we use them fitly and draw them forth to their just strength and nature by way of translation, or metaphor. But in this translation we must only serve neces- sity . . . or commodity, which is a kind of necessity: that is, when we either absolutely want a word to express by, and that is necessity; or when we have not so fit a word, and that is commodity. As when we avoid loss by it and escape obsceneness and gain in the grace and property, which helps significance. Metaphors farfet hinder to be understood, and affected lose their grace. Or when the person fetcheth his translation from a wrong place, as if a privy coun- cillor should at the table take his metaphor from a dicing house, or ordinary, or a vintner's vault; or a Justice of Peace draw his similitudes from the mathematics; or a divine from a bawdy house or taverns; or a gentleman of Northamptonshire, Warwickshire or the Midland, should fetch all his illustra- tions to his country neighbours from shipping and tell them of the main sheet and the boulin. Metaphors are thus many times deformed. . . . All attempts that are new in this kind are dangerous and somewhat hard before they be softened with use. A man coins not a new word without some peril and less fruit: for if it happen to be received, the praise is but moderate: if refused, the scorn is assured. Yet we must adventure: for things at first hard and rough, are by use made tender and gentle . . .

Custom is the most certain mistress of language, as the public stamp makes the current money. But we must not be too frequent with the mint, every day coining. Nor fetch words from the extreme and utmost ages, since the chief virtue of a style is perspicuity, and nothing so vicious in it as to need an interpreter. Words borrowed of antiquity do lend a kind of majesty to style and are not without their delight sometimes. For they have the authority of years and out of their intermission do win to themselves a kind of grace like newness. But the eldest of the present and newest of the past language is the best. For what was the ancient language, which some men so dote upon, but the ancient custom? Yet when I name custom, I understand not the vulgar custom, for that were a precept no less dangerous to language than life, if we should speak or live after the manners of the vulgar: but that I call custom of speech which is the consent of the learned, as custom of life which is the consent of the good. . . . A strict and succinct style is that where you can take away nothing without loss, and that loss to be manifest. The brief style is that which expresseth much in little. The concise style, which expresseth not enough, but leaves somewhat to be understood. The abrupt style, which hath many breaches, and doth not seem to end, but fall. The congruent and harmonious fitting of parts in a sentence hath almost the fastening and force of knitting and connection: as in stones well squared, which will rise strong a great way without mortar . . .

Language most shows a man: speak that I may see thee. It springs out of the most retired and inmost parts of us, and is the image of the parent of it, the mind. No glass renders a man's form or likeness so true as his speech.

* * *

The poet is the nearest borderer upon the orator, and expresseth all his virtues, though he be tied more to numbers; is his equal in ornament; and above him in his strengths. And (of the kind) the comic comes nearest, because in moving the minds of men and stirring of affections (in which oratory shows and especially approves her eminence) he chiefly excels. What figure of a body was Lysippus ever able to form with his graver, or Appeles to paint with his pencil, as the comedy to life expresseth so many and various affections of the mind? There shall the spectator see some insulting with joy; others fretting with melancholy; raging with anger; mad with love; boiling with avarice; undone with riot; tortured with expectation; consumed with fear: no perturbation in common life, but the orator finds an example of it in the scene.

5.21 FRANCIS BACON, *THE ADVANCEMENT OF LEARNING*

Bacon's later theory of 'idols', which he here calls 'false appearances', is first given public articulation here. His account of how they obstruct our understanding seems remarkably modern. Warning against the idols of the market place (language), of human nature (later called those of the tribe) and of the cave (our own minds) he aims to encourage a sceptical philosophical stance to the world and to language, which predates Descartes (see 6.16), and is similar to Montaigne (see 8.13). Culturally, it shows society a way of thinking anew about language, society and politics. It is a theory he elaborates further in the *Novum Organum* in 1620 (see 6.14). Text from: 1605 edition, pp. 56^r–57^v.

For the mind of man is far from the nature of a clear and equal glass, wherein the beams of things should reflect according to their true incidence; nay it is rather like an enchanted glass, full of superstition and imposture, if it be not delivered and reduced. For this purpose let us consider the false appearances that are imposed upon us by the general nature of the mind, beholding them in an example or two: as first in that instance which is the root of all superstition, namely that to the nature of the mind of all men it is consonant for the affirmative or active to affect more than the negative or privative. So that a few times hitting or presence, countervails oft-times failing or absence; as was well answered by Diagoras to him that showed him in Neptune's temple the great number of pictures of such as had scaped shipwreck, and had paid their vows to Neptune, saying, *Advise now, you that think it folly to invocate Neptune in tempest. Yea: but* (saith Diagoras), *where are they painted that are drowned?* Let us behold it in another instance namely, that the spirit of man, being of an equal and uniform substance, doth usually suppose and feign in nature a greater equality and uniformity than is in truth. Hence it cometh that the mathematicians cannot satisfy themselves except they reduce the motions of the celestial bodies to perfect circles, rejecting spiral lines and labouring to be discharged of eccentrics. Hence it cometh that whereas there are many things in nature as it were *monodica sui juris* [unique, of its own kind]; yet the cogitations of man do feign unto them relatives, parallels, and conjugates, whereas no such thing is; as they have feigned an element of fire, to keep square with earth, water and air, and the like. Nay it is not credible till it be opened, what a number of fictions and fantasies the similitude of human actions and arts together with the making of man *communis mensura* [the measure of all things common], have brought into natural philosophy . . . And therefore Veleius the Epicurean needed not to have asked why God should have adorned the heaven with stars, as if he had been an *aedelis* [architect], one that should have set forth some magnificent shows or plays. For if that great work master had been of an human disposition, he would have cast the stars into some pleasant and beautiful works and orders, like the frets in the roofs of houses; whereas one can scarce find a posture in square, or triangle, or straight line, amongst such an infinite number; so differing an harmony there is between the spirit of man and the spirit of nature.

Let us consider again the false appearances imposed upon us by every man's own individual nature and custom, in that feigned supposition that Plato maketh of the cave: for certainly if a child were continued in a grot or cave under the earth until maturity of age, and came suddenly abroad, he would have strange and absurd imaginations. So in like manner, although our persons live in the view of heaven, yet our spirits are included in the caves of our own complexions and customs, which minister unto us infinite errors and vain opinions, if they be not recalled to examination . . .

Elenchi magni, sive de idolis animi humani nativis et adventitiis [cautions against the idols of human nature and of the market place]. And lastly let us consider the false appearances that are imposed upon us by words, which are framed and applied according to the conceit and capacities of the vulgar sort: and although we think we govern our words and prescribe it well *loquendum ut vulgus sentiendum ut sapientes* [to speak as the people do, but think as wise men do]; yet certain it is that words, as a tartar's bow, do shoot back upon the understanding of the wisest and mightily entangle and pervert the judgement, so as it is almost necessary in all controversies and disputations to imitate the wisdom of the mathematicians in setting down in the very beginning the definitions of our words and terms, that others may know how we accept and understand them, and whether they concur with us or no. For it cometh to pass, for want of this, that we are sure to end there where we have begun, which is in questions and differences about words. To conclude therefore, it must be confessed that it is not possible to divorce ourselves from these fallacies and false appearances, because they are inseparable from our nature and condition of life.

5.22 HENRY WOTTON, *THE ELEMENTS OF ARCHITECTURE*

Wotton was English ambassador to Venice for James I, and held other civic posts. His work on architecture brought renaissance Italian principles to England for the first time, both theoretically, through his citation of Vitruvius, and practically by his descriptions and recommendations about building neo-classical seats in England. Text from: first edition, 1622, pp.1–10ff; 82–9; 95–123.

In architecture as in all other operative arts, the end must direct the operation. The end is to build well

Therefore first touching situation. The precepts thereunto belonging, do either concern the total posture (as I may term it) or the placing of the parts, whereof the first sort, howsoever usually set down by architects as a piece of their profession, yet are in truth borrowed from other learnings: there being between arts and sciences, as well as between men, a kind of good fellowship and communication of their principles.

For you shall find some of them to be merely physical, touching the quality and temper of the air: which being a perpetual ambient and ingredient, and the defects thereof incorrigible in single habitations (which I most intend), doth in those respects require the more exquisite caution: that it be not too gross; not too penetrative; not subject to any foggy noisomeness from fens or marshes near adjoining; nor to mineral exhalations from the soil itself; not undigested, for want of sun; not unexercised for want of wind, which were to live (as it were) in a lake or standing pool of air, as Alberti the Florentine architect doth ingeniously compare it.

Some do rather seem a little astrological, as when they warn us from places of malign influence, where earthquakes, contagions, prodigious births or the like are frequent without any evident cause; whereof the consideration is peradventure not altogether vain: some are plainly economical, as that the seat be well watered and well fuelled, that it be not of too steepy and incommodious access to the trouble both of friends and family; that it lie not too far from some navigable river or arm of the sea for more ease of provision and such other domestic notes.

Some again may be said to be optical: such I mean as concern the properties of a well chosen prospect: which I will call the royalty of sight. For as there is a lordship (as it were) of the feet, wherein the master doth much joy when he walketh about the line of his own possessions: so there is a lordship likewise of the eye, which being a ranging, and imperious, and (I might say) an usurping, sense, can endure no narrow circumscription; but must be fed both with extent and variety. Yet on the other side I find vast and indefinite views which drown all apprehension of the uttermost objects, condemned by good authors as if thereby some part of the pleasure (whereof we speak) did perish. Lastly I remember a private caution, which I know not well how to sort, unless I should call it political. By no means to build too near a great neighbour: which were in truth to be as unfortunately seated on the earth, as Mercury is in the heavens: for the most part ever in combustion or obscurity under brighter beams than his own.

From these several knowledges as I have said and perhaps from some other, do architects derive their doctrine about election of seats; wherein I have not been so severe as a great scholar of our time who precisely restraineth a perfect situation, at least for the main point of health . . . that is, in a word, he would have the first salutation of the spring. But such notes as these, wheresoever we find them in grave or slight authors, are to my conceit rather wishes than precepts; and in that quality I will pass them over. Yet I must withal say that in the seating of ourselves (which is a kind of marriage to a place) builders should be as circumspect as wooers . . .

The next in order is the placing of the parts: about which (to leave as little as may in my present labour, unto fancy, which is wild and irregular), I will propound a rule of mine own collection, upon which I fell in this manner. I had noted that all art was then in truest perfection when it might be reduced to some natural principle. For what are the most judicious artisans but the mimics of nature? This led me to contemplate the fabric of our own bodies, wherein the high architect of the world had displayed such skill as did stupefy all human reason. There I found the heart as the fountain of life placed about the middle, for the more equal communication of the vital spirits. The eyes seated aloft that they might describe the greater circle within their view. The arms projected on each side for ease of reaching. Briefly (not to lose ourselves in this sweet speculation) it plainly appeareth as a maxim drawn from the divine light, that the place of every part is to be determined by the use.

So then, from natural structure to proceed to artificial; and in the rudest things to preserve some image of the excellentest. Let all the principal chambers of delight; all studies and libraries, be towards the east, for the morning is a friend to the Muses. All offices that require heat, as kitchens, stillatories, stoves, rooms for baking, brewing, washing or the like, would be meridional. All that need a cool and fresh temper, as cellars, pantries, butteries, granaries, to the north. To the same side likewise all that are appointed for gentle motion, as galleries, especially in warm climes, or that otherwise require a steady and unvariable light, as *pinacotechia* (saith Vitruvius) by which he intendeth (if I may guess at his Greek as we must do often even at his Latin) certain repositories for works of rarity in picture . . .

I must here not omit to note that the ancient Greeks and the Romans by their example in their buildings abroad, where the seat was free, did almost religiously situate the front of their houses towards the south; perhaps that the master's eye when he came home might not be dazzled, or that being illustrated by the sun it might yield the more graceful aspect, or some such reason. But from this, the modern Italians do vary.

* * *

Every man's proper mansion house and home, being the theatre of his hospitality, the seat of self-fruition, the comfortablest part of his own life, the noblest of his son's inheritance, a kind of private princedom; nay, to the possessors thereof, an epitome of the whole world, may well deserve by these attributes according to the degree of the master, to be decently and delightfully adorned. For which end, there are two arts attending on architecture, like two of her principal gentlewomen, to dress and trim their mistress: picture and sculpture, between whom before I proceed any further, I will venture to determine an ancient quarrel about their precedency, with this distinction: that in the garnishing of fabrics, sculpture no doubt must have the preeminence, as being indeed of nearer affinity to architecture itself and consequently the more natural and more suitable ornament. But on the other side (to consider these two arts as I shall do philosophically, and not mechanically), an excellent piece of painting is to my judgement the more admirable object because it comes near an artificial miracle: to make divers distinct eminences appear upon a flat by force of shadows, and yet the shadows themselves not to appear; which I conceive to be the uttermost value and virtue of a painter, and to which very few have arrived in all ages.

. . . For picture is best when it standeth off, as if it were carved; and sculpture is best when it appeareth so tender, as if it were painted: I mean, when there is such a seeming softness in the limbs as if not a chisel had hewed them out of stone, or other material, but a pencil had drawn and stroked them in oil . . .

But this generality is not sufficient to make a good chooser without a more particular contraction of his judgement: therefore when a piece of art is set before us, let the first caution be not to ask who made it, lest the fame of the author do captivate the fancy of the buyer. For that excellent men do always excellently is a false conclusion; whereupon I observe among Italian artisans three notable phrases which well decipher the degrees of their works.

They will tell you that a thing was done *con diligente, con studio,* and *con amore.* The first is but a bare and ordinary diligence; the second is a learned diligence; the third is much more, even a loving diligence: they mean not with love to the bespeaker of the work, but with a love and delight in the work itself, upon some special fancy to this or that story. And when all these concur (particularly the last) in an eminent author, then perchance *Titianus fecit* [Titian painted it] . . .

The next caution must be (to proceed logically) that in judging of the work itself we be not distracted with too many things at once: therefore first (to begin with picture) we are to observe whether it be well drawn, or (as more elegant artisans term it) well designed; then whether it be well coloured, which be the two general heads; and each of them hath two principal requisites: for in well designing there must be truth and grace; in well colouring, force and affection; all other praises are but consequences of these.

Truth (as we metaphorically take it in this art) is a just and natural proportion in every part of the determined figure. Grace is a certain free disposition in the whole draught, answerable to that unaffected frankness of fashion in a living body, man or woman, which doth animate beauty where it is, and supply it where it is not.

Force consisteth in the roundings and raisings of the work, according as the limbs do more or less require it; so as the beholder shall spy no sharpness in the bordering lines, as when tailors cut out a suit . . . nor any flatness within the body of the figure, which how it is done, we must teach from a higher discipline. For the optics teach us that a plane will appear prominent and (as it were) embossed, if the parts furthest from the axel-tree, or middle beam of the eye, shall be the most shadowed. Because in all darkness there is a kind of deepness. But, as in the art of persuasion, one of the most fundamental precepts is the concealment of art, so here likewise, the sight must be sweetly deceived by an insensible passage from brighter colours to dimmer, which the Italian artisans call the middle tinctures. That is, not as the whites and yolks of eggs lie in the shell with visible distinction, but as when they are beaten and blended in a dish: which is the nearest comparison that I can suddenly conceive.

Lastly, affection is the lively representation of any passion whatsoever as if the figures stood not upon a cloth or board, but as if they were acting upon a stage: and here I must remember in truth with much marvel, a note which I have received from excellent artisans, that though gladness and grief be opposites in

329

nature, yet they are such neighbours and confiners in art, that the least touch of a pencil will translate a crying into a laughing face . . .

In sculpture likewise the two first are absolutely necessary, the third impertinent, for solid figures need no elevation by force of light or shadows. Therefore in the room of this we may put (as hath been before touched) a kind of tenderness, by the Italians termed *morbidezza*, wherein the chisel, I must confess, hath more glory than the pencil, that being so hard an instrument and working upon so unpliant stuff, can yet leave strokes of so gentle appearance.

The fourth, which is the expressing of affection (as far as it doth depend upon the activity and gesture of the figure) is as proper to the carver as to the painter, though colours, no doubt, have therein the greatest power; whereupon perchance, did first grow with us the fashion of colouring even regal statues, which I must take leave to call an English barbarism.

* * *

First, therefore touching picture, there doth occur a very pertinent doubt which hath been passed over too slightly, not only by some men, but by some nations, namely, whether this ornament can well become the outside of houses; wherein the Germans have made so little scruple that their best towns are the most painted, as Augusta and Nuremburg. To determine this question in a word: it is true that a story well set out with a good hand will everywhere take a judicious eye: but yet withal, it is as true that various colours on the out-walls of buildings have always in them more delight than dignity: therefore I would there admit no paintings but in black and white, nor even in that kind any figures (if the room be capable) under nine or ten foot high, which will require no ordinary artisan, because the faults are more visible than in small designs. In unfigured paintings the noblest is the imitation of marbles and of architecture itself, as arches, friezes, columns and the like.

Now for the inside: here grows another doubt, whether *grotesca* (as the Italians) or antique works (as we call it) should be received against the express authority of Vitruvius himself, Lib. 7.cap. 5, where *pictura* (saith he) *fit eius, quod est, seu potest est* [the only suitable picture is one which is possible], excluding by this severe definition all figures composed of different natures or sexes: so as a siren or a centaur had been intolerable in his eye. But in this we must take leave to depart from our master, and the rather because he spake out of his own profession, allowing painters (who have ever been as little limited as poets) a less scope in their imaginations, even than the gravest philosophers, who sometimes do serve themselves of instances that have no existence in nature. . . . I am for these reasons unwilling to impoverish that art, though I could wish such medley and motley designs, confined only to the ornament of friezes and borders, their properest place. As for other storied works upon walls, I doubt our clime be too yielding and moist for such garnishment: therefore leaving it to the dweller's discretion, according to the quality of his seat, I will only add a caution or two about the disposing of pictures within.

First, that no room be furnished with too many, which in truth were a surfeit of ornament, unless they be galleries or some peculiar repository for rarities of art.

Next, that the best pieces be placed not where there is the least, but where there are the fewest lights: therefore not only rooms windowed on both ends, which we call through-lighted, but with two or more windows on the same side, are enemies to this art; and sure it is that no painting can be seen in full perfection but (as all nature is illuminated) by a single light.

Thirdly, that in the placing there be some care also taken how the painter did stand in the working, which an intelligent eye will easily discover and that posture is the most natural: so as Italian pieces will appear best in a room where the windows are high, because they are commonly made to a descending light, which of all other doth set off men's faces in their truest spirit.

Lastly that they be as properly bestowed for their quality, as fitly for their grace: that is, cheerful painting in feasting and banqueting rooms; graver stories in galleries; landscapes and boscage and such wild works in open terraces or in summer houses (as we call them) and the like. . . . I will set down a few positive notes for the placing of sculpture, because the choosing hath been handled before.

That first of all it be not too general and abundant, which would make a house look like a cabinet, and in this point moral philosophy which tempereth fancies, is the superintendent of art.

That especially there be a due moderation of this ornament in the first approach; where our authors do more commend (I mean about the principal entrance) a Doric than a Corinthian garnishment. So as if the great door be arched, with some brave head cut in fine stone or marble for the key of the arch, and two incumbent figures gracefully leaning upon it towards one another, as if they meant to confer, I should think this a sufficient entertainment for the first reception of any judicious sight; which I could wish seconded with two great standing statues on each side of a paved way that shall leap up into the fabric, so as the beholder at the first entrance may pass his eye between them.

That the niches, if they contain figures of white stone or marble, be not coloured in their concavity too black: for though *contraris iuxta se posita magis illucescunt* [a negative juxtaposed with a positive is more illumined] (by an old rule) yet it hath been subtly and indeed truly noted that our sight is not well contented with those sudden departments from one extreme to another. Therefore let them have rather a duskish tincture, than an absolute black . . .

Now there are ornaments also without, as gardens, fountains, groves, conservatories, of rare beasts, birds and fishes. Of which ignobler kind of creatures, we ought not (saith our greatest master among the forms of nature) childishly to despise the contemplation, for in all things that are natural there is ever something that is admirable. Of these external delights a word or two.

First, I must note a certain contrariety between building and gardening: for as fabrics should be regular, so gardens should be irregular, or at least cast into a very wild regularity. To exemplify my conceit, I have seen a garden (for the manner perchance incomparable) into which the first access was a high walk like a terrace, from whence might be taken a general view of the whole plot below, but rather in a delightful confusion than with any plain distinction of the pieces. From this the beholder descending many steps, was afterwards conveyed again by several mountings and valings, to various entertainments of his sense and sight, which I shall not need to describe (for that were poetical): let me only note this, that everyone of these diversities was as if he had been magically transported into a new garden.

But though other countries have more benefits of sun than we, and thereby more properly tied to contemplate this delight, yet have I seen in our own, a delicate and diligent curiosity, surely without parallel among foreign nations, namely in the garden of Sir Henry Fanshaw, at his seat in Ware-park, where I well remember he did so precisely examine the tinctures and seasons of his flowers, that in their setting, the inwardness of those which were to come up at the same time should be always a little darker than the outmost, and so serve them for a kind of gentle shadow, like a piece not of nature, but of art.

5.23 JOHN MILTON, *AREOPAGITICA*

Milton's speech to Parliament against censorship was made during the debate in 1644, and afterwards printed. It is a suitable reminder of the still intimate link between Church, State and what can be spoken. Text from: 1644 edition, passim.

A speech for the liberty of unlicensed printing, to the Parliament of England 1644

I find ye esteem it to imitate the old and elegant humanity of Greece, than the barbaric pride of a Hunnish and Norwegian stateliness. And out of those ages to whose polite wisdom and letters we owe that we are not yet Goths and Jutlanders, I could name him who from his private house wrote that discourse to the Parliament of Athens that persuades them to change the form of democracy which was then established. Such honour was done in those days to men who professed the study of wisdom and eloquence, not only in their own country, but in other lands, that cities and signiories heard them gladly and with great respect if they had aught in public to admonish the State . . .

If ye be thus resolved, as it were injury to think ye were not, I know not what should withhold me from presenting ye with a fit instance wherein to show both that love of truth which ye eminently profess and that uprightness of your judgement which is not wont to be partial to yourselves; by judging over again that order which ye have ordained to regulate printing: that no book, pamphlet or paper shall be henceforth printed unless the same be first approved and licensed by such, or at least one of such, as shall thereto be appointed. . . . I shall now attend with such a homily as shall lay before ye, first the inventors of it to be those whom ye will be loath to own; next what is to be thought in general of reading, whatever sort the books be; and that this order avails nothing to the suppressing of scandalous, seditious and libellous books, which were mainly intended to be suppressed. Last, that it will be primely to the discouragement of all learning and the stop of truth, not only by dis-exercising and blunting our abilities in what we know already, but by hindering and cropping the discovery that might be yet further made, both in religious and civil wisdom.

I deny not but that it is of greatest concernment in the Church and Commonwealth to have a vigilant eye how books demean themselves as well as men; and thereafter to confine, imprison and do sharpest justice on them as malefactors. For books are not absolutely dead things, but do contain a potency of life in them to be as active as that soul was whose progeny they are; nay, they do preserve as in a vial the purest efficacy and extraction of that living intellect that bred them. I know they are as lively and as vigorously productive as those fabulous dragons' teeth, and being sown up and down may chance to spring up armed men. And yet, on the other hand, unless wariness be used, as good almost kill a man as kill a good book. Who kills a man kills a reasonable creature, God's image: but he who destroys a good book kills reason itself, kills the image of God, as it were in the eye.

* * *

Good and evil we know in the field of this world, grow up together almost inseparably; and the knowledge of good is so involved and interwoven with the knowledge of evil and in so many cunning resemblances hardly to be discerned, that those confused seeds which were imposed upon Psyche as an incessant labour to cull out and sort asunder, were not more intermixed. It was from out the rind of one apple tasted that the knowledge of good and evil, as two twins cleaving together, leaped forth into the world. And perhaps this is that doom which Adam fell into of knowing good and evil; that is to say, of knowing good by evil. As therefore the state of man now is: what wisdom can there be to choose, what continence to forbear, without the knowledge of evil? He that can apprehend and consider vice with all her baits and seeming pleasures, and yet abstain and yet distinguish, and yet prefer that which is truly better, he is the true wayfaring Christian.

I cannot praise a fugitive and cloistered virtue, unexercised and unbreathed, that never sallies out and sees her adversary, but slinks out of the race, where that immortal garland is to be run for, not without dust and heat. Assuredly we bring not innocence into the world, we bring impurity much rather; that which purifies us is trial, and trial is by what is contrary. That virtue therefore which is but a youngling in the contemplation of evil, and knows not the utmost that vice promises to her followers, and rejects it, is but a blank virtue, not a pure, her whiteness is but an excremental whiteness. Which was the reason why our sage and serious poet Spenser, whom I dare be known to think a better teacher than Scotus or Aquinas, describing true temperance under the person of Guyon, brings him in with his Palmer through the cave of Mamon and the bower of earthly bliss, that he might see and know, and yet abstain. Since therefore the knowledge and survey of vice is in this world so necessary to the constituting of human virtue, and the scanning of error to the confirmation of truth, how can we more safely and with less danger, scout into the regions of sin and falsity than by reading all manner of tractates and hearing all manner of reason? And this is the benefit which may be had of books promiscuously read . . .

But on the other side, that infection which is from books of controversy in religion is more doubtful and dangerous to the learned than to the ignorant; and yet those books must be permitted untouched by the Licenser. It will be hard to instance where any ignorant man hath been ever seduced by papistical book in English, unless it were commended and expounded to him by some of that clergy . . .

If we think to regulate printing thereby to rectify manners, we must regulate all recreations and pastimes, all that is delightful to man. No music must be heard, no song be set or sung but what is grave and Doric. There must be licensing dancers, that no gesture, motion or deportment be taught our youth but what by their allowance shall be thought honest; for such Plato was provided of: it will ask more than the work of twenty licensers to examine all the lutes, the violins and the guitars in every house; they must not be suffered to prattle as they do, but must be licensed what they may say. And who shall silence all the airs and madrigals that whisper softness in chambers? The windows also and the balconies must be thought on; there are shrewd books with dangerous frontispieces set to sale: who shall prohibit them? Shall twenty licensers? The villages also must have their visitors to inquire what lectures the bagpipes and the rebeck reads, even to the ballatry and the gamut of very municipal fiddler, for these are the countryman's *Arcadias* . . .

Next what more national corruption for which England hears ill abroad, than household gluttony: who shall be the rectors of our daily rioting? And what shall be done to inhibit the multitudes that frequent those houses where drunkenness is sold and harboured? Our garments also should be referred to the licensing of some more sober workmasters to see them cut into a less wanton garb. Who shall regulate all the mixed conversation of our youth, male and female together, as is the fashion of this country? Who shall still appoint what shall be discoursed, what presumed, and no further? Lastly who shall forbid and separate all idle resort, all evil company? These things will be and must be: but how they shall be least hurtful, how least enticing, herein consists the grave and governing wisdom of a State.

To sequester out of the world into Atlantic and Utopian politics which never can be drawn into use will not mend our condition: but to ordain wisely as in this world of evil in the midst whereof God hath placed us unavoidably. Nor is it Plato's licensing of books will do this, which necessarily pulls along with it so many other kinds of licensing as will make us all both ridiculous and weary and yet frustrate: but those unwritten or at least unconstraining laws of virtuous education, religious and civil nurture, which Plato there mentions as the bonds and ligaments of the Commonwealth, the pillars and the sustainers of every written statute: these they be which will bear chief sway in such matters as these, when all licensing will be easily eluded. Impunity and remissness, for certain, are the bane of a Commonwealth, but here the great art lies to discern in what the law is to bid restraint and punishment, and in what things persuasion only is to work . . .

And how can a man teach with authority, which is the life of teaching, how can he be a doctor in his book as he ought to be, or else had better be silent, whenas all he teaches, all he delivers is but under the tuition, under the correction of his patriarchal licenser to blot or alter what precisely accords not with the hidebound humour which he calls his judgement? When every acute reader upon the first sight of a pedantic licence will be ready with these like words to ding the book a quoit's distance from him: I hate a pupil teacher, I endure not an instructor that comes to me under the wardship of an over-seeing fist . . .

Nor is it to the common people less than a reproach: for if we be so jealous over them, as that we dare not trust them with an English pamphlet, what do we but censure them for a giddy, vicious and ungrounded people; in such a sick and weak state of faith and discretion as to be able to take nothing down but through the pipe of a licenser?

* * *

For if we be sure we are in the right, and do not hold the truth guiltily, which becomes not, if we ourselves condemn not our own weak and frivolous teaching and the people for an untaught and irreligious gadding rout, what can be more fair than when a man judicious, learned and of a conscience, for aught we know as good as theirs that taught us what we know, shall not privily from house to house, which is more dangerous, but openly by writing publish to the world what his opinion is, what his reasons, and wherefore that which is now thought cannot be sound? Christ urged it as wherewith to justify himself, that he preached in public: yet writing is more public than preaching; and more easy to refutation, if need be: there being so many whose business and profession merely it is to be the champions of truth, which if they neglect, what can be imputed, but their sloth or inability? . . .

There is yet behind of what I proposed to lay open, the incredible loss and detriment that this plot of licensing puts us to: more than if some enemy at sea should stop up all our havens and ports and creeks, it hinders and retards the importation of our richest merchandise, Truth: nay, it was first established and put in practice by antichristian malice and mystery on set purpose to extinguish, if it were possible, the light of Reformation and to settle falsehood; little differing from that policy wherewith the Turk upholds his Alcoran, by the prohibiting of printing. 'Tis not denied but gladly confessed we are to send our thanks and vows to heaven louder than most of nations, for that great measure of truth which we enjoy, especially in those main points between us and the Pope, with his appurtenances the prelates: but he who thinks we are to pitch our tent here and have attained the utmost prospect of reformation that the mortal glass wherein we contemplate can show us, till we come to beatific vision, that man by this very opinion declares that he is yet far short of truth.

Trust indeed came once into the world with her Divine Master, and was a perfect shape most glorious to look on: but when He ascended and his apostles after Him were laid asleep, then straight arose a wicked race of deceivers, who, as the story goes of the Egyptian Typhoon with his conspirators, how they dealt with the good Osiris, took the virgin truth, hewed her lovely form into a thousand pieces, and scattered them to the four winds. From that time ever since the sad friends of truth, such as durst appear, imitating the careful search that Isis made for the mangled body of Osiris, went up and down, gathering up limb by limb, still as they could find them. We have not yet found them all, Lords and Commons, nor ever shall do, till her Master's second coming: he shall bring together every joint and member and shall mould them into an immortal feature of loveliness and perfection. Suffer not these licensing prohibitions to stand at every place of opportunity, forbidding and disturbing them that continue seeking, that continue to do our obsequies to the torn body of our martyred saint . . .

Lords and Commons of England, consider what nation it is whereof ye are, and whereof ye are the governors: a nation not slow and dull, but of a quick, ingenious and piercing spirit, acute to invent, subtle and sinewy to discourse, not beneath the reach of any point, the highest that human capacity can soar to. Therefore the studies of learning in her deepest sciences have been so ancient and so eminent among us that writers of good antiquity and ablest judgement have been persuaded that even the school of Pythagoras and the Persian wisdom took beginning from the old philosophy of this island . . .

Yet that which is above all this, the favour and the love of heaven, we have great argument to think in a peculiar manner propitious and propending towards us. Why else was this nation chosen before any other, that out of her, as out of Sion, should be proclaimed and sounded forth the first tidings and trumpet of reformation to all Europe? And had it not been the obstinate perverseness of our prelates against the divine and admirable spirit of Wycliff, to suppress him as a schismatic and innovator, perhaps neither the Bohemian Huss and Jerome, no nor the name of Luther or of Calvin had ever been known . . .

Behold now this vast city: a city of refuge, the mansion house of liberty, encompassed and surrounded with His protection; the shop of war hath not there more anvils and hammers waking to fashion out the plates and instruments of armed Justice in defence of beleaguered Truth, than there be pens and heads there sitting by their studious lamps, musing, searching, revolving new notions and ideas wherewith to present, as with their homage and their fealty, the approaching reformation: others as fast reading, trying all things, assenting to the force of reason and convincement. What could a man require more from a nation so pliant, and so prone to seek after knowledge? What wants there to such a towardly and pregnant soil, but wise and faithful labourers to make a knowing people, a nation of prophets, of sages, and of worthies?

5.24 JOHN MILTON, *THE REASON OF CHURCH GOVERNMENT*

Here Milton makes a plea for a public but populist art, which should be supported by the reforming party. Text from: first edition, 1641, book 2, preface.

That what the greatest and choicest wits of Athens, Rome or modern Italy, and those Hebrews of old did for their country, I, in my proportion, with this over and above, of being a Christian, might do for mine; not caring to be once named abroad, though perhaps I could attain to that, but content with these British Islands as my world; whose fortune hath hitherto been that; if the Athenians, as some say, made their small deeds great and renowned by their eloquent writers, England hath her noble achievements made small by the unskilful handling of monks and mechanics.

Times serves not now, and perhaps I might seem too profuse to give any certain account of what the mind at home, in the spacious circuits of her musing, hath liberty to propose to herself, though of highest hope and hardest attempting; whether that epic form whereof the two poems of Homer and those other two of Virgil and Tasso are a diffuse, and the book of Job a brief, model: or whether the rules of Aristotle herein are strictly to be kept or nature to be followed, which in them that know art, and use judgement, is no transgression, but an enriching of art; and lastly what king or knight before the conquest might be chosen in whom to lay the pattern of a Christian hero. And as Tasso gave to a prince of Italy his choice whether he would command him to write of Godfrey's expedition against the infidels, or Belisarius against the Goths or Charlemagne against the Lombards; if to the instinct of nature and the emboldening of art aught may be trusted, and that there be nothing adverse in our climate, or the fate of this age, it haply would be no rashness from an equal diligence and inclination to present the like offer in our own ancient stories; or whether those dramatic constitutions, wherein Sophocles and Euripides reign, shall be found more doctrinal and exemplary to a nation.

The Scripture also affords us a divine pastoral drama in the Song of Solomon, consisting of two persons and a double chorus, as Origen rightly judges. And the Apocalypse of St. John is the majestic image of a high and stately tragedy, shutting up and intermingling her solemn scenes and acts with a sevenfold chorus of hallelujahs and harping symphonies . . .

. . . Teaching over the whole book of sanctity and virtue, through all the instances of example, with such delight to those especially of soft and delicious temper, who will not so much as look upon truth herself unless they see her elegantly dressed; that whereas the paths of honesty and good life appear now rugged and difficult, though they be indeed easy and pleasant, they will then appear to all men both easy and pleasant, though they were rugged and difficult indeed. And what a benefit this would be to our youth and gentry may be soon guessed by what we know of the corruption and bane which they suck in daily from the writings and interludes of libidinous and ignorant poetasters; who having scarce ever heard of that which is the main consistence of a true poem, the choice of such persons as they ought to introduce, and what is moral and decent to each one, do for the most part lay up vicious principles in sweet pills to be swallowed down and make the taste of virtuous documents harsh and sour.

But because the spirit of man cannot demean itself lively in this body without some recreating intermission of labour and serious things, it were happy for the Commonwealth if our magistrates, as in those famous governments of old, would take into their care not only the deciding of our contentious law cases and brawls; but the managing of our public sports and festival pastimes; that they might be, not such as were authorised a while since, the provocations of drunkenness and lust, but such as may inure and harden our bodies by martial exercises to all warlike skill and performance; and may civilise, adorn and make discreet our minds by the learned and affable meeting of frequent academies and the procurement of wise and artful recitations; sweetened with eloquent and graceful enticements to the love and practice of justice, temperance and fortitude; instructing and bettering the nation at all opportunities, that the call of wisdom and virtue may be heard everywhere, as Solomon saith: *she crieth without, she uttereth her voice in the streets, in the top of high places, in the chief concourse, and in the openings of the gates.* Whether this may not be, not only in pulpits, but after another persuasive method, at set and solemn paneguries, in theatres, porches, or what other place or way may win most upon the people, to receive at once both recreation and instruction, let them in authority consult.

5.25 WILLIAM DAVENANT, 'PREFACE' TO *GONDIBERT*

Davenant's *Gondibert* was a long romantic epic: his preface articulates a theory of pleasurable poetic reading and writing, which he evidently felt was missing from the society of the Commonwealth. Text from: first edition, 1651, pp. 1–3; 10; 24; 45–51.

The author's preface to his much honoured friend Mr. Hobbes

First give me leave (remembering with what difficulty the world can show any heroic poem, that in a perfect glass of nature gives us a familiar and easy view of ourselves) to take notice of those quarrels which the living have with the dead; and I will . . . begin with Homer, who though he seems to me standing upon the poets' famous hill, like the eminent sea-mark, by which they have in former ages steered, and though he ought not to be removed from that eminence, lest

338

posterity should presumptuously mistake their course; yet some (sharply observing how his successors have proceeded no further than a perfection of imitating him) say that as sea-marks are chiefly useful to coasters, and serve not those who have the ambition of discoverers, that love to sail in untried seas; so he hath rather proved a guide for those whose satisfied wit will not venture beyond the track of others; than to them who affect a new and remote way of thinking, who esteem it a deficiency and meanness of mind to stay and depend upon the authority of example . . .

His successor to fame (and consequently to censure) is Virgil, whose toils nor virtue cannot free him from the peevishness (or rather curiosity) of divers readers. He is upbraided by some (who perhaps are affected antiquaries, and make priority of time the measure of excellence) for gaining his renown by the imitation of Homer; whilst others (no less bold with that ancient guide) say he hath so often led him into heaven and hell, till by conversation with Gods and ghosts he sometimes deprives us of those natural probabilities in story which are instructive to human life; and others affirm (if it be not irreverence to record their opinion) that even in wit he seems deficient by many omissions, as if he had designed a penance of gravity to himself and to posterity. And by their observing that continued gravity, methinks they look upon him as on a musician composing of anthems, whose excellence consists more in the solemnness than in the fancy and upon the body of his work: as on the body of a giant whose force hath more of strength than quickness and of patience than activity.

. . . And surely poets (whose business should represent the world's true image often to our view) are not less prudent than painters, who when they draw landscapes, entertain not the eye wholly with even prospect and a continued flat, but (for variety) terminate the sight with lofty hills whose obscure heads are sometimes in the clouds . . .

When I considered the actions which I meant to describe (those inferring the persons) I was again persuaded rather to choose those of a former age than the present; and in a century so far removed, as might preserve me from their improper examinations, who know not the requisites of a poem, nor how much pleasure they lose (and even the pleasures of heroic poesy are not unprofitable) who take away the liberty of a poet and fetter his feet in the shackles of an historian. For why should a poet doubt in story to mend the intrigues of fortune by more delightful conveyances of probable fictions, because austere historians have entered into bond to truth? An obligation which were in poets as foolish and unnecessary as is the bondage of false martyrs who lie in chains for a mistaken opinion: but by this I would imply that truth narrative and past is the idol of historians (who worship a dead thing); and truth operative and by effect continually alive, is the mistress of poets and hath not her existence in matter but in reason.

* * *

Yet to such painful poets some upbraid the want of extemporary fury or rather, inspiration, a dangerous word which many have of late successfully used; and inspiration is a spiritual fit derived from the ancient ethnic poets who then, as they were priests, were statesmen too and probably loved dominion and as their well-dissembling of inspiration begot them reverence then, equal to that which was paid to laws, so these who now profess the same fury may perhaps by such authentic example pretend authority over the people.

* * *

Others may object that poesy on our stage, or the heroic in music (for the latter was anciently used) is prejudicial to a state as begetting levity and giving the people too great a diversion by pleasure and mirth. To these (if they be worthy of satisfaction) I reply that whoever in government endeavours to make the people serious and grave (which are attributes that may become the people's representatives, but not the people) doth practise a new way to enlarge the State by making every subject a statesman: and he that means to govern so mournfully (as it were without any music in his dominion) must lay but light burdens on his subjects; or else he wants the ordinary wisdom of those, who to their beasts that are much loaden, whistle all the day to encourage their travel. For that supreme power which expects a firm obedience in those who are not used to rejoicing but live sadly, as if they were full preparing for the funeral of peace, hath little skill in contriving the lastingness of government, which is the principal work of art, and less hath that power considered nature, as if such new austerity did seem to tax even her, for want of gravity in bringing in the spring so merrily with a musical variety of birds. And such sullen power doth forget that battles (the most solemn and serious business of death) are begun with trumpets and fifes, and anciently were continued with more diversity of musics. And that the Grecian laws (laws being the gravest endeavour of human counsels for the ease of life) were long before the days of Licurgus (to make them more pleasant to memory) published in verse; and that the wise Athenians (dividing into three parts the public revenue) expended one in plays and shows to divert the people from meeting to consult of their rulers' merit and the defects of government; and that the Romans had not so long continued their empire but for the same diversions at a vaster charge.

Again it may be objected that the precepts of Christian religion are sufficient towards our regulation by appointment of manners, and towards the ease of life by imposing obedience: so that the moral assistance of poesy is but vainly intruded. . . . For poesy which (like contracted essences seems the utmost strength and activity of nature) is as all good arts, subservient to religion, all marching under the same banner, though of less discipline and esteem. And as poesy is the best expositor of nature (nature being mysterious to such as use not to consider), so nature is the best interpreter of God and more cannot be said of religion. And when the judges of religion (which are the chiefs of the Church) neglect the help of moralists in reforming the people (and poets are of all moralists the most useful) they give a sentence against the law of nature. For nature performs all things by correspondent aids and harmony . . .

I cannot also be ignorant that divers (whose conscious melancholy amazes and discourages others' devotion) will accuse poets as the admirers of beauty; and inventors or provokers of that which by way of aspersion they call love. But such, in their first accusation seem to look carelessly and unthankfully upon the wonderful works of God; or else through low education or age become incompetent judges of what is the chief of his works upon earth. And poets when they praise beauty are at least as lawfully thankful to God as when they praise seas, woods, rivers, or any other parts that make up a prospect of the world. Nor can it be imagined but that poets in praising them, praise wholly the Maker; and so in praising beauty . . .

They who accuse poets as provokers of love are enemies to nature: and all affronts to nature are offences to God, as insolencies to all subordinate officers of the crown are rudenesses to the King. Love (in the most obnoxious interpretation) is nature's preparative to her greatest work, which is the making of life. And since the severest divines of these latter times have not been ashamed publicly to command and define the most secret duties and entertainments of love in the married, why should not poets civilly endeavour to make a friendship between the guests before they meet, by teaching them to dignify each other with the utmost of estimation. And marriage in mankind were as rude and unprepared as the hasty elections of other creatures, but for acquaintance and conversation before it: and that must be an acquaintance of minds not of bodies; and of the mind, poesy is the most natural and delightful interpreter.

When neither religion (which is our art towards God); nor nature (which is God's first law to man, though by man least studied); nor when reason (which is nature and made art by experience) can by the enemies of poesy be sufficiently urged against it, then some (whose forwardness will not let them quit an evil cause) plead written authority. . . . This authority (which is but single too) is from Plato: and him some have maliciously quoted, as if in his feigned Commonwealth he had banished all poets. But Plato says nothing against poets in general; and in his particular quarrel (which is to Homer and Hesiod) only condemns such errors as we mentioned in the beginning of this preface when we looked upon the ancients. And those errors consist in their abasing religion by representing the gods in evil proportion and their heroes as unequal characters, and so brought vices into fashion by intermixing them with the virtues of great persons. Yet even during this divine anger of Plato he concludes not against poesy, but the poems then most in request.

5.26 INIGO JONES, *STONEHENGE RESTORED*

Jones's fanciful and forceful account of the origin of Stonehenge neatly illustrates the contemporary interest in antiquarianism, neo-classical architecture, and the assertion of historical links between the old Roman empire and the new English one. Text from: 1651 edition, pp. 1; 11–12; 65–71.

Being naturally inclined in my younger years to study the arts of design, I passed into foreign parts to converse with the great masters thereof in Italy; where I applied myself to search out the ruins of those ancient buildings, which in despite of time itself, and violence of barbarians, are yet remaining. Having satisfied myself in these and returning to my native country, I applied my mind more particularly to the study of architecture. Among the ancient monuments whereof, found here, I deemed none more worthy the searching after than this of Stonehenge: not only in regard of the founders thereof, the time when built, the work itself, but also for the rarity of its invention; being different in form from all I had seen before: likewise of as beautiful proportions, as elegant in order and as stately in aspect as any.

King James in his progress the year one thousand six hundred and twenty, being at Wilton and discoursing of this antiquity, I was sent for by the right honourable William, then Earl of Pembroke, and received there his Majesty's command to produce out of mine own practice in architecture and experience in antiquities abroad, what possibly I could discover concerning this of Stonehenge.

* * *

Touching the manner of the buildings of the ancient Britons and of what materials they consisted, I find them so far short of the magnificence of this antiquity that they were not stately nor sumptuous, neither had they anything of order or symmetry, much less of gracefulness and decorum in them, being only such as Ovid (relating to the first age of the world) makes mention of. . . . Thus Englished by Arthur Golding:

> their houses were the thicks
> And bushy queaches, hollow caves and hurdles made of sticks.

To like purpose Vitruvius. *In the first age of the world* (saith he) *men lived in woods, caves and forests, but after they had found out the use of fire, and by the benefit thereof were invited to enter into a certain kind of society. . . . Some of them began to make themselves habitations of boughs, some to dig dens in mountains; other some, imitating the nests of birds, made themselves places of loam and twigs, and such like materials to creep into, and shroud themselves in.* Directly after which manner of workmanship were the houses of the ancient Britons.

* * *

You cannot but remember in what manner the ancient inhabitants of this island lived before reduced to civility by the Romans I have formerly delivered: also how they were first instructed by them in several arts and sciences, whereof the Britons, wholly ignorant before the Romans' arrival here and teaching them. I have given you in like manner a full description of this antiquity whereby doubtless it

342

[Stonehenge] doubtless appears to you, as in truth it is, a work built with much art, order and proportion. That the ancient Britons before the discovery of this island by the Romans could not be the founders thereof, by the former reasons, I suppose is clearly manifested. For where art is not, nothing can be performed by art . . .

It rests now to endeavour the discovering by whom Stonehenge built, in what time, and for what use anciently erected . . .

Touching the founders of Stonehenge. Among the Egyptian antiquities or those eastern nations from whom the Grecians deduced their learning, I find not any such composure ever used: or with the Greeks themselves mention made of any work conformable to this in point of order (as the most conversant in those histories cannot contradict). I read nevertheless in Pausanius of a temple amongst the Eleans erected without walls. . . . *I saw* (saith he) *in the market place of the Eleans, a temple of a new form, a low thing without walls, having the roof supported with props of oaken timber* (instead it seems of columns) *neatly wrought.* He remembers a temple also in Attica sacred to Jove without a roof. The Thracians (as I read likewise) used to build temples dedicated to Sol, of a round form, open in the middle, and also without a roof: by the form or roundness thereof they signified the sun's figure; by making them open and roofless they expressed his surmounting and dilating light equally to all things . . .

Howsoever, considering what magnificence the Romans in prosperous times anciently used in all works, both public and private; their knowledge and experience in all arts and sciences; their powerful means for effecting great works; together with their order in building and manner of workmanship accustomed amongst them; Stonehenge in my judgement was a work built by the Romans and they the sole founders thereof. For if look upon this antiquity as an admired and magnificent building, who more magnificent than the Romans? . . . If consider the art and elegant disposition thereof, all arts and sciences (we must know) were in full perfection with them, and architecture which amongst the Greeks was youthful only and vigorous, under the Romans their empire grown to the full height became manly and perfect, not in inventions and elegancy of forms alone, but also in exquisiteness of art and excellency of materials. . . . If take notice of their power and ways by which they effected such goodly structures, their means were not ordinary according to the common custom of other people: and why? Because, besides particular artisans practised in several arts, they employed in those their works whole bodies of their own armies and whatever nations subdued by them . . .

If observe their orders in building, the only order of architecture which Italy may truly glory in the invention of is the Tuscan order, so called because first found out by the Tuscans, that in a more than ordinary manner they might reverence their deities in temples composed thereof. . . . Which order, though first used by the Tuscans, certain it is the Romans took from them and brought it in use with other arts in several parts of the world as their conquests led them on. Now of this Tuscan order, a plain, grave and humble manner of building, very solid and strong, Stonehenge principally consists. So that, observing the order whereof

343

Stonehenge built, there being no such elements known in this island as distinct orders of architecture until the Romans introduced them, the very work itself, of so great antiquity, declares the Romans founders thereof. Who that hath right judgement in architecture knows not the difference and by the manner of their works, how to distinguish Egyptian, Greek and Roman structures of old, also Italian, French and Dutch buildings in these modern times? Is not our shipping by the mould thereof, known throughout the world English built? . . . And in all likelihood the Romans for so notable a structure as Stonehenge made choice of the Tuscan rather than any other order, not only as best agreeing with the rude, plain, simple nature of those they intended to instruct, and use for which erected; but also because presuming to challenge a certain kind of propriety therein, they might take occasion thereby to magnify to those then living the virtue of their ancestors for so noble an invention, and make themselves the more renowned to posterity for erecting thereof, so well ordered a building.

Besides, the order is not only Roman, but the scheme also: consisting of four equilateral triangles inscribed within the circumference of a circle, by which this work Stonehenge formed, was an architectonical scheme used by the Romans . . .

Moreover, whatever footsteps of the Romans found in other places of this island, it's not inconsiderately to be passed over that in Wiltshire, the county (as is said before) where our Stonehenge remains, Roman antiquities are most perspicuous, not only by the apparent testimonies of the coins of their emperors in divers places digged up, but by several their encamping places yet to be seen, as Leckham, in times of yore a seat of the Romans; the place also where old Salisbury now showeth itself . . .

But it is objected if Stonehenge a Roman work, how comes it no Roman author makes mention of it? I answer their historians used not to commit to writing every particular work or action the Romans performed: if so, how vast would their volumes have been? Stonehenge, 'tis granted, is much admired by us; yet how far more admirable works were the Romans founders of, not mentioned in any of their ancient stories?

6

SCIENCE AND MAGIC

INTRODUCTION

Francis Bacon is a key figure in the intellectual history of the seventeenth century: he marks the dividing line between a modern view of environment and nature and a premodern one. But unlike Copernicus or Galileo he made no scientific discoveries; unlike Descartes, or his own fellow-countrymen Oughtred and Napier, he saw mathematics as a narrow discipline with no scientific future; and unlike Harvey he did not seriously practise his trumpeted experimentalism. Even the much cited experiment which caused his death (the attempt at freezing a chicken which brought on pneumonia) has become something of a historical joke. But Bacon's writing had four significant features, which in combination may explain the reverence with which he was treated by later seventeenth-century scientists, such as Boyle or Newton, even where they had scarcely read him.[1] First, he had an overarching philosophical vision about the role of the scientist in a modern society, combined with an intellectual excitement about the natural world. Second, he coupled human and material development with scientific advancement: a link between knowledge and utility, or technology, which is recognisably modern. Third, he argued cogently for a scientific method based on empirical observation, data collection and inductive reasoning. And fourth, he shared with other writers, such as Galileo and Descartes (6.11, 6.16), the view that nature was ruled internally by discoverable laws: in contradistinction to the older Aristotelian and Christian view that nature was organic (for example, Albertus Magnus and Roger Bacon, 6.1, 6.7) and moved according to a divine purpose (see Crooke and Burton, 6.12 and 6.13). This is the first noticeable shift towards a belief in a mechanical universe (see 6.14). In all these areas he has been heralded as paradigmatic of the modern Western rationalist assumptions about the place and function of human control and exploitation of the natural environment.[2]

Yet if we read Bacon's works with this reputation in mind he can seem curiously old-fashioned, even incomprehensible, to us. His own collections of 'facts', the natural histories he wrote in the 1620s, are all compilations from literary and fantastical sources, many of them medieval and classical, and combined in an eclectic fashion that is more medieval than modern.[3] Such collections were typical of the fashionable renaissance intellectual; but the mark of encyclopedic cataloguers, not scientific modernists.[4] Similarly, even some of his statements about nature and natural philosophy read as if they have more in common with the alchemical and magical *Book of Secrets* (6.1), than with twentieth-century particle physics. Yet this is precisely why he must be a key figure to a contemporary reader. The co-existence, even interdependence, of magical and alchemical traditions with 'scientific' discoveries has often been remarked.[5] Thus the empirical investigation of nature; the vision of magus or scientist as unveiler of nature's secrets; the accurate technical use of instruments, of weighing and gauging and producing effects; are all shared by alchemy, natural magic and natural philosophy. The elision between these roles, of magus and natural philosopher, is particularly clear in Agrippa's writing (6.2). Many of the famous names in natural philosophy, Kepler, John Dee (6.3), even Newton, also carried out investigations which today we would classify as 'magic': Kepler and Dee believed in an animate world full of animate spirits, and used mathematics to try to uncover them; Newton was deeply involved in alchemy. So, while it has been pointed out[6] that the important scientists of the period scrupulously defined their work as distinct from that of magicians or alchemists, it is important to understand that this distinction was only just being made during this period. 'Science' as we understand it, or 'natural philosophy' as Bacon's contemporaries knew it, was part of a broad field of knowledge: indeed, the contemporary meaning of 'science' was 'knowledge', its referential field was not narrowed to cover simply natural science until the eighteenth century.

Despite the excitement generated among intellectuals by new discoveries, such as Copernican heliocentrism, Vesalius's anatomy, Galileo's axioms of motion or Descartes's mechanical philosophy that the world of nature could be fully explained by mathematics, most people's views about the natural world did not change. Not only did they remain theistic, but were often superstitious as well.[7] It was God's will if the sun was obscured through an eclipse, or the harvest failed. Magical charms might help prevent the latter, but natural philosophy did not seem to offer either an explanatory system to replace that of an interventionist God, nor technical advances that could convince people through results, until the eighteenth century. Medicine and astrology are good examples of the slow advancement of a scientific or rationalist paradigm.

The predominant medical philosophy and practice remained Aristotelian and Galenic: Galen (see 6.6) used Aristotle's belief that nature was purposive and that the human was a microcosm of the universal frame of things, made up of the four elements, earth, air, fire and water. In human beings, these four elements manifested themselves as four humours, blood, phlegm, black bile and yellow bile, controlled by the liver, and disease was defined as an imbalance of these humours. All diagnoses and cures, whether medicinal or physical (such as blood-letting), were offered as a means of returning the body to its ideal humorous balance. This method-ology remained the medical philosophy and practice until well into the eighteenth century; in some cases even longer. Culpeper's translation and exposition of Galen in this collection, for example (6.6) illustrates this, as do the extracts from Crooke and Burton (6.12, 6.13). Thus, despite Harvey's discovery of the circulation of the blood and the importance of the lungs (6.15), medical practice continued to believe in the centrality of the liver and its humours. Scientific discovery, then, was virtually meaningless until education and technical developments placed it in a wider social and industrial revolution.

Similarly, the continued, even increasing, popularity of astrology can be measured through the sale of almanacs[8] (see part 4). Their claims to be able to predict events in people's and nations' lives, is based upon a funda-mentally pre-rationalist view of the world, in which not only did the microcosm of daily lives and our localised natural world echo the wider macrocosm of the heavens, but the world was animated by teleological purpose and secret influences, which could be sought out by the astrologer (or magus, or alchemist, or scientist). For most men, women and children of the early modern period, the almanac's contents summed up their view of the natural world, and their relation to it: the world was animate and unpre-dictable, but certain prayers, charms or actions might bring parts of it under your control. Koyre's description of the changed world view of the late seventeenth century as 'the mathematization of nature'[9] is only true for a handful of elite philosophers and scientists. Changes in popular conscious-ness, so much harder to measure, were also much slower.

Equally, there is no one moment, or even series of moments, which a historian can say was the scientific revolution. Many of the so-called discov-eries actually emerged from re-readings of newly found or newly edited classical texts: in 1543 two texts were published which often mark the commencement point of this revolution. These were Copernicus's *De Revolutionibus Orbium Coelestium* [on the revolutions of the celestial planets] and Vesalius's *De Humani Corporis Fabrica* [on the fabric of the human body]. In each case, both men took as the starting point work done by classical writers in their field: Ptolemy in the case of Copernicus, and Galen in the case of Vesalius. Copernicus argued that Ptolemy's hypothesis on geocentrism was mathematically wrong, but claimed that other ancient authors, such as Plutarch, had led him to his 'new' hypothesis of a helio-centric universe.[10] Thus, although this did initiate (eventually) a shift in metaphysical perspective, its source was the ancient texts and knowledge of the Greeks and Romans. Similarly, Vesalius claims that his work builds upon the writings and findings of Galen, whose physiological view of the human body remained unchallenged. Vesalius's innovation was in the exact and empirical investigation of the body, and his technical and perspective drawings which ensured the success of his text as heuristic tool for future generations. Digges was the first to translate Copernicus's ideas into English (see 6.4), and Vesalius's drawings were quickly incorporated into other medical publications in England, although no English translation of his work was made. Epicurus, Lucretius and the pre-Socratics provided ways of thinking and theories which led to Descartes's and Gassendi's advocacy of a particulate and mechanical universe (see 6.16, 6.18 and 6.23). Thus the populist notion of the scientific revolution as a revolutionary break with the past is untenable. Similarly, the continuity of much work from and within medieval universities to those of the mid and late renaissance, such as that on optics, hydraulics, machines, mining, agriculture, military technology, draughtsmanship and perspective, tells us that the discoveries and inventions of the sixteenth and seventeenth century were often the culmination of earlier research and thinking. This has been demonstrated, for example, in the work of Galileo on motion.[11]

Nevertheless, despite these caveats, it is also true to say that there is a discernible intellectual shift between 1550 and 1660. 1550 saw the publication in English of the pseudo Albertus Magnus, *Book of Secrets* (6.1), an observably medieval and magical account of the natural world, and the human place within that. 1660 saw the first formal meetings of the group that was to become the Royal Society of London for Improving of Natural Knowledge in 1662 by royal charter, whose observably Baconian aims were listed as: 'the advancement of the knowledge of natural things and useful arts by experiments to the glory of God the creator and for application to the good of mankind'.[12] Men such as John Wilkins, Kenelm Digby, John Evelyn, Robert Hooke and Robert Boyle (see 6.17, 6.18 and 6.23), all of whom had been actively engaged in experimentation, research and writing of natural philosophy for the previous twenty years, were active founders and members. What they shared was not only a recognisably 'scientific' approach to the study and exploitation of nature, but a common philosophical premise: that the universe was subject to discoverable, rational, mathematical laws, and that it was the task of the natural scientist to uncover these laws. The language and methodologies of Gilbert, of Galileo, of Bacon, Descartes and of Harvey (6.9, 6.11, 6.14, 6.16, 6.19) had become the accepted methodology of scientific enterprise.

This shift from a verbal and literate culture (based on the word of God and interpretations of texts of the ancients) to a mathematical and numerical one (based on the mechanical operations of particles in space) is a definitive change, a revolution in the way in which humans viewed and controlled the world around them. Thus, although the moment of revolution does not exist, comparison of texts across these hundred years can tell us much about the comparative social and intellectual climates of the sixteenth and seventeenth centuries, such a comparison enables us to see 1550 as pre-modern, and 1660 as modern.

6.1 PSEUD. ALBERTUS MAGNUS, *THE BOOK OF SECRETS*

The Book of Secrets was thought to have been composed by Albertus Magnus, the medieval philosopher and magus, although it is now known it was a forgery. It proclaims secret virtues and effects to be found in herbs and minerals, and was much quoted by early chemical writers, including Paracelsus. To the late-twentieth-century audience, as with other books which advised treatment according to herbal or mineral concoctions, it appears to mix the pragmatic with the fantastic. Text from: fos A2^r–A3^r; C1^r–^{v}; C4^v–C5^v.

Of the virtues of certain herbs

Aristotle, the prince of philosophers, saith in many places that every science is of the kind of good things. But notwithstanding, the operation sometime is good, sometime evil: as the science is changed to a good or to an evil end, to which it worketh. Of the which saying, two things be concluded: the one, and the first is that the science of magic is not evil, for by the knowledge of it evil may be eschewed and good followed. The second thing is also concluded, forasmuch as the effect is praised for the end, and also the end of science is dispraised when it is not ordained to good or to virtue. It followeth then that every science or operation is sometime good, sometime evil . . .

The first herb is called . . . with Englishmen, *marigold*: whose interpretation is of *elios*, that is the sun, and *tropos*, that is alteration or change, because it is turned according to the sun. The virtue of this herb is marvellous: for if it be gathered, the sun being in the sign of Leo in August, and be wrapped in the leaf of a laurel or bay tree, and a wolf's tooth be added thereto, no man shall be able to have a word to speak against the bearer thereof, but words of peace. And if anything be stolen, if the bearer of the things before named lay them under his head in the night, he shall see the thief . . .

The fourth herb is named . . . of Englishmen *celandine*. This herb springeth in the time in the which the swallows and also the eagles maketh their nests. If any man shall have this herb with the heart of a mole, he shall overcome all his enemies and all matters in suit, and shall put away all debate. And if the before named herb be put upon the head of a sick man, if he should die he shall sing anon with a loud voice, if not he shall weep.

The fifth herb is named . . . of Englishmen *periwink*, when it is beaten unto powder with worms of the earth, wrapped about it and with an herb called *sempervina*, in English houseleek, it induceth love between man and wife if it be used in their meats . . .

Of the virtues of certain stones

If thou wilt know whether thy wife is chaste or no

Take the stone which is called magnes in English, the loadstone, it is of saddle blue in colour, and it is found in the sea of Inde, sometime in parts of Allmain, in the province which is called East France. Lay this stone under the head of a wife, and if she be chaste, she will embrace her husband; if she be not chaste, she will fall anon forth of the bed. Moreover, if this stone be put brayed and scattered upon coals in four corners of the house, they that be sleeping shall flee the house and leave all . . .

If thou wilt provoke sorrow, fear, terrible fantasies and debate

Take the stone which is called onyx, which is of black colour. And the kind is best which is full of white veins. And it cometh from Inde, unto Araby, and if it be hanged upon the neck or finger, it stirreth up anon sorrow or heaviness in a man, and terrors and also debate, and this hath been proved by men of late time . . .

If thou wilt overcome thy enemies

Take the stone which is called adamas: in English speech, a diamond, and it is of shining colour and very hard, insomuch that it cannot be broken but by the blood of a goat, and it groweth in Arabia or in Cyprus. And if it be bound to the left side, it is good against enemies, madness, wild beasts, venomous beasts and evil men, and against thy dying . . .

If thou wilt overcome beasts and interpret or expound all dreams and prophecy of things to come

Take the stone which is called esmundus or asmadus, it is of divers colours, it putteth out all poison and maketh a man to overcome his adversaries and giveth prophesying and the interpretation of all dreams, and maketh a man to understand dark questions, hard to understand or be assailed.

6.2 CORNELIUS HENRY AGRIPPA, OF THE UNCERTAINTY AND VANITY OF SCIENCES

Agrippa was a philosopher and occultist and in this work he rejects the occult, arguing that God alone can provide certain and effective knowledge. Nevertheless, his discussion of natural philosophy and natural magic tells us much about contemporary beliefs and practices. Text from: English translation, 1569, pp. 1; 55–6; 63ᵛ–64ᵛ.

It is an ancient and almost an agreeable and common opinion, of all the philosophers by the which they think that every science doth bring unto man some divinity, according to the capacity and value of them both; so that oftentimes beyond the limits of humanity they may be reckoned among the fellowship of the God. From hence arose the divers and infinite commendations of sciences, with which every man doth endeavour, with no less eloquent than long discourse, to exalt and extol above the heavens these arts and disciplines in the which by continual exercise every man hath whetted the strength of his wit. Notwithstanding, I being persuaded with other kind of reason, am of opinion that there can chance to the life and salvation of our souls, nothing more hurtful and pestilent than these arts and sciences.

* * *

Of natural magic

Men think that natural magic is nothing else but a singular power of natural knowledges which therefore they call the greatest profoundness of natural philosophy, and absolutest perfection thereof, and showeth what is the active part of natural philosophy, which with the aid of natural virtues, according to the mutual and convenient applying of them, doth publish works exceeding all the capacity of admiration. The which magic was much used of the Egyptians, and of the Indians, where there was abundance of herbs, of stones, and other things thereunto belonging. They say that Jerome made mention thereof, writing to Paulinus, where he saith that Appollonius Tyana was a magician or a philosopher, as the Pythagoreans were. And the magicians were of this sort which went to worship Christ when he was born, visiting him with gifts. . . . Natural magic, then, is that which having intentively beheld the forces of all natural things and celestial, and with curious search sought out their order, doth in such sort publish abroad the hidden and secret powers of nature; coupling the inferior things with the qualities of the superior, as it were certain enticements by a natural joining of them together, that thereof oftentime do arise marvellous miracles: not so much by art as nature, whereunto this art doth proffer herself a servant, when she worketh these things. For the magicians, as very diligent searchers of nature, bringing the things which be prepared by nature, applying and setting active things to passive, very oftentimes before the time by nature appointed to bring forth effects; which of the common sort be accounted miracles. Whereas, for all that they be but natural works, nothing else coming between but the foretaking of time: as if a man in the month of March would cause roses to spring, and ripe grapes; beans sown, or parsley within few hours to grow into a perfect plant; and greater things than these, as clouds, rain, thunder, beasts of divers sorts, and infinite transformations of things, of which kind Roger Bacon doth boast that he hath done many with pure and natural magic . . .

Of mathematical magic

There be moreover other very prudent and adventurous searchers of nature, which without natural virtues, with the mathematical disciplines alone, the influences of the heavens being put thereto, do promise that they are able to bring forth things like to the works of nature: as bodies that go and speak, which for all that, have not the virtues of the soul: as the wooden dove of Architas was, which flew; and the image of Mercury that spake; and the brazen head forged by Albert the great, which as it is said, did speak. Boethius did excel in these things, a man of passing profound wit and divers learning: to whom Cassiodorus writing of these things, saith: thou art determined to know difficult matters and to show miracles: with the passing skill of thy art metals do bellow, Diomedes bloweth aloud in brass, the brazen serpent hisseth, birds be counterfeited, and they that have no proper voice be heard to utter sweetness of song . . .

Of witching magic

There is another kind of natural magic which is termed witching or medicinal which is done with potions, charmed drinks, for love; and divers poisoning medicines such a one as Democritus is read to have made, whereby happy and fortunate children may be begotten, and another whereby we may well understand the voices of birds . . .

Of natural philosophy

But it is now more than time to go to further matters, and to trace out the opinions of philosophy, the things which search nature and the sciences, which with subtle syllogisms seek out the beginnings and ends of things. . . . But if any will assemble together all the philosophers, nevertheless, it cannot be known among them which ought to be called the better sect, and to whose opinions we should rather obey: they do so much strive and disagree among themselves in all things and do maintain this perpetual strife from age to age. . . . And although philosophy disproveth and judgeth of all things, yet she is certain of nothing: wherefore I know not whether I should account philosophers among beasts or among men: they seem to surmount brutish beasts because they have reason and understanding; but how shall they be accounted men, whose reason cannot persuade no constant and certain thing, but doth always waver in mutable opinions; whose understanding, doubtful at every matter knoweth not what it should hold or follow, and that this is true we will now at large declare.

Of the principles of natural things

There is a very grievous battle fought among the gravest philosophers concerning the principles of natural things, whereupon all this science is grounded, and yet the matter is before the judge. They allege persuadings and invincible reasons of contraries, which of them hath spoken best. For Thales Milesius judged, the first wise man by the oracles of Apollo, that all things would be made of water. Anaximander, his auditor and successor in the school, said that the beginnings of things be infinite. Anaximenes his scholar affirmed that the air was an infinite beginning of things. Hyparchus and Heraclitus Ephesius, the fire; to these after a sort do Archelaus the Athenean and Anaxagoras the Clasomenian agree, that the beginnings were infinite, as it were certain small and confused parts, but afterward set in order by the will of God. Xenophanes said that one was all things, and the same not moveable; Parmenides hot and cold; as the fire which moveth and the earth which fashioneth; Leucippus, Diodorus and Democritus, the full and the empty. Diogenes the free said that it was the air which hath yet in it the divine reason. Pythagoras the Samian would that number should be the beginning of things. . . . Empedocles the Agrigentine, strife, friendship, and the four elements. Epicurus the beams of the sun, and the empty; Plato and Socrates, God, the form conceived in the mind, and the matter. Zeno, God, the matter and the elements. Aristotle, the matter to the appetite of the form by privation.

6.3 JOHN DEE, 'PREFACE' TO *EUCLID'S ELEMENTS*

John Dee, magus, mathematician, alchemist and astrologer to Elizabeth I, was an active writer, translator and practitioner of natural and mathematical science. He patronised other mathematicians, geographers and cosomographers. One such, Henry Billingsley, had translated the *Euclid*, to which Dee wrote this preface. Text from: first edition, trans. Henry Billingsley, 1570, fos i–Aii.

How immaterial and free from all matter number is, who doth not perceive? Yea, who doth not wonderfully wonder at it? . . . O comfortable allurement! O, ravishing persuasion! To deal with a science whose subject is so ancient, so pure, so excellent, so surmounting all creatures, so used of the almighty and incomprehensible wisdom of the creator in the distinct creation of all creatures, in all their distinct parts, properties, natures, and virtues by order and most absolute number brought from nothing to the formality of their being and state. By number's property therefore . . . we may both wind and draw ourselves into the inward and deep search and view of all creatures' distinct virtues, natures, properties and forms; and also, farther, arise, climb, ascend and mount up (with speculative wings) in spirit to behold in the glass of creation the form of forms, the exemplar number of all things numerable, both visible and invisible, mortal and immortal, corporal and spiritual . . .

Anthropography is the description of the number, measure, weight, figure, situation and colour of every diverse thing contained in the perfect body of man. . . . If the description of the heavenly part of the world had a peculiar art called astronomy; if the description of the earthly globe hath his peculiar art called geography; if the matching of both hath his peculiar art, called cosmography, which is the description of the whole and universal frame of the world, why should not the description of him who is the less world and from the beginning called *microcosmus* (that is the less world), and for whose sake and service all bodily creatures else were created, who also participates with spirits and angels, and is made to the image and similitude of God, have his peculiar art? . . . Whereby good proof will be had of our harmonious and microcosmical constitution. The outward image and view hereof, to the art of painting, to sculpture, and architecture (for church, house, fort or ship) is most necessary and profitable for that it is the chief base and foundation of them. Look in Vitruvius, whether I deal sincerely for your behoof or no. Look in Albert Durer *De Symmetria humani corporis* . . .

The art of navigation demonstrateth how by the shortest good way, by the aptest direction, and in the shortest time a sufficient ship between any two places (in passage navigable) assigned, may be conducted: and in all storms and natural disturbances chancing, how to use the best possible means whereby to recover the place first assigned. What need the master pilot hath of other arts here before recited, it is easy to know: as of hydrography, astronomy, astrology and horometry. Presupposing continually the common base and foundation of all: namely arithmetic and geometry. So that he be able to understand and judge his own necessary instruments and furniture necessary, whether they be perfectly made or no, and also can (if need be) make them himself: as quadrants, the astronomer's ring, the astronomer's staff, the astrolabe universal, an hydrographical globe, charts hydrographical (true, not with parallel meridians), the common sea compass, the compass of variation, the proportional and paradoxal compasses (of me invented for our two Muscovy master pilots at the request of the company). . . . And also be able to calculate the planets' places for all times.

6.4 THOMAS DIGGES, *PERFECT DESCRIPTION OF THE CELESTIAL ORBS*

Thomas Digges, son of the astrologer and inventor Leonard Digges, was a renowned mathematician and engineer, a consultant on several voyages to the north-west passage, and was the first Englishman to adopt the Copernican heliocentric hypothesis. He translated and edited Copernicus's *De Revolutionibus Coelestium* (first published in Latin in 1543). The preface and expository diagram alone are included here, given the technical nature of the translation itself (see figure 1). Text from: Leonard Digges, *A Prognostication of Right Good Effect, corrected and augmented by Thomas Digges*, 1576 edition, Appendix, fos M1–M3.

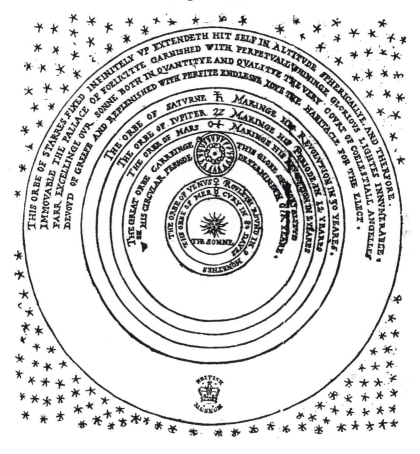

Figure 1 Perfect Description of the Celestial Orbs

Preface to the reader

In this our age one rare wit (seeing the continual errors that from time to time more and more have been discovered, besides the infinite absurdities in their theorics[1] which they have been forced to admit that would not confess any mobility in the ball of the earth) hath by long study, painful practice, and rare invention, delivered a new theoric or model of the world, showing that the earth resteth not in the centre of the whole world, but only in the centre of this our mortal world or globe of elements which environed and enclosed the moon's orb, and, together with the whole globe of mortality, is carried yearly round about the sun, which like a king in the middest of all reigneth and giveth the laws of motion to the rest, spherically dispersing his glorious beams of light through all this sacred celestial temple; and the earth itself to be one of the planets having his peculiar and straying courses turning every twenty-four hours round about his own centre whereby the sun and great globe of fixed stars seem to sway about and turn, albeit indeed they remain fixed. So many ways is the sense of mortal man abused, but reason and deep discourse of wit having opened these things to Copernicus and the same being with demonstrations mathematical most apparently by him to the world delivered, I thought it convenient together with the old theoric also to publish this, to the end such noble English minds (as delight to reach above the baser sort of men) might not be altogether defrauded of so noble a part of philosophy. And to the end it might manifestly appear that Copernicus meant not as some have fondly excused him to deliver these grounds of the earth's mobility only as mathematical principles feigned, and not as philosophical truly answered, I have also delivered from him both the philosophical reasons by Aristotle and others produced to maintain the earth's stability, and also their solutions and insufficiency, wherein I cannot a little commend the modesty of that grave philosopher Aristotle, who seeing (no doubt) the insufficiency of his own reasons in seeking to confute the earth's motion, useth these words: *de his explicatum est ea qua potuimus facultate* [the explanation for these things is according to our ability], howbeit his disciples have not with like sobriety maintained the same. Thus much for my own part in this case will I only say, there is no doubt but of a true ground truer effects may be produced than of principles that are false, and of true principles falsehood or absurdity cannot be inferred. If therefore the earth be situate immoveable in the centre of the world, why find we not theorics upon that ground to produce the effects as true and certain as these of Copernicus? Why cast we not away those *circulos aequantes* [equal circles] and motions irregular, seeing our own philosopher, Aristotle himself, the light of our universities, hath taught us, *simplicis corporis simplicem oportet esse motum* [a simple motion belongs to a simple body]. But if contrary be found, impossible (the earth's stability being granted) but that we must necessarily fall into these absurdities, and cannot by any means avoid them. Why shall we so much dote in the appearance of our senses, which many ways may be abused, and not suffer ourselves to be directed by the rule of reason, which the great God hath given us as a lamp to lighten the darkness of our understanding and the perfect guide to lead us to the golden branch of verity amid the forest of errors? . . .

In the midst of this globe of mortality hangeth this dark star or ball of earth and water, balanced and sustained in the midst of the thin air only with that propriety, which the wonderful workman hath given at the creation to the centre of the globe with his magnetical force vehemently to draw and hale unto itself all such other elementate things as retain the like nature. This ball every twenty-four hours by natural, uniform and wonderfully smooth motion rolleth round, making with his period our natural day, whereby it seems to us that the huge infinite immoveable globe should sway and turn about.

The moon's orb that environeth and containeth this dark star and other mortal, changeable, corruptible elements and elementate things, is also turned around every 29 days 31 minutes 50 seconds 8 thirds 9 fourths and 20 fifths: and this period may aptly be called the month. The rest of the planets' motions appear by the picture and shall more largely be hereafter spoken of.

Herein good reader, I have waded farder than the vulgar sort's demonstrative and practice, and God sparing life I mean, though not as a judge to decide, yet at the mathematical bar in this case to plead in such sort as it shall manifestly appear to the world whether it be possible upon the earth's stability to deliver any true or probable theoric, and then refer the pronouncing of sentence to the grave senate of indifferent discreet mathematical readers.

Farewell and respect my travail as thou shalt see them tend to the advancement of truth and discovering the monstrous loathsome shape of error.

6.5 REGINALD SCOTT, *THE DISCOVERY OF WITCHCRAFT*

Scott's *Discovery of Witchcraft* attempted to bring reason to the witch scare and the persecution of old women for minor offences. Although he does argue that he believes in the existence of some witches, the main import of his argument is that most accusations are scare stories, or maliciously motivated. The importance of this view is that he suggested that reason would allow people to understand and order the natural world. Text from: first edition, 1584, fos Aii^r–A^w; Bii^r–B^w; pp. 291–2.

Epistle to Sir Roger Manwood, Lord Chief Baron of Her Majesty's Court of the Exchequer

Howbeit it is natural to unnatural people and peculiar unto witchmongers to pursue the poor, to accuse the simple, and to kill the innocent, supplying in rigour and malice towards others that which they themselves want in proof and discretion, or the other in offence or occasion. But as a cruel heart and an honest mind do seldom meet and feed together in a dish, so a discreet and merciful magistrate and a happy commonwealth cannot be separated asunder. How much then are we bound to God, who hath given us a queen, that of justice is not only the very perfect image and pattern, but also of mercy and clemency under God, the mere fountain and body itself? Insomuch as they which hunt most after blood in these duties have least authority to shed it. Moreover sith I see that in cases where lenity might be noisome and punishment wholesome to the commonwealth, there no respect of person can move you, no authority can abash you, no fear, no threats can daunt you in performing the duties of justice.

In that respect again I find your Lordship a fit person to judge and look upon this present treatise. Wherein I will bring before you, as it were to the bar, two sorts of most arrogant and wicked people; the first challenging to themselves, the second attributing unto others, that power which only appertaineth to God: who only is the creator of all things; who only searcheth the heart and reins;[2] who only knoweth our imaginations and thoughts; who only openeth all secrets; who only worketh great wonders; who only hath power to raise up and cast down; who only maketh thunder, lightning, rain, tempests, and restraineth them at his pleasure; who only sendeth life and death, sickness and health, wealth and woe; who neither giveth nor lendeth his glory to any creature . . .

And although some say that the devil is the witch's instrument to bring her purposes and practices to pass; yet others say that she is his instrument to execute his pleasure in any thing, and therefore to be executed. But then (methinks) she should be injuriously dealt withal and put to death for another's offence: for actions are not judged by instrumental causes; neither doth the end and purpose of that which is done depend upon the mean instrument. Finally, if the witch do it not, why should the witch die for it? But they say that witches are persuaded and think that they do indeed those mischiefs; and have a will to perform that which the devil commiteth: and that therefore they are worthy to die. By which reason everyone should be executed that wisheth evil to his neighbour, etc. But if the will should be punished by man, according to the offence against God, we should be driven by thousands at once to the slaughter house or butchery. For whosoever loatheth correction shall die. And who should escape execution if this loathsomeness (I say) should extend to death by the civil laws? Also the reward of sin is death. Howbeit everyone that sinneth is not to be put to death by the magistrate. But (my Lord) it shall be proved in my book and your Lordship shall try it to be true, as well here at home in your native country, as also abroad in your several circuits, that besides them that be . . . plain poisoners, there will be found among our witches only two sorts: the one sort being such by imputation, as so thought of by others (and these are abused and not abusers); the other by acceptation as being willing so to be accounted (and these be mere cozeners).

Cahine, treating of these magicians, calleth them cozeners, saying that they use their juggling knacks only to amaze or abuse the people; or else for fame: but he might rather have said for gain . . . in ancient time the learned were not so blockish as not to see that the promises of magicians and enchanters were false, and nothing else but knavery, cozenage and old wives' fables . . .

And because I know your Lordship will take no counsel against innocent blood, but rather suppress them that seek to imbrue their hands therein, I have made choice to open their case unto you, and to lay their miserable calamities before your feet, following herein the advice of that learned man Brendus, who saith . . . if any admonish the magistrate not to deal too hardly with these miserable wretches that are called witches, I think him a good instrument raised up for this purpose by God himself.

But it will perchance be said by witchmongers, to wit, by such as attribute to witches the power which appertaineth to God only, that I have made choice of your Lordship to be a patron to this my book, because I think you favour mine opinions, and by that means may the more freely publish any error or conceit of mine own; which should rather be warranted by your Lordship's authority, than by the word of God, or by sufficient argument. But I protest the contrary and by these presents I renounce all protection and despise all friendship that might serve to help towards the suppressing or supplanting of truth: knowing also that your Lordship is far from allowing any injury done unto man, much more an enemy to them that go about to dishonour God, or to embezzle the title of his immortal glory. But because I know you to be perspicuous and able to see down into the depth and bottom of causes, and are not to be carried away with the vain persuasion or superstition, either of man, custom, time or multitude, but moved with the authority of truth only: I crave your countenance herein, even so far forth, and no further, than the law of God, the law of nature, the law of this land and the rule of reason shall require. Neither do I treat for these poor people any otherwise but so as with one hand you may sustain the good and with the other suppress the evil: wherein you shall be thought a father to orphans, an advocate to widows, a guide to the blind, a stay to the lame, a comfort and countenance to the honest, a scourge and terror to the wicked.

Epistle to the readers

But Robin Goodfellows ceaseth now to be much feared, and popery is sufficiently discovered; nevertheless, witches' charms and conjurers' cozenages are yet thought effectual. Yea, the gentiles have espied the fraud of their cozening oracles and our cold prophets and enchanters make us fools still, to the shame of us all, but specially of papists, who conjure everything and thereby bring to pass nothing. They say to their candles: I conjure you to endure for ever, and yet they last not a paternoster while the longer. They conjure water to be wholesome both for body and soul: but the body (we see) is never the better for it, nor the soul any whit reformed by it. And therefore I marvel that when they see their own conjurations confuted and brought to nought, or at the least void of effect, that they (of all other) will yet give such credit, countenance and authority to the vain cozenages of witches and conjurers; as though their charms and conjurations could produce more apparent, certain and better effects than their own.

But my request unto all you that read my book shall be no more but that it would please you to confer my words with your own sense and experience, and also with the word of God. If you find yourselves resolved and satisfied, or rather reformed and qualified in any one point or opinion, that heretofore you held contrary to truth, in a matter hitherto undecided and never yet looked into, I pray you take that for advantage, and suspending your judgement, stay the sentence of condemnation against me and consider of the rest at your further leisure. If this may not suffice to persuade you, it cannot prevail to annoy you; and then that which is written without offence may be overpassed without any grief.

. . . Christ himself in his gospel never mentioned the name of a witch. And that neither he nor Moses ever spake any one word of the witch's bargain with the devil, their hagging, their riding in the air, their transferring of corn or grass from one field to another, their hurting of children or cattle with words or charms, their bewitching of butter, cheese, ale, etc.; nor yet their transubstantiation; insomuch as the writers hereupon are not ashamed to say that it is not absurd to affirm that there were no witches in Job's time. The reason is that if there had been such witches then in being, Job would have said he had been bewitched. But indeed, men took no heed in those days to this doctrine of devils; to wit, to these fables of witchcraft, which Peter saith shall be much regarded and hearkened unto in the later days [1 Pet. 4.1].

Howbeit, how ancient soever this barbarous conceit of witches' omnipotence is, truth must not be measured by time: for every old opinion is not sound. Verity is not impaired, how long soever it be suppressed: but is to be searched out in how dark a corner soever it lie hidden. . . . Finally, time bewrayeth old errors, and discovereth new matters of truth . . .

God that knoweth my heart is witness and you that read my book shall see that my drift and purpose in this enterprise tendeth only to these respects. First that the glory and power of God be not so abridged and abased as to be thrust into the hand or lip of a lewd old woman: whereby the work of the creator should be attributed to the power of a creature. Secondly that the religion of the gospel may be seen to stand without such popish trumpery. Thirdly, that lawful favour and Christian compassion be rather used towards these poor souls than rigour and extremity. Because they, which are commonly accused of witchcraft are the least sufficient of all other persons to speak for themselves, as having the most base and simple education of all others: the extremity of their age giving them leave to dote, their poverty to beg, their wrongs to chide and threaten (as being void of any other way of revenge), their humour melancholical to be full of imaginations, from whence chiefly proceedeth the vanity of their confessions; as that they can transform themselves and others into apes, owls, asses, dogs, cats etc.: that they can fly in the air, kill children with charms, hinder the coming of butter etc.

And for so much as the mighty help themselves together and the poor widows' cry, though it reach to heaven, is scarce heard here upon earth: I thought good (according to my poor ability) to make intercession, that some part of common rigour and some points of hasty judgement may be advised upon. For the world is now at that stay (as Brennius in a most godly sermon in these words affirmeth), that even as when the heathen persecuted the Christians, if any were accused to believe in Christ, the common people cried *ad leonum* [to the lions]: so now if any woman, be she never so honest, be accused of witchcraft, they cry, *ad ignum* [to the fire] . . .

Cardanus from the mouth of his own father reporteth that one Barnard, a poor servant, being in wit very simple and rude, but in his service very necessary and diligent (and in that respect dearly beloved of his master) professing the art

360

of witchcraft, could in no wise be dissuaded from that profession, persuading himself that he knew all things and could bring any matter to pass, because certain country people resorted to him for help and counsel, as supposing by his own talk that he could do somewhat. At length he was condemned to be burned: which torment he seemed more willing to suffer, than to lose his estimation in that behalf. But his master having compassion upon him and being himself in his prince's favour, perceiving his conceit to proceed of melancholy, obtained respite of execution for twenty days. In which time (saith he) his master bountifully fed him with good fat meat and with four eggs at a meal, as also with sweet wine: which diet was best for so gross and weak a body. And being recovered so in strength that the humour was suppressed, he was easily won from his absurd and dangerous opinions, and from all his fond imaginations; and confessing his error and folly, from the which before no man could remove him by any persuasion, having his pardon, he lived long a good member of the Church; whom otherwise the cruelty of judgement should have cast away and destroyed.

... Neither hath God given remedies to sickness and griefs by words or charms: but by herbs and medicines which he himself hath created upon earth and given men knowledge of the same; that he might be glorified for that therewith he doth vouchsafe that the maladies of men and cattle should be cured etc. And if there be no affliction nor calamity, but is brought to pass by him, then let us defy the devil, renounce all his works, and not so much as once think or dream upon this supernatural power of witches: neither let us prosecute them with such despight, whom our fancy condemneth, and our reason acquiteth: our evidence against them consisting in impossibilities, our proofs in unwritten verities, and our whole proceedings in doubts and difficulties.

Now because I mislike the extreme cruelty used against some of these silly souls (whom a simple advocate having audience and justice might deliver out of the hands of the inquisitors themselves), it will be said that I deny any punishment at all to be due to any witch whatsoever. Nay, because I bewray the folly and impiety of them which attribute unto witches the power of God, these witchmongers will report that I deny there are any witches at all: and yet behold (say they) how often is this word, witch, mentioned in the Scriptures? Even as if an idolater should say in the behalf of images and idols, to them which deny their power and godhead, and inveigh against the reverence done unto them: how dare you deny the power of images, seeing their names are so often repeated in the Scriptures? But truly, I deny not that there are witches or images: but I detest the idolatrous opinions conceived of them, referring that to God's work and ordinance, which they impute to the power and malice of witches; and attributing that honour to God, which they ascribe to idols. But as for those that in very deed are either witches or conjurers, let them hardly suffer such punishment as to their faults is agreeable, and as by the grave judgement of law is provided.

* * *

361

What secrets do lie hidden and what is taught in natural magic, how God's glory is magnified therein, and that is nothing but the work of nature

In this art of natural magic God Almighty hath given many secret mysteries: as wherein a man may learn the properties, qualities and knowledge of all nature. For it teacheth to accomplish matters in such sort and opportunity as the common people thinketh the same to be miraculous, and to be compassed none other way but only by witchcraft. And yet in truth, natural magic is nothing else but the work of nature. For in tillage, as nature produceth corn and herbs, so art being nature's minister, prepareth it. Wherein times and seasons are greatly to be respected . . .

But as many necessary and sober things are herein taught: so doth it partly (I say) consist in such experiments and conclusions as are but toys, but nevertheless lie hid in nature, and being unknown do seem miraculous, specially when they are intermeddled and corrupted with cunning illusion or legerdemain, from whence is derived the estimation of witchcraft. But being learned and known, they are condemned and appear ridiculous: for that only is wonderful to the beholder whereof he can conceive no cause nor reason. . . . And therefore a man shall take great pains herein and bestow great cost to learn that which is of no value and a mere juggling knack. Whereupon it is said that a man may not learn philosophy to be rich, but must get riches to learn philosophy: for to sluggards, niggards and dizzards the secrets of nature are never opened. And doubtless a man may gather out of this art that which being published shall set forth the glory of God, and be many ways beneficial to the commonwealth: the first is done by the manifestation of his works, the second by skilfully applying them to our use and service.

What strange things are brought to pass by natural magic

The daily use and practice of medicine taketh away all admiration of the wonderful effects of the same. Many other things of less weight, being more secret and rare, seem more miraculous. . . . Wherein it may not be denied but nature showeth herself a proper workwoman. But it seemeth impossible that a little fish, being but half a foot long, called remora or remiligio, or of some, echeneis, stayeth a mighty ship with all her lead and tacking, and being also under sail. And yet it is affirmed by some many and so grave authors, that I dare not deny it: specially because I see as strange effects of nature otherwise, as the property of the loadstone, which is so beneficial to the mariner and of rhubarb, which only meddleth with choler and purgeth neither phlegm nor melancholy, and is as beneficial to the physician as the other to the mariner.

6.6 GALEN AND CULPEPER, *ART OF PHYSIC*

Galen's humoural theory of disease constructed physical identity and medical treatment: here Culpeper expounds Galen, demontrating a continued allegiance to the physiology of humours throughout the early modern period (see also Burton and Crooke). Text from: translated and edited by Nicholas Culpeper 1652, pp. 5–8; 52–7.

Of healthful bodies

A body is said to be healthful when it is in good natural temper, when the seven natural things, viz. spirits, elements, complexions, humours, members, virtues, operations, keep a good decorum, then is a body simply said to be in health. . . . Thus Galen.

Culpeper's comment

I shall here explain a little Galen's meaning in those words of his: *seven natural things*.

1. Spirit: taken in a physical sense is an airy substance very subtle and quick, dispersed throughout the body from the brain, heart and liver by the nerves, arteries and veins, by which the powers of the body are stirred up to perform their office and operation.

2. An element is a body pure, simple, unmixed from which all natural things have their original, they are held to be in number four: fire, air, water, earth; their operations are active, as heat and cold; passive as dryness and moisture.

3. Complexions are the operations of these elements upon man's body, as when the fire prevails the body is choleric; when the air he is sanguine; when the water he is phlegmatic; when the earth, he is melancholy.

4. Humours are: 1. Choler, whose receptacle is the gall; 2. blood, whose seat is the liver; 3. phlegm, placed in the lungs; 4. melancholy, which keeps his court in the spleen. Thus you see how elements, complexions and humours are subservient the one to other, even as the spirits, soul and body are . . . in the microcosm.

5. Members or limbs are simple or compound, principal or subservient. First, simple members are: 1. bones; 2. cartilages; 3. ligaments; 4. veins; 5. arteries; 6. nerves; 7. tendons; 8. panides; 9. fat; 10. flesh; 11. skin. Secondly, compound members are: 1. head; 2. heart; 3. liver; 4. lungs; 5. legs; 6. arms; 7. hands. Thirdly, principal members are: 1. brain; 2. heart; 3. liver; 4. testicles. Fourthly, members subservient are: 1. nerves to carry the animal spirits; 2. arteries to carry the vital spirit; 3. veins to carry the natural spirit; 4. spermatic vessels to carry the procreative spirit.

6. Virtues are that whereby these act the body, and these are vital, natural and animal. I forbear writing of them, there being a treatise of them . . .

7. Operations of these upon the body of man are first the animal virtue causeth: 1. imagination, apprehension, fancy, opinion, consent, etc. in the two former ventricles of the brain. 2. Judgement, esteem, reason, reformation, disposing,

discerning, in the middle ventricle of the brain. 3. Calling to mind what is to come, remembrance of what is past in the hinder ventricle of the brain. Secondly the vital virtue moveth: 1. joy, hope, mirth, singing, by dilating the heart; 2. sadness, sorrow, fear, sighing etc., by compressing the heart.

Thirdly the natural virtue: 1. altereth food into chile, chile into blood and humours; blood into flesh. 2. Joineth, formeth, engendereth, increaseth and nourisheth the body of man.

* * *

Sanguine complexion

Description

A man or woman in whose body heat and moisture abounds is said to be sanguine of complexion: such are usually of a middle stature, strong composed bodies, fleshy but not fat, great veins, smooth skins, hot and moist in feeling, their body is hairy, if they be men they have soon beards, if they be women it were ridiculous to expect it; there is a redness intermingles with white in their cheeks, their hair is usually of a blackish brown, yet sometimes flaxen, their appetite is good, their digestion quick, their urine yellowish and thick, the excrements of their bowels, reddish and firm, their pulse great and full, they dream usually of red things and merry conceits.

Conditions

As for their conditions, they are merry cheerful creatures, bountiful, pitiful, merciful, courteous, bold, trusty, given much to the games of Venus, as though they had been an apprentice seven years to the trade; a little thing will make them weep, but so soon as 'tis over, no further grief sticks to their hearts.

Diet and exercise fitting

They need not be very scrupulous in the quality of their diet, provided they exceed not in quantity because the digestive virtue is so strong.

Excess in small beer engendereth clammy and sweet phlegm in such complexions, which by stopping the pores of the body engenders quotidian agues, the cholic and stone, and pains in the back.

Inordinate drinking of strong beer, ale, and wine breeds hot rheums, scabs and itch, St. Anthony's fire, quinsies, pleurisies, inflammations, fevers, and red pimples.

Violent exercise is to be avoided because it inflames the blood and breeds one-day fevers.

Choleric complexion

Description

We call that man choleric in whose body heat and dryness abounds or is predominant, such persons are usually short of stature, and not fat, it may be because the heat and dryness of their bodies consumes radical moisture, their skin rough and hot in feeling, and their bodies very hairy, the hair of their heads is yellowish, red or flaxen for the most part, and curls much, the colour of their face is tawny or sunburnt, they have some beards, they have little hollow hazel eyes, their concoction is very strong insomuch that they are able to digest more than they appetite [*sic*], their pulse is swift and strong, their urine yellow and thin, they are usually costive, they dream of fighting, quarrelling, fire and burning.

Conditions

As for conditions, they are naturally quick witted, bold, no way shame-faced, furious, hasty, quarrelsome, fraudulent, eloquent, courageous, stout-hearted creatures, not given to sleep much, but much given to jesting, mocking and lying.

Diet and exercise etc.

A choleric man is oftener hurt by much fasting and much drinking than by much eating, for much fasting weakens nature in such people, and fills the body full of choleric humours and breedeth adust[3] humours; let such eat meats hard of digestion as beef, pork, etc., and leave dainties for weaker stomachs.

Moderate drinking of small beer doth him good, for it cools the fiery heat of his nature, moisteneth the body which is dried by the heat of his complexion and relieves radical moisture; but let a man of such a complexion fly from wine and strong beer as fast as he would from a dragon, for they inflame the liver, and breed burning and hectic fevers, choler and hot dropsies, and bring a man to his grave in the prime of his age.

Much exercise is likewise bad for choleric people, and breeds inflammation and adustion of blood, the yellow jaundice, consumptions, fevers, costiveness and agues.

Melancholy complexion

Description

A melancholy person is one [in] whose body cold and dryness is predominate; and not such a one as is sad sometimes as the vulgar dream; they are usually slender and not very tall, of swarthy duskish colour, rough skin, cold and hard in feeling, they have very little hair on their bodies, and are long without beards, and sometimes they are beardless in age, the hair of their heads is dusky brown usually and sometimes dusky flaxen, their appetite is far better than their concoction usually, by reason appetite is caused of a sour vapour sent up by the spleen, which is the seat of melancholy, to the stomach; their urine is pale, their dung of a clayish colour and broken, their pulse slow, they dream of frightful things black, darkness, and terrible businesses.

Conditions

They are naturally covetous, self-lovers, cowards, afraid of their own shadows, fearful, careful, solitary, lumpish, unsociable, delight in being alone, stubborn, ambitious, envious, of a deep cogitation, obstinate in opinion, mistrustful, suspicious, spiteful, squeamish, and yet slovenly, they retain anger long and aim at no small things.

Diet and exercise fitting

By all means let melancholy men avoid excess both in eating and drinking, let them avoid all means hard of digestion, especially such as are students or lead a sedentary life; let them use meats that are light of digestion, and drink often at meat. Excess either in meat or strong liquor causeth crudities and rawness at the stomach, idle and strange imaginations and fancies, a stinking breath, headache, toothache, forgetfulness, shortness of breath, consumptions, phtisics,[4] third day agues, the colic and iliac passions and dropsies.

Much exercise is very profitable for such, not only because it helpeth digestion, but also because it distributeth the vital spirits throughout the body and consumeth those superfluous vapours by insensible transpiration, which causeth those idle fancies and imaginations in men.

Phlegmatic complexion

Description

Such people in whom coldness with moisture abounds are called phlegmatic, yet are usually not very tall, but very fat: some you shall find almost as thick as they are long, their veins and arteries are small, their bodies without hair, and they have but little beards; their hair is usually flaxen or light brown, their face white and pale, their skin smooth, cold and moist in touching; both appetite and digestion is very weak in them, their pulse little and low, their urine pale and thick, but their excrements of their bowels usually thin, they dream of great rains, water and drowning.

Conditions

As for conditions, they are very dull, heavy and slothful, like the scholar that was a great while learning a lesson but when once he had it, he had quickly forgotten it. They are drowsy, sleepy, cowardly, forgetful creatures, as swift in motion as a snail, they travail (and that's but seldom) as though they intend to go fifteen miles in fourteen days, yet are they shamefaced and sober.

Diet and exercise fitting

People of this complexion of all other ought to use a very slender diet, for fasting cleanseth the body of those gross and uncocted humours which phlegmatic people are usually as full of as an egg is of meat. What they do eat, let it be of light digestion, a cup of strong beer, and now and then a cup of wine is no ways unwholesome for them of this complexion that are minded to keep their bodies in health.

Much meat and drink fills their bodies full of indigestion, wind and stitches, quotidian agues and dropsies, falling-sickness and gouts, rheums and catthars.

Much exercise is very healthful for them unless they love their laziness better than their health, for by that means gross humours are made thin and expelled by sweat, the memory is quickened and the skin clarified.

6.7 ROGER BACON, *THE MIRROR OF ALCHEMY*

Roger Bacon's alchemical work, originally written in the fourteenth century, remained current well into the seventeeth century amongst followers of alchemy. It provided a way of classifying metals in a pre-atomic age. Text from: first edition translated into English, 1597, pp. 2–5; 54–7; 58–9; 64–5.

Of the natural principles and procreation of minerals

. . . I will perfectly declare the natural principles and procreation of minerals: where first it is to be noted that the natural principles in the mines are *argent-vive* and *sulphur*. All metals and minerals, whereof there be sundry and divers kinds, are begotten of these two. But I must tell you that nature always intendeth and striveth to the perfection of gold: but many accidents, coming between, change the metals, as it is evidently to be seen in divers of the philosophers' books. For according to the purity and impurity of the two aforesaid principles, argent-vive and sulphur, pure and impure metals are engendered: to wit, gold, silver, steel, lead, copper and iron: of whose nature, that is to say, purity and impurity, or unclean superfluity and defect, give ear to that which followeth.

Of the nature of gold

Gold is a perfect body, engendered of: argent-vive, pure, fixed, clear, red; and of sulphur clean, fixed, red, not burning: and it wanteth nothing.

367

Of the nature of silver

Silver is a body clean, pure and almost perfect, begotten of argent-vive, pure, almost fixed, clear and white; and of such a like sulphur. It wanteth nothing save a little fixation, colour and weight.

Of the nature of steel

Steel is a body clean, imperfect, engendered of argent-vive pure, fixed and not fixed clear, white outwardly, but red inwardly; and of the like sulphur. It wanteth only decoction or digestion.

Of the nature of lead

Lead is an unclean and imperfect body, engendered of argent-vive impure, not fixed, earthy, drossy, somewhat white outwardly and red inwardly; and of such a sulphur in part burning. It wanteth purity, fixation, colour and firing.

Of the nature of copper

Copper is an unclean and imperfect body, engendered of argent-vive, impure, not fixed, earthy, burning, red not clear; and of the like sulphur. It wanteth purity, fixation and weight: and hath too much of an impure colour and earthiness not burning.

Of the nature of iron

Iron is an unclean and imperfect body, engendered of argent-vive impure, too much fixed, earthy, burning, white and red not clear; and of the like sulphur. It wanteth fusion, purity and weight. It hath too much fixed unclean sulphur and burning earthiness. That which hath been spoken every alchemist must diligently observe.

* * *

An excellent discourse of the admirable force and efficacy of art and nature

Some there are that ask whether of these twain be of the greatest force and efficacy: nature or art. Wherto I make answer and say that although nature be mighty and marvellous, yet art using nature for an instrument, is more powerful than natural virtue, as it is to be seen in many things. But whatsoever is done without the operation of nature or art is either no human work, or if it be, it is fraudulently and colourably performed: for there are some that by a nimble motion and show of members, or through the diversity of voices and subtility of instruments, or in the dark and by consent, do propose unto men diverse things to be wondered at that have indeed no truth at all. The world is everywhere full of such fellows. For jugglers cog[5] many things through the swiftness of their hands, and others with variety of voices, by certain devices that they have in their bellies, throats or mouths, will frame men's voices far off or near, as it pleaseth them, as if a man spake at the same instant: yea they will counterfeit the sounds of brute beasts. But the causes hidden in the grass, or buried in the sides of the earth prove it to be done by a human force and not by a spirit, as they would make men believe. In like manner, whereas they affirm things without life to move very swiftly in the twilight of the evening or morning, it is altogether false and untrue. As for consent, it can feign anything that men desire, according as they are disposed together. In all these, neither physical reason nor art, nor natural power, hath any place: and for this cause it is most abominable, sith it condemneth the laws of philosophy and contrary to all reason, invocateth wicked spirits that by their help they may have their desire . . .

Now concerning charms, characters and such like trumperies that are used in these days. I adjudge them to be all false and doubtful; for some are without all show of reason, whereof the philosophers have made mention in the works of nature and art, to the end they might conceal secrets from the unworthy, as if it were altogether unknown that the load-stone could attract iron, and one desirous to work this feat before the people should make characters and pronounce charms that by this means he might bring it to pass: this work of his should be erroneous and deceitful. After this manner there are many things hidden in the philosophers' books, wherein a wise man must be aware, that neglecting the charms and characters, he only attend and make trial of the work of nature and art. And then he shall perceive things living and without life to concur and agree in nature, for the conformity and likeness of their natures, and not by virtue of the charm or character. Whereas the simple people suppose many things to be wrought by magic, which are nothing else but the secrets of art and nature. Yea the magicians themselves do vainly repose such confidence in their charms and characters as though they should receive power from them, that in the meantime they forsake the work of art and nature. And by this means both these kind of men are deprived of the benefit of wisdom. . . . It must not be forgotten that the skilful physician and any other of what profession so ever, may to good purpose use charms and characters, though they be feigned after the opinion of Constantine's the physician: not as charms and characters could work anything, but that the medicine might be the more willingly and readily received and that the mind of the patient might be excited, become more confident, and be filled with joy: for the soul thus affected is able to renew many things in his own body, insomuch that it may recover his former health thorough the joy and hope it hath conceived. If therefore the physician for the magnifying of his work, do administer any such thing, that his patient may not despair of his health, it is not to be abhorred.

* * *

Now will I begin to recount unto you strange things performed by art and nature, and afterwards I will show you the causes and manners of things, wherein shall be nothing magical: so that you shall confess all magic powers to be inferior to these, and unworthy to be compared with them. And first of all by the figuration of art itself, there may be made instruments of navigation without men to row in them; as huge ships to brook the sea, only with one man to steer them, which shall sail far more swiftly than if they were full of men; and chariots that shall move with an unspeakable force, without any living creature to steer them, such as the crooked chariots are supposed to have been, wherein in old time they used to fight; yea instruments to fly withal, so that one sitting in the middle of the instrument, and turning about an engine, by which the wings being artificially composed, may beat the air after the manner of a flying bird. Besides, there may be made a small instrument in quantity to lift up and let down things of great weight, than which there is nothing more commodious to weigh with. For by an instrument of three fingers high and three fingers broad and less quantity, may a man rid himself and his companions from all danger of imprisonment, and lift them up and let them down. Yea, such an instrument may easily be made where a man may violently draw unto him a thousand men, will they nill they, and any other thing.

Moreover instruments may be made wherewith men may walk in the bottom of the sea or rivers without bodily danger, which Alexander the Great used, to the end he might behold the secrets of the seas, as the ethic philosopher reporteth; and these have been made not only in times past, but even in our days. And it is certain that there is an instrument to fly with, which I never saw, nor know any man that hath seen it, but I full well know by name the learned man that invented the same. In a word, a man may make an infinite sort of such things: as bridges over rivers without posts or pillars, and instruments and engines never heard of before.

But physical figurations are far more strange: for in such manner may we frame perspects and looking-glasses, that one thing shall appear to be many, as one man shall seem a whole army; and divers suns and moons, yea as many as we please, shall appear at one time: for in such wise sometimes are the vapours figured that two or three suns and two moons appear together in the air, as Pliny witnesseth in the second book of his *Natural History*.

6.8 JOHN GERARD, *HERBAL*

Gerard's *Herbal* was a particularly popular and comprehensive one, first published in 1597. It provides a fine, accurate, line-drawn illustration for each entry, a classification system, based on continental models, and an account of the medicinal and household uses of all herbs. Text from: first edition, 1597, preface, fos A7ᵛ–A8ʳ; pp. 299–301; 316–18.

To the courteous and well-willing reader

... In the expert knowledge of herbs, what pleasures still renewed with variety? What small expense? What security? And yet what an apt and ordinary means to conduct man to that most desired benefit of health? Which as I devoutly wish unto my native country, and to the careful nursing mother of the same, so having bent my labours to the benefiting of such as are studiously practised in the conversation thereof, I thought it a chief point of my duty thus out of my poor store, to offer up these my far-fetched experiments, together with mine own country's unknown treasure, combined in this compendious herbal (not unprofitable, though unpolished) unto your wise constructions and courteous considerations. ... I list not seek the common colours of antiquity, when notwithstanding the world can brag of no more ancient monument than paradise and the garden of Eden: and the fruits of the earth may contend for seniority, seeing their mother was the first creature that conceived and they themselves the first fruit she brought forth. Talk of perfect happiness or pleasure and what place was so fit for that as the garden place where Adam was set to be the herbalist? Whither did the poets hunt for their sincere delights but into the garden of Alcinous, of Adonis, and the orchards of Hesperides? Where did they dream that heaven should be but in the pleasant garden of Elysium? Wither do all men walk for their honest recreation but thither where the earth hath most beneficially painted her face with flourishing colours? And what season of the year more longed for than the spring, whose gentle breath enticeth forth the kindly sweets and makes them yield their fragrant smells? Who would therefore look dangerously up at planets, that might safely look down at plants?. ... The science is nobly supported by wise and kingly favourites. The subject thereof so necessary and delectable that nothing can be confected, either delicate for the taste, dainty for smell, pleasant for sight, wholesome for body, conservative or restorative for health, but it borroweth the relish of an herb, the savour of a flower, the colour of a leaf, the juice of a plant or the decoction of a root: and such is the treasure that this my treatise is furnished withal wherein though mine art be not able to countervail nature in her lively portraitures, yet have I counterfeited likeness for life, shapes and shadows for substance, being ready with the bad painter to explain the imperfections of my pencil with my pen, choosing rather to score upon my pictures such rude marks as may describe my meaning, than to let the beholder to guess at random and miss. I have here therefore set down not only the names of sundry plants, but also their natures, their proportions and properties, their affects and effects, their increase and decrease, their flourishing and fading, their distinct varieties and various qualities, as well, of those which our own country yieldeth, as of others which I have fetched further, or drawn out by perusing divers Herbals set forth in other languages.

* * *

Containing the description, place, time, names, nature and virtues of all sorts of herb for meat, medicine or sweet smelling use

Of corn rose or wild poppy

The description

The stalks of wild poppy be black, tender and brittle, somewhat hairy. The leaves are cut roundabout with deep gashes like those of succory or of rocket; the flowers grow forth at the tops of the stalks, being of a beautiful and gallant red colour with blackish threads compassing about the middle part of the head: which being fully grown, is lesser than that of garden poppy. The seed is small and black.

There is also a lesser kind hereof, with smaller leaves, not so deeply snipped about the edges, but a little nicked or toothed; in other points agreeing with the former, saving that the flowers of this are somewhat doubled.

The place

They grow in arable grounds among wheat, spelt, rye, barley, oats and other grains, and in the borders of fields.

The time

The fields are garnished and overspread with these wild poppies in June and August.

The names

Wild poppy is called . . . in Latin *papauer erraticum*: Gaza termeth it *papauer fluidum*; in shops *papauer rubrum*. Of l'Obelius *papauer rhaeus*, because the flower thereof soon falleth away, which name *rhaeus* may for the same cause be common, not only to these but also to the others, of it be so called of the speedy falling of the flowers: but if it be surnamed *rhaeus* of the falling away of the seed (as it appeareth) then shall it be proper to all the rest whose flowers do not only quickly fall away, but the seed also: in French, *cocquelicot, consanons, panot suavage* . . .

The nature

The faculty of the wild poppy is like to that of the other poppies: that is to say cold and causing sleep.

The virtues

Most men being led rather by false experiments than reason, commend the flowers against the pleurisy, giving to drink as soon as the pain cometh either the distilled water or syrup mace by often infusing the leaves. And yet many times it happeneth that the pain ceaseth by that means, though hardly sometimes, by reason that the spittle cometh up hardly and with more difficulty, especially in those that are weak and have not a strong constitution of body. Baptista Sadus might be counted the author of this error: who hath written that most men have given the flowers of this poppy against the pain of the sides, and that it is good against the spitting of blood.

It is manifest that this wild poppy is that of which the composition *Diacodium* is to be made: as Galen hath at large entreated in his seventh book of medicines according to the place affected.

* * *

Of rhubarb

The description

Flowering rhubarb   Touching the rhubarb used in shops of the form or bigness of the plant itself, or of the leaves and flowers, we find nothing set down in the old writers; Dioscorides hath expressed a certain likeness, substance and colour of the roots only, and yet but of that rhubarb which groweth in those places that are beyond the strait of Constantinople called the black sea, and Pontus Euxinus, or also Maeotis, called the white sea.

The greatness of the roots of rhubarb (and as it is very like, of the whole plant itself also) doth not a little vary according to the difference of the regions, ground, and weather, which (as we must ever now and then repair) be oftentimes great cases of alteration and differences in plants.

But seeing there is extant a picture of the green rhubarb with his flowers, stalk, and roots, it shall not be amiss to set forth his description likewise.

Rhubarb hath a green thick stalk a foot high, garnished with many leaves, of two spans long, sometimes longer or shorter according to their age; narrow towards the stem, broad and round at the top like a pear, bowing backwards towards the ground, covered over with a certain down or woolliness when they be young and green, but when they be old of a pale yellowish colour: out of the middle of the leaves there groweth up a slender stalk bearing flowers, consisting of five little leaves confusedly placed upon the small branches without order, which turn from white to yellow, in shape like the garden violet, but greater and of a strong unpleasant savour. The root groweth two or three hands deep in the ground, wrapped in a bark of a dark brown colour, sometimes as big as the calf of a man's leg, sometimes lesser; from the main root shoot forth many threads and small shoots, which spread far abroad in the earth, whereby it increaseth . . .

The place

It is brought out of the country of Sina (commonly called China) which is towards the east in the upper part of India, and that India which is without the river Ganges: and not all *ex scenitarum provincia* (as many do unadvisedly think), which is in Arabia, the happy, and far from China: it groweth on the sides of the river Rha as Amianus Marcellus saith, which river springeth out of the Hyperborei mountains in the high northern parts and running through Muscovy, it falleth into the Caspian or Hircan sea, as also upon the banks of the river Rha, now called Volga.

The choice

The best rhubarb is that which is brought from China fresh and new, of a light purplish red with certain veins and branches of an uncertain variety of colour, commonly whitish: but when it is old the colour becometh ill favoured by turning yellowish or pale, but more, if it be worm eaten: being chewed in the mouth it is somewhat gluey and clammy and of a saffron colour, which being rubbed upon paper or some white thing, showeth the colour more plainly: the substance thereof is neither hard or closely compacted, nor yet heavy: but something light and as it were in a middle between hard and loose and something spongy: it hath also a sweet and pleasant smell. The second in goodness is that which cometh from Barbary. The last and worst from Bosphorus and Pontus.

The names

It is commonly called in Latin, *rha barbarum* . . .

The temperature

Rhubarb is of a mixed substance, temperature and faculty: some of the parts thereof are earthy, binding and drying; others thin, airous, hot and purging.

The virtues

Rhubarb is commended of Dioscorides against windiness, weakness of the stomach and all griefs thereof, convulsions, diseases of the spleen, liver and kidneys, groin and inward grumblings of the gut, infirmities of the bladder and chest, swelling above the heart, diseases of the matrix, pain in the huckle bones, spitting of blood, shortness of breath, yaxing or the hicks, the bloody flux, the last proceeding of raw humour, firs in ague, and against the bitings of various beasts.

Moreover, he saith that it taketh away black and blue spots and [?] tetors or ring worm if it be mixed with vinegar and the place anointed therewith.

Galen affirmeth it to be good for burstings, cramps and convulsions and for those that are very short-winded and that spit blood.

But touching the purging faculty, neither Dioscorides nor Galen hath written anything because it was not used in those days to purge with. Galen held opinion that the thin aireous parts do make the binding quality of more force; not because it doth resist the cold and earthy substance, but by reason that it carrieth the same, and maketh it deeply to pierce and thereby to work the greater effect, the dry and thin essence containing in itself a purging force and quality to open obstructions, but helped and made more facile by the subtile and aerous parts . . .

The purgation which is made of rhubarb is profitable and fit for all such as are troubled with choler and for those that be sick of sharp and tertian fevers, for them that have the yellow [?] thunders and bad livers.

It is a good medicine against the pleurisy, inflammation of the lungs the squinancy or squincy, madness, frenzy, inflammation of the kidneys, bladder and all the inward parts and especially against Saint Anthony's fire, as well outwardly as inwardly taken.

Rhubarb is undoubtedly an especial good medicine for the liver and infirmities of the gall, for besides that it purgeth forth choleric and naughty humours, it removeth stoppings out of the conduits.

It also mightily strengtheneth the entrails themselves, insomuch as rhubarb is justly termed of divers, the life of the liver: for Galen in his first book of the method or manner of curing, affirmeth that such kind of medicines are most fit and profitable for the liver as have joined with a purging and opening quality, an astringent or binding power. The quantity that is to be given is from one dram to two: and in the infusion, from one and a half to three.

It is given or steeped, and that in hot diseases, with the infusion or distilled water of Cycote, endive or some other of like nature and likewise in whey: and if there be no heat, it may be given in wine.

It is also oftentimes given being dried at the fire, but so that the least or no parts thereof at all be burned; and being so used it is a remedy for the bloody fluxes and all kinds of [?] leaks: for it both purgeth away naughty and corrupt humours, and likewise withal stoppeth the belly.

The same being dried after the same manner doth also stay the overmuch flowing of the monthly sickness, and stoppeth blood in any part of the body, especially that which cometh through the bladder: but it should be given in a little quantity, and mixed with some other binding thing.

Mesues saith that Rhubarb is an harmless medicine, and good at all times and for all ages and likewise for children and women with child.

6.9 WILLIAM GILBERT, *OF MAGNETISM*

Gilbert, physician to Elizabeth I, published *De Magnete* in 1600, aimed at a learned European audience. In England, Bacon viewed it as an unimportant work, unnecessarily glorifying one small practical discovery. Text from: trans. E. Fleury Mottelay, 1893, pp. 12ff.

The loadstone possesses parts different in their natural powers, and has poles conspicuous for their properties

The many qualities exhibited by the loadstone itself, qualities hitherto recognised yet not well investigated, are to be pointed out in the first place, to the end the student may understand the powers of the loadstone and of iron, and not be confused through want of knowledge at the threshold of the arguments and demonstrations. In the heavens, astronomers give to each moving sphere two poles; thus do we find two natural poles of excelling importance even in our terrestrial globe, constant points related to the movement of its daily revolution, to wit, one pole pointing to Arctos (Ursa) and the north; the other looking toward the opposite part of the heavens. In like manner the loadstone has from nature its two poles, a northern and a southern; fixed, definite points in the stone, which are the primary termini of the movements and effects, and the limits and regulators of the several actions and properties. It is to be understood, however, that not from a mathematical point does the force of the stone emanate, but from the parts themselves; and all these parts in the whole, while they belong to the whole, the nearer they are to the poles of the stone, the stronger virtues do they acquire and pour out on other bodies. These poles look toward the poles of the earth, and move toward them and are subject to them. The magnetic poles may be found in every loadstone, whether strong, and powerful (male, as the term was in antiquity) or faint, weak and female; whether its shape is due to design or to chance, and whether it be long, or flat, or four-square, or three-cornered, or polished; whether it be rough, broken off, or unpolished: the loadstone ever has and ever shows its poles.

* * *

One loadstone appears to attract another in the natural position; but in the opposite position repels it and brings it to rights

First we have to describe in popular language the potent and familiar properties of the stone; afterward, very many subtle properties, as yet recondite and unknown, being involved in obscurities, are to be unfolded; and the causes of all these (nature's secrets being unlocked) are in their place to be demonstrated in fitting words and with the aid of apparatus. The fact is trite and familiar, that the loadstone attracts iron; in the same way, too, one loadstone attracts another. Take the stone on which you have designated the poles, N and S, and put in its vessel so that it may float; let the poles lie just in the plane of the horizon, or at least in a plane not very oblique to it; take in your hand another stone the poles of which are also known, and hold it so that its south pole shall lie toward the north pole of the floating stone, and near it alongside; the floating loadstone will straightway follow the other (provided it be within the range and dominion of its powers) nor does it cease to move nor does it quit the other till it clings to it, unless by moving your hand away you manage skilfully to prevent the conjunction.

6.10 FRANCIS BACON, *THE ADVANCEMENT OF LEARNING*

Bacon's *Advancement of Learning* was dedicated to King James in the hope of encouraging royal investment in schemes for scientific change and an educational programme to initiate it. Here Bacon articulates the distinction between theological and natural knowledge which was to inspire natural scientists of the subsequent two centuries to investigate nature without fear of divine or theological disapproval. Text from: first edition, 1605, pp. 1–4.

In the entrance to the former of these, to clear the way, and as it were to make silence, to have true testimonies concerning the dignity of learning to be better heard without the interruption of tacit objections; I think good to deliver it from the discredits and disgraces which it hath received, all from ignorance, but ignorance severally disguised: appearing sometimes in the zeal and jealousy of divines; sometimes in the severity and arrogancy of politiques; and sometimes in the errors and imperfections of learned men themselves.

I hear the former say that knowledge is of those things which are to be accepted of with great limitation and caution; that the aspiring to overmuch knowledge was the original temptation and sin whereupon ensued the fall of man; that knowledge hath in it somewhat of the serpent, and therefore where it entereth into a man it makes him swell: *scientia inflat*; that Solomon gives a censure, *there is no end of making books, and that much reading is weariness of the flesh;* and again in another place, *that in spacious knowledge there is much contristation, and that he that increaseth knowledge, increaseth anxiety* [Eccles. 12.12; 1.18]; that Saint Paul gives a caveat, *that we be not spoiled through vain philosophy* [Coloss. 2.8]; that experience demonstrates how learned men have been arch-heretics, how learned times have been inclined to atheism, and how the contemplation of second causes doth derogate from our dependence upon God, who is the first cause.

To discover then the ignorance and error of this opinion and the misunderstanding in the grounds thereof, it may well appear these men do not observe or consider that it was not the pure knowledge of nature and universality, a knowledge by the light whereof man did give names unto other creatures in paradise, as they were brought before him, according unto their proprieties, which gave occasion to the fall; but it was the proud knowledge of good and evil, with an intent in man to give law unto himself, and to depend no more upon God's commandments, which was the form of the temptation. Neither is it any quantity of knowledge, how great soever, that can make the mind of man to swell; for nothing can fill, much less extend the soul of man, but God and the contemplation of God; and therefore Solomon, speaking of the two principal senses of inquisition, the eye and the ear, affirmeth *that the eye is never satisfied with seeing, nor the ear with hearing* [Eccles. 1.8]; and if there be no fullness, then is the continent greater than the content; so of knowledge itself, and the mind of man, whereto the senses are but reporters, he defineth likewise in these words, placed after the kalendar or Ephemerides, which he maketh of the diversities of times and seasons for all actions and purposes; and concludeth thus: *God hath made all things beautiful, decent, in the true return of their seasons; also he hath placed the world in man's heart, yet cannot man find out the work which God worketh from the beginning to the end*: declaring not obscurely, that God hath framed the mind of man as a mirror or glass, capable of the image of the universal world, and joyful to receive the impression thereof, as the eye joyeth to receive light; and not only delighted in beholding the variety of things and vicissitudes of times, but raised also to find out and discern the ordinances and decrees, which throughout all those changes are infallibly observed. And although he doth insinuate that the supreme or summary law of nature, which he calleth *the work which God worketh from the beginning to the end*, is not possible to be found out by man; yet that doth not derogate from the capacity of the mind, but may be referred to the impediments as of shortness of life, ill conjunction of labours, ill tradition of knowledge over from hand to hand, and many other inconveniences, whereunto the condition of man is subject. For that nothing parcel of the world is denied to man's inquiry and invention, he doth in another place rule over, when he saith: *the spirit of man is as the lamp of God, wherewith he searcheth the inwardness of all secrets* [Prov. 20.27]. If then such be the capacity and receipt of the mind of man, it is manifest that there is no danger at all in the proportion of quantity of knowledge, how large soever, lest it should make it swell or outcompass itself; no, but it is merely the quality of knowledge, which, be it in quantity more or less, if it be taken without the true corrective thereof, hath in it some nature of venom or malignity, and some effects of that venom, which is ventosity or swelling. This corrective spice, the mixture whereof maketh knowledge so sovereign, is charity. . . . And as for the third point, it deserveth to be a little stood upon, and not to be lightly passed over: for if any man shall think by view and inquiry into these sensible and material things to attain that light whereby he may reveal unto himself the nature or will of God, then indeed is he spoiled by vain philosophy: for the contemplation of God's creatures and works produceth (having regard to the works and creatures themselves) knowledge; but having regard to God, no perfect knowledge, but wonder, which is broken knowledge. And therefore it was most aptly said by one of Plato's school, *that the sense of man carrieth a resemblance with the sun, which (as we see) openeth and revealeth all the terrestrial globe; but then again it obscureth and concealeth the stars and celestial globe: so doth the sense discover natural things, but it darkeneth and shutteth up divine.* . . . To conclude therefore, let no man upon a weak conceit of sobriety, or an ill-applied moderation think or maintain that a man can search too far, or be too well-studied in the book of God's word, or in the book of God's works, divinity or philosophy but rather let men endeavour an endless progress or proficience in both; only let men beware that they apply both to charity and not to swelling; to use and not to ostentation; and again, that they do not unwisely mingle or confound these learnings together.

And as for the disgraces which learning receiveth from politiques, they be of this nature: that learning doth soften men's minds and makes them more unapt for the honour and exercise of arms; that it doth mar and prevent men's dispositions for matter of government and policy in making them too curious and irresolute by variety of reading, or too peremptory or positive by strictness of rules and axioms, or too immoderate and over-weening by reason of the greatness of examples, or too incompatible and differing from the times by reason of the dissimilitude of examples; or at least it doth divert men's travails from action and business, and bringeth them to a love of leisure and privateness; and that it doth bring into states a relaxation of discipline, whilst every man is more ready to argue than to obey and execute . . .

But these and the like imputations have rather a countenance of gravity, than any ground of justice: for experience doth warrant that both in persons and in times there hath been a meeting and concurrence in learning and arms, flourishing and excelling in the same men and the same ages. For as for men, there cannot be a better, nor the like instance as of the pair, Alexander the Great and Julius Caesar the dictator whereof the one was Aristotle's scholar in philosophy, and the other was Cicero's rival in eloquence. . . . Neither can it otherwise be: for as in man the ripeness of strength of the body and mind cometh much about an age, save that the strength of the body cometh somewhat the more early, so in states, arms and learning, whereof the one correspondeth to the body, the other to the soul of man, have a concurrence or near sequence in times.

And for matter of policy and government, that learning should rather hurt than enable thereunto, is a thing very improbable: we see it is accounted an error to commit a natural body to empiric physicians, which commonly have a few pleasing receipts whereupon they are confident and adventurous, but know neither the causes nor the complexions of patients, nor peril of accidents, nor the true method of cures: we see it is a like error to rely upon advocates or lawyers which are only men of practice and not grounded in their books, who are many times easily surprised when matter falleth out besides their experience, to the prejudice of the causes they handle: so by like reason, it cannot be but a matter of doubtful consequence if States be managed by empiric statesmen, not well mingled with men grounded in learning . . .

And as for those particular seducements or indispositions of the mind for policy and government, which learning is pretended to insinuate; if it be granted that any such thing be, it must be remembered withal that learning ministereth in every of them greater strength of medicine or remedy that it offereth cause of indisposition or infirmity . . .

And for the conceit that learning should dispose men to leisure and privateness and make men slothful; it were a strange thing if that which accustometh the mind to a perpetual motion and agitation should induce slothfulness; whereas contrariwise it may be truly affirmed that no kind of men love business for itself but those that are learned . . .

And if any man be laborious in reading and study and yet idle in business and action, it groweth from some weakness of body, or softness of spirit . . .

And that learning should take up too much time or leisure, I answer the most active or busy man that hath been or can be, hath (no question) many vacant times of leisure, while he expecteth the tides and turns of business . . .

Again, for that other conceit that learning should undermine the reverence of laws and government, it is assuredly a mere depravation and calumny, without all shadow of truth. For to say that a blind custom of obedience should be a surer obligation than duty taught and understood, it is to affirm that a blind man may tread surer by a guide than a seeing man can by a light. And it is without all controversy that learning doth make the minds of men gentle, generous, maniable, and pliant to government; whereas ignorance makes them churlish, thwart and mutinous: and the evidence of time doth clear this assertion, considering that the most barbarous, rude and unlearned times have been most subject to tumults, sedition and changes.

6.11 GALILEO GALILEI, *THE STARRY MESSENGER*

Galileo's discovery of the powerful telescope and of the stars around Jupiter was announced to the world in this publication, first written in Latin, and it swiftly became a matter for intellectual discussion in London. His sparse style, which deliberately eschews references to forbears, and concentrates on the reported observations of natural phenomena, and the probable deductions he has made, was unlike that of any natural philosopher before him, and provided a model for subsequent scientific and philosophical writing. Text from: *The Sidereal Messenger of Galileo Galilei*, ed. and trans. Edward Strafford Carlos, London, Rivingtons, 1880, pp. 1–20.

About ten months ago a report reached my ears that a Dutchman had constructed a telescope by the aid of which, visible objects, although at a great distance from the eye of the observer, were seen distinctly as if near; and some proofs of its most wonderful performances were reported, which some gave credence to, but others contradicted. A few days after, I received confirmation of the report in a letter written from Paris by a noble Frenchman, Jacques Badovere, which finally determined me to give myself up first to inquire into the principle of the telescope, and then to consider the means by which I might compass the invention of a similar instrument, which a little while after I succeeded in doing, through deep study of the theory of refraction: and I prepared a tube, at first of lead, in the ends of which I fitted two glass lenses, both plane on one side, but on the other side, one spherically convex and the other concave. Then bringing my eye to the concave lens, I saw objects satisfactorily large and near, for they appeared one-third of the distance off and nine times larger than when they are seen with the natural eye alone. I shortly afterwards constructed another telescope, with more nicety, which magnified objects more than sixty times. At length, by sparing neither labour nor expense, I succeeded in constructing for myself an instrument so superior that objects seen through it appear magnified nearly a thousand times, and more than thirty times nearer than if viewed by the natural powers of sight alone.

It would be altogether a waste of time to enumerate the number and importance of the benefits which this instrument may be expected to confer, when used by land or sea. But without paying attention to its use for terrestrial objects, I betook myself to observations of the heavenly bodies; and first of all, I viewed the moon as near as if it was scarcely two semi-diameters of the earth distant. After the moon I frequently observed other heavenly bodies, both fixed stars and planets, with incredible delight; and when I saw their very great number, I began to consider about a method by which I might be able to measure their distances apart . . .

Now let me review the observations made by me during the two months just past, again inviting the attention of all who are eager for true philosophy to the beginnings which led to the sight of most important phenomena.

Let me first speak of the surface of the moon, which is turned towards us. For the sake of being understood more easily, I distinguish two parts in it, which I call respectively the brighter and the darker. The brighter part seems to surround and pervade the whole hemisphere, but the darker part, like a sort of cloud, discolours the moon's surface and makes it appear covered with spots. Now these spots, as they are somewhat dark and of considerable size, are plain to everyone, and every age has seen them, wherefore I shall call them great or ancient spots, to distinguish them from other spots, smaller in size, but so thickly scattered that they sprinkle the whole surface of the moon, but especially the brighter portion of it. These spots have never been observed by anyone before me; and from my observations of them, often repeated, I have been led to that opinion which I have expressed, namely that I feel sure that the surface of the moon is not perfect smooth, free from inequalities and exactly spherical, as a large school of philosophers considers with regard to the moon, and the other heavenly bodies, but that, on that contrary, it is full of inequalities, uneven, full of hollows and protuberances, just like the surface of the earth itself, which is varied everywhere by lofty mountains and deep valleys.

The appearances from which we may gather these conclusions are of the following nature: on the fourth or fifth day after new moon, when the moon presents itself to us with bright horns, the boundary which divides the part in shadow from the enlightened part does not extend continuously in an ellipse, as would happen in the case of a perfectly spherical body, but it is marked out by an irregular, uneven, and very wavy line . . . for several bright excrescences, as they may be called, extend beyond the boundary of light and shadow into the dark part, and on the other hand pieces of shadow encroach upon the light: nay, even a great quantity of small blackish spots, altogether separated from the dark part, sprinkle everywhere almost the whole space which is at the time flooded with the sun's light, with the exception of that part alone which is occupied by the great and ancient spots. I have noticed that the small spots just mentioned have this common characteristic always and in every case, that they have the dark part towards the sun's position, and on the side away from the sun they have brighter boundaries, as if they were crowned with shining summits. . . . Now is it not the case, on the earth before sunrise that while the level plain is still in shadow, the peaks of the most lofty mountains are illuminated by the sun's rays? After a little while does not the light spread further, while the middle and larger parts of those mountains are becoming illuminated, and at length when the sun has risen, do not the illuminated parts of the plains and hills join together? The grandeur, however, of such prominences and depressions in the moon seems to surpass both in magnitude and extent the ruggedness of the earth's surface, as I shall hereafter show.

* * *

I have now finished my brief account of the observations which I have thus far made with regard to the moon, the fixed stars and the galaxy. There remains the matter, which seems to me to deserve to be considered the most important in this work, namely that I should disclose and publish to the world the occasion of discovering and observing four planets, never seen from the very beginning of the world up to our own times, their positions, and the observations made during the last two months about their movements and their changes of magnitude; and I summon all astronomers to apply themselves to examine and determine their periodic times, which it has not been permitted me to achieve up to this day, owing to the restriction of my time. I give them warning, however, again, so that they may not approach such an inquiry to no purpose, that they will want a very accurate telescope, and such as I have described in the beginning of this account.

On the 7th day of January in the present year, 1610, in the first hour of the following night, when I was viewing the constellations of the heavens through a telescope, the planet Jupiter presented itself to my view, and as I had prepared for myself a very excellent instrument, I noticed a circumstance which I had never been able to notice before, owing to want of power in my other telescope, namely, that three little stars, small but very bright, were near the planet; and although I believed them to belong to the number of fixed stars, yet they made me somewhat wonder, because they seemed to be arranged exactly in a straight line, parallel to the elliptic, and to be brighter than the rest of the stars, equal to them in magnitude. The position of them with reference to one another and to Jupiter was as follows.

On the east side there were two stars, and a single one towards the west. The star which was furthest towards the east and the western star, appeared rather larger than the third.

I scarcely troubled at all about the distance between them and Jupiter, for, as I have already said, at first I believed them to be fixed stars; but when on January 8th, led by some fatality, I turned again to look at the same part of the heavens, I found a very different state of things, for there were three little stars all west of Jupiter, and nearer together than on the previous night, and they were separated from one another by equal intervals.

At this point, although I had not turned my thoughts at all upon the approximation of the stars to one another, yet my surprise began to be excited, how Jupiter could one day be found to the east of all the aforesaid fixed stars, when the day before it had been west of two of them: and forthwith I became afraid lest the planet might have moved differently from the calculation of astronomers, and so had passed those stars by its own proper motion. I therefore waited for the next night with the most intense longing, but I was disappointed of my hope, for the sky was covered with clouds in every direction.

But on January 10th the stars appeared in the following position with regard to Jupiter: there were two only, and both on the east side of Jupiter, the third, as I thought, being hidden by the planet. They were situated just as before, exactly in the same straight line with Jupiter, and along the zodiac.

When I had seen these phenomena, as I knew that corresponding changes of position could not by any means belong to Jupiter, and as moreover, I perceived that the stars which I saw had been always the same, for there were no others either in front or behind, within a great distance along the zodiac: at length, changing from doubt into surprise, I discovered that the interchange of position which I saw belonged not to Jupiter, but to the stars to which my attention had been drawn, and I thought therefore that they ought to be observed hencefor-ward with more attention and precision.

Accordingly on January 11th I saw an arrangement of the following kind, namely, only two stars to the east of Jupiter, the nearer of which was distant from Jupiter three times as far as from the star further to the east; and the star furthest to the east was nearly twice as large as the other one; whereas on the previous night they had appeared nearly of equal magnitude. I therefore concluded and decided unhesitatingly that there are three stars in the heavens moving about Jupiter, as Venus and Mercury round the sun; which at length was established as clear as daylight by numerous other subsequent observations. These observations also established that there are not only three, but four, erratic sidereal bodies performing their revolutions round Jupiter.

6.12 HELKIAH CROOKE, *MICROCOSMOGRAPHIA*

Crooke popularised the discoveries and writings of the sixteenth and seventeenth-century anatomists and physiologists, writing for the barber-surgeons. He typically includes a survey of the medical and philosophical literature, from Galen and Aristotle onwards, which is omitted here. His style is in stark contrast to that of Galileo or Bacon, both contemporaries. Text from: first edition, 1615, pp. 3–7;14–15; 26.

The excellency of man is declared by his parts, namely the mind and the body, and first what is the dignity of the soul

In the inauguration or coronation of a prince there is nothing more stately or magnificent than to have his style rehearsed by men of greatest nobility, every one adding somewhat thereto till the whole number of his seigneuries and honours are heaped upon him; if therefore we list to search what and how magnificent have been the acclamations of all ages, we shall find in the records of antiquity, that man in whom the sparks of heavenly fire and seeds of the divine nature are (as appeareth both by the Majesty imprinted in his face and by the frame of his body, which was made upright and looking toward heaven) was of the wise and prudent priests of the Egyptians, styled a reverend and admirable creature. . . . [by] Pythagoras, *the measure of all things*. Plato *the wonder of wonders*. Theophrastus, *the pattern of the whole universe*. Aristotle, *a politic creature framed for society*. . . . Finally, all men with one consent, call him, *microcosmus, or the little world*. For his body is, as it were a magazine or storehouse of all the virtues and efficacies of all bodies, and in his soul is the power and force of all living and sensible things . . . for that, being the image and resemblance of the whole world, he can suddenly (Proteus like) transform himself into any particular thing . . .

Of the dignity and wonderful frame of man's body

As the soul of man is of all sublunary forms the most noble, so his body, the house of the soul, doth so far excel, as it may well be called . . . the measure and rule of all other bodies. There be many things which set forth the excellency of it, but these especially among others. The frame and composition which is upright and mounting toward heaven, the moderate temper, the equal and just proportion of the parts, and lastly, their wonderful consent and mutual concord, as long as they are in subjection to the law and rule of nature: for so long in them we may behold the lively image of all this whole universe, which we see with our eyes (as it were) shadowed in a glass or deciphered in a table . . .

Now the . . . due proportion, composition or correspondency of the parts of man's body, with respect each to other, and of them all to the whole, is admirable. This alone for a pattern do all workmen and arts' masters set before them: to this, as to Polyclitus' rule,[6] do the surveyors, master carpenters and masons refer all their plots and projects; they build temples, houses, engines, shipping, forts, yea and the ark of Noah, as it is recorded, was framed after the measure and proportion of man's body. For as the body of man is in length three hundred minutes, in breadth fifty, in height thirty; so the length of the ark was three hundred cubits, the breadth fifty, and the height thirty. Moreover in this proportion of his parts, you shall find both a circular figure, which is of all other the most perfect, and also a square, which in the rest of the creatures you shall not observe. For the navel being placed in the middle of the whole body, and as it were in the centre, if you lay a man upon his back, and as much as may be, labour to spread both his hands and feet, and keeping one end of the compass unmoved and set upon his navel, do turn about the other end, you shall come unto both the thumbs, toes of the feet, and the middle finger of the hands: and if in any part this proportion fail, you may imagine there is a defect in that part. . . . For as in that celestial part the sun is predominant, by whose motion, beams and light all things have their brightness, lustre, and beauty, so in the middest of the chest the heart resideth, whose likeness and proportion with the sun is such and so great, as the ancient writers have been bold to call the sun the heart of the world, and the heart the sun of man's body. For even as by the perpetual and continual motion of the sun and by the quickening and lively heat thereof, all things are cheered and made to flourish, the earth is decked and adorned, yea crowned, with flowers, brings forth great variety of fruits and yields out of her bosom innumerable kinds of herbs. . . . So in like manner by the perpetual motion of the heart and by the vital heat thereof, this little world is refreshed, preserved, and kept in vigour and good life: neither can anything therein be either fruitful or fit and disposed to bring forth unless that mighty and puissant power of the heart do afford and yield an effectual power of fecundity. The vital faculty floweth from the heart as from the fountain, the celestial faculty from heaven.

* * *

How profitable and behoveful anatomy is to the knowledge of man's self

It is no doubt an excellent thing for a man to attain to the knowledge of himself, which thing anatomy and dissection of bodies doth teach us, and as it were point out unto us with the finger; but there is another far more divine and useful profit of anatomy than the former, proper and peculiar to us to whom the light of the Gospel hath shined, namely the knowledge of the immortal God. That high father and creator of all things, who only by himself hath immortality, dwelling in that light that is clearer than all lights, unto which there is no access, whom no man can either see with his eyes, or comprehend with his mind; that eternal father (I say) cannot be known but by his effects: and all the knowledge of God that can be had must be derived not *a priori* but *a posteriori*, not from any cause or matter proceeding, but from the effects and things subsequent.

So we read in the sacred Scriptures that Moses could not endure the bright shining face of God, his eyes were so dazzled therewith. *The invisible things of God* (saith the Apostle) *are known by those things that are visible* [Romans]. Who is it therefore that will not honour, reverence and admire the author and workman of so great a work if he do attentively advise with himself how wonderful the fabric and structure of man's body is? *I will praise thee, o Lord* (saith that Kingly prophet) *because I am wonderfully made.* Phidias his Minerva, Apelles his Venus, Polyclitus his rule,[7] are admired by antiquity and therefore great and high honours have been decreed unto them. . . . They did imitate in the works of nature that which is of least respect and regard, namely, the outward face and feature: for their works are but dumb, without motion or life. But by the view of anatomical dissection, we see and are able to distinguish the variable and divers motions of man's body, and those also very strange and sometime uncouth.

Some of the ancient writers have dignified the frame of man's body with the name and title of the book of God. . . . For even in the smallest and most contemptible creature there is matter enough of admiration; but yet in the frame of man's body there is (I know not what) something more divine, as wherein appeareth not only the admirable power of God, but his wisdom even past all belief, and his infinite and particular goodness and bounty to man.

For his power is not only visible but palpable also, in that of so small a quantity of seed, the parts whereof seem to be all homogeny or of one kind, and of a few drops of blood, he hath framed so many and so divers particles: above two hundred bones, cartilages yet more, many more ligaments, a number of membranes numberless, the pipes or trunks of the arteries, millions of veins, sinews more than thirty pair, muscles almost four hundred, and to conclude, all the bowels and inward parts. His incredible wisdom appeareth in the admirable contabulation or composition of the whole, made of so many parts so unlike one to another. Enter thou, whosoever thou art (though thou be an atheist, and acknowledgest no God at all), enter I beseech thee into the sacred tower of Pallas, I mean the brain of man, and behold and admire the pillars and arched cloisters of that princely palace, the huge greatness of that stately building, the pedestals or bases, the porches and goodly frontispiece, the four arched chambers, the bright and clear mirror, the labyrinthean mazes and web of the small arteries, the admirable trainings of the veins, the draining furrows and watercourses, the living ebullitions, and springings up of the sinews, and the wonderful fecundity of that white marrow of the back, which the wise man in the Book of the Preacher, or *Ecclesiastes* calleth the silver cord. From the brain turn the eye of thy mind to the gates of the sun, and windows of the soul, I mean the eyes, and there behold the brightness of the glittering crystal, the purity and neat cleanness of the watery and glassy humours, the delicate and fine texture of the tunicles,[8] and the wonderful and admirable volubility of the muscles in turning and rolling of the eyes. Mark and observe also the art and curious workmanship appearing in the inward part of the ear, how exquisitely it is made and trimmed with labyrinths, windings, little windows, a sounding tympan or timbrel; three small bones, a stirrup, an anvil and a hammer; the small muscles, the nerve or sinew of hearing, and the cartilaginous or gristle passage, prepared for conveying all sounds unto the sense. Look upon the unweariable and agile motions, the conquering power, the frame and composition, the muscles, the proper and peculiar kind of flesh, the membranes, the veins and sinews, and the bridle, as it were, all easily distinguished within the compass of that little body, or rather little member of the body, the tongue, wherewith we bless God and wherewith we curse men.

Consider and observe the heart, his two ventricles, ears as many, four notable vessels, which as Hippocrates saith are as it were . . . the fountains and wellsprings of the human nature, and the rivers and sources whereby the whole body is watered and refreshed: besides eleven gates or entrances; the admirable and intricate textures of the vessels of the liver; the separation and division of the currents of the arteries and the veins; and in a word, consider the admirable structure of all the parts, animal, vital and natural, wilt thou not cry out, . . . o admirable architect! O, unimitable workman! And wilt thou not with the inspired prophet sing unto the creator this hymn: *I praise thee (O, Lord) because thou hast showed the greatness of thy wisdom in fashioning of my body?*

Lastly the infinite goodness and bounty of God shineth in this excellent workmanship, inasmuch as he hath so well provided for all the parts that every one hath her proper and peculiar use, and yet all are so fitted and knit together in such an harmony and agreement that every one is ready to help another, and any one of them being ill affected, the rest are immediately drawn to a sympathy and participation with it.

* * *

Of the definition of anatomy

Tomh is a Greek word and signifieth section or cutting. Hence comes *anatomia*, a diligent and curious section, undertaken to get knowledge or skill by. For *anatomia* is to cut with great diligence. Now there is amongst physicians a double acception of anatomy either it signifieth the action which is done with the hand, or the habit of mind, that is, the most perfect action of the intellect. The first is called practical anatomy, the latter theoretical or contemplative. The first is gained by experience, the second by reason and discourse: the first we attain only by section and inspection, the second by the living voice of a teacher, or by their learned writings; the first we call historical anatomy, the second scientifical; the first is altogether necessary for the practice of anatomy, the second is only profitable, but yet this profit is oftentimes more beneficial than the use itself of anatomy; the first looketh into the structure of the parts, the second into the causes of structure and the actions and uses therefrom proceeding.

6.13 ROBERT BURTON, *THE ANATOMY OF MELANCHOLY*

Burton's *Anatomy*, first published in 1626, was revised six times during his lifetime, and expanded with each edition. He attempted to anatomise diseases of the brain, with lengthy digressions tracing other writers and sources on the topic. Here he places the understanding of disease within an orthodox, strictly Protestant and biblical framework. Text from: first edition, pp. 1–20.

Man's excellency, fall, miseries, infirmities; the causes of them

Man, the most excellent and noble creature of the world *the principal and mighty work of God, wonder of Nature,* as Zoroaster calls him . . . the *marvel of marvels,* as Plato; *the abridgement and epitome of the world,* as Pliny; *microcosmus,* a little world, a model of the world, sovereign lord of the earth, viceroy of the world, sole commander and governor of all the creatures in it; to whose empire they are subject in particular, and yield obedience; far surpassing all the rest, not in body only, but in soul . . . created to God's own image, to that immortal and incorporeal substance, with all the faculties and powers belonging unto it; was at first pure, divine, perfect, happy, *created after God in true holiness and righteousness*; fitted for divinity, free from all manner of infirmities, and put in paradise, to know God to praise and glorify Him, to do His will . . . to propagate the Church.

But this most noble creature . . . o pitiful change! is fallen from that he was, and forfeited his estate, become *miserabilis homuncio*, a castaway, a caitiff, one of the most miserable creatures of the world, if he be considered in his own nature, an unregenerate man, and so much obscured by his fall that (some few relics excepted) he is inferior to a beast. . . . *He must eat his meat in sorrow*, subject to death and all manner of infirmities, all kind of calamities . . .

The impulsive cause of these miseries in man, this privation or destruction of God's image, the cause of death and diseases, of all temporal and eternal punishments, was the sin of our first parent Adam, in eating of the forbidden fruit, by the devil's instigation and allurement. His disobedience, pride, ambition, intemperance, incredulity, curiousity; from whence proceeded original sin and that general corruption of mankind, as from a fountain flowed all bad inclinations and actual transgressions, which cause our several calamities inflicted upon us for our sins. And this, belike, is that which our fabulous poets have shadowed unto us in the tale of Pandora's box, which, being opened through her curiosity alone, filled the world full of all manner of diseases . . . .

Now the instrumental causes of these our infirmities are as diverse as the infirmities themselves; stars, heavens, elements, etc., and all those creatures which God hath made, are armed against sinners. They were indeed once good in themselves, and that they are now many of them pernicious unto us, is not in their nature, but our corruption, which hath casued it. For, from the fall of our first parent Adam, they have been changed, the earth accursed, the influence of stars altered, the four elements, beasts, birds, plants are now ready to offend us. *The principal things for the use of man, are water, fire, iron, salt, meal, wheat, honey, milk, oil, wine, clothing, good to the godly, to the sinners turned to evil* (Ecc. 39.26). *Fire, and hail and famine, and dearth, all these are created for vengeance* (Ecc. 39.29).

The heavens threaten us with their comets, stars, planets, with their great conjunctions, eclipses, oppositions, quartiles, and such unfriendly aspects; the air with his meteors, thunder and lightning, intemperate heat and cold, mightly winds, tempests, unseasonable weather; from which proceed dearth, famine, plague, and all sorts of epidemedical diseases, consuming infinite miriads of men. At Cairo in Egypt every third year (as it is related by Boterus and others), 300,000 die of the plague, and 200,000 in Constantinople every fifth or seventh at the utmost . . .

Our intemperance it is that pulls so many several incurable diseases upon our heads, that hastens old age, perverts our temperature and brings upon us sudden death. And last of all, that which crucifies us most, is our own folly, madness . . .

weakness, want of government, our facility and proneness in yielding to several lusts, in giving way to every passion and perturbation of the mind: by which means we metamorphose ourselves and degenerate into beasts . . .

The definition, number, division of diseases

What a disease is, almost every physician defines. Fernelius calleth it an *affection of the body contrary to nature*; Fuchsius and Crato, *an hindrance, hurt, or alteration of any action of the body, or part of it* . . .

How many disaeases there are, is a question not yet determined: Pliny reckons up 300 from the crown of the head to the sole of the foot: elsewhere he saith . . . their number is infinite. Howsoever it was in those times, it boots not; in our days I am sure the number is much augmented . . .

For besides many epidemical diseases unheard of, and altogether unknown to Galen and Hippocrates, as *scorbutum*, smallpox, *plica*, sweating sickness, *morbus Gallicus*, etc., we have many proper and peculiar to every part.

No man amongst us so sound, of so good a constitution, that hath not some impediment of body or mind . . . we have all our infirmities, first or last, more or less. . . . Paracelsus may brag that he could make a man live 400 years or more, if he might bring him up from his infancy, and diet him as he list; and some physicians hold, that there is no certain period of man's life; but it may still by temperance and physic be prolonged . . .

Division of the diseases of the head

These diseases of the mind, forasmuch as they have their chief seat and organs in the head, are commonly repeated amongst the diseases of the head, which are divers, and vary much according to their site. For in the head, as there be several parts, so there be divers grievances, which . . . are inward or outward (to omit all others which pertain to eyes and ears, nostrils, gums, teeth, mouth, palate, tongue, weasel, chops, face, etc.) belonging properly to the brain, as baldness, falling of hair, furfur, lice, etc. Inward belonging to the skins next to the brain, called *dura* and *pia mater*, as all headaches, etc., or to the ventricles, cauls, kells, tunicles, creeks, and parts of it, and their passions, as *caro*, vertigo, incubus, apoplexy, falling sickness. The diseases of the nerves, cramps, stupor, convulsion, tremor, palsy; or belonging to the excrements of the brain, catarrhs, sneezing, rheums, distillations; or else those that pertain to the substance of the brain itself, in which are conceived frenzy, lethargy, melancholy, madness, weak memory, *sopor* or coma, *vigilia* [sleeplessness] and *vigil coma*. Out of these again I will single such as properly belong to the fantasy, or imagination, or reason itself, which Laurentius calls the diseases of the mind; and Hildesheim, *morbos imaginationis aut rationis laesae* [diseases of the imagination, or of injured reason], which are three or four in number, frenzy, madness, melancholy, dotage, and their kinds: as hydrophobia, lycanthropia, St. Vitus's dance, possession of devils.

6.14 FRANCIS BACON, *THE GREAT INSTAURATION*

Bacon's *Great Instauration*, written in Latin and published in 1620, was dedicated to James I, in a vain attempt to obtain royal patronage for some of Bacon's empirical projects. Its aim was not to describe experiments, or publish new discoveries, but to set forth a new scientific method for discovery. Bacon thus pleads for an intellectual revolution, which must precede any scientific one. Text from: *The Works of Francis Bacon*, ed. J. Spedding *et al.* (1857–74), vol. IV, pp. 13–14; 16–17; 47–55; 78; 95.

Preface

It seems to me that men do not rightly understand either their store or their strength, but overrate the one and underrate the other. Hence it follows that either from an extravagant estimate of the value of the arts which they possess, they seek no further; or else from too mean an estimate of their own powers, they spend their strength in small matters and never put it fairly to the trial in those which go to the main. These are as the pillars of fate set in the path of knowledge: for men have neither desire nor hope to encourage them to penetrate further. And since opinion of store is one of the chief causes of want, and satisfaction with the present induces neglect of provision for the future, it becomes a thing not only useful, but absolutely necessary that the excess of honour and admiration with which our existing stock of inventions is regarded be in the very entrance and threshold of the work, and that frankly and without circumlocution stripped off and men be duly warned not to exaggerate or make too much of them. For let a man look carefully into all that variety of books with which the arts and sciences abound, he will find everywhere endless repetitions of the same thing, varying in the method of treatment, but not new in substance, insomuch that the whole stock, numerous as it appears at first view, proves on examination to be but scanty. And for its value and utility, it must be plainly avowed that that wisdom which we have derived principally from the Greeks, is but like the boyhood of knowledge, and has the characteristic property of boys: it can talk, but it cannot generate, for it is fruitful of controversies but barren of works. So that the state of learning as it now is appears to be represented to the life in the old fable of Scylla, who had the head and face of a virgin, but her womb was hung round with barking monsters, from which she could not be delivered. For in like manner the sciences to which we are accustomed have certain general positions which are specious and flattering: but as soon as they come to particulars, which are as the parts of generation, when they should produce fruit and works, then arise contentions and barking disputations, which are the end of the matter, and all the issue they can yield. Observe also that if sciences of this kind had any life in them, that could never have come to pass which has been the case now for many ages, that they stand almost at a stay, without receiving any augmentations worthy of the human race: insomuch that many times not only what was asserted once is asserted still, but what was a question once is a question still, and instead of being resolved by discussion is only fixed and fed, and all the tradition and succession of schools is still a succession of masters and scholars, not of inventors and those who bring to further perfection the things invented. In the mechanical arts we find it not so: they, on the contrary, as having in them some breath of life, are continually growing and becoming more perfect. As originally invented they are commonly rude, clumsy and shapeless: afterwards they acquire new powers and more commodious arrangements and constructions . . .

And if there be any who have determined to make trial for themselves and put their own strength to the work of advancing the boundaries of the sciences, yet have they not ventured to cast themselves completely loose from received opinions or to seek their knowledge at the fountain: but they think they have done some great thing if they do but add and introduce into the existing sum of science, something of their own, prudently considering with themselves that by making the addition they can assert their liberty, while they retain the credit of modesty by assenting to the rest. But these mediocrities and middle ways so much praised in deferring to opinions and customs, turn to the great detriment of the sciences. For it is hardly possible at once to admire an author and to go beyond him: knowledge being as water which will not rise above the level from which it fell. Men of this kind therefore amend some things, but advance little, and improve the condition of knowledge, but do not extend its range. Some indeed there have been who have gone more boldly to work and taking it all for an open matter and giving their genius full play, have made a passage for themselves and their own opinions by pulling down and demolishing former ones: and yet all their stir has but little advanced the matter, since their aim has been not to extend philosophy and the arts in substance and value, but only to change doctrines and transfer the kingdom of opinions to themselves: whereby little has indeed been gained, for though the error be the opposite of the other, the causes of erring are the same in both. And if there have been any who, not binding themselves either to other men's opinions or to their own, but loving liberty, have desired to engage others along with themselves in search, these, though honest in intention, have been weak in endeavour. For they have been content to follow probable reasons, and are carried round in the whirl of arguments and in the promiscuous liberty of search have relaxed the severity of inquiry. There is none who has dealt upon experience and the facts of nature as long as is necessary. Some there are indeed who have committed themselves to the waves of experience, and almost turned mechanics: yet these again have in their very experiments pursued a kind of wandering inquiry, without any regular system of operations. And besides they have mostly proposed to themselves certain petty tasks, taking it for a great matter to work out some single discovery, a course of proceeding at once poor in aim and unskilful in design. For no man can rightly and successfully investigate the nature of anything in the thing itself: let him vary his experiments as laboriously as he will, he never comes to a resting place, but still finds something to seek beyond. And there is another thing to be remembered, namely that all industry in experimenting has begun with proposing to itself certain definite works to be accomplished, and has pursued them with premature and unseasonable eagerness: it has sought, I say, experiments of fruit, not experiments of light; not imitating the divine procedure, which in its first day's work created light only and assigned to it one entire day, on which day it produced no material work, but proceeded to that on the days following.

* * *

Aphorisms concerning the interpretation of nature and the kingdom of man

I. Man being the servant and interpreter of nature can do and understand so much and so much only as he has observed in fact or in thought of the course of nature: beyond this he neither knows anything nor can do anything.

II. Neither the naked hand nor the understanding left to itself can effect much. It is by instruments and helps that the work is done, which are as much wanted for the understanding as for the hand. And as the instruments of the hand either give motion or guide it, so the instruments of the mind supply either suggestions for the understanding, or cautions.

III. Human knowledge and human power meet in one: for where the cause is not known the effect cannot be produced. Nature to be commanded must be obeyed, and that which in contemplation is as the cause, is in operation as the rule.

IV. Towards the effecting of works all that man can do is to put together or put asunder natural bodies. The rest is done by nature working within.

V. The study of nature with a view to works is engaged in by the mechanic, the mathematician, the physician, the alchemist, and the magician: but by all (as things now are) with slight endeavour and scanty success.

VI. It would be an unsound fancy and self-contradictory to expect that things which have never yet been done, can be done except by means which have never yet been tried.

VII. The productions of the mind and hand seem very numerous in books and manufactures. But all this variety lies in an exquisite subtlety and derivations from a few things already known: not in the number of axioms.

VIII. Moreover, the works already known are due to chance and experiment rather than to sciences: for the sciences we now possess are merely systems for the nice ordering and setting forth of things already invented, not methods of invention or directions for new works.

IX. The cause and root of nearly all evils in the sciences is this: that while we falsely admire and extol the powers of the human mind, we neglect to seek for its true helps.

X. The subtlety of nature is greater many times over than the subtlety of the senses and understanding: so that all those specious meditations, speculations and glosses in which men indulge are quite from the purpose, only there is no one by to observe it.

XI. As the sciences which we now have do not help us in finding out new works, so neither does the logic which we now have help us in finding out new sciences.

XII. The logic now in use serves rather to fix and give stability to the errors which have their foundation in commonly received notions, than to help the search after truth. So it does more harm than good.

XIII. The syllogism is not applied to the first principles of sciences, and is applied in vain to intermediate axioms, being no match for the subtlety of nature. It commands assent therefore to the proposition, but does not take hold of the thing.

XIV. The syllogism consist of propositions, propositions consist of words, words are symbols of notions. Therefore if the notions themselves (which is the root of the matter) are confused and over-hastily abstracted from the facts, there can be no firmness in the superstructure. Our only hope therefore lies in a true induction.

XV. There is no soundness in our notions, whether logical or physical. Substance, quality, action, passion, essence itself are not sound notions: much less are heavy, light, dense, rare, moist, dry, generation, corruption, attraction, repulsion, element, matter, form and the like: but all are fantastical and ill-defined . . .

XVIII. The discoveries which have hitherto been made in the sciences are such as lie close to vulgar notions, scarcely beneath the surface. In order to penetrate into the inner and further recesses of nature, it is necessary that both notions and axioms be derived from things by a more sure and guarded way, and that a method of intellectual operation be introduced altogether better and more certain.

XIX. There are and can be only two ways of searching into and discovering truth. The one flies from the senses and particulars to the most general axioms, and from these principles, the truth of which it takes for settled and immoveable, proceeds to judgment and to the discovery of middle axioms. And this way is now in fashion. The other derives axioms from the senses and particulars, rising by a gradual and unbroken ascent, so that it arrives at the most general axioms last of all. This is the true way, but as yet untried.

XX. The understanding left to itself takes the same course (namely the former) which it takes in accordance with logical order. For the mind longs to spring up to positions of higher generality, that it may find rest there, and so after a little while wearies of experiment. But this evil is increased by logic, because of the order and solemnity of its disputations . . .

XXII. Both ways set out from the senses and particulars and rest in the highest generalities: but the difference between them is infinite. For the one just glances at experiment and particulars in passing, the other dwells duly and orderly among them. The one, again, begins at once by establishing certain abstract and useless generalities, the other rises by gradual steps to that which is prior and better known in the order of nature.

XXIII. There is a great difference between the Idols of the human mind and the Ideas of the divine. That is to say, between certain empty dogmas and the true signatures and marks set upon the works of creation as they are found in nature . . .

XXXIV. Even to deliver and explain what I bring forward is no easy matter: for things in themselves new will yet be apprehended with reference to what is old . . .

XXXVI. One method of delivery alone remains to us, which is simply this: we must lead men to the particulars themselves, and their series and order; while men on their side must force themselves for awhile to lay their notions by and begin to familiarise themselves with facts.

XXXVII. The doctrine of those who have denied that certainty could be attained at all has some agreement with my way of proceeding at the first setting out: but they end in being infinitely separated and opposed. For the holders of that doctrine assert simply that nothing can be known: I also assert that not much can be known in nature by the way which is now in use. But then they go on to destroy the authority of the senses and understanding: whereas I proceed to devise and supply helps for the same.

XXXVIII. The idols and false notions which are now in possession of the human understanding and have taken deep root therein, not only so beset men's minds that truth can hardly find entrance, but even after entrance obtained, they will again in the very instauration of the sciences, meet and trouble us, unless men being forewarned of the danger fortify themselves as far as may be against their assaults.

XXXIX. There are four classes of idols which beset men's minds. To these for distinction's sake I have assigned names, calling the first class, *Idols of the Tribe*; the second *Idols of the Cave*; the third, *Idols of the Marketplace*; the fourth, *Idols of the Theatre*.

XL. The formation of ideas and axioms by true induction is no doubt the proper remedy to be applied for the keeping off and clearing away of idols. To point them out, however, is of great use: for the doctrine of idols is to the interpretation of nature, what the doctrine of the refutation of sophisms is to common logic.

XLI. The Idols of the Tribe have their foundation in human nature itself, and in the tribe or race of men. For it is a false assertion that the sense of man is the measure of things. On the contrary, all perceptions as well of the sense as of the mind are according to the measure of the individual and not according to the measure of the universe. And the human understanding is like a false mirror, which receiving rays irregularly, distorts and discolours the nature of things by mingling its own nature with it.

XLII. The Idols of the Cave are the idols of the individual man. For everyone (besides the errors common to human nature in general) has a cave or den of his own, which refracts and discolours the light of nature: owing either to his own proper and peculiar nature; or to his education and conversation with others; or to the reading of books and the authority of those whom he esteems and admires; or to the differences of impressions, accordingly as they take place in a mind preoccupied and predisposed or in a mind indifferent and settled; or the like. So that the spirit of man (according as it is meted out to different individuals) is in fact a thing variable and full of perturbation and governed, as it were, by chance. Whence it was well observed by Heraclitus that men look for sciences in their own lesser worlds, and not in the greater or common world.

XLIII. There are also idols formed by the intercourse and association of men with each other, which I call Idols of the Marketplace, on account of the commerce and consort of men there. For it is by discourse that men associate, and words are imposed according to the apprehension of the vulgar. And therefore the ill and unfit choice of words wonderfully obstructs the understanding. Nor do the definitions or explanations wherewith in some things learned men are wont to guard and defend themselves, by any means set the matter right. But words plainly force and overrule the understanding and throw all into confusion, and lead men away into numberless empty controversies and idle fancies.

XLIV. Lastly there are idols which have immigrated into men's minds from the various dogmas of philosophies, and also from the wrong laws of demonstration. These I call Idols of the Theatre: because in my judgement all the received systems are but so many stage-plays, representing worlds of their own creation after an unreal and scenic fashion.

* * *

LXXX. To this it may be added that natural philosophy, even among those who have attended to it, has scarcely ever possessed especially in these later times, a disengaged and whole man (unless it were some monk studying in his cell or some gentleman in his country-house) but that it has been made merely a passage and bridge to something else. And so this great mother of the sciences has with strange indignity been degraded to the offices of a servant, having to attend on the business of medicine or mathematics, and likewise to wash and imbue youthful and unripe wits with a sort of first dye, in order that they may be the fitter to receive another afterwards. Meanwhile let no man look for much progress in the sciences, especially in the practical part of them, unless natural philosophy be carried on and applied to particular sciences and particular sciences be carried back again to natural philosophy. For want of this, astronomy, optics, music, a number of mechanical arts, medicine itself, nay, what one might more wonder at, moral and political philosophy and the logical sciences, altogether lack profoundness and merely glide along the surface and variety of things.

* * *

C. But not only is a greater abundance of experiments to be sought for and procured, and that too, of a different kind from those hitherto tried: an entirely different method, order and process for carrying on and advancing experience must also be introduced. For experience, when it wanders in its own track, is, as I have already remarked, mere groping in the dark and confounds men rather than instructs them. But when it shall proceed in accordance with a fixed law, in regular order, and without interruption, then may better things be hoped of knowledge.

6.15 WILLIAM HARVEY, *ON THE MOTION OF THE HEART AND BLOOD*

Harvey's discovery of the motion of the heart, through anatomy, was one of the major physiological observations of the century. It was first published in Latin in 1628, and only translated into English in the nineteenth century, although he expounded the theory in later works written in English (such as *Anatomical Exercitations* in the 1650s). Text from: William Harvey, *Works*, trans. Robert Willis, London, 1847, pp. 45–7.

Thus far I have spoken of the passage of the blood from the veins into the arteries and of the manner in which it is transmitted and distributed by the action of the heart . . . What remains to be said upon the quantity and source of the blood is of so novel and unheard of character that I do not only fear injury to myself from the envy of a few, but I tremble lest I have mankind at large for enemies, so much does wont and custom that become as another nature, and doctrine once sown . . . and respect for antiquity, influence all men: still, the die is cast and my trust is in my love of truth . . .

When I surveyed my mass of evidence, whether derived from vivisections, and my various reflections on them, or from the ventricles of the heart and the vessels that enter into and issue from them, the symmetry and size of these conduits, for nature doing nothing in vain would never have given them so large a relative size without a purpose; or from the arrangement and intimate structure of the valves in particular, and of the other parts of the heart in general, with many things besides, I frequently and seriously bethought me, and long revolved in my mind, what might be the quantity of blood which was transmitted, in how short a time its passage might be effected, and the like; and not finding it possible that this could be supplied by the juices of the ingested aliment, without the veins on the one hand becoming drained and the arteries on the other getting ruptured through the excessive charge of blood, unless the blood should somehow find its way from the arteries into the veins, and so return to the right side of the heart; I began to think whether there might not be *a motion, as it were, in a circle*. Now this I afterwards found to be true, and I finally saw that the blood, forced by the action of the left ventricle into the arteries was distributed to the body at large, and its several parts, in the same manner as it is sent through the lungs, impelled by the right ventricle into the pulmonary artery, and that it then passed through the veins and along the vena cava, and so round to the left ventricle in the manner already indicated. Which motion we may be allowed to call circular. . . . The various parts are nourished, cherished, quickened, by the warmer, more perfect, vaporous, spirituous and, as I may say, alimentative blood; which, on the contrary, in contact with these parts becomes cooled, coagulated, and, so to speak, effete; whence it returns to its sovereign the heart, as if to its source, or to the inmost home of the body, there to recover its state of excellence or perfection. . . . The heart consequently is the beginning of life; the sun of the microcosm, even as the sun in his turn might well be designated the heart of the world: for it is the heart by whose virtue and pulse the blood is moved, perfected, made apt to nourish, and is preserved from corruption and coagulation.

6.16 RENÉ DESCARTES, *DISCOURSE OF METHOD*

Descartes's work was written in 1637, and translated into English during the intellectual ferment of the English Civil War. Its style and philosophical approach, although related to those of both Bacon and Montaigne, was refreshingly free of dogma and authority, and influenced contemporary thinking and writing about science (see, for example, Kenelm Digby). Text from: translated by Thomas Newcombe, 1649, 7–15; 26–31; 50–5 (parts I, II, III).

I have been bred up to letters from mine infancy, and because I was persuaded that by their means a man might acquire a clear and certain knowledge of all that's useful for this life, I was extremely desirous to learn them. But as soon as I had finished all the course of my studies, at the end whereof men are usually received amongst the rank of the learned, I wholly changed my opinion, for I found myself entangled in so many doubts and errors, that methought I had made no other profit in seeking to instruct myself but that I had the more discovered mine own ignorance. Yet I was in one of the most famous schools in Europe; where I thought, if there were any on earth, there ought to have been learned men. I had learnt all what others had learnt, even unsatisfied with the sciences which were taught us; I had read over all books (which I could possibly procure) treating of such as are held to be the rarest and the most curious. Withal, I knew the judgement others made of me, and I perceived that I was no less esteemed than my fellow students, although there were some amongst them that were destined to fill our masters' rooms. And in fine, our age seemed to me as flourishing and as fertile of good wits as any of the preceding, which made me take the liberty to judge of all other men by myself, and to think that there was no such learning in the world, as formerly I had been made believe.

Yet did I continue the esteem I had of those exercises which are the employments of the Schools: I knew that languages which are there learnt are necessary for the understanding of ancient writers; that the quaintness of fables awakens the mind; that the memorable actions in history raise it up, and that being read with discretion, they help to form the judgement; that the reading of good books is like the conversation with the honestest persons of the past age who were the authors of them, and even a studied conversation, wherein they discover to us the best only of their thoughts; that eloquence hath forces and beauties which are incomparable; that poetry hath delicacies and sweets extremely ravishing; that the mathematics hath most subtle inventions, which very much conduce as well to content the curious as to facilitate all arts and to lessen the labour of men; that those writings which treat of manners contain divers instructions and exhortations to virtue which are very useful; that theology teacheth the way to heaven; that philosophy affords us the means to speak of all things with probability and makes herself admired by the least knowing men; that law, physic and other sciences bring honour and riches to those who practise them; finally that it's good to have examined them all, even the falsest and the most superstitious, that we may discover their just value and preserve ourselves from their cheats.

But I thought I had spent time enough in the languages and even also in the lecture of ancient books, their histories and their fables. For 'tis even the same thing to converse with those of former ages, as to travel. It's good to know something of the manners of several nations that we may not think that all things against our mode are ridiculous or unreasonable, as those are wont to do who have seen nothing. But when we employ too long time in travel we at last become strangers to our own country, and when we are too curious of those things which we practised in former times, we commonly remain ignorant of those which are now in use. Besides, fables make us imagine divers events possible which are not so: and that even the most faithful histories, if they neither change or augment the value of things, to render them more worthy to be read at least, they always omit the basest and less remarkable circumstances; whence it is that the rest seems not as it is; and that those who form their manners by the examples they thence derive are subject to fall into the extravagancies of the Paladins of our romances, and to conceive designs beyond their abilities.

I highly prized eloquence and was in love with poetry: but I esteemed both the one and the other, rather gifts of the mind than the fruits of study. Those who have the strongest reasoning faculties and who best digest their thoughts to render them more clear and intelligible, may always the better persuade what they propose, although they should speak but a corrupt dialect, and had never learnt rhetoric. And those whose inventions are most pleasing and can express them with most ornament and sweetness, will still be the best poets, although ignorant of the art of poetry.

Beyond all, I was most pleased with the mathematics for the certainty and evidence of the reasons thereof; but I did not yet observe their true use, and thinking that it served only for mechanic arts, I wondered that since the grounds thereof were so firm and solid, that nothing more sublime had been built thereon. As on the contrary, I compared the writings of the ancient heathen which treated of manners, to most proud and stately palaces which were built only on sand and mire, they raise the virtues very high and make them appear estimable above all the things in the world; but they do not sufficiently instruct us in the knowledge of them ...

I reverenced our theology, and pretended to heaven as much as any; but having learnt as a most certain truth that the way to it is no less open to the most ignorant than to the most learned, and that those revealed truths which led thither were beyond our understanding, I durst not submit to the weakness of my ratiocination. And I thought that to undertake to examine them and to succeed in it, required some extraordinary assistance from heaven and somewhat more than man. I shall say nothing of philosophy but that seeing it hath been cultivated by the most excellent wits which have lived these many ages, and that yet there is nothing which is undisputed, and by consequence which is not doubtful. I could not presume so far as to hope to succeed better than others. And considering how many different opinions there may be on the same thing maintained by learned men, and yet that there never can be but one only truth, I reputed almost all false which had no more than probability in it.

As for other sciences, since they borrow their principles from philosophy, I judged that nothing which was solid could be built upon such unsound foundations; and neither honour nor wealth were sufficient to invite me to the study of them. For (I thank God) I found not myself in a condition which obliged me to make a trade of letters for the relief of my fortune. And although I made it not my profession to despise glory with the Cynic, yet did I little value that which I could not acquire but by false pretences. And lastly, for unwarrantable studies, I thought I already too well understood what they were, to be any more subject to be deceived either by the promises of an alchemist, or by the predictions of an astrologer, or by the impostures of a magician, or by the artifice or brags of those who profess to know more than they do.

By reason whereof as soon as my years freed me from the subjection of my tutors, I wholly gave over the study of letters and resolving to seek no other knowledge but what I could find in myself or in the great book of the world, I employed the rest of my youth in travel to see courts and armies, to frequent people of several humours and conditions, to gain experience, to hazard myself in those encounters of fortune which should occur: and everywhere to make such a reflection on those things which presented themselves to me that I might draw profit from them.

* * *

And having since observed in my travels that all those whose opinions are contrary to ours are not therefore barbarous or savage, but that many use as much or more reason than we; and having considered how much one man with his own understanding, bred up from his childhood among the French or the Dutch becomes different from what he would be had he always lived amongst the Chinese or the Cannibals; and how even in the fashion of our clothes the same thing which pleased ten years since and which perhaps will please ten years hence, seems now to us ridiculous and extravagant. So that it's much more custom and example which persuades us than any assured knowledge; and notwithstanding, that plurality of voices us a proof of no validity in those truths which are hard to be discovered; for that it's much more likely for one man alone to have met with them than a whole nation; I could choose no man whose opinion was to be preferred before another's; and I found myself even constrained to undertake the conduct of myself.

But as a man that walks alone and in the dark, I resolved to go so softly and use so much circumspection in all things, that though I advanced little I would yet save myself from falling. Neither would I begin quite to reject some opinions which formerly had crept into my belief, without the consent of my reason, before I had employed time enough to form the project of the work I undertook, and to seek the true method to bring me to the knowledge of all those things of which my understanding was capable.

I had a little studied, being young, of the parts of philosophy, logic and of the mathematics, the analysis of the geometricians, and algebra. Three arts of sciences which seemed to contribute somewhat conducing to my design: but examining them, I observed that as for logic, its syllogisms and the greatest part of its other rules, serve rather to expound to another the thing they know, or even as Lullius's art,[9] to speak with judgement of the things we are ignorant of, than to learn them ... they have made a confused and obscure art which perplexeth the mind, instead of a science to instruct it. For this reason I thought I ought to seek some other method which, comprehending the advantages of these, they might be exempt from their defects. And as the multitude of laws often furnisheth excuses for vice, so a State is far better policed when having but a few, they are very strictly observed therein. So instead of the great many precepts whereof logic is composed, I thought these four following would be sufficient for me, if I took but a firm and constant resolution not once to fail in the observation of them.

The first was never to receive any thing for true but what I evidently knew to be so: that's to say, carefully to avoid precipitation and prevention and to admit nothing more into my judgement but what should so clearly and distinctly present itself to my mind, that I could have no reason to doubt it.

The second, to divide every one of these difficulties which I was to examine, into as many parcels as could be, and, as was requisite the better to resolve them.

The third, to lead my thoughts in order, beginning by the most simple objects and the easiest to be known, to rise by little and little, as by steps, even to the knowledge of the most next, and even supposing an order among those which naturally do not proceed one the other.

And the last, to make everywhere such exact calculations and such general reviews that I might be confident to have omitted nothing.

Those long chains of reasons (though simple and easy) which the geometricians commonly use to lead us to their most difficult demonstrations, gave me occasion to imagine that all things which may fall under the knowledge of men, follow one the other in the same manner.

* * *

I know not whether I ought to entertain you with the first meditations which I had there, for they are so metaphysical and so little common that perhaps they will not be relished by all men: and yet that you may judge whether the foundations I have laid are firm enough, I find myself in a manner obliged to discourse them. I had long since observed that as for manners it was sometimes necessary to follow those opinions which we know to be very uncertain, as much as if they were indubitable, as is before said. But because that then I desired only to intend the search of truth, I thought I ought to do the contrary and reject as absolutely false all wherein I could imagine the least doubt, to the end I might see if afterwards anything might remain in my belief, not at all subject to doubt. Thus because our senses sometimes deceive us, I would suppose that there was nothing which was such as they represented it to us. And because there are men who mistake themselves in reasoning, even in the most simple matters of geometry and make therein paralogisms, judging that I was as subject to fail as any other man, I rejected as false all those reasons which I had before taken for demonstrations. And considering that the same thoughts which we have waking may also happen to us sleeping, when as not any one of them is true, I resolved to feign that all those things which ever entered into my mind were no more true than the illusions of my dreams. But presently after I observed that whilst I would think that all was false, it must necessarily follow that I who thought it must be something. And perceiving that this truth, *I think therefore I am*, was so firm and certain that all the most extravagant suppositions of the Sceptics was not able to shake it, I judged that I might receive it without scruple for the first principle of the philosophy I sought.

Examining carefully afterwards what I was, and seeing that I could suppose that I had no body, and that there was no world, not any place where I was: but for all this I could not feign that *I was not*; and that even contrary thereto, thinking to doubt the truth of other things, it most evidently and certainly followed that *I was*. Whereas if I had ceased to think, although all the rest of whatever I had imagined were true, I had no reason to believe that *I had been*. I knew then that I was a substance, whose whole essence or nature is but to *think*; and who, to *be*, hath need of no place, nor depends on any material thing. So that this *me*, to wit, my soul, by which I am what I am, is wholly distinct from the body and more easy to be known that it; and although *that* [the body] were not, *it* [the soul] would not therefore cease to be what it is.

After this I considered in general what is requisite in a proposition to make it true and certain: for since I had found out one which I knew to be so, I thought I ought also to consider wherein that certainty consisted: and having observed that there is nothing at all in this *I think therefore I am*, which assures me that I speak the truth, except this: that I see most clearly that to think one must have a being, I judged that I might take for a general rule that those things which we conceive clearly and distinctly are all true, and that the only difficulty is punctually to observe what those are which we distinctly conceive.

In pursuance whereof, reflecting on what I doubted, and that consequently my being was not perfect, for I clearly perceived that it was greater a perfection to know than to doubt, I advised in myself to seek from whence I had learnt to think on something which was more perfect than I; and I knew evidently that it must be of some nature which was indeed more perfect. As for what concerns the thoughts I had of divers other things without myself, as of heaven, earth, light, heat and a thousand more, I was not so much troubled to know whence they came, for that I observed nothing in them which seemed to render them superior to me; I might believe that if they were true they were dependencies from my nature, as far forth as it had any perfection; and if that were not, I made not account of them; that is to say, that they were in me because I had something deficient. But it could not be the same with the *Idea* of a being more perfect than mine: for to esteem of it as of nothing was a thing manifestly impossible. And because there is no less repugnancy that the more perfect should succeed from and depend upon the less perfect, than for something to proceed from nothing, I could no more hold it from myself: so as it followed that it must have been put into me by a nature which was truly more perfect than I, and even which had in it all the perfections whereof I could have an *Idea*, to wit (to explain myself in one word): God. Whereto I added, that since I knew some perfections which I had not, I was not the only being which had an existence (I shall under favour, use here freely the terms of the schools), but that of necessity there must be some other more perfect whereon I depended, and from whom I had gotten all what I had.

6.17 JOHN WILKINS, *THE DISCOVERY OF A WORLD IN THE MOON*

Wilkins was one of the group of scientists and thinkers who during the Civil War as warden of Wadham College, Oxford, encouraged experimentation, scientific discussion and the development of natural philosophy; during which period Boyle began to develop his chemical experiments and theories (see 6.23). Text from: first edition, 1638, epilogue.

The propositions that are proved in this discourse

1. That the strangeness of this opinion is no sufficient reason why it should be rejected, because other certain truths have been formerly esteemed ridiculous and great absurdities entertained by common consent.

2. That a plurality of worlds does not contradict any principle of reason or faith.

3. That the heavens do not consist of any such pure matter which can privilege

them from the like change and corruption, as these inferior bodies are liable unto.

4. That the moon is a solid, compacted, opacous[10] body.

5. That the moon hath not any light of her own.

6. That there is a world in the moon hath been the direct opinion of many ancient, with some modern, mathematicians, and may probably be deduced from the tenets of others.

7. That those spots and brighter parts which by our sight may be distinguished in the moon do show the difference betwixt the sea and land in that other world.

8. That the spots represent the sea, and the brighter parts the land.

9. That there are high mountains, deep valleys, and spacious plains in the body of the moon.

10. That there is an atmosphere or an orb of gross vaporous air, immediately encompassing the body of the moon.

11. That as their world is our moon, so our world is their moon.

12. That 'tis probable there may be such meteors belonging to that world in the moon as there are with us.

13. That 'tis probable there may be inhabitants in this other world, but of what kind they are is uncertain.

6.18 KENELM DIGBY, *TWO TREATISES*

Digby was another of the group of philosophers and scientists who knew Wilkins and Boyle; he addressed this *Treatise* to his son, and attempted to use the Cartesian method to prove the existence of the soul. Text from: first edition, 1645, Book I, pp. 1–2; 9–11; 421–23; Book II, preface.

The first treatise, declaring the nature and operation of bodies

In delivering any science the clearest and smoothest method and most agreeable to nature is to begin with the consideration of those things that are most common and obvious and by the dissection of them to descend by orderly degrees and steps (as they lie in the way) unto the examination of the most particular and remote ones. Now in our present intended survey of bodies the first thing which occurreth to our sense in the perusal of it is its *quantity*, bulk or magnitude: and this seemeth by all mankind to be conceived so inseparable from a body as when a man would distinguish a corporeal substance from a spiritual one (which is accounted indivisible) he naturally pitcheth upon an apprehension of its having bulk, and being solid, tangible and apt to make impression upon our outward senses, according to that expression of Lucretius, who studying nature in a familiar and rational manner, telleth us *tangere enim et tangi niso corpus nulla potest res* [for nothing can touch or be touched except by the sense]. And therefore in our inquiry of bodies we will observe that plain method which nature teacheth us and will begin with examining *what quantity is*, as being the first and primary affection . . .

. . . I conceive it will not be amiss before we enter the explication of it, to consider how the mystery of discoursing and expressing our thoughts to one another by words (a prerogative belonging only to man) is ordered and governed among us: that so we may avoid those rocks which many and for the most part such as think they spin the finest threads, do suffer shipwrack against in their subtlest discourses. The most dangerous of all, which assuredly is when they confound the true and real nature of things, with the conceptions they frame of them in their own minds. By which fundamental miscarriage of their reasoning, they fall into great errors and absurdities: and whatsoever they build upon so ruinous a foundation, proveth but useless cobwebs or prodigious chimeras. It is true words serve to express things, but if you observe the matter well, you will perceive they do so only according to the pictures we make of them in our own thoughts, and not according as the things are in their proper natures . . .

Of quantity

Among those primary affections which occur in the perusal of a body, quantity (as I have observed in the precedent chapter) is one, and in a manner the first and the root of all the rest. Therefore (according to the caution we have been so prolix in giving, because it is of so main importance) if we aim at right under-standing the true nature of it, we must examine what apprehension all kinds of people (that is mankind in general) maketh of it. By which proceeding we do not make the ignorant multitude judge of that learning which groweth out of the consideration of quantity, but only of the natural notion which serveth learned men for a basis and foundation to build scientifical superstructures upon. For although sciences be the works and structures of the understanding governed and levelled by the wary and strict rules of most ingenuous artificers, yet the ground upon which they are raised are such plain notions of things as naturally and without any art do present themselves to every man's apprehension . . .

If then anyone be asked what quantity there is in such a thing, or how great it is, he will presently in his understanding compare it with some other thing (equally known by both parties) that may serve for a measure unto it: and then answer that it is as big, or twice as big, or not half so big, or the like: in fine, that it is bigger or lesser than another thing, or equal to it . . .

Wherefore when we consider that quantity is nothing else but the extension of a thing, and that this extension is expressed by a determinate number of lesser extensions of the same nature (which lesser ones are sooner and more easily apprehended than greater, because we are first acquainted and conversant with such; and our understanding graspeth, weigheth and discerneth such more steadily; and maketh an exacter judgement of them); and that such lesser ones are in the greater which they measure as parts in a whole; and that the whole, by comprehending those parts, is a mere capacity to be divided into them: we conclude, that quantity or bigness is nothing else but divisibility, and that a thing is big by having a capacity to be divided, or (which is the same) to have parts made of it.

* * *

The conclusion of the treatise

. . . I am persuaded that by this summary discourse (short indeed in regard of so large a scope, however my lame expressions may peradventure make it appear tedious) it appeareth evidently that none of nature's greatest secrets, whereof our senses give us notions in the effects, are so overshaded with an impenetrable veil, but that the diligent and wary hand of reason might unmask them and show them to us in their naked and genuine forms, and delight us with the contemplation of their native beauties: if we had as much care and constancy in the pursuit of them as we daily see men have in the heaping up of wealth, or in striving to satisfy their boundless ambitions, or in making their senses swim in the muddy lake of base and contemptible pleasures. For who shall thoroughly consider and weigh what we have hitherto said, will plainly see a continual and orderly progress from the simplest, highest and most common conception that we frame of a body in general, unto the furthest and most abstruse effects that in particular are to be found in any body whatsoever: I mean any that is merely corporeal, without mixture of a nobler nature; for hitherto we have not moved, nor so much as looked out of that orb: he shall find one continued thread, spun out from the beginning to the end. He will see that the various twisting of the two species of bodies: rare and dense, do make the yarn, of which all things and actions within the sphere of matter are woven . . .

. . . one of our chief endeavours hath been to show that those actions which seem to draw strongly into the order of bodies, the unknown nature of certain entities named *qualities*, either do or may proceed from the same causes which produce those known effects, that all sides agree do not stand in need of any such mystical philosophy. And this being the main hinge upon which hangeth and moveth the full and clear resolving of our main and great question, *of the immortality of the soul*; I assure myself the pains I have taken in this particular will not be deemed superfluous or tedious: and withal I hope I have employed them with so good success as henceforward we shall not be any more troubled with objections drawn from their hidden and incomprehensible nature.

* * *

This then was it that obliged me to go so far about and to show in common how all those effects which are so much admired in bodies, are, or may be made and continued by the sole order of quantitive parts and local motion: this hath forced us to anatomise nature and to begin our dissection with what first occurreth unto our sense from a body. In doing which, out of the first and most simple notions of bigness or quantity, we found out the prime division of bodies into rare and dense; then finding them to be the qualities of dividing and of being divided (that is of local motion) we gained knowledge of the common properties of gravity and levity; from the combination of these we retrieved the four first qualities and by them the elements. When we have agreed how elements were made, we examined how their action and composition raiseth those second qualities, which are seen in all mixed bodies and do make their divisions. Thence proceeding into the operations of life, we resolved they are composed and ordered merely by the varieties of the former: nay that sense and fantasy (the highest things we can discern out of man) have no other source but are subject to the laws of parts and of rarity and density; so that in the end we became assured of this important maxim: *that nothing whatsoever we know to be a body can be exempted from the declared laws and orderly motions of bodies*: unto which let us add two other positions, which fell also within our discovery: the first, *that it is constantly found in nature that none of the bodies we know do move themselves, but their motion must be founded in some thing without them*; the second, *that no body moveth another unless itself be also moved*: and it will follow evidently out of them (if they be of necessity and not prevaricable) that some other principle beyond bodies is required to be the root and first ground of motion in them.

6.19 WILLIAM HARVEY, *ANATOMICAL EXERCITATIONS*

Harvey here shows that the female hen egg provides form as well as matter to the generation of life: thus empirically disproving the old Aristotelian and Galenical view that the female was inessential to generation. Text from: 1653 edition, fos A4^v–a5^r; 162–3; 383–6.

All physicians, following Galen, teach that out of the seed of male and female mingled in coition, according to the predominant power of this or that, the child resembles either this, or that parent, and is also either male or female. And sometimes they pronounce the male's seed to be the efficient cause, and the female's the material; and sometimes again the clean contrary.

But Aristotle (nature's most diligent searcher) affirms that the male and female are the principles of generation, and that she contributes the matter and he the form; and that forthwith after coition, there is formed in the womb out of the menstruous blood the vital principle and first particle of the future foetus (namely, the heart in creatures that have blood).

But that these are false and rash assertions will soon appear and will like clouds instantly vanish (when the light of anatomical dissection breaks forth) nor will they require any elaborate confutation, when the reader instructed by his own eyes shall discover the contrary by ocular inspection; and shall also understand how unsafe and degenerate a thing it is to be tutored by other men's commentaries without making trial of the things themselves; especially since nature's book is so open and legible . . .

Since therefore in the generation of animals (as in all other things of which we covet to know anything) every inquisition is to be derived from its causes, and chiefly from the material and efficient, it seems fit to me, looking back on perfect animals (namely by what degrees they are begun and completed) to retreat as it were from the end to the beginning; that so at last when there is no place for further retreat we may be confident we have arrived at the principles themselves; and then it will appear out of what first matter, by what efficient, and what procession the plastic power hath its original; and then also what progress nature makes in this work. For both the first and remoter matter appears the clearer (being stripped naked, as it were) by negation; and whatsoever is first made in generation, that is, as it were, the material cause of that which succeedeth. So, for example, a man was first a boy (because from a boy he grew up to be a man); before he was a boy, he was an infant; and before an infant an embryo.

Now we must search further, what he was in his mother's womb, before he was his embryo or foetus whether three bubbles; or some rude and undigested lump; or a conception or coagulation of mixed seed; or whether anything else, according to the opinion of writers?

In the same manner, before a hen or cock came to perfection (and that is called a perfect animal, that can beget its like) there was a chicken, before that chicken, there is seen in the egg an embryo or foetus.

* * *

By those very arguments which contend to prove the male to be the principle of generation and the primary efficient; the energy or efficiency of the female seems to be confirmed and ratified: for that is to be counted the primary efficient in which the reason of the foetus and form of the production is most eminent, and whose apparent similitude is discovered in the foetus, and also which hath an existence itself before, and then generates. Since therefore the form, reason, and similitude of the foetus is no less (nay more) in the female than in the male, and she also is in being before, as a primary mover, we may well conclude that the female is as eminent an efficient of generation as the male.

And though Aristotle truly say that the conception or egg assumes no part of its body from the male, but only its form, species and soul, and that the female contributes only the body and quantity [*De. Gen. Anim.* 2.4]. Yet it doth no way appear to the contrary but that the female doth contribute in some sort both form, species and soul (and not the matter singly). As is evident in the hen, which produceth eggs without a male (as the trees bear their fruits, herbs and seed without any distinction of sexes at all). And Aristotle himself confesses that even a subventaneous egg hath a soul. The female therefore must be the efficient cause of the egg.

* * *

That an egg is the common original of all animals

Animals, saith Aristotle, have this in common together with plants, that some do

407

spring out of seed, and some of their own accord: for as plants do either arise from the seed of other plants, or else spring up of their own accord, having attained some principle fit for their production, and some of them do attract aliment to themselves out of the earth, and some again are bred in other plants; so some animals are generated by the cognation or affinity of their form; and some of their own accord, no seed at all proceeding which is of kin to them: whereof some are generated out of putrefied earth or plants (as several insects) others are begotten in animals themselves, and out of the excrements of their parts [*Histor. Animal.* 1.1]. But this is common to all those (whether they be generated of their own accord, or else in other animals, or out of the putrefaction of their parts or their excrements), namely: to arise out of some principle fit for that purpose, and by some efficient contained in that principle. So that all living creatures must of necessity have a principle out of which, and by which, they are begotten. Give me leave to call this principle, *primordium vegetale*, the vegetal principle; namely, some corporeal substance having life in it *in potentia*, or something subsisting of itself, which is apt to be transformed into a vegetative form by some internal principle acting in it: namely such a principle as the egg and the seed of plants is: such is the conception of viviparous animals and the worm of insects, as Aristotle calls it; the principles of divers animals being also diverse, according to the diversity of which principles, the manner of the generation of animals is diverse likewise; and yet they all consent and agree in this; that they spring from a vegetal principal out of a matter endowed with an efficient or productive virtue, but differ in that this principle doth either result casually or of its own accord, or else proceed from something preexistent (as the fruit thereof). . . . For every principle which is only alive in potentia we (with Fabricius) do conceive ought to be called an ovum, an egg; and as for that principle which Aristotle called vermis, a worm, we do not at all distinguish it *ab ovo*, from an egg, and that because it looks like one to the eye, and also because that indistinction seems consonant to reason. For that vegetal prinicple which is alive in potentia is also an animal in potentia . . .

And Aristotle himself calls the very same things worms in one place, and eggs in another. . . . And indeed, everybody may see that the first rudiments of spiders, silkworms, and other insects are to be no less ranked in the classis and scale of eggs, than the spawn or eggs of fishes, which have softer shells, or of fishes which have no shells at all, and almost of all sort of fishes whatsoever: which spawn of theirs is not actually an animate body, but yet animals are begotten out of them.

6.20 JOHN WEBSTER, *THE EXAMINATION OF ACADEMIES*

Webster included a Baconian account of how natural philosophy should be taught and learned in his reform of educational provision (see 4.12). Text from: first edition, 1654, pp. 104–10.

Of some helps in natural philosophy

Now I come to lay down some expedients for the reformation and promotion of physical knowledge . . .

1. It cannot be expected that Physical Science will arrive at any wished perfection unless the way and means, so judiciously laid down by our learned countryman the Lord Bacon, be observed and introduced into exact practice. And therefore I shall humbly desire and earnestly press that his way and method be embraced and set up for a rule and pattern, that no Axioms may be received but what are evidently proved and made good by diligent observation and luciferous experiments; that such may be recorded in a general history of natural things . . .

2. How unfit and unsuitable is it for people professing the Christian religion, to adhere unto that philosophy which is altogether built upon Ethical principles, and indeed contrary and destructive to their tenets? So that I shall offer as a most fit expedient that some physical learning might be introduced into the Schools, that is grounded upon sensible, rational, experimental and Scripture principles . . .

3. That the philosophy of Plato, revived and methodised by Francisco Patritius, Marsilius Ficinus, and others; that of Democritus, cleared and in some measure demonstrated; by Renatio Descartes, Regius, Phoclydos, Holwarda, and some others; that of Epicurus, illustrated by Petrus Gassendus; that of Phliolaus, Empedocles and Parmenides, resuscitated by Telesius, Campanella and some besides; and that excellent Magnetical Philosophy found out by Doctor Gilbert, that of Hermes, revived by the Paracelsian school, may be brought into examination and practice, that whatsoever in any of them, or others of what sort soever, may be found agreeable to truth and demonstration, may be embraced and received; for there are none of them but have excellent and profitable things and few of them but may justly be equalised with Aristotle and the Scholastic learning; nay, I am confident upon due and serious perusal and trial, would be found far to excel them.

4. That youth may not be idly trained up in notions, speculations and verbal disputes, but may learn to inure their hands to labour and put their fingers to the furnaces, that the mysteries discovered by pyrotechny and the wonders brought to light by chemistry, may be rendered familiar unto them; that so they may not grow proud with the brood of their own brains, but truly to be taught by manual operations and ocular experiment that so they may not be sayers, but doers, not idle speculators, but painful operators; that so they may not be sophisters and philosophers, but sophists indeed, true, natural magicians, that walk not in the external circumference, but in the centre of nature's hidden secrets, which can never come to pass unless they have laboratories as well as libraries, and work in the fire, better than build castles in the air.

5. That the Galenical way of the medicinal art of Physic (a path that hath been long enough trodden to yield so little fruit) may not be the prison that all men must be enchained in, and ignorance cheating and impostorage maintained

by laws and charters, but that the more sure, clear and exquisite way of finding the true causes and certain cures of diseases, brought to light by those two most eminent and laborious persons, Paracelsus and Helmont, may be entertained, prosecuted and promoted; that it may no longer be disputable whether medicine (as it stands in the common road of use and form) be more helpful than hurtful, or kill more than it cures.

6.21 WILLIAM COLES, *ADAM IN EDEN*

Coles's scientific botany was classificatory and utilitarian, but shows little development from Gerard's *Herbal*, although it helped promote the contemporary interest in scientific gardening. Text from: first edition, 1657, Preface to the reader, fos a1ʳ; 19–20.

To the reader

To make thee truly sensible of that happiness which mankind lost by the fall of Adam is to render thee an exact *Botanic*, by the knowledge of so incomparable a science as the art of simpling[11] to reinstate thee into another Eden or a garden of paradise. For if we rightly consider the addresses of this divine contemplation of herbs and plants, with what alluring steps and paces the study of them directs us to an admiration of the supreme wisdom, we cannot but, even from these inferior things, arrive somewhat near unto a heavenly contentment: a contentment indeed next to that blessedness of fruition which is only in the other world. For all our pleasures here having but the fading aids of sense are beholding, or subjected to our human frailties, so that they must in respect of our expectations in some kind or other fall short. Nevertheless, most certain it is amongst all these transitory entertainments of our lives, there is none more suitable to the mind of man than this: for I dare boldly assert that if there be any one that is become so much an herbalist as to be delighted with the pleasant aspects of nature, so as to have walked a few turns in her solitary places, traced her alleys, viewed her several embroidered beds, recreated and feasted himself with her fragrances, the harmless delights of her fields and gardens: he it is that hath embraced one of the greatest terrestrial felicities. Hence it is that emperors, princes, heroes and persons of the most generous qualifications, have trod on their sceptres, slighted their thrones, cast away their purples, and laid aside all other exuberances of state, to court their mother earth in her own dressings: such beauties there are to be discerned in flowers; such curiosities of features to be found in plants. When God Almighty would have Adam to partake of a perfection of happiness, even then when he stood innocent, he could find none greater under the sun than to place him in a garden. Spenser, the prince of our English poets, seats all pleasures in the Garden of Adonis, as the more ancient did.

* * *

Of lavender

The name

I doubt very much whether this plant were at all known unto the Grecians, because I cannot find it in Dioscorides, or any ancient or modern Greek author to be so much as mentioned, though I have sought diligently for it. It is called in Latin *Lavandula* and *Lavendula*, and of some *Lavandea, quia lavacris experitur*, because it is used in baths and in washing of the hands, for the sweetness of the smell. The ordinary great lavender is called by Matthiolus, *Nardus Italica* and *Pseduonardus*; Tragus calleth it *spica* and *nardus germanica*; but most authors call the greater *lavendula maior et mas*, as they do the lesser, *minor et femina*. It is by some called *spikenard* . . . and by others the female of this here is called lavender, and spike the male.

The kinds

There are two sorts of lavender, as I said before, that is a greater and a lesser. Of the lesser there be three sorts: 1. small lavender or spike, with purplish blue flowers; 2. small white lavender or spike, with a white flower; 3. jagged lavender.

The form

Ordinary garden lavender hath a hard woody stem, parted into many small branches, whereon are set whitish long and narrow leaves, by couples one against another, from among which rise up naked square stalks with two leaves at a joint; and at the tops divers small husks standing round about them, formed in long round heads or spikes, with blueish gaping flowers, springing out of each of them; the root is woody and spreadeth in the ground; the whole plant is of a strong sweet smell, but especially the heads of flowers, which are much used to be put into linen and apparel, as also into nosegays or posies, because they are very pleasing and delightful to the brain, which is much refreshed with its sweetness, as on the contrary side it is very much offended with evil smells. I know not whether it would bear seed or no, it being so usually gathered by our country-women for the purposes aforesaid, before it come to maturity; and therefore it must necessarily be propagated by slips, as rosemary and sage usually is.

The place and time

The first sort is found in the gardens of most women that pretend to good housewifery, who bind it up in bundles, and either carry it to the market to sell, or else reserve it for their own use; but it and the second and third sort grow naturally in many places of Spain and Narbonne in France, from whence they have been translated into the gardens of those which are curious of all rare herbs and plants. . . . In those hotter countries they flower in February or March, but here in England they flower not till the beginning of July or the end of June, at the soonest. It prospereth best in an open and sunny place, and if the earth be stony, it groweth better.

The temperature

Lavender is hot and dry, and that in the third degree, and is of a thin substance, consisting of many airy and spiritual parts. Therefore it is good to be given any way against the diseases of the head and especially those which have their original or beginning not of abundance of humours, but chiefly of one quality only.

The virtues

The distilled water of lavender being sunned for a time, is not only sweet of smell and therefore comfortable to the brain, but also is good for the palsy and all other infirmities of the head, proceeding of cold, if the temples, the hollowness under the ears, and the nape of the neck be washed therewith, as the Catalepsis, which is a disease that taketh away all motion from the body, the megrim and the falling sickness: yea two or three spoonfuls of the water being drunk, recovereth the speech being lost, and reviveth them that are in a swound, and so it doth if it be but applied to the temples or nostrils to be smelt unto; but it is not safe to use it when the body is full of humours mixed with blood, because of the hot and subtle spirits wherewith it is possessed. A decoction made with the flowers of lavender, horehound, fennel and asparagus roots and a little cinnamon is very profitably used to help the falling sickness, and the giddiness or turning of the brain. Wherefore not without cause the herb is reckoned of Scholus Salerni amongst those things that cure the palsy . . .

That is to say, sage, castory (that is the stones of the beast called a castor), lavender, primrose, watercress and tansy cure and heal members infected with the palsy. So that though the flowers be of most virtue, yet the herb itself is good for the uses aforesaid: as also for apoplexies, lethargies, cramps, convulsions and gripings of the body proceeding of cold. It helpeth also the stopping of the milk, heateth the belly, and sendeth down the terms,[12] and if the same be holden often in the mouth it helpeth the ulcers and pains of the teeth; and the same water is excellent good for blisters of the mouth if the mouth be washed therewith. It being often smelled unto doth comfort and clear the sight, and if a shirt be but wetted in the water wherein lavender hath been boiled, and after dried, no louse will breed or abide therein as long as it keepeth the smell. The lesser lavender is much commended in all the diseases of the mother,[13] as the strangling or suffocation, the dislocation or displacing, etc.: for women to be bathed therewith, as also to help forward their travail.[14] The chemical oil drawn from lavender, usually called oil of spike, is good for the palsy, falling sickness, gouts of the joints, and of the feet, both taken at the mouth and also anointed: but it must be used cautiously, some few drops being sufficient to be given with other things, either for inward or outward griefs.

6.22 THOMAS MOUFFET, *THE THEATRE OF INSECTS*

Written during the reign of Elizabeth I by Thomas Mouffet, a supporter of Paracelsus, and much read throughout Europe, this text was updated, edited and illustrated in the seventeenth century, as the study and classification of insects became popular, with the invention of the microscope. Text from: 1658 edition, Epistle dedicatory.

. . . Thy mind being abstracted from the sad vexations of human life; and what time thou hast to spare from divine meditations, penetrating into all nature and the secrets of things, thou dost expatiate into the pleasant green gardens of various natural philosophy. Behold here is a most exquisite garland for thee gathered out of the most secret orchard of our great parent, which will not only feed the eyes, but will lead the singular acuteness of thy wit, which thou aboundest with, into her most hidden places. Thou being an excellent anatomist, I beseech thee try if thou canst dissect insects: the great Stagyrite[15] being thy guide, who did not disdain to search into the parts of animals. Thou shalt find in the little body of bees a bottle which is the receptacle of honey sucked from flowers, and their legs loaded with bitumen which sticks fast to make wax. Also in the tail there is a horny sting full of revenging poison, that is ready to draw forth as soon as the bee please; but the King of the swarm is said to want one, for there naturally belongs to the supreme power, who can overthrow all when he will at his pleasure, and there ought to be an imbred gentleness, whence it is that kings by their proper attribute are called fathers and pastors of the people. In gnats you shall observe their sounding trumpet that will suck blood out of animals, and will draw out moisture through the joints of the most solid wood and wine vessels. How wilt thou be pleased to see the small proboscis of butterflies wreathed always into a spiral line, after they have drawn forth nutriment from flowers, their extended large wings painted by nature's artificial pencil, with paints cannot be imitated: to which the very rainbow is scarce comparable . . .

What a pleasant spectacle will this be when the artificial hands carefully and curiously guide the most sharp pen knife and very fine instrument by direction of the sight! To behold the pipe of the grasshoppers that live upon dew and the organs of the shrill sound they make that in the heat of the dog-days importunately beats upon the ears of travellers; which are so framed that their concave belly is made vaulted under the diaphragm, over which is extended a cover of a thin and dry membrane, like to a drum, which lets in the air by an oblique turning, which being beaten by the regular and successive motion of their wings and stomach, coming in at a straight passage, and presently dilated, beating against the rough cast walls of the hollow place and refracted, makes a sound. To see the horns of the great beetles that are like to stags' horns, and with sharpest points are able to make wounds and the muscles that move them and tie them on exceeding fast. The rhinoceros is of the kind of great beetles. The swelling purse which is the matter of the silk, and is wound back again into many turnings by silk-worms which are chief of all caterpillars, of divers forms and colours: in which after the time destinated for the concoction of their food, which is gathered chiefly from mulberry leaves, a tenacious glue or jelly is reserved, until such time as their ventricle swelling and nature affecting to attain her end, the worm by degrees belcheth forth her spittle, the thread whereof growing firm by the air (which is provided to make garments for great men) this little creature dispenseth through her very narrow claws, and spinning with the motion of her head and of half her body, with the combing of it by the help of her forefeet, she first disposeth it for the strengthening of her dew of yarn, and after that upon her own sepulchre, where she must receive her transmutation. How the spider thrusts out her excrements by her lower parts of her body, which is drawn forth into a web, of which she, poor creature, frames nets with great labour, which are necessary to sustain her life; and with her long legs that end in sharp claws, she knits them into knots, being continually obnoxious to repair her work. In the uppermost cases of the green locusts which feed upon hedges, there are two scales that are hard as horn, the mutual rubbing together whereof by the ministration of the air beaten with their softer wings, make a very sharp sound. The head of all of this kind is armed, their hinder legs are hard, dry, long, by the vehement thrusting whereof against some firm object, with the help of their most strong tendons, they will cast their body a great way, being equally balanced, and is heavy enough for the proportion of it, like an arrow coming forth of a bow; as it happens to fleas that leap with a huge force. But which is yet more, besides their pincers, which are as sharp as keen razors, where is a direct passage from their mouth to their tail: the pylorus is compassed about with toothed bars that answer one the other with a thorny gomphosis,[16] wherewith they destroy whole fields with devouring fore-teeth, like chisels, and grind them as it were in a mill, and very suddenly they void it forth again: their hunger never ceases until the vile creatures have consumed whole countries which God is angry with, divine revenge commanding them, and brings to nought that people who ridiculously threaten heaven with destruction. You shall see the sharp spears that arm the mouth of the spider's phalangia and by the small wounds they make a strange venom enters and penetrates into the centre of the body and sticks fast to the deepest marrow . . . You shall behold the internal fire of glow-worms fastened to their tails and the torches of the Indian Coccuia[17] that shines in the night, and overcomes Cimmerean darkness. And moreover, if you take lenticular optic glasses of crystal (for though you have lynx his eyes, these are necessary in searching after atoms) you will admire to see the dark red colour of the fleas that are cuirasiers[18] and their back stiff with bristles, their legs rough with hair, and between two fore-yards there stands a hollow trunk to torture men, which is a bitter plague to maids, and is the greatest enemy to human rest, especially when that men would sleep . . .

... If you be pleased to reason deeper concerning insects, you shall find what will exercise you in the monarchical government of bees, the democratical of ants and the economical providence of them both: of that in gathering and laying up wax and honey; of this in replenishing her granaries and biting asunder the grains of corn at that end where they spring forth, lest the provision which is gathered with hard labour and laid up for winter, by the force of an inbred heat in their workhouse underground (which is hot whilst the winter lasts) should corrupt, being spoiled by a sudden production and a plague arising, together with a famine overspreading, should destroy the whole nest. Nor can you lightly pass over the architecture in framing the cells in the combs of wax, mathematically to an exact hexagon, in the hollow places of a wasps' nest, in the various chambers of the ant hill, and winding meanders, in the joining together whereof he saw granaries, chambers, hospitals, places of burial, besides the innumerable endowments of these indefatigable creatures, their functions and labours, and he could not admire or praise them sufficiently who had spent a long time in the contemplation of them, thinking it a work worth his pains, his whole life past being employed in this negligent and very idle business. Silk-worms, all caterpillars and spiders show their art in spinning, making snares for flies and pitching their nets to provide themselves victuals. The wood worms practise graving with the rasp of their mouths piercing into the timber; ants and bees amongst other insects will teach men piety toward old men, tired, sick men and their own children: oil beetles sacred to Apollo will teach them to love their offspring, who never cease for twenty-eight days to roll up and down a dung-pill (that is the receptacle of their seed) from east to west, following the sun's motion, until it be fit to hide in the ground for the production of their young, after the space of a lunar month, which nature hath assigned for the forming and excluding of this worm, which shall at length become a fly. Here take notice that the male hath a prolific seed without help of the female and can generate by itself putrefaction of fit matter interceding in a convenient matrix, though it be not animal. But (that which crowns all the meditations of a Christian man and carrieth him aloft) consider how the silk worm makes herself a tomb that is unpassable, by reason of her woven work that is most compacted within, in which the worm contracted into itself seems to die, and by a prodigious meta-morphosis it is born anew a butterfly, a more noble creature, which by the weaving of its wings flies up into the air toward heaven, whereas before its burial it lived a base creeping creature fastened to the earth and glued to the food of the ground.

6.23 ROBERT BOYLE, *THE SCEPTICAL CHEMIST*

Robert Boyle worked in Oxford both before and after the Protectorate on chemical, mechanical and physical experiments; he was a theoretical atomist, as well as an experimental chemist. He was instrumental in the founding of the Royal Society. Text from: first edition of 1661, pp. 37–8.

To proceed then with my propositions, I shall begin with this: *that it seems not absurd to conceive that at the first production of mixed bodies, the universal matter whereof they among other parts of the universe consisted was actually divided into little particles of several sizes and shapes variously moved.*

This . . . I suppose you will easily enough allow. For besides that which happens in the generation, corruption, nutrition and wasting of bodies, that which we discover partly by our microscopes of the extreme littleness of even the scarce sensible parts of concretes; and partly by the chemical resolutions of mixed bodies, and by divers other operations of spagyrical[19] fires upon them, seems sufficiently to manifest their consisting of parts very minute and of differing figures. And that there does also intervene a various local motion of such small bodies will scarce be denied; whether we choose to grant the origin of concretions assigned by Epicurus, or that related by Moses. For the first, as you well know, supposes not only all mixed bodies, but all others to be produced by the various and casual occursions of atoms, moving themselves to and fro by an internal principle in the immense, or rather infinite, vacuum. And as for the inspired historian,[20] he informing us that the great and wise author of things did not immediately create plants, beasts, birds etc., but produced them out of those portions of the preexistent, though created, matter (that he calls water and earth) allows us to conceive that the constituent particles whereof these new concretes were to consist were variously moved, in order to their being connected into the bodies they were, by their various coalitions and textures, to compose.

7

GENDER AND
SEXUALITY

INTRODUCTION

There are two main reasons for studying gender and sexuality in the early
modern era: first, it can tell us about one of the fundamental ways in which
people thought of and constructed their identity and themselves in any
period; and second, during this period most of the political theory, natural
philosophy, embryology, discovery and travel, even literary theory, began to
articulate theories through gender, either as metaphor or as a political
theory of hierarchy. Thus many earlier extracts, for example, James Stuart
(2.14), Gosson and Stubbes (5.7, 3.8), Charles I (2.20), Winstanley (2.23),
Hoby (3.3,5.2), Machievelli (2.10) and many others use gendered language
to describe both social distinctions and political effectiveness.

Reasons for this development have been much discussed in recent
years:[1] some historians see increasing misogyny as a displacement of anxieties about other social disruptions;[2] others have related it to a
development and even revival of a particular scientific mentality[3] in which
femininity represented nature and uncontrolled chaos, whilst masculinity
represented ordered reason; and some have linked it to the gradual development of a bourgeois economy and the ideology of the division of labour:
'separate spheres' placed men out at work in the marketplace, women at
home caring for home and children.[4]

Whatever the causes of the increased volume of material, both popular
and learned, about sexuality and gender and of the presence of a gendered
discourse in ostensibly unrelated discursive and intellectual fields, examination of these texts shows us that both sexuality and gender were key
markers of difference and of identity, and ones which were fought over as
part of a genuine ideological battle. The debate in James I's reign, for
example, about women's appropriate dress, was not simply a discussion

about fashion, but about appropriate gendered behaviour in society as a whole, as articulated and signified through dress (see 7.17). Joseph Hall's satiric poem about a young gallant in 1599 (7.15), is typically condemnatory of any man or woman cross-dressing or showing other visible signs of a fluid gender identity. The tracts on conduct (such as those by Dod and Cleaver, Brathwaite or du Bosc, 7.13, 7.21, 7.23) argued that women were only properly feminine when they conformed to theological and supposedly essentialist dictates. Writers such as Gosson and Stubbes (7.9 and 3.8) consequently could claim that men who adopted supposedly 'feminine' fashions were unmanly. It has been argued by many feminists that anxieties about appropriate gendered behaviour tend to occur when societies and economies are undergoing fundamental changes which threaten the status quo.[5] Thus it is possible to argue that the seventeenth century saw a hardening of ideas about gender into a much more conservative and essentialist view and version of what it was to be masculine and what it was to be feminine.[6] Continued reiteration of such views through sermons and conduct books suggests education in such ideas was a continuing battle (see, for example, 7.7, 7.8, 7.18, 7.19, 7.22).

There were two, perhaps contradictory, traditions of thinking about sexuality and gender during this period. The first was the combination of the teaching and ideology of the Christian Church and of the medical establishment; and the second was the developing theory of natural law, and the consequent educational philosophy associated with that. Western men and women's identity and consequent social role during the renaissance and early modern period were constrained by two very specific traditions and institutions: first, the Church and its theology; and second the medical establishment and its theories about male and female bodies. The way in which women were described by each of these discourses determined for middle-class and aristocratic women, in turn, their role in marriage, their relationship to all men, their roles in the work place, their access to education, their ability to speak in certain situations; and, in turn, the power of men in relation to women. Theology and physiology both portended to give true accounts about women based upon respective belief systems which structured all social belief and practice of the period, and which went for the most part unchallenged. These were first, that of Christian revelation of the truth of the universe through the text of the word of God, or The Bible; and second, that of 'scientific' and empirical truth which analysed anatomy and physiology supposedly objectively. Both these systems held that woman was 'objectively' and naturally inferior (see, for example, 7.8, 7.26, 7.28). Women and men who wished to challenge those beliefs could do so successfully only in one of two ways: either by reinterpreting either biblical or scientific evidence, or by demonstrating that what was claimed as 'natural' was in fact merely 'custom', or construction.

The Bible told men and women that women had caused the fall and were responsible for the entry of sin into the world through Eve; that they were hence subject to men because of their natural inferiority and because of their greater sinfulness (Genesis and St. Paul); that their role was confined to the home (Proverbs); and that they should be silent abroad, only asking questions of husbands and fathers (St. Paul). Man was the 'head', a symbolic image of the political hierarchy between men and women, but also of the physiological (man as rational head: woman as irrational body). Sermons, conduct books, poems, letters to daughters and wives continually reiterated these strictures about conduct to women and girls (see 7.5, 7.7, 7.18, 7.22). Church attendance and faith was nigh-on universal during the period, as we have seen in part 1, and in an age when belief in God and his word was virtually unquestioned, these strictures on identity and social role went for the most part unchallenged. Salvation for women would come through childbearing and in the next life: certainly not on earth (see Guillemeau and Gataker, 7.16, 7.18).

The one biblical exception to the unalloyed subordinate status accorded to women was the verse from Galatians: 'there is neither Jew nor Greek, there is neither bond nor free, there is neither male nor female: for ye are all one in Christ Jesus' (3.28). This phrase was used again and again by women practitioners and writers who wanted to defend their active involvement in religious and Church matters. Margaret Vivers based her argument in favour of women prophesiers on precisely this point (7.27). But in other hands (for example those of male preachers) it was often used to justify political and economic subordination on earth: your true reward would arrive in heaven. The work of Mary Cary (1.25), Anna Trapnel (1.26) and Katherine Chidley (7.25) in preaching and prophesying claimed that spiritual identity and its non-worldly imperatives, not gendered or social identity, justified the publication of their writings. Some writers (such as Castiglione, Guazzo and du Bosc, 7.6, 7.11, 7.23) permitted and encouraged courtly women to have a speaking role almost equal to their male counterparts in the intellectual and elite environment of the court.

Physiological explanations of how men and women were 'naturally' constructed were based on the ancient writings of Aristotle and Galen. Aristotle, for example, who was still widely cited in populist medical literature, described women as incomplete men. Galen (whose theory of the humours continued to influence medical accounts of how the body worked) argued that women were naturally hotter and moister, and hence more lustful, than men were. These views are discussed by Crooke (7.20), and still inform scientific writing in the 1650s (see 7.27). Despite anatomical discoveries during the sixteenth century, women were still often described as incomplete men; their womb as a 'seed bed' where men's powerful sperm constructed life. Women's identities were described as being determined by nature: men's as being above and beyond nature, or in control of nature. In this sense, then gender identity (that is how one's society created and sustained norms of behaviour relating to biological sex) was intimately connected to sexuality. By the 1650s, most anatomical writers were beginning to concur with Crooke (7.20) that both men and women were equally essential for procreation: but such 'knowledge' was still formulated in a discourse in which women were passive and men active.

One example of the gender bias in scientific investigation and accounts of sexuality may be seen in the fact that the function of the sperm in reproduction was first identified in the 1670s, and had been the focus of discussion and investigation for some decades. In contradistinction the existence and function of the ovum was not confirmed until 1827, despite Harvey's suggestions in his *Anatomical Exercitations* in 1657 that all life proceeded from an egg (see 6.19).

Physiology was used to justify women's confinement to the domestic sphere on the grounds of three issues: greater infirmity; the need to control their natural lusts; and because of supposedly lesser reason (see 7.7, 7.18, 7.22). It was also employed to justify different education systems (see 4.14); the double sexual standard (women's sexuality should be controlled, men's did not need to be, see 7.14, 7.3); and their exclusion from politics.

Turning to the second way in which challenges to the intellectual status quo could be made, that is that 'laws' were only customs or habits, resistance to and arguments against the conventional limitation of women's circumscription was very voluble from the mid seventeenth century onwards. It is important to see the period as one of debate about some of these issues, particularly as women and men gained education and literacy.

Thus, for example, the supposedly 'natural' law of woman's inferiority had been challenged by some of the political theorists who defended Elizabeth I's right to inherit the throne in 1558 (see 2.4). Some of the early religious martyrs, under Mary I, claimed spiritual equality on earth for men and women, by rereading and reinterpreting the Bible. During the Civil War, many women became preachers and visionaries of different sects (Cary, Trapnel and Chidley, for example); many travelled to America to preach, or to join religious communities which recognised equal public roles for men and women. Huge numbers of conduct manuals were published from the late sixteenth century onwards (mostly by men) advocating domestic duties, necessary submission to masculine authority, silence in public, and preaching chastity as the supreme virtue. But these conduct manuals, whilst advocating ideal gendered conduct, were premised on the fact that education and socialisation could and did affect behaviour: and this very premise provided the philosophical basis for many proto-feminist arguments by both men and women during the period, for example Tilney, Tattlewell and Tasso.

Masculinity, where it is discussed, is defined always in contradistinction to femininity: whether on matters of household duties, conduct, dress, social or political position (see 7.5, 7.12, 7.22.). Additional pictures of expected masculine behavioural norms can be found in some of the poems and ballads included here, which provide a fictional model of man-to-man conversations about how to bed, marry or flirt with women (for example, 7.3, 7.4, 7.14).

It is extremely difficult, if not impossible, to reconstruct an impression of sexual activity during the period, nevertheless, population studies, careful scrutiny of Church court records and parish records of births and marriages, as well as of medical advice books and diaries, has enabled some tentative conclusions to be reached. Thus, the work of Macfarlane and Houlbrooke[7] have shown that marriage happened quite late in life (at 28 for men, 26 for women), and that whilst illegitimate births remained relatively steady at about 4 per cent during this era,[8] it is estimated that about 20 per cent of brides were pregnant when they married in Church.[9] These figures show a pattern of premarital sex where the couple had agreed to marry: and given the relatively low illegitimacy rate, combined with the lack of contraception, suggest a surprisingly stable marital and sexual economy. Although contraceptive charms were sold and advertised, the only two effective contraceptives of the period were premature ejaculation and abortion. There is some evidence that both of these methods were practised:[10] indeed, Culpeper refers to both in his work *A Directory for Midwives* in 1651 (pp. 68ff; 113: but not included in this selection),[11] and midwives who were licensed by bishops in the mid seventeenth century had to swear not to dispose of foetuses 'in the jakes'. Non-heterosexual activity is rarely mentioned in the published literature, although references to catamites and sodomites does occur, and Jane Sharp's *The Midwive's Book* appears to refer obliquely to genital lesbian sex in 1671. But as recent gay and lesbian historians have pointed out, sodomy was used more as a term of political than sexual aberrancy, and referred to bestiality as much as to sex between men.[12] As with the public exhortations to women about appropriate behaviour, men and women who resisted through silence and in private go unrecorded by history.

7.1 ERASMUS, *IN LAUD AND PRAISE OF MATRIMONY*

Erasmus was a correspondent and friend of More and Vives, and a partici-pant in the debate about women's education and the humanist reform of morals. He wrote all his works in Latin, but they were widely available in England, in translation as well as the original. This epistle aims to persuade a young friend to marry. It was widely influential in reformation circles as a justification for priests to marry. Text from: first English translation, by Richard Tavernor, 1532 fos A4ᵛ–C2.

Now, Sir, if the other sacraments of Christ's Church be had in great veneration, who seeth not that much worship ought to be given to this, which was both ordained of God and first of all other? And the other in earth, this in paradise, the other for remedy, this for solace, the other were put to in help of nature which was fallen, only this was given to nature at the first creation. If we count the laws holy which be instituted of men, shall not the law of wedlock be most holy which we have received of him, of whom we have received life? And which began in manner even at one time with mankind? . . .

For nothing is so naturally given neither to men nor yet to any other kind of brute beasts, as that every one should preserve his kind from destruction and by propagation of posterity to make it as it were immortal, which without carnal copulation (as every man knoweth) cannot be brought to pass. And it seemeth a foul shame dumb beasts to obey these laws of nature, and men (after the manner of giants) to bid battle against nature, whose work, if we will behold with eyes not dazzling, we shall perceive that her will is that there be in every kind of things a certain spice of wedlock . . .

No man therefore have been counted a noble and worthy citizen, which hath not bestowed his diligence in begetting children and bringing them virtuously up. Among the Hebrews and Persians, he was most highly commended, that had most plenty of wives, as though the country were most bound to him, that with most children had enriched it. Do ye study to be more holy than was Abraham? . . . For if it have been well said of the old philosophers, if it have been not without cause confirmed of our divines, if it have been rightly everywhere pronounced as a proverb, that *God nor nature have made no thing frustrate or in vain*, why (I pray you) hath God given us these members? Why these pricks and provocations? Why hath he added the power of begetting, if bachelorship be taken for a praise? If one would give you a precious gift, as a bow, a garment, or a sword, ye should seem unworthy the thing ye have received, if either ye would not, or ye could not, use it. Whereas all other things be ordained by nature with most high reason, it is not likely that she slumbered and slept in making only this privy member. Nor I hear not him which will say unto me that the foul itching and pricks of carnal lust have come not of nature, but of sin. What is more unlike the truth? As though matrimony (whose office cannot be executed without these pricks) was not before sin. Moreover in other beasts I pray you from whence cometh those pricks and provocations? Of nature, or of sin? Wonder it is if not of nature! And as touching the foulness, surely we make that by our imagination to be foul, which of the self nature is fair and holy. Else, if we would weigh the thing, not by the opinion of the people, but by the very nature, how is it less foul (after the manner of wild beasts) to eat, to chew, to digest, to empty the belly, than to use the lawful and permitted pleasure of the body? But virtue (ye say) is to be obeyed rather than nature. As though that is to be called virtue which repugneth with nature, from whence if virtue hath not his first beginning, certes it cannot be it which may with exercise and learning be made perfect.

7.2 ROESSLIN, *THE BIRTH OF MANKIND*

Raynald's translation of Roesslin's texts was the first midwife's book published in English, and republished thirteen times before 1640. It was also distinguished by its illustrations, mostly from continental editions of Vesalius. It aimed at a popular audience, rather than a learned one, and hence was read by mothers and midwives. Text from: trans. Thomas Raynald, 1545, fos B2ʳff.

A prologue to the women readers

And think not the utility and profit of this first book, and knowledge thereof, to be little or of small value, but take it as the foundation and ground by the perseverance whereof your wits and understanding shall be illuminate and lightened, the better to understand how everything cometh to pass within your bodies in time of conception, bearing and of birth. And further, by the perfect knowledge of this book ye shall clearly perceive the reason of many diseases which happen peculiarly to women and the causes thereof, by which perseverance again ye shall have the readier understanding how to withstand and remedy the said infirmities or diseases. For note ye well that as there is no man, whatsoever he be, that shall become an absolute and perfect physician unless he have an absolute and perfect knowledge of all the inwards and outwards of man's and woman's body: even so shall ye never groundly understand the matters contained in the second book or any other communication or writing touching the same intent, except ye first have true and just cognisance in the first book. Again when that a woman cometh to a physician for counsel concerning something that may be amiss in the part, the answer of the physician and reasonable allegations of causes to the same infirmity is many times obscure, dark, and strange to be comprehended by the woman for lack of due knowledge of the situation, manner and fashion of the inwards. And truly when a person is sick or diseased in any part, it is half a comfort yea half his health, to understand in what part the disease is, and how that part lieth in his body. This knowledge also ministereth yet a further engine and policy to invent infinitely the better how the medicine should be applied and after the most profitable sort ministered and set to the diseased plot. To be short, all the wittiness and artificial crafty invention, and divers manners of ministrations in the noble science of physic proceedeth and springeth of the profound knowledge of anatomy.

* * *

Wherefore considering that there is nothing in this world so necessary, nor so good, holy or virtuous, but that it may by wickedness be abused, it shall be no great wonder though this little book, be made, written and set forth for a good purpose, yet by light and lewd persons be used contrary to godliness, honesty or the intent of the writer thereof. The abusion of this book (in my simple judgement) consisteth only in these two points: the one is, least that some wicked person should abuse such medicines as be here declared for a good purpose, to some devilish and lewd used. What I mean by the lewd use of them, they that have understanding right soon will perceive. The second point is least that this book happening into any light merchant's hands should minister matters unto such, to devise of these things at unset and unseemly times, to the derision or ashaming of such women as should be in presence. To these reasons can I make no better answer than hath been alleged before. Notwithstanding, yet I say that I trust, yea, and do not doubt, but that this book shall be so discreetly divided abroad that none of them shall fall in such persons' handling.

* * *

Yet another sort is there which would that neither honest nor unhonest men should see this book, for because (as they say) be a man never so honest, yet by reading here of things to them before unknown they shall conceive a certain loathsomeness and abhorring towards a woman. To these I answer that I know nothing in woman so privy nor so secret that they should need to care who knew of it, neither is there any part in woman more to be abhorred than in man. And if the knowledge of such things which commonly be called the woman's privities, should diminish the hearty love and estimation of a woman in the mind of man, then by this reason physicians' and surgeons' wives should greatly be abhorred and misbeloved of their husbands.

* * *

For truly as for my part considering the manifold daily and imminent dangers and perils the which all manner of women of what estate or degree so ever they be, in their labours do sustain and abide, yea many times with peril of their life (of the which there be so many examples needless here to be rehearsed), I thought it should be a very charitable and laudable deed and right thankfully to be accepted of all honourable and other honest matrons, if by my pains this little treatise were made to speak English. . . . So that to them which diligently will advert and give heed to the instructions of this little book, it may supply the room and place of a good midwife and advise them many times of sundry cases, chances, and remedies wherein peradventure right wise women and good midwives shall be full ignorant. And truly (as I have been credibly informed by divers persons worthy to be believed) there be sith the first setting forth of this book, right many honourable ladies and other worshipful gentlewomen, which have not disdained the oftener by the occasion of this book to frequent and haunt women in their labours, carrying with them this book in their hands and causing such part of it as doth chiefly concern the same purpose, to be read before the midwife and the rest of the women then being present, whereby oft times then all have been put in remembrance of that wherewith the labouring woman have been greatly comforted and alleviated of her throngs and travail.

7.3 *A DIALOGUE BETWEEN THE COMMON SECRETARY AND JEALOUSY, TOUCHING THE UNSTABLENESS OF HARLOTS*

This dialogue is a popular ballad form, extant in the 1550s, in which contemporary stereotypes about sexual and gendered behaviour of both men and women are delineated. Text from: Bodleian facsimile, passim.

Jealousy

What a world is this, I trow it be accurst
Fain would I marry, if that I durst
But I trow, sith the time that God was born,
So many honest men held of the horn.

Secretary

What is the matter, be ye in any doubt?
Pacify your mode let it all come out!
Discharge your stomach, avoid it forth
Sorrows in store be nothing worth.

Jealousy

Truth it is, I trust you will not be grieved
Though a small question to you be moved,
In a matter to me doubtful and diffuse,
Which I suppose ye have had in experience and use.

Secretary

What peradventure, but I will not promise you precisely,
To assail your question very wisely:
Now be it that ye say, I am of experience
So ye will be close, ye shall hear my sentence.

Jealousy

Then thus: she that hath a rolling eye,
And doth convey it well and wisely,
And thereto hath a wavering thought,
Trow you that this trull will not be bought?

Secretary

Yes, but take heed by the price ye have no loss:
A mad merchant that will give v. mark for a goose.
Beware a rolling eye, with wavering thought, mark that,
And for such stuff, pass not a dandyprat.[1]

Jealousy

She that is very wanton and nice,

425

Thinking herself marvellous wise,
And will come to him that doth her call:
Will she not wrestle for a fall?

Secretary

Yes surely, for a fall as flat as a cake,
And careth not how many falls she doth take.
There is no fall can make her lame:
For she will be sure of the best game.

Jealousy

She that doth make it all strange and quaint,
And looketh as she were a very saint
If a man in the dark doth her assay
Hath she any power to hold out nay, nay?

Secretary

Hold out yes: or it is pity she was born.
A horse, a wheelbarrow and a ram's horn:
(If the other things come, ye wot what I mean)
For all her holy looks she will convey it clean.[2]

Jealousy

She that doth love much dallying,
With divers men for fair speaking,
And thinketh not on her own shame:
Will not this wild fowl be made tame?

Secretary

Yes with good handling as I aim,
Even by and by ye shall her reclaim;
And make her tame as ever was turtle,
To suffer kissing and tickling under the kirtle.

Jealousy

She that is somewhat light of credence,
And to make her fresh, large of expense,
How say you, and her money do fail
Will she not lay to pledge her tail?

426

Secretary

Yes and if she be of that appetite,
She will both pledge and sell outright
Head piece, tail piece, and all four quarters,
To one or other, rather than fail to carters.

Jealousy

She that loveth to sit and muse,
And craftily can herself excuse,
When she is taken with a fault:
Will she not be won with a small assault?

Secretary

What needs assault? I dare say she will consent
That ye shall enter, by a reasonable pointiment.
And then take heed, for in keeping of this ward, and hold
Is more danger than in getting a thousand fold.

Jealousy

She that is of mind somewhat reckless,
Giving herself all to idleness,
And loveth to lie long in her bed:
Who waiteth a time, shall he not be sped?

Secretary

Time, nay, nay: wait if she be in good mood;
For out of the Church all times be good.
But pass not thereon though she say nay,
For so she will, when she hath best lust to play.

Jealousy

She that can no counsel keep,
And lightly will sob and weep,
Laugh again and wot not why:
Will she not be soon 'ticed to folly?

Secretary

The tears betoken a gracious courage,
And laughing doth all malice assuage.

When she is in that taking, mark well, mark:
Let slip, spare not for one course in her park.

Jealousy

She that is fair, lusty and young,
And can commune in terms with filed tongue;
And will abide whispering in the ear:
Think ye her tail is not light of the fear?

Secretary

By all these seemly touches methinketh surely
Her own tail she should occupy:
Sometime for need her honesty saved
She will wash often, or she be ones shaved.[3]

Jealousy

She that painteth her in staring apparel,
Use hot wines and daily fare well,
And loveth to sleep at afternoon tide:
Who list to strike, trow she will not stride?

Secretary

I cannot say if she will stride.
But if reason be offered, nothing shall fail beside:
For of truth, as frost engendereth hail,
Ease and rank feeding doth cause a lickerous[4] tail.

7.4 C. PYRRYE, *THE PRAISE AND DISPRAISE OF WOMEN*

This misogynist poem is typical of the attacks made on women in the
querelles des femmes debate, in which extreme views could be articulated
as part of a rhetorical exercise, in response to the question: what is
woman? Text from: 1551 edition (there is no date on title page; critical
opinion gives 1551 as date of poem), passim.

The Dispraise of Women

Examples plain and manifest,
  do teach it to be true:
For while all vice out of her breast,
  from time to time doth grow.

By reading histories thou shalt find,

what cruel bloody facts,
Committed were by womankind,
delighting in such acts.

Read Ovid, Virgil, understand
in them it doth appear,
How Medea with bloody hand
murdered her children dear.

How Paris stole the Grecian rape,
to Troy, and how that she
(Who was in deed of comely shape)
did willingly agree.

And how the Grecians sought the way,
to have her home again.
And thereby moved war to Troy,
which war ten years did reign.

How Scilla her father's house forsook,
what moved her to do so:
Her father's purple hair she took[5]
and gave it to his foe . . .

Also how Eve from joyful place,
(alas, alas the while)
Her posterity did deface,
and cast into exile.

Those and sundry more we find,
teaching us to beware:
In trusting of this monstrous kind,
whose mischief is not rare.

In time therefore take heed and learn,
this monster to eschew,
And eke with wisdom to discern,
her wicked witless hue.

7.5 VIVES, *THE OFFICE AND DUTY OF AN HUSBAND*

Vives, Spanish humanist and tutor to Mary I, wrote conduct and educational treatises for both men and women. He was interested in reforming both private and public ethical habits, as were other humanist writers such as Erasmus and More. Text from: trans. Thomas Paynell, London, 1553, fos A4ʳff; D8ᵛff; Q3ᵛff.

It seemed unto the auctor of nature when he laid the foundation of the ages and time that was to come, that all such beasts that were subject unto sickness and death, should at one generation and birth bring forth but few younglings to the end their generation might increase and endure for ever, and that they of a little beginning might multiply and arise unto an infinite multitude, and of mortal things obtain, as it were, an immortality. But all other beasts do indifferently (without any order or law) obey nature and give themselves unto procreation. And this is, as it were, an universal law, whereunto we do perceive and see, that all manner of beasts do willingly obey, although there be among these that live in society, and observe the holiness of matrimony so undefiledly, that they may well instruct and teach many thousands of men the chastity, charity the faith, the manner and the quality of matrimony, and in this number are swans, turtle-doves, crows and doves. But man being born to live in company, and in the communion of life, was bound by the auctor of nature with more exact and straighter laws of matrimony. Nor he would not that man untemperately should meddle with many women, nor that the woman should submit herself to many men. Therefore he bound them together in lawful marriage, and delivered her unto the man, not only for generation's sake, but also for the society and fellow-ship of life. And this is it, that Moses doth say in Genesis [Genesis 2.18] that the prudent and wise maker of the world said: It is not good that man should be alone, let us make him an help like unto himself. And how many utilities and profits do spring and issue of matrimony? First as all controversies and debates are removed and do cease among men when lands be occupied and possessed and by the power of the law granted and stablished: even so when the woman is lawfully married all such contentions do cease, which certainly would have grown among men, if women were common. For some would desire those that were beautiful and fair, and such as were most mighty and most in power, would judge all things to be as a reward of their fortitude and strength, in their power and dominion. And he that assayed her, would as though he had taken posses-sion, strongly resist and fight for her as for his own wife, whereupon should arise envy, hatred and debate. And man, the which (if he followeth his natural affec-tion and appetite) is a proud, a fierce and a desirous beast to be revenged, shall find many ways to accomplish his lust and to ensure and revenge, that he inter-preteth to be an injury, and shall associate and gather many unto him, either for fear, or by some benefit enticed, whereby partakings and factions should first arise, and afterwards war, and cruel battle, both at home and abroad, as old auctors do report to have chanced for women ravished, as for Helen Lacona, Tindaras's and Leda's daughter and for Lucretia and Virginia, Romans. And through Cava Julian's daughter we lost Spain. In England King Henry the second was driven out of his realm by his son for after that he had been long in love with Phillip's the French king's sister, and that she was sent into England and married unto him, his father being in love with his fair daughter in law, his son making war in Scotland, deflowered her. The young woman at the first coming home of her husband, opened unto him what had chanced and being moved therewith, drave out his father and occupied the kingdom. I let pass those things that Plutarch

430

doth write in his books of lovely narrations. Would God there were not so many examples as give occasions to every man to write, both of princes and private persons, how great contention and debate lechery hath caused. This was to many a man the way and occasion to overturn kingdoms and families, and of great and bitter perils and calamities among all nations. But God the inventor of matrimony and most provident father, having pity and compassion upon mankind, hath put a measure to this immoderate luxuriousness, printing the law of matrimony not in paper only, but in every man's heart. In the which matrimony he hath given to all nations (not only to those the which thorough humanity and good letters are instructed with rites and civil customs, but also to fierce and barbarous nations, being far from all good education and customs) so great benevolence and charity, that they which are married, induced through love, will not leave nor change their mates, and where there is no love, shamefastness doth take place, so that there is no man so far from the understanding of man, that is ignorant, that to be a thing most sclerate, and worthy to be hated and punished, to seek or to embrace any other, as long as matrimony endureth. And what a commodity the wife is unto the husband, in ordering of his house, and in governing of his family and household, and by this cities are edified, and builded. And she cometh, even as God sayeth into her husbands house as an helper like unto himself, and as a sure companion continuing unto the end of her life, a partaker of mirth and heaviness, the mother of their common children, the which keepeth his goods as her own, thinking none other goods to be hers but those, and keepeth them to leave them to her children, the which she loveth as herself. It cannot be spoken from how great a burden, and molestiousness the mind of man is lightened thereby, the which for the worthiness and dignity thereof, should not be molested with such inferior cures.

* * *

In the soul there is, as it were, two parts: the superior, wherein is judgement, counsel and reason, the which is called the mind. The inferior part is, in the which are the motions and perturbations, the which the Greeks call Pathi. The affections do grow of opinions, the which are more in one than in another after the disposition, the customs and usance of the body, age, health, manner, use of living, time, and place: the which do change and move the disposition of the body, and consequently do work in that part of the soul that is annexed unto the body, the which we call the inferior part, and therefore the affections, as the persuasions of things and opinions be, are common to all ages. But yet some of these are of more power in man, than in woman, and contrariwise in woman than in man. After that nature hath cast the see of man into the motherly and natural place, it incorporateth the same, and if it find sufficient heat, it bringeth forth a man child, if not a woman. So that when it wanteth that most excellent active and lively quality, the woman remaineth feeble and weak, not only in human generation, but also in all other proportion of her kind, and through such filthiness as increaseth in her (the which that feeble heat that is in her is not sufficient nor able to cast forth) she is less of stature, and more sickly than other be, and of this by and by (if she be not great bellied) she suffereth her menstruation: she is timorous also, for it is heat that encourageth the man, and maketh him bold and hardy, and through fear, she is covetous, and taught secretly by nature: she knoweth herself to be feeble, and needful of many things, and busy about many trifles, and like unto a ruinous house, that must be underset and upholden with many small props. And through fear she is full of suspicion, complaints, envious and troubled with many and diverse thoughts. And for lack of experience of things, of wisdom, and of knowing her own debility, she thinketh continually that she shall be despised, and therefore in this feeble and weak nature, anger and a desire to be revenged doth kindle as it were in flare continually. She loveth also to be gay and well apparelled, because she would not be condemned, and as impotent and subject to all casualties on every side: she doth seek whereunto she may lean and stay herself. And thou shalt easily perceive that certain of them do attribute unto glory things of no estimation, as to have some great man to her neighbour, or that some great and mighty prince did salute her, or call unto her. I will not speak of these things, the which unto many that would be seen to be most strongest are thought most precious, as of kindred, riches, beauty and friends. Of the self same fear doth superstition arise and grow, for as wisdom doth persuade and move a man to religion, so doth vain fear lead a man to superstition. Many women are full of words, partly thorough the variety of thought and affections, the which as they succeed one another, so they come unto their minds, and from thence unto the mouth: partly by suspicion and fear lest that by holding their peace they be not judged capable, or that through ignorance they known not what they say. All these foresaid things are of nature, and not of the women themselves, and therefore they are not only found in women, but also in such men as other of nature, or else by the first constitution and making of the body, the which cannot be changed, are women like, or become such through age, as children and aged persons, or by some other casualty, or chance, as they that are long diseased both in mind and body, nor yet all women have not these faults in like sort and manner, for there have been, and are yet not a few which are of a more strong and constant mind than many men be. And many such are spoken of among the gentiles, as Cleobulina, Hypparchia, Diotima, Lucretia, Cornelia graccorum, Portia, Chelia and Sulpitia. And among us there are innumerable martyrs, unto the which neither Athens the talker, nor Rome the conqueror may be compared. Nor Christ would not that even in our time we should be without an example the which should flow and descend unto our posterity, left and exhibited unto us by Catherine the Spaniard Queen of England, and wife unto King Henry the Eighth of most famous memory, of whom that may be more truly spoken of than that Valerius writeth of Lucrece, that there was in her feminine body a man's heart by the error and fault of nature . . .

But these things, the which are now known unto all men, shall be hereafter worthily and diligently declared. These things before rehearsed were spoken to this intent, to declare that as man cannot be changed, nor utterly delivered of his affections, so let no man hope to change a woman from her proper and native nature: make her better he may, but he shall never wholly annihilate her affections for as it is not in him to make of a woman no woman, so it is not in him to make of a man no man. And briefly to say, a man shall be continually a man, that is a feeble beast, impotent, mutable, subject unto infirmities and affections, inclining to evil, the which by learning may be amended, and impaired by evil customs. We must bear with these affections in women, as we bear with them in other our friends, except we do intend to avoid all company, and live solitariously in wilderness. And the affections of women ought more reasonably to be supported and born withal, than the affections of men, the which are fierce, and can hardly be tamed, or ruled, and thorough a false spice of liberty the which doth teach them, they refuse and disdainfully cast off the bridle. But as women are far more weaker than man, so they are far more meek and humble: therefore thou maist bring them under, and rule them other by manly power, or by sharpness of wit, by wisdom, or by the long use and experience of things.

* * *

Let not thy wife be over much eloquent, nor full of her short and quick arguments, nor have the knowledge of all histories, nor understand many things which are written, she pleaseth not me that giveth herself to poetry, and observing the art and manner of the old eloquence, doth study to speak facundiously. This holy and sincere institution shall increase thorough the good example of the husband, the which to inform and fashion the woman's life and his family withal, is of no less value and force than the example of a prince to inform the public manners and customs of a city, for every man is a king in his own house and therefore as it beseemeth a king to excel the common people in judgement and in example of life and in the execution and performance of the thing which he commandeth, so he that doth marry must cast off all childishness, and remember the saying of the poet, this age requireth another manner of life, and other manners, and so to take unto himself the counsel and mind of him that is aged to maintain the duty and office of an husband.

7.6 CASTIGLIONE, *THE COURTIER*

For an account of Castiglione's work see 3.3 and 4.2. Here Lord Julian explains how women courtiers should behave. Text from: trans. Thomas Hoby, 1561, fos Bb2ᵛ–4ʳ.

The Lord Julian proceeded: for a proof therefore (Madam) that your commandment may drive me to assay to do, yea, the thing I have no skill in, I shall speak of this excellent woman as I would have her. And when I have fashioned her after my mind, and can afterward get none other, I will take her as mine own after the example of Pygmalion. And whereas the Lord Gaspar hath said that *the very same rules that are given for the courtier, serve also for the woman*, I am of a contrary opinion. For albeit some qualities are common and necessary as well for the woman as the man, yet are there some other more meet for the woman than for the man, and some again meet for the man that she ought in no wise to meddle withal. The very same I say of the exercises of the body. But principally in her fashions, manners, words, gestures, and conversation (methink) the woman ought to be much unlike the man. For right as it is seemly for him to show a certain manliness full and steady, so doth it well in a woman to have a tenderness, soft and mild, with a kind of womanly sweetness in every gesture of hers, that in going, in standing, and speaking whatever she lusteth, may always make her appear a woman without any likeness of man. Adding therefore this principal to the rules that these lords have taught the courtier, I think well she may serve her turn with many of them, and be endowed with very good qualities, as Lord Gaspar saith. For many virtues of the mind I reckon be as necessary for a woman as for a man. Likewise, nobleness of birth, avoiding affectation or curiosity, to have a good grace of nature in all her doings, to be of good conditions, witty, foreseeing, not haughty, not envious, not ill tongued, not light, not contentious, not untowardly to have the knowledge to win and keep the good will of her lady, and of all others, to do well, and with a good grace, the exercises comely for a woman. Methink well beauty is more necessary in her than in the courtier, for (to say the truth) there is a great lack in the woman that wanteth beauty. She ought also to be more circumspect and to take better heed that she give no occasion to be ill-reported of, and so to behave herself that she be not only not spotted with any fault, but not so much as with suspicion, because a woman hath not so many ways to defend herself from slanderous reports as hath a man. But for so much as Count Lewis hath very particularly expressed the principal profession of the courtier, and willeth it to be in martial feats, methink also behoveful to utter (according to my judgement) what the gentlewoman of the palace ought to be: in which point when I have thoroughly satisfied, I shall think myself rid of the greatest part of my duty. Leaving therefore apart the virtues of the mind that ought to be common to her with the courtier, as, wisdom, nobleness of courage, steadiness, and many more; and likewise the conditions that are meet for all women, as, to be good and discreet, to have the understanding to order her husband's goods and her house and children when she is married and all those parts that belong to a good housewife: I say that for her that liveth in court, methink there belongeth unto her above all other things a certain sweetness in language that may delight, whereby she may gently entertain all kind of men with talk worthy the hearing, and honest and applied to the time and place and to the degree of the person she communeth withal, accompanying with sober and quiet manners and with the honesty that must always be a stay to all her deeds, a ready liveliness of wit, whereby she may declare herself far wide from all dullness, but with such a kind of goodness that she may be esteemed no less chaste, wise, and courteous, than pleasant, feat-conceited[6] and sober: and therefore must she keep a certain mean very hard, and (in a manner) derived of contrary matters, and come just to certain limits but not to pass them. This woman ought not therefore (to make herself good and honest) be so squeamish, and make wise to abhor both the company and the talk (though somewhat of the wantonest) if she be present, to get her thence by and by: for a man may lightly guess that she feigned to be so coy to hide that in herself, which she doubted others might come to the knowledge of: and such nice factions are always hateful. Neither ought she again (to show herself free and pleasant) speak words of dishonesty, nor use a certain familiarity without measure and bridle, and fashion to make men believe that of her that perhaps is not: but being present at such kind of talk, she ought to give the hearing with a little blushing and shamefastness. Likewise to eschew one vice that I have seen reign in many: namely to speak and willingly to give ear to such as report ill of other women.

7.7 *AN HOMILY OF THE STATE OF MATRIMONY*

For an account of the place of the *Homilies* of the Church of England, see 1.4 and 2.5. The *Homily on Matrimony* was read regularly during the Church year, as well as at weddings. Text from: 1562 edition, fos 255ᵛ–264ᵛ.

The word of Almighty God doth testify and declare whence the original beginning of matrimony cometh and why it is ordained. It is instituted of God to the intent that man and woman should live lawfully in a perpetual friendly fellowship, to bring forth fruit, and to avoid fornication. By which means a good conscience might be preserved on both parties, in bridling the corrupt inclinations of the flesh within the limits of honesty. For God hath straightly forbidden all whoredom and uncleanness and hath from time to time taken grievous punishments of this inordinate lust, as all stories and ages hath declared. Furthermore it is also ordained that the Church of God and his kingdom, might by this kind of life be conserved and enlarged, not only in that God giveth children by his blessing, but also in that they be brought up by the parents godly in the knowledge of God's word, that this the knowledge of God and true religion might be delivered by the succession from one to another, that, finally, many might enjoy that everlasting immortality. Wherefore, forasmuch as matrimony serveth as well to avoid sin and offence as to increase the kingdom of God, you, as all other which enter that state, must acknowledge this benefit of God, with pure and thankful minds, for that he hath so ruled your hearts, that ye follow not the example of the wicked world who set their delight in filthiness of sin, where both of you stand in the fear of God and abhor all filthiness. For that is surely the singular gift of God, where the common example of the world declareth how the devil hath their hearts bound and entangled in various snares, so that they in their wifeless state run into open abominations without any grudge of their conscience. Which sort of men that liveth so desperately and filthily, what damnation tarieth for them, Saint Paul describeth it to them saying: *neither whoremongers neither*

435

adulterers shall inherit the kingdom of God [1 Cor. 5]. This horrible judgement of God ye be escaped through his mercy, if so be that ye live inseparately, according to God's ordinance. And yet I would not have you careless without watching. For the devil will assay to attempt all things, to interrupt and hinder your hearts and godly purpose, if ye will give him any entry. For he will either labour to break this godly knot, once begun betwixt you, or else at the least he will labour to encumber it with divers griefs and displeasures.

And this is his principal craft, to work dissension of hearts of the one from the other: that whereas now there is pleasant and sweet love betwixt you he will in the stead thereof bring in most bitter and unpleasant discord. And surely that same adversary of ours doth, as it were from above, assault man's nature and condition. For this folly is ever from our tender age grown up with us: to have a desire to rule, to think highly by ourself, so that none thinketh it meet to give place to another. That wicked vice of stubborn will and self love is more meet to break and dissever the love of heart then to preserve concord. Wherefore married persons must apply their minds in most earnest wise to concord, and must crave continually of God the help of his Holy Spirit, so to rule their hearts and to knit their minds together that they be not dissevered by any division of discord. This necessity of prayer must be oft in the occupying and using of married persons, that oft time the one should pray for the other, lest hate and debate do arise betwixt them. And because few do consider this thing, but more few do perform it (I say to pray diligently) we see how wonderfully the devil deludeth and scorneth this state, how few matrimonies there be without chidings, brawlings, tauntings, repentings, bitter cursings and fightings. Which things whosoever doth commit, they do not consider that it is the instigation of the ghostly enemy, who taketh great delight therein: for else they would with all earnest endeavour, strive against these mischiefs, not only with prayer, but also with all possible diligence. Yea, they would not give place to the provocation of wrath, which stireth them either to such rough and sharp words or stripes, which is surely compassed by the devil, whose temptation, if it be followed must needs begin and weave the web of all miseries and sorrows.

* * *

Learn thou therefore, if thou desirest to be void of all these miseries, if thou desirest to live peaceably and comfortably in wedlock, how to make thy earnest prayer to God, that he would govern both your hearts by his Holy Spirit, to restrain the devil's power, whereby your concord may remain perpetually. But to this prayer must be joined a singular diligence whereof St. Peter giveth his precept saying: *you husbands deal with your wives according to knowledge, giving honour to the wife as unto the weaker vessel, and as unto them that are heirs also of the grace of life, that your prayers be not hindered* [1 Peter 3]. This precept doth particularly pertain to the husband. For he ought to be the leader and auctor of love, in cherishing and increasing concord, which then shall take place if he will use measurableness and not tyranny and if he yield some things to the woman. For the woman is a weak creature, not endued with like strength and constancy of mind, therefore they be the sooner disquieted, and they be the more prone to all weak affections and dispositions of mind, more than men be, and lighter they be, and more vain in their fantasies and opinions. These things must be considered of the man: that he be not too stiff, so that he ought to wink at some things, and must gently expound all things, and to forbear. Howbeit, the common sort of men doth judge, that such moderation should not become a man. For they say, that it is a token of womanish cowardness and therefore they think that it is a man's part to fume in anger, to fight with fist and staff. Howbeit, howsoever they imagine, undoubtedly St. Peter doth better judge what should be seeming to a man and what he should most reasonably perform. For he saith, reasoning should be used, and not fighting. Yea he saith more, that the woman ought to have a certain honour attributed to her, that is to say, she must be spared and born with, the rather for that she is the weaker vessel, of a frail heart, inconstant and, with a word, soon stirred to wrath. And therefore considering these her frailties, she is to be the rather spared. By this means, thou shalt not only nourish concord, but shalt have her heart in thy power and will. For honest natures will sooner be retained to do their duty, rather by gentle words then by stripes.

* * *

Thus all discommodities, as well worldly as ghostly, follow this froward testiness and cumbrous fierceness in manners, which be more meet for brute beasts than for reasonable creatures. Saint Peter doth not allow these things, but the devil desireth them gladly. Wherefore take the more heed. And yet a man may be a man, although he doth not use such extremity, yea though he should dissemble some things in his wife's manners. And this is the part of a Christian man, which both pleaseth God and serveth also in good use, to the comfort of their marriage state. Now as concerning the wife's duty. What shall become her? Shall she abuse the gentleness and humanity of her husband, and at her pleasure turn all things upside down? No, surely. For that is far repugnant against God's commandment. For thus does St. Peter preach to them: *ye wives be ye in subjection to obey your own husband*. To obey is another thing than to control or command, which yet they may do to their children and to their family. But as for their husbands, them must they obey, and cease from commanding and perform subjection. For this surely doth nourish concord very much, when the wife is ready at hand at her husband's commandment, when she will apply her self to his will, when she endeavoureth herself to seek his contentation and to do him pleasure, when she will eschew all things that might offend him. For thus will most truly be verified the saying of the poet: a good wife by obeying her husband shall bear the rule, so that he shall have a delight and a gladness, the sooner at all times to return home to her. But on the contrary part, when the wives be stubborn, froward and malapert, their husbands are compelled thereby to abhor and flee from their own houses, even as they should have battle with their enemies. Howbeit, it can scantly be, but that some offences shall sometime chance betwixt them, for no man doth live without fault, specially for that the woman is the more frail part. Therefore let them beware that they stand not in their faults and wilfulness: but rather let them acknowledge their follies, and say: *my husband, so it is, that by my anger I was compelled to do this or that, forgive it me, and hereafter I will take better heed.* Thus ought women the more readily to do, the more they be ready to offend. And they shall not do this only to avoid strife and debate: but rather in the respect of the commandment of God, as St. Paul expresseth it in this form of words: *let women be subject to their husbands, as to the Lord. For the husband is the head of the woman, as Christ is the head of the Church.* Here you understand that God hath commanded that ye should acknowledge the authority of the husband and refer to him the honour of obedience. And Saint Peter saith in that place before rehearsed that holy matrons did sometimes deck them selves, not with gold and silver, but in putting their whole hope in God, and in obeying their husbands as Sara obeyed Abraham, calling him Lord, whose daughters ye be (saith he) if ye follow her example [1 Peter 3]. This sentence is very meet for women to print in their remembrance. Truth it is, that they must specially feel the griefs and pains of their matrimony, in that they relinquish the liberty of their own rule, in the pain of their travailing, in the bringing up of their children: in which offices they be in great perils, and be grieved with great afflictions which they might be without if they lived out of matrimony. But Saint Peter saith that this is the chief ornament of holy matrons, in that they set their hope and trust in God, that is to say in that they refused not from marriage for the business thereof or the griefs and perils thereof: but committed all such adventures to God, in most sure trust of help, after that they have called on his aid. Oh, woman do thou the like and so shalt thou be most excellently beautified before God and all his angels and saints, and thou needest not to seek further for doing any better works. For obey thy husband, take regard of his requests and give heed unto him to perceive what he requireth of thee, and so shalt thou honour God, and live peaceably in thy house. And beyond this God shall follow thee with his benediction that all things shall well prosper both to thee and to thy husband. As the Psalm sayeth: *blessed is the man which feareth God, and walketh in his ways, thou shalt have the fruit of thine own hands, happy shalt thou be and well shall it go with thee. The wife shall be as a vine, plentifully spreading about thy house. Thy children shall be as the young springs of the olives about thy table. Lo thus shall that man be blessed* (saith David) *that feareth the Lord,* [Psalms 128]. This let the wife have ever in mind, the rather admonished thereto, by the apparel of her head, whereby is signified that she is under *covert* and obedience to her husband. And as that apparel is of nature so appointed to declare her subjection: so biddeth Saint Paul that all other of her raiment should express both shamefastness and sobriety. For if it be not lawful for the woman to have her head bare, but to bear thereon the sign of her power wheresoever she goeth: more is it required that she declare the thing that is meant thereby. And therefore the ancient women of the old world called their husbands Lords and showed them reverence in obeying them. But peradventure she will say, that those men loved their wives in deed. I know that well enough, and bear it well in mind. But when I do admonish you of your duties, then call not to consideration what their duties be. . . . For when I take in hand to admonish thy husband to love thee, and to cherish thee: yet will I not cease to set out the law that is appointed for the woman, as well as I would require of the man what is written for his law. Go thou therefore about such things as becometh thee only, and show thyself tractable to thy husband.

* * *

For if we be bound to hold out our left cheek for strangers which will smite us on the right cheek: how much more ought we to suffer an extreme and unkind husband? But yet I mean not that a man should beat his wife, God forbid that: for that is the greatest shame that can be, not so much to her that is beaten, as to him that doth the deed. But if by such fortune thou chancest upon such an husband, take it not too heavily, but suppose thou that thereby is laid no small reward hereafter, and in this lifetime no small commendation to thee, if thou canst be quiet. But yet to you that be men, thus I speak. Let there be none so grievous fault to compel you to beat your wives. . . . For if she be poor, upbraid her not; if she be simple, taunt her not, but be the more courteous. For she is thy body and made one flesh with thee. But thou, peradventure, wilt say that she is a wrathful woman, a drunkard, and beastly, without wit and reason. For this cause bewail her the more. Chafe not in anger, but pray to almighty God. Let her be admonished and holpen with good counsel, and do thou thy best endeavour that she may be delivered of all these affections. But if thou shouldst beat her, thou shalt increase her evil affections. For frowardness and sharpness is not amended with frowardness, but with softness and gentleness. Furthermore consider what reward thou shalt have at God's hand: for where thou mightest beat her, and yet for the respect of the fear of God thou wilt abstain and bear patiently her great offences, the rather in respect of that law which forbiddeth that a man should cast out his wife what fault soever she be cumbered with, thou shalt have a very great reward. And before the receipt of that reward, thou shalt feel many commodities: for by this means, she shall be made the more obedient, and thou, for her sake, shalt be made the more meek.

7.8 JOHN CALVIN, *A COMMENTARY UPON ST. PAUL'S EPISTLES TO THE CORINTHIANS*

Calvin's exegetical commentary and his sermons were widely used in churches. This extract is part of the commentary on 1 Corinthians 11.3–12; and 14.34–5. Numbers in the commentary refer to the verse numbers. Text from: translated Thomas Tymme, 1577, fos 128^{v}ff; 170^r–^{v}.

1 Corinthians 11.3–12

3. But I would have you know, that the head of every man is Christ; and the head of every woman is the man; and the head of Christ is God. 4. Every man praying or prophesying, having his head covered, dishonoureth his head. 5. But every woman that prayeth or prophesyeth with her head uncovered dishonoureth her head: for that is even all one as if she were shaven. 6. For if the woman be not covered, let her also be shorn: but if it be a shame for a woman to be shorn or shaven, let her be covered. 7. For a man indeed ought not to cover his head, forasmuch as he is the image and glory of God but the woman is the glory of the man. 8. For the man is not of the woman; but the woman of the man. 9. Neither was the man created for the woman; but the woman for the man. 10. For this cause ought the woman to have power on her head because of the angels. 11. Nevertheless, neither is the man without the woman, neither the woman without the man, in the Lord. 12. For as the woman is of the man, even so is the man also by the woman; but all things of God. 13. Judge in yourselves: is it comely that a woman pray unto God uncovered?

5. *Every woman that prayeth or prophesyeth.* This is the second proposition, how that the women ought to have their heads covered when they pray or prophesy, and that otherwise they do shame their head. For as the man by the profession of liberty honoureth his head, even so the woman by professing subjection, honoureth her husband. Wherefore on the contrary part the woman, if she uncover her head, casteth off her subjection, not without the contempt of the man. But this seemeth to be superfluous, that Paul forbiddeth the woman to pray with her head covered, seeing in another place he utterly restraineth women from speech in the congregation [1 Tim. 2.2]. Therefore it was not lawful for them to prophesy, no though their heads were covered. Whereupon it followeth that he reasoneth here in vain about the veil or covering . . .

7. . . . *And the woman is the glory of the man.* There is no doubt but that the woman is a notable ornament of the man. For it is a great honour that God hath appointed her to the man to be a companion and a helper of life, and hath made her subject to him, even as the body to the head: for that which Solomon speaketh concerning a careful and diligent wife, that she is a crown to her husband [Prov. 12.4], is true concerning the universal sex, if so be we respect the ordinance of God, which Paul commendeth here, teaching that the woman is therefore created that she may be the ornament of God.

8. *For the man is not of the woman.* He confirmeth with two arguments the preeminence which he had given to men over their wives. The first is that the woman taketh her original from the man, by order therefore she is the inferior or the latter. The second is that the woman is created for the man's sake: therefore she is subject unto him as the final work is to his cause. That the man is the beginning and the end of the woman it may appear out of the law: *it is not good for man that he be alone, let us make him an help [Genesis 2.17].* Again: *God took one of the ribs of Adam and made Eve . . .*

11. *Neither is the man without the woman.* This is added partly to restrain the men from triumphing over the women: and partly to comfort the women, lest they should take their subjection in evil part. Mankind, saith he, hath the preeminence over womankind for this cause: that they might be joined together between themselves with mutual benevolence, for the one cannot be without

other. But if they be separated they shall be as it were lame members of a torn body, therefore by this bond of mutual duty they agree together. When he saith in the Lord, he doth thereby calleth back the faithful to the Lord's institution seeing the wicked regard nothing but present necessity. For profane men if they might well spare and want their wives, would condemn the whole sex, not considering that they stand bound unto them by God's holy decree and ordinance. But the godly do know and acknowledge that the human sex is but one half part of mankind. They consider what this meaneth, *God made man, male and female created he them* [Genesis 5.2]. Thus willingly they acknowledge themselves betters to the weaker sex: and godly women in like manner consider of their dutiful obedience. Thus the man consisteth not without the woman, because otherwise he should be a head cut off from the body: neither doth the woman stand without the man, because then she would be a dead body. Therefore let the man show the duty of a head in governing her that is his wife: and let the woman show the duty of a body to her husband in helping him: and that not only in wedlock, but also when they are single persons. For I speak not here of the nuptial bed only, but also of those civil duties the which take place without matrimony. If any man like better to refer this to all mankind, I do not gainsay him: howbeit Paul, as he directeth his speech to everyone, so he seemeth to note specially the duty of every one.

12. *For as the woman is of the man.* If this be one of the causes why the rule is committed to the man, namely because the woman was taken out of him: so also this shall be the reason of friendly conjunction, because the man cannot defend and preserve himself without the woman. For this standeth always sure, *it is not good for man to be alone.* This saying of Paul may be referred to propagation, because men are not begotten of men alone, but also of women: but I comprehend this also, that a woman is a necessary help of the man because a solitary life is not expedient for man. This decree of God doth exhort us to embrace mutual fellowship. *But all is of God.* God is the beginning of both sex. Therefore they both ought with humility to embrace and hold the lot which the Lord hath appointed to them. Let the man moderately govern and not oppress his wife, which is given to him for a help. Let the woman be contented with subjection and let her not think scorn to be inferior to the more excellent sex. Otherwise they both shall cast off the yoke of God who hath appointed these degrees: and this is worse, that the man and the woman in forsaking their duty are rebellious against the ordinance of God, than if Paul had said that the one doth injury to the other.

1 Corinthians 14.34–5

34. Let your wives keep silence in the congregations: for it is not permitted unto them to speak; but let them be under obedience, as saith the law. 35. And if they will learn anything, let them ask their husbands at home: for it is a shame for women to speak in the congregation.

It appeareth that the Church of the Corinthians was polluted with this vice also: that women had leave to prate and babble in the holy assembly. Therefore he forbiddeth them to speak in public place, in the way of teaching or prophesying. But understand this of the ordinary function, or where the state of the Church is: for such necessity may happen as may require the voice of a woman: but Paul hath only respect to show what is most decent in a well ordered congregation.

34. *But let them be under obedience, as saith the law.* What maketh this subjection to the present purpose whereunto women are bound by the law? For some men may say they may be subject and yet not teach. I answer that the office of teaching is a jurisdiction or government in the Church, and therefore is contrary to subjection. For how unseemly a thing were it for the woman, which is subject to one member, to have jurisdiction over the whole body. . . . And truly in all places, where nature's honesty and good manner hath been kept, women in all ages have been excluded from public administration: and common sense teacheth that it is a very foul and unseemly thing for a woman to teach in a public place, because if she teacheth she hath government of all men, but it is meet that she be subject.

35. *If they will learn anything.* Least he might seem by his speech to cut off from women the liberty of learning, if they doubt of any matter he commandeth them to inquire privately, least publicly they move contention. When he saith *their husbands* he doth not forbid but that they may ask of the prophets if need require: for all husbands are not apt to give answer. But because he reasoneth here of external government he thinketh it sufficient to note what is uncomely, that the Corinthians may beware of the same. Nevertheless, it is the part of the discreet reader to weigh that the things whereof he treateth here are indifferent, in the which there is nothing unlawful but that which is contrary to comeliness and edification.

7.9 STEPHEN GOSSON, *THE SCHOOL OF ABUSE*

Gosson's attack on the theatre includes an assertion about ancient British manliness, perverted by contemporary excess. Text from: *The School of Abuse*, edited by E. Arber, English Reprints, 1868, pp. 38ff.

Bunducia,[7] a notable woman and Queen of England that time that Nero was emperor of Rome, having some of the Romans in garrison here against her, in an oration which she made to her subjects, seemed utterly to condemn their force and laugh at their folly. For she accounted them unworthy the name of men, or title of soldiers, because they were smoothly apparelled, soft lodged, daintily feasted, bathed in warm waters, rubbed with sweet ointments, strewed with fine powders, wine swillers, singers, dancers and players. God hath now blessed England with a Queen in virtue excellent, in power mighty, in glory renowned, in government politic, in possession rich, breaking her foes with the bent of her brow, ruling her subjects with shaking her hand, removing debate by diligent foresight, filling her chests with the fruits of peace, ministering justice by order of law, reforming abuses with great regard; and bearing her sword so even that neither the poor are trod underfoot, nor the rich suffered to look too high, nor Rome, nor France, nor tyrant nor Turk dare for their lives to enter the list. But we unworthy servants of so mild a mistress, unnatural children of so good a mother, unthankful subjects of so loving a prince, wound her royal heart with abusing her lenity, and stir Jupiter to anger to send us a stroke that shall devour us. How often hath her Majesty with the grave advice of her honourable counsel, set down the limits of apparel to every degree and how soon again hath the pride of our hearts overflown the channel? How many times hath access to the theatres been restrained, and how boldly again have we re-entered?. . .

I would read you a lecture of these abuses, but my school so increaseth that I cannot touch all, nor stand to amplify every point: one word of fencing, and so a conge to all kinds of plays. The knowledge in weapons may be gathered to be necessary in a commonwealth. . . . In Crete, Scythia, Persia, Thracia all the laws tended to the maintenance of martial discipline. Among the Scythians no man was permitted to drink of their festival cup which had not manfully killed an enemy in fight. I could wish it in England, that there were greater preferment for the valiant Spartans, than the sottish Helots; that our laws were directed to rewarding of those whose lives are the first that must be hazarded to maintain the liberty of the laws. The gentlemen of Carthage were not allowed to wear any more links in their chains than they had seen battles. If our gallants of England might carry no more links in their chains, nor rings on their fingers than they have fought fields, their necks should not be very often wreathed in gold, nor their hands emrodered with precious stones. If none but they might be suffered to drink out of plate that have in skirmish slain one of her Majesty's enemies, many thousands should bring earthen pots to the table. Let us learn by other men's harms to look to ourselves: when the Egyptians were most busy in their husbandry, the Scythians overran them; when the Assyrians were looking to their thrift, the Persians were in arms and overcame them; when the Trojans thought themselves safest, the Greeks were nearest; when Rome was asleep, the French men gave a sharp assault to the capitol.

7.10 EDMUND TILNEY, *THE FLOWER OF FRIENDSHIP*

In the form of a Castiglione-type dialogue, and dedicated to Queen Elizabeth, Tilney imagines a dialogue on marriage, including the humanists Vives and Erasmus at dinner. Text from: first edition, 1568, fos B5^r; D8^r; E2^{v}ff.

What then quoth Master Pedro, it is no part of my charge to dispraise women, but to speak the best of them, and to plant the Flower of Friendship between them and their husbands. Wherefore let love be rooted deeply in the man's heart towards the woman. Let her person be sought, not her substance, crave her virtues not her riches, then shall there be a joyful beginning, and a blessed continuance in amity, by which all things shall prosper, and come to happy end. Beware of hatred, be circumspect in love, which of them first taketh place, doth abide during life. And love grounded remaineth for ever, which being once gone, all other goodness followeth for company. Therefore to confirm this love, the married man must as much as he can, always abstain from brawling, lowering and grudging, especially when he is newly married. For if the wife first conceive hate, she will never receive love again. The husband then must be merry and pleasant with his wife, to make her the more in love with him at the beginning, so that if afterwards they chance to fall at square, it shall rise but of a sudden anger, which will be gone again as soon, and not of any old conceived malice. There be many men that boast much how they be served and feared . . . of their wives, but they marvellously deceive themselves. For much better were it, if they were better beloved and less feared. For whom the wife hateth, in fear she serveth, but whom she loveth, she gladly cherisheth. It is good reason that all women do labour to stand in the good grace of their husbands, but much more ought we men to foresee, that we fall not into the hatred of our wives. For if she once fasten her eyes on another, he shall enjoy her despite of her husband's beard. In this long and troublesome journey of matrimony, the wise man may not be contented only with his spouse's virginity, but by little and little must gently procure that he may also steal away her private will and appetite, so that of two bodies there may be made one only heart.

* * *

The office and duty of a married woman, for the preservation and continuance of this flower of friendship

There is another great maintainer of this *Flower*, and that is the goodly grace of obedience. For reason it is that we obey our husbands. God commandeth it and we are bound so to do. I know not, quoth the lady Isabella, what we are bound to do, but as meet is it, that the husband obey the wife, as the wife the husband, or at the least that there be no superiority between them, as the ancient philosophers have defended. For women have souls as well as men, they have wit as well as men, and more apt for procreation of children than men. What reason is it then that they should be bound, whom nature hath made free? Nay, among the Achaians, women had such sovereignty, their husbands obeyed. . . . Yea Plutarch saith, that the man swept the house, dressed the meat, and did all other necessaries, where the women governing the house and keeping the money, answered all matters and which worse was, they corrected them at their discretion. What did she, quoth master Gualter, and might she beat him too? Marry lo. Here is the matter, that some of our dames in this country take so much upon them. They think belike that they be in Achaia. But sure if I had been amongst those women: you would have done, quoth the Lady Isabella, as they did. For dogs bark boldly at their own master's door. Believe not daughter, quoth the Lady Julia, neither those ignorant philosophers, nor these fond customs. For contrary also to this, the Parthians, and Thracians accounted not of their wives, more than of slaves, so that after they had born them a dozen children, or more, they sold the mothers at the common markets or exchanged them for younger. Fie upon that law quothed the Lady Isabella. But what say you to the custom . . . of the Numidians and Lydians, where the women commandeth within doors and the men without? Yea marry quoth the Lady Aloisa, that was a just law, where the commanding was equal. Not so quoth the Lady Julia, for though it were better than the other two: yet not tolerable amongst us, neither was the sovereignty so equally divided, as you think. For if the woman keep always her house, as duty is, the man standeth ever at her commandment. For as long as she is within, though he command her without, the law bindeth her not to obey. Wherefore in my opinion all those barbarian customs are to be disannulled, and condemned of Christians. Ye say well madame, quoth M. Erasmus. For indeed both divine and human laws, in our religion, giveth the man absolute authority, over the woman in all places. And quoth the Lady Julia, as I said before, reason doth confirm the same, the man being as he is most apt for the sovereignty being in government, not only skill and experience to be required, but also capacity to comprehend, wisdom to understand, strength to execute, solicitude to prosecute, patience to suffer, means to sustain, and above all, great courage to accomplish, all which are commonly in a man, but in a woman very rare: then what blame deserve those men that do permit their wives to rule all, and suffer themselves to be commanded for company. A hard adventure, quoth Master Gualter, happeneth to that man which is matched with a maisterly shrew. For she being once past shame, not only blabbeth out all that she knoweth, but thundereth out that also, which her mad head conceiveth, or her fantastical brain dreameth of, and yet will she maintain that she is never angry, or speaketh without great cause. There be quoth the Lady Julia, some such women, but I do utterly condemn them. For this married woman whom I have taken upon me to describe, must of duty be unto her husband in all things obedient , and therefore if he, sometimes moved, do chance to chide her, she must forbear. In doing whereof he shall neither eat the more at his dinner, nor she have the less appetite to her supper. The wise woman must consider, that her husband chideth, either without reason, or hath good cause. If reason move him, then of duty she is bound to obey, if otherwise, 'tis her part to dissemble the matter. For in nothing can a wife show a greater wisdom, than in dissembling with an importunate husband. Her honesty, her good nature, and her praise is showed in nothing more than in tolerating of an indiscreet man, and to conclude as the woman ought not to command the man, but to be always obedient: so ought he not to suffer himself to be commanded of his wife . . .

The married woman must be also very careful and circumspect of her good name. For a good name is the flower of estimation, and the pearl of credit, which is so delicate a thing in a woman, that she must not only be good, but likewise must appear so. For you men are naturally so malicious, that you will judge as well of them you suspect, as of that which you see. The chiefest way for a woman to preserve and maintain this good fame, is to be resident in her own house. For an honest woman in soberness keeping well her house, gaineth thereby great reputation, and if she be evil, it driveth away many evil occasions, and stoppeth the mouths of the people. In keeping at home all things shall be better governed, her husband's heart better cheered, all evil suspicions dispelled, angers avoided, expenses diminished, and the great excess of apparel not required, wherein we are commonly so curious, that otherwise being naturally great savers, only therein are we as great wasters, which thing is avoided by the wife's honest keeping at home.

7.11 STEPHEN GUAZZO, *THE CIVIL CONVERSATION*

Guazzo's *Civil Conversation* sets out the proper role for a courtly woman, through dialogue. See 5.12 for an account of Guazzo's text. Text from: trans. George Pettie, 1586, fos 111ʳ–13.

Guazzo   If I remember the division which you made of the kinds of conversation, there remaineth no more for us to speak of, but the conversation with women.

Anniball   It was very meet this discourse should be reserved to the end, to refresh us, being weary with the long journey we have gone this day.

Guazzo   I doubt me that devising of this conversation instead of refreshment we shall feel greater travail and torment: or else I must say, that your taste differeth much from mine, for that I have always thought the conversation of women, not only vain and unprofitable, but dangerous and hurtful: and if you feel any spirit in you, repugnant to this my opinion, conjure it and drive it out of you by the virtue of three notable sentences: the first is that if the world could be maintained without women, we should live like God himself. The second that there is nothing in the world worse than a woman, be she never so good. The third that the naughtiness of a man is better than the goodness of a woman.

Anniball   These three sentences serve rather to keep in, than to cast out the spirit which is within me: and I see well you respect nothing but the outward bark. But if the sharpness of your understanding will pierce into the pith you shall find that those speeches have not been used in reproach of women, but in reproof of men's incontinency, and frailty. Who offend sooner in frequenting honest women, then naughty men? For that haunting the company of usurers, thieves, adulterers, slanderers and such like, of evil conversation, they will not suffer themselves so soon to be tempted and taken by their naughtiness, as in accompanying with women. For though they be never so chaste and honest, yet

446

men will be moved with a lascivious and disordinate desire towards them: which is verified by that which is said. Thou canst neither be more learned than David, neither more strong than Sampson, neither more wise than Solomon, who notwithstanding have fallen by means of women. Behold the very juice and true meaning of the sentences by you alleged, the which I will say once more, are more meet to keep in my spirit than cast him out. For if it be so that virtue consist in things difficult and uneasy, I think to do a virtuous act to conjure my senses to be quiet, and not to be moved anything with the presence and company of women: amongst whom I have gotten the habit to live in this my tranquillity of mind.

7.12 FRANCIS MERES, *GOD'S ARITHEMETIC*

Meres's work was an attempt to delineate the world in numerical terms: here he takes a detour to attack women's supposed faults in self-adornment. Text from: first edition, 1597, pp. 17ᵛ–18ᵛ.

I know of all points it pleaseth not to write against the pride of women, and if I tempered my pen to please, I would write none of this. But I must needs write, because I see that many who otherwise are good and virtuous, are overtaken here. Nay which of ye all is there (if ye will shrive yourselves) who is not longer in tricking up yourselves, than at your prayers; and what a shame is that among Christian women? Solomon was twenty years in building the temple and his own house: but he was but seven years in building the temple, and thirteen about his own house, and what a foul odds was that? Thirteen for himself, and but seven for God. But it is not so well with you, for if you divide the time of your attiring and your prayers into twenty parts, I think your attiring hath nineteen: with such trimming and setting, and smoothing and correcting, as if ye meant immediately to have your pictures taken, with such waiting, attendance, and solemnity, as if there were some solemn sacrifice to be performed, and so ye do, for ye make idols of your selves, and set up your image in a glass. Well, will ye have a glass to look in: look at Sarah, Abigail, and Rebecca, and in them ye shall see what is amiss in your selves, for what should I write of many other women more? Of Rachel, of Leah, of Ruth and Deborah, of Anna and Penninan, in them ye shall see how to behave yourselves toward God. In Rebecca ye shall see how to behave yourselves toward your children; in Sarah how toward your husbands; if they be good; in Abigail how, if they be bad. For love, wisdom, and obedience is the perfect beauty of a woman, and all other beauty is blackness, if ye be not fair within; which if ye be, then shall the King have pleasure in your beauty, and it shall appear that ye came out of paradise, and that ye be wives of God's making, and as in this life ye were joined with an earthly companion, so in the next ye shall be joined with Christ, the husband of the Church. Therefore love your husbands here, and if they reward it not, it shall be rewarded in heaven, be obedient unto them here, and ye shall be made equal with them in heaven: be humble and lowly here, and ye shall be exalted in heaven; be clothed with modesty here, and ye shall be clothed with honour in heaven; be patient here, and ye shall be crowned with glory in heaven; and as here for your bettering you did turn one into two, so there for your further bettering you shall turn two into one, and have unity and society with Christ for ever.

7.13 DOD AND CLEAVER, *A GODLY FORM OF HOUSEHOLD GOVERNMENT*

Both puritan clergymen wrote and preached extensively on marital conduct from the 1590s onwards. This book went through nine, extended, editions. It was first published in 1598. Text from: 1614 edition, fo. F7ʳ–F8; 04–P1.

But what need such as can live by their lands, to labour with their hands? What need had the woman that Solomon speaketh of? The conscience of doing good in the world should draw them to do that which no need driveth them unto. Remember that the virtuous woman *stretcheth out her hand to the poor and needy* (Prov. 21.20). She giveth not of her husband's, she giveth of her own: she found a way to do good without the hurt of her husband. St. Paul requireth that women should array themselves with good works [1 Tim. 2.10.], the comeliest ornament in the world, if women had spiritual eyes to discern it. Dorcas, in the Acts [9.36], teacheth wives how to get this array, for she made garments to cloth the naked and the poor. Thus might women find how to set themselves a work, though they could live of their own. But for such as have but a mean allowance, God thereby showeth that he will have them occupy themselves in some honest labour to keep them from idleness, and the evils that issue therefrom. They therefore must labour, if not to sell cloth as *Solomon*'s woman did, nor to clothe the poor as Dorcas did; yet to clothe her family, that they may not care for the cold. Let her avoid such occasions as may draw her from her calling. She must shake off sloth and love of ease. She must avoid gossiping further than the law of good neighbourhood doth require. St. Paul would have a woman a good *homekeeper*. The virtuous woman is never so well, as when she is in the middest of her affairs. She that much frequenteth meetings of gossips seldom cometh better home. Some count it a disgrace to come much abroad, lest they should be counted gossips, which name is become odious: but they must have tattlers come home to them to bring them news and to hold them in a tale, lest they should be thought to be idle without a cause. They perceive not how time runneth, nor how untowardly their business goeth forward while they sit idle. They know not that great tale bringers be as great carriers, and that such make their game of carrying and recarrying. The wise woman will be wary, whom she admitteth into her house to sit long there, knowing that their occupation is but to mark and carry. Towards her neighbours she is not sour, but courteous, not disdainful to the basest, but

448

affable with modesty; no scorner nor giber, but bearing with infirmities, and making the best of things; not ready to stomach them for every light matter, and so to look big, but passing by offences for unity's sake; not angry, but mild; not bold but bashful; not full of words, pouring out all in her mind and babbling of her household matters, that were more fitter to be concealed, but speaking upon good occasion, and that with discretion. Let her hear and see and say the best, and yet let her soon break off talk with such in whom she perceiveth no wisdom, nor favour of grace. Let her not be light to believe report nor ready to tell them again to fill the time with talk; for *silence* is far better then such unsavoury talk. Let her not be churlish, but helpful in all things to prevent breaches; or else to make them up again, if by the waywardness of others there be any made. Let her not be envious but glad of the good of others, nor fond of everything that she seeth her neighbour have, but wisely considering what is meet for her self and what her state will bear. Let her not be gawish[8] in apparel, but sober and modest: not nice nor coy, but handsome and housewifelike: no talker of other men's matters, nor given to speak ill of any for fear of the like measure.

* * *

What the duty of a wife is towards her husband

The duty is comprehended in these points; First that she reverence her husband. Secondly, that she submit herself and be obedient unto him. And lastly that she do not wear gorgeous apparel, beyond her degree and place, but that her attire be comely and sober, according to her calling. . . . The second point is that wives submit themselves and be obedient unto their own husbands, as to the Lord, because the husband is by God's ordinance the wife's head, that is her defender [Eph. 5.22; 1 Cor. 11; 14.4], teacher, and comforter: and therefore she oweth her subjection to him, like as the Church doth to Christ, and because the examples of Sarah, the mother of the faithful which obeyed Abraham [Gen. 18.12] and called him Lord, moveth them thereunto. This point is partly handled before in the first point, as also in the duty of the husband to the wife. As the Church should depend upon the wisdom, discretion and will of Christ and not follow what itself listeth: so must the wife also submit and apply herself to the discretion and will of her husband, even as the government and conduct of everything resteth in the head, not in the body. Moses writeth that the serpent was wise above all beasts in the field [Gen. 3.1], and that he did declare in assaulting the woman, that when he had seduced her, she might also seduce and deceive her husband. Saint Paul noting this among other the causes of the woman's subjection, doth sufficiently show that for the avoiding of the like inconveniences, it is God's will that she should be subject to her husband, so that she shall have no other discretion or will, but what may depend upon her head. The Lord also by Moses saith the same: *thy desire shall be subject to thy husband and he shall rule over thee*. This dominion over the wife's will doth manifestly appear in this, that God in old time ordained that if the woman had vowed anything unto God [Num. 30.7], it should notwithstanding rest in her husband to disavow it: so much is the wife's will subject to her husband. Yet it is not meant that the wife should not employ her knowledge and discretion which God hath given her in the help and for the good of her husband: but always as it must be with condition to submit herself unto him, acknowledging him to be her head, that finally they may agree in one, as the conjunction of marriage doth require . . .

Further there is a certain discretion and desire required of women to please the nature, inclinations and manners of their husbands, so long as the same import no wickedness. For as the looking-glass, howsoever fair and beautifully adorned, is nothing worth if it show that countenance sad which is pleasant; or the same pleasant that is sad: so the woman deserveth no commendation that (as it were) contrarying her husband when he is merry, showeth herself sad, or in sadness uttereth her mirth. For as men should obey the laws of their cities, so women the manners of their husbands. To some women a beck of her husband's is sufficient to declare that there is somewhat amiss that displeaseth him, and specially if she bear her husband any reverence. For an honest matron hath no need of any greater staff, but of one word, or sour countenance. Moreover a modest and chaste woman that loveth her husband, must also love her house, as remembering that the husband that loveth his wife, cannot so well like of the sight of any tapestry, as to see his wife in his house. For the woman that gaddeth from house to house to prate confoundeth her self, her husband and her family: Titus 2.5. But there are four reasons why the woman is to go abroad. First, to come to holy meetings according to the duty of godliness. The second, to visit such as stand in need, as the duty of love and charity doth require. The third for employment and provision in household affairs committed to her charge. And lastly, with her husband, when he shall require her, Gen. 20.1. The evil and unquiet life that some women have, and pass with their husbands, is not so much for that they commit with and in their persons, as it is for that they speak with their tongues. If the wife would keep silence when her husband beginneth to chide, he should not have so unquiet dinners, neither she the worse supper. Which surely is not so: for at the same time that the husband beginneth to utter his grief, the wife beginneth to scold and chafe: whereof doth follow that, now and then, most unnaturally, they come to handy-gripes,[9] more beast-like then Christian-like, which their so doing is both a great shame, and foul discredit to them both. The best means therefore that a wife can use to obtain, and maintain the love and good liking of her husband, is to be silent, obedient, peaceable, patient, studious to appease his choler if he be angry, painful and diligent in looking to her business, to be solitary and honest. The chief and special cause why most women do fail (in not performing this duty to their husbands) is because they be ignorant of the word of God, which teacheth the same.

7.14 TORQUATO TASSO AND HERCULE TASSO, *OF MARRIAGE AND WIVING*

This is a debate between the two brothers, in which each takes radically opposing views on marriage. It represents the conventional pro- and anti-marriage arguments found in the woman debate of the period. Text from: first edition, translated R. T., 1599, fos C3ᵛff; H2ᵛ; K3ʳff.

Hercule

But then by this argument a woman (that as Aristotle, prince of the peripatetics affirmeth) is so born, must needs be a creature, imperfect, corrupt and defiled. Let us not then bathe ourselves in such foul puddles.

After the same manner is woman born, through the defect of the virtue operative, or the working power of nature, as monsters are brought forth through defect, or through superabundance of matter, then is she born *per accidens*: but these accidental things are by the philosopher compared a little before unto the aforesaid things that have no being. And that this ens[10] may be changed from good to bad, and from bad to good, Aristotle teacheth Eudemius the same: and so by this rule *a woman* and *bad*, shall be (after a sort) synonymous, and by this means the one should import and be of as much force as the other. Every woman would willingly be a man, as every deformed wretch a goodly and fair creature; and every idiot and fool, learned and wise: but all natural instincts and motions move and bend from what is imperfect to what is perfect, and from what is lame and wanteth to what is full and overaboundeth. So then by this rule the same woman is convicted of imperfection and defect; she is loathed of the man that hath known her before carnally: whereas she on the contrary loveth the place where the fact was first done, as well as the man: this being a most manifest proof of a great loss unto him, and a sign of a kind of gain or dignity unto her. Then an unworthy and contemptible thing is a woman. She is the particular influence of the moon, as appeareth by the constitution and complexion of her body, conformable unto the same: and by the fullness and emptiness of both of them all at one time. But from the moon proceedeth nothing but bad qualities, as our natural philosophers well know: neither from a woman cometh anything that is good. They are as I should have told you before, of quality and complexion, cold and moist: the one appeareth by the softness of their flesh, and by the bigness and fullness of their breasts, strutting out like cow's udders: and the other is manifest through the thickness of their hair, and the smallness of their growth, and especially by the rawness of their blood which issueth oftentimes from them: and who are of such complexion (besides that for the most part it breedeth thick phlegm, drivelling spittle and smoking vapours coming from the stomach) are continually troubled with dropping distillations, with rheumatic catarrhs, with the solemn pain of the headache, with gouty swellings, with scurvy scabs, with loathsome pushes,[11] with mattery blains,[12] with filthy ructing[13] in the stomach, with the falling sickness, with the gnawing grief of the entrails, with the cruel colic, with the woeful iliack passion,[14] and such like sweet diseases, which as Aristotle in his ninth book *De Animalibus*, saith do force and infect the spirit to be sleepy and heavy; sluggish and slow; slothful and dull; unmindful and forgetful; simple and sottish; cold and chilly; unpleasing and unsavoury; fearful and timorous; astonished and amazed; malicious and envious; irksome and loathsome; carping and biting; fond and vain; curious and precise; insatiable and unsatisfied; jealous and suspicious; miserable and covetous; froward and petty; ignorant and assish; proud and insolent; bold and impudent; a great liar, and a smooth dissembler; she being not able to resist, but must needs alter the inclination and disposition of the body (according to the opinion of Plato, Xenocrates, Aristotle and of all philosophers) by reason of the sympathy and affinity that is betwixt her and the same.

* * *

Torquato Tasso

That it is good to take a wife, and that marriage is both honourable and necessary

If you shall please to think it worthy to place this my discourse as an attendance or follower of yours, you shall find that the one shall be no disparagement nor overthrow unto the other. But as in one and the self-same tree, those pears which are old are grafted with young and new pears, and as the apple by the apple, the fig by the fig, and the vine by the vine, receiveth and recovereth life again; so shall mine answer take life from yours, and in exchange, as it were, return back the same again unto you. And if my reasons shall in part seem contrary and repugnant unto yours, then shall it happen like unto those plants which are new grafted, upon which not alone is seen fruit of their own kind ... then (dear Hercules) let this friendly kind of grafting be in our contrary opinions, whilst most truly, though briefly I come unto the matter.

* * *

Oh, sweet conjoining of loyal hearts; oh, dulcet union of our souls together; oh, most lovely and nuptial knot; Oh, most chaste, pure and religious marriage yoke, who art rather a pleasing ease and a most welcome delight to support and bear, than any hard weight or grievous burden to sustain; rather a relieving comfort that upholdeth us everyway, than a troublesome labour that any way paineth us.

Thou first didst bring mankind to dwell in a house, enclosing him within a wall, causing him to build cities and towns to inhabit in, where before men lived like savage beasts in the woods and deserts, dispersed one from another.

Thou first didst alter dark caves into delightful chambers, and cold, snowy mountains into beautiful and goodly palaces and lodgings: thou madest that

452

lawful which (rightly) did please, and honest, that which everyone desired. Thou didst set just laws to human pleasures, and a laudable bridle to untamed head-long desires.

Through thee that came to be proper, which before was common; and that particular, which before was general; bringing that to be of account, which before was held of no esteem; by thee honour was conjoined unto delight, and pure chastity with perfect love; by thee came down from heaven loyal faith, and spotless modesty, and all other virtues; nay rather thou wert the first founder of the same, thy holy laws teaching men to take up defensible weapons in the honour of their wives, they learning by this means to become valiant. Thou taughtest others to assemble and gather together their friends, their kinfolks and subjects, filling the seas with sails and armed navies, and to fight many years in foreign coasts, or recover their wives whom they had lost. . . . Thou art the cause that fair ladies in their behaviours commit nothing worthy of reprehension. Thou art the root of godliness, whence springeth the branch of shamefastness, which is the only defence that nature hath given unto them to keep their reputation, to preserve their chastity, to maintain their honour, and to advance their praise.

To thee then is due all commendations proceeding from modest speeches. To thee is given the glory of every good work: and to thee is rendered all thanks for human felicity and happiness, for else our living without thee would be no other than woeful misery, heavy tribulation and grievous wretchedness, world without end: but thou turnest and convertest gall into honey, vinegar into wine, and loathsome bitterness into the sweetnesses of love, making us all happy by thy working. Sicknesses are less grievous unto us, adversity less noisome, health of body more precious and dear, and prosperity more pleasing and of better relish, only through thy operation and power. Thou dost lessen sorrows and increasest the delights of this life, making the troubles thereof seem less with thy mutual consolations and comforts, multiplying our pleasures with common and ordinary satisfactions and amends . . .

To conclude, thou art the cause that man, being as he is for the sovereignty of government fittest to rule, is endued with skill and experience to perform, with capacity to comprehend, with wisdom to understand, with strength to execute, with solicitude to prosecute, with patience to suffer, with means to sustain, and above all with a great courage to accomplish and bring to an end any enterprise: yet for all this, he is contented to be advised sometimes by his wife (though a weak woman) so dearly doth he love her, for in marriage love indifferent serveth not, nor love feigned prospereth not but right perfect love indeed knitteth loyal hearts in an indissoluble knot of amity, everlastingly to endure: and where such love is, there do the parties look for virtues and not for riches, and there as it is a joyful beginning amongst them, so is there as blessed a continuance and end, all things prospering with them, and sorting out happily, even unto their lives' end.

7.15 JOSEPH HALL, *VIRGIDEMIARUM*

Here Hall anatomises the contemporary gallant as having transgendered qualities. See 3.11 for an account of these satires. Text from: 1598 edition, Book IV, satire vi.

Satire vi

I wot not how the world's degenerate
That men or know, or like not their estate:
Out from the Gades up to the eastern morn,
Not one but holds his native state forlorn.
When comely striplings wish it were their chance
For *Canis'* distaff to exchange their lance:
And wear curled periwigs, and chalk their face.
And still are poring on their pocket glass,
'Tired with pin'd ruffles and fans and partlet strips,
And busks and verdingales about their hips;
And tread on corked stilts a prisoner's pace,
And make their napkin for their spitting place,
And gripe their waist with a narrow span,
Fond *Canis* that woudst wish to be a man;
Whose mannish housewives like their refuse state,
And make a drudge of their uxorious mate,
Who like a cot-queen freezeth at the rock,
Whiles his breech'd dame doth man the foreign stock.
Is't not a shame to see each homely groom
Sit perched in an idle chariot room,
That were not meet some panel to bestride,
Surcingled[15] to a galled hackney's side?
Each muckworm will be rich with lawless gain
Although he smother up mows of seven years' grain,
And hang'd himself when corn grows cheap again;
Although he buy whole harvests in the spring
And foist in false strikes to the measuring,
Although his shop be muffled in the light
Like a day dungeon, or Cimmerian night,
Nor full nor fasting can the carl take rest,
Whiles his george-nobles[16] lie rusten in his chest.
He sleeps but once and dreams of burglary,
And wakes and casts about his frighted eye,
And gropes for thieves in every darker shade,
And if a mouse but stir he calls for aid.
The sturdy ploughman doth the soldier see,
All scarfed with pied colours to the knee,
Whom Indian pillage hath made fortunate
And now he gins to loath his former state:

454

Now doth he inly scorn his kendal green,
And his patch'd cockers now despised been.
Nor list he now go whistling to the car,
But sells his team and settleth to the war.
O, war to them that never tried thee sweet;
When his dead mate falls grovelling at his feet,
And angry bullets whistlen in his ear
And his dim eyes see nought but death and drear:
O, happy ploughman, were thy weal well known;
O, happy all estates except his own.
Some drunken rhymer thinks his time well spent,
If he can live to see his name in print,
Who when he is once fleshed to the press,
And sees his handsel have such fair success.
Sung to the wheel, and sung unto the pail,
He sends forth thraves of ballads to the sale.
Nor then can rest: but volumes up bodg'd rhymes,
To have his name talk'd of in future times:
The brainsick youth that feeds his tickled ear
With sweet-sauc'd lies of some false traveller,
Which hath the Spanish *Decades*[17] read a while,
Or whetstone leafings of old Mandeville.
Now with discourses breaks his midnight sleep,
Of his adventures through the Indian deep,
Of all their massy heaps of golden mines,
Or of the antique tombs of Palestine;
Or of Damascus' magic wall of glass;
Of Solomon his sweating piles of brass,
Of the bird Rue that bears an elephant,
Of mermaids that the southern seas do haunt;
Of headless men; of savage cannibals;
The fashions of their lives and governals:
What monstrous cities there erected be,
Cairo, or the city of the Trinity,
Now are they dung-hill cocks that have not seen
The bordering Alps, or else the neighbour Rhein,
And now he plies the news-full grasshopper,
Of voyages and ventures to enquire.
His land mortgag'd; he sea-beat in the way
Wishes for home a thousand sithes a day;
And now he deems his home bred fare as lief
As his parch'd biscuit or his barrelled beef:
Mongst all these stirs of discontented strife,
O, let me lead an academic life:

To know much and to think we nothing know;
Nothing to have, yet think we have enough;
In skill to want, and wanting seek for more;
In weal nor want, nor wish for greater store;
Envy ye monarchs with your proud excess:
At our low sail, and our high happiness.

7.16 GUILLEMEAU, *CHILDBIRTH, OR THE HAPPY DELIVERY OF WOMEN*

The title page advertises its utilitarian purpose: 'wherein is set down the government of women in the time of their breeding child, of their travail, both natural and contrary to nature; and of their lying in. Together with the diseases which happen to women in those times, and the means to help them. To which is added a treatise of the diseases of infants, and young children, with the cure of them.' Text from: trans. London, 1612, preface.

The author's epistle introductory to the reader

Although that man be the most perfect and absolute of all other creatures nevertheless, so weak is he by nature, and so subject to infinite infirmities, that divine Hippocrates hath judged him to be even sickness itself from his very birth: he is not fit (saith he) to be employed in any business while he sucketh, because he wholly depends upon the help of another: afterward when he comes to more years, he grows stubborn, and unruly and wants a master to give him instruction: again when he is grown to the prime of his age, he becomes audacious and proud. At last in his declining time, he falls into misery, having nothing left him. but the remembrance of his labours ill bestowed.

Pliny noteth and experience shows it to be true that the ill scent only of a candle new put forth, is enough to destroy a child in the mother's womb, so that she may be forced to fall in travail, and be delivered before her time, unless her strength be the greater to resist the offence. And although the child stay the full time that nature hath prefixed him: yet commonly he is not able to get forth or come safely into the world (yea though the birth be natural) without the help not only of the other and himself: but also of the midwife and other women about her ready to receive and cherish him: and which is worst of all: if he be placed awry or else be weak and faint, or else if the midwife be at the farthest of her skill, then if they will save the child, and so consequently the mother from death, they must call a chirugeon to deliver her and bring the child into the world: which (that I may touch it by the way without taxing any) is commonly done too late either through the wilfulness of the kinsfolk, or obstinacy of the midwives.

But grant that the child comes into the world of itself, without the help either of chirugeon or midwife: yet (as it is commonly said) he draws his death after him: the which may be plainly perceived by the cries and laments which he

456

maketh as soon as he seeth the light, as if he craved for help and succour. For if he should continue in that case that he comes from his mother's womb, clogged with his bed or after-birth, without doubt this bed being putrefied, would infect the child, and at length kill it. Besides oftentimes if there were not help to make a free passage in the fundament, yard or other natural places, that are sometimes closed up there could neither sustenance be received, nor excrements expelled, which would cause the child to be stifled and choked up.

Many times also the head and other parts of the body (as the bones and the legs) happen to be ill-shapen, yea broken and out of joint, which would never come of themselves, into their proper and natural place. There, then, is it necessary that the chirugeon use his helpful and skilful hand: so that every man may plainly see the necessity and antiquity of his work: since that the first practice in chirgery that ever was done in the world was the Omphalotomia, or cutting of the navel, which Adam and Eve practised on their first child.

These therefore are the motives that have induced me to publish this discourse, and therein to treat of such diseases as happen to women with child.

And herein I have endeavoured to help them both in their natural and extraordinary travail: and to ease them in all such accidents as may happen unto them in their childbed, being the rather incited thereunto by reading the complaints of women related by Soranus . . .

O men, how ill do you bestow your time and pains! Alas we women die not, but are tormented even to death: for those that are accounted the most expert and skilful among you, take not that care of us which they should: you fill whole libraries with large volumes of every light and trivial disease of your own, making little or no mention at all of our cruel and insupportable torments.

I have purposed above fifteen years since to have written somewhat concerning this subject in my books of chirugery: but having more maturely considered thereof, I thought it fitter to write a treatise of it by itself: which it deserveth both for the difficulty of the subject, and for the variety of the matter which I was desirous to observe therein: and indeed this work excelleth all other, which are practised upon the body of man: whether ye respect the antiquity, necessity or dexterity thereof.

7.17 JOHN CHAMBERLAIN ON WOMEN'S DRESS

In 1620 James I asked the Bishop of London to preach against the contemporary fashion of masculine dress for women. Two pamphlets *Haec Vir* [the womanly man] and *Hic Mulier* [the manly woman], which capitalised on the debate, were published in the same year. Text from: *State Papers*, Dom. Jac. I, cxii, 36.

To Sir Dudley Carlton

My very good lord . . . the King went away to Tiballs on Tuesday without making any alteration, and on Monday goes to Roiston, and so on to Newmarket if the snow will give him leave, which hath fallen here every day or night since Monday, and no doubt is very deep in some places abroad. The prince went not with him by reason he was crazy upon some surfeit, but means to follow so soon as he is fully recovered. During the holy-days there was a flaw or some cross-speech at table twixt the Marquis Buckingham and Marquis Hamilton (wherein the Earl of Arundel had likewise his part) about an argument of selling of honours and abasing ancient nobility, by new advancements, wherein the Lord of Buckingham took himself to be aimed at, and so took exceptions, but the matter being misreported abroad and made worse than it was, the day before the King's going away, they both called together divers noblemen and gentlemen (among whom was Sir Horace Vere) and there complaining of the wrong done to their sincere amity and friendship, magnified one another and protested their unfeigned love and affection. Yesterday the bishop of London called together all his clergy about this town, and told him he had express commandment from the King to will them to inveigh vehemently and bitterly in their sermons against the insolency of our women, and their wearing of broad brimmed hats, pointed doublets, their hair cut short or shorn, and some of them stilettoes or poignards, and other such trinkets of like moment, adding withal that if pulpit admonitions will not reform them he would proceed by another course; the truth is the world is very far out of order, but whether this will mend it God knows. . . . So with the remembrance of my best service to my good lady I commend you to the protection of the Almighty. From London this 25th of January 1619.

February 12 1620

. . . Our pulpits ring continually of the insolence and impudence of women: and to help the matter forward the players have likewise taken them to task, and so too the ballads and ballad-singers, so that they can come no where but their ears tingle: and if all this will not serve, the King threatens to fall upon their husbands, parents or friends that have or should have power over them and make them pay for it.

7.18 THOMAS GATAKER, *TWO SERMONS*

Gataker's sermons are typical of others which prescribe fixed domestic roles for women, using theological justification. Text from: first edition, 1623, pp. 4–25; ii: 13–14, 39–40, 62–3.

i. A good wife's gift

But behold here a further evil than any of the former. An evil wife, a contentious woman (is) worse than any of them all. Husbands and wives are nearer than friends and brethren, or than parents and children. . . . The nearer the bond then, the greater the evil where it falleth out otherwise than it ought. *A foolish son* saith Solomon, *is the calamity of his father* [Proverbs 19.14]. And how is he his calamity? He is *filius pudefaciens* [Prov. 10.5, 7.2], such a one as shameth his parents and maketh them glad to hide their heads in the house. But an evil wife is *as the rain dropping* in through the tiles [Proverbs 19.13]: that maketh him weary of the house, that vexeth him so that it driveth him out of doors.

Yea *as a dropping on a rainy day* [Prov. 17.15], when it is foul without and it droppeth within. So that it maketh a man at his wits end, uncertain whether it would be better for him to be abroad in the rain, or to bide within doors in the dropping. And for this cause Augustine compareth *an evil conscience to a bad wife* (and it may seem that he pleased himself somewhat in the similitude, he maketh use so oft of it): which when a man hath many troubles and afflictions from without and would look home, hoping for some comfort from within, is much more troublesome to him than any of those his outward crosses are: is as a rock or a shelf to sea men in a storm, where they hoped to have found harbour and shelter against it [Prov. 19.13].

Yea further, not *as a dropping* only that driveth a man from his house and home, and that when it raineth: but as *a continual dropping* in such a day: so that a bad wife is worse than a quartane ague,[18] wherein a man hath two good days for one evil. He that hath an evil wife is as one that hath an evil soul; a guilty conscience that evermore sticketh by him, that every where accompanieth him; is a continual evil companion with him at bed and board, such as he cannot shift off or shun. And no marvel therefore if it be deemed the greatest temporal evil, because the most continual and the most inward, for a man to be matched with an evil wife, or a woman with an evil husband. For what is said of the one is as true of the other, the relation between them being alike . . .

Now this Solomon to show, as before he compared two great evils together, and found a bad wife to be the worse: so here he compareth two great benefits together [Psalm. 4.6], and affirmeth a good wife to be the greater.

House and possessions, wealth and riches, land and living is that that most men regard and look after: yea men are wont to seek wives for wealth. But saith Solomon *as a good name, so a good wife: a wise and a discreet woman is better than wealth,* her price is far above pearls: for house and possessions are the inheritance of the fathers, but *a prudent wife is of the Lord* [Proverbs 22.1; 31.10] . . .

So that two points then in Solomon's words here offer themselves unto us: the former: that *a good wife is God's gift* the latter: that *God's providence is more special in a wife than wealth.*

For the former: *a good wife is God's gift.* For *a prudent wife,* saith Solomon, *is of the Lord.* And *he that findeth a wife* (that is a *good wife* as, a name for a good name [Ecc. 7.1; Prov. 22.1; Genesis 11.4.]: as if *an evil wife were no wife,* deserved not the name of a wife) *hath found a good thing, and hath obtained a special favour from God.*

It was one of the first real and royal gifts that God with his own hand bestowed upon Adam. And it must needs be no small matter that God giveth with his own hand. The King's almoner may cast small silver about: but if the King give a man somewhat with his own hand out of his purse or pocket, it is expected it should be a piece of gold at least. The woman was God's own gift to Adam. And she was God's gift bestowed on him, to consummate and make up his happiness. Though he were at the first of himself happy, yet not so happy as he might be until he had one to partake with him in his happiness.

* * *

Yea hence let the wife learn what she is to strive to and labour for, that she may be indeed a good gift of God [1 Tim. 2.9, 10; 1 Pet. 3.4, 5]: not so much to deck and trick herself up to the eye, as to have her *inner man adorned* with holy skill and discretion, whereby to carry herself wisely and discreetly in that place and condition that God hath called her unto: that she may with *the wise woman* [Prov. 14.1] build up the house; and be *a crown* and a grace to him that hath her [Proverbs 12.4; 31.23]; that her husband and children may have cause to bless her, and to bless God for her and count it a blessed time when they came first together.

Let her consider what a fearful thing it is to be otherwise: for her that was made for a help [Gen. 2.18], to prove not an help but an hurt; for her that was given for a blessing, to prove a cross and a curse. As one saith of Eve, reft *from Adam as a rib, and shot by Satan at him as a shaft*, bestowed on him by God to consummate his felicity, but made by Satan's flight and her own default, the means of his extreme misery.

* * *

ii. A wife indeed

He that findeth a wife, findeth good; and obtaineth favour of God. [Prov. 18.22]

But how may a woman know then whether she be a wife or no?

I answer, read over the rules that St. Paul and St. Peter prescribe married women [Ephes. 22, 23; Coloss. 3.18; 1 Pet. 3.1–6], and examine thyself by them. Read over the description that Solomon's mother [Prov. 31.10.] maketh of a good wife, and compare thyself with it. There is set down a pattern and a precedent for thee. There is a looking glass for thee [Jam. 1. 23, 25; Psalm. 118], (as St. James speaketh of God's word in general) to see thyself in, and to show thee what thou art. And it were to be wished that as the philosopher[19] willed his followers *to view themselves oft in a glass*, that if they found themselves fair and comely they might be careful to have their carriage and courses correspondent, if otherwise they might strive by moral abilities to make amends for and recompense what were wanting that way: so that every married woman did, if not once a day, or once a week, yet once a month at least seriously look herself in this glass. Which it is to be feared that too many are therefore very loath to look into because they know how they shall find themselves there beforehand. . . .

And thus you see some few branches and rude lineaments of that goodness and beneficialness of this divine ordinance, which the spirit of God by the pen of Solomon here pointeth us unto. A good wife being, as you have heard:

> the best companion in wealth;
> the fittest and readiest assistant in work;
> the greatest comfort in crosses and griefs;
> the only warrantable and comfortable means of issue and posterity;
> a singular and sovereign remedy ordained by God against incontinency;
> and the greatest grace and honour, that can be, to him that have her.

In regard whereof even the very heathens themselves also, though led by the bare light of nature alone, yet have admired the excellency of this divine ordinance, and have worthily preferred it before all other external and temporal blessings whatsoever.

* * *

Now the consideration of these points may well serve partly for reprehension and partly also for admonition. For the former, it may first serve to reprove the practice of those that seek not at all, make no search or enquiry, but take wives as they stumble on them hand over head (as many do friends, whom a pint of wine drunk together, or a game of tennis, or a set at maw[20] maketh friends), as if they drew cuts or cast lots for them as some sometime have done. If thou wert to take a house, or hire but a servant . . . how careful wouldst thou be to make diligent enquiry of the commodities and discommodities, conveniences and inconveniences, easements and annoyances of the one who hath before dwelt in it, what neighbourhood about it, and the like: and of the qualities and conditions, vices or good parts of the other, whom he had formerly served, how behaved himself in their service, how likely to prove fit for thy service, and the like. And hast thou not much more cause to be careful, yea curious in thy enquiry concerning her, whom thou maist chance to make thy wife? That, so judgement, as it should do, may go before and lead affection and not follow and come after it. The rather since that thy house if upon trial thou mislike, thou maist leave: or thy servant if he please thee not, thou may put off again, up on a quarter, or half a year's warning at most. But thy wife there is no casting off again: she must all thy days abide by thee, all hers at least, like enough to last as long as thou livest [Matt. 19.5, 6; Rom. 7.2; 1 Cor. 7.10].

7.19 CORNELIUS LAPIDUS, *THE GREAT COMMENTARY OF CORNELIUS LAPIDUS*

Although Lapidus was a Catholic biblical commentator, his work was well known in England. His interpretation of the biblical injunctions about gender

was the contemporary convention, but he does insist on mutual dependency.
Text from: translated by W. F. Cobb, London, 1896, pp. 257–67.

1 Corinthians

Ver. 3 *But I would have you know that . . . the head of Christ is God. . . . Head* here has the meaning of lord, superior, or ruler. So God as being of a higher nature, is the head and ruler of Christ as man; while Christ as being of the same nature with the Church, is her head, and that, as St. Thomas says in four ways: (1) by reason of conformity of nature with other men, for Christ as man is the head of the Church; (2) by reason of the perfection of his graces; (3) by reason of his exaltation above every creature; (4) by reason of his power over all, and especially over the Church. So the man, St. Thomas says, is head of the woman in four ways: (1) He is more perfect than the woman, not only physically inasmuch as woman is but man with a difference, but also in regard to mental vigour, according to Eccles. 7.28: *one man among a thousand have I found; but a woman among all those have I not found.* (2) Man is naturally superior to woman, according to Eph. 5.22, 23: *wives submit yourselves to your own husbands, as unto the lord, for the husband is the head of the wife.* (3) The man has power to govern the woman, according to Gen. 3.16: *thy desire shall be to thy husband and he shall rule over thee.* (4) The man and woman enjoy conformity of nature, according to Gen. 2.18: *I will make him an help meet for him . . .*

Ver. 7 *But the woman is the glory of the man.* Woman was made of man to his glory, as his workmanship and image; therefore she is subject to him, and should be veiled in token of her subordination.

The woman, that is the wife, is the glory of the man, his glorious image because God formed Eve out of the man in his likeness so that the image might represent the man, as a copy the model. This image is seen in the mind and reason, inasmuch as the woman, like the man, is endowed with a rational soul, with intellect, will, memory, liberty, and is, equally with the man, capable of every degree of wisdom, grace and glory. The woman, therefore, is the image of the man, but only improperly: for the woman, as regards the rational soul, is man's equal, and both man and woman have been made in the image of God; but the woman was made from the man, and after him, and is inferior to him, and created like him merely. Hence the apostle does not say that *the woman is the image of the man,* but only *the woman is the glory of the man.* The reason is no doubt . . . that woman is a notable ornament of man as given to him for a means to propagate children and govern his family, and as the material over which he may exercise his jurisdiction and dominion. For man's dominion extends not only to inanimate things and brute animals, but also to rational beings, viz. to women and wives.

Vers. 8, 9. *For the man is not of the woman . . . but the woman for the man.* By two reasons he proves that the woman is the glory of man as her head. (1) That woman is of later date than man, produced from him, and consequently man is the source and principle from which woman sprang. (2) She was created to be a help to the man, the sharer of his life, and the mother of his children. As, then, man is the beginning from which, so he is the end for which, woman was made. Hence the woman is the glory of the man and not vice versa . . .

Ver. 11 *Nevertheless neither is the man without the woman, neither the woman without the man, in the Lord.* This is to be referred to ver. 9, not to the words immediately preceding, which by some Bibles are rightly put in a parenthesis. Having said in ver. 9 that the woman was created for the man the apostle, lest he might seem to have given to men an occasion for pride, to women of indignation, here softens the force of it by adding that in marriage neither can man be without woman nor woman without man. Each needs the other's help, and that *in the Lord*, that is by the will and disposition of the Lord.

7.20 HELKIAH CROOKE, *MICROCOSMOGRAPHIA*

For an account of Crooke's work see 6.12. Text from: second edition, 1631, pp. 270–6.

Of the difference of the sexes

Aristotle in his books of the history and generation of creatures doth often inculcate that the difference of sexes is most necessary unto perfect generation, which is also sufficiently proved by the final cause the most noble of all the rest, moving the other causes it self remaining immoveable. For as in the seed of a plant, the power of the whole tree is potentially included and contained, which notwithstanding never breaketh into act unless that act be stirred up by the heat of the earth, right so the seeds of the parents containing in them the idea or form of the singular parts of the body are never actuated, never exhibit their power and efficacy unless they be sown and, as it were, buried in the fruitful field or garden of nature, the womb of the woman.

It was therefore necessary that there should be a double creature, one which should beget in another, and another that should generate in itself: the first we call a male, the second a female. The male is originally the hotter and therefore the first principle of the work, and besides affordeth the greater part of the formative power or faculty. The female is the colder, and affordeth the place wherein the seed is conceived and the matter whereby the conception is nourished and sustained, which matter is made of the crude and raw remainders of her own aliment.[21] The place is the womb, which by a natural disposition looseneth the bonds wherein the spirit of the seed is fettered, and withal helpeth to add vigour and efficacy thereunto. For if the seed should be poured into any other part of the body it would not be as we use to say, conceived, but putrefied, not preserved but corrupted. The matter whereby the seed is nourished is the mother's blood. The excrement or surplusage rather the last aliment of the fleshy parts.

This difference of the sexes does not make an essential distinctions of the creature, the reasons are: first because (as Aristotle saith in his second book *De Generatione Animalium* and the fourth chapter and in his fourth book *De Historia Animalium* and the seventeenth chapter) in all creatures there is not this distinction or diversity of sexes. Secondly, because essential differences do make a distinction of kinds, now we know that the male and female are both one kind, and only differ in certain accidents. But what these accidental differences are is not agreed upon as yet.

The peripatetics think that nature ever intendeth the generation of a male, and that the female is procreated by accident out of a weaker seed which is not able to attain the perfection of the male. Wherefore Aristotle thinketh that the woman or female is nothing else but an error or abberation of nature, which he calleth by a metaphor taken from travellers which miss of their way, and yet at length attain their journey's end; yea he proceedeth further and saith that the female is a *by-work* or prevarication, yea the first monster in nature.

Galen in the sixth and seventh chapters of his fourteenth book *De Usu Partium* following Aristotle something too near, writeth that the formative power which is the seed of man being but one, doth always intend the generation of one, that is male; but if she err from her scope and cannot generate a male, then bringeth she forth the female which is the first and most simple imperfection of a male, which therefore he calleth a creature lame, occasional and accessory, as if she were not of the main, but made by the by.

Now herein he putteth the difference betwixt her and the male, that in males the parts of generation are without the body, in females they lie within because of the weakness of the heat which is not able to thrust them forth. And therefore he saith that the neck of the womb is nothing else but the virile member turned inward and the bottom of the womb nothing but the scrotum or cod inverted.

But this opinion of Galen and Aristotle we cannot approve. For we think that nature as well intendeth the generation of a female as of a male: and therefore it is unworthily said that she is an error or a monster in nature. For the perfection of all natural things is to be esteemed and measured by the end: now it was necessary that woman would be so formed or else nature must have missed of her scope because she intended a perfect generation, which without a woman cannot be accomplished.

Those things which Galen urgeth concerning the similitude of the parts of generation or their differing only in site and position, many men do esteem very absurd. Sure we are that they savour little of the truth of anatomy, as we have already proved in the book going before, wherein we have showeth how little likeness there is betwixt the neck of the womb and the yard, the bottom of it and the cod. Neither is the structure, figure, or magnitude of the testicles one and the same, nor the distribution and insertion of the spermatic vessels alike; wherefore we must not think that the female is an imperfect male differing only in the position of the genitals.

Neither yet must we think that the sexes do differ in essential form and perfection, but in the structure and temperature of the parts of generation.

The woman hath a womb ordained by nature as a field or seed-plot to receive and cherish the seed, the temper of her whole body is colder than that of a man because she was to suggest and minister matter for the nourishment of the infant. And this way Aristotle in the second chapter of his first book *De Generatione Animalium* seemeth to incline where he saith *that the male and female do differ as well in respect as in sense*: in respect because the manner of their generation is diverse: for the female generateth in herself, the male not in himself, but in the female: in sense, because the parts appear other and otherwise in the sexes. The parts of the female are the womb, and the rest which by a general name are called *matrices*, the parts of a man are the virile member and the testicles. And so much shall be sufficient to have been added concerning the difference of the sexes. But because there is more difference of the tempers in men and women, we will insist somewhat more upon the point.

* * *

That females are more wanton and petulant than males, we think happeneth because of the impotency of their minds: for the imaginations of lustful women are like the imaginations of brute beasts which have no repugnancy or contradiction of reason to restrain them. So brutish and beastly men are more lascivious, not because they are hotter than other men, but because they are brutish. Beasts do couple not to engender but to satisfy the sting of lust: wise men couple that they might not couple.

That women's testicles are hidden within their bodies is also an argument of the coldness of their temper, because they want heat to thrust them forth. Yet for all this we do not say that women do generate more than men, for they want the matter and the spirit. Indeed they have more blood, as we said even now, and that is by reason of their cold temperament which cannot discuss the reliques of the aliment: add hereto that the blood of women is colder and rawer than the blood of men. We conclude therefore that universally men are hotter than women, males than females, as well in regard of the natural temper as that which is acquired by diet and the course of life.

But now I had need here to apologise for my self in speaking so much of women's weakness: but they must attribute something to the heat of disputation, most to the current stream of our authors, least of all to me who will be as ready in another place to flourish forth their commendations as I am here to huddle over their natural imperfections.

7.21 RICHARD BRATHWAITE, *THE ENGLISH GENTLEMAN*

Brathwaite was a prolific advice-book writer and essayist. Here he outlines a man's duty within and to a family. Text from: first edition, 1630, pp. 154–5.

Vocation

If there be any that provideth not for his own, and namely for them of his household, he denieth the faith, and is worse than an infidel, saith the Apostle [1 Tim. 5.8]. Now how careful should we be to remove from us, so hateful a title as the name of infidel? Have we not our appellation from Christ? But in vain are we named after Christ if we do not follow Christ. We were not born to pass our time in an improvident or careless sensuality; we were not created only to cram ourselves and spend our days in security. *Man* (saith Job) *was born to labour, as the sparks to fly upward;* at least to provide for his own family, over which he is master, by relieving them outwardly with all necessaries and inwardly with all good and wholesome instructions. Now to propose you a form in what manner you are to demean yourself towards all degrees within your family, I shall little need, since the Apostle himself hath so notably laid down everyone's office or duty, where he showeth in what manner wives are to submit themselves unto their husbands; and again how husbands should love their wives, *even as Christ loved the Church, and gave himself for it* [Ephes. 6.10]. In the next ensuing chapter he declareth the duty of children in these words: *children obey your parents in the Lord, for this is right.* Then he descendeth to the duty of parents: and ye fathers, *provoke not your children to wrath, but bring them up in instruction and information of the Lord.* Then touching servants: *servants, be obedient unto them that are your masters, according to the flesh, with fear and trembling, in singleness of your hearts, as unto Christ.* Concluding the last duty with masters: *and ye masters do the same thing unto them, putting away threatening, and know that even your master also is in heaven, neither is there respect of person with him* . . . As every man's house is his castle, so is his family a private commonwealth, wherein if due government be not observed, nothing but confusion is to be expected. For the better prevention whereof, I have thought good to set down sundry cautions, as well for direction in affairs temporal as spiritual, which observed, it is not to be doubted but that God will give you all good success to your endeavours. First therefore, in affairs temporal I could wish you to observe this course: so to provide for the relief and supportance of your family, as you may not only have sufficient for yourselves, but also be helpful unto others; sufficient for yourselves in providing food and apparel, being all which Jacob desired of God; and helpful unto others in giving food and raiment to the fatherless, in providing relief for the desolate and comfortless, in harbouring the poor, needy and succourless, and briefly in ministering to the necessity of the saints, and all such as are of the family of faith.

7.22 WILLIAM GOUGE, *OF DOMESTICAL DUTIES*

Gouge was a popular London preacher, whose *Domestical Duties* were first published in 1622, and expanded in subsequent editions. It is an excellent guide to contemporary theological and social opinion about gendered roles. Text from: third edition, 1634, pp. 349–67.

Husbands' particular duties

Ephes. 5.25, etc. *Husbands, love your own wives even as Christ also loved the Church.* As the wife is to know her duty, so the husband much more, because he is to be a guide and good example to his wife; he is to dwell with her *according to knowledge* (1 Pet. 3.7). The more eminent his place is, the more knowledge he ought to have how to walk worthy thereof. Neglect of duty in him is more dishonourable unto God because by virtue of his place he is *the image and glory of God* [1 Cor. 11.7], and more pernicious not to his wife only, but also to the whole family, because of that power and authority he hath, which he may abuse to the maintenance of his wickedness, having in the house no superior power to restrain his fury; whereas the wife, though never so wicked, may by the power of her husband, be kept under and restrained from outrage . . .

Of that love which husbands owe their wives

This head of all the rest is expressly set down and alone mentioned in this and in many other places of Scripture, whereby it is evident that all other duties are comprised under it [Eph. 5.25, 28] . . .

Of an husband's hatred and want of love

Contrary hereunto is hatred of heart: which vice as it is very odious and detestable in itself, so much more when the wife is made the object thereof. As love provoketh an husband to do his wife what good he can; so hatred to do her what mischief he can. . . . Hence was it that a divorce was suffered to be made betwixt a man and his wife, in case he hated her [Deut. 24.3]: which law questionless was made for relief of the wife lest the hatred which her husband conceived against her should work her some mischief, if he were forced to keep her as his wife . . .

Of an husband's wise maintaining his authority

That these . . . are branches of an husband's love is evident by the place wherein God hath set him, which is a place of authority: for the best good that any can do, and so the best fruits of love which he can show forth to any, are such as are done in his own proper place, and by virtue thereof. If then an husband relinquish his authority, he disableth himself from doing that good and showing those fruits of love which otherwise he might. If he abuse his authority he turneth the edge and point of his sword amiss: instead of holding it over his wife for her protection, he turneth it into her bowels to her destruction, and so manifesteth thereby more hatred than love. . . . That an husband ought wisely to maintain his authority is implied under this apostolical precept, *husbands dwell with your wives according to knowledge*, that is, as such as are well able to maintain the honour

467

of that place wherein God hath set you: not as sots and fools without under-standing. The same is also implied under the titles of preeminence, which the Scripture attributeth to husbands, as *Lord, Master, head, guide, image and glory of God, etc.*

The honour and authority of God and of his son Christ Jesus is maintained in and by the honour and authority of an husband, as the King's authority is maintained by the authority of his Privy Council and other magistrates under him; yea, as an husband's authority is in the family maintained by the authority of his wife (*for as the man is the glory of God, so the woman is the glory of the man* [1 Cor. 11.7]).

The good of the wife herself is thus also much promoted, even as the good of the body is helped forward by the head's abiding in his place: should the head be put under any of the parts of the body, the body and all the parts thereof could not but receive much damage thereby; even so the wife and whole family would feel the damage of the husband's loss of his authority . . .

Of husbands' high account of wives

As authority must be well maintained, so must it be well managed. For which purpose two things are needful: 1. That an husband tenderly respect his wife. 2. That providently he care for her. An husband's tender respect of his wife is: inward, outward: inward in regard of his opinion of her, affection to her; outward in regard of his carriage towards her. For an husband's opinion of his wife, two things are to be weighed: her place, her person.

Her place is indeed a place of inferiority and subjection, yet the nearest to equality that may be: a place of common equity in many respects, wherein man and wife are, after a sort, even fellows and partners. Hence then it followeth that: *the husband must account his wife a yoke-fellow and companion* [1 Pet. 3.7] . . . . As a wife's acknowledgement of her husband's superiority is the groundwork of all her duties, so an husband's acknowledgement of that fellowship which is betwixt him and his wife, will make him carry himself much more amiably, familiarly, lovingly and every way as beseemeth a good husband towards her . . .

Of husbands' entire affection to their wives

An husband's affection to his wife must be answerable to his opinion of her: he ought therefore to delight in his wife entirely, that is, *so to delight in her as wholly and only delighting in her.* In this respect the prophet's wife is called the *desire* [Ezech. 24.16], or delight, or pleasure *of his eyes*: that wherein he most of all delighted, and therefore by a propriety so called . . .

Of husbands forbearing to exact all that they may

As a wife's reverence, so also her obedience must be answered with her husband's courtesy. In testimony whereof, *an husband must be ready to accept that wherein his wife showeth herself willing to obey him.* He ought to be sparing in exacting too much of her: in this case he ought so to frame his carriage towards her, as that obedience which she performeth may rather come from her own voluntary disposition, from a free conscience to God-wards, even because God hath placed her in a place of subjection, and from a wife-like love, than from any exaction on her husband's part, and as it were by force. . . .

Though the wife ought to go with her husband, and dwell where he thinks meet, yet ought not he (unless by virtue of some urgent calling he be forced thereto), remove her from place to place and carry her from that place where she is well settled, without her good liking . . .

Though she ought cheerfully to entertain what guests he bringeth into the house, yet ought not he to be grievous and burdensome therein unto her: the greatest care and pains for entertaining guests lieth on the wife; she ought therefore to be tendered therein.

If he observe her conscionable and wise, well able to manage and order matters about house, yet loath to do anything without his consent, he ought to be ready and free in yielding his consent, and satisfying her desire . . .

A general consent is especially required for ordering of household affairs, for it is a charge laid upon wives [1 Tim. 5.14]: *guide the house*; whereby it appeareth that the business of the house appertain and are most proper to the wife: in which respect she is called the *housewife*: so as therein husbands ought to refer matters to their ordering and not restrain them in every particular matter from doing anything without a special licence and direction. To exemplify this in some particulars, it appertaineth in peculiar to a wife: 1. to order the decking and trimming of the house [Pro. 31.21, 22]; 2. to dispose the ordinary provision for the family; 3. to rule and govern maidservants [Gen. 16.6]; 4. to bring up children while they are young, with the like [1 Tim. 5.10; Pet. 2.4]. These therefore ought he with a general consent to refer to her discretion, with limitation only of these two cautions: 1. That she have in some measure sufficient discretion, wit and wisdom and be not too ignorant, foolish, simple, lavish, etc. 2. That he have a general oversight in all, and so interpose his authority, as he suffer nothing that is unlawful or unseemly to be done by his wife about house, children, servants or other things. For: 1. The general charge of all lieth principally upon him. 2. He shall give an account unto God for all things that are amiss in his house. 3. The blame of all will also before men, lie upon him.

7.23 JACQUES DU BOSC, *THE COMPLETE WOMAN*

Jacques du Bosc was a French priest who published several works addressed at women, including this one. Its focus is unusually secular for the period, and aimed at gentry and courtly women. One edition was translated into English. Text from: English edition, translated 1639, Book I, pp. 17–8; 28–9; 51; 59–61; Book II, pp. 23–5; 43.

To say then, what seems to me at first most necessary, I should content myself to wish in women the three perfections which Socrates desired in his disciples: discretion, silence and modesty. These are so fair and necessary qualities in society that to judge the importance of them we need but only represent the vices opposite: imprudence, babble, and impudence. I would not have them think I purpose to take away the use of speech instead of ruling it. I should not do well to go about to frame a conversation of dumb persons, but to make a powerful war against vice, the most importunate and dangerous enemy in society. I only entreat those women who have not the inclination to speak little, to consider that if there be a time to speak something and also to say nothing, there is never any to speak all. That there is also danger to speak what is false in speaking much, but even to speak what is true, for so they may offend prudence or verity and both often together. That those who speak so much with others do never, as it were, speak with themselves, that they see not their thought, but when it is escaped from them, that they learn too late by repentance what sooner they might have learned through foresight, and that sorrow and shame always follow very close the discourses when prudence ushers not. That finally, the greatest part of those of their sex have less trouble to speak well than to say little, and that discretion is more difficult and necessary for them than eloquence . . .

Such as speak little as well as they who speak much should consider that modesty is necessary for silence and discourse; because it makes the one without contempt, and the other without guile or affection. And of what humour soever they be, to the end they may avoid the danger of being persecuted or debauched, it were good to seek ever the conversation of the best spirits, because they more easily pardon faults and better acknowledge the merit; and that of the most virtuous, because if libertines wrong not the conscience, they wound reputation; if they make them not vicious, they are made infamous.

There is nothing more necessary for women in conversation than to know well their own humour, to reform it if ill, or to polish it if good. It is the ground of all, what is of most importance. But seeing there are two sorts of them that may be good, each in his own kind, I think good in the entry of this discourse to compare them together, to note the better what is good or ill in either. And first, to point forth that which is most esteemed of in society, since the noblest scope we can propose therein is to have the gifts of the spirit which make us grateful. We must confess the pleasant humour therein hath a much greater advantage than the melancholy, which in truth is not amiss for sciences, but is too lumpish for discourse and too gross for witty conceits and apt replies. Pleasant humours have a great deal more grace with them and more liberty in all they do, and so are much better received in companies, as more kind in their affection, less forced in their carriages, and more innocent in their designs . . .

They who imagine that the piety of women is but a tenderness of complexion or a weakness of spirit are not of our opinion. And they offer them no less affront in despoiling them of this divine quality than if they plucked out their eyes. I should think how those who desire a wife without devotion, desire her also without pudicity. And that after they have robbed her of the feeling of piety, they purpose likewise to rob her of somewhat else. This is an old wily trick which took beginning with the world, and these libertines herein do no more with the women of this age than the devil practised with the first, when at the beginning he took away the fear of God from her to persuade her afterwards more easily to all other liberty . . .

Of chastity and courtesy

It is fit to join these two goodly qualities together to reduce them into a perfect temper, since there are some who become curst for being chaste, and others refuse nothing for being courteous. . . . Those women who imagine they cannot be honest and courteous at once skill not well the nature of virtues, since they are not contrary but diverse only, and their correspondency is too natural not to be able to subsist in one and the same subject . . .

But to tell some praises of chastity, it must needs be a divine quality, since even its very enemies make reckoning of it, and the most dissolute bear least respect to those who yield than who resist. We learn of poets that Daphne, resisting the wooings of Apollo was turned into a laurel, whereof he ever after wore his garlands; on the contrary that Io consenting to the ends of Jupiter, was changed into an heifer. How these two metamorphoses are different and how the refusal hath far more glorious marks than the consent. Respect accompanieth desire: contempt always attends possession. And it seems they are no longer amiable when they become amorous . . .

It is ill reasoning to say that a kind of timorousness withholds women more than virtue. If their inclination were ill, do they want solicitors? Experience shows that if they have any fear, it is to be vicious rather than to be blamed. Though men who have written books and proverbs, have done all things for their own advantage, yet they confess that chastity particularly appertains to women, since they who have it not are held for monsters. They would not so much wonder at it if this quality were not natural to them. There are men truly who have enjoyed this virtue, but in occasions where consideration and constraint have taken away all their merit . . .

Is it not a custom worthy of blame to see that men take to themselves all manner of licence without giving the least? One would say to see their tyranny that marriage was instituted but to put jailors upon wives, wherein there is a great deal of ingratitude as well as injustice to pretend a fidelity which they will not tender, especially being no less obliged to keep it. Women have wit enough and conscience to believe it would cost them too dear to revenge themselves by losing their virtue to take satisfaction of the vice of their husbands . . .

And especially to conserve more securely this virtue, it is good to give oneself always to some laudable exercise. Evil thoughts have no less power upon an idle spirit than enemies have on a man asleep, and I am fully of his opinion who calls this languishing repose the sepulchre of a living person: since if worms breed in a body without a soul, desires and passions are formed in a soul without employment. And if dishonest love be the trade of those women who spend not their time in any laudable thing, we may believe that chastity is conserved in employments as it is corrupted in ease. So likewise she whom our ancients took for the goddess of love, they also took for the mother of idleness. Diana hunts, Minerva studies, but Venus is idle and doth nothing.

Of learned women

... They that distrust a woman of letters are truly weak spirits who deserve what they fear so much, and who ground their suspicions on the reasons which ought to afford them the most security.

Besides, women who have some knowledge or reading afford great pleasure in conversation and receive no less in solitude when they are alone. Their idea hath somewhat to content them, while the ignorant are subject much to evil thoughts, because not knowing any laudable thing to busy their mind with ...

... They may not then imagine that speaking of this complete woman, whose image we set forth, we intend to paint you a mother of a family who can command her servants and who hath the care to comb and dress her children. Though we blame it not yet we must confess that music, history, philosophy and other such like exercises are more accommodate to our purpose than those of housewifery. And there is none so void of common sense that will not confess with me that without those good parts, though women have an excellent spirit, yet they shall have it full of naughty and fastidious things. Their good nature and good inclination remaining without effect for want of reading or conversation, when the tyranny of their mothers or husbands or else some other bar, hinders them to purchase those fair qualities whereof they are born capable.

For to say that the sciences are too obscure for women and that they cannot comprehend the arts in their principles and grounds, by reason the terms which are too hard for them to understand, in truth is strange error. It is a very extravagant opinion to think that reason speaks not all languages, and that sciences cannot as well be expressed in English as in Greek and Latin ...

It is easy to know a chaste women from her that is not so. For the vicious examines things to the least circumstance, her malice serves her as a pattern to judge evil; her experience and her purpose cause her to make ill interpretations of the best things.

7.24 MARY TATTLE-WELL AND JOAN HIT-HIM-HOME, *THE WOMEN'S SHARP REVENGE*

Written in response to John Taylor's Juniper and Crabtree Lectures, the authors' names are evidently pseudonymous and the rhetoric that of the controversy debate. There is no evidence whether the authors were women or men: but the use of the rhetorical personae of the two women, who defend women's rights offers men and women a language other than that of the Pauline injunctions, reiterated constantly in sermons and advice books, as this section demonstrates. Text from: first edition, 1640, pp. 67–77.

When we, whom they style by the name of weaker vessels, though of a more delicate, fine, soft and more pliant flesh, and therefore of a temper most capable of the best impression, have not that generous and liberal education, lest we should be made able to vindicate our own injuries, we are set only to the needle, to prick our fingers: or else to the wheel to spin a fair thread for our own undoings, or perchance to some more dirty and debased drudgery: if we be taught to read, they then confine us within the compass of our mother's tongue, and that limit we are not suffered to pass, or if (which sometimes happeneth) we be brought up to music, to singing and to dancing, it is not for any benefit that thereby we can engross unto ourselves, but for their own particular ends, the better to please and content their licentious appetites, when we come to our maturity and ripeness: and thus if we be weak by nature, they strive to make us more weak by our nurture. And if in degree of place low, they strive by their policy to keep us more under.

Now to show we are no such despised matter as you would seem to make us, come to our first Creation, when man was made of the mere dust of the earth, the woman had her being from the best part of his body, the rib next to his heart: which difference even in our complexions may be easily discerned. Man is of a dull, earthy and melancholy aspect, having fallows in his face and a very forest upon his chin, when our soft and smooth cheek are a true representation of a delectable garden of intermixed roses and lilies.

* * *

This captain Complement, with his page Implement, laid hard siege to the weak fortress of my frail carcass, he would swear that his life or death were either in my accepting or rejecting his suit; he would lie and flatter in prose, and cog and foist in verse most shamefully; he would sometimes salute me with most delicious sentences, which he always kept in syrup, and he never came to me empty mouthed or handed; for he was never unprovided of stewed anagrams, baked epigrams, soused madrigals, pickled roundelays, broiled sonnets, parboiled elegies, perfumed poesies for rings, and a thousand other such foolish flatteries, and knavish devices, which I suspected and the more he strived to overcome me or win me with oaths, promises and protestations, still the less I believed him; so that at last he grew faint at the siege, gave over to make any more assaults; and, vanquished with despair, made a small retreat. In like manner I wish all women and maids in general to beware of their gilded glosses; an enamoured toad lurks under the sweet grass, and a fair tongue hath been too often the varnish or embroidery of a false heart; what are they but lime-twigs of lust, and schoolmasters of folly? Let not their foolish fancy prove to be your brain sick frenzy, for if you note them, in all their speech or writings, you shall seldom or never have any word or syllable in the praise of goodness or true virtue to come from them: their talk shall consist either of wealth, strength, wit, beauty, lands, fashions, horses, hawks, hounds, and many other trivial and transitory toys, which as they may be used are blessings of the left hand, wherewith they entice and entrap poor silly young tender hearted females to be enamoured of their good parts (if they had any), but if men would lay by their tricks, flights, falsehoods and dissimulations, and (contrarily) in their conversing with us, use their tongues and pens in the praise of meekness, modesty, chastity, temperance, constancy and piety; then surely women would strive to be such as their discourses did tend unto: for we do not live in such an age of pollution that many a rich wicked man will spend willingly, and give more to corrupt and make spoil of the chastity, and honour of one beautiful untainted virgin than they will bestow (in charity) towards the saving of an hundred poor people from perishing by famine here, or from perdition in a worser place: and because they say women will always lie, I do wish that (in this last point I touched upon) they would make or prove me a liar.

Who but men have been the authors of all mischiefs? Had the firebrand of Troy (Paris) not stolen Helen from her husband King Menelaus, surely she had remained a wife in Sparta, and never been strumpeted in Phrygia: the ten years' siege and sacking of Ilion was never fought by women, but wrought by men: who but men are traitors, apostates, irreligious, sectaries, and schismatics? Alas, alas, these are vessels of vices and villainies, which the weak hands of brains of women could never broach. Who but men are extortioners, usurers, oppressors, thieves, perjured persons, and knights of the post? Who but men do write, print, divulge and scatter libels, rhymes, songs and pasquils against the known truth; against sovereign authority, against all law, equity and conformity to loyalty? Who but men have, and do set forth pestiferous pamphlets, emblems, and pictures of scurrility and nasty obsceneness? I am sure that Ovid and Aretine were no women, nor was there ever any woman found to be the authority for such base and vile inventions.

In one of their late wise ridiculous lectures, they do cast an aspersion upon us that we are mighty gossips, and exceeding scolds; to the first I answer that the most part of our meetings at gossipings are 'long[22] of the men, rather then to be imputed to us; for when children are born into the world (although men feel none of the misery) yet women have a more known sympathy and feeling of one another's pains and perils; and therefore in Christianity and neighbourly love and charity, women do meet to visit and comfort the weakness of such, as in those dangerous times do want it; and whereas they say that we tipple, and tittle-tattle more than our shares, I shall (before this discourse is ended) cast that ball back again in their teeths and emblazon them truly to be most vain and idle talkers; and that no living thing created is so sottish, senseless, brutish, and beastly, as most of them have been, and are daily, nightly and hourly in their drink: for their much talk (to no purpose) doth show that there is a running issue or fistula in their minds.

Man might consider that woman were not created to be their slaves or vassals, for as they had not their original sin out of his head (thereby to command him) so it was not out of his foot to be trod upon, but in a (medium) out of his side to be his fellow feeler, his equal and companion.

7.25 KATHERINE CHIDLEY, *THE JUSTIFICATION OF THE INDEPENDENT CHURCHES OF CHRIST*

Written in answer to a tract by Thomas Edwards, Chidley argues that 'the congregation of saints ought not to have dependency in government upon any other; or direction in worship from any other than Christ their head and law-giver', and uses this to claim that in spiritual matters women have equality with men. Text from: first edition, 1641, pp. 25–6.

In your third reason you affirm that toleration will breed divisions and schisms, disturbing the peace and quiet of churches and towns.

I answer, I have told you already we plead for no toleration that shall disturb the peace of churches or towns . . .

Again you say: *oh, how this will occasion disobedience!*

To this your lamentation I answer: oh, that you would remember the rule that every servant ought to count his master worthy of all honour and in the judgement of charity believe that persons professing the Gospel will learn that lesson.

Next you say: *oh, how will this take away that power and authority which God hath given to husbands, fathers and masters over wives, children and servants!*

To this I answer: oh, that you would consider the text in 1 Cor. 7, which plainly declares that the wife may be a believer and the husband an unbeliever, but if you have considered this text, I pray you tell me what authority this unbelieving husband hath over the conscience of his believing wife? It is true he hath authority over her in bodily and civil respects, but not to be a lord over her conscience, and the like may be said of fathers and masters: and it is the very same authority which the sovereign hath over all his subjects, and therefore it must needs reach to families: for it is granted that King hath power (according to the law) over the bodies, goods and lives of all his subjects, yet it is Christ the king of kings that reigneth over their consciences: and thus you may see it taketh away no authority which God hath given to them.

7.26 NICHOLAS FONTANUS, *THE WOMAN'S DOCTOR*

This text book is aimed at English physicians and lay readers. Text from: first edition, 1652, pp. 1–7.

Women were made to stay at home and to look after household employments, and because such business is accompanied with much ease, without any vehement stirrings of the body. Therefore hath provident nature assigned them their monthly courses, that by the benefit of those evacuations, the feculent and corrupt blood might be purified which otherwise as being the purest part of the blood, would liable to take poison should it remain in the body and putrefy, like the seed ejaculated out of its proper vessels. Hippocrates had a perfect understanding of these things, as may appear by those words, in his book, *De Locis in Homine* where he saith, that the matrix is the cause of all those diseases that happen to women; and it is no strange thing, which he speaketh, for the matrix hath a sympathy with all the parts of the body; as with the brain by nerves and membranes of the parts about the spine, from whence sometimes ariseth the pains in the fore part, and the hinder part of the head; with heart also, both by the spermatic and the epigastric arteries, or those that lie about the abdomen at the bottom of the belly, from hence cometh the pain of the heart, fainting and swounding fits, the passion of the heart, anxiety of mind, dissolution of the spirits, insomuch as you cannot discern whether a woman breathes or not, or that she hath any pulse; it hath likewise a consent with the breasts, and from hence proceed those swellings, that hardness, and those terrible cancers that afflict those tender parts, that a humour doth flow upwards from, the matrix to the breasts, and downwards again, from the breasts to the matrix, is the unanimous assertion of Galen, Hippocrates ... moreover it hath a sympathic with the liver, and thus the sanguification is perverted, and the body inclines to a dropsy; and with the stomach and kidneys also, as those pains which great-bellied women do feel, and the torments which some virgins undergo, when they have their courses, sufficiently witness. And lastly, Hippocrates hath taught us, that this consent holdeth with the bladder and the straight gut, for saith he, when that part is enflamed, then the urine cometh away by drops; and the patient hath frequent desires and solicitations to go to stool, but without any performance ...

Those diseases that are common both to widows and wives, both to barren women and women that are fruitful, as also to young maids and virgins, proceed from the retention or stoppage of their courses, as the most universal and most usual cause; when these come upon them in a due and regular manner, their bodies are preserved from most terrible diseases; but otherwise they are immediately subject to the falling sickness, the palsy, the consumption, the whites,[23] the mother, melancholy, burning fevers, the dropsy, inward inflammations of all the principal parts, the suppression of the urine, nauseating, vomiting, loathing of meat, yexing,[24] and a continual pain in the head, arising from ill vapours communicated from the matrix to the brain.

Wives are more healthful than widows or virgins, because they are refreshed with the man's seed, and ejaculate their own, which being excluded, the cause of the evil is taken away. This is evident from the words of Hippocrates, who adviseth young maids to marry, when they are thus troubled. That women have stones and seed, no true anatomist will deny. The women's seed, I confess, in regard of the small quantity of heat, is more imperfect than the seed of the man's, yet it is most absolute in itself, and fit for generation. Another cause also may be added, besides that which is alleged from Hippocrates, namely that married women by lying with their husbands, do loosen the passages of the seed, and so the courses come down more easily thorough them. Now in virgins it falls out otherwise, because the blood is stopped by the constipation and obstruction of the veins and, being stopped, putrefies, from which putrefaction gross vapours do arise, and from thence the heaviness of mind and dullness of spirit; a benumbedness of the parts; timorousness, and an aptness to be frighted, with a sudden propensity to fall into fits of the mother, by reason of much blood oppressing and burthening the heart; also continual anxiety, sadness, and want of sleep, with idle talking, and an alienation of the mind. But that which most commonly afflicts them is a difficulty and pain to fetch their breath, for the chest by a continual dilatation and compression, draweth the blood from the matrix to itself in a large proportion, and sometimes produceth asthmatical effects. But what shall we say concerning widows, who lie fallow and live sequestered from these venerous conjunctions? We must conclude that if they be young, of a black complexion and hairy, and are likewise somewhat discoloured in their cheeks, that they have a spirit of salacity, and feel within themselves a frequent titillation, their seed being hot and prurient, doth irritate and inflame them to venery, neither is this concupiscence allayed and qualified but by provoking the ejaculation of the seed: as Galen propounds the advice in the example of a widow who was afflicted with intolerable symptoms, till the abundance of the spermatic humour was diminished by the hand of a skilful midwife, and a convenient ointment. Which passage will also furnish us with this argument that the use of venery is exceeding wholesome if the woman will confine herself to the laws of moderation, so that she feel no wearisomeness, nor weakness in her body, after those pleasing conflicts.

Most certain it is, that barren women are more tormented with sickness, than those that are fruitful, because they who have children live in a more healthful condition, by reason of opening of the veins, and the coming away of the superfluous blood, which being of an earthy and feculent substance, must needs introduce prodigious symptoms in the bodies of other women, who have no seasonable means to vent and purge it out, and daily experience doth witness it to the private consideration of such women, that very many obstructions breed in their livers, mesenteries[25] and matrices. That women in childbed also, and such as nurse their own children, are subject to most bitter and vehement affects, Galen doth daily teach us, by an undeniable reason; for whereas the child in the womb is nourished by the sweetest, fattest, and most elaborate part of the menstruous blood, in its own nature filthy and dreggish, when the woman is delivered that blood is forcibly evacuated by a critical kind of motion and violent ebullition, whereupon the spirits are exhausted and the feeble creature is precipitated into mortal infirmities, as fainting fits, incredible torments and frequent soundings.

7.27 *THE SAINT'S TESTIMONY*

This is a vivid account of a trial of Quakers held at Banbury in July 1655, during which Margaret Vivers articulated a defence of both women's and men's rights to speak in public and to prophesy, an interesting contrast to Calvin's interpretation of the Pauline edict (see 7.8). Text from: first edition, 1656, pp. 14–16.

A testimony against false prophets and false teachers; and also the objection answered concerning the woman forbidden to speak in the Church

And after that they had confessed that they had Margaret Vivers (who had spoken to the priest in the steeplehouse, after that he had ended that day) there, neither for whoredom, felony nor theft, and words to that purpose, yet it was the mayor's mind that she should be there; but whether she had committed any offence or no, they could not tell (as they said, and words to that effect) and the man that kept her there upon such uncertainty, when they was about to put her in prison, and had her at the door, but did not put her in; for no law by her was transgressed at that time, as it was said, that could be proved for witnessing the truth in obedience to the command of the Lord (yet though they did not commit her to prison, other two they did, one that stood by, and another that was quietly passing up the street at that same time) and the man that had kept her in custody did object against a woman speaking in the Church; it was asked whether the spirit of God might not be permitted to speak in the temple of God yea or nay; the which by some was answered and granted that it might.

Answer. To the question about the woman forbidden to speak in the Church, and proved that the spirit of God may speak in his temple, either in the body of male or female, *let the woman keep silence in the Church*, as it is said, *and let God speak by his spirit in his temple,* 2 Cor. 6.16. *Either of male or female, whose bodies are the temples of God through the spirit,* 1 Cor. 3.16, 17. *So in Christ Jesus the spirit of God in male and female is both one,* Eph. 2.19, 20. Gal. 3.27, 28. And Paul he commended Phoebe in his Epistle to the Romans, which Phoebe was a servant of the Church which was at Cenchrea, Rom. 16.1 and in the same epistle he saluted Priscilla and also gave thanks with the churches for her labour, who had been a helper of him in Christ Jesus and she was a woman labourer in the gospel by the spirit of truth; so was there woman labourers with Paul in the gospel, which he writes of in his Epistle to the Philippians, as well as them he speaks of, whose names are written in the book of life, Rom.16.3, 4. Phil. 4.3.

So was there women guided by the spirit of the Lord, that were the Lord's prophetesses, as well as there were men that were his prophets; and the Lord spoke his word by his own spirit, in and through the one as well as the other: Miriam, Aaron's sister was a prophetess, and spake forth the praise of God, in that dispensation and administration, by the spirit of God that teacheth to prophesy, as well as the manifestation of it is given to profit withal, Exod. 15.20, 21. Isa. 8.16, 17; 1 Cor. 2.7.

And Deborah a prophetess by the spirit of the Lord which taught her to prophesy, she therewith judged Israel, and were a minister of justice amongst the Lord's people in her days, and in that dispensation, insomuch that the children of Israel came up to her for judgement, and did not despise the counsel of the Lord's spirit in a woman preacher, or a judge in Israel, and a prophetess of the Lord, Judg. the 4, 5, 6, 7,etc.

And in the days of Josiah, King in Israel, there was one Huldah a prophetess that lived in Jerusalem, a woman preacher, or one who by the spirit of the Lord, declared and spoke to the people the word of the Lord, and to her the priest and people went to enquire and hear the word of the Lord, according also to the king's command, 2 King. 22, 13, 14, 15, 16, 17 etc. Besides several other prophetesses as well as prophets, there was in the time of old among the Lord's people, as the prophetesses in Isaiah's time and in Nehemiah's time, so there was in the Apostle's time a man in Cesaria had four daughters that were virgins did prophesy Acts 21.8, 9. And at the coming of Christ when Simeon, that just man spoke of him, the light of the Gentiles and the glory of the people Israel, there was one woman, a widow of above four score years of age, that had no outward husband at home to ask, who was a preacher, or one that spoke of the Lord Jesus to all that looked for redemption in Jerusalem, Luke 2.36, 37, 38.

And Tryphena and Tryphosa and Peris (three virtuous godly women) did labour much in the Lord, which Paul (in his Epistle to the Romans) did salute and as the wife is in subjection to her husband, so is the Church subject unto Christ who is the head thereof, as the husband is the head of the wife; and Christ being the head of his spouse, or husband of his Church, the spouse of Christ united unto him, and betrothed in righteousness, both asketh of him, and staying at home taketh counsel with him, though the harlot from home, and the stranger unto him, knoweth it not and saith the Lord, *I will pour out of my spirit, that sons, and daughters, and handmaids also shall prophesy*; and who are they that are offended hereat now? That the Lord doth see but proud, covetous, self-seeking priests (who never knew God) amd their hearers that are deceived by them, and such in their nature who know not the sure word and spirit of prophecy, but are ignorant both of the mystery godliness, and so of him whose name is called the word of God, and knoweth neither the teachings of God, nor the life of the Scriptures, and the work of the spirit of God, who would not have him to be the same now that he was, and Christ to be the same yesterday, today, and for ever; who are such opposers of the work of the spirit of God, and persecutors of the servants of Jesus, in whom it is bringing, and brought, forth as their generation and seed of evil doers ever was; Matt. 23.33, 34, &c.

7.28 *THE COMPLETE MIDWIFE'S PRACTICE ENLARGED*

This gynaecological text claims authority from Louise Bourgeois (1563–1636), the midwife to Marie de Medici. It sets out contemporary beliefs about and attitudes towards sexuality. Text from: first edition, 1656, pp. 10–11; 35–6; 41–2.

Concerning the utility of the testicles and their parts

The structure of the testicles being thus known, it remains that we show you their use. This is first discovered from their situation. For of those creatures that have stones, some have them in their bodies, as fowl, others have them without, though not pendent; others have them hanging downwards, as men. Men therefore have their testicles without their bodies for two causes; first, because it is required that the testicles of the male should be bigger and hotter than those of the female, so that it were impossible for them to be contained with the body, because of their quantity. Besides, the seed of the male being the effective original of the creature, and therefore hottest, it is also required that the seed should be more abundant than could be contained in the testicles, were they placed within the body; for the seminal passages must have been less, and the veins themselves would not have afforded such plenty of matter as they now do. . . . The clitoris is a certain substance in the upper part of the great cleft, where the two wings concur, this in women is the seat of venereal pleasure: it is like the yard in situation, composition and erection, and hath something correspondent both to the prepuce[26] and glans in man. Sometimes it grows out to the bigness of the yard, so that it hath been observed to grow out of the body the breadth of four fingers.

This clitoris consists of two spongy and sinewy bodies, having a distinct original, from the bones of the pubes. The head of this is covered with a most tender skin, and hath a hole like the glans, though not quite through, in which, and in the bigness, it differs from the yard.

* * *

Of the stones in women

The stones of women although they do perform the same actions and are for the same use as mens, yet they differ from them in situation, substance, temperament, figure, magnitude and covering.

They are seated in the hollowness of the abdomen; neither do they hang out as in men, but they rest upon the muscles of the loins, and this for that cause that they might be more hot and fruitful; being to elaborate that matter which with the seed of men engenders men.

In this place arises a question not trivial; whether the seed of woman be the efficient or the material cause of generation? To which it is answered that though it have a power of acting, yet that it receives the perfection of that power from the seed of man.

* * *

Of the actions of the womb

The first use of the womb is to attract the seed by a familiar sympathy, just as the load stone draws iron.

The second use is to retain it, which is properly called conception.

The third is to cherish the seed thus attracted, to alter it, and change it into the birth, by raising up that power which before lay sleeping in the seed, and to reduce it from power into act. The fourth action of the womb is to send forth the birth at the time prefixed; the apt time of expulsion is when the expulsive faculty begins to be affected with some sense of trouble, that is when the birth afflicts and oppresses the womb with its own weight.

Besides these uses, it hath these moreover: to nourish the birth and to dilate itself, which it doth by the help of veins and arteries, which do fill more and more with matter, as nature requires.

The chiefest action of the womb and most proper to it, is the retention of the seed; without which nothing of other action could be performed for the generation of man.

8

EXPLORATION AND TRADE

INTRODUCTION

The chronology, titles, aims and content of the life's work of Richard Hakluyt the younger can tell us much about developing conceptions of nationhood, travel and discovery in this period. In 1582 he brought out his first publication *Divers Voyages Touching the Discovery of America*, dedicated to Sir Philip Sidney, and laying claim to a historiography of English endeavour and achievement on the world stage, comparable to that of Spain and Portugal celebrated in the translation by Richard Eden of Peter Martyr's *Decades* (extract 8.1). For the most part this was self-confessedly a very literary endeavour, although it inserted that endeavour into a current debate about the feasibility of planting America with a new colony. In 1589, the year after the success of the Spanish Armada, he published the first edition of a much larger work: *The Principal Navigations, Voyages and Discoveries of the English Nation*. Its tone echoes the strident rhetoric of national identity to be found in other historical and cultural writings of the 1580s: Holinshed's *Chronicles* (1577), Camden's *Britannia* (first edition, 1586), Stowe's *Chronicle of England* (1580) and into the fictional world of Shakespeare's early history plays. It was an extremely popular text.[1] He dedicated the work to Sir Francis Walsingham, Principal Secretary of the Privy Council, in an overt consociation with national State politics. Thus Hakluyt proudly (and exaggeratedly) proclaims:

it cannot be denied but, as in all former ages they have been men full of activity, stirrers abroad, and searchers of the most remote parts of the world, so in this most famous and peerless government of Her most excellent Majesty, her subjects in compassing the vast globe of the world more than once, have excelled all the nations and peoples of the earth.

In 1589, of course, he was referring here mainly to the circumnavigation of the world by Sir Francis Drake, the unsuccessful attempts by Martin Frobisher to find a north-west passage to Japan, and the successful trade treaty with Russia opened up by Anthony Jenkinson with the establishment of the Muscovy Company in 1555. When compared with the eight decades of successful plantation, conversion, ethnographical study, trade treaties and wealth of the Iberian powers (Spain and Portugal) in Africa, the Atlantic islands, South America and India, Hakluyt's patriotic fervour appears somewhat fevered. Nevertheless, the evident excitement (however bookish) associated with expansionist discovery informs all the writing in his collection.

In 1598, in an even more scholarly and far more extensive second edition of three volumes, Hakluyt extends his title to include the term 'traffic', meaning trade: *The Principal Navigations, Voyages, Traffics and Discoveries*, again dedicated to the Principal Secretary (now Sir Robert Cecil). Here Hakluyt delineates the recent adventures, trade treaties, privateering, encounters with Spanish ships, attempted plantations in Virginia, overland journeys to the Middle East, Persia and Japan, as part of a historical destiny which the English nation has been pursuing for five hundred years. (See 8.11 for the prefaces and 8.2, 8.4 and 8.5 for some examples of the texts included in his collection.)

However, Hakluyt combines this missionary and teleological zeal with a proto-mercantilist celebration of the economic benefits of trade and a (marginally) more hesitant plea to the monarch to support an imperial enterprise in Virginia. As with his previous prefaces, Hakluyt moves into the realm of propaganda with his description of Virginia in 1599:

> whereof is found of late to be so sweet and wholesome a climate, so rich and abundant in silver mines, so apt and capable of all commodities, and in a secret map of those parts made in Mexico for the King of Spain (which original with many others is in the custody of the excellent mathematician Mr. Thomas Harriot) as also in their intercepted letters come into my hand, bearing date 1595, they acknowledge the inland to be a better and richer country than Mexico itself.

Unfortunately, the truth of the historical record at this point shows that these letters were fictional and that the only English attempt at a plantation (that sponsored by Raleigh) at Roanoke had foundered through lack of commodities, crops and medicines in 1588 or 1589; and that no group of men or commercial company showed any interest in pursuing such a dangerous enterprise for another fifteen years, despite the attempts by both Raleigh and Harriot to get the funding for an expedition (see 8.9). Thus, despite Hakluyt's prophetic claims, and a theory of the necessary link between economic success and imperial expansion, he failed to obtain royal or privy councillor funding for any future enterprises like the ones he described of the recent past. Raleigh's attempts to prove the existence of El Dorado, somewhere in Guiana, and attempts to show that it would provide Elizabeth I with the kind of success the Spaniards had grasped through the conquering of the Incas (see 8.10) were discredited even by his contemporaries. Royal policy towards expansion remained cautious and sceptical, although all monarchs granted charters for exploration and exploitation of resources and trade, with a tax levy for the crown.[2]

The founding of the Virginia Company in 1606 (see 8.15), in which the Plymouth and London companies jointly received a patent from James I to establish two plantations in Virginia, was the real start of a continuous English plantation on north American soil. But Virginia was always teetering on the brink of financial and ecological disaster, for several reasons. First, the Company could never pay out the full dividends and land promised to shareholders (see 8.18). Second, it suffered from bad management and from settlers who were not committed to planting, but wanted a swift acquisition of local commodities, and gold if possible. And third, their relations with the native Americans worsened as the English acquired more land, and it became obvious that they intended to stay and colonise, rather than either share or trade with the locals. The Powhatan Confederacy (see 8.24) was formed with the specific aim of eradicating the English settlement to reclaim American land for its natives. But by this stage, tobacco had become a major cash crop, and English Virginia was able to recover its land, crops and settlers in a relatively short time. Other settlements which began to flourish at this time were those in Massachussetts, including that of the Pilgrim Fathers (8.20), a Catholic settlement in Maryland, and some in more northern parts of New England.[3]

The force which drove overseas expansion was primarily economic, although there was also the thrill of discovery for its own sake. But all the accounts which both Hakluyt and Samuel Purchas[4] publish, make direct links between the need for trade, cheap imports and how to effect these, with the prospect of travel and discovery. Even Drake's account of his circumnavigation of the world gives useful information about possible trading posts with Japan. The economic imperative was severalfold. First, a need to harvest the sea for more fish had driven boats to Newfoundland and the north American coast, and fish continued to be a necessary commodity for trade and food, particularly as the sea offered its commodities without any apparent cost. Thus Harriot and Smith both emphasise the crucial role of fish in their contemporary economy (8.9 and 8.24). Second, there was an increased demand for precious and industrial metals in Europe as a whole: and with the model of Spain and Portugal, all European nations looked for similar finds. Third, with a rapidly increasing population and domestic economic expansion the demand for luxury goods and consumer items boomed during the sixteenth century,[5] creating a taste and demand for raisins, wine, sugar, spices, tobacco and silk, among other commodities. Men like John Hawkins (see 8.4) gained their wealth through such trade, and then increased it by going into the slave trade.

England was learning how to manage an economy that functioned in an international system of trade. The conservative, and predominant, view of the time argued that excessive consumer demand drained the country of its bullion, and thence its wealth (represented by Wilson and Misselden here). James I and Charles I pursued this policy through proclamations restricting the export of bullion; and some of the excitement with which privateering appropriation of Spanish gold was greeted was because it was believed that direct importing of gold would strengthen the economy.[6] The trading consequence of this was that imports should be as cheap as possible (if not at no cost at all), and this was the declared aim of many joint stock companies, such as the Muscovy Company and the East India Company. Thus Gray's account of what can be stripped from Virginia, and his justification of acquisition, must be placed within this economic ideology. An emergent, nascent economic theory, later called mercantilism, argued that trade and exchange were the way to national wealth, both through export of native goods and the manipulation of exchange rates (see Gresham, de Malynes and Bacon). But despite this argument, the discovery of additional export markets was academic prior to the production of goods worthy to be exported. Thus, English and European economic expansion occurred mainly through acquisition and exploitation of the land and commodities of less developed nations,[7] gradually coming to depend on slave, unwaged labour to produce huge profits.

Images and accounts of native American or African populations usually denoted them as savages, although this term does not always have the negative connotations we assume. Readers of these texts will find writers struggling to find a language and images in which to express the wonder of a new world.[8] Thus Harriot's ethnographical account (8.9) and Montaigne's philosophical one (8.13), as well as Smith's geographical survey of settlements (8.19) give a different picture of the European encounter with America than that of Gray. The description of the strange disease which afflicted the natives after meeting the English in Harriot's *True Report* is a graphic reminder that it was European diseases that were mainly responsible for decimating the native population, rather than war or slavery.

The texts included in this section are limited to journeys to America, particularly those to Virginia, because of space constraints, readers who wish to consult further sources on other journeys of exploration and trade should consult the further reading list.

8.1 PETER MARTYR, *THE DECADES*

Martyr, a renowned European humanist, collected and published the available writings on the Americas in 1516. These were translated into English by

Richard Eden, son-in-law of Thomas More, in 1555. Text from: *The First Three English Books on America,* ed. E. Arber, 1885, pp. 65–7; 172ff.

Christopher Colonus (otherwise called Columbus) a gentleman of Italy, born in the city of Genoa, persuaded Fernando and Elizabeth, Catholic princes, that he doubted not to find certain islands of India near unto our ocean sea, if they would furnish him with ships and other things appertaining. Affirming that thereby not only the Christian religion might be enlarged, but Spain also enriched by the great plenty of gold, pearls, precious stones and spices which might be found there. At the length, three ships were appointed him at the king's charges: of the which one was a great caract with decks; and the other two were light merchant ships without decks, which the Spaniards call caravels. Thus he departed from the coasts of Spain about the calends of September in the year of Christ 1492 and set forward on his voyage, being accompanied with 220 Spaniards. The Fortunate Islands (as many think them to be, which the Spaniards call *Canariae,* found but of late days) . . . were called fortunate for the temperate air which is in them. For neither the coldness of winter is sharp unto them, nor the heat of summer intolerable . . .

From these islands Colonus directing his voyage towards the west, following the falling of the sun, but declining somewhat toward the left hand, sailed on forward thirty-three days continually, having only the fruition of the heaven and the water. Then the Spaniards which were accompanied with him began first to murmur secretly among themselves, and shortly after with words of reproach spake evil of Colonus their governor, and consulted with themselves, either to rid him out of the way, or else to cast him into the sea. Raging that they were deceived of a stranger, an outlandish man, a Ligurian, a Genoese, and brought into such dangerous places that they might never return again. And after thirty days were past they furiously cried out against him and threatened him that he should pass no further. But he ever with gentle words and large promises appeased their fury and prolonged day after day, sometime desiring them to bear with him yet awhile, and sometime putting them in remembrance that if they should attempt anything against him, or otherwise disobey him, it would be reputed for treason. Thus after a few days with cheerful hearts they espied the land long looked for. In this first navigation he discovered six islands, whereof two were exceeding great: of which the one he called Hispaniola and the other Johanna. But at that time he knew not perfectly that Johanna (otherwise called Cuba) was an island. As they coasted along by the shore of certain of these islands, they heard nightingales sing in the thick woods in the month of November. They found also great rivers of fresh water, and natural havens of capacity to harbour great navies of ships. Sailing by the coasts of Johanna from the north point to the west, he rode little less than eight hundred miles (for they call it a hundred and four score leagues) supposing that it had been the continent or firm land because he could neither find the land's end, nor any token of the end, as far as he could judge with his eye: wherefore he determined to return back again, being thereto partly enforced by the roughness of the sea. For the sea banks of the island of Johanna, by sundry windings and turnings, bend themselves so much toward the north that the north-north-east wind roughly tossed the ships by reason of the winter. Turning therefore the sterns of his ships toward the east, he affirmed that he had found the island of Ophir, whither Solomon's ships sailed for gold. But the description of the cosmographers well considered, it seemeth that both these and the other islands adjoining are the islands of Antillia. This island he called Hispaniola: on whose north side as he approached near to the land the keel or bottom of the biggest vessel ran upon a blind rock covered with water, and clove in sunder. But the plainness of the rock was a help to them that were not drowned. Making haste therefore with the other two ships to help them they brought away all the men without hurt. Here coming first aland they saw certain men of the island, who perceiving an unknown nation coming toward them, flocked together and ran all into the thick woods, as it had been hares coursed with greyhounds. Our men pursuing them, took only one woman, whom they brought to the ships: where filling her with meat and wine and apparelling her, they let her depart to her company. Shortly after a great multitude of them came running to the shore to behold this new nation, whom they thought to have descended from heaven. They cast themselves by heaps into the sea and came swimming to the ships, bringing gold with them, which they changed with our men for earthen pots, drinking glasses, points, pins, hawks' bells, looking-glasses and such other trifles. Thus growing to further familiarity, our men were honourably entertained of the king of that part of the island, whose name was Guaccanarillus: for it hath many kings, as when Aeneas arrived in Italy, he found Latium divided into many kingdoms and provinces, as Latium, Mezeutium, Turnum and Tarchontem, which were separated with narrow bounds, as shall more largely appear hereafter. At the eventide about the falling of the sun, when our men went to prayer and kneeled on their knees after the manner of the Christians, they did the like also. And after what manner soever they saw them pray to the cross, they followed them in all points as well as they could. They showed much humanity towards our men, and helped them with their lighters or small boats (which they called *canoas*) to unlade their broken ship: and that with such celerity and cheerfulness that no friend for friend, or kinsman for kinsman in such case moved with pity, could do more. Their boats are made only of one tree made hollow with a certain sharp stone (for they have no iron); and are very long and narrow. Many affirm that they have seen some of them with forty oars. The wild and mischievous people called *Cannibals* or *Caribs*, which were accustomed to eat man's flesh (and called of the old writers, *anthropophagi*) molest them exceedingly, invading their country, taking them captive, killing and eating them. As our men sailed to the islands of these meek and humane people, they left the islands of the cannibals in manner of the middest of their voyage toward the south. They complained that their islands were no less vexed with the incursions of these man-hunting cannibals when they go forth a-roving to seek their prey, than are other tame beasts, of lions and tigers. Such children as they take they geld to make them fat as we do cock chickens and young hogs, and eat them when they are well fed, of such as they eat they first eat the entrails and extreme parts, as hands, feet, arms, neck and head. The other most fleshy parts they powder for store, as we do pestles of pork and gammons of bacon. Yet do they abstain from eating of women and count it vile. Therefore such young women as they take they keep for increase, as we do hens to lay eggs. The old women they make their drudges. They of the islands (which we may now call ours) both the men and the women when they perceive the cannibals coming have none other shift but only to fly: for although they use very sharp arrows made of reeds, yet are they of small force to repress the fury of the cannibals: for even they themselves confess that ten of the cannibals are able to overcome a hundred of them if they encounter with them. Their meat is a certain root which they call *ages*: much like a navew[1] root in form and greatness, but of sweet taste, much like a green chestnut. They have also another kind of roots which they call *iucca*, whereof they make bread in like manner. They use *ages* more often roasted or sodden than to make bread thereof. But they never eat *iucca* except it be first sliced and pressed (for it is full of liquor) and then baked or sodden. But this is to be marvelled at that the juice of this root is a poison as strong as *aconitum* so that if it be drunk it causeth present death, and yet the bread made of the mass thereof is of good taste and wholesome, as all they have proved. They make also another kind of bread of a certain pulse called *panicum*, much like unto wheat, whereof is great plenty in the dukedom of Milan, Spain and Granada. But that of this country is longer by a span, somewhat sharp toward the end and as big as a man's arm in the brawn: the grains whereof are set in a marvellous order and are in form somewhat like a pease. While they be sour and unripe they are white, but when they are ripe they be very black. When they are broken, they be whiter than snow. This kind of grain they call *maizium*. Gold is of some estimation among them, for some of them hang certain small pieces thereof at their ears and nostrils. A little beyond this place our men went aland for fresh water, where they chanced upon a river whose sand was mixed with much gold. They found there no kinds of four-footed beasts except three kinds of little conies.[2] These islands also nourish serpents: but such as are without hurt. Likewise wild geese, turtle doves, and ducks, much greater than ours and as white as swans with heads of purple colour. Also popinjays, of the which some are green, some yellow, and some like them of India, with yellow rings about their necks, as Pliny describeth them. Of these they brought forty with them, of most lively and delectable colours, having their feathers intermingled with green, yellow and purple, which variety delighteth the sense not a little. Thus much I thought good to speak of popinjays (right noble prince) specially to this intent: that albeit the opinion of Christophorus Colonus (who affirmeth these islands to be part of India) doth not in all points agree with the judgement of ancient writers as touching the bigness of the sphere and compass of the globe as concerning the navigable portion of the same being under us, yet the popinjays and many other things brought from thence, do declare that these islands favour somewhat of India, either being near unto it, or else of the same nature. Forasmuch as Aristotle also, about the end of his book *De Caelo et Mundo* and likewise Seneca with diverse other authors not ignorant in cosmography, do affirm that India is no long tract by sea distant from Spain by the west ocean: for the soil of these islands bringeth forth mastix, aloes, and sundry other sweet gums and spices as doth India. Cotton also of the gossampine tree, as in India in the country of the people called Seres.

The languages of all the nations of these islands may well be written with our Latin letters. For they call heaven, *turei*; a house, *boa*; gold, *cauni*; a good man, *taino*; nothing, *mayani*. All other words of their language they pronounce as plainly as we do the Latin tongue. In these islands they found no trees known unto them but pineapple trees and date trees: and those of marvellous height and exceeding hard by reason of the great moistness and fatness of the ground, with continual and temperate heat of the sun, which endureth so all the whole year. They plainly affirm the island of Hispaniola to be the most fruitful land that the heaven compasseth about.

* * *

There is also another region in Hispaniola named Cotohy . . . this divideth the bounds of the provinces of Uhabo and Ciabo. It hath mountains, vales and plains. But because it is barren, it is not much inhabited. Yet is it richest in gold: for the original of the abundance of gold beginneth here: insomuch that it is not gathered in small grains and sparks as in other places, but is found whole, massy and pure, among certain soft stones and in the veins of rocks, by breaking the stones whereof they follow the veins of gold. They have found by experience that the vein of gold is a living tree: and that the same by all ways that it spreadeth and springeth from the root by the soft pores and passages of the earth, puteth forth branches even unto the uppermost part of the earth, and ceaseth not until it discover itself unto the open air; at which time it showeth forth certain beautiful colours in the stead of flowers, round stones of golden earth in the stead of fruits, and thin plates instead of leaves. These are they which are disparcelled throughout the whole island, by the course of the rivers, eruptions of the springs out of the mountains, and violent falls of the floods. For they think that such grains are not engendered where they are gathered, especially on the dry land, but otherwise in the rivers. They say that the root of the gold tree extendeth to the centre of the earth and there taketh nourishment of increase. For the deeper that they dig, they find the trunks thereof to be so much the greater as far as they may follow it, for abundance of water springing in the mountains. Of the branches of this tree, they find some as small as a thread, and other as big as a man's finger, according to the largeness or straightness of the rifts and cliffs. They have sometimes chanced upon whole caves sustained and born up as it were with golden pillars: and this in the ways by the which the branches ascend: the which being filled with the substance of the trunk creeping from beneath, the branch maketh itself way by which it may pass out. It is oftentimes divided by encountering with some kind of hard stone. Yet is it in other cliffs nourished by the exhalations and virtue of the root. But now perhaps you will ask me what plenty of gold is brought from thence. You shall therefore understand that only out of Hispaniola the sum of four hundred and sometimes five hundred thousand ducats of gold is brought yearly into Spain: as may be gathered by the fifth portion due to the King's exchequer. . . . In the last region toward the south, named *Guaccaiarima*, in the lordship of *Zauana*, they say there are certain wild men which live in the caves and dens of the mountains, contented only with wild fruits. These men never used the company of any other; nor will by any means become tame. They live without any certain dwelling places and without tillage or culturing of the ground, as we read of them which in old time lived in the golden age. They say also that these men are without any certain language. They are sometimes seen. But our men have yet laid hands on none of them. If at any time they come to the sight of men, and perceive any making toward them, they fly swifter than a hart. . . .

Let us therefore speak somewhat of the . . . tree called *copeia*: pitch is likewise gathered if it as of the pine tree, although some say that it is gathered by distilling or dropping of the wood when it is burnt. It is a strange thing to hear of the leaf thereof: and how necessary provision of nature is showed in the same. It is to be thought that this is the tree in the leaves whereof the Chaldeans (being the first finders of letters) expressed their minds before the use of paper was known. This leaf is a span in breadth, and almost round. Our men write in them with pins or needles or any such instruments made of metal or wood, in manner as well as on paper. It is to be laughed at what our men have persuaded the people of the island as touching this leaf. The simple souls believe that at the commandment of our men, leaves do speak and disclose secrets. They were brought to this credulity by this means. One of our men dwelling in the city of Dominica, the chief of the island, delivered to his servant (being a man born in the island) certain roasted conies (which they call *utias*, being no bigger than mice) willing him to carry the same to his friend which dwelt further within the island. This messenger, whether it were that he was thereto constrained through hunger, or enticed by appetite, devoured three of the conies by the way. He to whom they were sent writ to his friend in a leaf how many he received. When the master had looked a while on the leaf in the presence of the servant, he said thus unto him. *Ah, son, where is thy faith? Could thy greedy appetite prevail so much with thee as to cause thee to eat the conies committed to thy fidelity?* The poor wretch trembling and greatly amazed confessed his fault: and therewith desired his master to tell him how he knew the truth thereof. *This leaf* (quod he) *which thou broughtest me, hath told me all.* Then he further rehearsed unto him the hour of his coming to his friend, and likewise of his departing when he returned. And thus they merrily deceive these seely[3] souls and keep them under obedience: insomuch that they take our men for gods, at whose commandment leaves do disclose such things as they think most hid and secret.

8.2 *A BRIEF RELATION OF TWO SUNDRY VOYAGES MADE BY THE WORSHIPFUL MR. WILLIAM HAWKINS, 1530 AND 1532*

Hawkins was a politician, merchant and sailor, based in Plymouth, who expanded his trade in importing salt, wine, soap, sugar and pepper from Portugal and France, to adventures in Guinea and Brazil for dyewood (for the cloth industry) in 1530. His two journeys, in 1530 and 1532, took £23 worth of exports, and returned with £615 worth of Brazil wood and 'elephants' teeth'. Text from: Richard Hakluyt, *The Principal Navigations, Voyages, Traffics and Discoveries of the English Nation*, 1598–1600 edition, vol. 2, pp. 700–1.

Old Mr. William Hawkins of Plymouth, a man for his wisdom, valour, experience and skill, in sea causes much esteemed, and beloved of King Henry the Eighth, and being one of the principal sea-captains in the west parts of England in his time, not contented with the short voyages commonly then made only to the known coasts of Europe, armed out a tall and goodly ship of his own of burthen of 250 tons, called the *Paul* of Plymouth, wherewith he made three long and famous voyages unto the coast of Brazil, a thing in those days very rare, especially to our nation. He touched at the river of Sestos, upon the coast of Guinea, where he trafficked with the negroes, and took of them elephants' teeth and other commodities which that place yieldeth: and so arriving on the coast of Brazil, he used there such discretion and behaved himself so wisely with those savage people, that he grew into great familiarity and friendship with them. Insomuch that in his second voyage one of the savage kings of the country of Brazil was contented to take ship with him and to be transported hither into England: whereunto Mr. Hawkins agreed, leaving behind in the country as a pledge for his safety and return again, one Martin Cockeram of Plymouth. This Brazilian king being arrived, was brought up to London and presented to King Henry the Eighth, lying as then at Whitehall: at the sight of whom the King and all the nobility did not a little marvel, and not without cause: for in his cheeks were holes made according to their savage manner, and therein small bones were planted, standing an inch out from the said holes, which in his own country was reputed for a great bravery. He had also another hole in his nether lip, wherein was set a precious stone about the bigness of a pea: all his apparel, behaviour, and gesture were very strange to the beholders.

Having remained here the space almost of a whole year, Mr. Hawkins according to his promise and appointment, purposed to convey him again into his country: but it fell out in the way that by the change of air and alteration of diet, the said savage king died at sea, which was feared would turn to the loss of the life of Martin Cockeram his pledge. Nevertheless, the savages being fully persuaded of the honest dealing of our men with their prince, restored again the said pledge without any harm to him, or any man of the company: which pledge of theirs they brought home again into England, with their ship freighted and furnished with the commodities of the country. Which Martin Cockeram being an officer of the town of Plymouth, was living within these few years.

8.3 THOMAS GRESHAM, 'ADVICE ON EXCHANGE RATES'

Gresham was one of Elizabeth I's chief economic advisers, as well as a powerful merchant. He founded the Royal Exchange, and by the methods outlined below rescued English finances from considerable indebtedness to Antwerp financiers and merchants. Text from: J. W. Burgon, *The Life and Times of Sir Thomas Gresham*, London, 1839, vol. 2, pp. 334–6.

Written to William Cecil, Lord Teasurer, 1560

. . . With the like practice twice done in King Edward's time, I did raise the exchange from 16s. to 23s.4d.: whereby all foreign commodities and ours grew good cheap; and thereby we robbed all Christendom of their fine gold and fine silver: and by raising of the exchange and so keeping of it up, the fine gold and fine silver remains for ever within our realm. Sir, if you will enter upon this matter, you may in no wise relent, by no persuasion of the merchants. Whereby you may keep them *in fere* [in obligation] and in good order: for otherwise if they get the bridle, you shall never rule them.

I would presently the Queen's Majesty should give licence to our English merchants to ship, for the sooner they do begin, the sooner they will be laden: and for licence of long cloths, the Queen's Majesty to grant them liberally, and to let them suffer another way.

Sir, this matter is of so great importance, as it must be kept secret. For if the merchants have any inkling, they will never ship their goods; but dispatch them otherwise . . .

To conclude with this practice. First, you shall raise the exchange to the 'riching of the Queen's Majesty and the realm for ever.

Secondly, you shall defray the Queen's Majesty's debt.

Thirdly, you shall advance the Queen's homeward credit in such sort as you shall astonny King Philip and the French King, whereof latter her highness hath felt the commodity. Which matter is of so great importance for the Queen's Majesty's honour and for the profit of her realm, that I cannot express unto you: but refer me to the sequel thereof, which shall try all things, which I have attained unto by experience and proof thereof. For when the exchange was at 17s. I made them pay 20s. upon a cloth; and the next payment for every pound, 22s.: and to the hindrance and domage of no man. For, whereas it shall seem to the world and merchants that they shall be great losers, ere twelve months goeth about, they shall get for every penny lost, 2d., by the reason all foreign commodities (and ours) within the realm shall grow good cheap; as also all kinds of cattle and grain.

8.4 *THE VOYAGE MADE BY MR. JOHN HAWKINS . . . TO THE COAST OF GUINEA AND THE INDIES OF NOVA HISPANIA*

John Hawkins was the son of William Hawkins (8.2), and traded from Plymouth until 1560, importing goods from the Canaries. In 1560 he moved to London, a wealthy man, and set up a syndicate to exploit the economic possibilities in the slave trade. This extract describes his second journey, which was supported by William Cecil. Text from: Richard Hakluyt, *The Principal Navigations, Voyages, Traffics and Discoveries of the English Nation*, 1598–1600 edition: vol. 2, pp. 501–21.

Master John Hawkins with the *Jesus* of Lubeck, a ship of 700 and the *Solomon* a ship of 140, the *Tiger*, a bark of 50, and the *Swallow*, of 30 tons, being all well furnished with men to the number of one hundred three score and ten, as also with ordnance and victual requisite for such a voyage, departed out of Plymouth the 18 day of October in the year of our Lord 1564 with a prosperous wind.

The fourth of November they had sight of the island of Madeira and the sixth day of Tenerife, which they thought to have been the Canary. To speak somewhat of these islands, being called in old time, *insulae fortunatae* [the fortunate isles], by the means of the flourishing thereof, the fruitfulness of them doth surely exceed far all other: for they make wine better than any in Spain: for sugar, sweets, raisins of the sun and many other fruits, abundance; for resin and raw silk, there is great store . . .

The 29 we came to Cape Verde. These people are all black and are called negroes, without any apparel, saving before their privities: of stature goodly men.

The two and twentieth [of December] the captain went into the river called Callowsa, with the two barks, and the *John*'s pinnace, and the *Solomon*'s boat, leaving at anchor in the river's mouth, the two ships, the river being twenty leagues in where the Portuguese rode and dispatched his business, and so returned with two caravels laden with negroes.

The captain was advertised by the Portuguese of a town of the negroes where was not only great quantity of gold, but also that there were not above forty men and an hundred women and children in the town, so that he might get an hundred slaves: he determined to stay before the town three or four hours to see what he could do: and thereupon prepared his men in armour and weapon together, to the number of forty men well appointed, having to their guides certain Portugese. We landing boat after boat and divers of our men scattering themselves, contrary to the captain's will, by one or two in a company for the hope that they had to find gold in their houses, ransacking the same. In the meantime the negroes came upon them and hurt many, being thus scattered: whereas if five or six had been together they had been able, as their companions did, to give the overthrow of forty of them. While this was doing the captain, who with a dozen men, went through the town, returned, finding 200 negroes at the water's side, shooting at them in the boats and cutting them in pieces which were drowned in the water. Thus we returned back somewhat discomforted, although the captain in a singular wise manner carried himself with countenance very cheerful outwardly, having gotten by our going ten negroes, and lost seven of our best men and we had twenty-seven of our men hurt.

We departed with all our ships from Sierra Leone towards the West Indies and for the space of eighteen days we were becalmed, having now and then contrary winds, which happened to us very ill, being but reasonably watered, for so great a company of negroes and ourselves, which pinched us all; and that which was worse, put us in such fear that many never thought to have reached the Indies without great death of negroes and of themselves. But the Almighty God, who never suffereth his elect to perish, sent us the sixteenth of February the ordinary breeze, which is the north-west wind, which never left us, till we came to an island of the cannibals called Dominica, where we arrived the ninth of March, upon a Saturday. The cannibals of that island and also others adjacent are the most desperate warriors that are in the Indies, by the Spaniards' report, who are never able to conquer them, and they are molested by them not a little when they are driven to water there in any of those islands. Of very late, not two months past, in the said island, a caravel being driven to water, was in the night set upon by the inhabitants, who cut their cable in the hawser, whereby they were driven ashore, and so taken by them, and eaten.

We came to a place in the main called Cumana, whither the captain going in his pinnace, spake with certain Spaniards of whom he demanded traffic, but they made him answer they were but soldiers, newly come thither, and were not able to buy one negro: whereupon he asked for a watering place, and they pointed him a place two leagues off called Santa Fe, where we found marvellous good watering. Near about this place inhabited certain Indians, who the next day after we came thither, came down to us, presenting mill and cakes of bread, which they had made of a kind of corn called maize, in bigness of a pease, the ear whereof is much like to a teasel, but a span in length, having thereon a number of grains. Also they brought down to us hens, potatoes and pines, which we bought for beads, pewter whistles, glasses, knives and other trifles.

These potatoes be the most delicate roots that may be eaten and do far exceed our parsnips or carrots. These Indians being of colour tawny like an olive, having everyone of them both men and women, hair all black, and no other colour, neither men nor women suffering any hair to grow in any part of their body, but daily pull it off as it groweth. They go all naked, the men covering no part of their body but their yard,[4] upon the which they wear a gourd or piece of cane, made fast with a thread about their loins, leaving the other parts of their members uncovered, whereof they take no shame. The women also are uncovered, saving with a cloth which they wear a hand-breadth, wherewith they cover their privities both before and behind. These men carry every man his bow and arrows, whereof some arrows are poisoned for wars, which they keep in a cane together: the experience whereof we saw not once or twice, but daily, for they are so good archers that the Spaniards for fear thereof arm themselves and their horses with quilted canvas of two inches thick, and leave no place of their body open to their enemies saving their eyes, which they may not hide, and yet oftentimes are they hit in that so small a scantling: their poison is of such a force that a man being stricken therewith dieth within four and twenty hours.

The Indian women delight not when they are young in bearing of children, because it maketh them have hanging breasts which they account to be great deforming in them, and upon that occasion while they be young, they destroy their seed, saying that it is fittest for old women. Moreover, when they are delivered of child, they go straight to wash themselves, without making any further ceremony for it, not lying in bed as our women do. The beds which they have are made of cotton and wrought artificially of divers colours, which they carry about with them when they travel, and making the same fast to two trees, lie therein they and their women.

We passed between the mainland and the island called Tortuga, and sailed along the coast; the captain saw many Caribs on shore, and some also in their canoes, which made tokens unto him of friendship, and showed him gold; meaning thereby that they would traffic for wares. Whereupon he stayed to see the manners of them, and so for two or three trifles they gave such things as they had about them, and departed. But the Caribs were very importunate to have them come on shore, which if it had not been for want of wares to traffic with them, he would not have denied them, because the Indians which he saw before were very gentle people. These were no such kind of people as we took them to be, but more devilish and are eaters and devourers of any man they can catch . . .

We kept our course along the coast and came to a town called Burburata, where his ships came to an anchor, and he himself went ashore to speak with the Spaniards, to whom he declared himself to be an Englishman, and came thither to trade with them by the way of merchandise, and therefore required licence for the same. They were contented he should bring his ships into harbour, and there they would deliver him any victuals he would require. The next day divers of them came to cheapen, but could not agree of price, because they thought the price too high. Whereupon the captain perceiving they went about to bring down the price, did send for the principals of the town and made a show he would depart, declaring himself to be very sorry that he had so much troubled them, seeing now his pretence was to depart, whereat they asked him what cause moved him thereunto, seeing by their working he was in possibility to have his licence.

To the which he replied that it was not only a licence that he sought, but profit, which he perceived was not there to be had and therefore would seek further and withal showed him his writings what he paid for his negroes, declaring also the great charge he was at in his shipping and men's wages, and therefore to countervail his charges he must sell his negroes for a greater price than they offered. So they put him in comfort to sell better there . . .

The captain sailing by the shore in the pinnace came to the Rancheria, a place where the Spaniards used to fish for pearls and there spoke with a Spaniard who told him how far off he was from Rio de la Hacha: where, having talked with the King's treasurer of the Indies resident there, he declared his quiet traffic in Burboroata, and desired to have the like there also: but the treasurer made answer that they were forbidden by the Viceroy, who having intelligence of our being on the coast, did send express commission to resist us with all the force they could. Our captain replied that he was in an armada of the Queen's Majesty of England, and sent about other her affairs, but enforced by contrary winds to come into those parts where he hoped to find such friendship as he should do in Spain, in that there was amity betwixt their princes. But seeing that they would, contrary to all reason, go about to withstand his traffic, having the force that he hath, he therefore willed them to determine either to give him a licence to trade or else to stand to their own harms: so upon this it was determined he should have licence to trade, but they would give him such a price as was the one half less than he had sold for before. Whereupon the captain wrote to them a letter that they dealt too rigorously with him, to go about to cut his throat in the price of his commodities, which were so reasonably rated. But seeing they had sent him this to his supper, he would in the morning bring them as good a breakfast. In the morning he shot off a whole culverin[5] to summon the town, and preparing one hundred men in armour, went ashore, having in his great boat two falcons[6] of brass, which being perceived by the townsmen, they incontinent in battle array, with their drum and ensign displayed, marched from the town to the sands, of footmen to the number of a hundred and fifty, making great brags with their cries. Our captain perceiving them so bragful, commanded the two falcons to be discharged at them, which put them in no small fear. At every shot they fell flat to the ground, and as we approached near unto them they broke their array and dispersed. The horsemen also being about thirty, made as brave a show as might be, coursing up and down with their horses, their brave white leather targets in one hand, and their javelins in the other. But when we landed, they gave ground, for little they thought we would have landed so boldly: and therefore as the captain was putting his men in array they sent a messenger on horseback with a flag of truce: but the captain not well contented with this messenger, marched forwards. Upon this we made our traffic quietly with them . . .

They kept on their way along the coast of Florida and the fifteenth day came to an anchor, and so where the Frenchmen abode, ranging all the coast along, seeking for fresh water, anchoring every night, because we would overshoot no place of fresh water, and in the day time the captain in the ship's pinnace sailed along the shore, went into every creek, speaking with divers of the Floridians. They found sorrel to grow as abundantly as grass, and where their houses were great store of maize and mill, and grapes of great bigness, but of taste much like our English grapes. Also deer great plenty, which came upon the sands before them. Their houses are not many together, for in one house an hundred of them do lodge, they being made much like a great barn, having no place divided, but one small room for their king and queen. For the making of their fire, not only they but also the negroes do the same, which is made only by two sticks rubbing them, one against another. In their apparel the men only use deer skins, wherewith some only cover their privy members, othersome use the same as garments to cover them before and behind; which skins are painted some yellow and red, some black and russet, and every man according to his own fancy. They do not omit to paint their bodies also with curious knots or antic work, as every man in his own fancy deviseth.

The women also for their apparel use painted skins, but most of them gowns of moss, somewhat longer than our moss, which they sew together artificially, and make the same surplice-wise, wearing their hair down to their shoulders like the Indians . . .

. . . The ground yieldeth naturally grapes in great store, for in the time that the Frenchmen were there they made twenty hogsheads of wine. Also it yieldeth roots passing good, deer marvellous store, with divers other beasts and fowl serviceable to the use of man. These be things wherewith a man may live, having corn or maize wherewith to make bread, for maize maketh good savoury bread and cakes, as fine as flour. And this maize was the greatest lack they had because they had no labourers to sow the same, and therefore to them that should inhabit the land it were requisite to have labourers to till and sow the ground. The Indians with the head of maize roasted, will travel a whole day; in this order I saw three score of them feed, who were laden with wares and came fifty leagues off. The Floridians when they travel have a kind of herb, dried, who with a cane and an earthen cup in the end, with fire, and the dried herbs put together, do suck through the cane the smoke thereof, which smoke satisfieth their hunger and therewith they live four or five days without meat or drink. At the Frenchmen's first coming thither, they received for a hatchet two pound weight of gold, because they know not the estimation thereof: but the soldiers being greedy of the same, did take it from them, giving them nothing for it. How they came by this gold and silver the Frenchmen know not as yet. It seemeth they had estimation of their gold and silver, for it is wrought flat and graven, which they wear about their necks; other some made round like a pancake with a hole in the midst, to bolster up their breasts withal, because they think it a deformity to have great breasts. As for mines, either of gold or silver, the Frenchmen can hear of none. The Frenchmen obtained pearls of them of great bigness. The Spaniards used to keep daily fishing some two or three hundred Indians: and their order is to go in canoes or rather great pinnaces, with thirty men, whereof the one half be divers, the rest do open the same for the pearls. The oysters which have the smallest sort of pearls are found in seven or eight fathom water, but the greatest in eleven or twelve fathom.

Of beasts in this country, besides deer, foxes, hares, polecats, coneys, ounces,[7] and leopards, I am not able certainly to say: but it is thought that there are lions and tigers as well as unicorns.

8.5 *A DISCOURSE . . . BY ONE MILES PHILIPS*

Miles Philips was one of the company boat with John Hawkins, who with others was put ashore in the West Indies, after their famed defeat at San Juan de Ulloa (omitted here). Text from: Richard Hakluyt, *The Principal Navigations, Voyages, Traffics and Discoveries of the English Nation,* 1598–1600 edition, vol. 2, pp. 469–86.

Upon the coast of Guinea we obtained 150 negroes. There was a negro sent as an ambassador to our general, from a king of the negroes, which was oppressed with other kings his bordering neighbours, desiring our general to grant him succour and aid against those his enemies, which our general granted unto, and went himself in person aland, with the number of two hundred of our men, and the king which had requested our aid did join his force with ours, so that thereby our general assaulted and set fire upon a town in which there was at least the number of eight or ten thousand negroes, and they perceiving that they were not able to make any resistance sought by flight to save themselves, in which their flight there were taken prisoners to the number of eight or nine hundred, which our general ought to have had for his share. Howbeit the negro king falsifying his word and promise, secretly in the night conveyed himself away with as many prisoners as he had in his custody. But our general notwithstanding finding himself to have now very near the number of 500 negroes thought it best to depart with them, and such merchandise as he had from the coast of Africa, towards the West Indies, and therefore commanded with all diligence to take in fresh water and fuel, and so with speed to prepare to depart. In a storm we lost one of our ships, the *William and John*, of which ship and of her people we heard no tidings.

Upon the third day of February 1568 we departed from the coast of Africa, having the weather somewhat tempestuous, which made our passage the more hard: and sailing so for the space of fifty-two days, upon the 27 March 1568 we came in sight of an island called Dominica in the West Indies. From thence we departed for Cartagena, we could not obtain any traffic there, and so our general thought it best to depart from thence the rather for the avoiding of certain dangerous storms called the hurricanes, so the 24 of July 1568 we departed from thence, directing our course north: sailing toward Florida upon the 12 of August an extreme tempest arose, which dured for the space of eight days, in which our ships were most dangerously tossed and beaten hither and thither, so that we were in continual fear to be drowned, and in the end we were constrained to flee for succour to the port of St. Juan de Ulloa, or Vera Cruz, which is the port that serveth for the city of Mexico . . .

[He tells of their ships attacked by the Spanish fleet in port, and their escape, with loss of men, provisions and ships; and of the general's decision to leave some of the men on land, since the remaining ship could not carry them all.]

The next morning we thought it best to travel along by the sea coast to seek out some place of habitation: and so departing from an hill where we had rested all night, not having any dry thread about us (for all the night it rained cruelly) as we went from the hill and were come into the plain, we were greatly troubled to pass, for the grass and weeds that grew there higher than any man. On the left hand we had the sea, and upon the right hand great woods, so that of necessity we must needs pass on our way westward through those marshes, and going thus, suddenly we were assaulted by the Indians, a warlike kind of people.

These people are called *Chichimici*, they wear their hair long, even down to their knees, they do also colour their faces green, yellow, red and blue, which maketh them to seem very ugly and terrible to behold. These people keep wars against the Spaniards, of whom they have been oftentimes very cruelly handled: for with the Spaniards there is no mercy. They perceiving us at our first coming on land supposed us to have been their enemies the Spaniards, and having by their forerunners described what number we were and how feeble and weak, without armour or weapon, they suddenly raised a terrible and huge cry, and so came running fiercely upon us, shooting off their arrows as thick as hail, unto whose mercy we were constrained to yield, not having amongst us any kind of armour, nor yet weapon, saving one caliver[8] and two old rusty swords. When they perceived that we sought not any other than favour and mercy at their hands, and that we were not their enemies the Spaniards, they had compassion on us and came and caused us all to sit down. They came to all such as had any coloured clothes amongst us, and those they did strip stark naked, and took their clothes away with them, but those that were apparelled in black they did not meddle withal, and so went their ways and left us without doing us any further hurt, only in the first brunt they killed eight of our men. Shortly after they had left us stripped we thought it best to divide ourselves into two companies, and so being separated, half of us went under the leading of one Anthony Goddard, who is yet a man alive, and dwelleth at this instant in the town of Plymouth, whom before we chose to be captain over us all, and those which went under his leading, of which number I, Miles Philips, was one, travelled westward that way which the Indians with their hands had before pointed us to go. . . . We travelled on still westward sometimes through such thick woods that we were enforced with cudgels to break away the brambles and bushes from tearing our naked bodies; other sometimes we should travel through the plains in such high grass that we could scarce see one another, and as we passed in some places, we should have of our men slain and fall down suddenly being struck by the Indians which stood behind trees and bushes in secret places, and so killed our men as they went by, for we went scatteringly in seeking of fruits to relieve ourselves. We were also often greatly annoyed with a kind of fly, which the Spaniards call mosquitoes. They are scarce so big as a gnat: they will suck one's blood marvellously and if you kill them while they are sucking, they are so venomous that the place will swell extremely; but if you let them suck their fill, and go away of themselves, then they do you no other hurt but leave behind them a red spot somewhat bigger than a flea-biting. As we travelled thus for the space of ten or twelve days, our captain did oftentimes cause certain to go up into the tops of high trees to see if they could descry any town or place of inhabitants, but they could not perceive any. At length they descried a great river that fell from the north-west into the main sea, and presently after we heard an arquebus[9] shot off; which did greatly encourage us for thereby we knew that we were near to some Christians, and did therefore hope shortly to find some succour and comfort, and within the space of one hour after, as we travelled, we heard a cock crow, which was also no small joy unto us, and so we came to the north side of the river of Panuco: of this river we drank very greedily, for we had not met with any water in six days before, and as we were here by the river resting ourselves, we perceived many Spaniards upon the other side of the river, riding up and down on horseback: the Spaniards made out about the number of twenty horsemen, and embarking themselves in the canoes they led their horses by the reins swimming over after them, and being come over to that side of the river where we were, they saddled their horses and came very fiercely running at us. Our captain, Anthony Goddard, did persuade us to submit unto them, for being naked as we at this time were, and without weapon, we could not make resistance. They perceived us to be Christians and did call for more canoes, and carried us over by four and four in a boat, they understanding by our captain how long we had been without meat, imparted between two and two a loaf of bread made of that country wheat, which the Spaniards call maize, of the bigness of our half-penny loaves. This bread was very sweet and pleasant unto us, for we had not eaten any in a long time before, and what is it that hunger doth not make to have savoury and delicate taste?

When we were all come to the town, the governor there showed himself very severe unto us, and threatened to hang us all; and then he demanded what money we had, which in truth was very little: we accounted that amongst us all we had the number of five hundred pesos.

When he had taken all that we had, he caused us to be put into a little house much like a hogsty, where we were almost smothered. Many of our men had been hurt by the Indians at our first coming on land, whose wounds were very sore and grievous, desired to have the help of their surgeons to cure their wounds. The governor answered that we should have none other surgeon but the hangman, which should sufficiently heal us of all our griefs: and thus reviling us and calling us English dogs, and Lutheran heretics, we remained the space of three days in this miserable state, not knowing what should become of us.

Upon the fourth day, looking every hour when we should suffer death, there came a great number of Indians and Spaniards weaponed to fetch us out of the house and amongst them we espied one that brought a great many of new halters, at the sight whereof we made no other account but that we should presently have suffered death, and so crying and calling to God for mercy and forgiveness of our sins, we prepared ourselves, making us ready to die. When we were come out of the house with those halters they bound our arms behind us and so coupling us two and two together they commanded us to march on through the town, and so along the country from place to place towards the city of Mexico, which is distant the space of ninety leagues; having only but two Spaniards to conduct us, they being accompanied with a great number of Indians warding on either side with bows and arrows, lest we should escape. Upon the second day at night we came unto a town which the Indians call Nohele, and the Spaniards Santa Maria, in which town there is a house of white friars, which did very courteously use us, and gave us hot meat as mutton and broth, and garments also to cover ourselves withal, made of white baize: we fed very greedily of the meat. Our greedy feeding caused us to fall sick of hot burning agues. And here at this place one Thomas Baker one of our men died of a hurt: for he had been shot before with an arrow into the throat at the first encounter.

The next morrow about ten of the clock we departed from thence bound two and two together, and guarded as before, and so travelled on our way towards Mexico, till we came to a town named Mestitlan, where is a house of black friars, and in this town there are about the number of three hundred Spaniards both men, women and children. The friars sent us meat from the house ready dressed, and the friars and the men and women used us very courteously, and gave us some shirts and other such things as we lacked. Here our men were very sick of their agues and with eating of another fruit which did bind us so sore that for the space of ten or twelve days we could not ease ourselves ...

On our journey towards Mexico within two leagues of it, there was built by the Spaniards a very fair church called Our Lady's Church, in which there is an image of Our Lady of silver and gilt, being as high and as large as a tall woman, and before this image there are as many lamps of silver as there be days in the year, which upon high days are all lighted. Whensoever any Spaniards pass by this church, although they be on horseback, they will alight and come into the church, and kneel before the image: which image they call in the Spanish tongue *Nuestra Señora de Guadelupe*. At this place there are certain cold baths, the water thereof is somewhat brackish in taste, but very good for any that have any sore or wound. And every year once upon our Lady day, the people use to repair thither to offer and pray in that Church before the image, and they say that our Lady of Guadelupe doth work a number of miracles.

Here we met with a great number of Spaniards on horseback which came from Mexico to see us, both gentlemen and men of occupations, and they came as people to see a wonder. There was brought to us by the Spaniards from the market place great store of meat, sufficient to have satisfied five time so many as we were; some also gave us hats and some gave us money. Which place we stayed for the space of two hours, and from thence we were conveyed by water in two large canoes to an hospital. After our coming thither many of the company that came with me from Panuco died within the space of fourteen days. Soon after we were put altogether in Our Lady's hospital, in which place we were courteously used and visited oftentimes by virtuous gentlemen and gentlewomen of the city, who brought us divers things to comfort us withal, as suckets and marmalades, and that very liberally. In which hospital we remained for the space of six months, until we were all whole and sound of body, and then were appointed by the Viceroy to be carried unto the town of Texcoco, in which town there are certain houses of correction, like to Bridewell here in London. Into which place divers Indians are sold for slaves, some for ten years, and some for twelve. It was no small grief unto us when we understood that we should be carried thither, and to be used as slaves, we had rather be put to death. . . . Continuing thus straightly kept in prison there for the space of two months, at the length we agreed amongst ourselves to break forth of prison, come of it what would, for we were minded rather to suffer death than longer to live in that miserable state. And so having escaped out of prison, we knew not what way to fly for the safety of ourselves, the night was dark and it rained terribly, and not having any guide, we went we knew not wither, and in the morning at the appearing of the day we perceived ourselves to come hard to the city of Mexico, which is twenty-four English miles from Texcoco. The day being come we were espied by the Spaniards, and pursued and taken and brought before the Viceroy, and head justices, who threatened to hang us for breaking of the King's prison. Yet in the end they sent us into a garden belonging to the Viceroy and coming thither we found there our English gentlemen which were delivered as hostages when as our general was betrayed at San Juan de Ulloa, as is aforesaid; and with them we also found Robert Barret, the master of the *Jesus*, in which place we remained labouring and doing such things as we were commanded for the space of four months, having but two sheep a day allowed to suffice us all, being very near an hundred men, and for bread we had every man two loaves a day, of the quantity of one half-penny loaf. At the end of which four months, they having removed our gentlemen hostages, and the master of the *Jesus*, did cause it to be proclaimed that what gentleman Spaniard soever was willing or would have any English man to serve him should repair to the said garden and there take their choice: happy was he that could soonest get one of us.

The gentlemen that thus took us for their servants or slaves did new apparel us throughout, with whom we abode, doing such service as they appointed us unto, which was for the most part to attend upon them at the table, and to be as their chamberlains, and to wait upon them when they went abroad. In this sort we remained and served in the city of Mexico and thereabouts for the space of a year, and somewhat longer. Afterwards many of us were by our masters appointed to go to sundry of their mines and to be as overseers of the negroes and Indians that laboured there. In which mines many of us did profit and gain greatly: the Indians and negroes which wrought under our charge, upon our well using of them, would at times, as upon Saturdays when they had left work, labour for us, and blow as much silver as should be worth unto us three marks. Sundry weeks we did gain so much by this means besides our wages, that many of us became very rich: for we lived and gained thus in those mines some three or four years. As concerning those gentlemen which were delivered as hostages the said gentlemen were sent away into Spain with the fleet, where as I have heard it credibly reported, many of them died with the cruel handling of the Spaniards in the Inquisition house. Robert Barret, also master of *Jesus*, was sent away with the fleet into Spain the next year following, where afterwards he suffered persecution in the Inquisition and at the last was condemned to be burnt.

In the year of our Lord one thousand five hundred seventy four, the Inquisition began to be established in the Indies, very much against the minds of many of the Spaniards themselves. The Chief Inquisitor thought it best to call us that were Englishmen first in question, and so much the rather for that they had perfect knowledge and intelligence that many of us were become very rich, and therefore we were a very good prey to the Inquisitors: so that now began our sorrows afresh, for we were sent for and sought out in all places of the country and proclamation made upon pain of losing of goods and excommunication, that no man should hide or keep secret any Englishmen or any part of their goods . . .

I, Miles Philips and William Lowe were appointed to the Blackfriars to be an overseer of Indian workmen, who wrought there in building of a new Church: amongst which Indians I learned their language or Mexican tongue very perfectly, and had great familiarity with many of them, whom I found to be a courteous and loving kind of people, ingenious and of great understanding, and they hate and abhor the Spaniards with all their hearts, they have used such horrible cruelties against them, and do still keep them in such subjection and servitude, that they and the negroes also do daily lay in wait to practise their deliverance out of that thraldom. We served out the years that we were condemned for, with the use of our fool's coats, and we must needs confess that the friars did use us very courteously: for every one of us had his chamber with bedding and diet, and all things clean and neat: yea many of the Spaniards and friars themselves do utterly abhor and mislike of that cruel Inquisition, and would comfort us the best they could. We were then brought again before the Chief Inquisitor and had all our fool's coats pulled off and hanged up in the head Church, and every man's name and judgement written thereupon, with this addition, *an heretic Lutheran reconciled*. And there are also all their coats hanged up which were condemned to the galleys, with their names and judgements, and underneath his coat, *heretic Lutheran reconciled*, and also the coats and names of the three that were burnt, whereupon were written an *obstinate heretic Lutheran burnt*. Then were we suffered to go up and down the country and to place ourselves as we could, and yet not so free but that we very well knew that there was good espial always attending us and all our actions, so that we dared not once speak or look awry. David Alexander and Robert Cooke returned to serve the Inquisitor, who shortly after married them both to two of his negro women: Richard Williams married a rich widow of Biscay with 4,000 pesos: for mine own part I could never thoroughly settle myself to marry in that country although many fair offers were made unto me, but I could have no liking to live in that place where I must everywhere see and know such horrible idolatry committed, and durst not once for my life speak against it: and therefore I had always a longing and desire to this my native country. I made my choice to learn to weave grograins and taffetas, and so compounding with a silk-weaver, I bound myself for three years to serve him, and gave him a hundred and fifty pesos to teach me the science, and by this means I lived the more quiet and free from suspicion.

. . . And thus through the providence of Almighty God after sixteen years' absence, having sustained many and sundry great troubles and miseries, I came home to this my native country of England in the year 1582.

8.6 THOMAS WILSON, *A DISCOURSE UPON USURY*

Usury was increasingly seen as an evil necessity during the sixteenth century, given the expanding mercantile economy. The establishment of joint stock companies required some capital liquidity: but here Wilson voices the theological objections. Text from: 1572 edition, fos 362ff.

And therefore as Lucifer for pride fell down from heaven, so usurers for covetousness will fall down from earth to the dark dungeon of hell. And mark this ever: whatsoever he be that is a great usurer, is of a vile and base nature, and nothing of value in him. One saith that usury upon usury is villain usury, and no doubt they are no better than villeins or slaves, whosoever they be, that are great usurers, let them set never so good a countenance upon the matter.

All this notwithstanding, these wise worldly rich men, to cloak their sin and to bear out the matter as though their doings were lawful, do devise policies against God, and, seeking to mitigate offences, teach God what he hath to do. So were the stews devised as a common sink to scour cities, and maintained as tolerable to avoid further evil, being never punished in other countries, and much marvelled by strangers resorting hither that simple fornication is so severely punished here in England. But such devices are wicked policies and fetches directly against all godliness. For Saint Paul saith that no fornicator, no whore-monger, or unclean person shall inherit the kingdom of heaven. And as it is said for whoremongers, so saith the holy prophet King David, that no usurer who taketh overplus for his money or goods, for the very loan thereof, shall enter into the kingdom of heaven. To give alms and to lend freely are the fruits of charity, and two especial precepts of God, and plain tokens to know a faithful Christian from an infidel. But he that will do neither of these two things, as God hath commanded, can never be thought a good Christian . . .

And you, Master Civilian . . . you did allege certain lawyers of this time, and with them some godly divines, that thinks it were good to have some toleration to avoid further mischief, and to bridle the great greediness of certain covetous wretches, as that which you account to rise of a good mind and zeal . . .

And you Master Merchant, unto whom God hath lent great treasure of this world (for I tell you, you are but his steward), call to God that he will lend you grace in the middest of your wealth to learn and know him aright. Let not wealth choke your judgement and cloy your understanding. Beware how you cloak with God, do not under colour of bargain and sale practise usury as most men do. There be plain ways for men to take which are and hath been ever allowed. And this I say: he that liveth in his vocation truly and justly is an honest man. That grocer who selleth wholesome wares with good conscience is to be well esteemed. The draper that dealeth lawfully deserveth credit. The true tailor is an honest man in his calling. The goldsmith, the mercer and the haberdasher are all to be well liked, and so all others of any occupation that live justly in their trade. A merchant, of whatsoever calling he is, is to be accounted for honest, if he live with good fame and name by his lawful traffic or occupation. But I pray you, of what occupation is Goodman Usurer, or who would gladly be called one of the usurer's occupation? Or of what company or several hall or elsewhere are they in London? God grant all merchants to be otherwise occupied, and everyone to follow his lawful vocation, rather than to trade by this lewd craft or kind of living!

Some learned fathers, yea and some great philosophers also thinks it a thing almost impossible for a great rich merchant that is a mighty occupier, to be a good Christian. But I am not altogether of the mind, especially if the merchants that are great occupiers do live in any fear of God . . .

For if the merchant may be allowed to make gain of his money, he will rather use the certain and assured way than dangerously adventure the seas, and so the Queen shall lose her gain and right of inheritance, and the State shall be undone. The ploughman will no more turn up the ground for uncertain gain, when he may make an assured profit of his money that lieth by him. The artificer will leave his working, the clothier will cease his making of clothes, because these trades are painful and chargeable. Yea, all men will give themselves wholly to live an idle life by their money, if they have any. And although all cannot have money, yet if all those that have money will live by the loan thereof, all will be marred in the end. And amongst others, the gentleman will no more profess arms nor chivalry to advance his welfare, but selling his lands will have double gain by his money, and so give over housekeeping altogether, taking a chamber in London or elsewhere, instead of a house in his own country, as we see they do now commonly, the more is the pity, and the greater is their shame. Yea, the nobleman will no more defend the widow and fatherless, nor yet do judgement and justice, but live by his filthy gain, and lose thereby his dignity and estimation, as all those that do live by corrupt usury.

8.7 LETTERS PATENT TO SIR HUMPHREY GILBERT

Queen Elizabeth granted Gilbert a patent to settle Virginia in 1578, which was passed on to Raleigh after Gilbert's untimely death in 1583 in Newfoundland. The expedition of 1584 thus sailed under Raleigh's patronage (see 8.8). Text from: Hakluyt, *The Principal Navigations, Voyages, Traffics and Discoveries of the English Nation* III, pp. 17–8.

Elizabeth by the grace of God, Queen of England . . . know ye that . . . we have given and granted . . . for us, our heirs and successors . . . to our trusty and well-beloved servant, Sir Humphrey Gilbert of Compton . . . and to his heirs and assigns for ever, free liberty and licence . . . at all times forever hereafter to discover, find, search out, and view such remote, heathen and barbarous lands, countries and territories, not actually possessed of any Christian prince or people, as to him . . . shall seem good; and the same to have . . . and enjoy to him, his heirs and assigns for ever, with all commodities, jurisdictions and royal-ties, both by sea and land; and for the said Sir Humphrey, and all such as from time to time by licence of us . . . shall go and travel thither to inhabit or remain there, to build and fortify at the discretion of the said Sir Humphrey . . .

And further the said Sir Humphrey . . . shall have . . . and enjoy to him . . . all the soil of all such lands, countries and territories so to be discovered or possessed as aforesaid . . . to be had or used with full power to dispose thereof, and of every part thereof, in fee simple or otherwise according to the order of the laws of England, as near as the same convenient may be . . . paying unto us for all services, duties and demands the fifth part of all the ore of gold and silver that . . . shall be there gotten.

And for uniting in more perfect league and amity of such countries, lands and territories so to be possessed and inhabited as aforesaid, with our realms of England and Ireland, and for the better encouragement of men to this enter-prise, we do by these presents grant and declare that all such countries, so hereafter to be possessed and inhabited as aforesaid, from thenceforth shall be of allegiance to us, our heirs and successors, and we do grant to the said Sir Humphrey . . . and to all and every other person and persons being of our alle-giance . . . that with the assent of the said Sir Humphrey. . . shall now in this voyage for discovery or in the second journey for conquest, hereafter travel to such lands . . . as aforesaid . . . that they . . . shall and may have . . . all the privi-leges of free denizens and persons native of England and within our allegiance.

8.8 THE FIRST ENGLISH VOYAGE TO VIRGINIA

Subsequent to the granting of the Letters Patents for the exploration and settling of Virginia, Raleigh equipped and financed this expedition. Text from: Richard Hakluyt, *The Principal Navigations, Voyages, Traffics and Discoveries of the English Nation*, 1598–1600 edition, vol. 3, pp. 246–50.

The first voyage made to the coasts of America with two barks, captains Mr. Philip Amadas and Mr. Arthur Barlow, who discovered part of the country now called Virginia, in the year 1584. Sent to Sir Walter Raleigh, knight, at whose charge the voyage was set forth.

The 27 day of April 1584 we departed the West of England with two barks well furnished with men and victuals . . .

[July] . . . There came unto us divers boats and in one of them the king's brother, accompanied with forty or fifty men, very handsome and goodly people, and in their behaviour as mannerly and civil as any of Europe. The king is called Wingina, the country *Wingandacoa*, and now by her Majesty, Virginia. After he had made along speech unto us, we presented him with divers things, which he received very joyfully and thankfully.

The king is greatly obeyed, and his brothers and children reverenced; the king himself in person was at our being there, sore wounded in a fight which he had with the king of the next country, and was shot in two places through the body, and once clean through the thigh, but yet he recovered.

A day or two after this we fell to trading with them, exchanging some things that we had for chamois, buff and deer skins: when we showed him all our packet of merchandise, of all things that he saw, a bright tin dish most pleased him, which he presently took up and clapped it before his breast, and after made a hole in the brim thereof and hung it about his neck, making signs that it would defend him against his enemies' arrows: for those people maintain a deadly and terrible war with the people and king adjoining. We exchanged our tin dish for twenty skins worth twenty crowns or twenty nobles; and a copper kettle for fifty skins worth fifty crowns. They offered us good exchange for our hatchets and axes, and for knives, and would have given anything for swords: but we would not depart with any. After two or three days the king's brother came aboard the ships and drank wine and ate of our meat and of our bread, and liked exceedingly thereof; and after a few days overpassed he brought his wife with him to the ships, his daughter and two or three children. His wife was very well favoured, of mean stature, and very bashful: she had on her back a long cloak of leather with the fur side next to her body, and before her a piece of the same; about her forehead she had a band of white coral, and so had her husband many times; in her ears she had bracelets of pearls hanging down to her middle (whereof we delivered your worship a little bracelet) and those were of the bigness of good peas. The rest of her women of the better sort had pendants of copper hanging in either ear, and some of the children of the king's bother and other noble men have five or six in either ear; he himself had upon his head a broad plate of gold or copper, for being unpolished, we knew not what metal it should be, neither would he by any means suffer us to take it off his head, but feeling it, it would bow very easily.

Their boats are made of one tree, either of pine or of pitch trees: a wood not commonly known to our people, nor found growing in England. They have no edge tools to make them withal: if they have any they are very few, and those it seems they had twenty years since, which, as those two men declared, was out of a wreck which happened upon their coast of some Christian ship, being beaten that way by some storm and outrageous weather . . .

The king's brother had great liking of our armour, a sword and divers other things which we had, and offered to lay a great box of pearl in gage for them: but we refused it for this time, because we would not make them know that we esteemed thereof until we had understood in what places of the country the pearl grew.

He sent us every day a brace or two of fat bucks, coneys, hares, fish the best of the world. He sent us divers kinds of fruits, melons, walnuts, cucumbers, gourds, pease, and divers roots and fruits very excellent good, and of their country corn, which is very white, fair and well tasted, and groweth three times in five months: they cast the corn into the ground, breaking a little of the soft turf with a wooden mattock or pickaxe, ourselves proved the soil and put some of our pease in the ground and in ten days they were of fourteen inches high: they have also beans very fair of divers colours and wonderful plenty.

After they had been divers times aboard our ships, myself with seven more went twenty mile into the river: and the evening following we came to an island which they call Roanoke, distant from the harbour by which we entered seven leagues. And at the north end thereof was a village of nine houses, built of cedar and fortified round with sharp trees to keep out their enemies. The wife of Granganimo, the king's brother, came running out to meet us very cheerfully and friendly. When we were come in, having five rooms in her house, she caused us to sit down by a great fire and after took off our clothes and washed them, and dried them again: some of the women plucked off our stockings and washed them, some washed our feet in warm water.

She brought us into the inner room, where she set on the board standing along the house some wheat, like furmenty, sodden venison, and roasted; fish sodden, boiled and roasted; melons raw, and sodden; roots of divers kinds and divers fruits. Their drink is commonly water. We found the people most gentle, loving and faithful; void of all guile and treason; and such as live after the manner of the golden age. The people only care how to defend themselves from the cold in their short winter, and to feed themselves with such meat as the soil affordeth.

8.9 THOMAS HARRIOT, *A BRIEF AND TRUE REPORT OF THE NEW-FOUND LAND OF VIRGINIA*

Harriot was a young mathematician, chosen by Raleigh to accompany the first settlement to Roanoke in Virginia in 1585. He and John White (the artist) were commissioned to assess both ethnography and the possible exploitation of local commodities. Despite the failure of the settlement, White, Raleigh and Harriot believed the land had great potential, and his *Brief and True Report* was written to counteract negative publicity from some of the survivors of the first trip, and to seek further financial and political support for another voyage for the establishment of a permanent trading enterprise. Text from: first edition, 1588, fos B1ʳ–C2; E1–F2; F3ᵛ–F5ʳ.

Of merchantable commodities

Silk of grass or grass silk. There is a kind of grass in the country upon the blades whereof there groweth very good silk in form of a thin glittering skin to be stripped off. It groweth two foot and a half high or better: the blades are about two foot in length and half inch broad. The like groweth in Persia, which is in the self same climate as Virginia, of which very many of the silk works that come from thence into Europe are made. Hereof if it be planted and ordered as in Persia, it cannot in reason be otherwise but that there will rise in short time great profit to the dealers therein, seeing there is so great use and vent thereof as well in our country as elsewhere. And by the means of sowing and planting it in good ground, it will be far greater, better and more plentiful than it is. Although notwithstanding there is great store thereof in many places of the country growing naturally and wild . . .

Worm silk. In many of our journeys we found silk worms fair and great: as big as our ordinary walnuts. Although it hath not been our hap to have found such plenty as elsewhere to be in the country we have heard of, yet seeing that the country doth naturally breed and nourish them, there is no doubt but if art be added in planting of mulberry trees, and others fit for them in commodious places, for their feeding and nourishing; and some of them carefully gathered and husbanded in that sort as by men of skills known to be necessary, there will rise great profit in time to the Virginians, as thereof doth now to the Persians, Turks, Italians and Spaniards.

Flax and hemp. The truth is that of hemp and flax there is no great store in any one place together, by reason it is not planted, but as the soil doth yield it of itself; and howsoever the leaf and stem or stalk do differ from ours, the stuff by the judgement of men of skill is altogether as good as ours. And if not, as further proof should find otherwise, we have that experience of the soil, as that there cannot be showed any reason to the contrary but that it will grow there excellently well, and by planting will be yielded plentifully: seeing there is so much ground whereof some may well be applied to such purposes. What benefit hereof may grow in cordage and linens who cannot easily understand?

Alum. There is a vein of earth along the sea coast for the space of forty or fifty miles, whereof by the judgement of some that have made trial here in England is made good alum of that kind which is called red alum. The richness of such a commodity is so well known that I need not say anything thereof . . .

Pitch, tar, resin and turpentine. There are those kinds of trees which yield them abundantly and great store. In the very same land where we were seated, being fifteen miles of length, and five or six miles in breadth, there are few trees else but of the same kind; the whole land being full.

Sassafras. Called by the inhabitants, *winauk*, a kind of wood of most pleasant and sweet smell; and of most rare virtues in physic for the cure of many diseases. It is found by experience to be far better and of more uses than the wood which is called *guaiacum* or *lignum vitae*. For the description, the manner of using and the manifold virtues thereof, I refer you to the book of Monardus, translated and entitled in English, *The Joyful News from the West Indies*.

Cedar. A very sweet wood and fine timber, whereof if nests of chests be there made, or timber thereof fitted for sweet and fine bedsteads, tables, desks, lutes, virginals and many things else (of which there hath been proof made already) to make up freight with other principal commodities, will yield profit.

Wine. There are two kinds of grapes that the soil doth yield naturally: the one is small and sour of the ordinary bigness as ours in England: the other far greater and of himself luscious sweet. When they are planted and husbanded as they ought, a principal commodity of wines by them may be raised.

Oil. There are two sorts of walnuts, both holding oil, but the one far more plentiful than the other. When there are mills and other devices for the purpose, a commodity of them may be raised because there are infinite store. There are also three several kinds of berries in the form of oak acorns, which also by the experience and use of the inhabitants, we find to yield very good and sweet oil. Furthermore, the bears of the country are commonly very fat, and in some places there are many: their fatness because it is so liquid may well be termed oil and hath many special uses.

Furs. All along the sea coast there are great store of otters . . . which will yield good profit. We hope also of marten furs, and make no doubt by the relation of the people but that in some places of the country there are store; although there were but two skins that came to our hands. Lucerns[10] also we have understanding of, although for the time we saw none.

Deer skins. Dressed after the manner of chamois, or undressed, are to be had of the natural inhabitants thousands, yearly by way of traffic for trifles; and no more waste or spoil of deer than is and hath been ordinarily in time before.

Civet cats. In our travels there was found one to have been killed by a savage or inhabitant; and in another place the smell where one or more had lately been before: whereby we gather besides than by the relation of the people that there are some in the country: good profit will rise by them.

Iron. In two places of the country specially: one about fourscore and the other six score miles from the fort or place where we dwelt. We found near the waterside the ground to be rocky which by the trial of a mineral man was found to hold iron richly. It is found in many places of the country else. I know nothing to the contrary but that it may be allowed for a good merchantable commodity, considering there the small charge for the labour and feeding of men; the infinite store of wood: the want of wood and dearness thereof in England; and the necessity of ballasting of ships.

Copper. A hundred and fifty miles into the main in two towns we found with the inhabitants diverse small plates of copper that had been made as we understood, by the inhabitants that dwell farther into the country: where as they say are mountains and rivers that yield also white grains of metal which is deemed to be silver. For confirmation whereof at the time of our first arrival in the country, I saw with some others with me, two small pieces of silver grossly beaten . . .

Pearl. Sometimes in feeding on mussels we found some pearl, but it was our hap to meet with rags, or of a pied colour, not having yet discovered those places where we heard of better and more plenty. One of our company, a man of skill in such matters, had gathered together from among the savage people about five thousand: of which number he chose so many as made a fair chain, which for their likeness and uniformity in roundness, orientness and piedness of many excellent colours, with equality in greatness, were very fair and rare; and had therefore been presented to her Majesty, had we not by casualty and through extremity of a storm lost them with many things else in coming away from the country.

Sweet gums of divers kinds and many other apothecary drugs of which we will make special mention, when we shall receive it from such men of skill in that kind that in taking reasonable pains shall discover them more particularly than we have done, and than now I can make relation of, for want of the examples I had provided and gathered, and are now lost with other things by casualty before mentioned.

Dyes of divers kinds. There is shoemake, well known and used in England for black; the seed of an herb called *wasewowr*; little small roots called *chappaeor*; and the bark of the tree called by the inhabitants *tangomockomindge*: which dyes are for divers sorts of red: their goodness for our English cloths remain yet to be proved. The inhabitants use them only for the dyeing of hair and colouring of their faces and mantles made of deer skins; and also for the dyeing of rushes to make artificial works withal in their mats and baskets; having no other thing besides that they account of apt to use them for. If they will not prove merchantable there is no doubt but the planters there shall find apt uses for them, as also for other colours which we know to be there . . .

Of such commodities as Virginia is known to yield for victual and sustenance of man's life, usually fed upon by the natural inhabitants; as also by us during the time of our abode

Pagatowr, a kind of grain so called by the inhabitants; the same in the West Indies is called *maize*: Englishmen call it Guinea wheat or Turkish wheat, according to the names of the countries from whence the like hath been brought. The grain is about the bigness of our ordinary English pease, and not much different in form and shape, but of divers colours: some white, some red, some yellow and some blue. All of them yield a very white and sweet flour, being used according to his kind, it maketh a very good bread. We made of the same in the country some malt, whereof was brewed as good ale as was to be desired. So likewise by the help of hops thereof may be made as good beer. It is a grain of marvellous great increase, of a thousand, fifteen hundred, and some, two thousand fold.

* * *

The ground being thus set according to the rate by us experimented, an English acre . . . doth there yield in crop or offcome of corn, beans and peas, at the least two hundred London bushels . . . when as in England forty bushels of our wheat yielded out of such an acre is thought to be much . . .

Of the nature and manners of the people

It resteth I speak a word or two of the natural inhabitants, their natures and manners; leaving large discourse thereof until time more convenient hereafter: now only so far forth as that you may know how that they are in respect of troubling our inhabiting and planting, are not to be feared: but that they shall have cause both to fear and love us that shall inhabit with them.

They are a people clothed with loose mantles made of deer skins, and aprons of the same round about their middles, all else naked: of such a difference of statures only as we in England; having no edge tools or weapons of iron or steel to offend us withal, neither know they how to make any. Those weapons that they have are only bows made of witch hazel, and arrows of reeds; flat edged truncheons, also of wood, about a yard long; neither have they anything to defend themselves, but targets made of barks, and some armours of sticks wickered together with thread.

Their towns are but small and near the sea coast, but few, some containing but ten or twelve houses, some twenty, the greatest that we have seen have been but of thirty houses: if they be walled it is only done with barks of trees made fast to stakes, or else with poles only fixed upright and close one by another.

Their houses are made of small poles made fast at the tops in round form after the manner as is used in many arbories in our gardens of England, in most towns covered with barks and in some with artificial mats made of long rushes from the tops of the houses down to the ground. The length of them is commonly double to the breadth, in some places they are but twelve and sixteen yards long, and in other some we have seen of four and twenty.

In some places of the country one only town belongeth to the government of a *Wiroans*, or chief lord: in other some two or three, in some, six, eight and more; the greatest *Wiroans* that we had dealing with had but eighteen towns in his government, and able to make not above seven or eight hundred fighting men at the most. The language of every government is different from any other, and the farther they are distant the greater is the difference.

Their manner of wars amongst themselves is either by sudden surprising one another, most commonly about the dawning of the day, or moonlight; or else by ambushes, or some subtle devices. Set battles are very rare, except it fall out where there are many trees, where either part may have some hope of defence, after the delivery of every arrow, in leaping behind some or other.

If there fall out any wars between us and them, what their fight is likely to be, we having advantages against them so many manner of ways, as by our discipline, our strange weapons and devices else, especially by ordnance great and small, it may be easily imagined: by the experience we have had in some places, the turning up of their heels against us in running away was their best defence.

In respect of us they are a people poor and for want of skill and judgement in the knowledge and use of our things, do esteem our trifles before things of greater value. Notwithstanding in their proper manner considering the want of such means as we have, they seem very ingenious: for although they have no such tools, nor any such crafts, sciences and arts as we, yet in those things do they show excellency of wit. And by how much they upon due consideration shall find our manner of knowledges and crafts to exceed theirs in perfection and speed for doing or execution, by so much the more is it probable that they should desire our friendship and love, and have the greater respect for pleasing and obeying us. Whereby may be hoped, if means of good government be used, that they may in short time be brought to civility and the embracing of true religion.

Some religion they have already, which although it be far from the truth, yet being as it is, there is hope it may be the easier and sooner reformed.

They believe that there are many gods, which they call *montoac*, but of different sorts and degrees; one only chief and great god which hath been from all eternity. Who, as they affirm, when he purposed to make the world, made first other gods of a principal order to be as means and instruments to be used in the creation and government to follow; and after the sun, moon, and stars as petty gods and the instruments of the other order more principal. First they say were made waters, out of which by the gods was made all diversity of creatures that are visible or invisible.

For mankind they say a woman was made first, which by the working of one of the gods conceived and brought forth children. And in such sort they say they had their beginning . . .

They believe also the immortality of the soul, that after this life as soon as the soul is departed from the body according to the works it hath done, it is either carried to heaven the habitacle of gods, there to enjoy perpetual bliss and happiness; or else to a great pit or hole, which they think to be in the furthest parts of their part of the world toward the sunset, there to burn continually: the place they call *popogusso*.

For the confirmation of this opinion they told me two stories of two men that had been lately dead and revived again: the one happened but few years before our coming into the country, of a wicked man which having been dead and buried, the next day the earth of the grave being seen to move, was taken up again: who made declaration where his soul had been, that is to say very near entering into *popogusso*, had not one of the gods saved him and gave him leave to return again and teach his friends what they should do to avoid that terrible place of torment.

The other happened in the same year we were there, but in a town that was threescore miles from us, and it was told me for strange news that one being dead, buried and taken up again as the first, showed that although his body had lien dead in the grave, yet his soul was alive, and had travelled far in a long broadway, on both sides whereof grew most delicate and pleasant trees, bearing more rare and excellent fruits than ever he had seen before, or was able to express; and at length came to most brave and fair houses, near which he met his father that had been dead before, who gave him great charge to go back again and show his friends what good they were to do to enjoy the pleasures of that place, which when he had done he should after come again.

What subtlety soever be in the *Wiroances* and priests, this opinion worketh so much in many of the common and simple sort of people that it maketh them have great respect to their governors, and also great care what they do to avoid torment after death, and to enjoy bliss: although notwithstanding there is punishment ordained for malefactors, as stealers, whoremongers and other sorts of wicked doers; some punished with death, some with forfeitures; some with beating, according to the greatness of the facts.

And this is the sum of their religion, which I learned by having special familiarity with some of their priests. Wherein they were not so sure grounded, nor gave such credit to their traditions and stories, but through conversing with us they were brought into great doubts of their own, and no small admiration of ours, with earnest desire in many to learn more than we had means, for want of perfect utterance in their language to express.

Most things they saw with us, as mathematical instruments, sea compasses, the virtue of the loadstone in drawing iron, a perspective glass whereby was showed many strange sights, burning glasses, wild fire works, guns, books, writing and reading, spring clocks that seem to go of themselves, and many other things that we had, were so strange unto them and so far exceeded their capacities to comprehend the reason and means how they should be made and done that they thought they were rather the works of gods than of men, or at the leastwise they had been given and taught us of the gods. Which made many of them to have such opinion of us as that if they knew not the truth of God and religion already, it was rather to be had from us, whom God so specially loved than from a people that were so simple as they found themselves to be in comparison of us. Whereupon greater credit was given unto that we spake of concerning such matters.

Many times and in every town where I came, according as I was able, I made declaration of the contents of the Bible, that therein was set forth the true and only God and his mighty works, that therein was contained the true doctrine of salvation through Christ, with many particularities of miracles and chief points of religion as I was able then to utter, and thought fit for the time. And although I told them the book materially and of itself was not of any such virtue, as I thought they did conceive, but only the doctrine therein contained, yet would many be glad to touch it, to embrace it, to kiss it, to hold it to their breasts and heads, and stroke over all their body with it to show their hungry desire of that knowledge which was spoken of.

The *Wiroans* with whom we dwelt called *Wingina* and many of his people would be glad many times to be with us at our prayers, and many times call upon us both in his own town as also in others wither he sometimes accompanied us, to pray and sing psalms, hoping thereby to be partaker of the same effects which we by that means also expected.

Twice this *Wiroans* was so grievously sick that he was like to die, and as he laid languishing, doubting of any help by his own priests, and thinking he was in such danger for offending us and thereby or God, sent for some of us to pray and be a means to our God that it would please him either that he might live or after death dwell with him in bliss, so likewise were the requests of many others in the like case.

On a time also when their corn began to wither by reason of a drought which happened extraordinarily, fearing that it had come to pass by reason that in something they had displeased us, many would come to us and desire us to pray to our God of England that he would preserve their corn, promising that when it was ripe we also should be partakers of the fruit.

There could at no time happen any strange sickness, losses, hurts or any other cross unto them but that they would impute to us the cause or means thereof for offending or not pleasing us.

One other rare and strange accident, leaving others, will I mention before I end, which moved the whole country that either knew or heard of us, to have us in wonderful admiration.

There was no town where we had any subtle device practised against us, we leaving it unpunished or not revenged (because we sought by all means possible to win them by gentleness) but that within a few days after our departure from every such town, the people began to die very fast, and many in short space; in some towns about twenty, in some forty, in some sixty and in one six score, which in truth was very many in respect of their numbers. This happened in no place, that we could learn, but where we had been, where they used some practice against us, and after such time. The disease also so strange that they neither knew what it was, nor how to cure it; the like by report of the oldest men in the country never happened before, time out of mind. A thing specially observed by us as also by the natural inhabitants themselves.

Insomuch that when some of the inhabitants which were our friends, and especially the *Wiroans* Wingina had observed such effects in four or five towns to follow their wicked practices, they were persuaded that it was the work of our God, through our means, and that we by him might kill and slay whom we would without weapons, and not come near them.

And thereupon when it had happened that they had understanding that any of their enemies had abused us in our journeys, hearing that we had wrought no revenge with our weapons, and fearing upon some cause the matter should so rest, did come and entreat us that we would be a means to our God that they as others that had dealt ill with us might in like sort die: alleging how much it would be for our credit and profit, as also theirs, and hoping furthermore that we would do so much at their requests in respect of the friendship we profess them.

Whose entreaties although we showed that they were ungodly, affirming that our God would not subject himself to any such prayers and requests of men; that indeed all things have been and were to be done according to his good pleasure as he had ordained; and that we were to show ourselves his true servants, ought rather to make petition for the contrary that they with them might live together with us, be made partakers of his truth, and serve him in righteousness; but notwithstanding in such sort, that we refer that, as all other things, to be done according to his divine will and pleasure, and as by his wisdom he had ordained to be best.

Yet because the effect fell out so suddenly and shortly after according to their desires, they thought nevertheless it came to pass by our means, and that we in using such speeches unto them did but dissemble the matter, and therefore came unto us to give us thanks in their manner, that although we satisfied them not in promise, yet in deeds and effect we had fulfilled their desires.

This marvellous accident in all the country wrought so strange opinions of us that some people could not tell whether to think us gods or men, and the rather because that all the space of their sickness there was no man of ours known to die, or that was specially sick; they noted also that we had no women amongst us, neither that we did care for any of theirs.

Some therefore were of opinion that we were not born of women, and therefore not mortal, but that we were men of an old generation many years past, then risen again to immortality . . .

These their opinions I have set down the more at large that it may appear unto you that there is good hope they may be brought through discreet dealing and government to the embracing of the truth and consequently to honour, obey, fear and love us.

* * *

Seeing therefore the air there is so temperate and wholesome, the soil so fertile and yielding such commodities as I have before mentioned, the voyage also thither to and fro, being sufficiently experimented to be performed thrice a year with ease and at any season thereof; and the dealing of Sir Walter Raleigh so liberal in large giving and granting land there, as is already known, with many helps and furtherances else (the least that he hath granted hath been five hundred acres to a man only for the adventure of his person): I hope there remain no cause whereby the action should be misliked.

8.10 WALTER RALEIGH, *THE DISCOVERY OF GUIANA*

Written in 1596, after Raleigh's unsuccessful attempt to find the city of Manoa, the mythical El Dorado, in Guiana, Raleigh here attempts to persuade Elizabeth I to invest money in a large scheme of discovery and plantation. Text from: first edition, 1596, pp. 93–101.

For the rest, which myself have seen, I will promise these things that follow and know to be true. Those that are desirous to discover and to see many nations, may be satisfied within this river [the Orinoco], which bringeth forth so many arms and branches leading to several countries and provinces, above 2,000 miles east and west, and 800 miles south and north; and of these the most either rich in gold or in other merchandises. The common soldier shall here fight for gold and pay himself instead of pence, with plates of half a foot broad, whereas he breaketh his bones in other wars for provant and penury. Those commanders and chieftains that shoot at honour and abundance, shall find there more rich and beautiful cities, more temples adorned with golden images, more sepulchres filled with treasure than either Cortez found in Mexico, or Pizarro in Peru; and the shining glory of this conquest will eclipse all those so far extended beams of the Spanish nation. There is no country which yieldeth more pleasure to the inhabitants, either for these common delights of hunting, hawking, fishing, fowling and the rest, than *Guiana* doth. It hath so many plains, clear rivers, abundance of pheasants, partridges, quails, rails, cranes, herons, and all other fowl; deer of all sorts, porks, hares, lions, tigers, leopards and divers other sorts of beasts, either for chase or food. It hath a kind of beast called Cama or Anta, as big as an English beef, and in great plenty . . .

Where there is store of gold, it is in effect needless to remember other commodities for trade: but it hath towards the south part of the river great quantities of Brazil wood and of divers berries that dye a most perfect crimson and carnation. And for painting, all France or Italy or the East Indies yield none such. For the more the skin is washed, the fairer the colour appeareth, and with which, even those brown and tawny women spot themselves, and colour their cheeks. All places yield abundance of cotton, of silk, of *balsamum*, and of those kinds most excellent and never known in Europe: of all sorts of gums, of Indian pepper and what else the countries may afford within the land we know not, neither had we time to abide the trial and search. The soil besides is so excellent and so full of rivers as it will carry sugar, ginger, and all those other commodities which the West Indies hath.

The navigation is short, for it may be sailed with an ordinary wind in six weeks, and in the like time back again, and by the way neither lee shore, enemy's coast, rocks, nor sands, all which in the voyages to the West Indies and all other places, we are subject unto, as the channel of Bahama, coming from the West Indies, cannot be passed in the winter, and when it is at the best, it is a perilous and fearful place: the rest of the Indies for calms and diseases very troublesome, and the Bermudas a hellish sea for thunder, lightning and storms . . .

To conclude, Guiana is a country that hath yet her maidenhead: never sacked, turned, nor wrought; the face of the earth hath not been torn, nor the virtue and salt of the soil spent by manurance; the graves have not been opened for gold; the mines not broken with sledges; nor their images pulled down out of their temples. It hath never been entered by any army of strength and never conquered or possessed by any Christian prince. It is besides so defensible that if two forts be built in one of the provinces which I have seen, the flood setteth so near the bank, where the channel also lieth, that no ship can pass up but within a pike's length of the artillery, first of the one, and afterwards of the other. Which two forts will be a sufficient guard both to the empire of Inca, and to an hundred other several kingdoms lying within the said river, even to the city of Quito in Peru . . .

And I farther remember that Berrio[11] confessed to me and others (which I protest before her majesty, of God, to be true) that there was found among prophecies in Peru (at such time as the empire was reduced to the Spanish obedience) in their chiefest temples, amongst divers others which foreshadowed the loss of the said empire, that from *Inglatierra* those *Incas* should be again in time to come restored and delivered from the servitude of the said conquerors. And I hope, as we with these few hands have displanted the first garrison and driven them out of the said country, so her majesty will give order to the rest, and either defend it and hold it as tributary, or conquer and keep it as empress of the same. For whatsoever prince shall possess it shall be greatest; and if the king of Spain enjoy it, he will become unresistable. Her majesty hereby shall confirm and strengthen the opinions of all nations as touching her great and princely actions. And where the south border of Guiana reacheth to the dominion and empire of the Amazons, those women shall hereby hear the name of a virgin which is not only able to defend her own territories and her neighbours, but also to invade and conquer so great empires and so far removed.

8.11 RICHARD HAKLUYT, 'PREFACE' TO *THE PRINCIPAL NAVIGATIONS, VOYAGES, TRAFFICS AND DISCOVERIES OF THE ENGLISH NATION*

Hakluyt's three-volume work collected and published as many accounts as he could find of English journeys, trading and discoveries. His aim, as he explains here, was to use such accounts as stimuli to further economic and imperial expansion. Text from: second edition, 1598–1600, fos *4^r^–**2^v^.

A preface to the reader as touching the principal voyages

Having for the benefit and honour of my country zealously bestowed so many years, so much travail and cost to bring antiquities smothered and buried in dark silence to light, and to preserve certain memorable exploits of late years by our English nation achieved, from the greedy and devouring jaws of oblivion: to gather likewise, and as it were to incorporate into one body the torn and scattered limbs of our ancient and late navigations by sea, our voyages by land and traffics of merchandise by both: I do this second time (friendly reader) presume to offer unto thy view this discourse . . .

Be it granted that the renowned Portugal, Vasco da Gama, traversed the main ocean southward of Africa. Did not Richard Chancellor and his mates perform the like, northward of Europe? Suppose that Columbus, that noble and high-spirited Genoese, escried unknown lands to the westward of Europe and Africa: did not the valiant English knight Sir Hugh Willoughby; did not the famous pilots Stephen Burrough, Arthur Pet, and Charles Jackman accost Novaya Zemlya to the north of Europe and Asia? Howbeit you will say perhaps, not with the like golden success, not with such deductions of colonies, nor attaining of conquests. True it is that our success hath not been correspondent unto theirs: yet in this our attempt the uncertainty of finding was far greater, and the difficulty and danger of searching was no whit less . . .

To return to our voyages performed within the bounds of Russia, neither hath our nation been contented only thoroughly to search into all parts, but also to visit Kazan and Astrakhan. They have adventured their persons, ships and goods, homewards and outwards, fourteen times over the unknown and dangerous Caspian Sea; that valiant, wise and personable gentleman Mr. Anthony Jenkinson being their first ring-leader.

But that no man should imagine that our foreign trades of merchandise have been comprised within some few years there may he plainly see in an ancient testimony translated out of the Saxon tongue, how our merchants were often wont for traffic's sake, so many hundred years since to cross the wide seas.

* * *

The epistle dedicatory in the second volume. To the Right Honourable Robert Cecil 1599

Right honourable. After the coming in of the Normans and so downward for a space of above three hundred years, such was the ardent desire of our nation to visit the Holy Land and to expel the Saracens and Mahometans that not only great numbers of earls, bishops, barons and knights, but even kings, princes and peers of the blood royal with incredible devotion, courage and alacrity, intruded themselves into this glorious expedition. All these, either kings, kings' sons, or kings' brothers, exposed themselves with invincible courage to the manifest hazard of their persons, leaving their ease, their countries, wives and children, induced with a zealous devotion and ardent desire to protect and dilate the Christian faith. These memorable enterprises I have brought together in the best method and brevity that I could devise.

And here by the way if any man shall think that an universal peace with our Christian neighbours will cut off the employment of the courageous increasing youth of this realm, he is much deceived. There is under our noses the great and ample country of Virginia the inland whereof is found of late to be so sweet and wholesome a climate, so rich and abundant in silver mines, so apt and capable of all commodities, and in a secret map of those parts made in Mexico for the King of Spain (which original with many others is in the custody of the excellent mathematician Mr. Thomas Harriot), as also in their intercepted letters come unto my hand, bearing date 1595, they acknowledge the inland to be a better and richer country than Mexico itself. If upon a good and godly peace obtained, it shall please the Almighty to stir up Her Majesty's heart to continue with transporting one or two thousand of her people and such others as upon mine own knowledge will most willingly at their own charges become adventurers in good numbers with their bodies and goods, she shall by God's assistance in short space, work many great and unlooked for effects, increase her dominions, enrich her coffers and reduce many pagans to the faith of Christ.

This treatise containeth our ancient trade and traffic with English shipping to the islands of Sicily, Candia and Chios, which I find to have begun in the year 1511, and to have continued until the year 1552 and somewhat longer. But shortly after it was given over, by occasion of the Turk's expelling of the four and twenty governors of the Genoese out of the island of Chios and by taking the island wholly into his own hand; and afterward by his growing over-mighty and troublesome in those seas.

Lastly I have here put down the happy renewing and much increasing of our interrupted trade in all the Levant: the traffic of our nation in all the chief havens of Africa and Egypt; the voyages over land and by river through Aleppo, Babylon and Basra, and down the Persian Gulf to Ormuz, and then by the ocean sea to Goa, and even to the frontiers of the Empire of China. I have likewise set in order such voyages as our nation, and especially the worthy inhabitants of this city of London, have painfully performed without the Strait of Gibraltar, upon the coasts of Africa, about the Cape of Buona Speranza, to and beyond the East Indies. I have here set down the whole course of the Portugal carracks from Lisbon to the bar of Goa in India, with the sundry and infallible marks of approaching unto and doubling the Cape of Good Hope.

Because our chief desire is to find out ample vent for our woollen cloth, the natural commodity of this our realm, the fittest place I find for that purpose are the manifold islands of Japan and the northern parts of China, and the regions of the Tartars next adjoining. Therefore I have here inserted treatises of the said countries, one of which was printed in Latin in Macao, a city of China, in China-paper, in the year 1590, and was intercepted in the great carrick called *Madre de Dios* two years after, enclosed in a case of sweet cedar wood and lapped up almost an hundred fold in fine calicut-cloth, as though it had been some incomparable jewel.

8.12 CHARTER TO THE EAST INDIA COMPANY

Granted by Elizabeth I in 1601, and subsequently renewed regularly by her successors, the Charter to the East India Company was one of the cornerstones of developing English mercantilism. Text from: *Charters Granted to the East India Company from 1601*, London, 1773, pp. 3–7.

Whereas our most dear and loving cousins George, earl of Cumberland, and our well-beloved subjects Sir John Hart of London, knight [and 217 others] have . . . been petitioners unto us for our royal assent and licence to be granted unto them, that they at their own adventures, costs and charges . . . might adventure and set forth one or more voyages with convenient number of ships and pinnaces, by way of traffic and merchandise to the East Indies, in the countries and parts of Asia and Africa, and to as many of the islands, ports, cities, towns and places thereabouts as where trade and traffic may by all likelihood be . . . had: divers of which countries and many of the islands, cities and ports thereof have long since been discovered by others of our subjects, albeit not frequented in trade of merchandise: know ye therefore that we, greatly tendering the honour of our nation, the wealth of our people, and the encouragement of them and others of our loving subjects in their good enterprises, for the increase of our navigation and the advancement of lawful traffic to the benefit of our commonwealth, have . . . granted . . . [that they be] one body corporate and politic, in deed and name, by the name of the Governor and Company of Merchants of London Trading into the East Indies . . . and by that name . . . shall be at all times hereafter . . . capable in law to have . . . and retain lands, rents, privileges, liberties, jurisdictions, franchises and hereditaments of whatsoever kind . . .

[We grant them to] freely traffic and use the trade of merchandise by seas in and by such ways and passages . . . as they shall esteem and take to be fittest into and from the said East Indies in the countries and parts of Asia and Africa . . . as shall from time to time at any public assembly or court held by or for the said governor and company . . . limited and agreed, and not otherwise . . . so always the same trade be not undertaken nor addressed to any country . . . or place already in the lawful and actual possession of any such Christian prince or State as at this present is or any time hereafter shall be in league or amity with us, our heirs or successors, and who doth not or will not accept of such trade, but doth overtly declare . . . the same to be utterly against his or their goodwill and liking . . .

. . . [We grant] that the said East Indies . . . shall not be visited . . . by any other the subjects of us . . . during the said term for fifteen years, contrary to the true meaning of these presents. And by virtue of our prerogative royal, which we will not in that behalf have argued to brought in question, we straightly charge . . . all the subjects of us . . . that none of them, indirectly or directly, do visit . . . or trade . . . into or from any of the said East Indies . . . unless it be by . . . licence and agreement of the said governor.

8.13 MICHEL MONTAIGNE, 'OF CANNIBALS', *ESSAYS*

Montaigne's essay on cannibals was well known in its original French (first published in 1580): Florio's translation in 1603 brought it to a wider audience. It is characterised by its dispassionate insistence on a historical and international outlook as the means to combat narrow nationalism and racism. Text from: trans. John Florio, 1603, fos 2C^r–4D^r.

Now (to return to my purpose) I find (as far as I have been informed) there is nothing in that nation [America] that is either barbarous or savage, unless men call that barbarism which is not common to them. As indeed, we have no other aim of truth and reason than the example and idea of the opinions and customs of the country we live in. There is ever perfect religion, perfect policy, perfect and complete use of all things. They are even savage, as we call those fruits wild which nature of herself and of her ordinary progress hath produced. Whereas indeed, they are those which ourselves have altered by our artificial devices and diverted from their common order, we should rather term savage. In those are the true and most profitable virtues, and natural properties most lively and vigorous, which in these we have bastardised, applying them to the pleasure of our corrupted taste. And if notwithstanding in divers fruits of those countries that were never tilled, we shall find that in respect of ours they are most excellent and as delicate unto our taste, there is no reason art should gain the point of honour of our great and puissant mother nature. We have so much by our inventions surcharged the beauties and riches of her works that we have altogether over-choked her: yet wherever her purity shineth, she makes our vain and frivolous enterprises wonderfully ashamed . . .

All our endeavour or wit cannot so much as reach to represent the nest of the least birdlet, its contexture, beauty, profit, and use, no nor the web of a seely spider. *All things* (saith Plato) *are produced either by nature, by fortune, or by art. The greatest and fairest by one or other of the two first, the least and imperfect by the last.* Those nations seem therefore so barbarous unto me because they have received very little fashion from human wit, and are yet near their original naturality. The laws of nature do yet command them, which are but little bastardised by ours, and that with such purity as I am sometimes grieved the knowledge of it came no sooner to light, at what time there were men that better than we could have judged of it. I am sorry Licurgus and Plato had it not: for me seemeth that what in those nations we see by experience doth not only exceed all the pictures wherewith licentious poesy hath proudly embellished the golden age, and all her quaint inventions to feign a happy condition of man, but also the conception and desire of philosophy. They could not imagine a genuity so pure and simple, as we see it by experience; nor ever believe our society might be maintained with so little art and human combination. It is a nation, would I answer Plato, that hath no kind of traffic, no knowledge of letters, no intelligence of numbers, no name of magistrate, nor of politic superiority, no use of service, of riches or of poverty, no contracts, no successions, no partitions, no occupation but idle; no respect of kindred, but common; no apparel, but natural; no manuring of lands; no use of wine; corn or metal. The very words that import lying, falsehood, treason, dissimulations, covetousness, envy, detraction and pardon were never heard of amongst them. How dissonant would he find his imaginary commonwealth from this perfection? . . .

Furthermore they live in a country of so exceeding pleasant and temperate situation that as my testimonies have told me, it is very rare to see a sick body amongst them; and they have further assured me they never saw any man there either shaking with the palsy, toothless, with eyes dropping, or crooked and stooping through age. They are seated alongst the sea-coast, encompassed toward the land with huge and steepy mountains, having between both a hundred leagues or thereabout of open and champagne ground. They have great abundance of fish and flesh, that have no resemblance at all with ours, and eat them without any sauces, or skill of cookery, but plain boiled or broiled. The first man that brought a horse thither, although he had in many other voyages conversed with them, bred so great a horror in the land, that before they could take notice of him, they slew him with arrows. Their buildings are very long, and able to contain two or three hundred souls, covered with barks of great trees, fastened in the ground at one end, interlaced and joined close together by the tops after the manner of some of our granges; the covering whereof hangs down to the ground and steadeth them as a flank. . . . They spend the whole day in dancing. Their young men go ahunting after wild beasts with bows and arrows. Their women busy themselves therewhilst with warming of their drink, which is their chiefest office. Some of their old men in the morning before they go to eating, preach in common to all the household, walking from one end of the house to the other, repeating one self-same sentence many times, till he have ended his turn (for their buildings are a hundred paces in length) he commends but two things unto his auditory: first valour against their enemies, then lovingness unto their wives. They never miss (for their restraint) to put men in mind of this duty, that it is their wives which keep their drink luke-warm and well-seasoned. . . . They believe their souls to be eternal and those that have deserved well of their Gods to be placed in that part of heaven where the sun riseth, and the cursed toward the west in position. They have certain prophets and priests, which commonly abide in the mountains and very seldom show themselves unto the people; but when they come down there is a great feast prepared and a solemn assembly of many townships together (each grange as I have described maketh a village, and they are about a French league one from another). The prophet speaks to the people in public, exhorting them to embrace virtue and follow their duty . . .

They war against the nations that lie beyond their mountains, to which they go naked, having no other weapons than bows or wooden swords, sharp at one end as our brooches are. It is an admirable thing to see the constant resolution of their combats, which never end but by effusion of blood and murder: for they know not what fear or routs are. Every victor brings home the head of the enemy he hath slain as a trophy of his victory, and fasteneth the same at the entrance of his dwelling place. After they have long time used and entreated their prisoners well, and with all commodities they can devise, he that is master of them, summoning a great assembly of his acquaintance, tieth a cord to one of the prisoner's arms, by the end whereof he holds him fast with some distance from him, for fear he might offend him, and giveth the other arm, bound in like manner to the dearest friend he hath, and both in the presence of all the assembly kill him with swords: which done they roast and then eat him in common, and send some slices of him to such of their friends as are absent. It is not as some imagine, to nourish themselves with it (as anciently the Scythians wont to do), but to represent an extreme and inexpiable revenge. Which we prove thus: some of them perceiving the Portugals who had confederated them-selves with their adversaries, to use another kind of death when they took them prisoners, which was to bury them up to the middle, and against the upper part of the body to shoot arrows, and then being almost dead, to hang them up: they supposed that these people of the other world (as they who had sowed the knowledge of so many vices amongst their neighbours and were much more cunning in all kinds of evils and mischief than they) undertook not this manner of revenge without cause, and that consequently it was more smartful and cruel than theirs, and thereupon began to leave their old fashion to follow this. I am not sorry we note the barbarous horror of such an action, but grieved that prying so narrowly into their faults we are so blinded in ours. I think there is more barbarism in eating men alive, than to feed upon them being dead; to mangle by tortures and torments a body full of lively sense, to roast him in pieces, to make dogs and swine to gnaw and tear him in mammocks (as we have not only read, but seen very lately, yea and in our own memory, not amongst ancient enemies, but our neighbours and fellow citizens; and which is worse, under pretence of piety and religion)[12] than to roast and eat him after he is dead. Chrysippus and Zeno, arch-pillars of the Stoic sect have supposed that it was no hurt at all, in time of need, and to what end soever, to make use of our carrion bodies and to feed upon them, as did our forefathers, who being besieged by Caesar in the city of Alexia, resolved to sustain the famined of the seige with the bodies of old men, women and other persons unserviceable and unfit to fight . . .

And physicians fear not in all kinds of compositions availful to our health to make use of it, be it for outward or inward applications: but there was never any opinion found so unnatural and immodest that would excuse treason, treachery, disloyalty, tyranny, cruelty and such like, which are our ordinary faults. We may then well call them barbarous in regard of reasons's rules, but not in respect of us that exceed them in all kind of barbarism. Their wars are noble and generous and have as much excuse and beauty as this human infirmity may admit: they aim at nought so much and have no other foundation amongst them, but the mere jealousy of virtue. They contend not for the gaining of new lands: for to this day they yet enjoy that natural uberty and fruitfulness which without labouring toil doth in such plenteous abundance furnish them with all necessary things that they need not enlarge their limits. They are yet in that happy estate as they desire no more than what their natural necessities direct them: whatsoever is beyond it is to them superfluous. Those that are much about one age do gener-ally intercall one another brethren, and such as are younger they call children, and the aged are esteemed as fathers to all the rest. These leave this full posses-sion of goods in common, and without division to their heirs, without other claim or title but that which nature doth plainly impart unto all creatures, even as she brings them into the world . . .

Their language is a kind of pleasant speech and hath a pleasing sound and some affinity with the Greek terminations. Three of that nation, ignorant how dear the knowledge of our corruptions will one day cost their repose, security and happiness, and how their ruin shall proceed from this commerce, which I imagine is already well advanced (miserable as they are to have suffered themselves to be so cozened by a desire of new-fangled novelties and to have quit the calmness of their climate, to come and see ours) were at Rouen in the time of our late King Charles the ninth, who talked with them a great while. They were showed our fashions, our pomp, and the form of a fair city; afterward some demanded their advice and would needs know of them what things of note and admirable they had observed amongst us. They answered three things, the last of which I have forgotten, and am very sorry for it, the other two I yet remember. They said: *First, they found it very strange that so many tall men with long beards, strong and well-armed, as it were about the King's person* (it is very likely they meant the Switzers of his guard) *would submit themselves to obey a beardless child and that we did not rather choose one amongst them to command the rest.* Secondly . . . *they had perceived there were men amongst us full gorged with all sorts of commodities and others which, hunger starved and bare with need and poverty, begged at their gates; and found it strange these moieties so needy could endure such an injustice, and that they took not the others by the throat or set fire on their houses.*

8.14 JEAN BODIN, *SIX BOOKS OF A COMMONWEAL*

Bodin's political theorisation of a commonwealth was the most comprehensive of his age: here he delineates a liberal and transparent public finance system, advice few contemporary princes took to heart. Text from: 1606 English translation, pp. 649ff.

Of treasure

. . . Every commonweal therefore must provide to have their treasure built of a sure and durable foundation. There are only seven means in general for the making of a public treasure, in the which all other are contained. The first is by the revenues of the commonweal; the second by conquest from the enemy; the third by liberality and gift of friends; the fourth by the pensions and tribute of their allies; the fifth upon traffic; the sixth, upon merchants which bring in and carry out merchandise; and the seventh upon the subjects' imposts . . .

In old time the first article set down in the expenses of the treasure was for alms' deeds; the second for the king's house; and the third for reparations: but the order is quite changed. As for alms-deeds, the wise and ancient princes of the Hebrews have left this discipline to posterity, the which they received from the holy prophets, who said that the surest preservation and defence of the treasure were alms-deeds and liberality to the needy: the which they restrained to the tenth part of every man's goods, which should be employed upon the ministers of the Church and the poor. And if we will look advisedly into it, we shall not find any prince, State or family that hath flourished more in riches, honours and all happiness than those which had most care of the poor and needy. . . . And contrariwise we see great families, States, realms and empires come to poverty and ruin, having condemned the poor and abandoned the subject to the spoil of the soldier and the thefts of toll gatherers. . . . A fasting army can never observe good discipline, for what they want they will presume to take by force: the which cannot be done unless there be a great care had of the treasure. The king's house therefore entertained, the soldiers and the officers paid, and due rewards given to them that deserve them, it is great reason the poor should be remembered. And if the treasury be well furnished, a part should be employed to repair towns, to fortify upon the frontiers, to furnish places of strength, make the passages even, build bridges, fortify the ports, send ships to sea, build public houses, beautify temples, erect colleges for honour, virtue and learning: for besides necessity of reparations, it brings great profit to the commonweal. For by this means arts and artificers are entertained, the poor people are eased, the idle are set to work, cities are beautified and diseases expelled; finally, hatred against princes (which doth often times stir up the subjects to rebellion) is quite suppressed, when as the impositions which he hath levied, redounds not only to the general, but also to every private man's good. And therefore the emperor Alexander Severus was accustomed to leave many imposts and tolls to cities, to be employed in the necessary reparations thereof.

. . . But the greatest benefit and which doth most import the preservation of an estate is that the two greatest plagues of a commonweal, idleness and poverty, are banished: a very necessary thing in a popular and aristocratical State; and especially in those countries where they have great spirits and but barren soil . . .

Charles the Seventh did limit by a law what sum of money the king might take yearly to dispose at his pleasure: which sum being very little, seemed in those days exceeding great. There is nothing more profitable for the prince, nor necessary for the subjects than to have the rewards which they give, known and examined by their officers . . .

Of coins and the means how to prevent that they be not altered, nor falsified

Looking well into the best grounds and strongest supports of a commonweal, in my opinion he must exactly understand this point that will wisely settle an estate or reform the abuses: for that there is nothing that doth more trouble and afflict the poor people than to falsify the coins and to alter the course thereof: for both rich and poor, everyone in particular, and all in general, receive an infinite loss and prejudice, the which cannot precisely in every point be described, it breeds so many inconveniences. The coin may not be corrupted, no not altered, without great prejudice to the commonweal: for if money (which must rule the price of all things) be mutable and uncertain, no man can make a true estate of what he hath, contracts and bargains shall be uncertain, charges, taxes, wages, pensions, rates, interests and vacations shall be doubtful, fines also and amercements limited by the laws and customs shall be changeable and uncertain: to conclude, the estate of the treasure and of many affairs both public and private shall be in suspense. . . . The prince may not make any false money, no more than he may kill or rob, neither can he alter the weight of his coin to the prejudice of his subjects, and much less of strangers, which treat with him and traffic with his people, for that he is subject to the law of nations, unless he will lose the name and majesty of a king and be termed a counterfeiter of money.

8.15 JAMES I, CHARTER TO THE VIRGINIA COMPANY

In 1606 James I issued a new licence for the settling of Virginia in the form of the charter for the Virginia Company, which would subsequently manage the land and issue licences for its settlement. Text from: *The Federal and State Constitutions, Colonial Charters and other Organic Laws of the . . . United States*, edited by W. B. Poore, 2nd edn, 2 vols., Washington, 1878, II, pp. 1,888ff.

James, by the grace of God king of England, Scotland, France and Ireland, defender of the faith, etc. Whereas our loving and well-disposed subjects Sir Thomas Gates and Sir George Somers, knights; Richard Hakluyt, clerk, prebendary of Westminster; and Edward Maria Wingfield, Thomas Hanham and Ralegh Gilbert, esquires; William Parker and George Popham, gentlemen, and divers others of our loving subjects have been humble suitors unto us that we would vouchsafe unto them our licence to make habitation, plantation, and to deduce a colony of sundry of our people into that part of America commonly called Virginia . . . [and] are desirous to divide themselves into two several colonies and companies: the one consisting of certain knights, gentlemen, merchants and other adventurers of our city of London and elsewhere . . . and the other consisting of sundry knights, gentlemen, merchants and other adventurers of our cities of Bristol and Exeter, and of our town of Plymouth, and of other places . . . we greatly commending . . . so noble a work . . . do by these our Letters Patent graciously accept of and agree to their humble and well-intended desires . . .

And we do also ordain, establish and agree for us, our heirs and successors, that each of the said colonies shall have a council, which shall govern and order all matters and causes which shall arise, grow or happen to or within the same several colonies, according to such laws, ordinances, and instructions as shall be, in that behalf, given and signed with our hand or sign manual, and pass under the privy seal of our realm of England: each of which councils shall consist of thirteen persons to be ordained, made and removed from time to time according as shall be directed and comprised in the same instructions . . . and that also there shall be a council established here in England which shall . . . consist of thirteen persons to be for that purpose appointed by us, our heirs and successors, which shall be called our Council of Virginia, and shall from time to time have the superior managing and direction . . .

Also we do, for us, our heirs and successors, declare by these presents that all and every the persons, being our subjects, which shall dwell and inhabit within every part or any of the said several colonies and plantations, and every of their children which shall happen to be born within any of the limits and precincts of the said several colonies and plantations, shall have and enjoy all liberties, franchises, and immunities within any of our other dominions to all intents and purposes as if they had been abiding and born within this our realm of England.

8.16 ROBERT GRAY, *A GOOD SPEED TO VIRGINIA*

Gray's work was one of several public relations' activities commisioned by the Virginia Company to encourage more investors and shareholders, to sustain Jamestown, and a new charter (which was granted in 1609, reducing royal supervision). Its tone, in contradistinction to that of Harriot's for example (8.9), is one of triumphal self-justification for the plantation project. Text from: first edition, 1609, passim.

The heavens, saith David, even the heavens are the Lord's, and so is the earth, but he hath given it to the children of men (Psalm 113.16). Yet notwithstanding the fatherly providence, and large bounty of God towards man, so improvident and irrespective is man, that he had rather live like a drone and feed upon the fruits of other men's labours, whereunto God hath not entitled him, than look out and fly abroad, like the bee, to gather the pleasures and riches of the earth, which God hath given him to enjoy whereupon it comes to pass that although the Lord hath given the earth to the children of men, yet this earth which is man's fee simple by deed of gift from God, is the greater part of it possessed and wrongfully usurped by wild beasts, and unreasonable creatures, or by brutish savages which by reason of their godless ignorance and blasphemous idolatry are worse than those beasts which are of most wild and savage nature. As Ahab therefore sometimes said to his servants: 1 Kings. 22.13: *know ye not that Ramoth Geilad was ours, and we stay and take it not out of the hands of the King of Aram?* So may man say to himself: the earth was mine, God gave it me and my posterity, by the name of the children of men, and yet I stay and take it not out of the hands of beasts and brutish savages, which have no interest in it, because they participate rather of the nature of beasts than men . . .

But now God hath prospered us with the blessings of the womb, and with the blessings of the breasts, the sword devoureth not abroad, neither is there any fear in our streets at home. . . . And therefore we may justly say as the children of Israel say here to Joshua, we are a great people, and the land is too narrow for us: so that whatsoever we have been, now it behooves us to be both prudent and politic, and not to deride and reject good proffers of profitable and gainful expectation, but rather to embrace every occasion which hath any probability in it of future hopes. And seeing there is neither preferment nor employment for all within the lists of our country, we might justly be accounted as in former times, both imprudent and improvident, if we will yet sit with our arms folded in our bosoms, and not rather seek after such adventures whereby the glory of God may be advanced, the territories of our kingdom enlarged, our people both preferred and employed abroad, our wants supplied at home, his Majesty's customs wonderfully augmented, and the honour and renown of our nation spread and propagated to the ends of the world . . .

There is nothing more dangerous for the estate of commonwealths, than when the people do increase to a greater multitude and number than may justly parallel with the largeness of the place and country: for hereupon comes oppression and diverse kind of wrongs, mutinies, sedition, commotion and rebellion, scarcity, dearth, poverty, and sundry sorts of calamities, which either breed the conversion or eversion of cities and commonwealths. For even as blood, though it be the best humour in the body, yet if it abound in greater quantity than the state of the body will bear, doth endanger the body, and oftentimes destroys it: so although the honour of the king be in the multitude of people, Proverbs 14.28, yet when this multitude of people increaseth to over great a number, the commonwealth stands subject to many perilous inconveniences, for which cause many nations perceiving their people to increase above a due and proportionable number, they have sent their overflowing multitudes abroad into other countries and provinces to the end they might preserve their own in greater peace and prosperity. So we see husbandmen deal with his grounds when they are overcharged with cattle, he removes them from one ground to another, and so he provideth well both for his cattle and for his ground . . .

. . . And hereupon it is that many serviceable men give themselves to lewd courses, as to robbing by the highway, theft and cozening, sharking upon the land, piracy upon the sea, and so are cut off by shameful and untimely death. Others live profanely, riotously and idly, to the great dishonour of almighty God, the detriment of the commonwealth. Now our case standing thus, it behooveth everyone to devise a remedy for this misery. When there was no bread in Canaan, Jacob and his family sought into Egypt for corn to relieve themselves . . .

. . . Now then in next place we are to note the direction of Joshua, upon the aforesaid complaint of the children of Joseph, which is to enlarge their territories and dilate their borders, by destroying God's enemies. . . . From whence we may learn how odious those people are, in the sight of God which having no knowledge of him and his worship, give that honour to the insensible and unreasonable creature, which is only due to the omnipotent and almighty creator. For this cause hath almighty God overthrown the mightiest monarchies in the world . . .

The report goeth that in Virginia the people are savage and incredibly rude, they worship the devil, offer their young children in sacrifice unto him, wander up and down like beasts, and in manners and conditions, differ very little from beasts, having no art, nor science, nor trade to employ themselves, or give themselves unto, yet by nature loving and gentle, and desirous to embrace a better condition: o, how happy were that man which could reduce this people from brutishness to civility, to religion, to Christianity, to the saving of their souls: happy is that man and blest of God, whom God hath endued either with means or will to attempt this business, but far be it from the neither of the English to exercise any bloody cruelty amongst these people; far be it from the hearts of the English to give them occasion that the holy name of God should be dishonoured among the infidels, or that in the plantation of that continent they should give any cause to the world to say that they sought the wealth of that country above or before the glory of God and the propagation of his kingdom. I remember the practice of Christopher Columbus, which he used among the West Indians, to persuade them to receive his Spaniards to society and commerce, which was, he observed, that they were superstitiously given to worship the moon, and by the skill he had in astronomy, he foresaw that within three days the moon should be eclipsed: whereupon he called them together and told them that he had often used his best means to bring them to a civil and friendly converse with strangers, but they would not harken unto him, and therefore in the presence of them all, he called upon the moon to revenge such a barbarous people, which denied strangers to converse and commerce with them. Within three days after the moon was much darkened by reason of the eclipse, which when the Indians saw, they thought the moon to be angry with them, and fearing some plague would proceed from her displeasure, they were easily induced to do whatsoever Columbus would have them. In like manner should all men use their wits in the first place and weapons should always be the last means in all our projects. And therefore although the children of Joseph have an express commandment here in this place to destroy those idolaters and possess their land, yet forasmuch as we have no precept but by example, we must first try all means before weapons, and when we take them into our hands, necessity of preserving our own lives must rather move us to destroy the enemies of God, than either ambition, or greedi-ness of gain, or cruelty, or any private respect whatsoever . . .

The first objection is, by what right or warrant we can enter into the land of these savages, take away their rightful inheritance from them, and plant ourselves in their places, being unwronged or unprovoked by them. Some affirm, and it is likely to be true, that these savages have no particular propriety in any part or parcel of that country, but only a general residency there, as wild beasts have in the forests, for they range and wander up and down the country, without any law or government, being led only by their own lusts and sensuality, there is not *meum and tuum* amongst them: so that if the whole land should be taken from them, there is not a man that can complain of any particular wrong done unto him. But the answer to the foresaid objection is that there is no intendment to take away from them by force that rightful inheritance which they have in that country, for they are willing to entertain us, and have offered to yield into our hands on reasonable conditions, more land than we shall be able this long time to plant and manure: and out of all question upon easy composition with them, we may have as much of their country yielded unto us as we can or will desire, so that we go to live peaceably among them and not to supplant them. We desire not, neither do we intend to take anything from them, *ex pacto et jure foederis*: but to compound with them for that we shall have of them. And surely, except succession and election, there cannot be a more lawful entrance to a kingdom than this of ours.

Moreover all politicians do with one consent, hold and maintain that a Christian king may lawfully make war upon barbarous and savage people, and such as live under no lawful or warrantable government, and may make a conquest of them . . .

Their second objection is that this age will see no profit of this plantation. Which objection admit it were true, yet it is too brutish, and bewrays their neglect and uncurious respect of posterity: we are not born like beasts for ourselves, and the time present only, but besides many other things which may challenge an interest and right in us: posterity and the age yet ensuing have not the least part in our life and labours . . .

Others object the continual charges which will prove in their opinion very heavy and burdensome to those that shall undertake the said plantation. These like the dog in the manger neither eat hay themselves, neither will they suffer the oxen that would. They never think any charges too much that may any way increase their own private estate. They have thousands to bestow about the engrossing of a commodity, or upon a mortgage, or to take their neighbour's house over his head, or to lend upon usury: but if it come to a public good, they groan under the least burden of charges that can be required of them . . .

. . . Policy thus establishing religion, and religion guiding policy, provision must be made of men furnished with arts and trades most necessary for this business: artificers and tradesmen must be nourished and cherished, for without artificers and tradesmen a commonwealth cannot flourish nor endure. And therefore the magistrate must specially regard them and respect them, and they must so carry themselves that they may be respected and cherished of the magistrate. It is required at their hands that they be faithful, painful and honest in their callings: for if they be thus qualified the country itself will make them rich. Every trade hath his mystery, which is for the most part grounded upon deceit and fraud: but seeing the beginning of a commonwealth is now attempted, the foundation must not be laid upon fraud and deceit, for there can no good end be expected of an evil beginning. It is required likewise that they be painful in their trades, or else the commonwealth can have little use or comfort of them. And here our English tradesmen and artificers are to be advised that they be wary in taking the savages to be apprentices to teach them their trade, seeing there be means of employment sufficient besides to set many thousands on work; and therefore not necessary as yet to instruct them in our trades and mysteries.

Besides all this, industry must be also added to help art and nature, so that such as have no professed arts and trades must painfully employ themselves in some labour or other to the furthering of this plantation. A drone will in short space devour more honey than the bee can gather in a long time, and therefore the magistrate must correct with all sharpness of discipline those unthrifty and unprofitable drones which live idly. For there is a law given to the sons of Adam to labour, and to the daughters of Eve, with the sweat of their brows to get their living, and therefore it is an evangelical precept that they which will not labour must not eat. In Job's time there was a very strict order taken for such as lived idly, Job 30.5. *They were chased forth from among men, and every one shouted at them, as at a thief.* And surely such an order must be taken with those that will not live painfully in Virginia, the rather because meat and drink and such other necessary supplies of livelihood will be very precious there a while.

8.17 WILLIAM STRACHEY, *A TRUE REPORTORY OF THE WRACK*

George Somers, carrying Thomas Gates to be the new Governor of Virginia, was wrecked in the Bermudas: and this was one of the additional disasters for the Virginia Company's prospects of survival, both because it delayed or destroyed valuable provisions, and suggested to potential investors and colonists that the journey to Virginia itself was fraught with danger. Somers and his men rebuilt the wrecked ships, and went on to reach Virginia. Text from: *Purchas His Pilgrims*, 1625, xix, pp. 5–72.

On St. James his day, July 24, being Monday (preparing for no less all the black night before), the clouds gathering thick upon us and the winds singing and whistling most unusually, which made us to cast off our pinnace . . . a dreadful storm, and hideous, began to blow out from the out the north-east, which swelling and roaring, as it were by fits, some hours with more violence than others, at length did beat all light from heaven; which like an hell of darkness turned black upon us, so much the more fuller of horror, as in such cases horror and fear use to overrun the troubled, and overmastered senses of all, which (taken up with amazement) the ears lay so sensible to the terrible cries and murmurs of the winds, and distraction of our company, as who was most armed and best prepared was not a little shaken . . .

For four and twenty hours the storm in a restless tumult had blown so exceedingly as we could not apprehend in our imaginations any possibility of greater violence, yet did we still find it, only more terrible, but more constant, fury added to fury, and one storm urging a second more outrageous than the former; whether it so wrought upon our fears, or indeed met with new forces. Sometimes shrieks in our ship amongst women and passengers, not used to such hurly and discomforts, made us look one upon the other with troubled hearts and panting bosoms; our clamours drowned in the winds, and the winds in thunder. Prayers might well be in the heart and lips, but drowned in the outcries of the officers; nothing heard that could give comfort, nothing seen that might encourage hope . . .

Howbeit this was not all: it pleased God to bring a greater affliction yet upon us: for in the beginning of the storm we had received likewise a mighty leak. And the ship in every joint almost, having spewed out her oakum before we were aware (a casualty more desperate than any other that a voyage by sea draweth with it) was grown five foot suddenly deep with water above her ballast, and we almost drowned within, whilst we sat looking when to perish from above. This imparting no less terror than danger, ran through the whole ship with much fright and amazement, startled and turned the blood and took down the braves of the most hardy mariner of them all, insomuch as he that before happily felt not the sorrow of others, now began to sorrow for himself . . .

But see the goodness and sweet introduction of better hope by our merciful God given unto us. Sir George Summers, when no man dreamed of such happiness, had discovered and cried land. . . . We were inforced to run her ashore, as near the land as we could, which brought us within three quarters of a mile of shore . . .

We found it to be the dangerous and dreaded island or rather islands of the Bermuda: whereof let me give your ladyship a brief description before I proceed to my narration. And that the rather because they be so terrible to all that ever touched on them, and such tempests, thunders, and other fearful objects are seen and heard about them, that they be called commonly the Devil's Islands, and are feared and avoided of all sea travellers alive, above any other place in the world. Yet it pleased our merciful God to make even this hideous and hated place both the place of our safety and means of our deliverance.

And hereby also, I hope to deliver the world from a foul and general error: it being counted of most that they can be no habitation for men but rather given over to devils and wicked spirits; whereas indeed we find them now by experience to be as habitable and commodious as most countries of the same climate and situation: insomuch as if the entrance into them were as easy as the place itself is contenting, it had long ere this been inhabited as well as other islands. Thus shall we make it appear that truth is the daughter of time, and that men ought not to deny everything which is not subject to their own sense . . .

Sure it is that there are no rivers, nor running springs of fresh water to be found upon any of them: when we came first we digged and found certain gushings and soft bubblings, which being either in bottoms, or on the side of hanging ground, were only fed with rain water, which nevertheless, soon sinketh into the earth and vanisheth away . . .

In these dangers and devilish disquiets (whilst the Almighty God wrought for us and sent us miraculously delivered from the calamities of the sea, all blessings upon the shore, to content and bind us to gratefulness) thus enraged amongst ourselves, to the destruction each of other, into what a mischief and misery had we been given up had we not had a governor, with his authority to have suppressed the same?

8.18 *A BRIEF DECLARATION OF THE PRESENT STATE OF THINGS IN VIRGINIA*

This is an example of how the royal Council supervised the Virginia

Company, of the kinds of financial difficulties such a company could experience, and the method which the Council proposed to solve them. Text from: 1616 proclamation.

Statement made by His Majesty's Council of Virginia (1616)

When first it pleased God to move his Majesty's mind, at the humble suit of sundry his loving subjects, to yield unto them his gracious privilege for the Virginia plantation, it was a thing seeming strange and doubtful in the eye of the world, that such and so few undertakers should enterprise a charge of that weight, as rather beseemed a whole State and commonwealth to take in hand. But such was the success of their sundry attempts in the happy discovery of so goodly a land, the description of which, for the excellency of the climate and fertility thereof had soon obtained to lay such an assured ground of future hope, in the sense and understanding of all men rightly weighing it, that not long after their new Letters Patents with more ample privileges granted by his Majesty were almost filled with many hundred names, both honourable and others of all sorts, that gave their hands and consent to further and uphold that honourable action.

Upon which encouragement of so many worthy patrons the Company very deeply engaged themselves in sending men and ships, cattle and all kind of provisions with governors and captains, for peace and war, insomuch as no earthly means seemed then wanting for the speedy reducing of that barbarous nation and savage people to a quiet Christian commonwealth.

But such was the will of Almighty God, as the world well knoweth that this great hope and preparation, by many disasters on sea and land too long to be here recited, was in a manner clean defeated and there only remained a poor remnant of those men and women, cattle and provisions that escaped the danger and which are now remaining there to raise and build up that intended colony.

Which when those gentlemen the adventurers here saw and that the expectance of so great a preparation brought nothing home but adverse success and bad reports, they for the most part withdrew themselves in despair of the enterprise and so gave it over, not enduring to repair the ruins nor to supply what themselves had underwritten, to discharge the deep engagement whereinto the Company was drawn by their encouragement.

By whose unconstancy and irresolution, the hope of that plantation, together with the lives of our people there, had then utterly perished, had not God's secret purpose been more strongly fixed to uphold the same, by stirring up the minds and undaunted spirits of a very small remnant of constant adventurers, that with Sir Thomas Smith (their treasurer and governor from the beginning) in all that time of three years disaster, were never discouraged, nor withdrew themselves from weekly courts and meetings, yielding their purses, credit and counsel from time to time, to make new supplies, even beyond their proportion to uphold the plantation.

Insomuch as by the favourable assistance of God, who in his own wisdom doth often times effect the greatest ends by weakest means, it is now come to pass that our English colony there subsisteth in a very good and prosperous condition. They sow and reap their corn in sufficient proportion without want or impeachment; their kine multiply already to some hundreds; their swine to many thousands; their goats and poultry in great numbers; every man hath house and ground to his own use; and now being able to maintain themselves with food, they are also prepared and ready, once having the means, to set upon the minerals, whereof there are many sorts; as also to plant and sow such several kinds of seeds and fruits as may best befit the soil and climate, to make the land profitable to themselves and the adventurers.

This being a true relation of the present state and hope of things in Virginia, we thought good in this short manner to mention it by the way, as well to give those worthy governors in Virginia their deserved praise, for the unspeakable pains and hazards which they have endured there in framing the people and plantation to so happy a form, as also to withdraw the despairing thoughts of such old retired adventurers, that make no other reckoning, but whatsoever hath been spent, upon the name of Virginia to be lost and cast away; the special purpose of this our publication being to another end which for the further satisfying of all reasonable minded we will now in few words deliver.

It was published to the world, about seven years since, and the time is now expired, wherein we promised to cause a dividend to be made of the lands in Virginia, as well to every man's person that went himself to the plantation, as to every particular man that had adventured his money.

And inasmuch as we are now by the natives' liking and consent in actual possession of a great part of the country, the other part not as yet freed from encumber of woods and trees, nor thoroughly surveyed, whereby to make a dividend of the whole: yet of that part which is now fit for plantation, we intend, God willing, to begin a present division by lot to every man that hath already adventured his money or person. For every single share of twelve pound ten shillings, fifty acres of land, till further opportunity will afford to divide the rest, which we doubt not will bring at least two hundred acres to every single share.

This division is intended to be done by a new governor with commissioners and surveyors to be sent from hence to join with others that are there already to give every man his lot in due proportion, according to such indifferent directions as shall be given them in charge.

And forasmuch as this course of sending a governor with commissioners and a surveyor with men, ships, and sundry provisions for fortifications and other occasions, as all men may conceive, cannot be effected without great charge and expense to the Company; it is therefore thought requisite and determined that so many adventurers as will partake of this first dividend shall present their names, with their number of shares, into a book remaining at Sir Thomas Smith's, for that purpose, before the 25 of June next.

And they shall also promise under their hands, to contribute to the said charge, the sum of twelve pound ten shillings, to be paid within one month after subscription, whether his shares be more or less, except any man shall be pleased to adventure more, and for which twelve pound ten shillings (or more if he will) he shall also have a further dividend of land in proportion, as for all other his monies formerly adventured. But for such as are not able to lay down present money, if they shall desire favour, it is agreed for them that the treasurer may receive the one half of their said adventure in present money, after their under-writing, to furnish out the ships, and the other half at six months after that.

And that no man may hereafter excuse himself by ignorance, nor tax the Company for concealing their purpose, we declare to all men that this present division is to be only in the lands lying along the King's river on both sides and all about the new towns erected; in which so many as shall give in their names, as aforesaid, may have their parts, and those that will not, may at their pleasure forbear till hereafter to take their lot upon the same terms in places more remote.

The names of all such as will partake of this dividend shall be given in writing to the commissioners before they go hence, at whose return they shall bring with them a perfect map and description of the said lands and ground divided, that every man may see and know in what condition and where his land lieth, that accordingly he may dispose thereof at his pleasure, either by going himself in person to possess it, or by sending families to manure it for yearly rent, or for half the clear profits, as many others do.

And furthermore every man's portion allotted to him shall be confirmed as state of inheritance to him and his heirs for ever, with bounds and limits under the Company's seal, to be holden of his Majesty, as of his manor of East Greenwich, in *socage tenure*, and not in *capite*, according to His Majesty's gracious Letters Patents already granted to the Virginia Company in that behalf.

8.19 JOHN SMITH, *A DESCRIPTION OF NEW ENGLAND*

John Smith was a merchant adventurer: according to his own account he was a mercenary in Syria, sold into slavery in Turkey and escaped. He was instrumental in setting up the Virginia Company in 1606, and was among the group of men chosen to lead the settlement in Jamestown. By all accounts his resourcefulness, discipline, and practical skills were the key reasons for the survival of the colony. He returned to England in 1609; and subsequently took part in this exploratory voyage to New England. Text from: first edition, 1616, pp. 1–12.

In the month of April 1614 with two ships from London of a few merchants I chanced to arrive in New England a part of America, at the isle of Monahigan, in 43½ of northerly latitude: our plot was there to take whales and make trials of a mine of gold and copper. If those failed, fish and furs was then our refuge to make ourselves savers howsoever. We found this whale fishing a costly conclusion: we saw many and spent much time in chasing them, but could not kill any:

they being a kind of jubarts, and not the whale that yields fins and oil as we expected. For our gold, it was rather the master's device to get a voyage, that projected it, than any knowledge he had at all of any such matter. Fish and furs was now our guard: and by our late arrival and long lingering about the whales, the prime of both those seasons were past ere we perceived it: we thinking that their seasons served at all times: but we found it otherwise, for by the midst of June, the fishing failed. Yet in July and August some was taken, but not sufficient to defray so great a charge as our stay required. Of dry fish we made about 40,000, of cor fish about 7,000.

Whilst the sailors fished myself with eight or nine others of them might best be spared, ranging the coast in a small boat, we got for trifles near 1,100 beaver skins, 100 martens and near as many otters, and the most of them within the distance of twenty leagues.

We ranged the coast both east and west much further: but eastwards our commodities were not esteemed, they were so near the French who affords them better . . .

With these furs, the train, and cor-fish, I returned for England in the bark; where within six months after our departure from the Downs, we safe arrived back. The best of this fish was sold for five pound the hundred, the rest by ill usage betwixt three pound and fifty shillings.

The other ship stayed to fit herself for Spain with the dry fish, which was sold, by the sailors' report that returned, at forty royals[13] the quintal, each hundred weighing two quintals and a half.

New England is that part of America in the ocean sea opposite to Nova Albion[14] in the South Sea, discovered by the most memorable Francis Drake in his voyage about the world. In regard whereto this is styled New England, being in the same latitude. New France, off it, is northward, southwards is Virginia, and all the adjoining continent, with New Granado, New Spain, New Andalusia and the West Indies . . .

Florida is the next adjoining to the Indies, which unprosperously was attempted to be planted by the French. A country far bigger than England, Scotland, France and Ireland, yet little known to any Christian but by the wonderful endeavours of Ferdinando de Soto a valiant Spaniard, whose writings in this age is the best guide known to search those parts.

Virginia is no isle (as many do imagine) but part of the continent adjoining to Florida, whose bounds may be stretched to the magnitude thereof without offence to any Christian inhabitant. For from the degrees of 30 to 45 his Majesty hath granted his Letters Patents, the coast extending south-west and north-east about 1,500 miles; but to follow it aboard, the shore may well be 2,000 at the least: of which 20 miles is the most gives entrance into the Bay of Chesapeake, where is the London plantation; within which is a country (as you may perceive by the description in a book and map printed in my name of that little I there discovered) may well suffice 300,000 people to inhabit.

And southward adjoineth that part discovered at the charge of Sir Walter

Raleigh, by Sir Ralph Lane and that learned mathematician Master Thomas Harriot.

Northward six or seven degrees is the river Sadagahoc, where was planted the Western Colony by that honourable patron of virtue, Sir John Popham, Lord Chief Justice of England . . .

. . . Africa, had not the industrious Portugals ranged her unknown parts, who would have sought for wealth among those fried regions of black brutish nigers;[15] where notwithstanding all the wealth and admirable adventures and endeavours, more than 140 years, they know not one third of those black habitations? . . .

That part we call New England is betwixt the degrees of 41 and 45, but that part this discourse speaketh of stretcheth but from Pennobscot to Cape Cod; some seventy-five leagues by a right line distant each from other; within which bounds I have seen at least forty several habitations upon the sea coast, and sounded about twenty-five excellent good harbours; in many whereof there is anchorage for 500 sail of ships of any burden, in some of them for 5,000. And more than 200 isles overgrown with good timber, of divers sorts of wood, which do make so many harbours as requireth a longer time than I had to be well discovered.

The principal habitation northward we were at was Pennobscot. Southward along the coast and up the rivers we found, *Medadacut, Segocket, Pemmaquid, Nusconcus, Kenebeck, Sagadahoc* and *Aumoughcawgen;* and to those countries belong the people of *Segotago, Paghuntanuck, Pocopassum. Taughtanakagnet, Warbigganus, Nassaque, Masherosqueck, Wawrigweck, Moshoquen, Wakcogo, Passharanack, etc..* To these are allied the countries of *Aucocisco, Accominticus, Passataquack, Aggawom* and *Naemkeck.* All these, I could perceive, differ little in language, fashion or government, though most be lords of themselves, yet they hold the *Bashabes* of *Pennobscot* the chief and greatest among them.

The next I can remember by name are *Mattahunts,* two pleasant isles of groves, gardens, and corn fields, a league in the sea from the main. Then *Totant, Massachussett, Pocapawmet, Quonahassit, Sagoquas, Nahapassumkeck, Topeent, Seccasaw, Totheet, Nasnocomacack, Accomack, Chawum;* then *Cape Cod,* by which is *Pawmet* and the Isle of *Nawset,* of the language and alliance of them of *Chawum:* the others are called *Massachussetts,* of another language, humour and condition.

For their trade and merchandise, to each of their habitations they have divers towns and people belonging; and by their relations and descriptions more than twenty several habitations and rivers that stretch themselves far up into the country, even to the borders of divers great lakes where they kill and take most of their beavers and otters.

From *Pennobscot* to *Sagadahoc* this coast is all mountainous and isles of huge rocks but overgrown with all sorts of excellent good woods for building houses, boats, barks or ships; with an incredible abundance of most sorts of fish, much fowl and sundry sorts of good fruits for man's use.

Betwixt *Sagadahoc* and *Sawocatuck* there is but two or three sandy bays, but betwixt that and *Cape Cod* very many: especially the coast of the *Massachussetts* is so indifferently mixed with high clayey or sandy cliffs in one place, and then tracts of large long ledges of divers sorts and quarries of stones in other places so strangely divided with tinctured veins of divers colours: as free stone for building, slate for tiling, smooth stone to make furnaces and forges for glass or iron, and iron ore sufficient conveniently to melt in them. But the most part so resembleth the coast of Devonshire, I think most of the cliffs would make such limestone. If they be not of these qualities, they are so like they may deceive a better judgement than mine. All which are so near adjoining to those other advantages I observed in these parts, that if the ore prove as good iron and steel in those parts as I know it is within the bounds of the country, I dare engage my head (having but men skilful to work the simples there growing) to have all things belonging to the building, the rigging of ships of any proportion, and good merchandise for the freight within a square of 10 or 14 leagues; and were it for a good reward, I would not fear to prove it in a less limitation.

And surely by reason of those sandy cliffs and cliffs of rocks, both which we saw so planted with gardens and corn fields and so well inhabited with a goodly, strong and well proportioned people, besides the greatness of the timber growing on them, the greatness of the fish and the moderate temper of the air (for of twenty-five, not any was sick but two that were many years diseased before they went, notwithstanding our bad lodging and accidental diet) who can but approve this a most excellent place, both for health and fertility? And of all the four parts of the world that I have yet seen not inhabited, could I have but means to transport a colony, I would rather live here than any where, and if it did not maintain itself, were we but once indifferently fitted, let us starve.

The main staple from hence to be extracted for the present to produce the rest is fish, which, however it may seem a mean and a base commodity, yet who will but truly take the pains and consider the sequel, I think will allow it well worth the labour. It is strange to see what great adventures the hopes of setting forth men of war to rob the industrious, innocent, would procure; or such massy promises in gross; though more are choked than well fed with such hasty hopes. But who doth not know that the poor Hollanders, chiefly by fishing at a great charge and labour in all weathers in the open sea are made a people so hardy and industrious? And by the venting this poor commodity to the Easterlings[16] for as mean, which is wood, flax, pitch, tar, resin, cordage, and such like (which they exchange again to the French, Spaniards, Portingales and English etc., for what they want), are made so mighty, strong and rich, as no State but Venice, of twice their magnitude, is so well furnished with so many fair cities, goodly towns, strong fortresses; and that abundance of shipping and all sorts of merchandise, as well of gold, silver, pearls, diamonds, precious stones, silks, velvets, and cloth of gold; as fish, pitch, wood, or such gross commodities? What voyages and discoveries, east and west, north and south, yea about the world, make they? What an army by sea and land have they long maintained in despite of one of the greatest princes of the world? And never could the Spaniard will all his mines of gold and silver pay his debts, his friends and his army half so truly as the Hollanders still have done by this contemptible trade of fish. Divers (I know) may allege many other assistances. But this is their mine: and the sea the source of those silvered streams of all their virtue; which hath made them now the very miracle of industry.

8.20 EDWARD WINSLOW, *A RELATION OR JOURNAL OF THE PROCEEDINGS OF THE PLANTATION SETTLED AT PLYMOUTH, NEW ENGLAND*

Winslow was one of the chief leaders of the Mayflower voyage, along with William Bradford, John Carver and William Brewster. The Plymouth Company had obtained a patent from the Virginia Company to settle in New England, in return for profit from tenancies or quit rents. The advantage of such an agreement for the Pilgrim Fathers was that they could establish independent political and religious systems. Text from: first edition of 1622, pp. 1–3.

Wednesday the sixth of September the wind coming east-north-east, a fine small gale, we loosed from Plymouth; having been kindly entertained and courteously used by divers friends there dwelling; and after many difficulties in boisterous storms, at length by GOD's providence, upon the 9th of November following, by break of the day we espied land; which we deemed to be Cape Cod, and so afterward it proved. And the appearance of it much comforted us: especially seeing so goodly a land and wooded to the brink of the sea; it causes us to rejoice together and praise GOD that had given us once again to see land.

And thus we made our course south-south-west, purposing to go to a river ten leagues to the south of the Cape; but at night the wind being contrary, we put round again for the Bay of Cape Cod. And upon the 11th November we came to an anchor in the bay; which is a good harbour and pleasant bay; circled around, except in the entrance, which is about four miles over from land to land; compassed about to the very sea with oaks, pines, juniper, sassafras, and other sweet wood. It is a harbour wherein a thousand sail of ships may safely ride.

There we relieved ourselves with wood and water, and refreshed our people; while our shallop was fitted to coast the bay to search for a habitation.

There was the greatest store of fowl that ever we saw. And every day we saw whales playing hard by us. Of which, in that place, if we had instruments and means to take them we might have made a very rich return, which to our great grief we wanted. Our master and his mate, and others experienced in fishing, professed we might have made £3,000 or £4,000 worth of oil. They preferred it before Greenland whale fishing, and purpose the next winter to fish for whale here.

For cod, we assayed but found none. There is good store, no doubt, in their season.

Neither got we any fish all the time we lay there, but some few little ones on the shore. We found great mussels, and very fat and full of sea pearl; but we could not eat them for they made us all sick that did eat, as well sailors as passengers. They caused to cast and scour.[17] But they were soon well again.

The bay is so round and circling that before we could come to anchor we went round all the points of the compass. We could not come near the shore, by three-quarters of an English mile, because of shallow water, which was a great prejudice to us. For our people, going on shore, were forced to wade a bow-shot or two in going a-land; which caused many to get colds and coughs, for it was many times freezing cold weather.

This day, before we came to harbour, observing some not well affected to unity and concord, but gave some appearance of faction, it was thought good there should be an Association and Agreement that we should combine together in one body; and to submit to such government and governors as we should, by common consent, agree to make and choose; and set our hands to this that follows, word for word:

> In the name of GOD, Amen. We, whose names are underwritten, the loyal subjects of our dread Sovereign Lord King James, by the grace of GOD, of Great Britain, France and Ireland, King, Defender of the Faith, etc.
>
> Having undertaken for the glory of GOD and advancement of the Christian faith and honour of our King and country a voyage to plant the first colony in the northern parts of Virginia; do by these presents, solemnly and mutually in the presence of GOD and one of another, covenant and combine ourselves together into a civil body politic, for our better ordering and preservation; and furtherance of the ends aforesaid; and by virtue hereof, to enact, constitute and frame such just and equal laws, ordinances, acts, constitutions, offices, from time to time, as shall be thought most meet and convenient for the general good of the colony, unto which we promise all due submission and obedience.
>
> In witness whereof we have hereunder subscribed our names.[18]
> Cape Cod 11 November . . . 1620.

8.21 EDWARD MISSELDEN, *FREE TRADE*

Misselden was a merchant who subscribed to the economic theory that England's prosperity depended on the volume of bullion in the country; and therefore on the need to export native goods, and to restrict imports. Text from: first edition, 1622, pp. 104; 108–25.

For it is not the rate of exchanges, but the value of moneys, here low, elsewhere high, which cause their exportation: nor do the exchanges, but the plenty or scarcity of moneys cause their values. Or if I should grant that to be the cause which is not: yet it doth not follow that because the stranger, like enough, would be a deliverer here of money at a high rate, that therefore the English must take it. And then the consequence will be ill: for if the rate be such as the taker like not, then the deliverer is yet more thrust upon the exportation.

* * *

The mediate or remote causes of the want of money, I observed to be either domestic or foreign. The domestic, general or special. The general, the great excess of the kingdom in consuming the commodities of foreign countries in such abundance, to our own loss. And amongst those, the great excess in tobacco is none of the least: which if it might seem good to the high wisdom of his Majesty to restrain or at least to give a toleration of the Virginia and Bermudas only: there might a great deal of piety and policy showed in this remedy. For in the one respect, it would tend to a great enriching of that plantation, which so happily succeedeth through God's blessing; and in the other it would advantage the King and the kingdom in the redress of the disorder of the Spanish trade, and in bringing in treasure instead of that toy, more than the rent that is now raised to his Majesty for the same.

The superfluity of other commodities may be restrained by laws vestiary and sumptuary, according to the example of Germany and other our neighbour countries . . .

The remedy for the exportation of money out of Christendom by the trades before mentioned, dependeth much on the good conclusion hoped for between the Dutch and our nation. Whereby not only the Indian commodities which in those trades are principal may be bought much better cheap, and consequently spare a great deal of the treasure now issued out for the same: but also, the native commodities of either country, and as much as may be of every country, may be brought into trade and train with the Indians; and advanced in their use and price that so at last instead of money for wares, we may give wares for wares according to the law and nature of commerce . . .

Another remedy of this kind may be his Majesty's gracious protection of the Persian trade now so happily set on foot: that so neither envy of any at home, nor the power or policy of any abroad supplant us in the same. Whereby the cloth and tin and other the native commodities of this kingdom may be brought into use and commerce amongst the Persians also. Which through God's blessing and his Majesty's royal assistance may be a means to draw the whole trade of the Persian silk into this kingdom and make it the magazine thereof, for the supply of other nations, to the weakening of the Turk's power, the increase of trade in this commonwealth, and with it His Majesty's customs, the navigation and employment of the poor, to the great honour of the King and enriching of his kingdoms . . .

The remedy for usury may be plenty of money. For then men will have no such cause to take money at interest, as when money is scant. For as it is the scarcity of money that maketh the high rates of interest, so the plenty of money will make the rates low, better than any statute for that purpose. For although in the Netherlands it is lawful for a man to take twenty in the hundred if he can get it . . . yet there, commonly money is let at six or seven in the hundred, by reason of the plenty of money.

Or there is another remedy for usury, in giving liberty to the subjects, if so it may seem good to his Majesty's high wisdom, to buy and sell and to transport bills of debt from man to man, according to the custom of Germany and the Low Countries. Which is found to be an excellent means to supply men's wants in course of trade and tendeth also to the enlarging thereof. And for the extortion upon the poor above noted, if a stock of money were raised in manner of a Lombard, or otherwise in London, and in the Countries, where much poor depend on clothing and elsewhere where there is cause, whereby the multitudes of poor wherewith the kingdom swarmeth, might be from time to time supplied for a small consideration it would certainly give great encouragement to the poor to labour, it would set on work many fatherless children that are ready to starve, it would benefit the commonwealth by their labours, and it would be an acceptable work to Almighty God . . .

The trades considered apart, I reduced to such as tend to the fortification of the kingdom or maintenance of trade, the former I noted to be ordinance or munition . . .

The latter I reduced to fishing and clothing, as the nurseries of trade. For the fishing, the infinite treasure that strangers search out of our seas, the variety of trade that thereby they purchase, the multitude of mariners they breed, the fleets of shipping they maintain, methinks should every of them apart, or all of them together be unto us as so many provocations to rouse us up to the exercise thereof. Whereby His Majesty might receive such a toll or custom of them as other princes do in like case, and be once again lord and master of the seas . . .

The present domestic causes of the decay of clothing, I considered in the trade under clothier, or under merchant. Under the clothier I noted the ill making and false sealing of cloth, and both through the non-execution of the statute of 4. of the King;[19] the abuse whereof is grown to be very great. . . . Nevertheless, if it may please his Majesty, to commit the care of the execution of the statute to some of the principal cities and towns in the clothing counties, where broadcloths, kersies and perpetuanoes are made, and to make them overseers mentioned in the statute, instead of those ignorant and negligent searchers, with reasonable allowance for their pains, I am confident it would prove a singular remedy. For we have not only the example of the Low Countries, where this course is taken, but also here with us: as Worcester for that sort of cloths; Colchester for bays, and Canterbury for says. In all which places the former abuses are removed by this means; and the cloths, and bays and manufactures of those cities triumph in great credit and estimation. Which execution of the said statute is that rather to be committed to the care and charge of the principal cities and towns in the clothing counties, because by ancient statutes not repealed all cloths and kersies ought to be brought to the next city, borough or town corporate to be sealed, before they be put to sale. And if such cloths so sealed prove defective, that corporation or township that so hath sealed them shall forfeit the whole value thereof.

The reformation of which abuse will redound to the benefit of the clothier as well as the merchant. For none is more hurt with false cloth than that clothier which maketh true cloth, because his markets are always hurt by the cheapness that false cloth may be afforded at.

8.22 GERARD DE MALYNES, *THE MAINTENANCE OF FREE TRADE*

Malynes wrote this in response to Misselden, and dedicated it to James I, in an attempt to argue that traffic and exchange, and their manipulation, would make the nation wealthy. Text from: first edition, 1622, preface, pp. 82–105.

Traffic (most dread and gracious sovereign) by nature admirable and by art amiable, being the sole peaceable instrument to enrich kingdoms and commonweals, may properly be called the preeminent study of princes, the rather because the sacred wisdom hath approved this axiom: that a king is miserable (how rich soever he be) if he reigns over a poor people, and that that kingdom is not able to subsist (how rich and potent soever the people be) if the king be not able to maintain his estate. Both which (being relatives) are depending upon traffic and trade, which is performed under three simples or essential parts, namely commodities, moneys and exchange for moneys by bills. Whereupon having lately perused a treatise entitled *Free Trade, or the means to make trade flourish*, wherein the author either ignorantly or wilfully hath omitted to handle the predominant part of trade, namely the mystery of exchange, which is the public measure between us and other nations, according to which all our commodities are bought and sold in foreign parts: his only scope being to have the moneys of the kingdom enhanced in price, and the foreign coins made current within the realm at high rates (whereby great inconveniences will follow).

* * *

Of the remedy for all the former causes of the decay of trade

... The efficient cause of the transportation of our moneys is gain, and this gain ariseth by the undervaluation of our moneys in regard of the enhancing and overvaluation of foreign coin, so that the cause is extrinsic and comprised under the said exchange of moneys, and not intrinsic in the weight and fineness of the coin, which are considered in the course of true exchange between us and foreign nations; and thereupon it followeth that neither difference of weight, fineness of standard, proportion between gold and silver, or the proper valuation

545

of moneys can be any true causes of the exportation of our moneys; so long as a due course is held in exchange, which is founded thereupon.

Hence ariseth the facility of the remedy, by the reformation of exchange in causing the value of our money to be given in exchange, which cutteth off the said gain had by the said exportation and causeth (in effect) that the foreign coin beyond the seas shall not be received above the value although the enhancing thereof, or the embasing by alloy were altering continually. For take away the cause (gain) and the effect will cease.

All men of common understanding when they do hear of the raising of moneys beyond the seas, are ready to say we must do the like . . .

But let us suppose that this will be a sufficient remedy to enhance our moneys, as they do theirs, to embase our coin, as they do theirs, and to imitate overvaluation and undervaluation of gold and silver, as they do, requiring a continual labour, charge and innovation; is it not an excellent thing that all this can be done by the course of exchange with great facility? And that without enhancing of our moneys at home, or meddling with the weight and fineness of the sterling standard?

This is to be done only by his Majesty's proclamation, according to the statutes of exchanges, prohibiting that after three months next ensuing the same, no man shall make any exchanges by bills or otherwise, for moneys to be paid in foreign parts, or to be rechanged towards this realm under the true *par*, or value for value of our moneys, and the moneys of other countries in weight and fineness, but at the said rate or above the same, as merchants can agree, but never under the said rate, which shall be declared in a pair of tables publicly to be seen upon the Royal Exchange in London, according to the said proclamation, and the said table shall be altered in price, as occasions shall be ministered beyond the seas, in the general respective places of exchanges, either by the enhancing of moneys by valuation, or by embasing of the same by alloy, which by a vigilant eye may be observed, and will be a cause to make other nations more constant in the course of their moneys. And this will be executed more of course than by authority, because gain doth bear sway and command with most men . . .

. . . the merchant stranger, being here the deliverer of money generally, will easily be induced to make the most of his own, receiving by exchange more for the same beyond the seas; and the English merchant being the taker of the said moneys, will not be so injurious to the State as to give less beyond the seas, than the value of the money of the realm in exchange, contrary to the said proclamation; and if he would the deliverer will not let him have it. Besides that the taker's occasions are enforced by necessity, and he can be no loser, for by this direction he will sell his commodities beyond the seas accordingly . . .

This raising of money was augmented afterwards by Queen Elizabeth of blessed memory, in the highest degree, by one full third part, from 45 pence the ounce, unto 60 pence or 5 shillings sterling standard: but the exportation did never cease, because the course of exchange for money did run always under the value of the money, still affording a gain between the said exchange and money, which caused the said exportation. And so will it be still if this be not prevented by direction in a pair of tables much like unto the tables kept at Dover in the time of King Edward the Third, to receive the passengers' money, and by exchange *in specie* for it beyond the seas; which made them to leave their moneys within the realm; and this course of exchange so directed, is the only mean and way to restore England's wealth by importation of money and bullion, advancing the price of our native commodities and to prevent the transportation of our moneys: and all other remedies are defective, as experience will prove and demonstrate, if good things can be favoured.

The statute of employment must also be observed, to make the remedy more complete with a register also, to record the moneys which foreign mariners do receive for freight coming from Norway, and other places, which are above one hundred voyages in one year; as also many other ships, bringing corn into the northern and western parts of the realm, and exporting money for it.

The Turk, Persian and Russian have herein been more politic than we, keeping the price of their exchanges high, much above the valuation of their moneys. So that they have no trade by exchange, nor moneys, but only for commodities; whereby they prevent the overbalancing of foreign commodities with theirs, as also the exportation of their moneys: albeit the use of our commodities in those countries is very great.

* * *

The want of money coming by the consumption of foreign commodities may properly be termed overbalancing of commodities, which are more worn and used because of the quantity of them imported, proceeding also of the abuse of exchange as the efficient cause thereof, as aforesaid.

The excessive use of tobacco for so much as concerneth the importation thereof in lieu of treasure, will be much diminished by the late limitation of a quantity of Spanish tobacco lately established, to the end that the plantation of Virginia and the Bermudas may be advanced thereby . . .

The returns lately had from the East Indies will in part assuage the same, if merchants in the dispersing of those commodities will procure importation of money and bullion as (no doubt) they will do. And this will further be increased when the Hollanders and our merchants shall be at an end of their present controversies, which by his Majesty's high wisdom will soon be determined . . .

For a conclusion therefore let us note that all the said causes of the decay of trade in England are almost all of them comprised in one, which is the want of money; whereof we find the abuse of exchange to be the efficient cause, which maketh us to find out so easy a remedy, whereby the kingdom shall enjoy all the three essential parts of traffic under good and politic government, which will be free trade effectually or in deed.

8.23 FRANCIS BACON, *OF USURY*

First printed in 1625 this was a reasoned contribution to the debate on finance, which had first been offered to James I, when Bacon was Lord Chancellor. Text from: *The Essays*, 1625, fos 2H4–2I3.

. . . Few have spoken of usury usefully. It is good to set before us the incommodities and commodities of usury; that the good may be either weighed out or culled out; and warily to provide that while we make forth to that which is better, we meet not with that which is worse.

The discommodities of usury are: first that it makes fewer merchants. For were it not for this lazy trade of usury, money would not lie still but would, in great part, be employed upon merchandising, which is the *vena porta* [gate vein] of wealth in a State. The second, that it makes poor merchants. For as a farmer cannot husband his ground so well, if he sit at a great rent, so the merchant cannot drive his trade so well if he sit at great usury. The third is incident to the other two, and that is the decay of customs of kings or States, which ebb or flow with merchandising. The fourth, that it bringeth the treasure of a realm or State into a few hands. For the usurer being at certainties, and other at uncertainties, at the end of the game, most of the money will be in the box; and ever a State flourisheth when wealth is more equally spread. The fifth, that it beats down the price of land, for the employment of money is chiefly either merchandising or purchasing, and usury waylays both. The sixth, that it doth dull and damp all industries, improvements and new inventions wherein money would be stirring, if it were not for this slug. The last, that it is the canker and ruin of many men's estates, which in process of time breeds a public poverty.

On the other side, the commodities of usury are first, that howsoever usury in some respect hindereth merchandising, yet in some other it advanceth it. For it is certain that the greatest part of trade is driven by young merchants upon borrowing at interest. So as if the usurer either call in or keep back his money, there will ensue presently a great stand of trade. The second is that were it not for this easy borrowing upon interest, men's necessities would draw upon them, a most sudden undoing, in that they would be forced to sell their means (be it lands or goods) far under foot; and so, whereas usury doth but gnaw upon them, bad markets would swallow them quite up. As for mortgaging or pawning, it will little mend the matter, for either men will not take pawns without use, or if they do, they will look precisely for the forfeiture. I remember a cruel moneyed man in the country that would say, the devil take this usury, it keeps us from forfeitures of mortgages and bonds. The third and last is that it is a vanity to conceive that there would be ordinary borrowing without profit, and it is impossible to conceive the number of inconveniences that will ensue if borrowing be cramped. Therefore to speak of the abolishing of usury is idle. All States have ever had it, in one kind or rate or other. So as that opinion must be sent to *Utopia*.

To speak now of the reformation and reglement of usury: how the discommodities of it may be best avoided, and the commodities retained. It appears by the balance of commodities and discommodities of usury, two things are to be reconciled. The one, that the tooth of usury be grinded that it bite not too much; the other that there be left open a means to invite moneyed men to lend to the merchants for the continuing and quickening of trade. This cannot be done except you introduce two several sorts of usury: a less and a greater. For if you reduce usury to one low rate, it will ease the common borrower, but the merchant will be to seek for money. And it is to be noted that the trade of merchandise, being the most lucrative, may bear usury at a good rate: other contracts not so.

To serve both intentions, the way would be briefly thus: that there be two rates of usury, the one free and general for all, the other under licence only to certain persons, and in certain places of merchandising. First therefore let usury in general be reduced to five in the hundred, and let that rate be proclaimed to be free and current and let the State shut itself out to take any penalty for the same. This will preserve borrowing from any general stop or dryness; this will ease infinite borrowers in the country. This will, in good part, raise the price of land, because land purchased at sixteen years' purchase will yield six in the hundred, and somewhat more, whereas this rate of interest yields but five. This, by like reason, will encourage and edge industrious and profitable improvements, because many will rather venture in that kind than take five in the hundred, especially having been used to greater profit. Secondly, let there be certain persons licensed to lend to known merchants, upon usury at a higher rate; and let it be with the cautions following. Let the rate be even with the merchant himself somewhat more easy than that he used formerly to pay: for by that means all borrowers shall have some ease by this reformation, be he merchant or whosoever. Let it be no bank or common stock, but every man be master of his own money. Not that I altogether mislike banks, but they will hardly be brooked in regard of certain suspicions. Let the State be answered, some small matter, for the licence, and the rest left to the lender. For if the abatement be but small, it will no whit discourage the lender. For he, for example, that took before ten or nine in the hundred, will sooner descend to eight in the hundred than give over his trade of usury, and go from certain gains to gains of hazard. Let these licensed lenders be in number indefinite, but restrained to certain principal cities and towns of merchandising: for then they will be hardly able to colour other men's moneys in the country. So as the licence of nine will not suck away the current rate of five: for no man will send his moneys far off, nor put them unto unknown hands.

If it be objected that this doth, in a sort, authorise usury, which before was in some places but permissive, the answer is: that it is better to mitigate usury by declaration than to suffer it to rage by connivance.

8.24 JOHN SMITH, *ADVERTISEMENTS FOR THE UNEXPERIENCED PLANTERS OF NEW-ENGLAND*

John Smith wrote this for John Winthrop's Massachussetts plantation, which founded Boston in 1630. Smith's remarks elsewhere in this essay indicate his conviction that Winthrop had the necessary practical skills and political aims, unlike the adventurers of the early Jacobean period, to run and extend a successful plantation. Nevertheless, Smith is careful to explain that he does not agree with the possibility of separation from the Church of England. Text from: first edition, 1631, pp. 10–12; 29–32.

Our right to those countries, true reasons for plantations, rare examples

Many good religious devout men have made it a great question, as a matter in conscience, by what warrant they might go to possess those countries which are none of theirs, but the poor savages.

Which poor curiosity will answer itself: for God did make the world to be inhabited with mankind, and to have his name known to all nations, and from generation to generation: as the people increased they dispersed themselves into such countries as they found most convenient. And here in Florida, Virginia, New England and Canada is more land than all the people in Christendom can manure, and yet more to spare than all the natives of those countries can use and culturate. And shall we here keep such a coil for land and at such great rents and rates, when there is so much of the world uninhabited, and as much more in other places, and as good, or rather better than any we possess, were it manured and used accordingly.

If this be not a reason sufficient to such tender consciences, for a copper knife and a few toys, as beads and hatchets, they will sell you a whole country; and for a small matter their houses and the ground they dwell upon; but those of the *Massachussetts* have resigned theirs freely.

Now the reasons for plantations are many: Adam and Eve did first begin this innocent work, to plant the earth to remain to posterity, but not without labour, trouble, and industry. Noah and his family began again the second plantation; and their seed as it still increased, hath still planted new countries, and one country another; and so the world to that estate it is. But not without much hazard, travel, mortalities, discontents and many disasters. Had those worthy fathers and their memorable offspring not been more diligent for us now in these ages, than we are to plant that yet unplanted for the after livers; had the seed of Abraham, our saviour Christ Jesus and his Apostles exposed themselves to no more dangers to plant the Gospel we so much profess, than we, even we ourselves had at this present been as savages and as miserable as the most barbarous savage yet uncivilised.

The Hebrews, Lacedaemonians, the Goths, the Grecians, Romans and the rest, what was it they would not undertake to enlarge their territories, enrich their subjects and resist their enemies? Those that were the founders of those great monarchies, and their virtues were no silvered idle golden Pharisees, but industrious honest hearted publicans; they regarded more provisions and necessaries for their people than jewels, riches, ease and delight for themselves. Riches was their servants not their masters. They ruled as fathers not as tyrants; their people as children, not as slaves; there was no disaster could discourage them; and let none think they encountered not with all manner of encumbrances. And what hath ever been the work of the best great princes of the world but planting of countries, and civilising barbarous and inhumane nations to civility and humanity? Whose eternal actions fills our histories with more honour than those that have wasted and consumed them by wars.

Lastly, the Portugals and Spaniards that first began plantations in this unknown world of *America* till within this 140 years, whose everlasting actions before our eyes will testify our idleness and ingratitude to all posterity, and neglect of our duty and religion we owe our God, our King, and country; and want of charity to those poor savages whose country we challenge, use and possess: except we be but made to mar what our forefathers made; or but only tell what they did; or esteem ourselves too good to take the like pains where there is so much reason, liberty and action offers itself. Having as much power and means as others, why should English men despair and not do so much as any? Was it virtue in those heroes to provide that doth maintain us, and baseness in us to do the like for others to come? Surely no: then, seeing we are not born for ourselves but each to help other; and our abilities are much alike at the hour of our birth and minute of our death; seeing our good deeds or bad, by faith in Christ's merits, is all we have to carry our souls to heaven or hell; seeing honour is our lives' ambition, and our ambition after death to have an honourable memory of our life; and seeing by no means we would be abated of the dignity and glory of our predecessors, let us imitate their virtues to be worthily their successors; or at least not hinder, if not further, them that would and do their utmost and best endeavour.

* * *

Their great supplies, present estate and accidents, advantages

Who would not think but that all those trials had been sufficient to lay a foundation for a plantation; but we see many men many minds, and still new lords, new laws; for those 350 men with all their cattle that so well arrived, and promised so much, not being of one body, but several men's servants, few could command and fewer obey, lived merrily of that they had, neither planting or building any thing to any purpose, but one fair house for the Governor, till all was spent and the winter approached; then they grew many diseases, and as many inconveniences, depending only of a supply from England, which expected houses, gardens and corn fields ready planted by them for their entertainment.

It is true that Master John Winthrop, their now Governor, a worthy gentleman both in estate and esteem went so well provided (for six or seven hundred people went with him) as could be devised; but at sea such an extraordinary storm encountered his fleet, continuing ten days, that of two hundred cattle which were so tossed and bruised, threescore and ten died, many of their people fell sick, and in this perplexed estate after ten weeks, they arrived in New England at several times: where they found threescore of their people dead, the rest sick, nothing done: but all complaining and all things so contrary to their expectation that now every monstrous humour began to show itself.

And to second this, near as many more came after them, but so ill provided, with such multitudes of women and children as redoubled their necessities.

This small trial of their patience caused among them no small confusion, and put the Governor and his Council to their utmost wits. Some could not endure the name of a bishop, others not the sight of a cross nor surplice, others by no means the *Book of Common Prayer*. This absolute crew, only of the elect, holding all (but such as themselves) reprobates and castaways, now make more haste to return to Babel as they termed England, than stay to enjoy the land they called Canaan: somewhat they must say to excuse themselves.

Those he found Brownists,[20] he let go for New Plymouth: who are now betwixt four or five hundred, and live well without want.

Some two hundred of the rest he was content to return to England, whose clamours are as variable as their humours and auditors. Some say they could see no timber of two feet diameter, some the country is all woods; others they drunk all the springs and ponds dry, yet like to famish for want of fresh water; some of the danger of the rattle snake; and that others sold their provisions at what rates they pleased to them that wanted, and so returned to England great gainers out of others' miseries; yet all that returned are not of those humours.

Notwithstanding all this, the noble Governor was no way disanimated, neither repents him of his enterprise for all those mistakes, but did order all things with that temperance and discretion and so relieved those that wanted with his own provision, that there is six or seven hundred remained with him, and more than 1,600 English in all the country, with three or four hundred head of cattle.

As for corn they are very ignorant, if upon the coast of America they do not before the end of this October (for toys) furnish themselves with two or three thousand bushels of Indian corn, which is better than ours; and in a short time cause the savages to do them as good service as their own men, as I did in Virginia; and yet neither use cruelty nor tyranny amongst them; a consequence well worth putting in practice, and 'till it be effected they will hardly do well.

I know ignorance will say it is impossible, but this impossible task ever since the massacre in Virginia,[21] I have been a suitor to have undertaken but with 150 men to have got corn, fortified the country, and discovered them more land than they all yet know or have demonstrated; but the merchants' common answer was necessity in time would force the planters do it themselves, and rather thus husbandly to lose ten sheep than be at the charge of a halfpenny worth of tar.

Who is it that knows not what a small handful of Spaniards in the West Indies subdued millions of the inhabitants, so depopulating those countries they conquered, that they are glad to buy negroes in Africa at a great rate, in countries far remote from them; which although they be as idle and as devilish people as any in the world, yet they cause them quickly to be their best servants. Notwithstanding, there is for every four or five natural Spaniards, two or three hundred Indians and negroes, and in Virginia and New England more English than savages that can assemble themselves to assault or hurt them, and it is much better to help to plant a country than unplant it and then replant it; but there Indians were in such multitudes, the Spaniards had no other remedy; and ours such a few and so dispersed it were nothing in a short time to bring then to labour and obedience.

8.25 THE NAVIGATION ACT

This protectionist measure, passed under the Commonwealth in 1651, was ultimately unenforceable and detrimental to trade. Nevertheless, it is indicative of foreign and economic policy in the interregnum. Text from: C. Firth and R. Rait, *Acts and Ordinances of the Interregnum*, London, 1911, vol. 2, pp. 559–61.

For the increase of the shipping and the encouragement of the navigation of this nation, which under the good providence and protection of God is so great a means of the welfare and safety of this Commonwealth: be it enacted by this present Parliament and the authority thereof, that . . . no goods or commodities whatsoever of the growth or manufacture of Asia, Africa or America, or any part thereof; or of any islands belonging to them, or which are described or laid down in the usual maps, or cards of those places, as well of the English plantations as others, shall be imported or brought into this Commonwealth of England, or into Ireland, or any other lands, islands, plantations or territories to this Commonwealth belonging, or in their possession, in any other ship or ships, vessel or vessels whatsoever, but only in such as do truly and without fraud belong only to the people of this Commonwealth, or the plantations thereof, as the proprietors or right owners thereof; and whereof the master and mariners are also for the most part of them of the people of this Commonwealth, under the penalty of the forfeiture and loss of all the goods that shall be imported contrary to this act; as also of the ship (with all her tackle, guns and apparel) in which the said goods or commodities shall be brought in and imported; the one moiety to the use of the Commonwealth, and the other moiety to the use and behoof of any person or persons who shall seize the goods or commodities, and shall prosecute the same in any court of record within this Commonwealth.

And it is further enacted by the authority aforesaid, that no goods or commodities of the growth, production, or manufacture of Europe, or of any part thereof, shall . . . be imported or brought into this Commonwealth of England . . . in any ship or ships, vessel or vessels whatsoever, but in such as do truly and without fraud belong only to the people of this Commonwealth as the true owners and proprietors thereof, and in no other, except only such foreign ships and vessel as do truly and properly belong to the people of that country or place of which the said goods are the growth, production or manufacture; or to such ports where the said goods can only be, or most usually are first shipped for transportation . . .

And it is further enacted by the authority aforesaid that no sort of cod fish, ling, herring, pilchard to any other kind of salted fish, usually fished for and caught by the people of this nation; nor any oil made, or that shall be made of any kind of fish whatsoever, nor any whale-fins, or whale-bones, shall henceforth be imported into this Commonwealth . . . but only such as shall be caught in vessels that do or shall truly and properly belong to the people of this nation, as proprietors and right owners thereof; and the said fish to be cured and the oil aforesaid made by the people of this Commonwealth under the penalty and loss expressed in the first branch of this present Act; the said forfeit to be recovered and employed as is there expressed.

And it is further enacted by the authority aforesaid that no sort of cod, ling, herring or pilchard or any other kind of salted fish whatsoever, which shall be caught and cured by the people of this Commonwealth, shall be from and after the first of February, one thousand six hundred fifty three, exported from any place or places belonging to this Commonwealth in any other ship or ships, vessel or vessels, save only in such as do truly and properly appertain to the people of this Commonwealth, as right owners, and whereof the master and mariners are for the most part of them English, under the penalty and loss expressed in the said first branch of this present Act; the said forfeit to be recovered and employed as is there expressed.

Provided always that this Act nor anything therein contained extend not, or be meant to restrain, the importation of the commodities of the Straits,[22] or Levant seas, laden in the shipping of this nation as aforesaid, at the usual ports or places for loading of them heretofore, within the said Straits or Levant seas, though the said commodities be not of the very growth of the said places.

Provided also that this Act nor anything therein contained extend not to, nor be meant to restrain, the importing of any East India commodities laden in the shipping of this nation, at the usual port of places for loading of them . . .

Provided also that it shall and may be lawful to and for any of the people of this Commonwealth in vessels or ships to them belonging, and whereof the master and mariners are of this nation as aforesaid, to load and bring in from any ports of Spain and Portugal, all sorts of goods and commodities that have come from, or any way belonged unto, the plantations or dominions of either of them respectively . . .

Lastly, that this Act therein contained, extend not to bullion, nor yet to goods taken, or that shall be taken, by way of reprisal by any ship or ships having commission from this Commonwealth.

Provided that this Act or anything therein contained shall not extend nor be construed to extend to any silk or silk wares, which shall be brought by land from any part of Italy.

CHRONOLOGY

Date	Political/Social Events	Religion and the Church	Education	Literature and culture	Science and magic	Trade, Empire and exploration
Chronology 1530–1662		d. = dies b. = born				
1530s	Henry's divorce of Catherine precipitates separation from Catholic Church	Coverdale Bible (1535) Great Bible (1539); English Bible to be in every Church; dissolution of monasteries (1536–9) Tyndale's translations available from Continental presses. Calvin's *Institutes* (1536)	Elyot, *The Governor* (1531). End of monastic colleges (1536)	Wyatt active as poet; Bale, *King John* (1538)		Inca empire overthrown (1531–3); voyages made by William Hawkins to trade slaves
1540–1546		Council of Trent opens 1545, to discuss Catholicism's response to Protestant reforms	Lily's *Brevissima Institutio* compulsory text in grammar schools; his *Grammar* pub. 1542. Trinity College, Camb. founded	Surrey's poems circulating in ms. Lindsay, *Satire of the Three Estates*; Hall, *Chronicle* (1542)	Copernicus's *De Revolutionibus* and Vesalius' *De Corpore Humani* published 1543	1539–42 Portuguese explore North America
1547	Henry VIII dies; Edward VI accedes under protectorate of Somerset	*Certain Sermons or Homilies* (1st ed)	Priests orderd to buy Erasmus, *Paraphrases* to improve their Scriptural knowledge	Earl of Surrey executed		

Date	Political/Social Events	Religion and the Church	Education	Literature and culture	Science and magic	Trade, Empire and exploration
1548	Edward's reign characterised by radical Protestantism; Crowley's *A . . . Petition against the Oppressors of the Poor Commons*	Book of Common Prayer (1st ed) (work of Cranmer)		Hall, *Union of . . . York and Lancaster*		
1549	Revolts against enclosures begin: corn famine 1549–51	Act of Uniformity and new Prayer Book introduced	Reform of university statutes; survey of educational institutions. Some schools protected by parliament	Wyatt, *Certain Psalms*. State censorship re-introduced		
1550	William Cecil made secretary of state	Latimer preaching		Vasari, *Lives of the Artists*		
1551	Edward has ex-Protector Somerset tried and executed for treason	Privy Council orders removal of plate from all churches				Muscovy Company chartered
1552		Book of Common Prayer (revised, 2nd ed.); 2nd ed. of *Homilies*				

Date	Chronology 1530–1662 Political/Social Events	d. = dies b. = born Religion and the Church	Education	Literature and culture	Science and magic	Trade, Empire and exploration
1553	Edward VI dies; Mary I accedes			Wilson, *Art of Rhetoric*; Udall, *Ralph Roister Doister*		
1554	Lady Jane Grey executed; Mary marries Philip of Spain	Catholic Church re-established: married clergy to be deprived of benefices	Trinity and St. John's colleges, Oxford, founded			
1555	Latimer and Ridley burned at stake for refusing to reconvert	Peace of Augsburg allows religious self-determination in German states: Cranmer deprived of archbishopric		*Mirror for Magistrates* (first ed.)		Eden translates Martyr's *Decades*
1556	Corn famine: worst harvest of century	Burning of Cranmer; Pole made archbishop				Plan to extend Pale in Ireland by plantation of counties Laois and Offaly
1557	War with France		Gonville and Caius, Cambridge, founded	Tottel's *Miscellany* (*Songs and Sonnets*); Stationer's Company incorporated: holds printing monopoly		Laois and Offaly renamed 'Queen's County' and 'King's County'

	Chronology 1530–1662	d. = dies b. = born				
Date	**Political/Social Events**	**Religion and the Church**	**Education**	**Literature and culture**	**Science and magic**	**Trade, Empire and exploration**
1558	Calais surrendered to France. Mary I dies; Elizabeth I accedes	Church of England re-established. Pole removed as archbishop. Protestant riots in Scotland	1558–1603 136 Grammar schools founded	Marguerite de Navarre, *Heptameron*		
1559	Act of Supremacy: Knox and Aylmer debate question of female monarchs. First parliament debates Elizabeth's marriage	Act of Uniformity: second edition of *Homilies*		Foxe's *Acts and Monuments*; *Queen's Injunctions* reiterate censorship		
1560	Gresham advising Queen on exchange rates and economic policy	Geneva Bible. Civil religious wars in Scotland. Many Marian exiles become protestant bishops		*Gorboduc*		Dublin parliament passes Act of Uniformity outlawing Catholicism
1561		First English translation of Calvin's *Institutes*	Becon' *Catechism*	Hoby trans. *The Courtier*; Awdeley, *The Fraternity of Vagabonds*		
1562	French wars of religion begin. English currency re-coined	Jewel, *Apology for the Church of England*		Daniel b.		John Hawkins begins slave trade with Africa

Date	Chronology 1530–1662 Political/Social Events	Religion and the Church	Education	Literature and culture	Science and magic	Trade, Empire and exploration
		d. = dies b. = born				
1563	Plague in London, first Poor Law: Statute of Artificers	*Thirty-Nine Articles.* Radical protestant attempts to reform prayer book are defeated		Drayton b.		
1564	Dearth and inflation. Robert Dudley made Earl of Leicester	Calvin, d. Many clergy deprived for refusing to wear surplices		Shakespeare, b. Marlowe, b. Michaelanglo, b.	Galileo, b.	Court of High Commission established in Ireland to enforce conformity. Riots against English plantation
1565	Elizabeth's summer progress to Coventry	Dean of Christ Church, Oxford, and President of Magdalen college suspended for nonconformity	Oxford receives new statutes stipulating BA curriculum	Golding trans. *Metamorphoses*		St. Augustine founded by Spain in Florida
1566	Parliament debates bills on simony and pluralism, and the succession. Elizabeth makes progresses to Oxfordshire	Parker's *Book of Advertisements* lays down rules for licensing approved preachers, and conducting services		Gascoigne, *Supposes*		

| | Chronology 1530–1662 | d. = dies
b. = born | | | | |
Date	Political/Social Events	Religion and the Church	Education	Literature and culture	Science and Magic	Trade, Empire and exploration
1567	First revolt in Netherlands suppressed by Spaniards	First separatist congregation discovererd in London. More clergy suspended for refusing to wear surplices		Campion, b. Nashe, b.		
1568	Mary Queen of Scots flees to England, after abdicating	The Bishop's Bible. Douai college founded to train English priests				Defeat of Hawkins by Spaniards at San Juan de Ulloa
1569	Revolt of Northern Earls suppressed		Thomas Cartwright professor of divinity at Cambridge	Spenser, *Visions of Bellay*, *Visions of Petrarch*	Agrippa, *Of the ... Vanity of ...Sciences*	
1570		Pope excommunicates Elizabeth I	Ascham, *The Schoolmaster.*		Dee, trans. Euclid's *Elements*	
1571	Parliament legislates against recusants. Cecil made Lord Burghley	Foxe's *Acts* to be placed in all Cathedral and collegiate churches; Fitz's separatist covenant and petition to Parliament. Cartwright loses Cambridge chair				

Date	Political/Social Events	Religion and the Church	Education	Literature and culture	Science and magic	Trade, Empire and exploration
	Chronology 1530–1662	d. = dies b. = born				
1572	Admonition to Parliament	Massacre of St. Bartholomew's. Roger's *Displaying of a Horrible Sect* attacks Familists. Puritans in parliament try to introduce parish independence		Jonson, b. Dekker, b. Donne, b.; actors not under aristocratic patronage declared vagabonds		
1573	Walsingham and Thomas Smith made Secretaries of State	Cartwright goes into exile				Earl of Essex granted plantation rights over County Antrim. Drake brings plundered treasure to Plymouth
1574	Re-issue of statutes of apparel	First priests arrive from Douai; exiled William Travers advocates presbyterianism				
1575	New poor law. Queen's progresses at Kenilworth, Worcester, Lichfield and Reading	Parker dies: Grindal made Archbishop of Canterbury		Tasso, *Gerusalemme Liberata*; Gascoigne, *Posies, Notes of Instruction*		Essex's army massacres inhabitants of Rathlin Island

Date	Political/Social Events	Religion and the Church	Education	Literature and culture	Science and Magic	Trade, Empire and exploration
1576	Wentworth claims Parliamentary right of freedom of speech	Wentworth attacks clerical abuses: sent to tower. Grindal challenges Queen's opposition to 'prophesyings'		The Theatre built	Digges translates Copernicus	Frobisher resumes exploration for north-west passage
1577	Christopher Hatton made vice chamberlain of the privy council	Grindal suspended; Aylmer bishop of London and to enforce Royal orders to suppress prophesying		Peacham, *The Garden of Eloquence*; The Curtain and Blackfriars theatres open. Holinshed, *Chronicle*	Burton, b.	Drake's first voyage to circumnavigate the world
1578	Queen's progress to Norwich brings plague to city	Hanging of Catholic priests begins		Lyly, *Euphues*; Sidney, *The Lady of May*. Tyler, trans, *The Mirror of Princely Deeds*		Patent awarded to Gilbert to settle Virginia
1579	Alencon negotiations begin	English Jesuit college founded in Rome		Gosson, *School of Abuse*; North trans. Plutarch; Spenser; *The Shepherd's Calendar*; Sidney, *Defence of Poesy*; *Astrophil and Stella* circulate in ms.		Skirmishes with Irish rebels continue

Chronology 1530–1662						
					d. = dies	
					b. = born	

Date	Social/Political Events	Religion and the Church	Education	Literature and Culture	Science and magic	Trade, Empire and exploration
1580	Raleigh and Spenser in Ireland (latter as Lord Lieutenant's secretary)	Campion and Parsons sent to England as part of Jesuit mission		Montaigne, *Essais*, vol.1–2; Sidney's *Arcadia* begun		Lord Grey appointed Lord Deputy of Ireland: crushes rebellion and massacres many
1581	Alencon arrives in England to complete marriage negotiations: which fail	Recusancy laws against Catholic laity strengthened; Campion executed	Mulcaster, *Positions*	Peele, *The Arraignment of Paris*; Pettie, trans, *Guazzo's Civil Conversation*; Tasso, *Gerusalemme Liberata*		
1582	Raleigh becomes Elizabeth's favourite	Presbyterian classes meet in East Anglia				Hakluyt, *Voyages* (1st ed). Lord Grey recalled
1583	Buchanan, *De Jure Regni, in Scotland,* argues that deposition of a tyrannical monarch is legal. Smith, *De Republica Anglorum* delineates the structure and constitution of the English *polis*	Grindal dies, Whitgift archbishop of Canterbury: criticised for 'Roman Inquisition' tactics by Burghley. Execution of three separatists at Bury St. Edmunds		Stubbes, *Anatomy of Abuses*	John Dee's house destroyed by mob fearful of his magical powers	Irish rebellion crushed

Date	Political/Social Events	Religion and the Church	Education	Literature and culture	Science and magic	Trade, Empire and exploration
					d. = dies b. = born	
					Chronology 1530–1662	
1584	Assassination of William of Orange. Puritan campaign through parliament for further Church reform	Whitgift issues revised articles and secures most clergy's subscription to them	Emmanuel College founded (puritan leanings)	Cambridge University Press founded; Lyly, *Campaspe, Sappho and Phao*; Raleigh active as poet	Scott, *Discovery of Witchcraft*	Raleigh sets sail for Virginia. John Perot as Lord Deputy of Ireland reveals further plantation plans
1585	Leicester's expedition to Netherlands. Philip II orders seizure of all English ships in Atlantic ports	Whitgift pursues campaign to prevent puritans being elected to parliament. Catholic priests banished, all Englishmen in seminaries recalled.				Raleigh founds first English colony in Virginia at Roanoke
1586	Decree of Star Chamber tightens press censorship. Severe harvest failure and famine	Pope proclaims crusade against England. Wentworth continues parliamentary campaign to replace Book of Common Prayer with Genevan *Form of Prayer*		Monteverdi; *First Book of Madrigals*; Sidney d.; Webbe, *Discourse of English Poetry*; Kyd, *Spanish Tragedy*; Camden *Remains of Britain* (1st ed)		Roanoke evacuated by Drake

	Chronology 1530–1662	d. = dies b. = born				
Date	Political/Social Events	Religion and the Church	Education	Literature and culture	Science and magic	Trade, Empire and exploration
1587	Mary Queen of Scots executed. Hatton becomes Lord Chancellor	Wentworth imprisoned after attempt to introduce Parliamentary bill abolishing Church of England		Marlowe, *Tamburlaine*		Drake's attack on Cadiz
1588	Spanish Armada defeated	Marprelate controversy: anti-episcopal debates from secret presses		Lyly, *Endimion*	Hobbes, b.	Harriot, *A Brief Report . . . of Virginia*
1589	Secret Marprelate press discovered	Bancroft's St. Paul's sermon claims bishops rule by divine right		Puttenham, *The Art of English Poesy*; Nashe, *Anatomy of Absurdity*; Marlowe, *Jew of Malta*; *Dr. Faustus*; Greene, *Menaphon*, *Friar Bacon*		Further campaigns to restore order in Ireland
1590	Walsingham, d.	Campaign against puritan ministers led by Whitgift and Bancroft (bishop of London). Margaret Hoby's Diary begins		Spenser, *The Faerie Queene (1–3)*; Shakespeare, *The Comedy of Errors* (1590–2); Sidney, *Arcadia (p)*; Peele, *The Old Wive's Tale*		

Date	Chronology 1530–1662		Religion and the church	Education	Literature and culture	Science and magic	Trade, Empire and exploration
		d. = dies b. = born					
	Political/Social Events						
1591	Robert Cecil becomes privy councillor. Proclamation against vagrant soldiers classifies them as vagrants		Perkins, *The Golden Chain*. Puritans of the Marprelate controversy (inc. Cartwright) are accused of treason in Star Chamber		Harrington trans. *Orlando Furioso*; Shakespeare, *Henry VI*; Harrington trans. *Orlando Furioso*. Herrick, b.		Raleigh, *A Report about the Flight of the Isles of Azores*
1592	Essex recalled to court, when Raleigh falls from favour after secret marriage, and is imprisoned. Plague shuts down many towns		Southwell's *An humble supplication to her Majesty* pleads for toleration towards loyal Catholics		Rose theatre opened; Marlowe, *Edward II*; Shakespeare, *Richard III*; Nashe, *Pierce Penniless*, *Summer's Last Will and Testament*. First of Lord Mayor's petitions against stage plays		
1593	Plague in London. Parliament meets: brings in severe fines against Catholics. Wentworth raises question of succession: imprisoned and dies. Essex made privy councillor		Hooker, *Ecclesiastical Polity*, books 1–4		Marlowe, *Hero and Leander*; Shakespeare, *Venus and Adonis*; Theatre closed due to plague; Marlowe d. Drayton, *Idea*. Herbert, b.		

Date	Political/Social Events	Religion and the Church	Education	Literature and culture	Science and magic	Trade, Empire and exploration
	Chronology 1530–1662	d. = dies b. = born				
1594	Bad harvests begin. Celebration of Elizabeth's 30 years on throne. Lord Mayor holds conference on problem of rogues in London	Aylmer, d.		*Titus Andronicus; Taming of the Shrew; Love's Labour's Lost; The Spanish Tragedy;* Admiral's Men and Chamberlain's Men consolidated; Daniel, *Delia*		
1595	Apprentices and masterless men riot in Southwark. Proclamation against Unlawful Assembly issued	Execution of Robert Southwell. University of Cambridge riven by predestination controversy. Whitgift issues Lambeth Articles, re-stating Calvinist position. Elizabeth stops further debate		Donne's early poems and Shakespeare's sonnets in circulation; Spenser, *Amoretti, Epithalamion;* Campion, *Poemata*		Voyage to West Indies by Drake and Hawkins, both die. Raleigh's voyage to Guiana. Tyrone rebellion in Ireland

	Chronology 1530–1662	d. = dies b. = born				
Date	Political/Social Events	Religion and the Church	Education	Literature and culture	Science and magic	Trade, Empire and exploration
1596	Building of suburban houses in Middlesex banned. Robert Cecil principal royal secretary. Very bad harvest: proclamation prohibiting grain exports. Riots in Oxfordshire against enclosures and grain prices.		Sidney Sussex College founded	Spenser, *The Faerie Queene* (books 4–6); *Four Hymns*; *Merchant of Venice*; John Davies, *Orchestra*. Plays banned due to plague		Raleigh, *Discovery of Guiana*; Spenser, *View of the Present State of Ireland*
1597	English campaign in Low Countries. Grain riots in Kent, Sussex, Norfolk			Chapman, *Humorous Day's Mirth*; *Henry IV (1)*; Bacon, *Essays* (1st ed)	James Stuart, *Demonology*; Roger, Bacon *The Mirror of Alchemy* (trans); *Gerard's Herbal*	
1598	Stow, *Survey of London*; Poor Law established, and confirmed in 1601. Legislation reverses some enclosures			*Henry IV* (2); Jonson, *Every Man in His Humour*; Marlowe, *Hero and Leander*		Hakluyt's *Principal Navigation's . . . .* published 1598–1600 in 3 vols. Defeat of English by Irish rebels

Date	Political/Social Events	Religion and the Church	Education	Literature and culture	Science and magic	Trade, Empire and exploration
	Chronology 1530–1662	**d. = dies b. = born**				
1599	Essex campaign in Ireland; James Stuart, *Basilikon Doron*; *The True Law of Free Monarchies*	Bishops order burning of satires and erotic material		Hall, *Virgimediarum*; Marston, *Scourge of Villany*; Shakespeare, *Julius Caesar*; *Much Ado About Nothing*, Jonson, *Every Man out of His Humour*. Globe Theatre built		Essex defeated in Ireland: negotiates with Tyrone without assent of Queen
1600	Mountjoy sent to Ireland: Essex under house arrest in London			*As You Like It, Twelfth Night*; Jonson, *Cynthia's Revels*; Heywood, *Fair Maid of the West*. Fortune Theatre built; Hooker, d; Nashe d.	Gilbert's *De Magnete* published in Latin	
1601	Essex open rebellion in London, trial and execution; Queen attacked in Parliament over monopolies	Dent, *The Plain Man's Pathway to Heaven*		Dekker, *Satiromastix*; Jonson, *Poetaster*; Shakespeare, *Hamlet*; Campion, *Book of Airs* Holland trans. Pliny		East India Company chartered. Spanish fleet lands in Ireland
1602			Bodleian library founded and opened	*Troilus and Cressida*; Campion, *Art of English Poesy*		Mountjoy defeats Irish

Date	Chronology 1530–1662 Political/Social Events	Religion and the Church	Education	Literature and culture	Science and magic	Trade, Empire and exploration
1603	Elizabeth I dies, James I accedes. Mountjoy completes conquest of Ireland. Plague in London kills 22% of the population; Raleigh sent to prison for treasonous plotting on the matter of the succession	Millenary petition to James I demands puritan reforms of doctrine and practice of Church	Camden endows Oxford Professorship of ancient history; Earl of Derby donates land for botanical garden for scientific study	Daniel, *Defence of Rhyme*; Jonson, *Sejanus*; Shakespeare, *All's Well that Ends Well*; *Othello*; Florio trans. Montaigne's *Essays*. Theatre companies come under royal patronage	William Gilbert d.	
1604	James I declared King of Great Britain; peace with Spain; first parliament 1604–1610. Bacon, *Brief Discourse . . . Happy Union*	Hampton Court Conference; new Canons establish and enforce greater conformity	1604–1625 83 Grammar schools founded	Marston, *The Malcontent*, *The Dutch Courtesan*; Shakespeare, *Measure for Measure*; Dekker and Middleton, *Honest Whore*; Dekker and Webster, *Westward Ho*		James I, *Counterblast to Tobacco*
1605	Gunpowder plot	Bancroft Archbishop of Canterbury	Bacon, *Advancement of Learning*	Camden, *Remains*; Chapman, Jonson and Marston, *Eastward Ho*; Marston, *Dutch Courtesan*; Middleton, *A Mad World My Masters*; Shakespeare, *King Lear*; Jonson, *Masque of Blackness*	Bacon, *Advancement of Learning*	George Weymouth explores New England coast

Date	Chronology 1530–1662 Political/Social Events	d. = dies b. = born Religion and the Church	Education	Literature and culture	Science and magic	Trade, Empire and exploration
1606	Courts uphold King's right to raise extra-parliamentary levies (Bate's case); Bodin's *Six Books of a Commonweal* trans.			*Revenger's Tragedy*; Jonson, *Volpone*; Shakespeare, *Macbeth*; Dekker, *Seven Deadly Sins of London*; Lyly, d.; Golding, d.		London and Plymouth companies chartered to settle Virginia
1607	Midlands rising against enclosures			Shakespeare, *Antony and Cleopatra*; Middleton, *Your Five Gallants*. Camden, *Remains* (2nd ed)		First English settlement at Jamestown, Virginia. Sagadahoc settlement fails
1608	Robert Cecil appointed Lord Treasurer. Parliament rejects union with Scotland			King's Men lease Blackfriars Theatre; Fletcher, *Faithful Shepherdess*; Shakespeare, *Timon of Athens*; Milton, b.		
1609				Jonson, *Epicoene*, Shakespeare, *Coriolanus, Pericles*		Virginian voyage shipwrecked in Bermuda: Jamestown endures 'starving time'. Gray, *A Good Speed to Virginia*

Date	Chronology 1530–1662 Political/Social Events	d. = dies b. = born Religion and the Church	Education	Literature and culture	Science and magic	Trade, Empire and exploration
1610	Parliament debates impositions; Arabella Stuart imprisoned for secret marriage	Archbishop Bancroft dies		Jonson, *Alchemist*; Dekker and Middleton, *Roaring Girl*; Shakespeare, *Cymbeline*; Heywood, *Golden Age*; Milton, b.	Galileo's *Starry Messenger* published in Latin	
1611	Robert Carr made Viscount Rochester; baronetcies for sale by monarch at £1095	Authorised version of the Bible published; George Abbot becomes Archbishop of Canterbury		Heywood, *Silver Age, Bronze Age*; Jonson, *Catiline*; Shakespeare, *Winter's Tale, Tempest*; Tourneur, *Atheist's Tragedy*; Donne, *Anatomy of the World*; Middleton, *A Chaste Maid in Cheapside*; Lanyer, *Salve Deus Rex Judaeorum*		
1612	Marriage arranged between Princess Elizabeth and Elector Palatine Frederick; death of Prince Henry		Brinsley's *Ludus Literarius* sets out ideal curriculum for grammar schools	Bacon, *Essays* (2nd ed); Webster, *White Devil*; Heywood, *Apology for Actors*; *Iron Age*		

Date	Chronology 1530–1662					
		d. = dies				
		b. = born				
	Political/Social Events	Religion and the Church	Education	Literature and culture	Science and magic	Trade, Empire and exploration
1613	Marriage of Elizabeth to Frederick; Frances Howard divorce approved and she marries Somerset; Overbury dies			Jonson, *The Irish Masque*; Drayton, *Polyolbion*, Webster, *Duchess of Malfi*		
1614	Addled parliament, dissolved over impositions, and not called until 1621; plans to marry Charles to Spanish Infanta			Overbury, *Characters*; Raleigh, *History of the World*; Jonson, *Bartholomew Fair*; second Globe built	Napier invents logarithms	Peace concluded between Powhatan Confederacy and Jamestown settlers. First tobacco shipment exported to England
1615	Arrest of Somersets for murder of Overbury			Middleton, *More Dissemblers Besides Women*; Jonson, *Golden Age Restor'd*	Crooke (King's physician), *Microcosmographia*	John Smith's explorations of New England coast
1616	Trial and conviction of Somersets; King raises money by selling peerages; James I publishes his complete *Works*; Coke dismissed as Chief Justice		Ladies hall in Deptford active (school for young women) - performed masque at court	Jonson publishes his *Works*; Shakespeare, d.; Chapman, *Whole Works of Homer*; Inigo Jones begins work on Queen's house, Greenwich		Raleigh released for final expedition to Guiana; *A Brief Declaration of the Present State of things in Virginia*

Chronology 1530–1662

d. = dies
b. = born

Date	Political/Social Events	Religion and the Church	Education	Literature and culture	Science and magic	Trade, Empire and exploration
1617	George Villiers (new favourite of James) becomes Earl of Buckingham; negotiations for Spanish marriage proceed			Fletcher, *The Mad Lover*, Webster *The Devil's Law Case*		
1618	Francis Bacon made Lord Chancellor; beginning of Thirty Years War; Lord Cranfield begins attempted reform of royal finances			Declaration of Sports. Jonson, *Pleasure Reconciled to Virtue*; Cowley, Lovelace, b.		Execution of Raleigh; Virginia Charter of Liberties granted
1619	Queen Anne dies; Frederick accepts crown of Bohemia	Synod of Dort: James's delegation to back Anti-Arminianism	Oxford University establishes chairs in geometry, astronomy, natural philosophy and anatomy	Daniel, d. 1619–1622, building of Banqueting House by Inigo Jones	Harvey discovers circulation of the blood	
1620	Frederick exiled from Bohemia by Catholic imperial forces: English Protestant party lobbies for war. Controversies over women dressing as men, and general extravagance at court			Jonson, *News from the New World*; *Pan's Anniversary*; Campion, d.	Bacon, *Novum Organum*; Crooke, *Microcosmographia* (2nd ed)	Pilgrim Fathers found colony at Plymouth, New England

Date	Chronology 1530–1662 Political/Social Events	Religion and the Church	Education	Literature and culture	Science and magic	Trade, Empire and exploration
		d. = dies b. = born				
1621	Business parliament: impeaches Bacon, and claims right to advise king on all subjects	Donne becomes Dean of St. Paul's		Van Dyck's first visit to England; Mary Herbert, d; Marvell, b.; Dekker, Ford, Rowley, *Witch of Edmonton*; Massinger, *New Way to Pay Old Debts, Maid of Honour*	Burton, *Anatomy of Melancholy*	
1622	Misselden and de Malynes debate Free Trade		Peacham, *The Complete Gentleman*	Middleton, *The Changeling, Women Beware Women*; Moliere, b., Wotton, *Elements of Architecture*		Massacre at Jamestown by Powhatan confederacy; Winslow, *Relation...of the Plantation settled at Plymouth*
1623	Buckingham and Charles sail secretly to Madrid to pursue Spanish marriage plans			William Byrd, d.; Daniel, *Works*		
1624	Fourth parliament: attacks on proposed alliance with Spain, and pressure for war alliance with Protestant powers of Europe; Richelieu chief minister in France			Donne, *Devotions*; Middleton, *Game at Chess*; Rowley and Webster, *Cure for a Cuckold*; Massinger, *Parliament of Love*; Fletcher, *Wife for a Month*; *Rule a Wife and Have a Wife*		Collapse of Virginia Company

	Chronology 1530–1662	d. = dies b. = born				
Date	Political/Social Events	Religion and the Church	Education	Literature and culture	Science and magic	Trade, Empire and exploration
1625	Death of James, accession of Charles I, who marries Henrietta Maria. First parliament at Oxford attacks Buckingham,		1625–1660 59 grammar schools founded	Heywood, *English Traveller*; Massinger, *Unnatural Combat*; Shirley, *Love Tricks*. Bacon, *Essays* (3rd ed)		
1626	Second Parliament dissolved. Forced Loan	York House Conference		Jonson, *Staple of News*; Massinger, *Roman Actor*; Shirley, *Wedding*	Bacon, d.	
1627	War against France			Middleton, d.; Davenant, *Cruel Brother*; Massinger, *Great Duke of Florence*		
1628	Third parliament produces Petition of Right. Buckingham assassinated	Laud becomes Bishop of London	Mrs. Thend's School in Stepney (girls' boarding school)	Davenant, *Albovine*; Ford, *Lover's Melancholy*; Shirley, *Witty Fair One*	Harvey, *On the Motion of the Heart and Blood*	
1629	Parliament dissolved, after refusal to grant impositions: not recalled until 1640	Andrewes, XCVI *Sermons*		Rubens visits England; Jonson, *New Inn*; Ford, *Broken Heart*		Massachusetts Bay Company founded

Date	Chronology 1530–1662 d. = dies b. = born Political/Social Events	Religion and the Church	Education	Literature and culture	Science and magic	Trade, Empire and exploration
1630	Future Charles II born. Exchequer confirms King's right to fine landowners who had not received knighthoods on his succession		Laud as Chancellor of Oxford university makes lecture attendance compulsory, and strengthens powers of colleges	Heywood, *Fair Maid of the West 2*; Charles purchases Raphael cartoons		Boston founded by emigrating puritans, along with ten other settlements
1631	Successive bad harvests: food riots		Powell, *Tom of all Trades*	Massinger, *Believe as You List*; Shirley, *Humorous Courtier*; Heywood, *England's Elizabeth*; Donne d.; Dryden b.		
1632	Locke b. Wentworth appointed Lord Deputy of Ireland			Ford, *Love's Sacrifice*, *'Tis Pity She's a Whore*; Jonson, *Magnetic Lady*; Massinger, *City Madam*; Shirley, *Hyde Park*; Donne, *Death's Duel*. Van Dyke settles in England. Dekker, d.		Maryland founded

Date	Chronology 1530–1662 Political/Social Events	Religion and the Church	Education	Literature and culture	Science and magic	Trade, Empire and exploration
		d. = dies b. = born				
1633	Charles visits Scotland and decides to introduce new Prayer Book. Book of Sports re-issued. Prynne sent to Tower for writing *Histriomastix*	Laud becomes Archbishop of Canterbury; abolition of fees of impropriations		Heywood, *Maidenhead Well Lost*; Jonson, *Tale of a Tub*, Ford, *Perkin Warbeck*; Herbert, *The Temple*; Herbert, d.		
1634	Ship money levied on maritime counties	Laud commences new Visitations in England and Wales to ensure and impose conformity		Brome and Heywood, *Late Lancashire Witches*; Davenant, *Love and Honour, Wits*; Milton, *Comus*		Demand for Massachusetts Charter to be public
1635	Judges declare ship money legal: levied on whole country			Davenant, *The Platonic Lovers*; Browne, *Religio Medici*; Quarles, *Emblems*		Restoration of monopoly of Company of Merchant Adventurers
1636		Book of canons imposed on Scotland		Brome, *Antipodes*; Cowley, *Sylva*		First English settlements on Connecticut river

Date	Political/Social Events	Religion and the Church	Education	Literature and culture	Science and magic	Trade, Empire and exploration
		d. = dies b. = born				
1637	Trial of Hampden for refusal to pay ship money	Prynne, Bastwick and Burton tried by Laud, then branded and ears cut off for anti-Episcopal publications. Riots in Scotland against imposition of new Prayer Book		Shirley, *The Royal Master*	Descartes, *Discours sur la Methode*	New Haven founded. Anne Hutchinson expelled from Massachusetts
1638		Scottish National Assembly reject Prayer Book and abolish bishops		Milton, *Lycidas*; Davenant, *Britannia Triumphans, Lminalia, Unfortunate Lovers*; Suckling, *Goblins* Quarles, *Hieroglyphics*	Wilkins, *The Discovery of a world in the Moon*	
1639	First Bishops War against Scotland	Fuller, *Holy War*		Carew, *Poems*; Brome, *Mad Couple Well Matched*; Shirley, *Politician*; Henry Wotton, d.		Crown formally acknowledges Virginia Assembly
1640	Short Parliament; second war with Scotland; Long Parliament meets until 1648	Hall, *Episcopacy by Divine Right*; Root and Branch petition; Laud impeached		Brome, *Court Beggar*; Shirley, *Imposture*; Jonson, *Timber; The Underwood*. Ford, Massinger, Burton, d. Aphra Behn, b. Censorship breaks down		

Chronology 1530–1662

| | Chronology 1530–1662 | | | | d. = dies
b. = born | |

Date	Political/Social Events	Religion and the Church	Education	Literature and culture	Science and magic	Trade, Empire and exploration
1641	Grand Remonstrance; execution of Strafford	Milton, *Of Reformation*	Manchester and York petition Parliament to establish northern university	Brome, *Jovial Crew;* Shirley, *Cardinal;* Killigrew, *Parson's Wedding;* Quarles, *Threnodes*		
1642	Outbreak of civil war: battle of Edgehill. Hobbes, *De Cive*	Milton, *Reason of Church Government.* Bishops excluded from House of Lords	Comenius, *A Reformation of all Schools:* urging Pym to establish scientific college	Theatres closed; Denham, *Cooper's Hill;* Peacham, *Art of Living in London*	Galileo d; Newton, b.	
1643	Pym, Hampden, Falkland die; Louis XIV ascends French throne	Westminster Assembly of Divines		Censorship re-introduced; Milton, *Doctrine and Discipline of Divorce*		Rhode Island granted charter by Parliament
1644	Covenant imposed on all adult males; Royalist Parliament at Oxford	Celebration of Christmas forbidden	Milton, *Of Education*	Milton, *Areopagitica*		
1645	New Model Army formed; Battle of Naseby. Clubmen petitions to Parliament against civil war.	Prayer Book and Anglican rites abolished: new Directory of Worship established. Laud executed		Howell, *Epistolae Ho Elianae;* Waller Poems; Milton, *Poems*	Digby, *Two Treatises*	

	Chronology 1530–1662				d. = dies b. = born	
Date	Political/Social Events	Religion and the Church	Education	Literature and culture	Science and magic	Trade, Empire and exploration
1646	End of first civil war after King's surrender: army mutinies over lack of pay	Parliament abolishes bishops. Edwards, *Gangraena (2nd ed)*		Suckling, *Fragmenta Aurea*; Crashaw, *Steps to the Temple*; Vaughan, *Poems*		
1647	Army captures King; debate political freedom: Leveller demands expressed, but mutinies crushed. King escapes	Laws against celebration of Easter and other festivals; Levellers' Agreement of the People demands religious and political liberty		Playing resumes briefly; Beaumont and Fletcher folio published. Andrews, *Private Devotions*; Cowley, *The Mistress*	More, *Philosophical Poems*	
1648	Thirty Years War ends; Pride's Purge; second civil war begins. Second *Agreement of the People* published. Filmer, *Anarchy of a Limited or Mixed Monarchy*			Herrick, *Hesperides*		

Date	Political/Social Events	Religion and the Church	Education	Literature and culture	Science and magic	Trade, Empire and exploration
	Chronology 1530–1662	d. = dies b. = born				
1649	Charles I tried and executed; England declared a commonwealth, monarchy and House of Lords abolished; Gauden, *Eikon Basilike*; Milton, *Tenure of Kings and Magistrates*; Cromwell campaigns in Ireland. Winstanley, *True Levellers' Standard*; Diggers' colonies established. Levellers' leaders arrested	Rump Parliament denies Army demands for religious toleration. Coppe, *A Fiery Flying Roll*		Lovelace, *Lucasta*; Milton, *Eikonoklastes*;	Descartes translated into English	Maryland grants religious toleration
1650	Cromwell conquers Ireland; adultery punishable by death; Charles II recognised by Scots	Church attendance not compulsory; Baxter, *The Saints' Everlasting Rest.* Blasphemy Act against non-conformity passed		Vaughan, *Silex Scintillans*; Marvell, 'Horatian Ode'. Weekly government newspaper established, *Mercurius Politicus.*	Descartes d.	
1651	Hobbes, *Leviathan*; Charles crowned in Scotland: defeated at Worcester and flees to France. Acts for selling off Royalist lands passed.	Cary, *A New.. Map.. of New Jerusalem's Glory*		Davenant, *Gondibert*; Cleveland, *Poems*; Vaughan, *Olor Iscanus*; Jones, *Stonehenge Restored*		Navigation Act: causes war with Dutch; Virginia acknowledges authority of Parliament

Date	Political/Social Events	Religion and the Church	Education	Literature and culture	Science and magic	Trade, Empire and exploration
	Chronology 1530–1662	d. = dies b. = born				
1652	Winstanley, *Law of Freedom* addressed to Cromwell			Crashaw, *Carmen Deo Nostro*		Settlement of Ireland Act
1653	Rump Parliament dissolved, Barebones Parliament sits; Cromwell becomes Lord Protector under Instrument of Government	Lay patronage of Church livings abolished; some religious toleration allowed	Dell, *A Trial of Spirits* attacks privileges of Oxbridge; Webster's *Acedemarium*	Shirley, *Cupid and Death*	Harvey, *Anatomical Exercitations*; Walton, *Complete Angler*	
1654	War against Dutch ends	Anna Trapnel's *Report and Plea*			Webster, *The Examination of Academies*	
1655	Rule of the Major-Generals; Jews re-admitted to England			Waller, *Panegyric to My Lord Protector*; Marvell, *First Anniversary of . . . The Lord Protector*		
1656	After elections, Major Generals exclude over 100 new MPs. Harrington, *Oceana*	Arrest of James Nayler for 'horrid blasphemy' after entering Bristol on an ass. Quakers active		Davenant, *Siege of Rhodes*, *First day's entertainment at Rutland House*; Cowley, *Poems*		First Quakers arrive in New England

| Date | Chronology 1530–1662 | | | | | |
	Political/Social Events	Religion and the Church	Education	Literature and culture	Science and magic	Trade, Empire and exploration
					d. = dies b. = born	
1657	Humble Petition and Advice asks Cromwell to be king			Lovelace d.	Harvey d.; Coles, *Adam in Eden*	
1658	Cromwell dies: son Richard succeeds as Lord Protector: Rump Parliament and Generals disagree over government			Davenant, *Cruelty of the Spaniards in Peru*; Browne, *Urn Burial, Garden of Cyrus*; Purcell b.	Enlarged reprint of Mouffet's *Theatre of Insects*	
1659	Protectorate abolished: Rump Parliament recalled		Hoole, *A New Discovery of the old Art of Teaching School*; Van Schurmann, *The Learned Maid*	Suckling, *Last Remains*; Lovelace, *Lucasta, Posthume Poems*		
1660	Declaration of Breda: Charles II restored to throne at request of Parliament and General Monk. Act of Indemnity and Oblivion	Bishops restored; Declaration of Indulgence	Stationer's Company to give a copy of every book to Bodleian library by statute	Theatres re-open; Pepys *Diary* 1660–69. Dryden, *Astraea Redux*	Royal Society founded	

Date	Political/Social Events	Religion and the Church	Education	Literature and culture	Science and magic	Trade, Empire and exploration
		Chronology 1530–1662		d. = dies b. = born		
1661	Bodies of Cromwell and others exhumed and publicly hanged; Corporation Act; Act against Tumultuous Petitioning; Quaker Act, Solemn League and Covenant to be burned	Savoy Conference: bishops reject compromise with Presbyterians		Act for censoring Press	Boyle, *Sceptical Chemist*	
1662		Act of Uniformity; introduction of new Prayer Book				

NOTES

1 RELIGION

Editor's introduction

1 See Morrill, J. (1982), pp. 89–94.
2 See Lake, P. (1987), pp. 32–76.
3 Cited in Cross, C. (1979), p. 79.
4 For a lucid discussion of the historiographical debate and literature, see Todd, M. (1995), pp. 1–10.
5 See Dickens, A. G. (1989), passim, and Collinson, P. (1983).
6 That is, government by the election of elders and presbyters, as in the Church of Scotland and Geneva.

Religion

1 Before.
2 Before.
3 That is, wrote up her notes after listening to it.
4 Beef broth.
5 The popular puritan preacher and writer, William Perkins; it is not known which text she was reading.
6 Thomas Cartwright, puritan divine and academic, whose Cambridge lectures in 1570 sparked the Vestiarian controversy: he advocated purity of doctrine and simplicity of ritual.
7 The custody of an ecclesiastical benefice.
8 *Declaration Concerning Sports*, see 3.20.

2 POLITICS

Editor's introduction

1 Both Whig and Marxist: for example, Neale, J. E. (1953); Gardiner, S. R. (1903) and Hill, C. (1958).
2 See Russell, C. (1971 and 1990) and Elton, G. R. (1982).

3 See Russell, C. (1990); Sharpe, K. (1993) and Burgess, G. (1992), chapter 2.
4 See Todd, M. (1995), pp. 1–10 for a summary of such revisions.
5 See Underdown, D. (1987), chapter 5; Cust, R. (1987), pp. 60–90 and Cust, R. and Hughes, A. (1989).
6 See Lake, P. (1987), pp. 32–76; Underdown, D. (1987) and Cust, R. (1987).
7 It was the invasion of England by Scotland in the late 1630s, and the rebellion of the Irish in 1641 which precipitated the final crisis in England.
8 See Quintrell, B. (1993), pp. 45–85.
9 See Cross, C. (1979), chapter 3.
10 Underdown, D. (1987), p. 106.
11 See Ingram, M. (1988).
12 See Zagorin, P. (1969).
13 This is a theme taken up in the cultural sphere by Collinson, P. (1983).
14 See Schochet, G. (1975).

Politics

1 Made their property.
2 A reference to More's *Utopia*.
3 Compressed.
4 Scarcely.
5 Process of giving help (*OED* cites first use 1670).
6 Restrain (obs).
7 Messages sent by ambassadors (obs.).
8 High or medium.
9 Reward.
10 Going to [Scot.].

3 SOCIETY AND SOCIAL LIFE

Editor's introduction

1 See Wrightson, K. (1986), pp. 190ff.
2 Whether imbued through Hollywood or historians such as Laslett, P. (1983).
3 See Wrigley, E. A. and Schofield, R. S. (1981).
4 For example Houlbrooke, R. (1979); Thirsk, J. (1967); Underdown, D. (1987); Wrightson, K. and Levine, D. (1979).
5 See Slack, P. (1984a).
6 See Houlbrooke, R. (1979); Quaife, G. (1979) and Underdown, D. (1987).
7 See Brown, E. H. Phelps and Hoskins, S. (1981); Slack, P. (1984b), pp. 221–42 and Thirsk, J. (1967).
8 The phrase is Margaret Spufford's (1974).
9 See Underdown, D. (1987); Wrightson, K. and Levine, D. (1979) and parts 1 and 2 of this book.

Society and social life

1 Prostitutes frequenting the bank of the Thames.
2 A trader or maker of bows.

3 All Hallows' Eve.
4 Softer.
5 Slippers.
6 Evidently London: the first part (*muni*) meaning city, the second (*dnol*) is Lond backwards.
7 Brooches.
8 Left-over material.
9 Reckoning for taxation.
10 Early.
11 Cooked dish.
12 Bailiffs.

4 EDUCATION

Editor's introduction

1 See Watson, Foster (1908).
2 See Stone (1975), i, 91–2.
3 See Wright, L.B. (1935) and Watson, Foster (1908), for example.
4 See Cressy, D. (1980) and Simon, J. (1966).
5 See Cressy, D. (1980).
6 See Lacqueur, T. (1976) and Spufford, M. (1979).
7 See Sharpe, J. A. (1987), pp. 254–69.
8 See Lacqueur, T. (1976) and Capp, B. (1979).
9 See Spufford, M. (1979) and Capp, B. (1979).
10 Lacqueur, T. (1976).
11 See Webster, C. (1975) and Hill, C. (1980).
12 See Watson, Foster (1908).
13 See Gardiner, D. (1929) and Kamm, J. (1965).
14 That is, the fathers of students were husbandmen, glovers, clothworkers, tradesmen and craftsmen: see Stone, L. (1975), i, pp. 91–2.
15 See Hill, C. (1980), chapter 1; and Webster, C. (1975).
16 See Feingold, M. (1984).

Education

1 A blemish.
2 Eradicate.
3 Caution.
4 Drawn.
5 Illuminating.
6 Nuzzled (obs).
7 That of men.
8 Wares.
9 In other words, if she is well born.
10 Rank.
11 Find the space for it.
12 The imparting of knowledge.
13 That of Ramus, the French logician who set forth a system of philosophical inquiry to answer and represent any problem.

14 Here Bacon is following the classical model of dialectic, wherein invention of matter is followed by judgement, and then delivery.
15 Honing.
16 Ramparts.
17 Of the *Commedia dell Arte*.
18 The most renowned and used of all grammar books.
19 George Buchanan.
20 Dispensary.
21 Humanist educationalist and writer of handbooks on grammar and rhetoric in education in the sixteenth century.
22 Francis Bacon.
23 That is, his work in Parliament for the parliamentary cause.
24 Those who board.
25 Provide money for.
26 That is, of the sentence *whether a maid may be a scholar*.

5 LITERARY AND CULTURAL THEORIES

Editor's introduction

1 The portrait is held by the National Portrait Gallery, London.
2 See King, J. (1982), pp. 122–61; Baugh, A. C. (1978), pp. 199–253.
3 See Caspari, F. (1954) and Greene, T. (1982).
4 See Greenblatt, S. (1980); Huizinga, J. (1955) and Jardine, L. (1996).
5 See Peterson, D. (1990); Norbrook, D. (1984); Sinfield, A. (1983) and Waller, G. (1986).
6 See King, J. (1982), pp. 35–86; Peterson, D. (1990), chapters 1 and 2 and Watt, T. (1991), pp. 131–257.
7 See Javitch, D. (1978).
8 See Altman, J. (1978); Lanham, R. (1976) and Waller, G. (1986).
9 See Altman J. (1978) and Howell, A. C. (1956).
10 See Altman, J. (1978).
11 See Greene, T. (1982) and Waller, G. (1986).
12 See Patterson, A. (1987).
13 See Hill, C. (1985), pp. 32–72.

Literary and cultural theories

1 In *The Mirror of Princely Deeds*.
2 Proud horses.
3 Ply for trade as a prostitute.
4 To make a citizen of.
5 A labourer in the Cornish tin mines.
6 John Taylor.
7 Francis Bacon.

6 SCIENCE AND MAGIC

Editor's introduction

1 See Hall, A. R. (1983) and Webster, C. (1975).
2 See Thomas, K. (1984); Webster, C. (1975) and Whitney, C. (1986).
3 See, for example, *Sylva Sylvarum* (1628), or *The History of Winds*.
4 Such as Burton's account of melancholy.
5 See, for example, Thorndike, L. (1941), vol. 5, pp. 23ff; Pagel, W. (1958), pp. 340ff and Rossi, P. (1968).
6 For example by Hall, A. R. (1983), pp. 1–19.
7 See Mcfarlane, A. (1970) and Thomas, K. (1971).
8 See Thomas, K. (1971), pp. 335–461.
9 Koyre, A. (1957), pp. 1ff.
10 See Hall, A. R. (1983), chapter 2.
11 See Drake, Stillman (1978), pp. 69–71 and Hall, A. R. (1983), pp. 96–114.
12 Translated by Webster (1975), p. 88.

Science and magic

1 Theories.
2 The kidneys (lit.): used to describe the seat of the affections.
3 Drying.
4 Wasting disease of the lungs.
5 Cheat.
6 A Greek sculptor.
7 All famous ancient Greek sculptors.
8 Membrane enclosing an organ.
9 Raymund Lull devised a logical system by which one could divide up and expound on any philosophical question.
10 Opaque.
11 The making of medicines.
12 Menstruation: he suggests it might be used as an abortifient.
13 Of the womb.
14 Childbirth.
15 Aristotle.
16 Articulation of a joint.
17 Insects which include the cochineal.
18 Any insect having armour (used metaphorically).
19 Pertaining to alchemy.
20 Moses.

7 GENDER AND SEXUALITY

Editor's introduction

1 See Wiesner, M. (1993), chapter 1.
2 See Underdown, D. (1987); Henderson, K. Usher and McManus, B. (1985) and Woodbridge, L. (1984).

3 See Harding, S. and Hintikka, M. B. (1983); Keller, E. Fox, (1985); Merchant, C. (1980) and Sawday, J. (1995), pp. 230–70.

4 See Clark, A. (1919, 1992); Mitchell, J. (1971) and Wiesner, M. (1993).

5 See, for example, Faludi, S. (1990), chapter 1.

6 See Lacqueur, T. (1990), chapter 3; Sawday, J. (1995), pp. 266–70 and Wiesner, M. (1993), chapter 1.

7 Houlbrooke, R. (1984) and Macfarlane, A. (1986).

8 See Quaife, G. R. (1979) and Sharpe, J. A. (1980).

9 See Quaife, G. R. (1979) and Sharpe, J. A. (1980).

10 See Crawford, P. (1993), pp. 82ff; Quaife, G. R. (1979) and Sharpe, J. A. (1980).

11 It is included in Aughterson, K. (1995).

12 See Bray, A. (1982); Goldberg, J. (1992) and Sedgewick, E. (1985).

Gender and sexuality

1 Small coin.

2 That is, try to arrange an abortion.

3 As a whore.

4 Lustful.

5 In Ovid's *Metamorphoses*, 8, the story is told of Scylla's father's kingdom, which is dependent on his retention of his one lock of purple hair: his daughter steals it to give to Minos, with whom she falls in love.

6 Gracefully intelligent.

7 Variant of Boadicea.

8 Gaudy.

9 Fisticuffs.

10 Essence.

11 Pimples.

12 Sores full of matter (or pus).

13 Belching.

14 Colic.

15 Girthed.

16 Coin of the value of half-crown.

17 Of Peter Martyr (see part 8).

18 A fever in which the paroxysms occur every four days.

19 Socrates.

20 A card game.

21 Partly digested food.

22 Belong, meaning due to.

23 A term used to describe any disease which produced vaginal discharge.

24 Hiccuping.

25 A fold in the peritoneum and alimentary canal: here used to mean abdominal obstructions.

26 The foreskin.

NOTES

8 EXPLORATION AND TRADE

Editor's introduction

1 See Wright, L. B. (1935).
2 See Chaudhuri, K. N. (1965)
3 See Middleton, R. (1996), pp. 51–113 for a more detailed account of the pattern and time of settlement.
4 Purchas continued the tradition of editing and publishing English voyages, with two editions of *Purchas his Pilgrims* in 1613 and 1625.
5 See Andrews, K. R. (1984), pp. 1–39.
6 See Clay, C. G. A. (1984) and Davis, R. (1973).
7 See Andrews, K. R. (1984), pp. 5–6.
8 See Elliot, J. H. (1970), for an account of different understandings of the new world.

Exploration and trade

1 Rapeseed plant.
2 Rabbits.
3 Foolish.
4 Penis.
5 A canon.
6 Canons.
7 A lynx.
8 Musket.
9 Small musket.
10 Lynxes.
11 His source for describing the city of Manoa as El Dorado.
12 During the civil wars in France between the Huguenots and Catholics in the 1560s and 1570s.
13 20 shillings.
14 Drake's name given to California on his circumnavigation of the globe.
15 Sixteenth-century word for negroes.
16 Eastern Germany.
17 Vomiting and purging.
18 Forty-one adult males, of the sixty-five male passengers, covenanted their agreement.
19 The fourth year of his reign.
20 A term used to describe any separatist.
21 In March 1622 much of the Jamestown plantation was destroyed in an attack by the Powhatan Confederacy, which had become disillusioned with the broken promises of English settlers, and convinced that their lands were under permanent threat.
22 Of Gibraltar.

593

SELECT BIBLIOGRAPHIES

1 RELIGION

Collinson, P. (1983) *The Religion of Protestants*, Oxford, Oxford University Press.

Cross, C. (1979) *Church and People 1450–1660*, London, Fontana.

Dickens, A. G. (1989) *The English Reformation* (revised edition), London, Batsford.

Lake, P. (1987) 'Calvinism and the English Church', *Past and Present*, 114: pp. 32–76.

Morrill, J. (1982) 'The Church in England, 1642–49', in Morrill, J. *Reactions to the English Civil War*, London, Macmillan.

Todd, M. (1995) *Reformation to Revolution: Politics and Religion in Early Modern England*, London, Routledge.

Further secondary sources in print

Acheson, R. J. (1990) *Radical Puritans in England 1550–1660*, Harlow, Longman.

Cressy, D. and Ferrell, Lori (1996) *Religion and Society in Early Modern England*, London, Routledge.

Elton, G. R. (1982) *The Tudor Constitution* (2nd edition), Cambridge, Cambridge University Press.

Foster, Andrew (1994) *The Church of England 1570–1640*, Harlow, Longman.

Kenyon, J. P. (1986) *The Stuart Constitution*, Cambridge, Cambridge University Press.

Sheils, W. J. (1989) *The English Reformation*, Harlow, Longman.

2 POLITICS

Burgess, G. (1992) *The Politics of the Ancient Constitution: an introduction to English political thought*, Basingstoke and London, Macmillan.

Collinson, P. (1983) *The Religion of Protestants*, Oxford, Oxford University Press.

Cross, C. (1979) *Church and People 1450–1660*, London, Fontana.

Cust, R. (1987) *The Forced Loan and English Politics 1626–1628*, Oxford, Oxford University Press.

Cust, R. and Hughes, A. (1989) eds. *Conflicts in Early Stuart England*, London, Longman.

Elton, G. R. (1986) *The Parliament of England 1559–1581*, Cambridge, Cambridge University Press.

Gardiner, S. R. (1903) *History of the Commonwealth and Protectorate*, 4 vols, London, Longmans, Green and Co.

Hill, C. (1958) *Puritanism and Revolution*, Oxford, Oxford University Press.

Ingram, M. (1988) *Church Courts, Sex and Marriage in England 1570–1640*, Cambridge, Cambridge University Press.

Lake, P. (1987) 'Calvinism and the English Church', *Past and Present*, 114: pp. 32–76.

Neale, J. E. (1953) *Elizabeth I and her Parliaments*, 2 vols, London, Cape.

Quintrell, B. (1993) *Charles I 1625–1640*, London, Longman.

Russell, C. (1971) *The Crisis of Parliaments: English History, 1509–1660*, Oxford, Oxford University Press.

—— (1990) *The Causes of the English Civil War*, Oxford, Oxford University Press.

Schochet, G. (1975) *Patriarchalism in Political Thought*, Oxford, Basil Blackwell.

Sharpe, K. (1993) *The Personal Rule of Charles I*, New Haven, Princeton University Press.

Todd, M. (1995) *Reformation to Revolution: Politics and Religion in Early Modern England*, London, Routledge.

Underdown, D. (1987) *Revel, Riot and Rebellion*, Oxford, Oxford University Press.

Zagorin, P. (1969) *The Court and the Country: The Beginning of the English Revolution*, London, Routledge.

Further secondary sources in print

Acheson, R. J. (1990) *Radical Puritans in England 1550–1660*, Harlow, Longman.

Barnard, T. (1982) *The English Republic 1649–1660*, Harlow, Longman.

Elton, G. R. (1982) *The Tudor Constitution* (2nd edition), Cambridge, Cambridge University Press.

Graves, M. (1987) *Elizabethan Parliaments 1559–1601*, Harlow, Longman.

Kenyon, J. P. (1986) *The Stuart Constitution*, Cambridge, Cambridge University Press.

Wootton, D. (1986) *Divine Right and Democracy: An Anthology of Political Writing in Stuart England*, Harmondsworth, Penguin.

3 SOCIETY AND SOCIAL LIFE

Brown, E. H. Phelps and Hoskins, S. (1981) *A Perspective of Wages and Prices*, London, Methuen.

Houlbrooke, R. (1979) *Church Courts and People During the English Reformation*, Cambridge, Cambridge University Press.

Laslett, P. (1983) *The World We have Lost Further Explored* London, Methuen.

Quaife, G. (1979) *Wanton Wenches and Wayward Wives: Peasants and Illicit Sex in Early Seventeenth-Century England*, London, Croom Helm.

Slack, P. (1984a) *Rebellion, Popular Protest and Social Change in Early Modern England*, Cambridge, Cambridge University Press.

—— (1984b) 'Poverty and Social Regulation in Elizabethan England', in Haigh, C. ed. *The Reign of Elizabeth*, London, Macmillan.

Spufford, M. (1974) *Contrasting Communities: English Villages in the Sixteenth and Seventeenth Centuries*, Cambridge, Cambridge University Press.

Thirsk, J. (1967), *The Agrarian History of England and Wales, vol. 4, 1500–1640*, Cambridge, Cambridge University Press.

Underdown, D. (1973) *Somerset in the Civil War and Interregnum*, London, David and Charles.

—— (1987) *Revel, Riot and Rebellion*, Oxford, Oxford University Press.

Wrightson, K. (1986) 'The Social Order of Early Modern England: Three Approaches', in Bonfield, L. *et al.* eds, *The World we Have Gained: Histories of Population and Social Structure*, Oxford, Oxford University Press.

Wrightson, K. and Levine, D. (1979), *Poverty and Piety in an English Village: Terling 1525–1700*, New York.

Wrigley, E. A. and Schofield, R. S. (1981) *The Population History of England 1541–1871: A Reconstruction*, London, Edward Arnold.

Further secondary sources in print

Coward, B. (1988) *Social Change and Continuity in Early Modern England 1550–1750*, Harlow, Longman.

Cressy, D. and Ferrell, Lori (1996) *Religion and Society in Early Modern England*, London, Routledge.

4 EDUCATION

Capp, B. (1979) *Astrology and the Popular Press: English Almanacs 1500–1800*, London, Faber.

Cressy, D. (1980) *Literacy and the Social Order: Reading and Writing in Early Modern England*, Cambridge, Cambridge University Press.

Feingold, M. (1984) *The Mathematicians Apprenticeship: Science, Universities and Society in England 1560–1640*, Cambridge, Cambridge University Press.

Gardiner, D. (1929) *English Girlhood at School: A Study of Women's Education Through Twelve Centuries*, Oxford, Oxford University Press.

Hill, C. (1980) *Intellectual Origins of the English Revolution* (revised edition), Oxford, Oxford University Press.

Kamm, J. (1965) *Hope Deferred: Girls' Education in English History*, London, Methuen.

Lacqueur, T. (1976) 'The Cultural Origins of Popular Literacy in England 1550–1850', *Oxford Review of Education*, 2, pp. 255–75.

Sharpe, J. A. (1987) *Early Modern England: A Social History*, London, Edward Arnold.

Simon, J. (1966) *Education and Society in Tudor England*, Cambridge, Cambridge University Press.

Spufford, M. (1979) 'First Steps in Literacy: The Reading and Writing Experiences of the Humblest Seventeenth-Century Spiritual Autobiographers', *Social History* 4, pp. 407–36.

Stone, L. (1964) 'The Educational Revolution in England, 1560–1640', *Past and Present*, 28: pp. 41–80.

—— (1975) ed. *The University in Society*, vol. 1, Princeton and London, Princeton University Press.

Watson, Foster (1908) *The Grammar Schools to 1660: Their Curriculum and Practice*, Cambridge, Cambridge University Press.

Webster, C. (1975) *The Great Instauration: Science, Medicine and Reform 1626–1660*, London, Duckworth.

Wright, L. B. (1935) *Middle Class Culture in Elizabethan England*, Ithaca, New York, Cornell University Press.

Further secondary source in print

Cressy, D. (1975) *Education in Tudor and Stuart England*, London, Arnold.

5 LITERARY AND CULTURAL THEORIES

Altman, J. (1978) *The Tudor Play of Mind: Rhetorical Inquiry and the Development of Elizabethan Drama*, Berkeley, University of California Press.

Baugh, A. C. (1978) *A History of the English Language* (revised edn), London, Routledge.

Caspari, F. (1954) *Humanism and the Social Order in Tudor England*, Chicago, Chicago University Press.

Greenblatt, S. (1980) *Renaissance Self-Fashioning*, Chicago, Chicago University Press.

Greene, T. (1982) *The Light in Troy: Imitation and Discovery in Renaissance Poetry*, New Haven, Yale University Press.

Hill, C. (1985) 'Censorship and English Literature', *Writing and Revolution in 17th Century England*, Brighton, Harvester, pp.32–72.

Howell, A. C. (1956) *Logic and Rhetoric in England 1500–1700*, Princeton, Princeton University Press.

Huizinga, J. (1955) *Homo Ludens*, New York, Beacon.

Jardine, L. (1996) *Worldly Goods: A New History of the Renaissance*, London, Macmillan.

Javitch, D. (1978) *Poetry and Courtliness in Renaissance England*, Princeton, Princeton University Press.

King, J. (1982) *English Reformation Literature: The Tudor Origins of the Protestant Tradition*, Princeton, Princeton University Press.

Lanham, R. (1976) *The Motives of Eloquence: Literary Rhetoric in the Renaissance*, New Haven, Yale University Press.

Norbrook, D. (1984) *Poetry and Politics in the English Renaissance*, London, Routledge.

Patterson, A. (1987) *Censorship and Interpretation*, University of Wisconsin Press.

Peterson, D. (1990) *The English Lyric from Wyatt to Donne* (second edn), East Lansing, Michigan College Press.

Sinfield, A. (1983) *Literature in Protestant England 1550–1660*, Beckenham, Croom Helm.

Waller, G. (1986) *English Poetry of the Sixteenth Century*, New York, Longman.

Watt, T. (1991) *Cheap Print and Popular Piety 1550–1640*, Cambridge, Cambridge University Press.

Further secondary source in print

Rivers, I. (1979) *Classical and Christian Ideas in English Renaissance Poetry*, London, Routledge.

6 SCIENCE AND MAGIC

Drake, Stillman (1978) *Galileo at Work: His Scientific Biography*, Chicago, University of Chicago Press.

Hall, A. R. (1983) *The Revolution in Science 500–1750*, London, Longman.

Koyre, A. (1957) *From the Closed World to the Infinite Universe*, Baltimore, John Hopkins University Press.

Mcfarlane, A. (1970) *Witchcraft in Tudor and Stuart England: A Regional and Comparative Study*, London, Routledge.

Pagel, W. (1958) *Paracelsus: An Introduction to Philosophical Medicine in the Era of the Renaissance*, Basel and New York, Karger.

Rossi, P. (1968) *Francis Bacon: From Magic to Science*, London, Routledge, Penguin.

Thomas, K. (1971) *Religion and the Decline of Magic*, London, Harmondsworth.

—— (1984) *Man and the Natural World*, London, Allen Lane.

Thorndike, L. (1941) *History of Magic and Experimental Science*, New York, Columbia University Press.

Webster, C. (1975) *The Great Instauration: Science, Medicine and Reform 1626–1660*, London, Duckworth.

Whitney, C. (1986) *Francis Bacon and Modernity*, New Haven, Yale University Press.

Further secondary source in print

Carey, J. (1996) ed. *The Faber Book of Science*, London, Faber.

7 GENDER AND SEXUALITY

Bray, A. (1982) *Homosexuality in Renaissance England*, London, Gay Men's Press.

Clark, A. (1919, 1992) *The Working Life of Seventeenth-Century Women*, London, Routledge.

Crawford, P. (1993) 'Sexual Knowledge in England 1500–1750', in Porter, R. and Teich, M. eds. *Sexual Knowledge, Sexual Science: The History of Attitudes to Sexuality*, Cambridge, Cambridge University Press, pp. 82–106.

Faludi, S. (1990) *Backlash*, London, Chatto and Windus.

Goldberg, J. (1992) *Sodometries: Renaissance Texts, Modern Sexualities*, Stanford, Stanford University Press.

Harding, S. and Hintikka, M. B. (1983) eds *Discovering Reality: Feminist Perspectives on Epistemology, Metaphysics, Methodology and Philosophy of Science*, Dordrecht, Kluwer Academic.

Houlbrooke, R. (1984) *The English Family 1450–1700*, London and New York, Longman.

Keller, E. Fox, (1985) *Reflections on Gender and Science*, New Haven, Yale University Press.

Lacqueur, T. (1990) *Making Sex: Body and Gender from the Greeks to Freud*, Cambridge, Mass., Harvard University Press.

Macfarlane, A. (1986) *Marriage and Love in England. Modes of Reproduction 1300–1800*, Oxford, Basil Blackwell.

Merchant, C. (1980) *The Death of Nature*, San Francisco, Harper and Row.

Mitchell, J. (1971) *Woman's Estate*, Harmondsworth, Penguin.

Quaife, G. R. (1979) *Wanton Wenches and Wayward Wives: Peasants and Illicit Sex in Early Seventeenth-century England*, London, Croom Helm.

Sawday, J. (1995) *The Body Emblazoned: Dissection and the Human Body in Renaissance Culture*, London, Routledge.

Sedgewick, E. (1985) *Between Men: English Literature and Male Homosocial Desire*, New York, Columbia University Press.

Sharpe, J. A. (1980) *Defamation and Sexual Slander in Early Modern England: the Church Courts at York*, Borthwick Paper 58, York, Borthwick Institute of Historical Research.

Underdown, D. (1987) *Revel, Riot and Rebellion: Popular Politics and Culture in England 1603–1660*, Oxford, Oxford University Press.

Wiesner, M. (1993) *Women and Gender in Early Modern Europe*, Cambridge, Cambridge University Press.

Woodbridge, L. (1984) *Women and the English Renaissance*, Chicago, University of Illinois Press.

Further secondary sources in print

Aughterson, K. (1995) *Renaissance Woman: Constructions of Femininity*, London, Routledge.

Henderson, K. Usher and McManus, B. (1985) *Half Humankind: Contexts and Texts of the Controversy about Women in England 1540–1640*, Urbana, University of Illinois Press.

Keeble, N. H. (1994) *The Cultural Identity of Seventeenth-Century Woman: A Reader*, London, Routledge.

8 EXPLORATION AND TRADE

Andrews, K. R. (1984) *Trade, Plunder and Settlement: Maritime Enterprise and the Genesis of the British Empire*, Cambridge, Cambridge University Press.

Chaudhuri, K. N. (1965) *The East India Company: The Study of an Early Joint Stock Company 1600–1640*, London, Frank Cass.

Clay, C. G. A. (1984) *Economic Expansion and Social Change: England 1500–1700* Cambridge, Cambridge University Press.

Davis, R. (1973) *English Overseas Trade 1500–1700*, London, Macmillan.

Elliot, J. H. (1970) *The Old World and the New 1492–1650*, Cambridge, Cambridge University Press.

Middleton, R. (1996) *Colonial America* (second edition), Oxford, Basil Blackwell.

Wright, L. B. (1935) *Middle Class Culture in Elizabethan England*, Ithaca, NY, Cornell University Press.

Further secondary sources in print

Columbus, Christopher (1969) *The Four Voyages*, Harmondsworth, Penguin.

Diaz, Bernal (1963) *The Conquest of New Spain*, Harmondsworth, Penguin.

Hakluyt, Richard (1972) *Voyages and Discoveries*, Harmondsworth, Penguin.

INDEX

Made in the USA
Middletown, DE
07 August 2015